Handbook of Research on Electronic Surveys and Measurements

Rodney A. Reynolds
Azusa Pacific University, USA
(on leave from Pepperdine University, USA)

Robert Woods
Spring Arbor University, USA

Jason D. Baker
Regent University, USA

IDEA GROUP REFERENCE
Hershey · London · Melbourne · Singapore

Acquisitions Editor:	Michelle Potter
Development Editor:	Kristin Roth
Senior Managing Editor:	Jennifer Neidig
Managing Editor:	Sara Reed
Copy Editor:	Angela Thor
Typesetter:	Sara Reed
Cover Design:	Lisa Tosheff
Printed at:	Yurchak Printing Inc.

Published in the United States of America by
Idea Group Reference (an imprint of Idea Group Inc.)
701 E. Chocolate Avenue, Suite 200
Hershey PA 17033
Tel: 717-533-8845
Fax: 717-533-8661
E-mail: cust@idea-group.com
Web site: http://www.idea-group-ref.com

and in the United Kingdom by
Idea Group Reference (an imprint of Idea Group Inc.)
3 Henrietta Street
Covent Garden
London WC2E 8LU
Tel: 44 20 7240 0856
Fax: 44 20 7379 0609
Web site: http://www.eurospanonline.com

Library of Congress Cataloging-in-Publication Data

Handbook of research on electronic surveys and measurements / Rodney A. Reynolds, Robert Woods and Jason D. Baker, editors.
    p. cm.
  Includes bibliographical references.
  Summary: "This book is the comprehensive reference source for innovative knowledge on electronic surveys. It provides complete coverage of the challenges associated with the use of the Internet to develop online surveys, administer Web-based instruments, and conduct computer-mediated assessments. This combination of how-to information about online research coupled with profiles of specific measures makes it an indispensable reference"--Provided by publisher.
  ISBN 1-59140-792-3 (hardcover) -- ISBN 1-59140-793-1 (ebook)
  1. Surveys--Methodology--Computer programs. 2. Interviewing--Computer programs. 3. Internet questionnaires. 4. Behavioral assessment--Computer programs. 5. Social sciences--Research--Statistical methods--Computer programs. I. Reynolds, Rodney A. II. Woods, Robert, 1970- III. Baker, Jason D. IV. Title: Electronic surveys and measurements.
  HA31.2.H347 2007
  001.4'33--dc22
                        2006019157

British Cataloguing in Publication Data
A Cataloguing in Publication record for this book is available from the British Library.

All work contributed to this handbook is new, previously-unpublished material. The views expressed in this handbook are those of the authors, but not necessarily of the publisher.

List of Contributors

Table of Contents

Section II
Survey Software

Section III
Instrument Profiles of Interest to Survey Researchers

Detailed Table of Contents

Section I
Usage of Online Surveys and Measurements

Consideration of conceptual, ethical, and methodological issues associated with various computer-based survey techniques.

The chapter offers a very hands-on approach to stages of Web survey design that new and returning survey researchers will find useful.

With a historical perspective on the development of electronic survey capabilities, the author offers insights into practical issues on converting from traditional survey forms to electronic survey forms and procedures.

This innovative chapter provides clear insight into the processes of doing online research through the lens of case studies.

This synthesis of survey research practices and Web site design practices allows for the establishment of a set of "best practices" principles for researchers to follow when constructing online questionnaires.

Combining traditional mail surveys with online survey methods afford a number of opportunities to improve the quality of research. Particular attention is offered on the task of increasing response rates to surveys.

This chapter offers specific directions for working through the Web page construction and the programming needed to optimize the online survey process.

The specific research challenges addressed in the chapter are response rates, sampling, and controlling the data collection environment.

A key argument here is that the requirement of representativeness limits the usefulness and validity of online surveys.

This chapter advances the case and the processes for researchers to demonstrate the empirical evidence of the equivalence of electronic and offline measures.

This chapter is a report on quantitative data on the similarities, differences, and potential problems when using electronic or conventional surveys.

This chapter moves beyond the basic ethical challenges of online research to present the solutions adopted by different organizations. An examination of the actual applications of research ethics in online surveys revealed serious ongoing ethical problems.

This chapter explores issues related to legal and sociocultural perspectives that should concern the international survey researcher.

The argument in this chapter is that doing research on or about the Internet requires consideration of the goals unique to Internet use (as opposed to general media use). The chapter presents factor analytic data on a measure of Internet dependency.

This chapter explains common online advertising metrics for measuring advertising effectiveness and encourages consideration of alternative models for the measurement of advertising effects.

After consideration of business measures and the uniqueness of electronic business and research environments, this chapter turns to address the evolving nature on electronic commerce and, thus, the evolving research environment for those interested in e-commerce.

This chapter reviews public relations measures and the development of online surveys and measurements in public relations. Consideration is also given to the future of measurement in public relations.

As different groups expand into electronic surveys, they increasingly need to adapt existing measures in their field. This chapter reviews a number of measures from religion and spirituality research relevant to future research interests.

With increasing use of computer-mediated group communication, there is an increasing need for group process measures and application of those measures in the online environment. This chapter offers conceptual explication of a measure of disagreement, and then explains how to employ that measure in the context of online group discussions.

A key concept in the information age is the capacity to handle cognitive load. This chapter reviews the conceptual and operational approaches to cognitive load, and suggests applications for both traditional and electronic-based research.

This chapter synthesizes and summarizes advances in information search and research techniques as applied to the computer-mediated communication research area.

This chapter is a state-of-the-art review of who is doing what research in the computer-mediated communication research area.

Section II
Survey Software

The authors introduce and explain a software tool that can facilitate mail, e-mail, and Web-based surveys.

The authors introduce and explain a Web-based tool for survey construction, and demonstrate the application in training and development assessments.

The author explains a Web-based tool for survey construction and compares the tool with other such tools.

The authors describe a Web portal dedicated to survey research. The portal includes various resources of particular interest to those who do Web-based surveys.

The authors explain a Web-based tool for survey construction and data management that offers flexibility in formatting, design, and implementation of interactive surveys.

The authors compare the technical functions, the graphical representation, and the usability of two major online survey tools developed in Germany.

The author describes the features, functions, and implementation of a survey software product that supports project management, survey authoring and design, and multiple electronic and paper data collection technologies. The discussion centers on applications of the software to research on schools, higher education, government, business, and healthcare.

The author discusses free software that may be useful to survey researchers.

Section III
Instrument Profiles of Interest to Survey Researchers

The author discusses the various methods for and uses of analyses of patterns of linkages between Web pages.

The author describes a battery of scales that "map" the experiential feeling resulting from a Web page encounter.

The author discusses coding procedures that can help identify problems and false assumptions in survey data.

The author describes the end-user computing satisfaction instrument. The instrument is common in studies on electronic uses and effects.

The author reviews various perspectives on the measurement of Web credibility.

The author describes and comments on a key assessment tool for evaluating online learning experiences.

The authors describe a scale for assessing media user's degree of personal identification with a celebrity.

The author reviews the TAM measure of perceived usefulness and perceived ease of use of computer technology as predictors of intent and actual use.

The authors describe a scale for assessing media user's perceptions of relationship with celebrities.

The author describes a measure that is useful for exploring the fit between the person and the organization, the need for organizational culture change, distinguishing subcultures, and the potential fit for planned organizational mergers.

The author describes the measurement of the sense of "flow" (complete and total immersion in an activity), and the implications of flow for e-commerce.

The author describes a measure of communication apprehension (CA). CA has profound effects on individual performance and personal relationships.

The authors describe a measure for assessing the degree of reactance (overvaluing denied alternatives) to messages.

The authors report on the concepts and closed-ended measures for surprise, anger, fear, sadness, guilt, happiness, contentment.

The authors discuss a measure to assess preferences to listen for people, action, content, and time.

The authors describe a measure of leaders for their love, empowerment, vision, humility, trusting, serving, and altruism.

The authors report on short-form measures of aggression. The measures tap dimensions of anger, hostility, verbal aggression, physical aggression, and indirect aggression.

The authors report on a seven-dimension instrument useful in person-job fit analysis.

The author discusses an online service offering over 500 measures and tests ranging from substantial to fun uses.

The author reports on a self-report measure of the tendency to approach or avoid initiating communication.

The author details a measure of leaders who lead by modeling, inspiring, challenging, enabling, and encouraging.

The authors present an efficient short-form measure for extraversion, neuroticism, and psychoticism. Research based on electronic platforms tends to require such efficient measures.

The author details a measure of the fear people experience when interacting with others from different cultural groups.

The authors describe a newly developed 14-item inventory designed as a refinement of the Bem sex role inventory.

The author reports on a refined measure of Internet motives. The dimensions are: entertainment, convenience, interpersonal/communication utility, and social utility.

The author reviews a measure of state communication anxiety (in contrast with generalized trait anxiety).

Foreword

The Internet has become a part of the research process. Many younger scholars who use the Internet to do research, whose graduate studies commenced after the Internet diffused to universities, barely know of the research processes, controversies, and problems that preceded the Net. Sometimes this is a great loss: Many methodological and ethical issues that now appear to be Internet-related were addressed in the long pre-Internet era, and elude the Internet-native generation. Many more senior researchers whose foci do not involve Internet-based phenomena must think creatively, and no less skeptically, whether there are sampling, stimulus presentation, or instrumentation advantages that online techniques can offer that will economize, enhance, or extend what they can do with traditional media and data-gathering methods (see Watt, 1999). Internet-enabled research, whether it focuses on Net-related or unrelated phenomena, offers great advantages and abilities but, which methods and which measures? What have others done that can be replicated, co-opted, or remodeled? The *Handbook of Research on Electronic Surveys and Measurements* will help researchers sort out the otherwise confusing and disparate approaches that have been and could be used to get useful data.

Electronically supported research methods can and do focus on at least four domains, each with its own methodological genre and issues.

Online measures about off-line phenomena. Much attention has been paid to methods of facilitating research using online resources when the focus of the research has nothing topically related to the Internet. In this domain, the Internet is a medium only, taking its place among slide projectors, telephones, and print questionnaires. These include Web-based questionnaire forms, computer interfaces that measure reaction times to different stimuli, eye-tracking sensors, and other adaptations. Research is accruing that evaluates whether new interfaces introduce new errors; whether electronic interfaces remove systematic distortions (e.g., they encourage greater disclosiveness and reduce social desirability biases; Richman, Kiesler, Weisband, & Drasgow, 1999), or whether they encourage more mindless, response set repetitions. These are critical questions. It is clear, however, that such systems facilitate research, removing the steps between raw information acquisition and data entry into statistical analysis formats. That step is not merely a temporal and financial cost; manual data entry also involves potential transcription error. Their economic efficiencies and ease of use cannot be doubted.

Online measures about online phenomena. Online transactions have created a host of sufficiently novel behavior that occurs in no other venue the way it occurs online; demanding methods to evaluate it. We educated ourselves very quickly that inferences about Web site visitation from Web site "hit" data are fraught with validity and reliability error, but we have learned just as quickly to treat clickstream data carefully, and sometimes in controlled experimental ways, to suit novel hypotheses. Studying how

Web sites link to one another has opened up not only new methods of search-engine design, but vast sociometries of association and identification. Studying basic email and discussion boards yields new artifacts to analyze, from the use and meaning of emoticons, to sensitivity, to time stamps. How people respond to rule violations in virtual communities tells us not only about these important species of human behavior, but about rules, communities, and behavior writ large.

Online measures about online variations. The field of human computer interaction (HCI) has moved from analyzing single-user human-factors-type usability to discovering how to facilitate social interaction, feedback systems, the utility of notifications about others' behaviors, and ways to monitor various systems', transactions', and partners' progress in interdependent activities. The experimental approach that HCI has long used has become a mainstay in testing alternative site designs, evaluating users' responses, and evaluating different versions of information provision, in fields ranging widely from virtual libraries to community health applications. Retrospective research, data-mining, and triangulation allow experts to learn why some online services work whereas others do not, and new research methods allow strong conclusions to be made without resort to armchair speculation or coolness judgments.

Online measures about online action. In the words of Zuboff (1988), when you automate, you informate: electronic methods to facilitate users' behavior have built-in methods to track those behaviors, and whether the tracking of those behaviors is for good or for bad is not inherent. While marketers develop sophisticated methods to measure and use the crumbs we leave behind on our travels through the Internet forest, the measurement of presence and associations, messaging and replying, offers researchers potential profiles about people's concerns and social structures through stark empirical glimpses. Ten-years ago we viewed estimates of Usenet news readership, to learn among other things that 8,100 people used presumably uncooperative hands to read the arthritis online support group (Reid, 1995). Now, Microsoft's experimental Netscan tool (http://netscan.research.microsoft.com) shows us not only that alt.support.arthritis had 147 different writers last month (as well as every other Usenet newsgroup), that they generated 1,258 messages altogether, 1,104 of which were replies; we can see who are the central contributors, what kinds of questions and answers have online longevity, and a host of other extrapolations from innocuous user activity. We may learn more about what online discussion groups really do for people—rather, what people do for people when they share with one another online—as new methods to harness data are slowly caught up with by new ways to make sense of the traces people inadvertently leave. (We could crudely estimate gender ratios if we wished, on the basis of posters' names, since in many cases, those show, too.)

As new phenomena and new techniques have developed, there have been missteps and concerns. For instance, in taking advantage of the low-cost, high-volume potential of a Web-based survey offered to any and all takers, Internet Addiction researchers posed exceedingly lengthy questionnaires online, with exhaustive new scales, personality measures, and concurrent validity measures for comparison. It may be no surprise that a large proportion of those who completed the voluntary, hour-long questionnaire revealed high scores on compulsive Internet use. Unfortunately, these most probably skewed samples were extrapolated to the whole Internet-using population, making good headlines if not good science.

Other concerns have arisen about the ethics of research that new techniques and new behaviors enable. For instance, it has been questioned whether a researcher really knows if a research participant, contacted only via the Internet, understands informed consent information without the traditional oral and handwritten agreement, and perhaps the head nod, that accompany face-to-face interviews (as if these artifacts actually guarantee understanding; see Walther, 2002). What of the case that many participants in virtual communities believe that researchers should not be privy-indeed have no right-to read, analyze, and above all reproduce the comments they exchanged in the seemingly confidential spaces of their virtual fora (Hudson & Bruckman, 2004) despite the fact that many of the very spaces they inhabit are, by design, publicly and openly accessible. Virtual communities simply would not work were people not privy to the Internetworked storage and reproduction of those very comments. U.S. law appears to allow researchers the use of such things (Jacobson, 1999), so it is not a matter of researchers' rights, but it is an emotional issue where, right or wrong, researchers must tread carefully.

New, online methods for old behaviors; new methods for new behaviors; measures assessing online presence and activity; and comparative methods, are different species of research approaches, and these four types merely scratch the surface of what is known and what is to be developed in exploring the online world. In this respect, The *Handbook of Research on Electronic Surveys and Measurements* is more than needed, as are the theories and revelations these methods will help us illuminate.

Joseph B. Walther
Michigan State University, USA

REFERENCES

Hudson, J. M., & Bruckman, A. (2004). "Go away": Participant objections to being studied and the ethics of chatroom research. *The Information Society, 20*, 127-139.

Jacobson, D. (1999). Doing research in cyberspace. *Field Methods, 11*, 127-145.

Reid, B. (1995, Apr 1). *USENET Readership report for Mar 95*. Retrieved December 1, 1995, from Usenet news (now Google Groups), news.lists.

Richman, W., Kiesler, S., Weisband, S., & Drasgow, F. (1999). A meta-analytic study of social desirability distortion in computer-administered questionnaires, traditional questionnaires, and interviews. *Journal of Applied Psychology, 84*, 754-775.

Walther, J. B. (2002). Research ethics in Internet-enabled research: Human subjects issues and methodological myopia. *Ethics and Information Technology, 4*, 205-216.

Watt, J. H. (1999). Internet systems for evaluation research. In G. Gay & T. L. Bennington (Eds.), *Information technologies in evaluation: Social, moral, epistemological, and practical implications* (pp. 23-44). San Francisco: Jossey-Bass.

Zuboff, S. (1988). *In the age of the smart machine: The future of work and power*. New York: Basic Books.

Joseph B. Walther is a professor in the Department of Communication and the Department of Telecommunication, Information Studies, and Media at Michigan State University. Dr. Walther is one of the foremost authors on computer-mediated communication. His research explores how the Internet impacts the ways we coordinate and relate to one another. His theories and findings examine the development of relationships online, how computer networks alter routines and requirements for successful collaboration, and how virtual teammates blame each other for their own misuses of time and technology. He has been the chair of the Organizational Communication and Information Systems division of the Academy of Management, and the Communication and Technology division of the International Communication Association.

Preface

Just like the electronic technology world, the frequency, breadth, and depth of electronic surveys and measures is expanding exponentially. Researchers and research consumers are rapidly transitioning to demands and expectations for sophisticated uses of electronic surveys and measures. There can be little question about the need to learn about electronic surveys.

The habits and opportunities for research with electronic platforms has become a completely independent area of research and advanced study. Employers are increasingly seeking individuals who can assist with designing survey tools that take advantage of developing technology and software. It is no longer enough to know just the technology or the software. Researchers, students, and consumers are increasingly sophisticated in their expectations. If we want to use electronic surveys to study people, we need to know more about how people respond to and react to electronic surveys.

One particular task the research community faces is the demand to shift and adapt the body of existing paper and pencil measurement tools onto electronic technology capabilities. It is not really much of an issue any more to observe that electronic options increase the potential and complexities for doing research. It is also not very useful to observe that some conventional research areas or measures are best done (or only validated) in traditional settings with those established tools. Research participants are less and less willing to answer and respond to older survey research practices and settings.

Developing technological abilities for electronic surveys and measurements have created a recent growth industry in online survey services. Researchers with limited programming knowledge could design and pilot test surveys in a day. The next day, the researcher could draw samples (with sophistication far beyond older practices). By the end of the week, not only can the data collection be complete, but also the statistical analyses done (again with amazing sophistication) and strategically potent presentational materials constructed (and also tested for effectiveness). Our need is rapidly moving on to how to prepare for such abilities by practically any person with any potential motive.

This handbook helps us move toward coping with and adjusting to a sophisticated world of research capabilities. There is no promise here of definitive answers. We are not even sure enough of the most relevant questions yet. Therefore, the modest goal with this volume is to help move us all along toward clarifying the central issues we need to address on electronic surveys and measurements.

The authors of the chapters in this book are representatives from some of the most innovative private and public programs that study, develop, or directly use research based on electronic surveys and measurements. Just reading the list of authors and their biographies is inspiring. The insights of their individual and their collective wisdom certainly justifies spending some time with this volume. Both novice and sophisticated researchers will find useful materials here.

The handbook is divided into three sections: usage of online surveys and measurements; survey software; and specific measurements.

In Section I: Usage of Online Surveys and Measurements, the focus is on the details of using online surveys to do research. In these chapters, the readers will encounter details (at various levels) on issues related to various types of electronic surveys and research. Some of the chapters carefully contrast electronic surveys and research with related methods. Some of the chapters here directly address ethical issues related to electronic surveys. Several of the later chapters in this section direct the reader to broader issues that should be of particular concern to researchers who use electronic-based communication platforms.

In Section II: Survey Software, the focus is on software services and programs that should be of strong value to those who do research with, on, or about electronic-based communication platforms. While readers will know about one or two survey software programs, most readers will be well impressed with the variety of software and programming options covered in the second section of the book.

In Section III: Instrument Profiles of Interest to Survey Researchers, the focus is on specific measurements or measurement processes related to or of value for survey research on or about the use of electronic-based communication platforms. The intention with the chapters in this section is to provide short and efficient introductions to particular measurement options. Readers should find resources here so central to their own research efforts that they will want to keep the entire volume well within a quick reach. Several of the authors for this volume hope to find an economically viable option for offering a database with downloadable versions of the measures profiled here. We also hope to add to that database of downloadable files on a regular basis.

Rodney A. Reynolds
Azusa Pacific University, USA
(on leave from Pepperdine University, USA)

Robert Woods
Spring Arbor University, USA

Jason D. Baker
Regent University, USA

Acknowledgments

We thank God for successful completion of this project. We are thankful for the support of our colleagues, publisher and student assistants as we labored on this project. Our colleagues provided solid contributions to this handbook and demonstrated a commitment to excellence throughout the editorial process. Our editorial representatives, particularly Kristin Roth, demonstrated patience and extreme cooperation as we went through the different stages of development and production. Sara Reed also provided valuable support throughout the process. Several graduate research assistants, including but not limited to Melissa Macaskill and Sharon Berry, provided important administrative and research support at key moments along the way. Last, and certainly not least, we thank our families for their continued support behind the scenes in ways that allow us to pursue such scholarly projects. To all of these key players we extend our deepest gratitude.

Section I
Usage of Online
Surveys and Measurements

In this first section of the Handbook of Research on Electronic Surveys and Measurements, the focus is on the details of using online surveys to do research. In these 23 chapters, the readers will encounter details (at various levels) on issues related to online surveys and research. Several of the later chapters in this section direct the reader to broader issues that should be of particular concern to researchers who use electronic-based communication platforms.

Chapter I
E–Survey Methodology

Karen J. Jansen
University of Virginia, USA

Kevin G. Corley
Arizona State University, USA

Bernard J. Jansen
The Pennsylvania State University, USA

ABSTRACT

With computer network access nearly ubiquitous in much of the world, alternative means of data collection are being made available to researchers. Recent studies have explored various computer-based techniques (e.g., electronic mail and Internet surveys). However, exploitation of these techniques requires careful consideration of conceptual and methodological issues associated with their use. We identify and explore these issues by defining and developing a typology of "e-survey" techniques in organizational research. We examine the strengths, weaknesses, and threats to reliability, validity, sampling, and generalizability of these approaches. We conclude with a consideration of emerging issues of security, privacy, and ethics associated with the design and implications of e-survey methodology.

INTRODUCTION

For the researcher considering the use of electronic surveys, there is a rapidly growing body of literature addressing design issues and providing laundry lists of costs and benefits associated with electronic survey techniques (c.f., Lazar & Preece, 1999; Schmidt, 1997; Stanton, 1998). Perhaps the three most common reasons for choosing an e-survey over traditional paper-and-pencil approaches are (1) decreased costs, (2) faster response times, and (3) increased response rates (Lazar & Preece,

1999; Oppermann, 1995; Saris, 1991). Although research over the past 15 years has been mixed on the realization of these benefits (Kiesler & Sproull, 1986; Mehta & Sivadas, 1995; Sproull, 1986; Tse, Tse, Yin, Ting, Yi, Yee, & Hong, 1995), for the most part, researchers agree that faster response times and decreased costs are attainable benefits, while response rates differ based on variables beyond administration mode alone.

What has been lacking in this literature, until recently, is a more specific and rigorous exploration of e-survey methodology. In this chapter, we focus on the methodological issues associated with designing and conducting e-surveys. We include additional issues relating to these methodological areas gathered from our own experience in conducting e-survey research. We begin by defining the domain of electronic surveys, and develop a typology of the various e-survey approaches that are possible with today's technology. This typology is important because methodological issues can vary depending on whether we are employing an e-mail, Web-based, or point-of-contact survey; yet these different approaches have frequently been treated synonymously in the literature (e.g., Simsek & Veiga, 2000; Stanton, 1998). We then review what we know and what we do not know about e-survey data reliability, validity, and generalizability. Finally, we consider several emerging concerns associated with designing and implementing computer-based surveys including survey security, ethical issues associated with how and when data is captured, and privacy concerns. A version of this chapter was presented at the 2000 Academy of Management Annual Meeting (Corley & Jansen, 2000).

We define an electronic survey as one in which a computer plays a major role in both the *delivery* of a survey to potential respondents and the *collection* of survey data from actual respondents. We use the term mixed-mode surveys (c.f., Schaefer & Dillman, 1998) to describe surveys that offer alternative response formats (e.g., e-mail solicitation with an option to print and return a paper-and-pencil survey).

A Typology of E-Surveys

One can categorize the collection of survey data via computers into three main categories based upon the type of technology relied upon to distribute the survey and collect the data: (1) point of contact; (2) e-mail-based; and (3) and Web-based. Disk by mail was once a common method (Higgins, Dimnik, & Greenwood, 1987; Witt & Bernstein, 1992), but it is used less so now.

Point-of-contact involves having the respondent fill out an e-survey on a computer provided by the researcher, either on-site or in a laboratory setting (Synodinos, Papacostas, & Okimoto, 1994), for organization members who do not use computers in their jobs (Rosenfeld, Booth-Kewley, Edwards, & Thomas, 1996). Point-of-contact surveys have also been popular among researchers wishing to have tight control over the context of the study (i.e., lab based).

The second electronic data collection technique is the e-mail-based survey. E-mail-based surveys are generally defined as survey instruments that are delivered through electronic mail applications over the Internet or corporate intranets (Kiesler & Sproull, 1986; Sproull, 1986). E-mail-based surveys are generally seen as being delivered more cheaply and faster than traditional paper-and-pencil surveys; however, they still require the researcher to manually code the data into a database after receiving completed surveys. Researchers have extensively used e-mail surveys within corporations and online user groups (Corman, 1990; Kiesler & Sproull, 1986; Mehta & Sivadas, 1995; Sproull, 1986; Thach, 1995).

The final form of electronic survey, and the technique currently receiving the most interest from researchers (e.g., Stanton, 1998; Zhang, 2000), is the Web-based survey. They are generally defined as those survey instruments that physically reside on a network server (connected to either an organization's intranet or the Internet), and that can be accessed only through a Web-browser (Green, 1995; Stanton, 1998). Because a Web-based survey is actually created through the use of a coding language, the potential exists for the survey to change based upon previously answered questions (e.g., providing a different set of questions based on reported tenure in the organization). In addition, these surveys can use animation, voice, and video to enhance the user's experience. For example, one study provided a sidebar of events that occurred in the year of the respondent's self-reported birth date to assist the respondent with recall as well as to maintain motivation to respond to the survey (Witte, Amoroso, & Howard, 2000). Finally, Web-based surveys are often connected directly to a database where all completed survey data is categorized and stored for later analysis (Lazar & Preece, 1999; Schmidt, 1997). Web-based surveys can be either sampled or self-selected. The sampled category describes respondents who were chosen using some sampling method (i.e., randomly selected from larger population), notified of the chance to participate, and directed to the survey's Web site. In contrast, the self-selected category includes those respondents that happen across the survey in the course of their normal browsing (e.g., search results, Web advertisement, etc.) and are not proactively solicited by the researcher.

REVIEW OF THE LITERATURE

A rapidly expanding body of literature on electronic survey techniques reflects a growing concern among researchers as to the methodological issues associated with their use (Couper, 2000; Dillman, 1978, 1991; Fink, 1995; Fowler, 1995; Krosnick, 1999; Sudman, Bradburn, & Schwarz, 1996). Much of this literature has focus on the methodological issues of e-surveys, or comparing Web vs. other survey methods (Leece, Bhandari, Sprague, Swiontkowski, Schemitsch, Tornetta et al., 2004). These issues include the following sections.

Reliability

Recent work (e.g., Davis, 1999; Richman, Kiesler, Weisband, & Drasgow, 1999) has found a strong degree of measurement equivalence between computer-based and paper-and-pencil formats, although others report lower response rate (Crawford, Couper, & Lamias, 2001). There appear to be techniques to improve response rates, however (Fowler, 1995). Data quality is also a unique

threat to e-surveys; however, recent automation tools (e.g., Jansen, 1999, 2004; Witte et al., 2000) allow for data checking.

Validity

According to Cook and Campbell (1979), selection is a threat to validity when an effect may be attributed to the differences between the kinds of people in each experimental group. Instrumentation is a threat when an effect might be due to a change in the measuring instrument between pretest and posttest, rather than due to the treatment's differential effect at each time interval (Cook & Campbell, 1979). A pervasive threat is in actually changing an e-survey between time periods and administrations. The electronic development and maintenance of the survey makes it quite simple (and tempting) to make changes during the course of data collection, especially when multiple waves of data are collected over time; for example, see Zhang (2000) and Jansen (1999).

Sampling and Generalizability

As with traditional survey methods, decisions regarding sampling and generalizability are important ones when considering the use of e-surveys. The interested reader can find more detailed information about specific survey methodologies in Simsek and Veiga (2000) for e-mail surveys, and Witte et al. (2000) and Kaye and Johnson (1999) for Web-based surveys.

Emerging Issues

The issues of reliability, validity, and sampling and generalizability are similar to those encountered when using a traditional pencil-and-paper survey. The presence of technology does provide additional issues that must be considered in order to effectively collect survey data electronically, namely security/access, privacy, and ethics. With security, a researcher must be able to restrict access to only those people solicited to participate. Prior research has summarized the privacy issues associated with Internet survey research (Cho & LaRose, 1999); the ethical dilemmas in how data is captured electronically and how those procedures are communicated to the respondent.

IMPLICATIONS AND ADDITIONAL CONSIDERATIONS

A researcher must then decide which e-survey approach is best suited for the particular research project under consideration. No one e-survey type is inherently better than the others. Each approach has its benefits and drawbacks, especially when considering issues of time, money, and target population. The following section outlines the benefits and drawbacks of each approach as a way to summarize our discussion of the methodological implications of e-surveys (see Table 1).

The point-of-contact approach provides several benefits to organizational researchers. First, their use circumvents most software compatibility and

computer access problems. Second, they ensure that all respondents, regardless of computer access or position in the organization, complete the identical instrument. This approach can also afford the researcher (if the programming know-how is available) the ability to take advantage of increasingly advanced technology to provide multiple-question formats on the instrument, or to have data captured directly into a database program. The drawbacks to this approach can be consequential though, and should be taken into consideration before designing a project around point-of-contact technology. These drawbacks include the cost of supplying the equipment to the respondents, scheduling their time to interact with the equipment, the potential for time-consuming development of the instrument as well as the time-consuming task of meeting with all of the respondents, and finally, this approach may limit the number of respondents a researcher can reach in a given amount of time.

E-mail surveys provide the researcher with the ability to reach a large number of potential respondents quickly and relatively cheaply,

Table 1. Benefits and drawbacks of e-survey approaches

Approach	Benefits	Drawbacks
Web-based (both solicited and non-solicited; *italicized applies to non-solicited only*)	• Turnaround time (quick delivery and easy return) • Ease of reaching large number of potential respondents • Can use multiple question formats • Data quality checking • Ease of ensuring confidentiality • Can provide customized delivery of items • Can capture data directly in database	• Time-consuming development • Potential for limited access within target population • Potential for technology problems to decrease return rate • Security issues may threaten validity or decrease return rate • *Lack of control over sample* • *Potential for bias in sample*
Email-based (both embedded and attached; *italicized applies to attached only*)	• Turnaround time (quick delivery and easy return) • Ease of reaching large number of potential respondents	• Possibility of incompatible software • Potential for limited access within target population • Confidentiality issues may decrease return rate • *Respondents comfort level with software and attachment process*
Point of Contact	• No software compatibility issues • Fewer computer access issues • Access to populations without computers • Identical instrument across all respondents • Technology available for multiple question formats • Potential to capture data directly in database	• Cost of equipment • Scheduling time with respondents • Finding acceptable location • Potentially time-consuming development • Potential for time consuming data collection effort • May not be able to reach large sample

and to receive any completed surveys in a correspondingly short amount of time. However, as with all technology, there can be drawbacks that counter these benefits of time and money. E-mail surveys may be limited in the number of potential respondents they reach due to lack of access to a computer, to the Internet, or to an e-mail account. Issues of software compatibility must be addressed, along with the potential reliability issues present when differences in technological comfort exist among participants, especially for attached e-mail surveys. Finally, because e-mail messages usually contain some identifier of the sender, confidentiality issues may arise with e-mail surveys, serving to decrease the return rate.

Finally, Web-based surveys, while the most technologically advanced, also come with their own set of positives and negatives that must be weighed before implementation. On the benefit side, Web-based surveys are similar to e-mail-based surveys in that they provide a short turn-around time, and can reach a large number of potential respondents quickly. In addition, Web-based surveys can easily take advantage of advancing technology to provide multiple-question formats, direct database connectivity, data quality checking, customized instrument delivery, and guaranteed confidentiality, all of which can serve to improve the reliability of the data. The drawbacks can be serious, depending on the targeted population and goal of the research project, because they involve time-consuming development, limited access to potential users (only those with Internet access), potential technological problems, and the possibility of poor security threatening the validity of the study. In addition, self-selected Web surveys are likely to result in biased samples and provide little to no control over the sample.

Design and Planning Considerations

Regardless of which type of e-survey is chosen, there are two additional design considerations that should be explored. First, the choice of a particular survey methodology does not imply that solicitation and follow-up requests use the same approach. We encourage researchers to consider using mixed-mode designs, in keeping with the unique requirements of the study and the target population (c.f., Lazar & Preece, 1999; Sproull, 1986).

The second consideration focuses on different approaches for planning for, and coping with, technical malfunctions. Simsek and Veiga (2000) state that an "advantage of a WWW survey is that it is always present and available while [e-mail] is inherently episodic." In actuality, of course, both forms of delivery suffer from the same threats (transmission errors, network availability, or network overload), while point of contact can have its own technical troubles. As a recommendation, we caution researchers to consider the possibility of their occurrence early in the survey design process, and the impact outages can have on subsequent response rates and substantive research issues. A second recommendation is that care should be taken to design user-friendly and informative error screens or instructions when the survey is unavailable. Additional fail-safes can be designed, such as providing alternate routes or means of completing the survey when it is inaccessible.

Once researchers get beyond the obvious benefits associated with using e-surveys, we must acknowledge the importance of careful design, development, and testing, which we may not be as familiar with in developing paper-and-pencil surveys. Software is now available to help create HTML forms (Birnbaum, 2000), and many firms are emerging that specialize in the design and development of electronic surveys. Some of these alternatives may be quite costly, and care must be taken that the survey and database design represent the researcher's desires. However, if used appropriately, these services can help to offset the time and knowledge requirements associated with effectively designing and implementing a computer-based survey.

CONCLUSION

Researchers attempting to take advantage of organizations reaching the point where computers and Internet access are common, and organizational members are comfortable interacting with electronic media, are beginning to use computer-based surveys as a way to reach large numbers of respondents quickly and inexpensively. However, the design and implementation of e-surveys involves unique methodological issues that researchers must consider. We have addressed the various electronic techniques, and clarified their methodological implications in the hope that the changing technologies faced by researchers do not result in a growing suspicion of e-survey data, but instead serve to raise the standards of what we consider to be a strong survey methodology.

REFERENCES

Birnbaum, M. H. (2000). SurveyWiz and FactorWiz: JavaScript Web pages that make HTML forms for research on the Internet. *Behavior Research Methods, Instruments, & Computers, 32*(2), 339-346.

Cho, H., & LaRose, R. (1999). Privacy issues in Internet surveys. *Social Science Computer Review, 17*(4), 421-434.

Cook, T. D., & Campbell, D. T. (1979). *Quasi-experimentation: Design and analysis issues for field settings.* Boston: Houghton Mifflin Company.

Corley, K. G., & Jansen, K. J. (2000). *Electronic survey techniques: Issues and implications.* Paper presented at the Academy of Management Annual Meeting, Toronto, Canada.

Corman, S. R. (1990). Computerized vs. pencil and paper collection of network data. *Social Networks, 12*, 375-384.

Couper, M. (2000). Web surveys: A review of issues and approaches. *Public Opinion Quarterly, 64*(4), 464-494.

Crawford, S. D., Couper, M. P., & Lamias, M. J. (2001). Web surveys: Perceptions of burden. *Social Science Computer Review, 19*(2), 146 - 162.

Davis, R. N. (1999). Web-based administration of a personality questionnaire: Comparison with traditional methods. *Behavior Research Methods, Instruments, & Computers, 31*(4), 572-577.

Dillman, D. A. (1978). *Mail and telephone surveys.* New York: John Wiley & Sons.

Dillman, D. A. (1991). The design and administration of mail surveys, *Annual Review of Sociology* (pp. 225-249). Palo Alto, CA: Annual Reviews.

Fink, A. (1995). *The survey handbook* (Vol. 1). Thousands Oaks, CA: Sage.

Fowler, F. J. (1995). *Improving survey questions: Design and evaluation* (Vol. 38). Thousand Oaks, CA: Sage Publications.

Green, T. M. (1995). *The refusal problem and nonresponse in on-line organizational surveys.* Unpublished doctoral dissertation, University of North Texas, Denton, TX.

Higgins, C. A., Dimnik, T. P., & Greenwood, H. P. (1987). The DISKQ survey method. *Journal of the Market Research Society, 29*, 437-445.

Jansen, K. J. (1999). *Momentum in organizational change: Toward a multidisciplinary theory.* Unpublished doctoral dissertation, Texas A&M University, College Station, TX.

Jansen, K. (2004). From persistence to pursuit: A longitudinal examination of momentum during the early stages of strategic change. *Organization Science, 15*(3), 276-294.

Kaye, B. K., & Johnson, T. J. (1999). Research methodology: Taming the cyber frontier. *Social Science Computer Review, 17*(3), 323-337.

Kiesler, S., & Sproull, L. S. (1986). Response effects in the electronic survey. *Public Opinion Quarterly, 50*, 402-413.

Krosnick, J. A. (1999). Survey research. *Annual Review of Psychology, 50*, 537-367. Annual Reviews.

Lazar, J., & Preece, J. (1999). Designing and implementing Web-based surveys. *Journal of Computer Information Systems, 39*(4), 63-67.

Leece, P., Bhandari, M., Sprague, S., Swiontkowski, M. F., Schemitsch, E. H., Tornetta, P., Devereaux, P., & Guyatt, G. H. (2004). Internet vs. mailed questionnaires: A randomized comparison. *Journal of Medical Internet Research, 6*(3), e30.

Mehta, R., & Sivadas, E. (1995). Comparing response rates and response content in mail vs. electronic mail surveys. *Journal of the Market Research Society, 37*(4), 429-439.

Oppermann, M. (1995). E-mail surveys: Potentials and pitfalls. *Marketing research, 7*(3), 28.

Richman, W. L., Kiesler, S., Weisband, S., & Drasgow, F. (1999). A meta-analytic study of social desirability distortion in computer administered questionnaires, traditional questionnaires, and interviews. *Journal of Applied Psychology, 84*(5), 754-775.

Rosenfeld, P., Booth-Kewley, S., Edwards, J. E., & Thomas, M. D. (1996). Responses on computer surveys: Impression management, social desirability, and the big brother syndrome. *Computers in Human Behavior, 12*(2), 263-274.

Saris, W. E. (1991). *Computer-assisted interviewing, 80.* Newbury Park: Sage.

Schaefer, D. R., & Dillman, D. A. (1998). Development of a standard e-mail methodology: Results of an experiment. *Public Opinion Quarterly, 62*, 378-397.

Schmidt, W. C. (1997). World-wide Web survey research: Benefits, potential problems, and solutions. *Behavior Research Methods, Instruments, & Computers, 29*(2), 274-279.

Simsek, Z., & Veiga, J. F. (2000). The electronic survey technique: An integration and assessment. *Organizational Research Methods, 3*(1), 92-114.

Sproull, L. S. (1986). Using electronic mail for data collection in organizational research. *Academy of Management Journal, 29*(1), 159-169.

Stanton, J. M. (1998). An empirical assessment of data collection using the Internet. *Personnel Psychology, 51*, 709-725.

Sudman, S., Bradburn, N. M., & Schwarz, N. (1996). *Thinking about answers: The application of cognitive processes to survey methodology.* San Francisco: Jossey-Bass Publishers.

Synodinos, N. E., Papacostas, C. S., & Okimoto, G. M. (1994). Computer-administered vs. paper-and-pencil surveys and the effect of sample selection. *Behavior Research Methods, Instruments, and Computers, 26*(4), 395-401.

Thach, L. (1995). Using electronic mail to conduct survey research. *Educational Technology, March-April*, 27-31.

Tse, A. C. B., Tse, K. C., Yin, C. H., Ting, C. B., Yi, K. W., Yee, K. P., & Hong, W. C. (1995). Comparing two methods of sending out questionnaires: E-mail vs. mail. *Journal of the Market Research Society, 37*(4), 441-446.

Witt, K. J., & Bernstein, S. (1992). *Best practices in disk-by-mail surveys.* Paper presented at the Fifth Sawtooth Software conference, Sun Valley, ID.

Witte, J. C., Amoroso, L. M., & Howard, P. E. N. (2000). Research methodology: Method and representation in Internet-based survey tools —Mobility, community, and cultural identity in

Survey2000. *Social Science Computer Review, 18*(2), 179-195.

Zhang, Y. (2000). Using the internet for survey research: A case study. *Journal of the American Society for Information Science, 51*, 57-68.

KEY TERMS

Electronic Survey: Survey in which a computer plays a major role in both the *delivery* of a survey to potential respondents and the *collection* of survey data from actual respondents.

E-Mail-Based Surveys: Survey instruments that are delivered through electronic mail applications over the Internet or corporate intranets.

Mixed-Mode Surveys: Surveys that offer alternative response formats (e.g., e-mail solicitation with an option to print and return a paper-and-pencil survey).

Point-of-Contact Survey: Having the respondent fill out an e-survey on a computer provided by the researcher, either on-site or in a laboratory setting.

Web-Based Survey: Survey instruments that physically reside on a network server (connected to either an organization's intranet or the Internet) and that can be accessed only through a Web browser.

Chapter II
Web Survey Design

Qingxiong Ma
Central Missouri State University, USA

Mary McCord
Central Missouri State University, USA

ABSTRACT

The Web survey design chapter covers the process of creating a Web (online) survey system. Along with technical requirements, the chapter gives instruction and examples for four stages of Web survey design: determine survey requirements, design initial survey system, pilot test, and system modification. In the determine survey requirements section, the authors direct the reader through steps that design a questionnaire form with data types that will meet the survey requirements. The chapter includes examples of design and coding procedures to be used for Web surveys. In the design initial survey system stage, issues such as user interface design, database design, and application interface design are covered, and recommendations are given. After the survey system is built, the chapter outlines procedures for a pilot test, giving solutions for debugging the system, and how to increase response rate. The chapter ends with methods to revise the system before its final use.

INTRODUCTION

According to Kerlinger (1986), research employs surveys to discover sociological or psychological variables' incidence, distribution, and interrelations. To conduct a survey, researchers today have several different options to choose from, ranging between the traditional paper-and-pencil survey to a Web-based survey. A Web-based survey has advantages over other survey types in that it sharply reduces the cost of data collection, eliminates the interviewer (and their bias) completely (Tourangeau, Couper, & Conrad, 2004), increases responses to sensitive questions (Turner, Ku, Rogers, Lindberg, Pleck, & Sonenstien, 1998), can incorporate images, audio, and video (Couper, Tourangeau, & Kenyon, 2004), and offers higher quality data due to built-in checks that prohibit respondent errors (Dillman, 2000; McCullough, 1998). In a population where each member has Web access, a Web survey can achieve comparable response rates (Kaplowitz, Hadlock, & Levine, 2004).

In this chapter, we define a Web survey as a type of survey using Web technology and server-client architecture. Many surveyors also integrate

Web technology with e-mail to inform participants of the Web address. There are several options for generating Web-based surveys. A Web survey author may develop the entire system themselves (self-development), or use commercial survey services (commercial development). Here, we assume you want to implement a pure self-developed and self-administered Web survey system.

A self-designed and administered survey system has many advantages over commercial survey systems. Researchers have more control over the system. It is easier to monitor the survey and back up the database regularly, and it is flexible so the researcher can fix unexpected problems promptly. Self-designed and administered systems can more easily comply with an organization's security policy, and make the system stable and reliable. For example, a survey designer may choose to host the Web survey on a Linux machine, which is widely recognized as a more secure system than other systems such as Windows. It also allows the researcher to better protect the respondents' privacy, because the researcher has actual control on what data to collect, and how to handle the collected data after the research is completed. Finally, it is cost effective if the researcher possesses the necessary hardware and software. If you have a nice, working computer and fast, Internet access, there is basically no financial cost involved to develop and administer the system.

This chapter provides guidelines for designing a Web survey system. It is for researchers who are not familiar with online surveys, but are interested in them and intend to deploy this approach in their research. To be practical and meaningful, we will design a Web-based survey system for computer icon research as an illustration.

Chapter at a Glance

This chapter will help you do the following:

- Determine survey requirements
- Design initial survey system

- Pilot test
- System modification

DETERMINE SURVEY REQUIREMENTS

The first stage in designing a Web survey system is preparation. Generally, as a designer, two categories of requirements need to be considered: content or questionnaire design, and technical design.

Content Consideration

Just as in paper-based surveys, the researcher must outline the objectives of the survey, determine questions to conceptualize the variables in the research problem, determine question types, determine the sample method, and consider scales and anchors (Bailar & Lanphier, 1978). For human-subject related research, the survey generally includes at least three parts. Part one has two pages, a cover letter page and demonstration page. Part two is the main question part, which is directly related to research questions in your study. Last is part three, which is a "thank you" page.

Technical Considerations

Technically, you need a computer that can be used as the server to run the survey system. You also need to have fast Internet access. Generally, the software configuration on the server can follow Table 1. If you have Windows (i.e., Windows XP) installed on your system, we recommend you use IIS (Internet Information Service) as the Web server. Correspondingly, you should use MS SQL server or Access as the database management system. For researchers with little computer experience, the Microsoft Windows system is easy to configure due to its familiar user interface. However, a Linux-based system is

Table 1. Software configuration on the server

Operating system	Windows	Linux/Unix
Web servers	IIS	Apache
Database systems	SQL server or Access	MySQL
Web-editing applications	FrontPage, Dreamweaver,	Dreamweaver
Scripting languages	ASP with VBscript or Javascript	PHP, Cold Fusion
Object-oriented language	ASP.net with VB.net, C#, or C++	JSP with Java

cheaper, more secure, and has lower requirements on the server hardware.

You are assumed to understand basic HTML code and know how to use MS FrontPage and Access database management applications.

DESIGN INITIAL SURVEY SYSTEM

Initial survey system design includes user interface design, database design, and application interface design.

Human Interface Design

The principle effort in the Web survey process concerns transforming paper-based instruments or main-question pages into Web forms, and incorporates user interface design. The tools that can be used for this purpose include MS FrontPage, Dreamweaver, Flash, or Cold Fusion software. The following are some general guidelines:

1. The designer should consider what kind of form component should be used to collect the data in the Web form. Although most of the questions can be directly transformed from paper based to Web based, some questions need to be redesigned. Some survey questions can be presented in a shorter way. For example, questions about educational background or working experience can be transformed into radio button, check box, or pull-down components. Of those, the pull-down menu will save space and makes the survey physically look short. Generally, for close-ended questions, a radio button, check box, or pull-down menu are generally used; for open ended questions, a text box is most appropriate.

2. Split long surveys into multiple pages. This division has two benefits. One benefit is that because long forms can easily make people tired, shortening the form avoids respondent fatigue, and thus reduces the drop-out rate. Another advantage is that it can minimize data loss. Since participants are very busy and they might be interrupted at any time during the survey completion process, short forms with more chances of submission allow more data to be saved.

3. Spelling, nice font, and appropriate background colors are important factors to consider. A good interface design reflects your professionalism to the users, and might increase the data quality and response rate. Although color and font features are easily implemented in a Web-based survey, their use has to be carefully planned. The interface design should appeal to the sample subjects, because different user groups have different interface preferences. For example, children like a colorful and animated interface, while professional adults like a white or solid background. In addition to color or font, the use of images should be very carefully weighed. If the images clarify the question (a brand image, etc.) it should be used, but otherwise, visual embellishments do not increase motivation or decrease fatigue of respondents, and definitely affects their answers (Couper et al., 2004).

4. Last, but not least, put the status bar on each page so that participants are aware of their

Figure 1. Create Web prototype using tools such as FrontPage

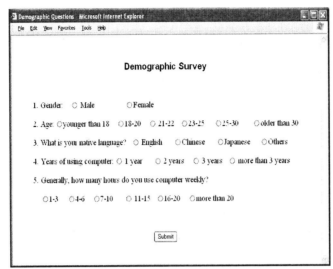

Figure 2. HTML code

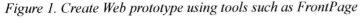

progress and can decide whether they have enough time to complete the survey before they give up.

Designing the initial system is important. It not only determines how the questions will be presented to the participants, but also determines the structure of the database, which will be discussed next. Figure 1 is the screen print of demographic questions designed by using FrontPage; Figure 2 is the cleaned HTML code for this page.

Database Design

When designing the database, the following questions should be asked:

1. What database system should be used? The decision can be made based on Table 1. In our example, since we use IIS Web server on a Windows XP, we can either use SQL Server or Access. SQL server is more powerful and has better performance for an online system,

but it also requires better hardware. If you do not have a powerful computer and only have a small number of participants in your survey, you can use Access. In the example, we used Access as our database management system.

2. The researcher codes each question in the interface (Web form) and matches them to field names in the related database. For example, "Q1" refers to the first question in both the form field of the Web survey and the field name of the database table. Therefore, the designer must decide the variable's (field/column) name, width, and data type. Generally, column names should be short and easy to understand.

3. How many tables should be created? Generally, one table is simplest to create and easiest to use for data analysis. In the example, we have multiple tables because we have different subject groups. Storing their responses separately will make the data analysis process simpler and easier. Although it is possible to design a fully functional Web-based database system, it is not the purpose of this chapter, and not addressed here. To simplify the database related activity, we will only allow the users to add or update records.

Figure 3 is the screen print of MS Access table design view for the example's database design.

Application Interface Design

This part lets the Web server save the data collected from participants into the database. Following Table 1, there are two kinds of scripting language you can choose: ASP and PHP. Our example used ASP. However, if it is a Linux-Apache environment, PHP is your better choice. Although there are many tutorials on the topics of "ASP" or "PHP programming" that can help you create online survey systems, we will show you the technique through an example.

After the participants click the "submit" button, two tasks are expected to be accomplished: the data in the Web-page form should be saved into the database and a new Web page should be displayed. In our example, the next page after the demographic questions page holds questions about icons, and is named En_P_Q01.asp. Figure 4 shows the interface.

This process is illustrated by the following three steps:

1. rename the HTML files as asp files.
2. open the HTML file of the demographic

Figure 3. Microsoft Access database

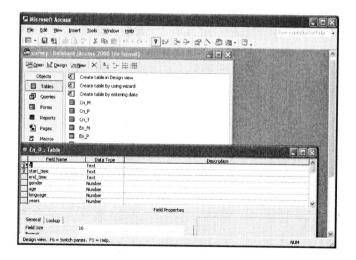

Figure 4. First question page

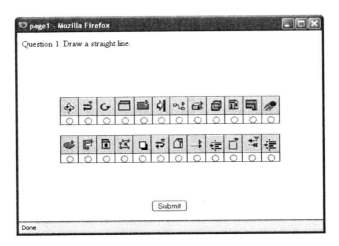

Figure 5. Database connection code example in ASP

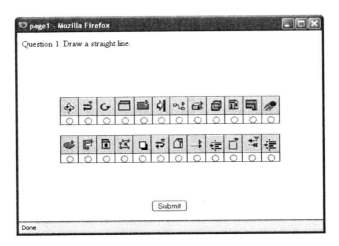

questions page (Figure 2) and change the <form> tag into <form method="POST" action=En_P_Q01.asp>. This means after a user clicks the submit button, the Web server should execute the file En_P_Q01.asp

3. open the HTML file (En_P_Q01.asp) and insert appropriate scripting code in the head part. The code for our example is displayed in Figure 5.

The code is an example of ASP script using VBscript. The same function can also be accomplished by PHP script. The purpose of each

statement is explained in the comments (the words after the symbol '). In Figure 5, the major parts are separated by a blank line, and the function and purpose of each part is "commented" out. Further knowledge on VBscript and ASP are available online. Many tutorials are written on how to access databases (Kroenke, 2005, p.146).

To save the response for the first question in the sample, several options can be used. One way is to use the same approach as that explained in the example for demographic questions, by rewriting the query statement in Figure 5. Since there is only one value to store, and in order to reduce the chances of database access and eliminate similar coding again and again, a hidden input textbox can be used to pass the value.

PILOT TEST

The survey instrument has to be pretested through a pilot study before administrating the final survey. The purpose of a pilot study is to evaluate the instrument for content validity and to identify any potential problems, such as understandability and operationability. Because the use of the computer itself may have an impact on instrument reliability, the survey should be both pretested and implemented online (Litaker, 2003). In order to increase response rates, a mailing protocol should be designed, and some incentive to the respondents should be provided (Tuten, Galesic, & Bosnjak, 2004).

The system should be tested with different browsers before soliciting the participants.

Often beginning Web-survey designers are shocked that the forms they carefully and beautifully made preview fine in FrontPage, but display quite differently in a Web browser other than MS Internet Explorer. DreamWeaver avoids these discrepancies among browsers. Of course, the forms could be coded directly in HTML, but that is usually outside the range of a beginner's skill.

When using business e-mails to contact participants, the time and day to send is critical. Since it is a business e-mail account rather than private, most people check it during working hours. Experience indicates that Monday through Thursday has the highest response rate, decreasing dramatically along a weeklong timeline. Generally, most of the respondents fill out the survey on the first day. The number of responses by the second day is reduced to about half, and the third day is almost half again. After the third day, there are almost no replies. Since your survey request might be buried in the spam, it could be very easily overlooked. In the initial contact e-mail, it should indicate that the results of the study would be available free for respondents upon request, and it might offer an incentive, such as ten percent of the respondents to be randomly selected to receive $25 in cash for participation.

Screen the Initial Responses

The purpose of screening the initial responses is to identify the following issues. For example:

1. How many respondents had multiple submissions?
2. How many respondents started the survey; how many of them gave up and did not complete the survey?
3. What is the initial response rate?
4. When is the best time to solicit participation?

Some respondents may complete the questionnaire several times. If two responses share the same IP address and are submitted with the same Web browser, you can assume they are from the same respondent. Respondents may resubmit because in order to make sure the survey instrument is submitted successfully, they click the submit button more than once. The other possible reason is confusion about how an incentive that was offered will operate. Respondents may believe that by submitting multiple surveys, their chance of winning will increase. Make it clear in your introductory page(s) that respondents can enter the drawing only once, and any other entry will be removed.

Antispamming programs may block e-mails that include a $ sign and /or outside link(s) or e-mails, a sender's name or e-mail address that is not listed in the receiver's e-mail system, or an e-mail with repeated subject or content. In order to avoid the chance that your initial contact be blocked on the server before it reaches the expected receiver, use different subjects and send each message one by one. A high turnover rate in some business areas may reduce your response rate. In addition, many organizational policies do not allow employees to respond to unsolicited mail surveys. Many organizations are very sensitive and concerned that answering an unsolicited online survey might expose the business's security policies and practices, which may facilitate computer hackers to attack their systems. Some candidates may fear that answering an unsolicited e-mail may expose their personal information, while others may justifiably be concerned about viruses and cookies that may be downloaded from a Web-based survey.

SURVEY SYSTEM MODIFICATION

The system design process is iterative. This revision process also has two aspects: content and technical design.

Content Revision

Based on the feedback from the respondents in the pilot study, some modifications may need to be made to the instrument. For example, some respondents may find a question unclear, or its scale may be confusing. You should pretest your instrument until a final version is achieved. Look for items with high missing rates. These may be the items that need to be revised.

Once the content is eliciting the quality and type of response you want, you must validate the instrument. This is done through factorial analysis, which is beyond the scope of this chapter. A way to bypass issues of validity and reliability is to use previously tested instruments.

Technical Revision

There are four main issues involved in revising a Web survey technically: client/server data valida-tion, security, system performance, and availability and testing with different browsers and Web-server configurations.

Data Validation

Considering the anonymity of respondents using the Internet, data validation is a concern. Data validation can be implemented on both client and server sides. On the client side, data validation requires the respondent to answer certain critical form items before they are allowed to submit the form. For example, if an item is still blank, and the respondent hits the "submit" button, a box or window asking them to return and answer question # "x" will appear. This feature should be used carefully, since overuse can lead to respondent frustration and survey abandonment. On the other hand, if some questions are not answered because of forgetfulness, a reminding message box is very helpful. This function can be easily implemented by using Web-editing tools such as MS FrontPage.

Sometimes it is necessary to differentiate data from respondents in case some of them submit multiple times. Thus, more information about the respondents can be collected. Some "hidden" fields, including information on IP addresses, the name and version of the Web browsers used, and submission time for each form, can signal multiple responses. This is only for survey validation purposes. This information would not be used for research analysis or reported in the research. This function can be implemented on the server side.

System Availability, Performance, and Security

Technically, collecting data using e-mails and Web surveys has two concerns. First, the electronic survey resides on a machine (Linux, Windows, etc.). If many people access the system at the same time, the system might freeze. Thus, you should reconfigure the maximum number of sessions accessing the Web server to a certain number such as 50 or 100. You should make sure the server is available 24 hours a day, 7 days a week. You should close unnecessary access ports, and use some kind of firewall to protect your server.

Second, the fewer times the database is accessed, the better. The server might be very busy during data collection. If the server has low performance, data might be lost, or participants might experience some unexpected difficulties such as system freezing or "server busy" error messages. Thus, in order to have a faster and more stable system, you should reduce the number of database connections (form submissions).

Third, the link used to collect the data should be secure. The best way to relieve respondent's fears of privacy violations is to use a Secure Socket Link or some other form of secure link that resists hacking.

REFERENCES

Bailar, B. A., & Lanphier, C. M. (1978). A pilot study to develop survey methods to assess survey practices. *American Statistician, 32*(4), 130-133.

Couper, M. P., Tourangeau, R., & Kenyon, K. (2004). "Picture this!" *Public Opinion Quarterly, 68*(2), 255-267.

Dillman, D. A. (2000). *Mail and Internet surveys: The tailored design method.* New York: John Wiley & Sons.

Kaplowitz, M. D., Hadlock, T. D., & Levine, R. (2004). A comparison of Web and mail survey response rates. *Public Opinion Quarterly, 68*(1), 94-101.

Kerlinger, F. N. (1986). *Foundations of behavioral research* (3rd ed.). Fort Worth: Holt, Rinehart and Winston, Inc.

Kroenke, D. M. (2005). *Database concepts* (2nd ed). Englewood Cliffs, NJ: Pearson/Prentice Hall.

Litaker, D. (2003). New technology in quality of life research: Are all computer-assisted approaches created equal?. *Quality of Life Research, 12*, 387-393.

McCullough, D. (1998). Web-based market research ushers in a new age. *Marketing News, 32*(19), 27-28.

Tourangeau, R., Couper, M. P., & Conrad, F. (2004). Spacing, position, and order: Interpretive heuristics for visual features of survey questions. *Public Opinion Quarterly, 68*(3), 368-393.

Turner, C. F., Ku, L., Rogers, S. M., Lindberg, L. D., Pleck, J. H., & Sonenestein, F. L. (1998). Adolescent sexual behavior, drug use, and violence: Increased reporting with computer survey technology. *Science, 280*(5365), 867-874.

Tuten, T. L., Galesic, M., & Bosnjak, M. (2004). Effects of immediate vs. delayed notification of prize draw results on response behavior in Web surveys. *Social Science Computer Review, 22*(3), 377-385.

KEY TERMS

Client Side Data Validation: Using a program's function to validate that the user's input is within certain parameters or requirements before the data is submitted to the server.

Database Management System: Special software to create and maintain a database and enable applications to extract the data they need without having to create separate files or data definitions.

Hidden Fields: Web controls such as a text box that does not show to the end user, but functionally can pass a value between Web pages.

Self-Designed/Self-Administrated Survey System: A survey system developed completely by the author and under the author's control.

Software Configuration: The software that makes up a system. To "configure" software is to choose options between different sets of systems (i.e., a "Windows"-based system or "Linux"-based system).

Web Editor: A tool or application that can be used to create, edit, and publish Web pages or Web sites. Most tools include a human interface editor and an HTML editor.

Web Server: A computer that stores Web documents and makes them available to the rest of the world. A server may be dedicated, meaning its sole purpose is to be a Web server, or nondedicated, meaning it can be used for basic computing in addition to acting as a server.

Web Survey: A type of survey using Web technology and server-client architecture.

Chapter III
Opportunities and Constraints of Electronic Research

Lynne D. Roberts
Crime Research Centre, University of Western Australia, Australia

ABSTRACT

In the past decade, many paper-and-pencil surveys and measures have been converted into electronic formats for administration via the Internet. In this paper, the evolution of methods of administering surveys and measures is briefly traced. This is followed by an outline of the major opportunities and constraints associated with conducting surveys and measures within the electronic environment. The paper concludes with a consideration of the appropriate situations for use of electronic surveys and measures.

BACKGROUND

Methods of administering surveys and measures have changed over time. Up until the 1970s, face-to-face interviewing was the dominant form of surveying. With the widespread acceptance of the telephone, telephone surveys became the standard methodology in the 1980s and 1990s, although mail surveys were also widely used (Dillman, 2000). The use of stand-alone computers enabled these methodologies to be advanced through the use of computer-assisted interviewing and computer-assisted testing (Epstein & Klinkerberg, 2001).

The Internet can be seen as providing a further stage in the evolution of survey and measure administration. With the introduction of the Internet, early electronic surveys were conducted using e-mail, typically in a text-only format (Topp & Palowski, 2002). The introduction of Hypertext Markup Language 2 (HTML 2) in 1994 provided the means for form-based surveys and measures on the World Wide Web, with the first academic surveys administered on the World Wide Web in 1995 (Birnbaum, 2004). Since this time, the growth of research studies conducted on the World Wide Web has been exponential (Birnbaum & Reips, 2005). A decade on from the first Internet surveys, it is timely to examine the advantages and disadvantages of electronic surveys and measures.

OPPORTUNITIES

The Internet provides a range of unique opportunities for the administration of surveys and measures. These are summarised in Table 1 and expanded.

Sampling

The Internet provides researchers with an additional or alternative source of research participants. Recruitment for research purposes can be conducted online through various methods including Web sites, postings to online communities, and e-mail. Alternatively, there are specialised commercial services that will select and contact samples from within their existing subject pools (Kraut, Olson, Banaji, Bruckman, Cohen, & Couper, 2004).

The Internet provides access to worldwide samples (Mitchell, Paprzycki, & Duckett, 1994, Smith & Leigh, 1997) without the problems associated with managing international time differences and working schedules (Foster, 1994). This reduces the reliance on college students or other

Table 1. Opportunities associated with electronics surveys and measures

- Sampling:
    - Access to world wide populations
    - Access to specialized and hidden populations
    - Potential for increased statistical power
- Potential savings:
    - Time
    - Resources
    - Costs
- Unique capabilities
    - Multimedia graphics and sound
    - Programmability
- Reduction in errors
    - Item completion
    - Automated data entry
- Advantages to the research participant
    - Convenience
    - Voluntary nature of participation enhanced
    - Tailored questions
    - Immediate feedback possible

local groups as research participants (Kraut et al., 2004). Even within a defined population (e.g. members of an organisation), different samples may be obtained using electronic recruitment and surveying (Ross, Tikkanen, & Mansson, 2000).

The Internet also provides increased access to hidden or specialised populations. For example, Duncan, White, and Nicholson (2003) used the World Wide Web to successfully recruit and survey "successful" illicit drug users (i.e. those not presenting for treatment or arrested), producing the largest known sample of this group (nearly 2,000 in the first 3 months of the survey). The large sample sizes enabled by Internet research can provide the researcher with increased statistical power (Hewson, Laurent, & Vogel, 1996).

Savings in Time, Resources, and Costs

The electronic administration of surveys and measures can be fast, as well as resource- and cost-efficient. Online recruitment reduces the time and cost associated with the recruitment of subjects (Kraut et al., 2004). The dispatch and turn-around time in electronic research is faster than that for off-line research (Kiesler & Sproull, 1986; Mitchell et al., 1994; Thach, 1995). Distribution lists can be set up on e-mail programs to send surveys to large groups simultaneously. Where all stages of the survey process (contact, response, and follow up) are conducted electronically, substantial savings can be made in the amount of time taken for fielding a survey (Fricker & Schonlau, 2002).

Internet research removes the need for a physical laboratory and the continued presence of researchers/research assistants. The requirements for physical space, resources, and paper are diminished. The reduction of paper used is an environmentally friendly measure (Schuldt & Tooten, 1994). The time and resources associated with data entry are reduced or removed.

The major additional costs of administering survey and measures electronically are the fixed costs of hardware, software, programming, and determining sampling frames, (Fricker & Schonlau, 2002; Simsek & Veiga, 2001). However, once established, there are minimal variable costs for each new research subject (Kraut et al., 2004; Simsek & Veiga, 2001). For example, Cobanoglu, Warde, and Moreo (2001) compared the cost of fax, mail, and electronic administration of a survey for a sample of 100. The fixed costs associated with design were higher for the electronic survey than other modes, but the variable costs (e.g., printing, organising, and sending surveys) per unit in the electronic condition were nil, providing Web surveys with the lowest overall cost. The price differential would increase rapidly with larger sample sizes.

Unique Capabilities

There are unique capabilities associated with the use of electronic surveys and measures. First, surveys and measures administered via the Internet can utilise multimedia graphics and sound. The use of visually attractive Web sites, interesting material, a high-speed site, and incentives for participation may increase participation (Reips, 1996). Second, electronic surveys and measures are programmable. Complex item branching based on previous responses can be used to ensure the content of surveys and measures remain relevant to respondents (Rosenfeld, Booth-Kewley, & Edwards, 1993; Tingling, Parent, & Wade, 2003) and survey questions and response options can be randomised (Fricker & Schonlau, 2002).

Reduction in Errors

Online research can reduce errors associated with survey completion and data entry. There are fewer item completion mistakes, and fewer items left blank in electronic responding (Kiesler & Sproull, 1986; Stanton, 1998; Truell, 2003). Missing data can be reduced or eliminated by programming World Wide Web surveys to give prompts or not

go onto the next question until a response has been given (Rhodes, Bowie, & Hergenrather, 2003) and validiation checks are possible to ensure that responses given are within range (Braithwaite, Emery, de Lusignan, & Sutton, 2003). The order in which respondents see questions can be controlled (Tingling et al., 2003). Automated data entry (data from World Wide Web surveys can be automatically written to a database) removes the errors associated with manual data entry, as there is no need for human transcription (Batanic, 1997). All these factors serve to improve the accuracy and completeness of the data obtained.

Advantages to the Research Participant

Electronic surveys and measure provide four main advantages to research participants. The first of these is convenience. The research can be conducted in the research participant's own home or office. There is no requirement to physically attend the researcher's environment. Second, the voluntary nature of participation is enhanced in online research. Reips (1996) argued that the ecological validity of research is increased, as the individual takes part in their own surroundings rather than in an artificial laboratory. Removed from the demand characteristics associated with the researcher's presence, individuals are free to decide whether or not they wish to participate (Foster, 1994; Reips, 1996), and can participate at their own leisure (Hewson et al., 1996). It is far easier for a research participant to withdraw consent and discontinue an experiment when sitting alone in front of their computer, than it is to walk out of an experiment in front of an experimenter and, possibly, peers. This has the potential to improve the quality of data collected, as "forced" research participation is removed. Third, electronic surveys and measures can be programmed to ensure respondents are asked only to respond to questions that are relevant to them (based on their previous responses), making the experience more enjoyable and less tedious. Finally, it is possible in some circumstances for the respondent to be given immediate feedback upon completion of the survey or measure (e.g. results of a personality test).

Constraints

While electronic surveys and measures present a range of opportunities for researchers, their use needs to be tempered by the constraints imposed. Possible constraints to the successful conduct of electronic surveys and measures are summarised in Table 2 and expanded upon.

Results Not Generalizable to the Population

The population of Internet users is not representative of the general population, although differences are diminishing rapidly, particularly in westernised countries, as more people go online. Using the

Table 2. Constraints associated with electronics surveys and measures

- Results not generalizable
    - Coverage error
    - Sample biases
- Poor response rates
- Possible non-equivalence of measures
- Lack of control over research setting
- Technological limitations
    - Hardware
    - Software
    - Technical knowledge
- Limitations imposed by service providers
    Time
    Cooperation and goodwill
- Limitations of the researcher
    - Technical knowledge
    - Netiquette
- Limitations of the research participants
    - Computer literacy
    - Hardware and software compatibility
    - Distractions

Internet as the only source of recruitment will restrict the samples selected to those who have Internet access, and the technical proficiency and comfort level required to complete electronic surveys and measures (Kiesler & Sproull, 1986; Thach, 1995). Because of the coverage error associated with the mismatch between Internet users and the general population, it is not possible to generalise the results from Internet samples to the general population as some groups within the general population will not be represented (Best & Krueger, 2002; Couper, 2001; Fricker & Schonlau, 2002; Kypri, Stephenson, & Langley, 2004).

Even if we take "all Internet users" as our population of interest, there is currently no sampling frame that can be used to obtain a random sample, reducing the generalizability of the results due to the potential bias of samples obtained (Kraut, et al., 2004). Further potential bias in results may be due to self-selection. Less frequent Internet users are both less likely to respond and more likely to make a late response (Lukawetz, 2000, cited in Birnbaum, 2004). One option to overcome these potential biases in samples is to conduct analyses separately for each substratum of the sample (Birnbaum, 2004).

Poor Response Rates

Response rates are of key importance because the potential for nonresponse error increases as response rates fall. Where surveys or measures are advertised widely online, there may be no way of estimating the response rate. Even where response rates can be calculated, electronic surveys have been associated with lower response rates and higher drop-out rates than traditional surveys (Fricker & Schonlau, 2002; Kraut et al., 2004). In the 1990s the mean response rate to Internet surveys was estimated at 39.6% (Cook, Heath, & Thompson, 2000), with response rates declining over time (Sheehan, 2001). This decline has been attributed to increased surveying and spam, the threat of viruses, and that the novelty aspect of completing surveys online has passed (Sheehan, 2001).

Possible Nonequivalence of Measures

Not all measures retain their equivalence across paper-and-pencil and electronic modes of administration, threatening the reliability and validity of research. Speeded tests and measures of beliefs, cognitions, and affect towards computers are particularly susceptible to measurement nonequivalence. For a comprehensive review of this literature, see Roberts (this volume).

Lack of Control Over the Research Setting

Where surveys and measures are administered electronically and completed by respondents in their own environment, researchers have no control over the research setting. This means they cannot tailor instructions to an appropriate level for an individual, clear up any misunderstandings (unless contacted by e-mail), or ensure the survey or measure is completed in an environment free from distractions.

TECHNOLOGICAL LIMITATIONS

Researchers require a range of computer equipment, software, and large, fast, reliable servers to conduct electronic surveys and measures. They also require, or need access to, someone who has the technical knowledge to operate the equipment and to program measures and surveys (Topp & Palowski, 2002). Technology is fallible, and connection to the Internet can never be guaranteed for any particular point in time. Overseas links can go down, net-splits can occur, and servers can crash. These situations are often beyond the researcher's control, but may impact negatively upon the research process.

Software applications can place constraints on the layout and content of online surveys and measures. Internet users vary in the Internet software used, and programs used may not always be compatible with the software used by the researcher. For example, the format of e-mail questionnaires may change between sending and receipt if incompatible programs are used (Batinic 1997; Oppermann, 1995). The layout and presentation of World Wide Web surveys takes longer than paper-and-pencil surveys, and this may be particularly the case where effort is extended to make sure that surveys are readable across software programs (Thach, 1995).

Limitations Imposed by Service Providers

In addition to the limitations of the technology itself, Internet service providers and their representatives can constrain Internet-based research. Time limitations are imposed by service providers on some Internet accounts, particularly during busy periods. Some Internet service providers may cut off access if the user has been "idle" (has not sent a command over the Internet) for a specified period of time. This means that some research participants may lose their connection while completing a survey or measure. Research is reliant on the cooperation and good will of server and site administrators. Administrators can remove or alter surveys, measures, or Internet access.

Limitations of the Researcher

The use of electronic surveys and measures will be affected by the researcher's familiarity and comfort level in using the Internet and the particular software applications. The etiquette of Internet usage has been termed "netiquette." Online researchers need to comply with the prevailing netiquette in their dealings with Internet users. While scientific surveys are more readily accepted by the Internet public than commercial e-mail surveys (Batinic

& Bosnjak, cited in Batinic, 1997), mail-outs to large numbers of addresses obtained from Internet sources (e.g. from newsgroups) may be regarded as "spam attacks." In retaliation, Internet users may refuse to participate in research, or flame or mail bomb the message sender (Batinic, 1997; Foster, 1994; Mehta & Sivadis, 1995). Researchers need to familiarise themselves with the prevailing netiquette to identify potential "breaches" in their research process.

Limitations of the Research Participants

Research participants must have computer and Internet access, be computer literate, and have hardware and software compatible with that of the researcher in order to participate in electronic surveys (Fricker & Schonlau, 2002). Internet users may find their ability to respond to surveys and measures constrained by their typing speed, their ability to express their ideas in writing, and their experience on the Internet and with the software being used. Research participants may be subject to both distractions in their off-line environment (e.g., interruptions, phone calls) and distractions in their virtual environment (e.g., instant messages or e-mails from other users). The research participant may choose to engage in other activities simultaneously, diminishing their attention to the completion of the research.

Sabotage Attempts

It is possible for an individual to easily respond multiple times to online surveys and measures. Methods to prevent multiple submissions include asking people to refrain from answering more than once, removing incentives for multiple submissions, programming the server to accept only one submission per IP address, and supplying individual passwords. Multiple submissions can be detected through examining identifiers such as IP addresses and passwords (Birnbaum, 2004).

CONCLUSION

In this chapter, the opportunities and constraints of electronic surveys and measures have been outlined. The decision on whether or not to use electronic surveys and measures in any particular situation should be made after consideration of the opportunities and constraints as they apply to the proposed research. The first consideration is whether the population of interest can be "captured" through electronic recruitment. Where a representative sample of the general population is required (e.g., epidemiological surveys), the coverage error is likely to be too high to justify recruitment through the Internet. In contrast, where access is required to a hidden/specialised population, it may prove ideal. Care needs to be taken to adopt an approach that will maximise the response rate. A second major consideration is the skills and knowledge of the researcher, and their access to the computing equipment, software, back-up, and programming skills required for the proposed research. A further consideration is whether the proposed survey/measure has established measurement equivalence across modes of administration. Where measurement equivalence has not been established, additional time and resources need to be allocated. If, after a consideration of the constraints, electronic surveys and measures seem a viable option, they offer a raft of opportunities for researchers.

REFERENCES

Batinic, B. (1997). *How to make an Internet-based survey?* Paper presented at SoftStat '97, 9th Conference on the Scientific Use of Statistical Software, Heidelberg, Germany. Retrieved March 30, 1998, from http://www.psychol.uni-giessen. de/~Batinic/survey/faq_soft.htm

Best, S. J., & Krueger, B. (2002). New approaches to assessing opinion: The prospects for electronic mail surveys. *International Journal of Public Opinion Research, 14*(1), 73-92.

Birnbaum, M. H. (2004). Methodological and ethical issues in conducting social psychology research via the Internet. In C. Sansone, C. C. Morf, & A. T. Panter (Eds.), *Handbook of methods in social psychology* (pp. 359-382). Thousand Oaks, CA: Sage.

Birnbaum, M. H., & Reips, U.-D. (2005). Behavioral research and data collection via the Internet. In R. W. Proctor & K. P. L. Vu (Eds.), *Handbook of human factors in Web design* (pp. 471-491). Mahwah, NJ: Lawrence Erlbaum Associates.

Braithwaite, D., Emery, J., de Lusignan, S., & Sutton, S. (2003). Using the Internet to conduct surveys of health professionals: A valid alternative? *Family Practice, 20*(5), 545-551.

Cobanoglu, C., Warde, B., and Moreo, P. J. (2001). A comparison of mail, fax, and Web-based survey methods. *International Journal of Market Research, 43*(4), 441-452.

Cook, C., Heath, F., & Thompson, R. L. (2000). Meta-analysis of response rates in Web- or Internet-based surveys. *Educational and Psychological Medicine, 60*(6), 821-836.

Couper, M. P. (2001). Web surveys: A review of issues and approaches. *The Public Opinion Quarterly, 64*, 464-494.

Dillman, D. A. (2000). *Mail and Internet surveys: The tailored design method* (2nd ed.). New York: John Wiley & Sons, Inc.

Duncan, D. F., White, J. B., & Nicholson, T. (2003). Using Internet-based surveys to reach hidden populations: Case of nonabusive illicit drug users. *American Journal of Health Behavior, 27*(3), 208-218.

Epstein, J., & Klinkenberg, W. D. (2001). From Eliza to Internet: A brief history of computerized assessment. *Computers in Human Behavior, 17*, 295-314.

Foster, G. (1994). Fishing with the net for research data. *British Journal of Educational Technology, 25*, 91-97.

Fricker, R. D., & Schonlau, M. (2002). Advantages and disadvantages of Internet research surveys: Evidence from the literature. *Field Methods, 14*(4), 347-367.

Hewson, C. M., Laurent, D., & Vogel, C. M. (1996). Proper methodologies for psychological and sociological studies conducted via the Internet. *Behavior Research Methods, Instruments, and Computers, 28*, 186-191.

Kiesler, S., & Sproull L. S. (1986). Response effects in the electronic survey. *Public Opinion Quarterly, 50*, 402-413.

Kraut, R., Olson, J., Banaji, M., Bruckman, A., Cohen, J., & Couper, M. (2004). Psychological research online: Report of Board of Scientific Affairs' Advisory Group on the Conduct of Research on the Internet. *American Psychologist, 59*, 105-117.

Kypri, K., Stephenson, S., & Langley, J. (2004). Assessment of nonresponse bias in an Internet survey of alcohol use. *Alcoholism: Clinical and Experimental Research, 28*(4), 630-634.

Mehta, R., & Sivadas, E. (1995). Comparing response rates and response content in mail vs. electronic mail surveys. *Journal of the Market Research Society, 37*, 429-439.

Mitchell, T., Paprzycki, M., & Duckett, G. (1994). *Research methods using computer networks.* Retrieved June 30, 1996, from http://www.uni.loeln.de/themen/cmc/text/mitchell.94.txt

Oppermann, M. (1995). E-mail surveys-Potential and pitfalls. *Marketing Research: A Magazine of Management and Applications, 7*(3), 28-33.

Reips, U. (1996, October). *Experimenting in the WWW*. Paper presented at the 1996 Society for Computers in Psychology Conference. Chicago, IL.

Rhodes, S. D., Bowie, D. A., & Hegrenrather, K. C. (2003). Collecting behavioral data using the World Wide Web: Considerations for researchers. *Journal of Epidemiology and Community Health, 57,* 68-73.

Roberts, L. D. (2006). Equivalence of electronic and offline measures. In R. A. Reynolds, R. Woods, & J. D. Baker (Eds.), *Handbook of Research on Electronic Surveys and Measurements*. Hershey, PA: Idea Group Reference.

Rosenfeld, P., Booth-Kewley, S., Edwards, J. E., & Thomas. M. D. (1993). Computer-administered surveys in organizational settings: Alternatives, advantages, and applications. *American Behavioral Scientist, 36,* 485-511.

Ross, M. W., Tikkanen, R., & Mansson, S-A. (2000). Differences between Internet samples and conventional samples of men who have sex with men: Implications for research and HIV interventions. *Social Science & Medicine, 51,* 749-758.

Schuldt, B. A., & Tooten, J. W. (1994). Electronic mail vs. mail survey response rates. *Marketing Research: A Magazine of Management and Applications, 6,* 36-39.

Sheehan, K. B. (2001). E-mail survey response rates: A review. *Journal of Computer-Mediated Communication, 6*(2). Retrieved January 10, 2005 from http://www.ascusc.org/jcmc/vol6/issue2/sheehan.html

Simsek, Z., & Viega, J. F. (2001). A primer on Internet Organizational surveys. *Organizational Research Methods, 4*(3), 218-235.

Smith, M. A., & Leigh, B. (1997). Virtual subjects: Using the Internet as an alternative source of subjects and research environment. *Behavior*

Research Methods, Instruments, and Computers, 29(4), 496-505.

Stanton, J. M. (1998). An empirical assessment of data collection using the Internet. *Personnel Psychology, 51,* 709-725.

Thach, L. (1995). Using electronic mail to conduct survey research. *Educational Technology, 35,* 27-31.

Tingling, P., Parent, M., & Wade, M. (2003). Extending the capabilities of Internet-based research: Lessons from the field. *Internet Research, 13*(3), 223-235.

Topp, N. W., & Palowski, B. (2002). Online data collection. *Journal of Science Education and Technology, 11*(2), 173-178.

Truell, A. D. (2003). Use of Internet tools for survey research. *Information Technology, Learning, and Performance Journal, 21*(1), 31-37.

KEY TERMS

Coverage Error: Any mismatch between the target population and the sampling frame. Coverage errors for Internet-based surveys are large where the target population is the general population, because Internet research excludes the proportion of the population who do not have Internet access.

Dropouts: People who commence a survey or measure but do not complete it. The number of dropouts in electronic research may increase when the measure/survey design is not user-friendly, is lengthy, or where there are technical difficulties.

Item Branching: Conditional rules used to direct a respondent to the next relevant item, based on their response to one or more previous items in a survey or measure. Item branching can be used to skip questions, increase or decrease the difficulty of items, or terminate the survey/measure.

Netiquette: The etiquette, or social rules, associated with communicating online. Netiquette may vary across virtual environments.

Response Rates: A measure of the number of people completing research compared to the number of people in the sample. There are many methods of calculating response rates including raw response rate (completed/total sample), adjusted response rate (completed/total sample minus those who do meet criteria), and participation rate (completed/total sample minus those not contactable). Low response rates are problematic as respondents may differ from nonrespondents.

Sample Representativeness: Refers to the extent to which characteristics observed within the sample are present in the population.

Sampling Error: The error associated with surveying/measuring from a sample of the population rather than the whole population.

Self-Selection: Where individuals can elect to "opt-in" to a survey. Self-selection is a form of selection bias because it may result in systematic differences between participants and nonparticipants. For example, only people who have strong views on the subject matter of a survey may choose to participate.

Chapter IV
Electronic Data
Collection Methods

Mohini Singh
RMIT University, Australia

Stephen Burgess
Victoria University, Australia

ABSTRACT

This chapter discusses the application of new technologies to scholarly research. It highlights the process, benefits, and challenges of online data collection and analysis with three case studies: the online survey method, online focus groups, and e-mail interviews. The online survey method is described as it was undertaken to collect and collate data for the evaluation of e-business in Australia. The online focus group research is described as it was applied to complete research on e-commerce with small business. The e-mail interviews applied to collect information from a virtual community of global respondents to assess the impact of interaction between members on B2C e-commerce. The research process, its advantages and disadvantages, are elaborated for all three e-research methods

INTRODUCTION

Information systems research, like most other research, addresses "how do we know what we know" and "how do we acquire knowledge" (Klein, Hieschheim, & Nissen, 1991). As emphasised by Mumford (1991), research is undertaken to make things better for the community as a whole. Depending on the epistemology that guides the research, information systems research can be embarked on by utilising both qualitative and quantitative methods. In this chapter, we discuss three online data collection methods: the online survey method, online focus groups, and online interviews via e-mail, by presenting them as three case studies. These case studies were research methods that were utilised to accomplish information systems research.

Popular traditional methods of collecting data in both qualitative and quantitative methods have been interviews, survey methods, and focus groups. However, recent developments in technology have made a significant impact on information systems and other social science research by automating the processes. Innovative tools and technologies can be applied to case study research, focus groups, surveys, as well as analysis of data, making research an interesting experience. Application of the Internet, electronic mail, chat, online discussion boards, and other tools are increasingly applied to research to capitalise on the benefits of reduced costs, quick responses, reaching out to a larger population sample, and easier data analysis. However, e-research methods that are new and unproven, and akin to innovations such as business to consumer (B2C) e-commerce, need acceptance by the respondents for expediency and application.

In this chapter, we present and discuss three e-research methods: online surveys, online focus groups, and e-mail interviews. The automated research processes, technologies applied, the approach, and benefits and challenges of these methods are discussed with three case studies.

The first case study is about an online survey undertaken to collect and collate data for the evaluation of e-business in Australia. The use of HTML pages, generating a tracking number to allow respondents to complete the survey at a later time, presentation of the Web pages, use of radio buttons and drop down menus, ability to capture all information by not allowing the respondent to proceed unless an answer to all questions was provided, are discussed at length, together with their implications for research. The benefits of linking HTML pages to a database for capturing responses and transporting it to statistical packages for analysis are explained. Although the advantages of technology applications to the research process are indisputable, this paper highlights the reasons why this method has not replaced traditional methods of data collection, and why mixed methods of data collection are more popular than electronic methods.

The second case study is an online focus group research undertaken to assist the completion of a Delphi study with online expert panels to understand the development of e-commerce in small business. Advantages of online focus groups in

enhancing Delphi studies, and reduced errors in responses for analysis and completion of research are explicated.

The third case study is an example of e-mail interviews carried out with a focus group (virtual community) with global participants. The focus group comprised virtual community members of an e-business. Responses to e-mail interviews were collated and analysed using the software package, NVIVO. The e-mail interview process, data collation, and analysis of responses, together with advantages and disadvantages of this method, are discussed at length in this paper.

An emphasis on issues for research identified from the analysis of the three electronic methods of data collection and an analysis is presented in the following section of the chapter. Future research trends with applications of technology, their impact on the research process, uptake and acceptance issues, bias, and infrastructure issues form the gist of this chapter.

LITERATURE REVIEW

The Internet and the World Wide Web continue to grow at a phenomenal rate. Their presence and applications have extended from defence systems to business, government, education, finance, and other sectors of the globe. The Internet is ubiquitous, and has an astoundingly increasing adoption rate. Widespread networking, together with the ease of publishing multimedia material on the Web, supports exchange of high quality documents including erudite data and information. The Internet and other new technologies such as voice recognition systems, e-mail systems, Internet telephony, and other innovative communication technologies, have enabled e-research both amongst industry and academia.

The Web sites and Web pages are potential sources of data in their own right, as well as supporting both quantitative and qualitative research (Bryman, 2004). Ethnographic studies on the

Internet, observed by Bryman, are possible if the cyberspace is observed as a place. Ethnography of life on the Internet entails participant observation that, according to Markham (as cited in Bryman, 2004), can be likened to interviews. However, the Internet has enabled online surveys, focus groups, and interviews for data gathering as well.

With the widespread adoption of e-mail among corporate, scholastic, and government populations, dissemination of survey material among such populations is now a lot easier (Smith, 1997). Smith also explains that e-mail research is an economic alternative to labour intensive and expensive face-to-face and/or telephone interviews. Despite some anomalies, Smith emphasised that e-mails are rapidly becoming an indispensable tool for gathering detailed information on selected populations. However, Pitkow, and Recker (1995) are of the opinion that e-mail-based surveys require a user to perform text entry that does not have a consistent structure, making it difficult for data collation and analysis. Responses to data have to be entered by humans (researchers), who are error prone.

Persuasive arguments for using e-mail surveys are extreme cost reduction, quick turnaround, ability to facilitate interaction between the researcher and respondent, collapsed geographic boundaries for research, user (respondent) convenience, and candid and extensive response quality (Cobanoglu, Warde, & Moreo, 2001; Mann & Stewart, 2002; Pitkow & Recker, 1995; Smith, 1997). E-mail is a significant method of Internet communication, and it is widely used (Chaffey, 2004).

Survey research is a popular form of enquiry (Alreck & Settle, 1995); however, online surveys via the Web using fill-in forms are, to some extent, replacing postal questionnaire surveys due to the advantages of reduced costs; point-and-click responses; structured responses; using an electronic medium for data transfer and collation; presenting questions visually for reinspection and review; imposing loose time constraints; access to surveys made easy via radio buttons; quick responses; and the ability to incorporate high quality images, complex graphs, audio, video, and animated graphics (Bauman & Airey, 2003; Cobanoglu et al., 2001; Pitkow & Recker, 1995; Smith, 1997). Taylor (2000) is of the opinion that online research is based on volunteer or convenient sampling rather than probability sampling, captures the unedited voice of the respondents, and is more effective in addressing sensitive issues.

Focus-group research method is a form of group interview in which there are several participants, a facilitator or moderator, a tightly defined topic for the questions, and the joint construction of meaning from interaction within the group (Bryman, 2004). Online focus groups, as described by Bryman (2004), can be synchronous and asynchronous. Synchronous focus groups are in real time, with contributions made more or less immediately after previous contributions (whether from the moderator or other participants). The only difficulty with this is if the participants are in different time zones. For asynchronous groups, the moderator might ask a question and then send an e-mail. The group members may respond later. Both synchronous and asynchronous focus groups can use conferencing software, e-mails, and Web sites. Bryman also emphasises that online focus groups will not replace their face-to-face counterparts. Instead, they are likely to be employed in connection with certain types of research topics where dispersed and inaccessible people are required to participate in the focus group.

Online focus group research is widely deployed to support Delphi studies. A Delphi study typically has no physical contact between participants, iterations (or "rounds" of refinement), controlled feedback (where results of the previous round are provided to respondents), and a statistical presentation of the group response (ASTEC, 1996).

Key aspects of a Delphi study typically are (ASTEC, 2000; Koenig, Heinzl, & von Poblotzki, 1995; Williamson, 2000):

- Sets of questions or issues are identified for the study.
- A panel of experts is used for obtaining data.
- There are two or more rounds where participants are requested to respond, in writing, to a shared document that summarises the evolving consensus and views of other participants.
- At the end of each round, a summary of the results of the previous round is prepared by the investigators and communicated to the participants.
- An opportunity is provided for respondents to reevaluate responses given in previous rounds in the light of the views of others.
- There is a systematic attempt to produce a consensus of opinion, as well as identify opinion divergence.
- It is most common for a consensus to develop, but if there is divergence, then this is identified and explained.
- The process terminates when consensus amongst participants has been reached or opinions have been stabilised so that they are unlikely to change further.

Computer-based Delphi studies allow for greater exploration of notions than "pencil-and-paper" responses that may be limited by the size of the study. It is easier to protect the anonymity of respondents and, especially if the discussion is conducted online, participants have more freedom about when they choose to respond and what they respond to (Williamson, 2000).

Advantages of online focus groups are they are cheaper than face-to-face interviews; participants who would normally be inaccessible can more easily be involved; interviewees and focus group participants can read what they had written in their replies; participants can better fit interviews in their own time, and do not have to travel to attend a focus group session; interviews do not have to be audio recorded, eliminating in-

terviewee apprehension about speaking and being recorded; accuracy of transcript is guaranteed; shy and quiet participants are likely to come to the fore, and overbearing participants are less likely to predominate; participants are less likely to be influenced by characteristics like age, ethnicity, or appearance and, similarly, participants are less likely to be affected by characteristics of interviewers or moderators (Bryman, 2004).

Although there are several important advantages of online focus group research, the disadvantages are that only people with access to online facilities can participate, and sometimes it is difficult for an interviewer to develop a rapport with interviewees. Probing is more difficult, and in asynchronous interviews, a longer time is required with the risk of discontinuance from the interviewees. The researcher cannot always be sure that the respondent is who he/she claims to be (Bryman, 2004).

E-mail research enables repeat participation and works well with focus groups. A traditional focus group described by Alreck and Settle (1995) typically consists of 8 to 12 people seated around a conference table with a group moderator who focuses their discussion on a series of topics or issues of interest to the research sponsor. Focus groups provide qualitative information rather than quantitative, and focus group research is regarded as exploratory (Alreck & Settle, 1995).

Technology has also enabled mix-mode research, employing more than one method of collecting data. Cobanoglu et al. (2001) are of the opinion that mixed-mode research usually yields a higher response rate. They further explain that mixed-mode research is especially useful when developing technologies are not widely available. Mixed-mode research may entail phone, fax, e-mail, and Web surveys. Cooper and Schindler (2003) advocate that mixed-mode research is utilised when earlier choices of research methods do not turn out to be satisfactory. They also suggest that although this method will incur the costs of the combined modes, the flexibility of tailoring a method to the unique situation is often an acceptable trade-off.

Although technology-based research has numerous advantages, it also has limitations. Smith (1997) is of the opinion that these methods lack cosmetic features such as a precise layout and font styles, it is difficult to include monetary and other tangible incentives, technological ability is sometimes unpredictable, and the extent of use is limited to a homogeneous society. Taylor (2000) advocates that online surveys generate more "don't knows" and "not sures" because respondents can see these options (as opposed to hearing these options), and that raw online data substantially underrepresent some groups. Response rates to some Web surveys have been more than mail surveys, whereas drastically less in others (Smith, 1997).

Literature on technology-based research is sparse, portraying views based on specific applications and outcomes. Due to the evolving nature of new technologies, new applications to research will result; however, more scholarly research is required on these methods to support their use in academic research.

METHOD

Three case studies are presented in this chapter from three separate research projects. The first case study is from an online survey undertaken in Australia to evaluate the value of e-business. The second case study in this chapter is research conducted via e-mail interviews with Amazon.com's virtual community members (a focus group) to understand their role in an e-business. All case studies presented and discussed in this chapter are exploratory studies investigating new ways of collecting, collating, and analysing data. Case studies included in this chapter are an interpretation of learning from the process and outcome.

CASE STUDIES

The three case studies are presented in the following section, describing the process and analysis of data. Advantages and disadvantages of each application are also included.

Case One: Online Survey of E-Business Organisations

Introduction

This research was accomplished via an online survey method and a mail survey method. Online surveys were considered to be the apt method of investigating e-business organizations since they are technology (Internet) based. Online surveys are quick, convenient, enable unlimited reach, seek a response to all questions, and responses are downloadable into a database and transportable to statistical packages for analysis. However, due to a disappointing response to online surveys, a mail survey was implemented to complete the research project.

Research Process

A set of questions to evaluate the performance of e-business in Australia was initially developed in MSWord. The questionnaire was developed in nine parts, with part one comprising of questions about the organization, and part two including questions to establish e-business development at the organization. These were open-ended, straightforward questions to ease the respondent to complete the rest of the questionnaire. Part three comprised of eight questions to measure operational measures, with a space to fill in a number to indicate the percentage of improvement. Parts four and five were presented as Likert scales to identify the improvements achieved from customers, suppliers, processes, internal orientation, and systems integration. Part six included nine questions soliciting a "yes" or "no" response to establish the online developments in transaction capabilities. Parts seven, eight, and nine were presented on Likert scales to determine the financial performance, e-business benefits, and problems encountered.

These questions were discussed and checked for validity with a number of colleagues in the School of Business Information Technology at RMIT University. Responses of other academics and researchers were taken into account, and the questions accordingly modified. Once we were satisfied that the questions would capture the value of e-business in Australia, a programmer was employed to convert the Word document file to HTML pages.

The questionnaire commenced with a brief explanation of how to proceed with the survey: about a random number (tracking number) that would be created by the system to enable respondents to note and use to complete the questionnaire at a later time or date if they wished. With this tracking number, they could start where they had left. A statement to ensure anonymity and security of data and information was also included.

The HTML pages were made up of one or more parts of the questionnaire, depending on the number of questions in each part of the survey, and the type of responses sought for the set of questions. Respondents were expected to provide answers with radio buttons, choosing an option from the drop down menus, or filling in a word or phrase in the space provided. Attention was given to the background colour of the HTML forms to ensure that it was pleasant to the eye, and all questions were legible and acceptably formatted to correspond to the section of the pages accessible on each screen. The whole questionnaire was presented in six HTML pages. At the end of each page, the respondent was asked to select the "submit" button and proceed to the next. The questionnaire was designed so that a respondent could not proceed to the next page unless he or she provided an answer to all questions on the page.

Sample Population

A database of e-business organizations was obtained from the University library. Business Who's Who (http://bwww.dnb.com/au/default.asp) is a database that lists Australian Businesses. E-business organizations were sorted initially by http://* and, at a glance, 1,390 company names were obtained. It was further sorted to see if all the top 500 companies were include in the list with http://* and >1000, on the assumption that these organizations would have adopted e-business and that they would have more than 1000 employees.

Dissemination Process and Responses Received

An e-mail was sent to 1,390 companies requesting them to participate in the project and pointing them to the URL for the survey. A short explanation of the objectives of the research and its importance was also included. Responses received included 407 bounced back e-mails, 9 auto responses of out of office, 14 replies asking us to take them off the mailing list, 17 polite e-mails asking us to take them off the list as it was their company policy not to respond to surveys, 22 rather rude e-mails of a variety of reactions were received within a week. Some of these were:

- "My time is valuable – $75 per hour. Please don't waste it unless you can pay for it."...
- "Sorry I can receive your e-mail, but I can't access the website. In order to do that, we need to use a separate machine which is dedicated for the Internet use. Sorry I can't help you."...
- "If you wish us to participate in a survey either put it in your e-mail or attach it. We do not chase around strange websites";

- "We do not wish to participate, kind regards"
- "Thank you but we do not wish to participate. Please remove us from your mailing list/database."

Usable responses were only 15. From the database, we could see that 22 had started, but did not complete the survey. With such a low response, at the end of a fortnight, a reminder e-mail was sent to 899 companies asking them to ignore the e-mail if they had already responded, as we had no way of predicting who would have responded. At the end of another 2 weeks, the number of usable responses went up to 32. With such a low response rate, an investigation of the company Web sites was undertaken to see if they were e-business organizations by clicking on the URL's of each business in the database. This eliminated another 175 companies. The dot.com crash did have an impact on Australian organisations as well.

Case One: Mail Survey

With 32 responses the findings would not have been valid; therefore, we sent the same questionnaire, word processed as a mail survey, to 724 companies. A polite note to thank them if they had already responded to the survey, the URL for the survey if they wished to respond online, a stamped envelope for the response, and assurance of security of data were mailed with a hard copy of the questionnaire in the mail out. The letter was addressed to the e-business manager. In the month following the mail out of the survey, the online responses increased to 91, and valid hard-copy responses received were 78. This research analysis is therefore based on a response rate of 23.3%.

Data Collation

The responses to the online questionnaire were transferred to a database created in MySQL. Each page in the questionnaire was represented as a table in the database, and each response to a question was recorded as an element in the table. The database was designed to store both numeric and alphanumeric data. The reason for using MySQL was that it was freely available, could handle a large database, it has been tried and tested as a database server, and could be linked to the HTML files on a Unix server via php scripts. It was a proven technology, easy to use and maintain, and supported by the University Information Technology infrastructure. The information from the database was transferred to spreadsheet in Excel, and the data from the paper responses were recorded on the same spreadsheet. Although this was very time consuming, it was important to have all data collated in the same format before it was imported in SPSS (a statistical package for analysis).

Assumptions

That all e-business organization managers would be computer literate and "click" oriented;

- That all e-business organization would be "high-tech" organizations with automated processes and communications.

Findings

From case study one, the following findings about online surveys are evident:

- Technology supports scholarly research, which is easier than more traditional methods;
- New technology "clicks" is still very new and unproven; therefore, it is not utilised to its full potentia;
- Procedure for setting up an online survey is the same as a traditional survey; the difference is in the dissemination process;
- The process of collating data from online surveys is simplified by integrated technologies;

- Tools employed to collect data (radio buttons, drop down menus, filling in gaps) are user friendly and user convenient;
- It is possible to capture an answer to all questions, making the research findings more meaningful;
- Although there is evidence of bias in the population surveyed online, technology leaders are shy to adopt automated systems;
- Response rate with technology-based research is poor;
- Negative and rude e-mails are clear indications of unfamiliarity of innovations in research and resistance to change;
- Mixed research methods (e-mail, mail survey, and HTML pages) are more promising than e-research; and
- Respondents can remain anonymous with online surveys.

Challenges

Getting respondents to accept online questionnaires (first experience, unable to follow instructions, a lack of trust, difficult to share information).

Case Two: Delphi Online Expert Panels

Introduction

This case actually describes two very similar instances of use of the Delphi technique and online expert panels for the purposes of testing and refining a model representing business strategies that small businesses could adopt when establishing a Web presence. The first instance occurred at Monash University, Australia in 2001, where one of the authors used the technique to conduct an expert panel comprising six experts from various backgrounds. The second instance is occurring at the time of writing (2005), where a PhD student of the author is conducting a similar method of

data collection, taking into account lessons learned from the first instance in 2001.

Research Process and Sample Population

In the 2001 study, six Australian academics with a research background in one or more areas of small business, the strategic use of information technology, and/or electronic commerce, were invited (and agreed) to participate in the study. It is not possible to claim that the viewpoints of these academics were representative of the viewpoints of all worldwide, or even Australian, academics in their respective areas. However, the participants were regarded as experts in their fields by their teaching and research records in their respective fields, and that their input to the study was very useful in refining the conceptual model that had been developed from the literature in those areas. In 2005, the five participants again had varied backgrounds that related to the areas being covered by the model (small business, electronic commerce and, in this instance, developing countries, as this was a focus of the study).

These particular studies suited the use of the Delphi technique based on Williamson's (2000) ideas that:

- The development of the model benefits from subjective judgements on a collective basis.
- The individuals and organisations contributing to the process come from diverse backgrounds with respect to experience and expertise (small business, information technology, electronic commerce, developing countries).
- More individuals are needed than can effectively interact in a face-to-face environment.

The "electronic" study also assisted to resolve some of the problems of the Delphi study that were discussed earlier. Delphi studies can be slow, costly, and time consuming, especially when having to gather experts together. This problem was reduced with the use of electronic communication. In the 2001 study, an online bulletin board was used to conduct the study. In the 2005 instance, a listserve is being used. This means that experts do not have to gather in one place. Another problem is the chance of participants misunderstanding the written input. This was reduced in the rounds of data collection by providing summarised versions of the overall responses, identifying consensus or divergence at each stage. In relation to the panel of experts being too like-minded, it was identified earlier that focus group members for each study were selected from different fields. In relation to anonymity, there are significant differences between the two instances. In 2001, each respondent was offered the chance to view summary results of the study as an incentive for participating, but remained anonymous. Each participant could view previous responses of all participants without knowing who they were, and the summary of each round reduced the chance of "investigator bias." However, this also meant that participants had the opportunity to comment upon responses from other participants, so the contributors were not exactly contributing on an equal basis in relation to when and how they made their responses. This was of little concern, as the main reason for the use of the technique was to establish if there was any discourse to act upon and to achieve eventual consensus. The same aim was there in 2005, but the difference is that the use of the listserve meant that the participants were not anonymous to each other. This technique was selected in the hope that one participant's response would turn up in the e-mail inbox of other participants and would prompt them to respond, which appears to be the case.

Outcomes

In 2001, the outcome of the study resulted in a more complex model than was originally proposed, with extra feedback loops added in for small business operators to revisit what they had carried out earlier in the planning process. In the 2005 study, the model is being refined according to feedback from the experts: in this instance providing more detail to its operation.

Data Analysis

The use of the Delphi technique using small online expert panels means that data analysis is fairly easy. Respondents' comments (usually one major set of comments per respondent per round) are analysed for themes, a summary of the responses is prepared, and the model revised to show in the new data collection "round" to respondents. The fact that there are a number of rounds allows for the reporting of the results and the development of the model to occur in a systematic fashion.

Advantages of the online focus group method include being able to solicit responses from participants electronically without having to ask them to be present at a particular location, being able to complete a Delphi study in a much shorter period of time, and data collection and collation was better managed without the need for too much transcription.

The only disadvantage was keeping all the participants engaged till the end.

Case Three: E-Mail Interviews with Amazon.com Virtual Community

Introduction

This research (Singh & Rose, 2004) was accomplished via e-mail interviews with a cohort of virtual community members at a large, well-established e-business, Amazon.com. The objectives of the e-mail interviews were to understand the interviewees' experiences of being a virtual community member (product reviewer and customer of Amazon.com), to discover the roles of virtual communities in e-businesses, and to understand information (about products) diffusion process via a virtual community.

Why Amazon.com

Amazon.com was selected because it is a large, well-established e-business that has existed since 1995. The product reviews from its virtual community members are a feature that has existed since 1995 and used as a sales enhancement technique. The virtual community features consist of a publicly available homepage for every Product Reviewer, which other B2C e-businesses (Barnes & Noble, EBay, Dymocks, Angus and Robertson, Buy.com, eToys, iVillage, eTrade) did not have, and publicly available e-mail addresses for Product Reviewers (virtual community members), which enabled the collection of interview data.

E-Mail Interviews

The research was carried out through the use of interviews via e-mail. This method allowed for data to be gathered from respondents around the world who are members of Amazon.com's virtual community. The use of e-mail interviews was appropriate for this research because virtual community members at Amazon.com are contactable only via e-mails, and they are from different parts of the world. These reviewers provide a publicly available information source on the usage of community at the Amazon.com Web site. This research was conducted in two parts. The aim of Part one, e-mail interviews, was to understand the interviewee's experiences as a virtual community member (product reviewer and customer), and to determine the contribution a virtual community makes to an e-business by understanding the information diffusion process about new products.

The interview questions in the e-mail comprised two sections addressing issues in relation to an interviewee as a prospective customer and the reviewer as a product reviewer. There were four and three questions in each section respectively.

Population Sample

At the time of the interviews, the Amazon.com virtual community consisted of 500 members. This was identified from the Amazon.com Web site (http://www.Amazon.com.com.com/exec/obidos/tg/cm/top-reviewers-list/-/1/ref=cm_tr_trl_top/103-8089675-7444662). However, only 84 of these reviewers publicly listed their e-mail addresses on the product review home page. Therefore, the questionnaire was sent to 84 of the 500 virtual community members.

Pilot Testing

The interview questions were pilot tested with seven postgraduate research students in the School of Business Information Technology at RMIT University. These students had substantial experience and knowledge of the Web, Internet, information technology, and research issues. Their responses were incorporated according to which minor modifications were made to the questionnaire.

E-Mail Interview Process

An introductory e-mail was sent on the 3rd of November 2001 to 84 members of Amazon's virtual community. This e-mail briefly explained the aims and objectives of the research project, and RMIT University ethics information. Twenty-three respondents replied agreeing to participate in the project. On November 19, 2001, the first set of questions was e-mailed to the 23 Amazon.com virtual community members. Within 5 days of sending the e-mail out, 14 replies were received. On November 27, 2001, the first questionnaire was sent again to the 9 members who did not respond. By December 9th, all 23 responses for the first set of questions were received.

The second part of the research aimed to further explore two major themes analysed from the first part of the research. On December 10, 2001, the second set of questions were sent to the same 23 interviewees. Within a period of 3 days, 15 people responded. On December 13, 2001, the second set of questions were resent to 8 interviewees who had not replied previously, gently reminding them of the importance of their response. Within 4 days another 3 replies were received. By December 17th, 18 responses for the second set of questions were received. The second questionnaire comprised two sections. The first five e-mail questions determined interviewee's experiences of interaction with other virtual community members. Section two was made up of technology questions regarding the Web site features. This part consisted of four questions.

Data Analysis

A software package, called Nvivo, was used to carry out thematic data analysis. The Nvivo software is designed to run on the Windows operating system and, therefore, has a user-friendly interface. It enables thematic analysis of data on a computer. It uses the abstract concept of a node to represent a category. The process of coding a document involves discovering and creating nodes. The software automatically creates a node for which it generates a name.

All interview e-mail transcripts received were imported into the Nvivo software. The first stage was coding of the documents. The actual process of coding an interview transcript involved reading the e-mail document on the screen and highlighting key words or phrases. Once a suitable text passage was highlighted, a node was created and a name given to the node, which represented the concept that described the highlighted text. After moving on to another e-mail response, if similar text was encountered, then the node was used again by selecting the relevant text and dragging it onto the node. Therefore, the process of coding the documents involved the decision to either create a new node (to represent a new concept) or reuse an existing node (for the reappearance of a concept in the text). The Nvivo software includes the ability to generate reports on all codes. This report contains information such as the full node name (for a tree node), and the number of characters, paragraphs, and documents coded for the node. The report can then be exported into a text file for reporting, or a spreadsheet such as Excel for generating graphs to show trends.

Assumption

This research was based on the following assumptions:

- Amazon.com reviewers were also Amazon's customers;
- That the Amazon.com hierarchical ranking of reviewers (http://www.Amazon.com.com/exec/obidos/tg/cm/top-reviewers-list/-/1/ref=cm_aya_bb_tr/104-0068777-0349564) represents a ranking of the most influential members of the online store's virtual community;
- That the respondents (virtual community members at Amazon.com) had e-mail skills, which meant that they were able to express their views electronically and had access to computers and the Internet; and
- That all reviewers gave an honest response.

Findings

The findings of the third case study are:

- E-mail interviews work well with small research projects (fewer questions on the screen).

- It is a successful research method that works well with focussed groups;
- It is easy to identify nonrespondents and send them reminders without annoying the others, therefore respondents are not anonymous;
- Unstructured responses to e-mail can be collated with software such as Nvivo for qualitative analysis.
- It is cost effective;
- Requires less effort, as one e-mail can be sent to the group by creating group lists;
- Enabled research with a cohort of respondents from different parts of the world (researcher was in Australia and the respondents were in different parts of the world); and
- If questionnaires are not very long, they do not have to be attached and can be sent as an e-mail.

Discussion

From the three case studies presented previously, a number of issues regarding electronic research methods for scholarly research were identified. These are discussed in the following section of the chapter.

Benefits

Technology is an Enabler of Electronic Research

With the application of technology, the case studies mentioned have clearly illustrated automated research processes of data collection, data collation, analysis and reporting. Electronic questionnaires are not entirely a new concept as they were used as early as 1985 (Sekaran, 1992) via data disks and personal computers hooked to networks using a computer package called CAPPA. However, the ease of questionnaire dissemination and integrated research processes supported by the Internet, which is ubiquitous, can be amalgamated with front-end and back-end systems, as illustrated in the first case study, and have further enhanced scholarly research.

Global Reach

Electronic research enables a researcher to obtain responses from people in different parts of the same country as well as to people in different parts of the world. International respondents can add richness to data for research analysis. As illustrated in the second case study, the research would not have been possible, as the virtual community members did not provide addresses other than their e-mails.

Cost Effective

With e-mails and online surveys, the costs of paper, printing, photocopying, and postage are drastically depleted. Although costs have to be incurred to set up e-research, once set up, it can be easily adapted to other projects with minor modifications to the software. Communication via e-mails contributes to substantial cost savings. It also helps continued contacts, allows for easily expressed gratitude, and supports increased response rates. Gentle reminders via e-mails, illustrated in case two, managed an excellent response rate.

Convenience

The use of e-mail for disseminating a research questionnaire is convenient because one e-mail is sent to many recipients by grouping them. "Group lists" are features supported by all e-mail software. With this method, the recipients are blind copied so anonymity is maintained and the researcher has to do it once only. The laborious tasks of folding paper, sealing envelopes, placing stamps on the envelopes, opening mailed responses, are not required in technology-based research. All files are stored electronically, again reducing the need for space, people, and filing.

Quick Response

Through the use of e-mails and online survey questions, returning the response is accomplished with the click of a mouse or by pressing a key on the keyboard. The respondents' time with folding paper, sealing the envelope, and sending it back is not necessary. The researcher is able to receive responses quicker via technology than by post, or face-to-face interviews.

Enhanced Responses

To achieve a satisfactory response rate, it is a better and cheaper way of sending out reminders than the postal system. For the research participants, sending back responses are managed with the click of a mouse in electronic research. Response rates determine the success of a research project.

Data Collation

As explained in the case studies, data collation and analysis processes are far superior in technology-supported research. Computing tools and techniques enable sophisticated approaches for data management, transfer, analysis, presentation, and reporting. Electronic research methods ease data collation processes with integrated technologies such as e-mails, HTML pages, databases, spreadsheets, reporting software, and other applications that smartly combine, and support data transfer and analysis without having to re-entering it.

E-Mail Research is a Practical Means of Gathering Data

The e-mail infrastructure already exists in most organizations, virtual communities, businesses, the education sector, and in private homes, making it a very practical tool to use for research. It is also possible to obtain e-mail addresses of different groups of people from directories, Web sites, and other publications. Application of e-mail to research is illustrated in both the case studies presented.

Online Focussed Group Research

Focussed group research is increasingly replacing surveys and face-to-face interviews with individuals. It is well supported with advancements in technology and, as illustrated in the second case study, works well as an electronic research method.

Challenge

The most important challenge apparent from the first case study is *respondent (user) acceptance* of technology-based research. For an acceptable response rate to meaningful scholarly research, it is imperative that users accept technology for their responses. Akin to B2C e-commerce, where the success is dependent on consumer acceptance, the success of electronic research methods is dependent on respondent acceptance. It is very clear from the first case study that in spite of all the benefits of electronic research methods, they are only feasible if users accept it as a means of responding. Although strategies for enhancing respondent acceptance are a further research issue, it is highly likely that the acceptance rate can be improved by using the approaches used for any innovation diffusion. Communication, education programs, promotion, assurance of secure transaction and trust, and familiarity with technology may assist acceptance.

- **Biased Population:** Technology-based research has a very strong bias, enabling responses only from those who have access to and knowledge of technology.
- **Technical Knowledge:** It is evident from the case studies that technical knowledge is required to set up and manage online research.

CONCLUSION

This chapter shows how quantitative research can be managed via online surveys, and qualitative research can be managed using e-mail interviews and online focus groups. It reveals that technology application has been extended to areas of scholarly research, although it is not very widely discussed. Technology-based research is an economic alternative to traditional methods. The value of technology-based research lies in reduced costs, quick responses, technology-supported data collation, analysis and reporting, easy dissemination of questionnaires, and easy-to-do follow-up and repeat research. Technology can be combined with applications such as Web sites, listserves, bulletin boards, and e-mails in various forms for scholarly as well as market research. The new trends in scholarly research are increasingly becoming technology dependent, despite its low user acceptance rates. The current research trend is a combination of technologies to support surveys, focus group research, and e-mail interviews, or the use of mix-methods for eliciting responses. Further research into strategies for user acceptance of technology-based research, keeping them engaged, anonymity, and motivation is required for electronic research methods in scholarly applications.

REFERENCES

Alreck, P. L., & Settle, R. B. (1995). *The survey research handbook.* Irwin McGraw-Hill.

ASTEC [Australian Science and Technology Council]. (1996). *Developing long-term strategies for science and technology in Australia: Findings of the study: Matching science and technology to future needs 2010.* Department of Industry, Science and Resources. Retrieved January 21, 2000, from http://www.astec.gov.au/astec/future/findings/index.html

Bauman, S., & Airey, J. (2003). *Effective use of the Internet for survey research.* Wirthlin e-Solutions. Retrieved May 21, 2003, from http://www.wirthlin.webaxxs.com/wintellitech/casro.htm

Bryman, A. (2004). *Social research methods* (2nd ed.). Oxford University Press.

Chaffey, D. (2004). *E-business and e-commerce.* Pearson Education Limited.

Cobanoglu, C., Ward, B., & Moreo, P. J. (2001). A comparison of mail, fax and Web-based survey methods. *International Journal of Market Research, 43,* 441-452.

Cooper, D., & Schindler, P. (2003). *Business research methods* (8th ed.). Columbus, OH: McGraw Hill.

Eaton, B. (1997). Internet surveys: Does WWW stand for 'Why waste the work?', *Quirk's Marketing Research Review*, June, Retrieved May 21, 2003, from http://www.quirks.com/article_print.asp?arg_articleid=244

Klein, H. K., Hieschheim, R., & Nissen, H. E. (1991). A pluralist perspective of the information systems research arena', information systems research: Contemporary approaches and emergent traditions. In *Proceedings of the IFIP TC8/WG 8.2 Working Conference on Information Systems Research Arena of the 90' Challenges, Perceptions and Alternative Approaches*, North-Holland, Netherlands.

Kochtanek, T. R., & Hein, K. K. (1999). Delphi study of digital libraries. *Information Processing & Management, 35,* 245-254.

Koenig, W., Heinzl, A., & von Poblotzki, A. (1995). *Major research subjects of business information systems science: The next ten years.* Institute of Business Information Systems Science, Frankfurt University. Retrieved January

21, 2000, from http://www.wiwi.uni-frankfurt.de/~ansgar/iwi9502/ iwi9502.html.

Lai, V. S. (2001). Issues of international information systems management: A perspective of affiliates. *Information & Management, 38*, 253-264.

MacElroy, B. (2000). Measuring response rates in online surveys. *Quirk's Marketing Research Review*, April. Retrieved May 21, 2003, from http://www.quirks.com/article_print.asp?arg_articleid=583

Mann, C., & Stewart, F. (2002). *Internet communication and qualitative research: A handbook researching online*. London: Sage.

Mumford, E. (1991). Information systems research—Leaking craft or visionary vehicle?'. In *Proceedings of the IFIP TC8/WG 8.2 Working Conference on Information Systems Research Arena of the 90' Challenges, Perceptions and Alternative Approaches* (pp. 21-49). North-Holland, The Netherlands.

Pitkow, J., & Recker, M. M. (1995). Using the Web as a survey tool: Results from the second WWW user survey. *Journal of Computer Networks and ISDN systems, 27*(6). Retrieved May 21, 2003, from http://www.cc.gatech.edu/gvu/user_surveys_2z-paper.html

Sekaran, U. (1992). *Research methods for business: A skill-building approach*. John Wiley and Sons, Inc.

Singh, M., & Rose, A. (2004, April 28-29). Electronic data collection methods: A discussion of online surveys and e-mail interviews. In *Proceedings of the Fourth European Conference on Research Methodology for Business and Management Studies (ECRM 2004)*, UK [CD ROM].

Smith, C. B. (1997). Casting the net: Surveying an Internet population. *JCMC, 3*(1). Retrieved May 21, 2003, from http://www.ascusc.orf/jcmc/vol3/issue1/smith/html

Taylor, H. (2000). Does Internet research work?: Comparing online survey results with telephone survey. *International Journal of Market Research, 42*, 51-63.

Williamson, K. (2000). Research methods for students and professionals: Information management and systems. *Topics in Australasian Library and Information Studies, No.16*. Centre for Information Studies, Charles Sturt University, Wagga Wagga, Australia.

KEY TERMS

Electronic Research Methods: Research methods undertaken using technologies. These include surveys via the Internet and the World Wide Web, online focus groups, and e-mail interviews. Electronic research methods automate the research processes of data collection, collation, and analysis. They are cost effective, convenient, solicit quick responses, support global reach, and encourage participation from people and complete responses. However, it entails a bias: only those with technology access and knowledge can respond.

E-Mail Interviews: Interviews undertaken via e-mails. An e-mail interview can incorporate a set of questions in one e-mail or an attached file with semistructured questions. It is convenient, time efficient, and enables input from participants around the world.

Online Focus Groups: Refer to group interviews with participants via technology. These can be synchronous or asynchronous. where contributions are made by participants, but are kept within the bounds of the topic by a focus group facilitator (in a similar manner to that which would occur with a face-to-face focus group). The advantage that focus groups have over other forms of data collection is that thoughts and ideas not previously considered by the researcher can often be generated by the "group" discussion. Online groups provide two further advantages. One is that they can help to solve the problems involved in trying to organise a focus group of participants that are great distances apart. The other advantage is that the focus groups can be organised in such a way that participants are anonymous.

Online Surveys: Survey research undertaken via the Internet and the World Wide Web. A URL, with the research questions as fill-in-forms pro-grammed in HTML, is presented. The responses are captured in a database linked to the HTML pages. Online surveys can incorporate spaces for responses, list boxes, or radio buttons. Pages can be programmed to solicit responses to all questions by restricting submission without answers, thereby enriching data collection. Online surveys are fast replacing postal questionnaire surveys.

Chapter V
Online–Questionnaire Design Guidelines

Joanna Lumsden
NRC Institute for Information Technology, IIT e-Business, Canada

ABSTRACT

As a new medium for questionnaire delivery, the Internet has the potential to revolutionize the survey process. Online (Web-based) questionnaires provide several advantages over traditional survey methods in terms of cost, speed, appearance, flexibility, functionality, and usability. Designers of online questionnaires are faced with a plethora of design tools to assist in the development of their electronic questionnaires. Little if any support is incorporated, however, within these tools to guide online questionnaire designers according to best practice. In essence, an online questionnaire combines questionnaire-based survey functionality with that of a Web page/site. As such, the design of an online questionnaire should incorporate principles from both contributing fields. Drawing on existing guidelines for paper-based questionnaire design, Web site design (paying particular attention to issues of accessibility and usability), and existing but scarce guidelines for electronic surveys, we have derived a comprehensive set of guidelines for the design of online questionnaires. This article introduces this comprehensive set of guidelines as a practical reference guide for the design of online questionnaires.

INTRODUCTION

As a new medium for questionnaire delivery, the Internet has the potential to revolutionize the survey process. Online (Web-based) questionnaires provide several advantages over traditional survey methods in terms of cost, speed, appearance, flexibility, functionality, and usability (Bandilla, Bosnjak, & Altdorfer, 2003; Dillman, 2000; Kwak & Radler, 2002). Online questionnaires can also provide many capabilities not found in traditional paper-based questionnaires: they can include pop-up instructions and error messages; they can incorporate links; and it is possible to encode difficult skip patterns, making such patterns virtually invisible to respondents. Despite this, and the introduction of numerous tools to support online questionnaire creation, current electronic survey design typically replicates that of paper-based questionnaires, failing to harness the full power of the electronic delivery medium. Worse, a recent environmental scan of online questionnaire design tools found that little, if any, support is incorporated within these tools to guide questionnaire designers according to best practice (Lumsden & Morgan, 2005). This article introduces a comprehensive set of guidelines as a practical reference guide for the design of online questionnaires.

BACKGROUND

Online questionnaires are often criticized in terms of their vulnerability to the four standard survey error types: coverage, nonresponse, sampling, and measurement errors. Although, like all survey errors, coverage error ("the result of not allowing all members of the survey population to have an equal or nonzero chance of being sampled for participation in a survey" (Dillman, 2000, p. 9)) also affects traditional survey methods, it is currently exacerbated in online questionnaires as a result of the digital divide. That said, many developed countries have reported substantial increases in computer and Internet access and/or are targeting this as part of their immediate infrastructure development (OECD, 2001; OECD, 2002). Indicating that familiarity with information technologies is increasing, these trends suggest that coverage error will rapidly diminish to an acceptable level (for the developed world at least) in the near future, and positively reinforce the advantages of online questionnaires.

Nonresponse errors occur when individuals fail to respond to the invitation to participate in a survey or abandon a questionnaire before completing it. Given today's societal trend towards self-administration (Dillman, 2000), the former is inevitable, irrespective of delivery mechanism. Conversely, nonresponse as a consequence of questionnaire abandonment *can* be relatively easily addressed. Unlike traditional questionnaires, the delivery mechanism for online questionnaires makes it difficult for respondents to estimate the

length of a questionnaire and the time required for completion[1], thus increasing the likelihood of abandonment. By incorporating a range of features into the design of an online questionnaire, it is possible to facilitate such estimation —and indeed, to provide respondents with context sensitive assistance during the response process —and thereby reduce abandonment while eliciting feelings of accomplishment (Crawford, Couper, & Lamias, 2001).

For online questionnaires, sampling error ("the result of attempting to survey only some, and not all, of the units in the survey population", (Dillman, 2000, p. 9)) can arise when all but a small portion of the anticipated respondent set is alienated (and so fails to respond) as a result of, for example, disregard for varying connection speeds, bandwidth limitations, browser configurations, monitors, hardware, and user requirements during the questionnaire design process. Similarly, measurement errors ("the result of poor question wording or questions being presented in such a way that inaccurate or uninterpretable answers are obtained" (Dillman, 2000, p. 11)) will lead to respondents becoming confused and frustrated.

Sampling, measurement, and nonresponse errors are likely to occur when an online questionnaire is poorly designed. Individuals will answer questions incorrectly, abandon questionnaires, and may ultimately refuse to participate in future surveys; thus, the benefit of online questionnaire delivery will not be fully realized. To prevent errors of this kind[2], and their consequences, it is extremely important that practical, comprehensive guidelines exist for the design of online questionnaires. Many design guidelines exist for paper-based questionnaire design (e.g., American Statistical Association, 1999; Belson, 1981; CASRO, 1998; Fink, 1995; Jackson, 1988; Lindgaard, 1994; Oppenheim, 1992; Taylor-Powell, 1998); the same is not true for the design of online questionnaires (Dillman, 2000; Norman, Lee, Moore, Murry, Rivadeneira, Smith, & Verdines, 2003; Schonlau, Fricker, & Elliott, 2001). The guidelines presented in the remainder of this article address this discrepancy.

COMPREHENSIVE DESIGN GUIDELINES FOR ONLINE QUESTIONNAIRES

In essence, an online questionnaire combines questionnaire-based survey functionality with that of a Web page/site. As such, the design of an online questionnaire should incorporate principles from both contributing fields. Hence, in order to derive a comprehensive set of guidelines for the design of online questionnaires, we performed an environmental scan of existing guidelines for paper-based questionnaire design (e.g., American Statistical Association, 1999; Belson, 1981; CASRO, 1998; Fink, 1995; Jackson, 1988; Lindgaard, 1994; Oppenheim, 1992; Taylor-Powell, 1998) and Web site design, paying particular attention to issues of accessibility and usability (e.g., Badre, 2002; Brewer, 2001; Coyne & Nielsen, 2001; Coyne & Nielsen, 2002; Dillman, 1978; Hinton, 1998; Kothari & Basak, 2002; Lynch & Horton, 1997; National Cancer Institute, 2002; National Institute on Aging and the National Library of Medicine, 2001; Stover, Coyne, & Nielson, 2002; Stover & Nielsen, 2002; W3C, 1999). Additionally, we reviewed the scare existing provision of online questionnaire design guidelines (Dillman, 2000; Norman et al., 2003; Schonlau et al., 2001). Principal amongst the latter is the work of Dillman (2000). Expanding on his successful *Total Design Method* for mail and telephone surveys (Dillman, 1978), Dillman introduced, as part of his *Tailored Design Method* (Dillman, 2000), 14 additional guidelines specifically aimed at directing the design of online questionnaires. Albeit seminal, Dillman's guidelines do not incorporate much of the relevant guidance uncovered as part of our environmental scan. We therefore propose, after collating, filtering, and integrating the disparate

guidelines, a comprehensive set of guidelines for online questionnaire design that, although stemming from Dillman's guidelines, are more encompassing. These guidelines are concerned with the interface to a questionnaire as it appears to respondents; they do not provide support for the back-end architecture of the questionnaire in terms of database structures, connectivity, security, communication protocols, and so forth. It should be stressed that the following are *guidelines*; by following them, one is more likely to develop a questionnaire that adheres to principles of best practice and is, therefore, more usable by the target respondent group: one is not, however, *guaranteed* a good questionnaire, since that depends on the individual developer. It is also important to note that none of the guidelines are particularly innovative in their own right; each has been drawn from the aforementioned sources covered by the environmental scan. What is novel, however, is the fact that applicable guidelines from these disparate sources have been collated into a unified set that is presented methodically in order to comprehensively support online questionnaire design.

Figure 1. A design process for online questionnaires

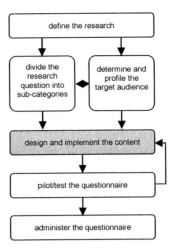

Design Process

To systematically design and implement an online questionnaire, a sequence of logical steps needs to be completed. Drawing on, and combining, accepted processes for paper-based questionnaire and Web site design, Figure 1 highlights the breakdown of activities that contribute to the generation of an online questionnaire.

The process assumes predetermination that an online mechanism is appropriate for survey delivery. The guidelines primarily focus on support for the design and implementation of online questionnaire content; minimal support is given for the preliminary steps, and no support is given for the piloting and administration phases. Similarly, this process is only concerned with the design and delivery of the questionnaire, as opposed to the analysis of the results upon termination of the survey. With the exception of the *Design and Implement the Content* step, which is discussed in detail in a later, dedicated section, each of the steps is outlined *briefly* as follows.

- **Define the Research Question:** Identify the purpose of the questionnaire and write it out clearly. In so doing, this sets out the mission and objectives of the survey.

- **Divide the Research Question into Subcategories:** List, and arrange in a logical order, the categories and subcategories of issues that are to be addressed by the online questionnaire. Place appropriate questions within each category and order them logically.

- **Determine and Profile the Target Audience:** Questionnaires are generally designed with a given audience or response group in mind. In order that the content of a questionnaire can be appropriately designed and delivered, it is essential that the target audience be profiled, and their specific requirements identified[3]. This is especially true when an online questionnaire is intended to reach and elicit response from persons with disabilities or the elderly, given the level of technology that is involved. Within the following guidelines, special consideration for respondents with physical disabilities (principally visual) and elderly respondents have been included.

- **Pilot/Test the Questionnaire:** Traditional questionnaires should be piloted/tested prior to general release or administration to identify potential for misunderstanding of questions or instructions and, thereby, afford the researcher a greater degree of confidence in the responses obtained. The same is true for online questionnaires. Furthermore, rigorous testing can help eliminate the presence of "bugs" within the source code of online questionnaires that, if gone unnoticed, can impact on online questionnaire use to the extent of abandonment and/or corruption of results. After piloting/testing, an online questionnaire should be amended to incorporate necessary changes, additions, or bug fixes. Thereafter, it should be repiloted before being administered. This process of piloting and changing the online questionnaire should be iterative until such time as the questionnaire is in the best possible position for administration; this process reflects good user interface design practice.

- **Administer the Questionnaire:** Once the online questionnaire has been designed and refined via iterative piloting/testing, it is ready to administer. Online questionnaires can be administered in several ways, depending on the target audience. Notification of the questionnaire and calls for response should be published in media most appropriate for the target audience. Such media include e-mail, newsprint, fliers, advertisements on radio and television, and person-specific correspondence. The process of profiling the target audience should serve to identify which media best suit the context and goals of the given questionnaire.

Design and Implement the Content

When designing and implementing an online questionnaire, there are many contributing factors to take into consideration such as layout or organization, formatting, the structure of the questions themselves, and technical requirements. The following guidelines address each of these aspects in turn. Regarding each of the following, decisions should be made in light of the target audience profile that has been identified for the survey.

General Organization

The following guidelines relate to the overall structure or organization of online questionnaires. This is shown in Figure 2: a welcome page should be used to motivate respondents to participate in the survey; where authenticated participation is required, a log in facility must be provided to allow respondents to enter pre-issued PIN numbers and passwords; a short introductory page should be used to present some general information about the survey, including any specific directions to

Figure 2. Organizational structure of online questionnaires

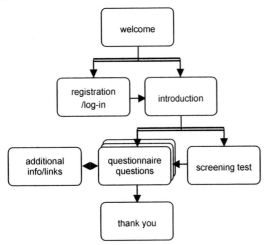

be followed by the respondents; if a screening test is required for a survey, this would typically be delivered before proceeding to the main question-focused sections of the online questionnaire; finally, it is important to remember to conclude every online questionnaire with acknowledgement to the respondents for their time and effort in completing the survey.

Issues of navigation and layout must also be addressed when designing online questionnaires. The following guidelines provide support for all organizational aspects of online questionnaire design, partitioned according to element of organization (including all the sections outlined in Figure 2).

1. **Welcome:** The site or domain name that takes respondents to this page should be easy for the target audience to remember, and should reflect the purpose of the questionnaire (it is advisable to register several domain names, all of which will bring potential respondents to this page). The welcome page should be designed to load quickly, and the organization administering the questionnaire (or on whose behalf it is being administered) should be clearly evident. The welcome screen should be motivational and emphasize the ease of responding; it should also make it evident to the respondent how to proceed. For questionnaires with password-restricted access, this should be made clear on the welcome screen to prevent wasting other users' time. Avoid the temptation to use animations and splash on the welcome page.

2. **Registration/Log in:** A registration or log-in screen is necessary when access to a questionnaire is to be restricted to specific people, and PIN numbers and passwords have been issued to the appropriate respondents. To prevent error messages, accept dashes and hyphens as part of a string of numbers (such as a telephone number). Furthermore, accept

all correct data and show respondents only the fields that have been erroneously omitted or completed incorrectly, explaining to them what they are required to do to resolve the situation. Both of these approaches alleviate user frustration and so will increase the likelihood of continued respondent participation. Do not rely on the use of the '*' (as is typical in Web-based forms) to indicate required fields since this is read as "star" by assistive technology, thus confusing the respondent and diluting the meaning that it was included to convey. Sufficient time should be provided to enable disabled users to read and complete the registration forms before automatic timeout. If error messages are unavoidable, present them in a clear, nonthreatening manner so as to prevent alarming elderly users.

3. **Introduction:** This should comprise a brief, but strong, explanation of what the survey is about. It should also outline all security and privacy practices associated with the survey being conducted in order to reassure respondents. Where appropriate, this information might also or alternatively be included within the registration/log-in page.

4. **Screening Test:** The location of the screening test is open to debate, depending on the nature and extent of the test. If screening is very simple, it should be located within the Introduction Page; if more extensive, it should be assigned a page of its own, but be clearly linked into the preceding and succeeding pages. Screening tests are advisable to prevent offence or insult, and to maintain public relations; if a respondent fails a screening test do not deny him/her the chance to complete the questionnaire, as this can be detrimental to his/her sense of worth and willingness to participate in the future—instead, simply discard or set aside his/her contribution.

5. **Questionnaire Questions:** In general, questions should be presented in a conventional format, similar to accepted paper-based standards. Later sections provide guidelines as to the specific types of questions. However, there are a number of important issues concerned with the number and order of appearance of questions, namely:

   a. The total number of questions included in a questionnaire should not exceed 60. More than 60 questions will increase the likelihood of abandonment of an online questionnaire.

   b. Initial questions should be routine, easy-to-answer questions designed to ease a respondent into a questionnaire. In particular, the first question should be engaging and easily answered to hook the respondent. If a screening test is being incorporated into the questionnaire, this type of question *may* constitute all or part of the test.

   c. Delicate, tricky, or the most important questions should appear approximately one third of the way through a questionnaire at a point at which a respondent has settled into the questionnaire but is not yet bored.

   d. Sometimes it is of value to repeat (slightly reworded) questions within a questionnaire; in particular, this technique is used to assess consistency of response, and to determine whether a respondent is answering in a manner that he/she thinks is desired rather than answering with honesty. Such questions should appear far enough apart that respondents are likely to have forgotten exactly how they answered the first time.

   e. Open-ended questions should appear before closed-ended questions on the same topic to prevent influencing respondents with the fixed option choices of the closed-ended questions.

f. If appropriate, open-ended questions should be reserved for placement at the two thirds point of the questionnaire to provide variation that will maintain the respondents' interest for the remainder of the questionnaire.

6. **Additional Information/Links:** To ensure that the main content of the questionnaire remains as simple and uncluttered as possible, links to additional information relating to the subject of the questionnaire should be included on a separate page from which it should be easy to return to the main questionnaire, at the point at which the respondent left it.

7. **Thank You:** Every questionnaire should conclude by thanking the respondents for their time and effort. This gratitude should be expressed in a gentle, friendly tone. Additionally, this page should include the facility for respondents to e-mail feedback or comments to the questionnaire administrators.

Layout

As a reflection of the organization conducting the survey, online questionnaires should create a distinctive, positive visual impression that will (a) evoke in respondents feelings of trust about the organization conducting the survey, and (b) assist the respondents in the process of completing the questionnaire. The following guidelines support the general layout and structure of online questionnaires.

1. The question and answering process should be attractive; that is, uncluttered and easy to complete. The content of a questionnaire should be well presented and organized. Do not squeeze too much information onto each page, and align elements horizontally or vertically to make them easier to read.

2. A question should never be divorced from its response set; that is, a question and all elements of its response should appear on the same page/screen.

3. Within a questionnaire, questions relating to a given topic should be presented together and clearly sectioned from questions related to other topics. Section headings and subheadings that are meaningful and well designed should be used to clearly differentiate sections. Avoid using too many sections in any one questionnaire since this is likely to become confusing to the respondents and reflects poor questionnaire design and lack of focus.

4. Do not require that a respondent provide an answer to one question before moving on to the next question (the exception to this being screening questions); unless for very specific reasons, respondents should be able to interrupt and re-enter responses and move backwards and forwards throughout the entire questionnaire.

5. Some controversy exists regarding whether all questions in an online questionnaire should be colocated within a single scrolling page or dispersed across several, linked, nonscrolling pages. In its favor, a single page strategy negates the need for navigational links and buttons; it can, however, be frustrating for respondents to have to scroll excessively through long screens just to access different questions or answer choices, and it gives the impression that a questionnaire is too long to complete. To avoid excessive scrolling, list only a few questions per page, and provide clear and easy links to the preceding and succeeding pages of a questionnaire; be careful here, however, to avoid excessive numbers of pages with complex navigational aids. As a general rule, the decision to scroll or to segment a questionnaire into a series of pages should be determined on the basis of the content and size of a questionnaire: a

very short questionnaire covering a limited number of topics may be best presented as a whole using scrolling; a long questionnaire is likely to benefit from page-based segmentation. In either case, refer to *Navigation* for more specific advice on the associated navigational mechanism.

6. Frames can make pages difficult to read and print, increase load time, and cause problems for disabled users who rely on assistive technology; they should, therefore, not be used for online questionnaires.

7. **Forms and Fields:** By their very nature, questionnaires include elements common to forms; that is, layout and the use of fields for data entry. Users with disabilities can find forms and fields problematic, and so it is important that the following guidelines, which are relevant across all respondent groups, be taken into consideration when laying out these elements of a questionnaire:

   a. Locate field labels close to their associated fields so that respondents can easily make the association; this also prevents labels becoming lost when a screen is magnified by users with visual impairment.

   b. A "submit" (or similar) button should always be located adjacent to the last field on any given page so that it is easily identified by respondents at the point at which they have completed the question responses; this is again especially important for users of assistive technology since it goes some way to ensuring that such a button will not be overlooked when the screen is magnified.

   c. The tab order for key-based navigation around the fields in a questionnaire should be logical and reflect the visual appearance as far as is possible.

   d. Fields are most easily read if stacked in a vertical column, and any instructions

pertaining to a given field should appear *before* and not *after* the field if it is to be understood by users of assistive technology.

Navigation

Online questionnaires can incorporate several facilities to assist navigation around the Web site presenting the questionnaire. These include buttons, links, site maps, and scrolling, each of which will be discussed in detail. As a general rule, all mechanisms for navigation should be clearly identified and easy for respondents to find when interacting with a questionnaire. Although navigational aids are typically located at the top right-hand corner of Web pages and, as such, this is likely to be the first place respondents would look, what is important is that the aids appear consistently in the same place on each page of a questionnaire's Web site. Navigational elements associated with Flash are dealt with under the "Formatting" section.

1. **Buttons:** Buttons allowing a respondent to exit a questionnaire or to return to the previous section of a questionnaire should be consistently available on each page of the Web site; the exception to this would be where it is necessary to restrict respondents from backtracking and altering responses (although this in itself is not an advisable practice in online questionnaire design). Buttons should be used sparingly and only where absolutely necessary since they can be hard for respondents with disabilities to use; when they are used, sufficient space should be inserted between them to increase their usability by such users. Furthermore, buttons should be large enough that users with visual impairment can see them, and users with impaired motor function (including the elderly) can click on them; this often means including the area immediately surrounding

the button as part of the button so as to avoid frustrating users with impaired vision or motor skills. Two buttons that are advisable to assist elderly users are obvious buttons to help them navigate to the previous and next pages from their current position.

2. **Links:** Links are commonplace in Web sites and, as such, respondents with Web experience are likely to anticipate their inclusion within the Web site for a questionnaire. That said, with a focus on simplicity of design, avoid excessive use of links in online questionnaires (as a general rule, do not exceed 20 links per Web page). The following guidelines provide some support for the use of links when such facilities are necessary within online questionnaires:

   a. When using links in questionnaires, make sure that the placeholder text for the links is clearly identifiable. Label them descriptively so that respondents can discriminate between similar links. Use blue, bold, underlined text for unvisited links since this is likely to meet the expectation of respondents with Web experience. Indicate that a link has been visited by changing its color.

   b. Use text-based links rather than image links for ease of navigation; if images or icons must be used for links, provide a redundant text link next to the image.

   c. Clearly distinguish between links to locations within the same page, links to other pages within the same Web site, and links to external sources outside the Web site. This will help avoid orientation confusion amongst the respondents, and ensure that they are able to make an informed decision as to whether or not to follow any given link. Ensure that all links are accurate and work properly.

   d. Links to important information or those concerned with fundamental navigation around a Web site should be placed at the top of a page; it is often advisable to repeat the same links at the bottom of pages that require scrolling.

   e. Like buttons, the use of links should be restrained, to accommodate users with disabilities who can find them hard to use. When they are included, sufficient space should be left between them to increase their usability by special needs groups, and the areas immediately surrounding the links should be treated as part of the link because it is difficult for the likes of elderly users to hit small targets accurately.

   f. When blocks of links or navigational aids are included in a page, "skip links" should be used; these are links that allow a user with visual impairment who relies on assistive technology to skip over the navigational aids rather than listen to a description of them on every page. This reinforces the importance of implementing links and navigational aids in a consistent fashion on each page.

3. **Site Maps:** Site maps provide an overview of the entire Web site at a single glance. They help users navigate through a Web site, saving them time and frustration. Although the path through *most* questionnaires is likely to be ostensibly linear and, therefore, orientation should not be overly complex, the provision of a site map (typically for Web sites containing 20 or more pages) has the potential to contribute to positive reinforcement of a respondent's progression through a questionnaire. The following guidelines relate to the design and use of site maps:

   a. Create a clear link to the site map on every page, and label it "site map." Keep the site map short, simple, clear, and condensed into one page wherever possible. Minimize the site map's download time, ensuring that the most important information appears first.

b. Design the site map to complement, and be consistent with, the rest of the site, and to include all areas of the site. Only use graphics if they are essential to the respondents' understanding of the site map.

c. Design site maps, like all Web pages, to be scaleable.

4. **Scrolling:** Try to avoid the need for scrolling on Web pages comprising an online questionnaire: some people find scrolling hard to use and when scrolling is required, information can be hidden from, and therefore overlooked by, respondents. It is particularly important that the welcome page to the questionnaire fit into a single screen and not require scrolling. If the use of scrolling cannot be avoided, inform respondents of the need to scroll—do not assume that it will be obvious to them—which will help prevent respondent frustration and ensure that questions are completely answered. Scrolling can be avoided via the use of jump buttons that take the respondent to the next "screen full" of information or questions.

Formatting

There are several aspects of general formatting that are of concern to designers of online questionnaires including: text, color, graphics, feedback, and other miscellaneous factors. Guidelines pertaining to each of these are discussed in the following sections.

1. **Text:** There are a number of issues of importance when designing the textual content of an online questionnaire:

a. Fonts used should be readable and familiar, and text should be presented in mixed case or standard sentence formatting; upper case (or all capitals) should only be used for emphasis, for example, to highlight certain words such as titles, captions, and so forth.

b. Sentences should not exceed 20 words, and should be presented with no more than 75 characters per line. If elderly respondents are anticipated, then this limit should be reduced to between 50 and 65 characters per line. Paragraphs should not exceed 5 sentences in length.

c. Technical instructions (those being instructions related to the basic technical operation of the Web site delivering the questionnaire) should be written in such a way that nontechnical people can understand them.

d. Ensure that questions are easily distinguishable, in terms of formatting, from instructions and answers.

e. For each question type, be consistent in terms of the visual appearance of all instances of that type and the associated instructions concerning how they are to be answered; in particular, keep the relative position of the question and answer consistent throughout the questionnaire. Where different types of questions are to be included in the same questionnaire, each question type should have a unique visual appearance.

f. When designing for access by users with disabilities and the elderly, employ a minimum of size 12pt font, and ensure that the font color contrasts significantly with the background coloring; text should be discernable even without the use of color. It is advisable to test font colors and size with a screen magnifier to ensure usability prior to release.

g. If targeting an elderly audience, provide a text-sizing option on each page, use bold face but avoid italics, and left-justify the text. It is also advisable to increase the spacing between the lines of text for ease of reading by this respondent group.

h. Make sure that text is read (by screen readers) in a logical order; specifically, set the tab order on the pages. This is especially true for the actual questions in the questionnaire; think carefully about the order in which a visually impaired user will hear the elements of a question, including the instructions and response options.

2. **Color:** Color has more of an impact than most people might imagine (a considerable part of its influence being subconscious), and so it is important to use color wisely:

   a. Use consistent color coding throughout the questionnaire to reinforce meaning or information in an unambiguous fashion.

   b. Use a neutral background color that excludes patterns that can make text very hard to read.

   c. When pairing colors or using two colors in close proximity, endeavor to use colors of high contrast to ensure maximum discernability across the target audience. This is particularly important for questionnaires targeted at audiences over 35 years of age; when catering to an elderly audience, this is imperative (easily distinguishable colors are to be recommended like black and white). Specifically, do not use the following colors together since visual vibrations and afterimages can occur, and these are the most common color combinations to affect people who are color-blind: red and green; yellow and blue; blue and red; and blue and green. For elderly respondents, the triple combination of blue, yellow, and green should be avoided, since it can be hard for some senior respondents to discriminate between these colors if used together.

   d. When using color, keep in mind standard cultural color associations.

3. **Graphics:** In essence, graphics should be kept to a minimum, wherever possible, to enhance download time and increase the accessibility of online questionnaires across target audiences (especially users with disabilities). The following are some basic guidelines that should be considered if graphics must be included in an online questionnaire:

   a. Avoid cluttering the questionnaire with graphics. This is especially true for users with visual disabilities.

   b. When using graphics, try to use small graphics that will download quickly. Individual images should not exceed 5KB in size, and no single Web page should exceed 20KB of graphics in total.

   c. Wherever a graphic is used, it is essential to provide a text-only version of the Web page. Use progressive rendering to allow the text to download before the graphics and, thereby, help alleviate access time issues that might repel a potential respondent from taking part in the survey. Graphics should be assigned descriptive names; furthermore, an ALT tag should be used for images where the text can provide a comprehensive and effective description in no more than five words; if more than five words would be required to describe an image, place the description directly within the body of the questionnaire adjacent to the graphic to which it relates.

   d. Minimize the number of colors that are used in any single graphic, and do not use graphics that mimic (or resemble) other items on a typical Web site. Ensure that graphics can be understood without color.

   e. Do not blur pictures, grey out information, or overlap menus; use crisp, clear images to maximize accessibility for users with visual disabilities.

f. Do not associate multimedia and audio clips with graphics if plug-ins would typically have to be downloaded by the respondents in order to access the associated media. Make it easy for users to skip, without penalty, multimedia content.

4. **Flash:** In general it is advisable to avoid Flash (including blinking text) within Web sites for online questionnaires since, to operate, it requires certain browser versions and/or plug-ins. As one of the most recent additions to the repertoire of Web sites, Flash can be problematic for users of assistive technology; it is difficult for users with low vision to focus on images that are moving, and it is difficult for screen readers to interpret Flash. A site that uses Flash or animation is basically just a difficult site that is slow to load for users suffering visual impairment. The following are a collection of guidelines to consider, in respect of users with disabilities, if Flash is considered essential within an online questionnaire:

a. Always give users an option of using a Flash or non-Flash format.

b. Provide static navigation; that is, do not make the navigational facilities moving parts of the Flash where they disappear and reappear, and always include a way to navigate back to the location from which a user encountered the Flash.

c. Let users determine the amount of time text appears on screen; do not make text automatically change or disappear.

d. Include a "close window" option in all additional windows that open. Use such windows sparingly since it is hard for a user with vision impairment to know when and what additional windows have been opened.

5. **Tables and Frames:** Tables and frames are commonly used in Web site design for alignment and other aesthetic purposes. Whilst this is fine for "standard" users, tables and frames cause confusion for people with visual impairment using screen readers and Braille displays. As such, tables and frames should be avoided when it is necessary to accommodate such respondents. Where tables are used to convey structured information (rather than for aesthetic purposes), they should be kept short and simple; cells should read serially when in cell-by-cell mode. All information included within tables should be provided in straight text as well, and tables should also be summarized using standard text. Frames should also be thoroughly described, and a no-frame version should be an option for users in the affected groups.

6. **Feedback:** An online questionnaire is, in essence, the user interface to a software application. It is therefore important to consider the provision of feedback to respondents using a questionnaire. Well-designed feedback can determine whether a respondent will abandon completion of a questionnaire or will persevere with it.

a. With each new section (page) of a questionnaire, respondents should be given real-time feedback as to their degree of process through the questionnaire; this might take the form of a statement to the effect "Question x of y completed," or it may be more visual such as a progress bar. It is important that such progress indicators are accurate in their reflection of respondents' relative completion status, otherwise the respondents will cease to trust the feedback and may be more likely to abandon a questionnaire.

b. At all times, when accessing a Web site containing a questionnaire, respondents should be provided with clear indication of where they are relative to the Web site as a whole, and should be informed, using nontechnical language, whenever a processing delay has been encountered.

c. Respondents' answers to questions should be immediately visible to them in a clear and concise manner to reinforce the effect of their actions. Feedback relating to a user's action should appear in close proximity to where their action took place to cater to the restrictions of assistive technology.

7. **Miscellaneous:** The following guidelines relate to formatting that does not naturally fall within any of the previous categories:

   a. Total Web site content should remain below 60KB of text and graphics.

   b. A version of the questionnaire (as a whole), as well as all referenced articles or documentation (where possible), should be provided in an alternative format that would allow them to be printed in their entirety.

   c. All introductory pages in the survey Web site should include a date-last-modified notification as well as a copyright notice, if applicable.

Response Formats

Consideration must be given to the technical mechanisms used to facilitate responses to the various types of survey question; that is, electronic equivalents to the various paper-based response styles have to be selected to best meet the needs of the questionnaire and target audience. The following are guidelines in this respect:

1. **Matrix Questions:** Matrix formats can be used to condense and simplify a question if it involves many response options. They should, however, be used sparingly, as they require a lot of work to be done within a single screen or locus of the questionnaire and, since they are typically constructed out of radio buttons, can encounter the interaction issues (see later) identified as hurdles to the use of radio buttons themselves.

Additionally, it is hard to predict how such questions will appear on respondents' Web browsers, and the size and format of such questions demands a significant amount of screen real estate that cannot be guaranteed on smaller-scale technology.

2. **Drop-Down Boxes:** A drop-down box measures the height of one line of text when collapsed; it contains a list of response options from which a respondent can select one or more by expanding the drop-down box. Drop-down boxes are fast to download, but should be used sparingly—typically only when very long lists of response options are required. They can be difficult to use, not just by users with disabilities or the elderly, since they require two, very accurate mouse clicks; as such, they should only be used when the increased mouse action is cost-effective, and should be avoided when it would be faster to simply type the response directly. Where drop-down boxes are used, their usability can be enhanced by incorporating type-ahead look up, and avoiding a requirement for, or possibility of, multiple selections. It is important that the first option in the drop-down box is not visible by default since this can lead respondents, and that visual clues to indicate how the drop-box is used are clear and visible.

3. **Radio Buttons:** Radio buttons are, essentially, small circles that are placed next to the response options of a closed-ended question. Technologically, it is important to note that, by default, only one radio button within any given group of radio buttons can be selected at a time; that is, radio buttons are mutually exclusive within the set to which they belong. Check boxes allow many selections within a set, and so should be used when multiple-response options can be selected by respondents for any given question. Radio buttons are popular because they closely resemble paper-based questionnaire

answer formats. They can, however, be frustrating because they demand a relatively high degree of mouse precision, and users with limited computer experience often do not know how to provide and/or change their responses (providing an answer involves clicking on the radio button; changing an answer involves clicking on another one in the set). Thorough, clear instructions should be provided when using radio buttons, and no radio buttons should be filled in by default. Furthermore, like navigational buttons and links, radio buttons should be relatively widely spaced to allow the space surrounding each to be treated as part of the radio button, and thereby assist users with any form of motor impairment.

4. **Check Boxes:** As mentioned previously, check boxes (typically small squares that contain a tick mark when checked) allow for multiple rather than exclusive response selection. Like radio buttons, they also demand a relatively high degree of mouse precision, and it is important to be cognizant of the need to support interaction that is sympathetic to users with disabilities. Thorough, clear instructions should be provided when using check boxes, and again, no check boxes should be filled in by default. The advantage to using check boxes and radio buttons within the same questionnaire is that their appearance is visibly different and so, provided with proper instruction, respondents are given visual cues as to how to answer any question using either of the two response formats.

Question Type and Phrasing

The following guidelines relate, specifically, to the type and phrasing of the questions used within an online questionnaire. These guidelines should be considered carefully when phrasing questions for inclusion in a questionnaire.

General Guidance

1. **Sensitive Questions:** If including sensitive questions—such as questions asking about confidential, disturbing, or threatening issues—word them politely, considerately, and in such a way that a low-prestige answer is equally as acceptable as a high-prestige answer.

2. **Attitude Statements:** If asking respondents to reflect their attitude regarding a statement about a particular topic, avoid statements that are too direct; instead, use more indirect or oblique statements. Ensure that each of the possible response options covers only one issue, is relevant to the topic being addressed, is clear, and represents a personalized expression of feeling. Make every effort to avoid descriptive observations in the response options since these will have a tendency to lead the respondents. It is advisable to use proven, existing questions when measuring common concepts such as religiosity, politics, or user satisfaction.

3. **Phraseology:** It is best to phrase questions in the present tense using the active voice. Comprising familiar, simple words (unless addressing a specialist homogeneous audience), use precise, consistent, grammatically correct sentences to construct questions of not more than 20 words. Whenever a knowledge question is presented, the possible response options should include a "do not know" and a "no opinion" response choice. It is generally held to be the case that precise measurement options are preferable to general categories for accurate response elicitation: for example, precise occupation rather than general occupational categories should be used.

   The following should be avoided when composing questions (unless appropriate for a specialized, homogeneous target audience): acronyms; abbreviations; slang;

jargon; proverbs; technical expressions; colloquial expressions; popular sayings; long alternatives as possible responses; different alternatives that could all be true; words that imply different meaning to different people; a lot of information carrying words; and loaded or provocative words such as black, democratic, free, healthy, and so forth.

Questions should be phrased so that they avoid being double-barrelled, double negative, hypothetical, negative, leading or biasing, two-edged (i.e., containing two ideas); and demanding of major memory effort.

When users must make a choice, warn them that the choice is coming, tell them how many options they will be presented with, and keep all possibilities in the same vicinity. If using age-related terms such as "senior" or "elderly" within an online questionnaire, do not stereotype or be condescending when presenting information so as to avoid offending elderly respondents. When asking respondents about their occupation, be sure to include "retired" as an option.

Types of Question

There are several different types of question that can be included in an online questionnaire (see Figure 3); essentially, any question that is appropriate for traditional paper-based questionnaires can be incorporated in an online questionnaire. These include open- and closed-ended; ordinal; magnitude estimate; Likert scale; categorical or nominal; rank-order; and skip questions. This section outlines some guidelines for each type of question in turn. It is important to note that for each question, irrespective of type, clear instructions should be provided to the respondents to inform them how and where to mark their answers; never assume a respondent will know how to respond to a question without instruction.

- **Open- and Closed-Ended Questions:** There are two main types of question that can be included in a questionnaire: open-ended and closed-ended. Open-ended questions should be used when there are too many possible response options to practically list, or when the response possibilities are unknown at

Figure 3. Types of question

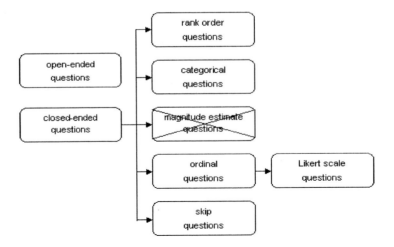

the time of administering the questionnaire. Alternatively, they should be used when it is important to capture the respondents' own words, or where the researcher does not want to impose response categories onto the respondents. Such questions gives the impression that the researcher is actively consulting each and every respondent, but the responses elicited are hard to analyse and, therefore, require more experience and skill on the part of the researcher to use effectively. Hence, it is advisable to use such questions sparingly; keep these questions to a minimum.

Closed-ended questions should be used when the goal is to obtain data that is ranked or rated, and when the researcher knows in advance how to order the ratings. These questions should be used when statistical data is required, and where the researcher would prefer to count the number of choices rather than analyse free text. Closed-ended questions incorporate a prespecified set of response choices and are generally used more frequently than open-ended questions in a survey. The response options listed for a closed-ended question should exhaust the possible answers to that question or, alternatively, include an "other —please specify" option. There are many different types of closed-ended question, guidance for the design and use of each of which is given in the following sections.

1.   **Rank-Order Questions:** This type of question requires the respondent to rank items in a list according to some criteria such as importance, for example. Given that people have a tendency to find ranking difficult, it is imperative that clear instructions are provided for these questions, and that such questions are kept to a minimum in any one questionnaire. Respondents should not be asked to rank more than three items in a list. Rank-order questions should be given a sufficiently distinct visual appearance so

that they can be differentiated from ordinal questions.

2.   **Categorical or Nominal Questions:** These questions require that a user chose one or more from a selection of categories listed as the response options. Categories listed should be all inclusive and exhaustive. They should also be meaningful within the context of the survey and useful categories for analysis. This question type is particularly useful for obtaining sensitive information like income.

3.   **Magnitude Estimate Questions:** Magnitude estimate questions are typically used in a survey when comparative judgements are required. However, it is unadvisable to use them within online questionnaires because, as a question type, they are generally only effective when the researcher is physically present to explain to respondents how to use such questions.

4.   **Ordinal Questions:** Only use ordinal questions when the topic is well defined and the response options represent a gradation along a single dimension. Use a meaningful, balanced scale to list the response options; the endpoints should be polar opposites of each other and the intervals between all points on the scale should be even. When listing options that could be open to interpretation, prevent confusion by specifying exactly what is meant by each (for example, if listing "Often" as an option indicate that this means "2-3 times a week" to avoid subjective interpretation of "often"). Although a neutral response category need only be included if it is meaningful or valid to do so, it is unadvisable to include only two options (the polar opposites of each other) because this effectively forces a respondent into indicating an extreme opinion that may inaccurately reflect less extreme opinions or ambivalence. It is generally accepted that ordinal questions work best when an odd number of response

options are presented; five or seven options have proven to be particularly effective, although it is possible to include more or less. When the negative response option to a question reflects potentially embarrassing or socially undesirable behaviour, it should be placed at the left hand (or first) end of the list of options.

5. **Likert Scale Questions:** These questions are really a specialized type of ordinal question, requiring respondents to indicate their level of agreement with a particular statement. When using this question type, a brief explanation of how respondents are to indicate their answers should be provided; it is best to provide this instruction per question since backward referencing in online questionnaires incurs greater cognitive load than for paper-based equivalents. Vary the wording of the response options to prevent encouraging a response-set (that is, where respondents answer questions in an automated fashion as a result of anticipated response options). Place the response option for the strongest level of agreement at the right-hand end of the option list, which is best laid out horizontally. As with ordinal questions, it is generally accepted that Likert scale questions work best when an odd number of response options are presented; five or seven options have proven to be particularly effective, although it is possible to include more or less.

6. **Skip Questions:** This type of question is primarily used to determine, on the basis of an individual respondent's answer, which of the following questions a respondent should jump (or "skip") to when question path is response directed. Although it is advised that these questions should not be used in self-administered paper-based questionnaires, technology permits them to be included in online questionnaires in such a manner that respondents are not burdened with determin-

ing where to skip to; skip questions can, and should, all be automated to the extent that a respondent need not even be aware that they are answering skip questions: complex skip patterns should appear invisible to them. When using skip questions, provide thorough directions that encourage marking of answers and being able to click to the next applicable question.

If it is deemed necessary to make skip questions explicit within online questionnaires, they should be distinct from all other question types, should include a training instruction, and reminder instructions should be used within the remainder of the questionnaire, where appropriate, to ensure correct question paths are maintained.

General Technical Guidelines

Although all of the above relate to the technicalities of online questionnaire design, there are some additional aspects that should be taken into consideration when developing online questionnaires:

1. **Privacy and Protection:** Ethically, it is important to ensure that respondents' privacy and perception of privacy are protected; it is especially important to encrypt the survey data and, in most cases, anonymize the data received.

2. **Computer Literacy:** In general, design with the less-knowledgeable, low-end computer user in mind; provide specific instructions to show users how to take each necessary step to respond to the survey without being condescending to this category of user and insulting to more experienced users. Do not assume prior knowledge or preconceptions in terms of technological know-how or expectations. Try to eliminate the need for double-clicks since these can be very difficult for users with motor impairment, including

the elderly; instead, use single-click activation.

3. **Automation:** Unlike paper-based questionnaires, many aspects of online questionnaires can be automated, most noticeably skip questions. It is important to weigh up the costs of automating elements of a questionnaire before including them in the design; when automation *is* included, it is vital that it be designed carefully so as to avoid disorientating or confusing respondents, and it is imperative that the automation is correct (it will frustrate respondents if automatically completed responses are filled in incorrectly).

4. **Platforms and Browsers:** Always ensure, via rigorous testing, that the questionnaire operates effectively across all platforms and within all browsers. As a general rule, use only a portion of the capacity of the most advanced browsers in order to maximize the chance that all recipients of the questionnaire are likely to respond.

5. **Devices:** Given increasing portability of technology and mobility of information access, it is important to design all elements of the online questionnaire to be scaleable, and to test the effect of viewing them on different scales of device. It is unlikely that many respondents would choose to complete a lengthy questionnaire on a handheld device, but equally, this cannot be discounted. Nor can the range of sizes to which a respondent might resize their desktop browser be anticipated; so a well-designed and tested online questionnaire needs to take this into consideration.

6. **Assistive Technology:** If users with visual impairment are to be included in a target audience, it is imperative that the design of the questionnaire be tested with assistive technology—in particular screen magnifiers and readers—to ensure that it is accessible to such an audience. The following guidelines

provide some support to help achieve this requirement:

a. Pages should not be overcrowded, and screen readers should be told how to read initials or acronyms.

b. Activity should be isolated to one area of the screen, and the need for scrolling should be minimized.

c. Wherever possible, avoid using pop-up windows, rollover text, cascading menus, and new browser windows; if pop-up windows are used, make sure that the default option is the most forgiving, and if new browser windows are opened, make sure that a simple means to get back to the original is provided.

FUTURE WORK

The above presents a *comprehensive* set of guidelines for the *design* of online questionnaires; there is scope for their expansion to cover areas other than simply the "user interface" design of the online questionnaire. For example, they could be expanded to include guidance related to the back-end setup of online questionnaires; that is, the architecture of the questionnaire in terms of database structures, connectivity, security, communication protocols, and so forth. Additionally, drawing on statistical protocols, guidance could be incorporated to support questionnaire design in terms of valid postsurvey analysis methods, as well as to support the postsurvey analysis process itself. Similarly, linguistic research findings could be incorporated to support better questionnaire wording.

The plethora of online questionnaire design tools on the market has essentially made online questionnaire design and delivery possible for novices; that is, people with no knowledge concerning *good* practice for such surveys. It is imperative that guidelines, such as these presented here (and their possible extensions), are incorporated into these tools to better guide the development of online questionnaires by such novice users; this is the focus of current research activities.

CONCLUSION

The previous sections have outlined a series of *guidelines* for the design of online questionnaires. Following these guidelines should help avoid some of the hurdles or pitfalls currently found in many online questionnaires, and potentially increase response rates and quality of responses; it does not, however, guarantee an effective questionnaire that will elicit a higher-than-average response rate. Such a guarantee is infeasible and unrealistic since the quality of a questionnaire is, ultimately, the responsibility of the person(s) designing the questions within the questionnaire, for which limited guidance can, at this point, be offered.

REFERENCES

American Statistical Association. (1999). *American Statistical Association series: What is a survey?* Retrieved July 7, 2003, from http://www.amstat.org/sections/srms/brochures/designquest.pdf

Badre, A. N. (2002). *Shaping Web usability: Interaction design in context.* Boston, MA: Pearson Education Inc.

Bandilla, W., Bosnjak, M., & Altdorfer, P. (2003). Self-administration effects? A comparison of Web-based and traditional written self-administered surveys using the ISSP Environment Module. *Social Science Computer Review, 21*(2), 235-243.

Belson, W. A. (1981). *The design and understanding of survey qestions.* UK: Gower Publishing Co. Ltd.

Brewer, J. (2001, January 4). *How people with disabilities use the Web* (Report W3C). [Working draft].

Brewer, J. (2001), *How people with disabilities use the Web.* W3C Technical Report (Working Draft). Accessed January 4, 2005.

CASRO (1998). *Council of American Survey Research Organization guidelines for survey research quality.* Retrieved 7th July 2003, from http://www.casro.org/guidelines.cfm

Coyne, K. P., & Nielsen, J. (2001). *Beyond ALT text: Making the Web easy to use for users with disabilities.* Fremont, CA: Nielsen Norman Group.

Coyne, K. P., & Nielsen, J. (2002). *Web usability for senior citizens.* Fremont, CA: Nielsen Norman Group.

Crawford, S. D., Couper, M. P., & Lamias, M. J. (2001). Web surveys: Perceptions of burden. *Social Science Computer Review, 19*(2), 146-162.

Dillman, D. A. (1978). *Mail and telephone surveys: The total design method.* New York: Wiley-Interscience.

Dillman, D. A. (2000). *Mail and Internet surveys: The tailored design method.* New York, NY: John Wiley & Sons, Inc..

Fink, A. (1995). *How to ask survey questions.* Thousand Oaks, CA: Sage Publications.

Hinton, S. M. (1998, April 14-18). From home page to home site: Effective Web resource discovery at the ANU. In *Proceedings of Seventh International World Wide Web Conference (WWW7)*, Brisbane, Australia, The Australian National University.

Jackson, W. (1988). *Research methods: Rules for survey design and analysis.* Scarborough: Prentice-Hall.

Kothari, R., & Basak, J. (2002, May 7-11). Perceptually automated evaluation of Web page layouts.

In *Proceedings of Eleventh International World Wide Web Conference*, Honolulu, Hawaii. IBM India Research Laboratory.

Kwak, N., & Radler, B. (2002). A comparison between mail and Web surveys: Response pattern, respondent profile, and data quality. *Journal of Official Statistics, 18*(2), 257-274.

Lindgaard, G. (1994). *Usability testing and system evaluation.* London: Chapman & Hall Inc.

Lumsden, J., & Morgan, W. (2005, May 15-18). Online questionnaire design: Establishing guidelines and evaluating existing support. In *Proceedings of International Conference of the Information Resources Management Association (IRMA '2005),* San Diego.

Lynch, P. J., & Horton, S. (1997). *Web style guide.* Yale Center for Advanced Instructional Media, Italy.

National Cancer Institute (2002). *National Cancer Institute's research-based Web design and usability guidelines.* Retrieved June 10, 2003, from http://usability.gov/guidelines/index.html

National Institute on Aging and the National Library of Medicine (2001). *Making your Web site senior friendly.* Retrieved June 19, 2003, from http://www.nlm.nih.gov/pubs/checklist.pdf

Norman, K. L., Lee, S., Moore, P., Murry, G. C., Rivadeneira, W., Smith, B. K., & Verdines, P. (2003). *Online survey design guide.* University of Maryland. Retrieved June 17, 2003, from http://lap.umd.edu/survey_design/tools.html

OECD. (2001). *Bridging the „digital divide": Issues and policies in OECD countries.* Organisation for Economic Cooperation and Development. Retrieved July 3, 2003, from http://www.oecd.org

OECD. (2002). *Organisation for economic cooperation and development ITC database.* Organisation for Economic Cooperation and Development. Retrieved July 2, 2003, from http://www.oecd.org/EN/statistics/0,,EN-statistics-13-nodirectorate-no-no--13,00.html

Oppenheim, A. N. (1992). *Questionnaire design, interviewing and attitude measurement.* London: Pinter Publishers.

Schonlau, M., Fricker, R. D., & Elliott, M. N. (2001). *Conducting research via e-mail and the Web.* RAND. Retrieved June 16, 2003, from http://www.rand.org/publications/MR/MR1480/

Stover, A., Coyne, K. P., & Nielsen, J. (2002). *Designing usable site maps for Web sites.* Fremont, CA: Nielsen Norman Group.

Stover, A., & Nielsen, J. (2002). *Accessibility and usability of flash for users with disabilities.* Fremont, CA: Nielsen Norman Group.

Taylor-Powell, E. (1998). *Questionnaire design: Asking questions with a purpose* (Report G3658-2). University of Wisconsin - Extension, Wisconsin, May.

W3C (1999). *Web content accessibility guidelines 1.0.* Retrieved une 8, 2003, from http://www.w3.org/TR/1999/WAI-WEBCONTENT-19990505

KEY TERMS

Assistive Technology: Software and hardware specifically designed to allow users with disabilities to successfully interact with a computer and the software applications running on a computer.

Browser (or Web Browser): A software application that is used to locate and display Web pages, for example, Netscape Navigator and Microsoft Internet Explorer.

Domain Name: A name that identifies the location on a network (e.g., the Internet) where a resource is located. Domain names are used in URLs (uniform resource locators—the global address of documents and other resources on the World Wide Web) to identify particular Web pages. For example, in the URL http://www.idea-group.com/encyclopedia/, the domain name is idea-group.com.

Online Questionnaire: A questionnaire that is delivered over the Internet using Web-based technology.

Platform: The underlying hardware or software configuration of a system.

Site Map: A hierarchical visual model of the pages of a Web site that helps users navigate through the Web site; it is similar to a table of contents in a book.

User Interface: The medium for communication between a user and a computer application; it comprises a set of components (e.g., menus and buttons) by which a user communicates with a software application, and components by which the application communicates feedback to the user.

Web Page: A single document on the World Wide Web that is uniquely identified via a URL.

Web Site: A location on the World Wide Web that is owned and managed by an individual, company, or organization; typically comprises one or more Web pages.

ENDNOTES

[1] In the absence of appropriate measures to address this.

[2] The research presented in this article is not concerned with coverage errors which are orthogonal to good questionnaire design; mixed-mode delivery is suggested as a means to combat such errors.

[3] Only when the characteristics of the survey's targeted respondents have been ascertained is it possible to decide on the level of specificity of questions and to ensure that the questions are structured in a manner most appropriate for all of the target audience. As a general rule, unless the survey is being targeted at a specialized, homogeneous group, questions should be phrased to accommodate a reading age of approximately 10 to 11 years. As for newsprint journalism, this goes some way to ensuring the maximum degree of audience comprehension. When questionnaires are required to be multi-lingual, it is important to ensure that all translations are meaningful. Note that, beyond this, the guidelines presented here are not intended to advise on the linguistic merits of survey questionnaires.

Chapter VI
Dual–Mode Electronic Survey Lessons and Experiences

Michael Lang
National University of Ireland, Galway, Ireland

ABSTRACT

This chapter presents a number of insights gained from a dual-mode survey of software designers recently conducted in Ireland. It describes the sampling method, pilot test procedures, response patterns, and the mechanisms engaged to authenticate participants and to filter duplicate responses. An outline is also given of how various factors with potentially beneficial affects on response rates were considered, as well as a breakdown of costs. Finally, the paper concludes with a summary of the main lessons learned.

INTRODUCTION

A substantial problem with survey-based research in recent years is dropping response rates, now typically of the order of 10% for postal questionnaires. Web-based surveys are less costly to implement than mail surveys, and have been found to yield faster, more complete and more accurate responses (Klassen & Jacobs, 2001; McCoy & Marks Jr., 2001; Schaefer & Dillman, 1998). In addition, they offer the advantages of real-time response validation, automated data entry, and programmable context-sensitive skip patterns. It would, therefore, appear that the Web has the potential to be the saviour of survey-based research. However, the rigorous execution of a Web-based survey necessitates a thorough consideration not just of methodological issues, but also technological, ethical, and cultural aspects (Lang, 2002). This chapter reports on the experiences gained from a recent dual mode (Web+mail) survey of software designers in Ireland that yielded an overall response rate of 52% (45% usable).

Design and Administration of Survey Instrument

Sampling Procedures

In software design research, as in other domains, the definition of accurate sampling frames is often difficult. The starting point in compiling our sample was to collate a list, drawing from several industry databases, that included software development organizations as well as large organizations likely to have internal IT departments (e.g., banks). This list was then systematically refined by visiting the Web sites of these organizations to (1) filter out those organizations not engaged in the sort of activities we were interested in, and (2) verify contact names and addresses. The eventual sample comprised 438 organizations.

When selecting a research sample, it is important that all members of a population have a fair and equal chance of being included or else "coverage" error may occur, potentially giving rise to bias (e.g., demographically skewed data). For Web-based surveys of the general public, coverage error is likely to be high because respondents are typically younger, better educated, more computer-oriented, and more affluent than society as a whole (Batagelj & Vehovar, 1998; Zhang, 1999). However, this was not a problem for us because our survey was aimed at software designers, all of whom had access to and were familiar with the Web.

Pilot Testing

Web-based technologies are continuously changing at a rapid pace, and users are adopting these changes at different rates. It is, therefore, imperative that Web-based surveys be adequately pilot tested on a variety of browsers and operating systems. What the designer of a Web survey sees on his screen may be very different to what the respondent sees because of differences between device characteristics, visual distances, text wrapping, fonts, special characters, plug-ins and media formats, and support for languages such as Java, Javascript, and CSS (Bertot & McClure, 1996; Dillman & Bowker, 2001; Smith, 1997; Stanton & Rogelberg, 2001).

For our survey, the following measures were executed

- The questionnaire was tested in various browsers (Microsoft Internet Explorer

v5.0, v6.0; Netscape Navigator v4.7, v6.2; Mozilla; Konqueror; Opera), operating systems (Microsoft Windows 95, 98, NT, 2000; Red Hat Linux; Apple Macintosh OS7), and screen resolutions (800×600, 1024×768, 1152×864). According to global Web statistics from http://www.thecounter. com over the period of the survey, these tests covered about 95% of all permutations;
- All HTML and CSS code was tested using the W3C validation service (see http://validator.w3.org/);
- As the Web server was a Linux machine (i.e., case sensitive file names), it was necessary to ensure that the URL and username-password would function correctly, regardless of whether they were typed in lower case, upper case, or the most likely combinations thereof. The Web server was also configured to return customized error pages rather than the unhelpful "404 File Not Found" default message;
- The Web server was apollo.university.edu[1], but an alias of http://www.apollo.university. edu was also set up because some users might expect a URL to commence with "http://www" and, therefore, experience an error if they wrongly entered it as a prefix;
- External access was tested to ensure there were no problems with firewalls or domain name servers;
- Web server performance was tested for download time, connection time, number of timeouts, and other critical parameters, using a monitoring tool from http://www. netmechanic.com;
- The e-mail merge message used in the second follow-up round was tested by sending it to colleagues in order to ensure that features such as text wrapping and clickable URL links worked properly in a variety of e-mail readers (e.g., Microsoft Outlook, Eudora, Mozilla Thunderbird, Webmail). Underscores were not used in URLs because

some e-mail readers automatically underline URLs, meaning that underscores could be mistaken as blank spaces;

• Before distribution, the questionnaire was pilot tested with a purposefully selected group using the "talk aloud protocol" advocated by Dillman (2000). A number of revisions were implemented across three rounds of testing.

Response Patterns

Respondents were mailed a package, giving them an option of responding by post or by Web. This package comprised a cover letter, stamped-addressed return envelope, and a professionally printed eight-page questionnaire (saddle-stitched booklet format). A sticker was affixed to the front of the paper questionnaire, giving the username, password, and URL to access the Web-based version.

After two follow-up rounds, a total of 215 valid responses were received. In addition, 23 questionnaires were returned undelivered or with a note that the organization had shut down. Only one response was solicited from each organization, but one company returned 2 separate responses. The overall response rate was, therefore, 52%[2]. However, 43 respondents indicated that they had no experience of the type of software design we were interested in, so should therefore not have been included in the population. Another 5 responses were insufficiently complete. Thus, the usable response rate is 45% based on the size of the true population[3]. A total of 167 usable responses were received in total (83 Web; 83 post; 1 other).

The response patterns are shown in Table 1 and Figure 1. Interestingly, although all of the survey participants were themselves Web designers, most of the responses received in the first 20 days were by mail; the number of usable postal responses received during that period was almost three times the number of Web responses. Consistent with experiences in other studies, most of the Web responses received in this first phase were in the initial 7 days (Comley, 1996; Schaefer & Dillman,

Figure 1. Survey response patterns

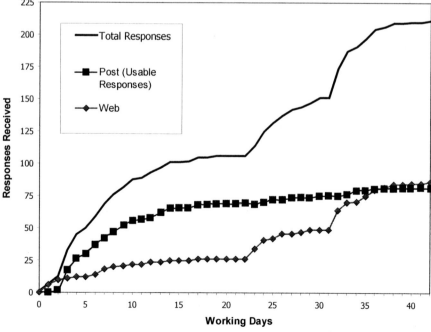

Table 1. Survey response patterns

Phase	Post (Usable)	Web	Other	Total
Day 0 to Day 10	56 (68%)	20 (24%)	1 (100%)	77 (46%)
Day 11 to Day 20	13 (16%)	4 (5%)	-	17 (10%)
Day 21 to Day 30	6 (7%)	20 (24%)	-	26 (16%)
Day 31 to Day 40	6 (7%)	37 (45%)	-	43 (26%)
After Day 40	2 (2%)	2 (2%)	-	4 (2%)
Total	83	83	1	167
Mean Response Time	12 days	24 days	-	19 days
Median	7 days	28 days	-	13 days

1998; Zhang, 1999). The average response time for postal responses was 12 days, which also accords with previous mixed-mode surveys (Comley, 1996; Schaefer & Dillman, 1998).

Follow-up reminders were issued by post on Day 22, the affect of which is clearly visible in Figure 1. This consisted of a one-page letter, reiterating the main points of the original cover letter, and again providing the Web URL. At the bottom of the page was a detachable slip whereby respondents could (a) request a replacement paper questionnaire or (b) specify a reason for not responding (thus giving insights into causes of non-response). Five participants requested replacement paper questionnaires, only one of whom subsequently submitted a response (notably, via the Web). Within 10 days of this initial follow-up, 6 usable responses were received by post (increase of 9%), and another 23 via the Web (increase of 88%). In addition, 20 detachable slips arrived by post with explanations for non-response; these are counted as valid but unusable postal responses, as shown in Figure 1.

A second follow-up was sent on Day 32, this time by e-mail. E-mail addresses were available for 221 of the 287 participants from whom responses had not been received, though 180 (81%) of these were of a general form such as info@ company.ie. A personalised message containing a respondent-specific URL link was generated us-

ing an e-mail merge tool. Within 10 days, 6 more usable responses were received by post (increase of 8%), and a further 37 via the Web (increase of 76%), as well as another 5 postal explanations of non-response.

Access Control and Treatment of Multiple Responses

If a Web-based survey is open to unsolicited, unidentifiable respondents, major doubts may hang over its validity (Dillman, 2000, p. 378). This is especially true where material incentives are being offered to participate because, in the absence of authentication mechanisms, fraudulent responses cannot be filtered out. We used a unique six-digit identifier that was embedded into the URL, for example, http://apollo.university.edu/survey/234567.php. Following the recommendation of Schleyer and Forrest (2000), the digits 0 and 1 were not used because of potential confusion with the letters "O" and "l". A password-protected directory was also used (username: "anonymous", password: "guest"). An added advantage of having a separate URL for each respondent was that it was possible to look at Web server logs to investigate access difficulties. It was discovered that 15 participants mistyped the username at least once, 11 of whom subsequently responded (8 by Web; 3 by mail). Two participants mistyped the

Table 2. Known causes of nonresponse (n=96)

Cause of nonresponse	Frequency
No or inadequate experience of the type of activity addressed by the survey	43 (45%)
Organization has shut down	23 (24%)
Too busy to respond	12 (13%)
Named contact person has left organization	8 (8%)
Organizational policy not to respond	4 (4%)
Problems loading Web survey	4 (4%)
Questionnaire received by person in inappropriate role	2 (2%)

password at first attempt, but both subsequently responded. There was one unsuccessful attempt to "hack" into the survey.

Another problem related to authentication is where a respondent either deliberately or inadvertently submits multiple responses to a Web-based survey (Klassen & Jacobs, 2001; Stanton & Rogelberg, 2001). We addressed this issue by recording a timestamp and the identifier for all responses. A number of "multiple" responses were indeed received, but it was clear from inspection of the data that, in most cases, what was happening was that respondents were clicking the "Next" button to have a preview of the screens, thus inadvertently submitting a response, or else the connection had timed out and a partially complete response was received. In such cases, all but the most recent responses were discarded.

Because the survey was dual-mode, it was also necessary to verify that no respondent used both modes. As the paper questionnaires had stickers affixed with the respondent's unique URL, it was

a simple procedure to cross-check for duplicates. One such case was found, explained by the fact that the respondent started the Web-based questionnaire, but dropped out and subsequently returned a completed paper questionnaire by mail.

Treatment of Factors with Potential Response Affects

Research on survey response affects reveals inconsistent findings; sometimes a particular strategy is found to be beneficial, elsewhere it might have a negligible affect (Dillman, 2000; Fox, Crask, & Kim, 1988). Because this was a high-stakes research project (a doctoral study), all possible measures, however marginal the potential affects, were taken to boost the response rate. Thirty-six percent[4] of non-responses can be explained, as shown in Table 2. It is also useful to examine causes of delayed response (Table 3), for late respondents might be regarded as surrogates for non-respondents.

Table 3. Known causes of delayed response (n=14)

Cause of delayed response (later than Day 20)	Frequency
Named contact person has left organization	8 (57%)
Prolonged absence abroad /off-site	3 (21%)
Named contact not in appropriate role; passed to colleague	2 (14%)
Initial mailing not received	1 (7%)

Major factors that have a positive impact on the response rate are the accuracy of the sampling frame and the follow-up procedures, both described earlier. Other possible factors, and explanations of how we treated them, are as follows:

- **Personalization of Correspondence** (McCoy & Marks Jr., 2001; Schaefer & Dillman, 1998; Smith, 1997): Of the 438 organizations, we had individual contact names for 425. The mail-out cover letter and postal follow-up bore a personalized greeting (e.g., "Dear John" rather than "Dear Sir/Madam") and each letter was personally signed. Recipients were asked to pass the questionnaire on to a colleague if they were not suitably placed to respond themselves. Although most of the follow-up e-mails were sent to general e-mail addresses, they were personalized insofar as possible (by personal greeting if to an individual address, or by "FAO: <*named contact*>" in the subject line if to a general address). In 47% of responding cases, the questionnaire was indeed completed by someone other than the addressee. Inspection of the causes of non-response and delayed response reveals that, in quite a few cases, the named contact had actually left the organization. Interestingly, the usable response rate from organizations with no named contact was 62% (8 of 13) as opposed to 45% overall. It is hard to draw clear lessons from this experience, but it seems that the absence of contact names is less of an issue for e-mail than it is for postal mail, because e-mail messages can be appropriately redirected more easily than written correspondence;

- **Use of Material Rewards:** Respondents were offered a summary report of the survey findings or inclusion in a prize raffle for UK£200 worth of Amazon.com gift certificates (11 separate prizes). One hundred and thirty one (78%) of the 167 respondents opted for the raffle; a slightly higher cohort of 134 (80%) requested a copy of the findings, while 19 (11%) declined both;

- **Clarity and Salience of Questions** (Dillman & Bowker, 2001; Lucas, 1991; McCoy & Marks Jr., 2001): The questions were drawn not just from the literature, but also from preliminary interviews with software designers in industry. Feedback from actual software designers was also incorporated during pilot tests;

- **Questionnaire Format:** In line with ESOMAR's (1999) principle of voluntary participation in Web surveys, no question was obligatory. Most of the questions were closed, requiring the respondent to select values from drop-down lists or to choose from a constrained set of checkboxes, although an "Other" textbox was always provided, where appropriate, to trap responses lying outside these prespecified sets. A number of introductory questions used textboxes for nominal data (e.g. job title, project cost), and two questions used larger textboxes for open-ended comments. Item response rates were as follows: drop-down lists/checkboxes 99%, "Other" category textboxes 8%, nominal data textboxes 94%, and open-ended comments textboxes 38%. For all questions, the item response rates of the Web survey were remarkably close to those of the postal survey. This is interesting, given that many questions in the paper version used 7-point Likert scales, for which drop-down lists were substituted in the Web version. No response-mode affect was therefore observed;

- The Web survey consisted of an introductory page and 11 consecutive screens, all of which were designed to fit within an 800 x 600 display without any need for scrolling. A screen-at-a-time design was preferred because this was found elsewhere to have better item-response rates than single-screen instruments (Klassen & Jacobs, 2001; Smith, 1997);

- **Good Visual Design and Web Survey Usability** (Dillman & Bowker, 2001; Lazar & Preece, 1999; McCoy & Marks Jr., 2001): A template and cascading style sheet (CSS) was used for the Web survey to ensure a consistent look-and-feel, thus minimizing the need for cognitive readjustments when navigating between screens. All Web screens had a progress indicator ("Screen *n* of 11"), all interface objects were clearly labelled ("Please select" for drop-down lists; "Next" and "Reset" for buttons), and the questions and response fields were separately color-coded so as to be visually distinct. The services of professional technical writers and graphic designers were engaged to assist with wording and visual layout;

- **Length of Questionnaire** (Batagelj & Vehovar, 1998; Bertot & McClure, 1996; Falconer & Hodgett, 1999; Farmer, 1998; Smith, 1997): Web-based surveys must be efficiently designed so as to minimize completion time and effort, ideally taking 15 minutes or less. We recorded timestamps for the start and finish screens, as well as each interim screen along the way. Six respondents took more than 30 minutes, taking breaks midway through. One extreme case started the questionnaire at the end of a working day and returned the following afternoon to complete it. Setting these outliers aside, the average completion time was 13 minutes;

- **Endorsement by a University or Professional Body, and Reputation of the Researcher:** This survey was a joint venture between two universities, and the logos of both were used on the cover letter, mail-out envelopes, and on all screens of the Web survey. All e-mail correspondence was from the university's domain (as opposed to an unfamiliar .com domain or freemail service

such as Yahoo or Hotmail), the Web survey was hosted within the university (as opposed to surveymonkey.com or other third-party), and e-mail signatures provided the URLs of researchers' "home" pages so that respondents could assure authenticity;

- **Web Server Uptime:** The server was constantly monitored to ensure that it was online, but by unfortunate accident, a power cable was severed by machinery on an adjacent construction site the morning after the initial follow-up notification, probably causing some Web responses to be lost;

- **Use of Return** SAEs (Dillman, 2000; McCoy & Marks Jr., 2001): In congruence with the theory of social exchange, stamped-addressed envelopes were included in the initial mail-out;

- **Advice of Cut-Off Dates:** The cover of the paper questionnaire mentioned a cut-off date, but no cut-off dates were included for the Web survey or mentioned in follow-ups because (1) it was anticipated that most would respond soon or not at all, and (2) it was felt that expiration of a cut-off date might dissuade late responses. By Day 45, all but three of the eventual tally of usable responses had been received, the late arrivals coming by post (Day 47; Day 90) and by Web (Day 50).

- **Confidentiality** (Lazar & Preece, 1999; Stanton & Rogelberg, 2001): Concerns about privacy and confidentiality can negatively impact response rates, but this was not an issue in this survey, as attested by the fact that 91% of respondents gave their names plus e-mail and/or telephone number in order to receive raffle prizes/summary report.

Survey Costs

The costs of implementing this survey are shown in Table 4, but this presents a misleading picture for two reasons. First, expenditure on incoming

Table 4. Survey costs

Expense item	Postal survey	Web survey
Stationery & printing	€ 465	€ 10
Outgoing postage	€ 394	-
Incoming postage (SAEs)	€ 344	-
Incentives (Amazon.com certificates)	€ 317	-
Total	€ 1520	€ 10

postage and incentives for the postal survey was not strictly necessary, and only incurred because of potentially beneficial affects on response rates. Second, the marginal costs of the Web-based version were nil because we had the necessary technical skills to design it ourselves (Dreamweaver, Photoshop), used software for which we already held licences or which was freely available (RedHat Linux, Apache, MySQL, PHP, Group-Mail), and hosted it on an internal Web server. The additional overhead of €10 represents merely the price of a box of stickers, used for affixing a unique URL to the front of each paper questionnaire. However, even after taking unnecessary costs away from the postal survey and adding development costs to the Web survey, it cost less than half the postal survey. For larger populations, this fraction decreases exponentially.

CONCLUSION

As with all other modes of survey research, valid, reliable responses cannot be expected from Web surveys unless careful attention has been given to sampling procedures and other critical aspects of research design. Notably, the European Society for Opinion & Marketing Research (ESOMAR) warn that:

Any Internet surveys which fall seriously below the high standards promoted by ESOMAR and other leading professional bodies will make it more difficult to use the medium for genuine research

and could seriously damage the credibility of such research, as well as being an abuse of the goodwill of Internet users generally. (ESOMAR, 1999)

A number of lessons can be drawn from our experiences:

* The design of a Web-based questionnaire calls not just for questionnaire design and testing skills, but also Web design and testing skills. With dual-mode surveys, it may be tempting to believe that there is no more to the Web-based version than merely porting a paper version directly to the screen. However, this is a gross over-simplification based on a poor understanding of Web design principles, and the conversion of a paper-based questionnaire to an online version should not be undertaken lightly;

* It would appear that, even amongst highly computer-literate populations, very many participants, when given the choice of mixed response modes, will opt for paper. This finding is consistent with previous mixed-mode studies (McCoy & Marks Jr., 2001; Zhang, 1999);

* Most of the responses to later rounds arrived via the Web, but there are a number of possible explanations: (1) replacement paper questionnaires were not sent in follow-up rounds, unless specifically requested, (2) the second follow-up round was by e-mail and contained a direct clickable URL to the Web survey, and (3) many participants, upon be-

ing reminded, might have opted for the Web survey because it was the most immediate medium and/or they might have discarded or mislaid the paper version;

- The absence of individual e-mail addresses was not a problem. Although 81% of e-mail addresses were of a general form (e.g. info@company.ie), the e-mail follow-up round boosted Web responses by 76%;

- If using password-protected folders, user-names and passwords that are likely to be misspelled (e.g., "anonymous") should be avoided. To an extent, we got away with this because respondents had the fall-back of a paper mode, but otherwise we might have lost 10% of responses;

- 17% of non-respondents indicated that they were either "too busy" or that it was "against policy" to respond to surveys. Hence, there is a greater need than ever for elegant questionnaire designs that prioritise the most salient questions and demand no more than 15 minutes of the respondent's time. Our initial follow-up letter mentioned that the average Web completion time at that point was 11 minutes, but this was obviously more than very many participants were willing or able to give;

- The use of material incentives means that authentication procedures need to be engaged, but in retrospect, it seems that there was no benefit in offering material incentives here because more respondents were interested in a copy of the survey findings than in a prize raffle, while 11% declined any reward;

- For both Web and postal modes, very high-item response rates were received for closed questions, with much lower rates for open-ended textboxes;

- If sending follow-up notifications for Web surveys, one should always check for scheduled network downtime or scheduled power outages, and ideally use a Web server with an uninterruptible power supply.

The potential of Web-based surveys has been dealt a serious blow by the spread of pernicious direct marketing and "spamming" technologies in recent years that have come to pervade all forms of electronic and traditional communications. Legislation has been recently introduced in the European Union (Directive 95/46 on Data Protection, Directive 2002/58/EC on Privacy and Electronic Communications) and the United States (Unsolicited Commercial Electronic Mail Act of 2001, CAN-SPAM Act of 2003) to protect privacy and restrict unscrupulous direct marketing, but in practice, these laws are difficult to enforce because of the borderless nature of cyberspace. More than ever, an aura of suspicion surrounds any stranger-to-stranger communication on the Internet, and the use of Web surveys for business-to-consumer research is likely to yield very low response rates, as well as being susceptible to coverage error. It would appear that Web-based surveys have most promise for intra-organizational research (including within the closed memberships of trade associations), but for all other contexts, it is likely that Web surveys need to be complemented by mail, telephone, and/or fax modes.

REFERENCES

Batagelj, Z., & Vehovar, V. (1998, May). *Technical and methodological issues in WWW surveys.* Paper presented at the 53rd Annual Conference of the American Association for Public Opinion Research (AAPOR), St. Louis, MO.

Bertot, J. C., & McClure, C. R. (1996, October). *Electronic surveys: Methodological implications for using the World Wide Web to collect survey data.* Paper presented at the 33rd American Society for Information Science (ASIS) Annual Meeting, Baltimore.

Comley, P. (1996, November). *The use of the Internet as a data collection method*. Paper presented at the ESOMAR/EMAC Symposium, Edinburgh, Scotland.

Dillman, D. A. (2000). *Mail and Internet surveys: The tailored design method* (2nd ed.). New York: Wiley.

Dillman, D. A., & Bowker, D. K. (2001). The Web questionnaire challenge to survey methodologists. In U.-D. Reips & M. Bosnjak (Eds.), *Dimensions of Internet science* (pp. 159-178). Lengerich, Germany: Pabst Science Publishers.

ESOMAR. (1999). ESOMAR guideline. Conducting marketing and opinion research using the Internet. *Journal of the Market Research Society, 41*, 439-441.

Falconer, D. J., & Hodgett, R. A. (1999, December). *Why executives don't respond to your survey*. Paper presented at the 10th Australasian Conference on Information Systems (ACIS), Wellington, New Zealand.

Farmer, T. (1998). *Using the Internet for primary research data collection*. InfoTek Research Group, Inc.

Fox, R. J., Crask, M. R., & Kim, J. K. (1988). Mail survey response rate: A metanalysis of selected techniques for inducing response. *Public Opinion Quarterly, 52*, 467-491.

Klassen, R. D., & Jacobs, J. (2001). Experimental comparison of Web, electronic and mail survey technologies in operations management. *Journal of Operations Management, 19*, 713-728.

Lang, M. (2002, April 29-30). *The use of Web-based international surveys in information systems research*. Paper presented at the European Conference on Research Methodology for Business and Management Studies (ECRM 2002), Reading, UK.

Lazar, J., & Preece, J. (1999). Designing and implementing Web-based surveys. *Journal of Computer Information Systems, 39*, 63-67.

Lucas, H. C., Jr. (1991). Methodological issues in information systems survey research. In K. L. Kraemer (Ed.), *The information systems research challenge: Survey research methods* (Vol. 3, pp. 273-285). Boston: Harvard Business School Press.

McCoy, S., & Marks Jr., P. V. (2001, August). *Using electronic surveys to collect data: Experiences from the field*. Paper presented at the 7th Americas Conference on Information Systems (AMCIS), Boston, MA.

Schaefer, D. R., & Dillman, D. A. (1998). Development of a standard e-mail methodology: Results of an experiment. *Public Opinion Quarterly, 62*, 378-397.

Schleyer, T. K. L., & Forrest, J. L. (2000). Methods for the design and administration of Web-based surveys. *Journal of the American Medical Informatics Association, 7*, 416-425.

Smith, C. B. (1997). Casting the net: Surveying an internet population. *Journal of Computer-Mediated Communication, 3*(1).

Stanton, J., & Rogelberg, S. G. (2001). Using Internet/Intranet Web pages to collect organizational research data. *Organizational Research Methods, 4*, 199-216.

Zhang, Y. (1999). Using the Internet for survey research: A case study. *Journal of the American Society for Information Science, 51*, 57-68.

KEY TERMS

CSS: Cascading style sheets, a mechanism for adding style (e.g. fonts, colors, spacing) to Web documents.

Firewall: A computer security mechanism used by organizations to enable internal users to make external connections to the Internet, but prevent external users connecting to the organization's internal computer systems.

Hypertext Markup Language (HTML): The language used to create Web documents.

IP Address: Every device connected to the Internet has an IP (Internet protocol) address, part of which identifies the organization or service provider through which that connection is channelled.

Linux: An open-source computer operating system, based on Unix. Many Web servers are based on the Linux platform.

Timestamp: A record of the time (date: hour: minute: second) at which an event occurred, based on the computer's in-built clock.

URL: uniform resource locator, the addressing convention used by the World Web Web (e.g., http://www.idea-group.com).

W3C: World Wide Web Consortium, an international body responsible for developing protocols, standards and guidelines for Web technologies (see http://www.W3C.org).

Web Server Logs: Files maintained by Web servers that automatically record all connection requests, detailing the IP address of the requestor, the pages visited, time and date, and any errors occurring (e.g. "file not found", "unauthorized access").

ENDNOTES

[1] For the sake of readability, a fictitious domain of university.edu is used in this write-up. However, the actual domain was buigalway.ie (National University of Ireland, Galway).

[2] (215 valid - 1 duplicate) / (438 sample size − 23 shutdowns) = 214 / 415 = 52%

[3] (215 valid - 1 duplicate - 43 irrelevant - 5 incomplete) / (438 sample size − 23 shutdowns − 43 irrelevant) =166 / 372 = 45%

[4] 96 explanations / (438 sample size − 166 usable − 5 insufficiently complete) = 96 / 267 = 36%

Chapter VII
Software Design
Tips for Online Surveys

John M. Artz
The George Washington University, USA

ABSTRACT

An online survey uses World Wide Web technology to deliver a survey instrument to a geographically dispersed audience, thus providing the benefits in elimination of mailing costs and an elimination of data entry costs. Both of these provide further secondary benefits such as elimination of follow-up mailing costs and fewer errors in data collection. This article explains the basics of constructing an online survey using World Wide Web technology, and provides some design tips for someone planning to construct such a survey. A simple online survey consists of three basic components. First, the survey is presented to the subject through a Web page that allows them to enter information or select options in response to questions. A simple HTML form will be used for this purpose. Second, a program is needed, on the Web server where the data will be stored, to take the values from the form and store them in a database. An active server page program will be used in this article for this purpose. This is, essentially, a program written in visual basic that takes values from the form and inserts them into a relational database. After a very simple example of each of these components is explained, some design tips will be provided that will make constructing, and exploiting an online survey much easier.

INTRODUCTION

An online survey uses World Wide Web technology to deliver a survey instrument to a geographically dispersed audience. The benefits of using this technology include the elimination of mailing costs (since instruments accessed via the Web do not have to be mailed out), and an elimination of data entry costs (since the values provided by the subjects are entered directly into a database).

Both of these provide further secondary benefits. For example, the elimination of mailing costs for the instrument also implies the elimination of mailing costs for follow-ups or reminders. And the elimination of data entry also eliminates data entry errors. The purpose of this article is to explain the basics of constructing an online survey using WWW technology, and to provide some design tips for someone planning to construct such a survey.

BACKGROUND

A simple online survey consists of three basic components. First, the survey is presented to the subject through a Web page that allows them to enter information or select options in response to questions. A simple HTML form will be used for this purpose. Second, a program is needed on the Web server, where the data will be stored, to take the values from the form and store them in a database. An active server page program will be used in this example for this purpose. This is, essentially, a program written in Visual Basic that takes values from the form and inserts them into a relational database. Finally, a database is needed to store the data. Finally, although it is not absolutely necessary, an example of a second active server page program will be provided. This second program will summarize the data in the database, and present it on a dynamically constructed Web page to show another benefit of online surveys: to provide up to the minute tallies of survey results. After a very simple example of each of these components is explained, some design tips will be provided that will make constructing and exploiting an online survey much easier.

The HTML Form

Figure 1 shows the rudiments of an HTML form. The entire form is enclosed within a <form> tag that would reside with the body of an HTML document. Users would invoke the form by typing in the URL or by clicking on a link to the form. Such a link could be included in an e-mail message sent out to potential subjects in order to make accessing the form easier.

Within the form tag is an "ACTION" parameter. This is where the program that will process the form is specified. In Figure 1, it refers to a program on the server called Surveyadd.asp (which will be discussed later) that resides in the Survey directory on a Web server with domain name MyServer.com.

Only one user input field is provided in the figure, but any number of input fields can be included. The one provided here is called a radio button. Other options commonly used in online surveys include checkbox, select menu, and text field. A checkbox is similar to a radio button in that the user selects an answer from a list. However, a checkbox allows multiple responses, whereas the radio button only allows one response.

Sometimes the number of potential responses is large. For example, if you ask the user to enter their state or zip code, a radio button listing all the possible states or zip codes would take up far too much space. So a drop down select menu would take up far less room on the screen. The user would click on the menu. The choice would be displayed. The user would select a choice, and the menu would disappear again.

Figure 1. The HTML form

```
<FORM METHOD=POST
ACTION="http://MyServer.com/Survey/Surveyadd.asp">
<b>Question 1: </b>
<INPUT TYPE=RADIO  NAME=Q1 VALUE = "1">Strongly Agree
<INPUT TYPE=RADIO  NAME=Q1 VALUE = "2">Agree Somewhat
<INPUT TYPE=RADIO  NAME=Q1 VALUE = "3">Neutral
<INPUT TYPE=RADIO  NAME=Q1 VALUE = "4">Disagree Somewhat
<INPUT TYPE=RADIO  NAME=Q1 VALUE = "5">Strongly Disagree
<INPUT TYPE=RADIO  NAME=Q1 VALUE = "6" CHECKED>No Opinion
<p>
<p>
<INPUT TYPE="submit" VALUE="Submit Survey">
<INPUT TYPE="reset" VALUE="Reset This Form">
</FORM>
```

If there are too many possible answers to be listed in a select menu, then a text field can be provided and the user can type in their specific answer. If the user needs to type in an answer that would exceed a single line, a text area can provide a larger input area with multiple lines.

(For a detailed explanation of these types of input fields and their parameters, see Deitel, Deitel, & Goldberg, 2004; Musciano & Kennedy, 2002; Niederst, 2002).

The Database

The database used for collecting this data is trivially simple. There is only one table called Responses. The Responses table has two fields: one that contains the question identifier, called Question, and one that contains the response to the question, called Response. If one were constructing a survey with 20 questions, there is a tendency to create a record with 20 fields, 1 for each response. Unfortunately, this makes the analysis of data more difficult. The 2-field design considers the capabilities of SQL for summarizing data and maximizes that capability. If a record with 20 fields were needed for another software package, it could be constructed from this basic design. So, this simple design offers maximum flexibility. Further, if questions were to be grouped for analysis, this design would also accommodate grouping. A second table could be set up with two columns—one for the question number and one for the category. The two tables could be joined and summarized by category. A second benefit of this simplified design is that it makes the active server page program a little easier, and anything that makes a program easier reduces the problem of programming errors. So simple is better: easier analysis and more reliable programming. The database actually used in constructing this example was Microsoft Access, although nothing would change if SQL Server or Oracle were used instead. The benefit of Microsoft Access is that it is easy to use, especially if the database is used directly for data analysis instead of using active server pages to tally the results. For an in-depth treatment of the functionality of Microsoft Access, see Balter (2003).

Figure 2. Active server page to update the database

```
Dim DBConnection
Set DBConnection = Server.CreateObject("ADODB.Connection")
 DBConnection.Open "FILEDSN=Survey.dsn"
Set RSRequest = Server.CreateObject("ADODB.RecordSet")

Dim RSRequest
RSRequest.Open "Responses", DBConnection, 1,2

For Each Field in Request.Form
 If Request.Form.Item(Field) < 6 Then
 RSRequest.AddNew
 RSRequest("Question") = Field
 RSRequest("Response") = Request.Form.Item(Field)
 RSRequest.Update
 End If
Next

DBConnection.Close
Set DBConnection = Nothing

Response.Write("<b>Thank you for Participating In the Survey<br></b>")
```

The Active Server Pages

When the user clicks the Submit button, the fields on the form are packaged up and sent to the server specified in the ACTION parameter. The program specified in that parameter is invoked and given the data from the form. This data must be taken by the specified program, parsed, and inserted into a database. Figure 2 shows such a program.

The first block of code sets up a connection between the program and a database that resides on the machine where the Web server is located. This database does not actually have to reside on the same machine, but using a database on another machine is a little more complicated. An ODBC name is established on the server machine, and all programs connect to the database using that ODBC name. The ODBC connection wizard can be found in the control panel of the server machine.

The next two lines of code use the DBConnection to create a record set object, RSRequest, that will be used by the program to insert records into the database. Once this record set object is created, inserting records into the record set is exactly the same as inserting records into the Responses table in the database.

When we set up the radio button on the HTML form, we allowed valid values of 1 through 5. If the user selected N/A, we assigned a value of 6. Hence, we go through each radio button and ask first if the value is less than 6. If it is less than 6, we use the field name (e.g., Q1) to populate the

Figure 3. Active server page to tally the survey results

```
Dim SQLString
Dim DatabaseConnection

SQLString = "Select Question, AVG(Response) as QAVG from Responses group by Ques-
tion"

Set DatabaseConnection = Server.CreateObject("ADODB.Connection")
 DatabaseConnection.Open "FILEDSN=Survey.dsn"
Set RS = Server.CreateObject("ADODB.RecordSet")
RS.Open SQLString, DatabaseConnection

If RS.EOF Then
 Response.Write("<b>No Surveys Sumitted</b>")
Else

Response.Write("<center><table border>")
Response.Write ("<TR><td>Question</td><td>Average<br>Response</td></tr>")

Do Until RS.EOF
 Response.Write ("<tr><td align=center>")
 Response.Write (RS("Question"))
 Response.Write ("</td><td align=center>")
 Response.Write (RS("QAVG"))
 Response.Write ("</TD></tr>")
 RS.MoveNext
Loop

Response.Write ("</table>")
Response.Write ("</center>")
End If

RS.Close
DatabaseConnection.Close
```

Question field, and the selected value to populate the Response field. So if the user selected the value of 3 on Q1, then Q1 would be assigned to Question and 3 would be assigned to Response. Note that carefully naming the fields on the HTML form makes the job of putting the data into the database much easier.

After we insert the values into the database, we close the database connection and send a response back to the user letting them know that their answer was successfully received and recorded in the database.

Figure 3 shows the code for an active server page that will execute an SQL query against the database and return an HTML table with the summarized results. A database connection is created as before, only this time it is opened with an SQL query. The query is executed and the results are returned in the record set. The remainder of the program reads the record set one record at a time, and uses the values from the fields to populate an HTML table that will be viewed by the person who initiated the query.

DESIGN TIPS

When designing an HTML form, some design tips are, hopefully, obvious. For example, even though multiple forms may be placed on an HTML page, it is never a good idea to do so. Each form would have its own Submit button, and the user would be confused with regard to how much is being submitted when the button is pressed. If the form is in a frame, the frame should be scrollable so that the user can scroll through the entire form and reach the Submit button. Other tips are less obvious.

For example, use radio suttons and select menus whenever possible because they force the user to choose from a limited set of answers. This improves the quality of the data and makes analysis easier. Radio buttons should be used when the number of choices can be easily listed on the page. Select menus allow for a longer list of choices without taking up valuable screen space. Checkboxes can be used when it is possible to select multiple choices. However, this makes the database design more difficult, and the program that updates the database more complicated.

When using radio buttons, always have a button for N/A, and do not insert N/A responses in the databases. This is important for two reasons. When a radio button is first displayed, no answer is selected. However, once the user selects an answer, it is not possible to unselect it. So if the user selects an answer and then decides that the question is not applicable, they are stuck with having to provide an answer any way. Further, the N/A response should be selected as the default selection so if the user skips over the question, it is read as a Not Applicable response. The N/A response is also important due to the way that SQL handles nulls (missing values). For example, if the values 1, 5, and null are averaged by SQL, the average would be 3. If the values 1, 5, and 0 are averages, the average would be 2.

Text fields can be used whenever the user must enter something that cannot be selected from a list. This reduces data quality and makes analysis more complicated, but sometimes it cannot be helped. When using a text field, use the size parameter to fix the box size, which gives the user some idea of how much information you expect to have entered. Further, use the maxsize parameter to limit the number of characters that can be entered. If the field in the database assumes that the user will enter a maximum of, say, 50 characters and the user enters 60, then the ASP updating the database will crash and the data will be lost. So if there is a limit of 50 characters, then the text field should limit the input.

Form fields should be named so that the names agree with the field names in the database. In the simple example provided here, this is not an issue. But if fields from the form have to be assigned directly to the corresponding fields in the database, then having the same names will make the programming must easier. Field values should also be chosen with an eye towards the database and future analysis. In the radio button shown in Figure 1, the values are integer values. This allows categorical analysis (e.g., 50% Strongly Agreed), cumulative analysis (e.g., 75% Agreed or Strongly Agreed), and averages (e.g., the average response was 1.8). If the values provided are strings, such as "Strongly Agreed" instead of 1, then the SQL and other programming necessary to analyze the data becomes more complicated. While some may chafe at using numerical averages on a Likert scale, it is, at least, important to know the consequences of not using numbers.

If the user tabs from one field to another on the form instead of using the mouse, then the fields will be visited in the order defined by the tab index. If tab indexes are not provided by the form designer, then default values will be assigned by the browser. So if a user is on the second choice on Question 1 and they hit the tab key, they may well jump to the fourth choice on Question 3. Since this would increase the user's confusion and frustration with the form, it is best to explicitly specify the tab order of the fields using the tab index parameter. The form designer should also tab through all of the fields to make sure that the tab order is correct.

The database should be normalized as much as possible to facilitate analysis, and the analytical capabilities of SQL should be considered as much as possible in both the database design and the form design. Putting data into a database and then trying to figure out how to exploit it is a formula for frustration. See Connolly and Begg (2005) for a short treatment of normalization and Bagui and Earp (2004), or Kline (2004) for an introduction to SQL, and Kriegel and Trukhnov (2003) for a more in-depth treatment.

If raw comments from the user are required, or allowed, a textbox should be used. A textbox allows the user to enter multiple lines of text and see all that they have written, unlike the text field, which allows a single line and requires the

user to cursor through the line one character at a time. However, the size of the textbox sends a subtle message to the user. If the textbox is 30 characters wide and 3 or 4 lines, it suggests brief comments are desired. If the textbox is 50 characters wide and 20 lines long, it suggests a brief essay is desired.

Finally, a word on response and security: a table can be set up in the database with a list of e-mail addresses and a corresponding number or some character sequence assigned to that e-mail address. When the user is contacted via e-mail and asked to fill out the survey form, they can be provided with this number or character sequence. This serves three purposes. First, you can keep a record of who has responded so that you do not bother respondents with follow-up e-mail messages. Second, it keeps visitors who are not in your sample from responding. And, third, it keeps respondents in the sample from skewing the results by repeatedly responding. On the down side, it allows you to connect responses with respondents. So if trust or confidentiality is an overriding issue, a more complicated scheme would have to be developed.

FUTURE TRENDS

Web technologies are in a constant state of evolution. Some of the design tips provided in this article, such as "name the fields in the form exactly the same as the fields in the database," may well become archaic over time. Others, such as "make sure that the size of the field on the form agrees with the size of the field in the database," are less likely to be overcome by technology. Others yet, such as "provide a Not Applicable option on radio buttons," will likely remain good advice regardless of how Web technologies evolve. We often find that technology defines the way we look at work. And, in the case of online surveys, this is no different. As Web technologies continue to evolve, the possibilities and the pitfalls of online surveys will also continue to evolve.

Due to the overwhelming benefits of doing surveys online, one would expect the future of online surveys to be very bright. It is likely that this technology is only beginning to be exploited. For example, beyond just surveys, it would be easy to construct panels to provide a longitudinal dimension to survey data. Panel members could be given user ids and passwords. They could then go to a site on some regular basis and fill out a survey providing results that were a measure of that moment in time. So the future trends should include greater use of online surveys and, increasingly, more support from Web technologies.

CONCLUSION

Online surveys vastly improve our ability to collect, store, and analyze survey data. By following some fairly simple design tips, we can further improve the ease with which this can be done.

REFERENCES

Bagui, S., & Earp, R. (2004). *Learning SQL: A step-by-step guide using Access*. Upper Saddle River, NJ: Addison-Wesley.

Balter, A. (2003). *Mastering Microsoft Office Access 2003*. Indianapolis, IN: Sam's Publishing.

Connolly, T., & Begg, C. (2005). *Database systems*, (4e). Addison-Wesley.

Deitel, H., Deitel, P., & Goldberg, A. (2004). *Internet & World Wide Web: How to program*. Upper Saddle River, NJ: Pearson /Prentice-Hall .

Kline, K. (2004). *SQL in a nutshell*. (2e). Sebastopol, CA: O'Reilly.

Kriegel, A., & Trukhnov, B. (2003). *SQL bible*. Indianapolis, IN: Wiley Publishing.

Musciano, C., & Kennedy, B. (2002). *HTML & XHTML: The definitive guide*. (5th ed.). Sebastopol, CA: O'Reilly.

Niederst, J. (2002). *HTML pocket reference* (2nd ed). Sebastopol, CA: O'Reilly.

KEY TERMS

Active Server Page: A program that executes on a Web server, providing some capabilities such as receiving data from an HTML form and inserting it in a database.

Hypertext Markup Language (HTML): The document formatting standard used on the World Wide Web.

HTML Form: An online data collection instrument defined using HTML tags.

Microsoft Access: A user friendly relational database for personal computers.

ODBC: Open database connection protocol, a platform independent protocol for connecting a program to a relational database.

Record Set: An object in an active server page program that acts as an intermediary between the program and the database. Typically, it corresponds to a table in the database, or contains the results of an SQL query.

Relational Database: A data repository in which data is stored in tables.

SQL: Structured query language, the language used to write queries against a relational database.

URL: Uniform resource locator, a standardized means of addressing Web pages.

Chapter VIII
Overcoming Challenges to Conducting Online Surveys

Jiali Ye
Georgia State University, USA

ABSTRACT

The widespread use of personal computers in the work place and at home has created a new opportunity of conducting research. With the increasing accessibility of the Internet and e-mail, using the new medium to distribute surveys is gaining popularity among researchers. The online survey, however, is a "double-edged sword," with the ability to access a large number of respondents at low costs, but the risk of increasing difficulties to evaluate the quality of the research (Couper, 2000). Concerns over response rates, sampling, and controlling the data collection environment have posed serious challenges to online survey researchers. The purpose of the present chapter is to offer suggestions for addressing these concerns. After a brief discussion on the formats of online surveys, the author will outline the challenges of conducting online surveys, and provide some strategies to overcome these challenges.

INTRODUCTION

Formats of Online Surveys

Internet-based research may appear in various forms, but generally there are two formats for online surveys: e-mail surveys and Web-based surveys.

E-mail surveys. According to Bachmann, Elfrink, and Vazzana (1996), e-mail questionnaires appeared almost simultaneously with the introduction of e-mail. E-mail surveys used to be restricted to population samples from within a company or a university. With the increasing number of e-mail users, e-mail surveys have been adopted by more business and academic communities. Conducting an e-mail survey involves several steps. First of all, researchers need to collect e-mail addresses of prospective respondents based on their research purposes. For example, some researchers used the technique of collecting e-mail addresses from listserves or newsgroups (Berge & Colins, 1996; Parks & Floyd, 1996). Then, questionnaires are sent by e-mails to users. Receivers can read the message, answer questions, and send the survey back to the researcher via e-mail.

Web-based surveys. One important feature of Web sites are forms that allow the user to select an option by clicking in small circles or boxes, or to type responses in a box. In a Web-based study, respondents are directed to a Web page containing a form (a questionnaire). They can fill out the form and then select an option to submit their answers. The answers then will be automatically passed to a program for scores, or sent to the researcher's e-mail. Compared to e-mail surveys, Web-based surveys are more standardized and convenient for users.

Challenges to Conducting Online Surveys and Improvement Strategies

Online surveys can be an effective and economic way to collect data. Miller and colleagues (Miller, Neal, Roberts, Baer, Cressler, Metrik, & Marlatt, 2002) noted that the superiority of Internet-based research to traditional methods lies in that "it potentially provides increased accessibility; capability for dynamic and interactive forms, which eliminate the viewing of irrelevant questions; and customized feedback tailored to the content of the responses" (p.56). When researchers use an online survey, they can enjoy a number of benefits linked to the Internet. However, they should also be prepared to face several challenges resulting from response rates, sampling, and control for data collection environment.

Response Rates

For surveys that do not identify the frame population: "the set of persons for whom some enumeration can be made prior to the selection of the sample" (Groves, 1989, p.82), it is impossible to find out response rates. However, e-mail surveys or Web-based surveys that use e-mails, or other personal contact methods to recruit respondents, have shown that an inadequate level of participation is very common for online surveys.

During the early stage of Internet research, the response rate of online surveys was its strength. At that time, online surveys were still limited to certain organizations. Sproull (1986) found that electronic mail surveys had response rates 20%

higher than paper surveys. As more and more researchers are targeting a wider range of Internet users, the response rate is increasingly becoming a problem. The response rates of Parks and Floyd's (1996) survey and Parks and Robert's (1998) survey on friendships formed on the Internet were only 35% and 20% respectively. Some marketing research achieved even lower response rates.

Researchers have used a variety of strategies to increase response rates. The following are some major strategies summarized from different studies:

Adopt recruiting tactics. Recruiting tactics are crucial to motivate people to participate in online surveys. Electronic prenotice has proven effective in increasing response rates. An e-mail that delivers the survey request can build trust and reduce uncertainty. An electronic reminder is another useful way to facilitate survey participation. Some people may not take the survey right after receiving the recruiting message. Researchers will get increased responses when they send follow-up e-mail reminders with the survey links included. Studies have suggested that sending follow-ups after initial survey requests may generate new waves of replies, even though the number of replies returned reduce with each follow-up (Zhang, 1999). Monetary or nonmonetary incentives can also have a positive effect in raising response rates. Depending on the nature of the study, incentives may range from small tokens or gift cards to Web shopping sites to free personal computers (Cho & LaRose, 1999). Prenotice, reminder, and incentives may be combined in a survey recruiting process to obtain the optimal result of response rates (Mehta & Sivadas, 1995)

In addition, the framing of the recruiting message also deserves deliberation. Dillman (2000) noted that personalized a e-mail invitation is positively related to response rates. One limitation of this technique is that names and titles of subscribers remain unknown (Zhang, 1999). This limitation may be decreased to a certain degree by carefully designed recruiting messages. Porter and Whitcomb (2003) found that in a recruiting message, both the statements of scarcity and a deadline when the survey Web site would be shut down have positive effects on response rates. The response rate was raised by almost 8 percentages by including a statement telling prospective respondents that they have been selected as part of a small group to participate in the study, and an announcement of the shut-down time of the Web site.

Improve survey design. Another desirable solution to low response rates is to improve the survey design itself. The researcher may adopt powerful tools to guide respondents through the survey and to motivate them to complete the task. Inappropriate hardware and software design may cause difficulties in computerized test. When the Web site has a level of technical sophistication that makes it difficult to get access to the survey, complete it, or submit it, respondents will be frustrated and unwilling to get involved in the study. The researcher needs to create relatively simple and technically uncomplicated designs that are compatible with different operating systems (Daley, McDermott, McCormack Brown, & Kittleson, 2003).

The content and length of the questionnaire can directly influence whether respondents are willing to provide answers. Users will only stay on a certain Web site if it is interesting or appealing, and this rule can be equally applied to online questionnaires (Gräf, 2002). If a questionnaire keeps asking for the same contents in a series of questions, respondents will soon feel bored. The length of a survey has been reported as a main factor to influence response behaviors (Tuten, Urban, & Bosnjak, 2002). The length of the questionnaire is positively linked to quitting rates and the likelihood of unreliability of answers. A golden rule given by Gräf (2002) is that no more than 25 opinions should be polled.

Protect respondents' privacy. Privacy concerns of Internet users may be a major reason for the reluctance of online survey participation. Privacy is a more sensitive issue for online surveys than for conventional survey methods because Internet users tend to see the computer as an extension of the self (Cho & LaRose, 1999). Online surveys are more likely to commit multiple violations of physical, informational, psychological, and interactional privacy. Thus, researchers need to try different means to minimize privacy invasion. For example, separate the consent from the survey, or offer multiple response options so that respondents may choose to return the questionnaire via other media (i.e., snail mail) (Cho & LaRose, 1999).

Reach targeted groups. Jackson and DeCormier (1999) suggested that targeting can increase responses. Finance-related questionnaires were sent to a sample of members from two financial newsgroups and two nonfinance newsgroups. Five hundred names were selected from each type of group. Although the nonfinance respondents achieved slightly higher response return rates (23%) than did the finance respondents (20%), 83% of the returned questionnaires from the finance groups were usable, compared to 54% of the returned questionnaires from the nonfinance groups. The researchers concluded that targeting is useful in collecting data online, especially for reaching marketing research. While it is true that targeting certain groups may increase the feeling of self-relevance of questions, the generalizability is limited, and researchers have to be cautious in interpreting the result because of the nonrandom sample.

Sampling

Sampling involves "(a) process of selecting a subset of cases in order to draw conclusions about the entire set" (Singleton & Straits, 1999, p.170). It is usually linked to the scientific goal of generalization. Various sources of potential bias related to sampling can cause threat to generalizability of the result of online surveys. For example, Internet users and nonusers differ in many aspects, such as education, income, race, and ethnicity.

In the late 1990s, this sampling bias was a main disadvantage of online surveys. The Internet users were primarily white, educated males. Over the past few years, the Internet users have been similar to the general population of developed countries. However, new concerns of sampling issues related to online surveys have emerged in recent years due to the high rate of nonresponses or unusable answers. Most online surveys got replies only from self-selected samples. These respondents are often more active on the Internet and interested in various forms of messages on the Web. Since self-selected respondents are relatively more homogeneous than randomly selected respondents, we may again question generalizability of the research result. To reduce sampling bias, researchers need to pay attention to the following aspects of sampling:

Accurately identify target population and sampling frame. Before selecting the sample, researchers need to have a clear picture of the target population. That is, they must clearly identify the population to which they would generalize their results (Singleton & Straits, 1999). After that, they can construct the sampling frame, the set of all cases from which the sample will be selected. In survey studies, sampling frame construction often amounts to establishing "an adequate listing—either of the population as a whole or of subgroups of the population" (p.139). Both the target population and the sampling frame should be carefully deliberated based on the category of online surveys.

Internet usage in survey research generally falls into two categories: (a) used for surveys that aim to explore features of Internet user populations; (b) used for surveys that are, by nature, a traditional type of research using the Internet as a data collection tool (Senior & Smith, 1999). If researchers are interested in characteristics of general Internet users or a special group of Internet users (e.g., online breast cancer support groups), an online survey is a desirable way, sometimes the only way, to reach these populations. For example, Parks and

Roberts' (1998) study explored relational topography in real-time text-based virtual environments known as MOOs. Conducting online surveys among Moo users was an appropriate method. If researchers use online surveys merely as an alternative to traditional forms of surveys, and the target population is not limited to Internet users, they have to consider the differences between users and nonusers. In such a case, in addition to the Internet, a researcher may consider using other survey collection methods, such as telephone or snail mail, to reach nonusers.

Carefully design sampling procedures. In spite of the difficulties to satisfy the requirement of generalizability in online research, some researchers have tried to recruit random samples with unique methods. Parks and Floyd's (1996) two-stage sampling procedure has been used as a good example for using random online samples (Döring, 2002). First, they randomly selected 24 newsgroups from published lists of groups. Then, 22 people were randomly chosen from lists of those who had posted messages to these groups. In the next step, the researchers sent surveys to prospective respondents by e-mail. About one third of the people contacted sent responses. The two-step procedure was replicated in many other online surveys. However, their low response rate allows the argument that among those who were randomly selected to receive questionnaires, only the self-selected samples chose to give a reply. Thus, to further solve the problem of sampling, researchers still need to consider tactics for increasing response rates.

Control for the Data Collection Environment

With Internet surveys, the actual data collection environment is impossible to control or monitor. Researchers cannot detect any random factors that can influence the respondent. Like traditional mail surveys, for online surveys, researchers can hardly tell whether it is the addressee who actually completes the survey or unintended respondents instead. Besides, the same respondents may submit answers multiple times, which can corrupt the data collected.

So far, the data collection supervision mainly relies on technical controls. For example, certain technical controls can be used to identify and control for potential multiple visits. Although it is hard to tell which particular Internet users have participated in a survey, it is possible to identify the unique IP address of the computer they are using. Some researchers log this information and screen out any multiple submissions from the same address (e.g., Buchanan & Smith, 1999). Sometimes, other identification methods are used to prevent multiple responses. In their online study, Knapp and Kirt (2003) used a software, deliberately programmed for the Web site, to admit only a respondent who had a valid access code. The access codes were randomly generated and checked for uniqueness so that no two codes were alike.

While technical control may effectively control the survey environment, some scholars argued that the placement of cookies or small identifying files on respondents' computers may raise serious Internet privacy concerns (Cho & LaRose, 1999). It is suggested that if such information has to be recorded, researchers need to make information included in the cookies visible to respondents.

CONCLUSION

Collecting data via the Internet has been shown to be viable and promising. As the use of the Internet expands, the prevalence of online surveys will continue to grow. Compared to traditional surveys, online surveys need more deliberation on construction, administration, and evaluation. This paper offers suggestions for minimizing problems resulting from response rates, sampling, and control over the data collection environment. Fast-changing Internet technology requires researchers

to continue to learn new technologies involved in Internet research, and explore ways to improve the effectiveness of this research tool.

REFERENCES

Bachmann, D., Elfrink, J., & Vazzana, G. (1996). Tracking the progress of e-mail vs. snail-mail. *Marketing Research, 8*(2), 31-35.

Berge, Z. L., & Collins, M. P. (1996). "IPCT Journal" readership survey. *Journal of the American Society for Information Science, 47(9),* 701-710.

Buchanan, T., & Smith, J. (1999). Using the Internet for psychological research: Personality testing on the World Wide Web. *The British Psychological society, 90*(1), 125-144.

Cho, H., & LaRose, R. (1999). Privacy issues in Internet surveys. *Social Science Computer Review, 17*(4), 421-434.

Couper, M. (2000). Web survey: A review of issues and approaches. *Public Opinion Quarterly, 64*(4), 464-494.

Daley, E. M., McDermott, R. J., McCormack Brown, K. R., & Kittleson, M. J. (2003). Conducting Web-based survey research: A lesson in Internet design. *American Journal of Health Behavior, 27*(2), 116-124.

Dillman, D. (2000). *Mail and Internet surveys: The tailored design method.* New York: John Wiley & Sons.

Döring, N. (2002). Studying online love and cyber romance. In B. Batinic, U. Reips, & M. Bosnjak (Eds.), *Online social sciences* (pp. 333-356). Seattle: Hogrefe & Huber Publishers.

Gräf, G. (2002). Assessing Internet questionnaires: The online pretest lab. In B. Batinic, U. Reips, & M. Bosnjak (Eds.), *Online social sciences* (pp. 49-68). Seattle: Hogrefe & Huber Publishers.

Groves, R. M. (1989). *Survey errors and survey costs*. New York, NY: John Wiley & Sons.

Jackson, A., & DeCormier, R. (1999). E-mail survey response rates: Targeting increases response. *Marketing Intelligence & Planning, 17*(3), 135-139.

Knapp, H., & Kirk, S. (2003). Using pencil and paper, Internet and touch-tone phones for self-administered surveys: Does methodology matter? *Computers in Human Behavior, 19*(1), 117-134.

Mehta, R., & Sivadas, E. (1995). Comparing response rates and response content in mail vs. electronic mail surveys. *Journal of the Market Research Society, 37*(4), 429- 39.

Miller, E., Neal, D., Roberts, L., Baer, J., Cressler, S., Metrik, J., & Marlatt, G. (2002). Test-retest reliability of alcohol measures: Is there a difference between Internet-based assessment and traditional methods? *Psychology of Additive Behaviors, 16,* 56-63.

Parks, M. R., & Floyd, K. (1996). Making friends in Cyberspace. *Journal of Communication, 46*(1), 80-97.

Parks, M. R., & Roberts, L. D. (1998). "Making MOOsic": The development of personal relationships on line and a comparison to their offline counterparts. *Journal of Social and Personal Relationships, 15,* 517-537.

Porter, S. R., & Whitcomb, M. E. (2003). The impact of contact type on Web survey response rates. *Public Opinion Quarterly, 67*(4), 579-588.

Senior, C., & Smith, M. (1999). The Internet … A possible research tool? *The Psychologist, 12*(9), 442-444.

Singleton, R. A., & Straits, B. C. (1999). *Approaches to social research* (3rd ed.). New York: Oxford University Press.

Sproull, L. S. (1986). Using electronic mail for data collection in organizational research. *Academy of Management Journal, 29*(1), 159-69.

Tuten, T., Urban, D., & Bosnjak, M. (2002). Internet survey and data quality: A review. In B. Batinic, U. Reips, & M. Bosnjak (Eds.), *Online social sciences* (pp. 7-26). Seattle: Hogrefe & Huber Publishers.

Zhang, Y. (1999). Using the Internet for survey research: A case study. *Journal of the American Society for Information Science, 51*(1), 57-68.

KEY TERMS

E-Mail Surveys: Surveys distributed and collected via e-mail. Conducting e-mail surveys usually involves composing e-mail contact lists, sending e-mails with the questionnaire to the prospective respondents, and receiving answers from the respondents.

Random Sample: A sample in which each member of a population has an equal chance of being included in the sample.

Response Rate: The proportion of people in the sample from whom completed questionnaires are received.

Self-Selected Sample: A sample that is collected by respondents volunteering their responses. In such a sample, respondents themselves decide whether to be included in a study.

Sampling: A process of taking any portion of a population as the representative of that population. Ideally, a sample provides unbiased reflection of a population.

Sampling Frame: The set of all cases from which the sample is actually chosen. Developing a sampling frame often amounts to getting an adequate listing of the whole population, or of subgroups of the population.

Web-Based Surveys: Surveys posted on Web sites. Respondents access a Web page containing a questionnaire. After filling out the questionnaire, they can select an option to submit the answer. The answers will be passed to a program for scores, or sent to the researcher's e-mail.

Chapter IX
Sampling in Online Surveys

Gerd Beidernikl

Center for Education and Economy Research & Consulting, Austria

Arno Kerschbaumer

Center for Education and Economy Research & Consulting, Austria

ABSTRACT

Online surveys have grown very popular in the past few years. They offer some major advantages compared to paper-and-pencil surveys. Nevertheless, some difficulties arise when online survey methods are applied: this especially concerns sampling and the question of representativeness. This article introduces the particularities of sampling in online surveys, and discusses the limitation of research settings (online surveys) for achieving population representativeness in the research sample.

INTRODUCTION

The World Wide Web, and its uncountable practical applications in every part of private and business life, has greatly affected and influenced social research. Using the Internet for both primary and secondary research has become a standard procedure in the social and psychological sciences worldwide. Online research itself is a widespread term used in different contexts including very different types of primary research such as Web surveys, Web interviews, Web experiments, Web observation, text and content analysis in the Internet, and the analysis of hard data such as logfiles (cf. Knapp 2003, p. 1). All these applications can be subsumed under "online research," as they collect data via the Web, but not all of them will be discussed in this chapter. In the following, we will concentrate on the Internet as a tool for the quantitative questioning of people and, therefore, the Internet as a new instrument for applying classical methods of social research.

Quantitative online survey tools offer a lot of advantages compared to paper-and-pencil questionnaires. To highlight the most obvious ones:

- Easy and cheap distribution of questionnaires among a high number of people via e-mail.
- The respondent is "guided" through the questionnaire. The survey becomes more than just a form to be filled in.
- The researcher can easily use multimedia such as pictures, sounds, flash animations, and even movies in the questionnaire as a stimulus.

- It is possible to give the questionnaire a logical structure using filter questions, ramifications, and so forth. The respondent only gets the questions suitable for him/her.
- It is possible to build in validation procedures (e.g., does the answer on question "driving license" match with the answer on question "age") and real-time checks (e.g., postal codes are checked if they are correct).

Different Types of Online Surveys

When talking about quantitative online surveys, we have to make a differentiation according to two main points:

- How is the survey carried out?
- How are the respondents invited or recruited?

The answer to these two questions helps to distinguish different forms of quantitative online surveys (cf. Mac Elroy 1999). In the first dimension "how is the survey carried out" we can intergrade the following types of surveys:

1. E-mail questionnaires
2. Web site surveys
3. (Interactive) Online questionnaires
4. Downloadable surveys
5. Bulletin boards

E-Mail Questionnaires

Without a doubt, the earliest method of conducting surveys over the Internet or over a company's internal system (intranet) is the text-based e-mail questionnaire. This kind of online survey simply uses the advantages of e-mail for sending out questionnaires. The receiver gets the questionnaire; fills in the questions, either directly into the file sent as an attachment or on a printout of the questionnaire; and returns the filled-in form via e-mail, or by using classical channels such as

fax or postal services. This type of survey can be generally thought of as an online form of paper-and-pencil surveys.

Web Site Surveys

Another possibility to do online surveys is to implement a survey directly on a Web site, programming it as an HTML page on the Web server. Every visitor to the Web site either directly sees the questionnaire, or an invitation to it opening up (popping up) in a separate Internet window (more or less suddenly when visiting a certain page) asking the visitor to the home page to participate in the survey. This kind of pop-up invitation attracts the attention of the home page visitor and, therefore, guarantees that a fixed Web site survey will not be overlooked. In most cases, this type of survey consists of just a few, maybe only one question, referring to actual topics. This type of research is often used as a kind of self-evaluation of Web sites, too (e.g., Did you find the information offered on this Web site useful?—Yes/No).

(Interactive) Online Questionnaires

This most advanced kind of online questionnaire is, nowadays, the most common type of online survey. In one or the other aspect, it might look quite similar to the fixed Web site and the pop-up survey (and there are a lot of similarities for sure as they represent former modes of online surveys), but they offer a lot more technical possibilities, and can be used in more research contexts (the two forms of online surveys explained before can be understood as the most simple forms of Web site surveys) (cf. Dannenberg; Barthel, 2002, p. 148f).

In general, these online questionnaires can be understood as programmed questionnaires on the Internet. These advanced surveys can be programmed directly in HTML or similar languages, but in most cases, the researchers use professional online questionnaire design software. These applications offer the possibility to design and build a survey (comparable to Web design tools such as Dreamweaver) in a very easy way, without the need for technical knowledge. Another difference is that the survey and its data are not implemented on a Web site, but normally on a special survey server of the providing survey tool company.

In the simplest case, these surveys consist of a one-page list of questions with checkboxes offering the possibility to mark one's answers. In more advanced cases, the test person is guided through the questionnaire in an interactive way. Multimedia such as pictures, sounds, or movies can be implemented in the survey, and the simple "filling in the form" is enhanced by a dynamic logical structure (e.g., the test person is guided through the questionnaire by using decision questions; the respondent, therefore, only sees the questions suitable for him/her), internal validation procedures (e.g., e-mail addresses or postal codes are checked in real time if they are correct), and real-time statistics (at the end of the survey the test person sees his/her own answers compared to former respondents).

The questionnaires can then be distributed in different ways: by e-mail containing a link to the survey site, or by implementing a link or a pop-up on a home page. Afterwards, the data from the filled-in forms can be downloaded as a data file from the survey site.

Downloadable Surveys

Downloadable surveys are a quite exotic form of surveys that is rarely used. In this case, the survey is downloaded from a Web page by the respondents. In most cases, the survey is a kind of self-extracting software that is installed on the user's own PC. The user fills in the questionnaire and, afterwards, the survey data is uploaded to the Internet again. This kind of survey is very time consuming and out of date, too. Nevertheless, in some psychological studies, this procedure is still used for specific test situations.

Bulletin Boards

Another exotic form of online survey is represented by bulletin boards. They mark the borderline of qualitative to quantitative online research. The technique involves inviting people to a specific Web site where a discussion board is posted. People can respond to the questions and can eventually see what others have posted. The researcher analyzes the answers given in these discussion boards due to specific criteria. The usage of this method might appear to be useful, for example, in a Delphi setting.

Recruitment

As already said, not only how the survey is carried out but also how the respondents are recruited is crucial. We can, in this regard, distinguish between two main options with two subdimensions each:

- Selection
  - Selective
  - Nonselective
- Recruiting
  - Active recruitment
  - Passive recruitment

The term selection refers to how the respondents are chosen. Selective means that the respondents are chosen, by the researcher, according to some specific criteria such as affiliation to a certain group (e.g., customers of a company). Nonselective means that the researcher passes on without such a selection resp. is not possible to select people according to criteria (e.g., all visitors of a home page).

Recruitment indicates how the respondents are invited to participate in the survey. Active, in this connection, means the respondent gets an individual invitation that asks him to participate. As an example, one could mention e-mail-invitations or pop-up windows. Passive means that the respondent is invited on a nonindividual basis. The best example might be a simple link on a home page saying: "Ongoing survey on XYZ: Please participate!". No one gets addressed actively. Participation depends on the particular interest and self-recruitment.

SAMPLING AND ONLINE SURVEYS

Carrying out a survey always has the aim to collect data about a certain population. In the easiest case, the population is small and, therefore, it is possible to question all relevant persons to get a complete picture of their opinions on a certain topic (complete survey) (cf. Diekmann, 2000, p. 324f). As group size increases, the difficulties to question everyone are increasing too (organizing the survey, costs of the survey, etc.). Although Web surveys offer a very good cost ratio for large surveys, it becomes obvious that at a certain stage, only a sample of people can be questioned. This especially concerns surveys that are aiming at being representative for the whole population of a city, a province or a country. In this case, conclusions about the whole population are drawn from the data collected from a sample of the population (sampled survey) (cf. Noelle-Neumann & Petersen, 1998, p. 229).

This leads to the question "how well a given sample represent the total population from which it was taken" and, therefore, whether the sampling is a valid procedure for ensuring representativeness or not. In the context of online surveys, one has to ask three basic questions:

1. Is the target group of the survey clearly defined, and has every individual access to the Internet?
2. Is it possible to invite these people individually (selectively and actively), based on a specified selection resp. sampling procedure to the survey?

3. Is this selection resp. sampling procedure in case of the underlying population suitable to collect representative data?

Question 1 is a crucial question when talking about sampling. In the case of some target groups (e.g., clients or employees of a company), the population is perfectly defined, and one can find out whether these people are contactable via the Internet or not (e.g., e-mail information in the customer database). In the case that a survey should be representative of a whole nation, the population can be defined as clearly (e.g., citizens of Austria, by a certain deadline, aged 18 or above), but the access to the Internet will be a problem as Internet access can not be guaranteed for every person in a nation (e.g., the Web-access ratio in Germany is about 50% (Faas, 2003, p. 59)) In other cases, the target group itself might be hard to define (e.g., Internet users) because there is a lack of background information on that population to give a valid picture of it.

Question 2 arises if the population can be defined as it was shown in the prior paragraph. Sampling procedures (random sampling, quota sampling) can be used in online surveys, in general, as they can be used in paper-based surveys, but that would include selectively and actively recruited respondents in the survey. In the case of a quote—sampling, the researcher needs further background information on the population to define the quotas and contact people fulfilling these criteria (cf. Technical University Berlin, 2000, p.17f). This again might be possible for certain target groups, but in most cases, this will be a problem.

Question 3 is the final question giving the answer if the researcher can expect representative results or not. We have already shown that it is not possible to reach representativeness for a whole population (nation, city, etc.) via online survey, as not everyone of this population can be expected to have access to the Web. At any rate, online surveys are restricted to WWW users. It is important to mention that even weighting the answers collected via the Web cannot establish representativeness. Weighting would have to be based on some attributes too, and there is no valid information on the differences between Internet users and nonusers in this connection (cf. Schoen, 2004, p. 28f). Systematic biases: Who is using the Web (no 50+, mainly young …)

For certain definable populations of WWW –users, for example, visitors to a home page, representativeness can be reached to a high amount. (Other problems, like a low participation rate in the survey, might arise, but are not discussed in this chapter). For even better-defined subgroups of WWW users (e.g., clients, employees of a certain company), the sampling procedure can definitely deliver representative results (even a total questioning of all members is possible).

Beside all these considerations on representativeness, one has always to remember that being representative is not necessary in every social research context. Especially, surveys with an explorative character might neglect the aim of being representative and, therefore, can easily be carried out via the Web.

Representativeness

Based on these basic assumptions on sampling in a survey, especially in an online setting, one has to think of how these basic preconditions of representativeness can be fulfilled for specific settings.

Representativeness for the whole population. It is not possible to be representative of the whole population by using online surveys. Not every group of persons can be reached via the WWW because the Internet penetration, even in Europe, is still low. Some population groups are underrepresented (e.g., elderly people, women) and, therefore, systematically neglected or even excluded from such a survey.

Representativeness for the Internet population. One could conclude that representativeness can be achieved at least for the population of WWW users. This assumption is incorrect for a few reasons: First of all, the population of WWW users is not clearly defined as there does not exist a complete directory of them; thus, it is impossible to draw a correct sample (cf. Bandilla, 1999, p. 9). Secondly, and consequently, inviting people to a study is mainly based on active but nonindividual invitations via pop-ups, banners, and so forth, instead of being based on invitations on an individual basis; therefore, samples are not drawn actively by the researcher. The respondents are chosen by self-recruitment (cf. Hauptmanns, 1999, p. 27). These self-recruitment processes underlie uncontrolled selection processes that cannot be controlled by the researcher and are therefore risky.

Representativeness for a certain population. For certain well-defined subgroups of people, online surveys seem to be a very good choice for carrying out a study as long as the recruitment takes place selectively and actively. If the whole population is defined, Internet access can be assured for every member of this target group and even contact information can be made available; surveys can be carried out that fit the high aim of representativeness. In other cases, even if the population is not defined but at least definable (e.g., visitors of a home page), representativeness can be reached to a high amount. In this connection, self-recruitment should be avoided as far as possible by using active invitation procedures, or recruiting certain target groups for an online survey off-line (e.g., via access panels. cf. Faas, 2003).

CONCLUSION

All in all, one can say the online surveys are, although of growing popularity, not able to substitute for classical off-line research instruments in every research situation. Although the community of WWW users is growing fast, representativeness in online surveys cannot be assured for the whole population. Furthermore, the absence of a boundary resp. directory of WWW users makes it impossible to draw correct samples. Online surveys based on Web sites run the risk of systematical distortions because of low participation rates and self-recruitment processes that can hardly be controlled by the researchers.

Online surveys offer advantages as well. But these advantages only make an impact in certain situations. The usage of online surveys can be recommended in three cases: First of all, for well-defined subgroups that can be completely defined and accessed via the Web and, where it is possible, to draw a correct sample; secondly, in cases where a nonrandom sample shall be drawn; and thirdly, in explorative research settings where representativeness is not necessary.

REFERENCES

Bandilla, W. (1999). WWW-Umfragen—Eine alternative Datenerhebungstechnik für die empirische Sozialforschung? In B. Batinic (Ed.), *Online-research. Methoden, Anwendungen und Ergebnisse* (pp. 9-19). Göttingen: Hogrefe.

Dannenbarg, B. (2002). *Effiziente Marktforschung*. Bonn: Galileo Business.

Diekman, A. (2000). *Empirische Sozialforschung*. Reinbeck: Rororo.

Faas, T. (2003). Offline Rekrutierte Access Panels: Königsweg der Online Forschung? *ZUMA-Nachrichten 53*, 58-76.

Hauptmanns, P. (1999). Grenzen und Chancen von quantitativen Befragungen mit Hilfe des Internet. In B. Batinic (Eds.), *Online-research. Methoden, Anwendungen und Ergebnisse* (pp. 45-54). Göttingen: Hogrefe.

Knapp, F. (2003). *Aktuelle Probleme der Online Forschung*. Retrieved June 30, 2006, from http://www.psyma-online.de

Mac Elroy, B. (1999). Comparing seven forms of online surveying. *Quirk's Marketing Research Review*, (0510).

Noelle-Neumann, E., & Petersen, T. (1998). *Alle, nicht jeder*. Berlin; Heiderlberg: Springer.

Schoen, H. (2004). Online Umfragen—schnell, billig, aber auch valide? *ZA-Information 54*, 27-29.

Technical University Berlin (2000). *Anwendungsbereiche, Validität und Representativität der Marktforschung über das Internet*. Retrieved June 30, 2006, from http://www.art-x.de/diplom/semi.pdf

KEY TERMS

Flash: A bandwidth friendly and browser independent vector-graphic animation technology. As long as different browsers are equipped with the necessary plug-ins, Flash animations will look the same.

HyperText Markup Language (HTML): Tthe authoring language used to create documents on the World Wide Web.

Interactivity: A dialogue between a human being and the computer. Unlike other forms of media, like print, radio, and television, the Web allows the visitor to shape the experience. Interactivity should improve the user's navigation of the content, improve reaction to the user's desires, help maintain the user's interest and finally improve the user's participation.

Log File: A file that lists actions that have occurred. For example, Web servers maintain log files listing every request made to the server. With log file analysis tools, it is possible to get a good idea of where visitors are coming from, how often they return, and how they navigate through a site.

Pop-Up: A pop-up is a graphical user interface (GUI) display area, usually a small window, that suddenly appears ("pops up") in the foreground of the visual interface. A pop-up window must be smaller than the background window or interface; otherwise, it is a replacement interface.

Representativeness: The degree to which data accurately and precisely represents a characteristic of a population, parameter variations at a sampling point, or an environmental condition. It is a qualitative parameter that is most concerned with the proper design of the sampling program.

Web Site: A site (location) on the World Wide Web. Each Web site contains a home page, which is the first document users see when they enter the site. The site might also contain additional documents and files. Each site is owned and managed by an individual, company, or organization.

Chapter X
Equivalence of Electronic and Off–Line Measures

Lynne D. Roberts
Crime Research Centre, University of Western Australia, Australia

ABSTRACT

This chapter explores the measurement equivalence of paper-and-pencil and electronic surveys and measures. After reviewing competing claims and the limitations of the research, there is a strong case that many measures do retain their psychometric equivalence across modes of administration, with the exception of speeded tests and measures that may be subject to social desirability response sets.

INTRODUCTION

Paper-and-pencil surveys and measures are frequently transformed into electronic formats for use. Many assume that because the questions remain identical that the two modes of administration can be used interchangeably, but is this the case? Does the mode of administration of surveys and measures make a difference to the results obtained? This chapter explores the measurement equivalence of paper-and-pencil and electronic surveys and measures. First, measurement equivalence is defined and methods of determining equivalence outlined. Next is an examination of the research literature pertaining to the extent and type of differences that have been found by modes of administration, and the reasons hypothesized to account for these differences. This is followed by an examination of the limitations of the research conducted to date. Finally, recommendations are provided for the electronic administration of paper-and-pencil surveys and measures.

BACKGROUND

Historically, many measures and surveys have been created in a paper-and-pencil format for interviewer or self-administration. The introduction of computers to the academic community enabled attempts to computerize many measures (Epstein & Klinkenberg, 2001). With the introduction of the Internet, a further stage in the evolution of measures has developed: the electronic distribution of surveys and measures. The introduction of Hypertext Markup Language 2 (HTML 2) in 1994 provided the means for the administration of form-based surveys and measures on the World Wide Web, with the first academic surveys administered on the World Wide Web in 1995 (Birnbaum, 2004).

What is Measurement Equivalence?

Measurement equivalence refers to the stability of a measure's factor structure across situations. When paper-and-pencil measures are converted for use in electronic environments, it is essential to maintain the psychometric properties of the measure. In order to determine measurement equivalence across modes of administration, an assessment of means, standard deviations, and structures resulting from the two modes of administration are required. In addition, the two results should be highly correlated to ensure they are both measuring the same concept (Taris, Bok, & Meijer, 1998). Statistical methods used to study the structural invariance of measures are confirmatory factor analysis and item response theory (Meade & Lautenschlager, 2004; Raju, Laffitte, & Byrne, 2002). A detailed account of the procedures involved in establishing measurement equivalence is beyond the scope of this article, but see Taris and colleagues (1998) for an eight-step procedure for determining structural invariance.

Are Electronic and Paper-and-Pencil Measures Equivalent?

Early measurement equivalence research compared paper-and-pencil and pre-Internet computer administered measures and surveys. The results obtained varied by the type of measure. Mead and Drasgow (1993) conducted a meta-analysis of computer vs. paper-and-pencil cognitive ability tests, based on 29 studies and 159 correlations. They concluded that speeded tests were affected by mode of administration (moderate effect size), but that timed power tests (tests that assess ability within a practical limitation of time) were

not. A suggested reason for the differences in speeded tests by mode of administration was the different motor skills required for computer and paper-and-pencil tests. In contrast to the cognitive tests, no differences were found in work-related noncognitive tests (King & Miles, 1995) and only minor differences found in nonaptitude psychological measures (Rosenfeld, Booth-Kewley, Edwards, & Thomas, 1993). Most differences found in personality tests such as the MMPI, EPI, 16PF, and CPI were attributable to the different response options offered, rather than the actual mode of administration, highlighting the need for instructions, presentation, and response formats to be kept equivalent (Rosenfeld et al., 1993). The measurement equivalence of computerized adaptive testing (where the level of subsequent items is determined by previous responses) has yet to be established (Epstein & Klinkenberg, 2001).

Survey responses may also be affected by mode of administration. Liefeld (1988) found that similar responses were obtained on multiple-choice and yes/no questions in computer-administered, personal interview, and self-completion measures. However, for questions where multiple responses could be selected, higher numbers of responses were selected in the computer-administered condition. Similarly, Mehta and Sivadas (1995) reported no differences in classification or attitudinal variables by mode of administration (e-mail vs. paper-and-pencil), but found that e-mail respondents write more comments than paper-and-pencil respondents. Keyboard design, screen size, screen illumination, and processing speed of respondents' computers do not affect survey responses (Rosenfeld, Doherty, Vicino, Kantor, & Greaves, 1989). However, responses can be affected by the programming of measures, such as the ability to scan, preview, review, or change answers (Kiesler & Sproull, 1986; Whitener & Klein, 1995). Thus, the programming of surveys and measures appears of more importance than the actual computer hardware used by research participants.

More recent studies comparing World Wide Web and paper-and-pencil surveys and measures have reported no significant differences on personality measures (Salgado & Moscoso, 2003), health related measures (Bressani & Downs, 2002; Ritter, Lorig, Laurent, & Matthews, 2004); attitudinal measures (Cronk & West, 2002; Meyerson & Tryon, 2003); organizational measures (Stanton, 1998) and ratings of physical and sexual attractiveness (Epstein, Klinkenberg, Wiley & McKinley, 2001). Reversing this trend, Barbiette and Weiss (2004) reported that measures of computer anxiety and computer self-efficacy lack measurement equivalence between electronic and paper-and-pencil modes of administration. Barbiette and Weiss argued that measures of beliefs, cognitions, and affect towards computers are likely to differ systematically between computer users and others.

A number of studies have examined respondents' attitudes to the computer administration of research. While some studies have reported favorable attitudes from respondents, and a preference for computer-administered questionnaires (Burke & Normand, 1987; Lukin, Dowd, Plake, & Kraft, 1985, Rosenfeld et al., 1989; Skinner & Allen, 1983), others have reported neutral attitudes (Finegan & Allen, 1994; Sproull, 1986). It is possible that attitudes towards computer administration reflect an individual's perception of their own computer competence and attitudes towards computers generally.

Prior to the introduction of the Internet, a body of research examined the effect of computer administration on impression management. While some research found no differences in social desirability responding between paper-and-pencil and computer administered surveys (Booth-Kewley, Edwards, & Rosenfeld, 1992; Finegan & Allen, 1994), others have noted less socially desirable responding on computer-administered surveys (Kiesler & Sproull, 1986). Rosenfeld et al. (1991) noted that is was high self-monitors who gave more socially desirable responses on

paper-and-pencil questionnaires than on computer surveys, with computer surveys eliciting higher candor in areas of greater sensitivity. Weisband and Kiesler (1996) conducted a meta-analysis of self-disclosure based on 39 studies and 100 measures between 1969 and 1994, concluding that computer administration increases self-disclosure. However, the size of this effect was found to be declining over time, a factor they attributed to the public's growing acceptance of, and knowledge about, computers.

Surveys and measures administered on the World Wide Web may further reduce the demand characteristics associated with off-line research by increasing both research participant and experimenter anonymity (Hewson, Laurent, & Vogel, 1996; Joinson, 1999; Smith & Leigh, 1997). This increased anonymity of responding to surveys online, in comparison to face-to-face surveys, results in decreased social desirability responding and social anxiety, and increased self-disclosure by research participants (Davis, 1999; Joinson, 1999).

In summary, the research to date suggests that many measures perform equivalently with paper-and-pencil and electronic submission. Two areas where measurement nonequivalence is likely are speeded tests, and measures of beliefs, cognitions, and affect towards computers. The most commonly found differences in other measures are a reduction in social desirability response sets, resulting in greater self-disclosure with electronic formats.

Limitations of Research to Date

The research to date on the measurement equivalence of electronic and paper-and-pencil surveys and measures has been subject to a number of limitations. First, some studies have used nonequivalent comparison groups. To determine the equivalence of electronic and paper-and-pencil measures, equivalent comparison groups must be used. Comparing the results from nonequivalent comparison groups is confounded by selection biases. The gold standard for the selection of equivalent comparison groups is random assignment to modes of administration (Epstein et al., 2001). For example, Ritter and colleagues (2004) recruited research participants through the Internet, and randomly assigned them to electronic or paper-and-pencil mode of administration.

Second, some studies have used inappropriate statistical analyses. In determining equivalence, it is not sufficient only to find no significant differences between groups. In addition, the factor structures of measures need to be examined to ensure they are equivalent (Epstein et al., 2001).

Finally, consideration needs to be taken of where surveys or measures are completed. There may be different demand effects associated with completing a survey/measure on the Internet in a classroom rather than in one's own home or workplace. For example, Cronk and West (2002) found that response rates in Internet surveys were affected by place of completion, with surveys completed at home having lower response rates than surveys completed in a classroom.

CONCLUSION

The equivalence of measures has been described as a "fundamental assumption of Internet (online) research" (Meyerson & Tryon, 2003, p. 614). Research to date suggests that many measures do retain their psychometric equivalence across modes of administration. This equivalence does not hold across all types of measures. Particular care needs to be taken with speeded tests, measures of beliefs, cognitions, and affect towards computers and measures that may be subject to social desirability response sets.

Researchers planning to use electronic versions of paper-and-pencil surveys and measures have a responsibility to ensure that measurement equivalence is not just assumed, but established in order to ensure that the reliability and valid-

ity of their research is not jeopardized. The first step in this process is to check whether previous researchers have examined the measurement equivalence of the measures of interest. If no previous examination of measurement equivalence by mode of administration has been undertaken this will need to be conducted by the researcher to meet the current standards for educational and psychological testing (American Educational Research Association, American Psychological Association, and National Council on Measurement in Education, 1999).

REFERENCES

American Educational Research Association, American Psychological Association, and National Council on Measurement in Education (1999). *Standards for educational and psychological testing*. Washington, DC: American Psychological Association.

Barbiette, F. G., & Weiss, E. M. (2004). Computer self-efficacy and anxiety scales for an Internet sample: Testing measurement equivalence of existing measures and development of new scales. *Computers in Human Behavior, 20*, 1-15.

Birnbaum, M. H. (2004). Methodological and ethical issues in conducting social psychology research via the Internet. In C. Sansone, C. C. Morf, & A. T. Panter (Eds.), *Handbook of methods in social psychology* (pp. 359-382). Thousand Oaks, CA: Sage.

Booth-Kewley, S., Edwards, J. E., & Rosenfeld, P. (1992). Impression management, social desirability, and computer administration of attitude questionnaires: Does the computer make a difference? *Journal of Applied Psychology, 77*, 562-566.

Bressani, R. V., & Downs, A. C. (2002). Youth independent living assessment: Testing the equivalence of Web and paper/pencil versions of the

Ansell-Casey Life Skills Assessment. *Computers in Human Behavior, 18*, 453-464.

Burke, M. J., & Normand, J. (1987). Computerized psychological testing: Overview and critique. *Professional Psychology: Research and Practice, 18*, 42-51.

Cronk, B. C., & West, J. L. (2002). Personality research on the Internet: A comparison of Web-based and traditional instruments in take-home and in-class settings. *Behavior, Research Methods, Instruments & Computers, 34*(2), 177-180.

Davis, R. N. (1999). Web-based administration of a personality questionnaire: Comparison with traditional methods. *Behavior Research Methods, Instruments, and Computers, 31*, 572-577.

Epstein, J., & Klinkenberg, W. D. (2001). From Eliza to Internet: A brief history of computerized assessment. *Computers in Human Behavior, 17*, 295-314.

Epstein, J., Klinkenberg, W. D., Wiley, D., & McKinley, L. (2001). Insuring sample equivalence across Internet and paper-and-pencil assessments. *Computers in Human Behavior, 17*, 339-346.

Finegan, J. E., & Allen, N. J. (1994). Computerized and written questionnaires: Are they equivalent? *Computers in Human Behavior, 10*, 483-496.

Hewson, C. M., Laurent, D., & Vogel, C. M. (1996). Proper methodologies for psychological and sociological studies conducted via the Internet. *Behavior Research Methods, Instruments, and Computers, 28*, 186-191.

Hinkle, J. S., Sampson, J. P., & Radonsky, V. (1991). Computer assisted vs. paper-and-pencil assessment of personal problems in a clinical population. *Computers in Human Behavior, 7*, 237-242.

Joinson, A. (1999). Social desirability, anonymith, and Internet-based questionnaires. *Behavior,*

Research Methods, Instruments & Computers, 31(3), 433-438.

Kiesler, S., & Sproull, L. S. (1986). Response effects in the electronic survey. *Public Opinion Quarterly, 50*, 402-413.

King, W. C., & Miles, E. W. (1995). A quasi-experimental assessment of the effect of computerizing noncognitive paper-and-pencil measurement: A test of measurement equivalence. *Journal of Applied Psychology, 80*, 643-651.

Liefeld, J. (1988). Response effects in computer-administered questioning. *Journal of Marketing Research, 25*, 405-409.

Lukin, M. E., Dowd, E. T., Plake, B. S., & Kraft, R. G. (1985). Comparing computerized vs. traditional psychological assessment. *Computers in Human Behavior, 1*, 49-58.

Mead, A. D. & Drasgow, F. (1993). Equivalence of computerized and paper-and-pencil cognitive ability tests: A meta-analysis. *Psychological Bulletin, 114*(3), 449-458.

Meade, A. W., & Lautenschlager, G. J. (2004). A comparison of item response theory and confirmatory factor analytic methodologies for establishing measurement equivalence/invariance. *Organizational Research Methods, 7*(4), 361-388.

Mehta, R., & Sivadas, E. (1995). Comparing response rates and response content in mail vs. electronic mail surveys. *Journal of the Market Research Society, 37*, 429-439.

Meyerson, P., & Tryon, W. W. (2003). Validating Internet research: A test of the psychometric equivalence of Internet and in-person samples. *Behavior Research Methods, Instrument & Computers, 35*(4), 614-620.

Raju, N. S., Laffitte, L. J., Byrne, B. M. (2002). Measurement equivalence: A comparison of methods based on confirmatory factor analysis and item response theory. *Journal of Applied Psychology, 87*(3), 517-529.

Ritter, P., Lorig, K., Laurent, D., & Matthews, K. (2004). Internet vs. mailed questionnaires: A randomized comparison. *Journal of Medical Internet Research, 6*(3):e29. Retrieved June 24, 2006 from http://www.jmir.org/2004/3/e29/

Rosenfeld, P., Booth-Kewley, S., Edwards, J. E., & Thomas. M. D. (1993). Computer-administered surveys in organizational settings: Alternatives, advantages, and applications. *American Behavioral-Scientist, 36,* 485-511.

Rosenfeld, P., Doherty, L. M., Vicino, S. M., Kantor, J., & Greaves, J. (1989). Attitude assessment in organizations: Testing three microcomputer-based survey systems. *Journal of General Psychology, 116,* 145-154.

Rosenfeld, P., Giacalone, R. A., Knouse, S. B., Doherty, L. M., Vicini, S. M., Kantor, J., & Greaves, J. (1991). Impression management, candor, and microcomputer-based organizational surveys: An individual differences approach. *Computers in Human Behavior, 7,* 23-32.

Salgado, J. F., & Moscoso, S. (2003). Internet-based personality testing: Equivalence of measures and assesses' perceptions and reactions. *International Journal of Selection and Assessment, 11,* 194-205.

Skinner, H. A., & Allen, B. A. (1983). Does the computer make a difference? Computerized vs. face-to-face vs. self-report assessment of alcohol, drug, and tobacco use. *Journal of Consulting & Clinical Psychology, 51,* 267-275.

Smith, M. A. & Leigh, B. (1997). Virtual subjects: Using the Internet as an alternative source of subjects and research environment. *Behavior Research Methods, Instruments, and Computers, 29*(4), 496-505.

Sproull, L. S. (1986). Using electronic mail for data collection in organizational research. *Academy of Management Journal, 29,* 159-169.

Stanton, J. M. (1998). An empirical assessment of data collection using the Internet. *Personnel Psychology, 51,* 709-725.

Taris, T. W., Bok, I. A., & Meijer, Z. Y. (1998). Assessing stability and change of psychometric properties of multi-item concepts across different situations: A general approach. *Journal of Psychology, 132,* 301-316.

Weisband, S., & Kiesler, S. (1996, April 14-22). Self-disclosure on computer forms: Meta-analysis and implications. *Proceedings of the CHI '96 Conference on Human-Computer Interaction,* Vancouver.

Whitener, E., & Klein, H. (1995). Equivalence of computerized and traditional research methods: The roles of scanning, social environment, and social desirability. *Computers in Human Behavior, 11*(1), 65-75.

KEY TERMS

Computerized Adaptive Testing: Testing administered by computer, where the level of subsequent items is determined by responses to previous items. This enables increased or decreased difficulty of items to match the level of the respondent.

Demand Characteristics: Cues within the research environment and/or researcher's behaviour that act to alert participants to expectations and/or desired responses or outcomes.

HyperText Markup Language (HTML): A data format used to create hypertext documents on the Internet. HTML documents can be used across platforms. HTML was introduced in 1990, with an updated version (HTML 2) released in

1994. HTML 2 enabled, for the first time, the means for the administration of form-based surveys and measures on the World Wide Web. See http://www.w3.org/MarkUp/html-spec/ for further information.

Measurement Equivalence: Refers to the stability of a measure's factor structure across situations or modes of administration. All existing surveys and measures adapted for electronic administration should have their measurement equivalence with the original paper-and-pencil version assessed. This is essential to ensure that equivalent results are obtained across modes of administration.

Mode of Administration: Surveys and measures can be administered across a variety of media.

The most common modes of administration of surveys are paper-and-pencil, person-to-person interviews, telephone interviews, and e-mail and Internet surveys. Measures (especially tests) may also be administered by stand-alone computer programs.

Response Sets: patterns of responding to items on a measure or survey that are independent of the questions asked. The response set most likely to vary across modes of administration is social desirability responding.

Social Desirability Responding: A type of response set where the individual responds in what they think is a socially appropriate manner in order to project a more favourable image of themselves.

Chapter XI
Electronic vs. Conventional Surveys

Rhonda Dixon
Victoria University, Australia

Rodney Turner
Victoria University, Australia

ABSTRACT

This chapter discusses the outcomes of two data collection methods involving questionnaires distributed to members of an organization. One group received a paper survey through the post, whilst the second group was asked to complete the survey online. The results indicated that although response rates were higher for the online group, there were no significant differences in the responses of the two groups. These results suggest that for targeted groups of the type involved in this study, either method can be used with confidence, but that the online method may result in higher return. However, the additional benefits of speed, convenience, and cost make the online method appealing.

INTRODUCTION

This study reviews Web-based surveys as a data collection method in comparison to paper-based surveys. This comparison is important at this point as, with the growth of the Internet and its availability, more and more researchers are looking to Web-based surveys as an additional means of research (Cobanoglu, Warde, & Moreo, 2001). Trends show that traditional paper-based surveys have declining response rates so "researchers must consider new ways to generate sufficient, valid data" (Griffis, Goldsby, & Cooper, 2003).

The chapter presents some results comparing responses to conventional survey methods with online survey methods involving participants with a common focus.

BENEFITS OF WEB-BASED SURVEYS

According to Perkins (2004), the benefits of Web-based surveys are

- **Instrument**
  - permits text, image, and sound
  - possibility of filtering questions
- **Sampling:** Can access larger and geographically broader samples
- **Human Resources:** Requires less resources, for example, no photocopying, folding, coding, verifying
- **Time Resources:** Improved, survey available 24-7, and shorter delivery time
- **Material Resources:** Requires less materials, for example, paper and stamps
- **Reduced Costs:** Less human and material resources required
- **Analysis**
  - Direct transmission of data, including coding and analysis
  - More complete replies to open-ended questions
  - Potential for customized feedback

Larger sample-size availability and time efficiencies were also supported by Eaton and Struthers (2002) and by Roztocki and Lahri (2003). Benefits such as reduced costs have been widely recognized by other authors in literature (Cobanoglu et al., 2001; Coderre, Mathieu, & St-Laurent, 2004; Eaton & Struthers, 2002; Griffis et al., 2003; McDonald & Adam, 2003; Roztocki & Lahri, 2003; Wilson & Laskey, 2003). These cost savings can increase significantly in larger sample sizes, for example, 500 plus (Cobanoglu et al., 2001; Wilson & Laskey, 2003).

In Web-based surveys, there is improved data capture and analysis because there is no need to enter the data manually. With manual data entry, there are risks of input errors (Griffis et al., 2003). Web-based surveys can be useful when traditional data collection methods are not feasible, for example, sensitive issues (Eaton & Struthers, 2002), or for targeted groups such as teenagers and business people (Wilson & Laskey, 2003).

Significant timesavings through response speed were identified in most literature (Cobano-

glu et al., 2001; Griffis et al., 2003; McDonald & Adam, 2003; Mehta & Sivadas, 1995; Sheehan & McMillan, 1999) except for Tse et al. (1995), who found no significant differences in response speed when the delivery methods were timed so that the participants received the surveys at the same time.

Another benefit mentioned by Griffis et al. (2003) and Cobanoglu et al. (2001), when comparing methods within a targeted group, was an improved response rate for Web-based surveys over mail surveys. Researchers consider response rate very important because a high response rate increases confidence in the survey's accuracy and thus, generalizability (Cobanoglu et al., 2001). In regard to improved response rates, however, many other authors in the literature disagreed. Dommeyer et al. (Dommeyer, Baum, & Hanna, 2002), McDonald and Adam (2003), Mehta and Sivadas (1995), Sheehan and McMillan (1999), Tse et al. (1995), and Wilson and Laskey (2003) all mentioned paper-based surveys as having a better response rate in comparison to Web-based surveys. Given the importance of the response rate to research, lower response rates are a major concern.

Response rates have been improved when a "mixed mode" (traditional data collection methods and Web-based combined) is used (Cobanoglu et al., 2001). There is even more improvement when the researcher combines the "mixed mode" with prenotification of the survey (Mehta & Sivadas, 1995; Sheehan & McMillan, 1999).

Issues Involving Web-Based Surveys

One of the main issues is the lower response rate with Web-based surveys. This problem could worsen once the "novelty" of the Web survey wears off (McDonald & Adam, 2003).

Another way of increasing response rates is to include some form of incentive, but this is more difficult to implement in Web-based surveys (Cobanoglu et al., 2001).

Web-based surveys have a significantly higher amount of "undeliverable" responses. People generally have more than one e-mail address, and also change their e-mail addresses more often than their regular mail address (Bradley, 1999; Cobanoglu et al., 2001; Dommeyer & Moriarty, 1999; McDonald & Adam, 2003). The importance of "reliable mailing lists" to reduce the number of undeliverable e-mail surveys was highlighted by McDonald and Adam (2003).

Literature showed that using Web-based surveys may not truly "represent" the targeted population (Dommeyer & Moriarty, 1999; Roztocki & Lahri, 2003; Tse et al., 1995; Wilson & Laskey, 2003), because not every participant may have Internet access, which limits the sample to Internet users. The survey may not be representative of the wider population (Dommeyer & Moriarty, 1999).

Even though Wilson and Laskey (2003) also raised the "representativeness" issue, they claim that Internet research may be more applicable to areas "where the subjects are more likely to be online, or are part of an easily accessible database list," indicating that for areas where routine Web access is assumed, then using the Web-based survey may reflect a representative sample.

Self-selection bias is a major issue. Web-based surveys, by their "voluntary" nature, have a potential for self-selection bias, thereby making generalization difficult (Eaton & Struthers, 2002).

Anonymity is a major concern, as it can affect the response rates and response quality (Coderre, Mathieu, & St-Laurent, 2004). E-mail surveys may allow for the respondent to be identified easily, for example, through the e-mail header (Mehta & Sivadas, 1995). Participant identification is less of a problem with coded forms. If respondents feel that they may be identified, they may reply with less candour or they may not to respond at all (Dommeyer et al., 2002; Dommeyer & Moriarty, 1999). Eaton and Struthers (2002) contradicted the fears about participant anonymity because participants in their Internet sample answered more candidly since they felt they had more anonymity.

Regarding response quality, some studies have found the response quality of Web-based surveys sometimes differ from paper-based surveys. Coderre, Mathieu, and St-Laurent (2004) performed three studies: two were comparable and one was not. The final study produced different results, as it was evaluating an Internet provider; therefore, many of the participants were already involved with that provider, influencing the result. Another study found differences in the nature of the responses. The online responses returned displayed less inclination to use the entire scale, and tended to use the end and middle points less (McDonald & Adam, 2003).

In 1995, Mehta and Sivadas found e-mail survey responses were often more "insightful," with respondents writing more. In comparison to paper-based surveys, Eaton and Struthers (2002) found that the Web-based surveys had harsher responses, and linked this to the Internet participants feeling that they had more anonymity.

A major question about Web-based surveys is; "Can we use Web-based surveys to predict the results of a paper-based survey?" Literature shows varying answers:

- Predictive validity was at least equal to other data collection methods (Coderre, Mathieu, & St-Laurent, 2004).
- McCoy et al. (2004) using the technology acceptance model (TAM), found that a Web-based survey could not be used to predict the results of a paper-and-pencil survey, and made the following recommendation:

In each case, the validity and reliability of the instruments cannot be assumed, but must be tested and re-proven before valid interpretations can be made from the data they are used to collect. (McCoy et al., 2004)

McCoy et al. (McCoy, Marks, Carr, & Mbarika, 2004) identified some other factors that may influence the results of the Web-based survey. These factors are:

- **Psychological Factors**
  - Level of computer knowledge of the participant
  - Researcher has no control over environment where survey is being filled out
- **Information Technology Factors**
  - Different browsers—therefore presentation may differ
  - Time lag—depends on connection speeds, could be frustrating if slow
- **Reliability Factors**
  - Internal consistency and stability

METHOD

The study reported here was of members of a social welfare organization in the State of Victoria, Australia. A targeted survey was used to compare the responses concerning the two methods of data collection. A paper-based survey was distributed to members concerning their attitudes to the services provided. Access to a Web-based version was provided to those members who had provided their e-mail contact.

Comparisons using the two data collection methods were carried out on questions that compared the awareness of services provided and performance in these areas. To minimise the chance of duplication of responses, those responding online were asked to indicate if they had also completed the survey using the paper-based version, and those who had were not included in the analysis. Apart from this extra question and layout of the two versions, the questionnaires were the same, enabling comparison of response rates to be made. Details of the questions used are included in the appendix.

Response rates were satisfactory for both methods of data collection: for the paper survey, 450 questionnaires were sent out and 115 were returned as usable (26% response rate); for the Web-based survey, 190 were sent requests to participate and 103 returns were received (54% response rate). Of the online returns, 13 indicated they had already completed the survey on paper, and these were excluded from the analysis of online responses and a response rate of .41%.

The online survey was developed using Microsoft Frontpage 2000© and data captured directly into an Access© database file. The data was transferred to SPSS R11 for statistical analysis after being merged with the data collected in the conventional method. The online form was posted on a Web site for two weeks, but most of the returns had been submitted within 7 days.

The survey included questions about demographic details of respondents and their organization, the services they subscribed to, and opinions about these services provided by the welfare organization to its members. Comparisons between the two collection methods were made on the opinion-related questions covering awareness of services and importance of them.

RESULTS

The results presented in Table 1 show the broad background of the respondents. Over half of the respondents indicated they were an organizational member; nearly 13% had individual membership, whilst about 25% responded as not applicable or simply did not answer. A breakdown of survey type against membership type is shown in Table 2.

The results presented in Table 2 are interesting given that, in the majority of cases, both distribution styles of the survey were delivered to the work address of the respondent. The paper version of the survey had nearly one third of private members responding, but none of this group responded to

Table 1. Summary of reported membership type

Membership type	Frequency	Percent
Not answered	18	8.8
Organisational member	127	62.0
Individual member	26	12.7
Not applicable or don't know	34	16.6
Total	205	100

Table 2. Survey type vs. membership type

		Membership type				
		Not answered	Organizational member	Individual member	Not applicable or don't know	Total
Survey type	Paper survey	9	80	26	0	115
	Online survey	9	47	0	34	90
Total		18	127	26	34	205

Table 3. Training and support needs

training and support needs	Mann-Whitney U	Z	Asymp. Sig. (2-tailed)
1a. Management of cost	5032	-0.35	0.73
1b. Management of budget	4889	-0.70	0.49
1c. Cashflow monitoring	4504	-1.65	0.10
1d. Preparation of accounting reports	4892	-0.69	0.49
2. Strategic planning	4963	-0.52	0.61
3. Government policy development	4589	-1.42	0.16
4. Human resources management (inc. volunteer management)	4998	-0.43	0.67
5. Organisational / program management and evaluation	4786	-0.94	0.35
6. Information technology and information systems (inc. web, networking, etc.)	5158	-0.04	0.97
7. Database development and management	5082	-0.23	0.82
8. Marketing	5030	-0.35	0.72
9. Media and public relations	4776	-0.97	0.33
10. Applying human rights framework	4928	-0.60	0.55
11. Research and policy development	4935	-0.58	0.56
12. Advocacy skills and campaign strategy	4849	-0.79	0.43
13. Fund submission writing and other fund raising	4891	-0.69	0.49
14. Dispute resolution	4442	-1.78	0.07
15. Stress and self management	4663	-1.24	0.21

the online survey. There was an equal number from each group who elected to not answer the question, but over one third of online respondents reported they did not know the membership type or that it was not applicable. These results may suggest that issues of privacy were underlying concerns for the online group, given the anecdotal problems surrounding spam mail.

Table 3 compares the responses from the two survey methods regarding the member training and support needs. In each case, the ranks of the paper-based responses were higher than were those of the online responses, but these differences are not statistically significant. Awareness and performance of services provided

Table 4. Comparison of the awareness of services and of performance of the services. (Responses that are significantly different are highlighted in bold.)

	aware			performance		
	Mann-Whitney U	Z	Asymp. Sig. (2-tailed)	Mann-Whitne y U	Z	Asymp. Sig. (2-tailed)
1. Monthly organisation publication Noticeboard	2195	-7.28	**0.00**	2800	-5.84	**0.00**
2. Quarterly organisation publication Just Policy	3187	-4.84	**0.00**	3600	-3.90	**0.00**
3. Annual organisation Congress	4283	-2.17	**0.03**	4962	-0.53	0.59
4.Organisation information resources (library, bookroom, guides & publications)	4427	-1.81	0.07	4586	-1.59	0.11
5. Organisation website	5089	-0.21	0.83	5150	-0.06	0.95
6. Sector development and education activities (e.g. seminars, workshops and governance support)	4492	-1.66	0.10	4661	-1.28	0.20
7. Negotiations with government on sector-wide issues (e.g. Funding and Service Agreements)	3994	-2.95	**0.00**	4807	-0.91	0.36
8. Input to government policy development through submissions, reports, consultations and collaborative projects	4601	-1.49	0.14	5174	0.00	1.00
9. Advocacy voice on social disadvantage issues	4992	-0.50	0.62	4805	-0.93	0.35
10. Organisation media profile on social justice issues	4969	-0.52	0.60	4832	-0.85	0.40
11. Analysis of government budget and economic policies	5084	-0.23	0.82	4783	-0.97	0.33
12. Adequate Income & Living Standards	4729	-1.11	0.27	4861	-0.78	0.44
13. Child and Family Issues	4858	-0.78	0.44	4490	-1.73	0.08
14. Disability Issues	5046	-0.32	0.75	4672	-1.28	0.20
15. Education and Training	5142	-0.08	0.94	4922	-0.66	0.51
16. Employment	4547	-1.54	0.13	4845	-0.86	0.39
17. Primary and Community Health	4723	-1.10	0.27	4939	-0.62	0.54
18. Housing	4740	-1.07	0.29	4855	-0.80	0.42
19. Indigenous & Reconciliation Issues	4780	-0.97	0.33	4664	-1.34	0.18
20. Justice	5123	-0.13	0.90	5087	-0.22	0.82
21. Tax Reform	4145	-2.52	**0.01**	5114	-0.16	0.88
22. Utilities (e.g. Electricity, Gas, Water)	4624	-1.35	0.18	4931	-0.62	0.54
23. Community Sector Development & Viability	4732	-1.09	0.28	4789	-0.97	0.33
24. Public Transport Issues	4314	-2.10	**0.04**	4293	-2.29	**0.02**
25. Women's Issues	4899	-0.68	0.50	5023	-0.40	0.69
26. Social / environmental sustainability	4247	-2.26	**0.02**	4650	-1.39	0.17

Table 4 shows the differences in awareness of the services provided by the organization and of the performances of these services according to the survey type. In each case, the ranks of the paper surveys were higher than the online responses. There is not a systematic pattern appearing in these results and, in the majority of cases, there is no statistical difference between the results for the two collection methods employed in this study.

DISCUSSION AND CONCLUSION

The distribution of responses to the two methods of survey delivery, as shown in Table 1 and Table 2, show some difference for the two distribution and collection methods.

The results presented in Table 3 and Table 4 suggest that, in the case of a targeted survey such as in this case, there is little statistical difference in responses, and that online surveys can yield similar results to those of conventionally distributed surveys. In terms of convenience and ease of data handling, online surveys do present a distinct advantage over the traditional methods of collection. The same conclusion may not be drawn, however, in the case of general surveys where self-selection problems may result in biased results (Dommeyer & Moriarty, 1999).

Where quick results are sought or where accessibility to the technology is not likely to affect the results, the use of online methods is attractive. There can be economic benefits (see for example Coderre, Mathieu, & St-Laurent, 2004) in using online surveys over paper-based surveys including savings in postage, survey duplication, and data entry being some of these. These benefits can be offset, though, by the potential for a growing rejection of online surveys because of privacy concerns and of the growth of spam mail. This seductively attractive method may mean a growth of this type of survey resulting in a type of survey fatigue (McDonald & Adam, 2003). In addition, it is often necessary for the online survey to be completed in a single session, whereas a paper survey can be revisited over a longer period and in places away from a computer.

REFERENCES

Bradley, N. B. (1999). Sampling for Internet surveys: An examination of respondent selection for Internet research. *Journal of the Market Research Society, 41*, 387-395.

Cobanoglu, C., Warde, B., & Moreo, P. J. (2001). A comparison of mail, fax and Web-based survey methods. *International Journal of Market Research, 43*, 441-452.

Coderre, F., Mathieu, A., & St-Laurent, N. (2004). Comparison of the quality of qualitative data obtained through telephone, postal and e-mail sur-

veys. *International Journal of Market* Research, *46*(3), 347-357.

Dommeyer, C. J., Baum, P., & Hanna, R. W. (2002). College students' attitudes toward methods of collecting teaching evaluations: In-class vs. online. *Journal of Education for Business, 78*, 11-15.

Dommeyer, C. J., & Moriarty, E. (1999). Comparing two forms of an e-mail survey: Embedded vs. attached. *International Journal of Market Research, 42*, 39-50.

Eaton, J., & Struthers, C. W. (2002). Using the Internet for organizational research: A study of cynicism in the workplace. *Cyber Psychology & Behaviour, 5*, 305-313.

Griffis, S. E., Goldsby, T. J., & Cooper, M. (2003). Web-based and mail surveys: A comparison of response, data, and cost. *Journal of Business Logistics, 24*, 237-258.

McCoy, S., Marks, P. V. Jr, Carr, C. L., & Mbarika, V. (2004). Electronic vs. paper surveys: Analysis of potential psychometric biases. *IEEE—HICSS 04—Proceedings of the 37th Hawaii International Conference on System Sciences.*

McDonald, H., & Adam, S. (2003). A comparison of online and postal data collection methods in marketing research. *Marketing Intelligence & Planning, 21*(2). 85-95.

Mehta, R., & Sivadas, E. (1995). Comparing responses rates and response content in mail vs. electronic mail surveys. *Journal of the Market Research Society, 37*, 429-439.

Perkins, G. H. (2004). Will libraries' Web-based survey methods replace existing non-electronic survey methods? *Information Technology and Libraries, 23*(3). 123-126.

Roztocki, N., & Lahri, N. (2003). Is the applicability of Web-based surveys for academic research limited to the field of information technology?

IEEE – HICSS '03 – Proceedings of the 36ᵗʰ Hawaii International Conference on System Sciences.

Sheehan, K. B., & McMillan, S. J. (1999). Response variation in e-mail surveys: An exploration. *Journal of Advertising Research, 39*(4), 45-54.

Tse, A. C. B, Tse, K.C., Yin, C. H., Ting, C. B., Yi, K. W., Yee, K. P., et al. (1995). Comparing two methods of sending out questionnaires: E-mail vs. mail. *Journal of the Market Research Society, 37*(4), 441-446.

Wilson, A., & Laskey, N. (2003). Internet-based marketing research: A serious alternative to traditional research methods? *Marketing Intelligence & Planning, 21*, 79-84.

KEY TERMS

Online Questionnaire: A survey method where distribution, completion, and collection of data is by access to the WWW.

Paper Questionnaire: A survey sent by conventional mailing.

Targeted Group: A group surveyed in which exists a common relationship amongst the group members.

Chapter XII
The Ethics of Online Surveys

Călin Gurău
Groupe Sup. de Co. Montpellier, France

ABSTRACT

Facilitated by the technological advancements in Internet applications, online surveys have become a powerful tool to collect primary data on a variety of topics. The ease with which the cyberspace medium facilitates these types of studies also raises issues about the ethical and legal dimensions of such research. The present paper attempts to investigate and present the main ethical issues related with online surveys, and the solutions implemented by various organisations for solving these ethical problems.

INTRODUCTION

The rapid growth of the online community, combined with the specific facilities offered by Internet applications, have significantly increased the popularity of online surveys. The Internet allows, nowadays, direct access to millions of people, as well as to billions of documents archived in the Internet collective memory. Another major appeal of online surveys is the significant decrease in the time and unit cost of conducting the survey (Hmieleski, 2000). The research environment has become more dynamic, demanding quicker data collections and results.

Usually, Internet research falls into three main categories:

- Studies that examine the opinions and the behaviour of people online, using the resources registered and archived in the Internet memory;
- Web sites that solicit people, actively or passively, to fill out questionnaires or participate in experimental tasks that measure psychological or behavioural constructs such as opinions, attitudes, memory, decision making, and reaction time; and
- Questionnaires sent and returned through e-mail applications.

Each of these research methods raises specific ethical issues. The ability of both researchers and their subjects to assume anonymous or pseudonymous identities online, the complexities of obtaining informed consent, the problems concerning privacy in cyberspace, and the blurred distinction between public and private domains, have the potential to create ethical problems in online surveys. The present paper attempts to investigate and present the main ethical issues related with online surveys, and the solutions implemented by various organisations for solving these ethical problems.

Advantages and Challenges of Online Surveys

Online surveys are used in many different areas of research: psychology, marketing, communication studies, and so forth, however, the advantages offered by Internet applications are common:

1. **Low Cost of Data Collection:** Online surveys are much cheaper than the classical data collection methods. Internet surveys cost only 10% of those conducted by phone, and just 20% of a classical mail survey (Komando, 2005). There are even Web sites that offer free survey tools: SurveyMonkey. com, for example, allows 10 questions on its free surveys and up to 100 responses per survey.

2. **Quick Data Collection:** The researchers that used online surveys reported a substantial reduction in the time required for data collection: 2-3 days in online surveys compared with 2-3 weeks with more traditional methods (Comley, 2002);

3. **Direct Input of Answers into Databases:** The answers provided online by participants can be directly loaded into data analysis software, thus saving time and resources associated with the data entry process (Ilieva, Baron, & Healey, 2002);

4. **Increased Quality of Answers:** Some researchers have reported that the answers collected though online surveys are more honest than the answers provided in classical surveys because of greater respondent anonymity (Comley, 2002; Sharp, 2002).

Online surveys are also associated with specific challenges, such as:

1. **Low Response Rate:** Some specialists (Komando, 2005) have reported a lower response rate in online surveys, in comparison with other traditional methods of data collection (e.g., telephone surveys), while other researchers have obtained very good response rates in online surveys (Comley, 2000). The success of an online survey might be dependent on the proper use of Internet technology, and on the choice of appropriate format (e-mail, Web, or pop-up survey).

2. **Sampling Problems:** Unless the researcher has access to an e-mail database of the entire population of study, the online surveys raise problems of sampling and sample representativity. In the case of Web questionnaires, the respondents self-select themselves, which can introduce specific biases in research findings (e.g., only the Internet users that have a specific type of browser are able to access the Web questionnaire). This problem can, however, be eliminated in pop-up or e-mail surveys (Comley, 2000; Ilieva et al., 2002).

3. **The Ethical and Legal Issues Associated with Online Surveys:** In the last 10 years, these issues have become important subjects for research and debate within the scientific community; however, the opinions are still divided concerning the ethical and legal standards that should be applied for online data collection.

The present study attempts to investigate the application of ethical principles in online surveys by answering to the following research objectives:

1. To define the main ethical principles relevant for online surveys.

2. To discuss the specific application of ethical principles to various types of online surveys.

3. To identify the practical implementation of ethical principles in active online surveys.

After a presentation of the research methodology used for data collection, the study presents the findings related to each of the above research objectives. The chapter concludes with a summary of the research findings and with propositions for future research.

Method

In order to answer the formulated research objectives, both secondary and primary data have been collected. In the first stage, an extensive desk research has been conducted, in order to access academic and professional papers or reports, presenting or debating the ethical issues concerning online surveys. The information provided a general picture of the main ethical principles involved in Internet research, and outlined the specificity of their application in various types of research.

In order to address the last research objective, in the second stage, 50 active online surveys have been randomly accessed on the Web, using the list of documents provided by the Google search engine to the keywords "online survey." The sites have been investigated in relation to the information categories provided to potential respondents, the facility to access them, and the way in which the standard ethical principles were applied in the survey.

The Ethical Principles of Online Surveys

A good starting point in creating ethical principles adapted for online surveys is the existing principles applied for classical research projects. The Belmont report outlines three major ethical principles for conducting research on human subjects: autonomy, beneficence, and justice (National Institutes of Health, 2004). In practice, their online application requires researchers to insure the confidentiality, security, privacy, and informed consent of participants.

Confidentiality, privacy, and informed consent are the cornerstones of ethical human research (Zimitat, & Crebert, 2002). Understanding and identifying the potential violation of any of these principles when using the Internet for research and evaluation is becoming more difficult as a result of increasing computer security measures, advances in the functionality of Web tools, and blurring boundaries between private and public communication spaces.

The application of ethical principles in online surveys implies the following:

1. To provide complete and unambiguous information regarding the identity of researcher/s, the purpose of the study and the use of the collected data, including the diffusion of the research results (the format and the level of details in which the results will be published, the people having access to the results);

2. To include a clear statement regarding the protection of participants' privacy (including information about the use of "cookies" or other Internet tools that collect data in a covert way) and to give the participants the opportunity to define the level of confidentiality they require;

3. To ensure the security of Internet connection and data transfer, informing the participants about any risks of data interception by a third party;

4. To openly present all the advantages or disadvantages related to the participation in the study; and

5. To provide contact information, allowing participants to obtain additional clarifications about the research project, and the methodology of data collection and analysis.

Some guidelines regarding the use of ethical statements in online surveys (Hom, 2004) recommend an adaptation of the ethical statements to the risks posed to participants by the research project:

One should not use overelaborate informed consent statements, extensive assurances of confidentiality, encryption, or digital signatures when risks are minimal. (Hom, 2004, p.1)

As with research in the real world, ethical concerns for participants depend on the type of research conducted. All types of research must adhere to the same basic ethical principles: protecting the privacy and autonomy of participants without inflicting harm. However, each type of online survey presents specific challenges at ethical level.

Studies of online forums. This type of study raises questions regarding the right of researchers to monitor, register, and analyse the Web-based interactions in a chat room or discussion forum without informing the participants of their actions. Some researchers consider that such data are in public domain, because most discussion forums are open to the public, while other researchers argue that people have the right to privacy and that scientists must obtain the consent of all the subjects involved before initiating the collection and the analysis of online data (Hutchinson, 2001; Zimitat, & Crebert, 2002).

The codes of ethics of many discussion forums explicitly prohibit the members to include in their messages any questionnaires or surveys. On the other hand, there are specific online forums that have a data collection purpose, openly declared in the forum presentation. Therefore, in theory, the researchers could identify and use only the discussion forums that specifically permit the collection and analysis of the information published by participants. However, in reality, it is impossible to implement efficient protection against the use of the data published in discussion forums, since

the presence of a researcher is often nonintrusive, and difficult to identify by site moderators.

Schrum (1995) suggests that researchers should approach the administrators of the online forum, provide them with detailed information regarding the proposed study, and obtain consent to conduct the research. On the other hand, posting information about researchers and the study undertaken on the online forum, can create the impression that researchers are part of the community rather than an alien presence (Cho & LaRose, 1999).

Web-based questionnaires. As Coomber (1997) has highlighted, there is little point in having a Web page and setting up an online survey and then passively "waiting" for eligible respondents to find the site: more active enrolment is needed to encourage users to complete an online survey. Usually, the Web questionnaires are applied in online communities (organisations, associations, universities), in which the Web site is frequently used by members, or in association with pop-up windows (Comley, 2000).

The use of questionnaires in online communities raises the question of power relations. For example, a professor that uses a Web questionnaire to collect information from students might apply an implicit pressure to increase participation. Often, these questionnaires do not contain any information regarding the scope of the survey, or the use of data collected, that limits significantly the capacity of participants to make an informed consent, and the privacy rules are very vague.

The use of pop-up windows can significantly increase the response rate of Web surveys (Comley, 2000). However, the widespread use of pop-up windows for online intrusive advertising has introduced negative perceptions concerning these Internet applications. Today, most antivirus or firewall software programmes contain options that actively block pop-up windows.

E-mail questionnaires. The use of e-mail questionnaires raises the problem of "spam." Internet users are intolerant of unsolicited communications, and invitations to participate in research are increasingly considered "spamming," resulting in online surveys often having lower response rates than onsite surveys (Witmer, Colman, & Katzman, 1999).

Therefore, the first ethical issue of e-mail questionnaires is obtaining the informed consent of participants to receive the e-mail questionnaire. Because of this, the application of an e-mail survey comprises at least two stages: in the first phase, an e-mail message is sent to the prospective participant, containing information about the identity of researchers, the purpose of the research project, and the specific use of the collected data, as well as an invitation to participate to the study; if the participant accepts, a second e-mail message is sent containing the e-mail questionnaire and instructions about completing and returning it.

In addition to this, the other ethical principles should be properly applied. The e-mail messages should contain clear specification about the security, privacy, and confidentiality of the data provided. Sometimes, in order to increase the response rate of participants, the researcher can promise to sent to respondents a summary of the findings; in this case, this promise should be strictly respected.

The Application of Ethical Principles in Active Online Surveys

The survey of 50 active online surveys has offered a direct insight into the practical application of ethical principles in Web questionnaires. The main limitation of this research methodology was the restricted access to just one type of online survey: the Web-based questionnaire. The sample size is also relatively small, although the study can be further extended in the future.

Fourteen of the investigated online surveys had a filtering system in place, in order to select only the qualified participants. In this case, the potential participants were first invited to enter a few basic pieces of personal information, such as age, gender, profession, address, as well as their

e-mail address. The selected participants were then sent a password in an e-mail message. The password gave them access to the Web-based questionnaire.

In the remaining 36 cases, the access to the online questionnaire was free.

In order to evaluate the application of the main ethical principles to the investigated online surveys, the presence of the following information categories was registered for each Web questionnaire:

a. information about researchers;
b. information about the research project (purpose, length, dissemination of results);
c. the use of collected data (storage, analysis, use, dissemination of results);
d. the security of data transmission;
e. the privacy of participants (use of cookies, level of anonymity);
f. the possibility to choose the level of confidentiality of the data transmitted;
g. the presentation of the main advantages/disadvantages of participating to the project; and
h. the incentives offered to participate in the survey, and the equitability of their application.

All the information categories presented are related with the principle of informed consent; while the information at letters d) and e) directly concern the application of the privacy principle, and those at letters c) and f) the confidentiality principle.

The findings presented in Table 1 present a very negative picture of the application of ethical principles to Web-based questionnaires. In general, the Web-based questionnaire with a preselection process applied, in a larger proportion, the ethical rules, by providing information about the researcher/s (85.7%), the research project (100%), the use of collected data (71.4%); the privacy protection of participants (100%), and the choice of the confidentiality level (78.5%).

Table 1. The practical application of ethical principles to active Web questionnaires

Type of questionnaire / Ethical information	Web questionnaire with pre-selection		Web questionnaires with free access		Total	
	N	%	N	%	N	%
Researcher	12	85.7	21	58.3	33	66
Research project	14	100	30	83.3	44	88
Use of collected data	10	71.4	18	50	28	56
Security	5	35.7	3	8.3	8	16
Privacy	14	100	27	75	41	82
Confidentiality	11	78.5	14	38.8	25	50
Advantages/ disadvantages	2	14.3	3	8.3	5	10
Incentives	8	57.1	9	25	17	34
Equity of incentives	4	28.5	3	8.3	7	14
Total of Web questionnaires	14	100	36	100	50	100

By comparison, the Web-based questionnaires with free access have lower percentages in all categories: only 58.3% of sites present information about researchers, 83.3% about the research project, 50% about the use of collected data, 75% about privacy, and only 38.8% permit the choice of the level of confidentiality.

The situation is critical in terms of a clear presentation of the advantages/disadvantages of participating in the survey; only 10% of the investigated sites contain this type of information. The presentation of data transfer security is equally weak, with 1% of the investigated sites providing this information.

A large percentage (76%) of the investigated surveys were posted on organisational Web sites (universities or associations) that required their members to participate in the survey in order to improve the quality of the service provided, or the interaction among members and the organisations. No other direct incentive was provided. Usually, on these sites, the information concerning the presentation of the project, the level of security, the confidentiality, and the balance of advantages/ disadvantages were vague or missing.

These findings show that the application of ethical principles is still weak in many Web-based questionnaires. The causes of this situation are difficult to assess, but the decentralised nature of

the Internet, and the lack of any regulatory body to set standards, and to control the application of ethical principles in online surveys, might explain this problem.

In order to solve this problem, some groups have already taken these preliminary steps for establishing ethical standards for online research, with, for example, the American Association for the Advancement of Science, (in conjunction with the Office for Protection from Research Risks), meeting in June 1999 to discuss the "Ethical and Legal Aspects of Human Subjects Research in Cyberspace." Their intentions were to highlight all relevant issues, and to lay the initial groundwork for further debates from other contributing bodies: professional bodies, educational institutions, online community groups, and political parties. The output of this initial meeting produced guidelines that addressed (Franklin & Siang 1999):

- the basic principles that should be adhered to when carrying out research involving human participants;
- issues surrounding any benefits or risks to participants;
- issues related to obtaining informed consent;
- privacy and confidentiality; and
- justice.

CONCLUSION

In order to reach a point where research participants are ethically and legally protected, and to promote the legitimacy of online research, it is extremely important that all aspects of the ethical, legal, and technical issues associated with this nascent area of research are explored and debated until a sound and rigorous policy framework is established.

This chapter attempted to outline the main problems regarding the application of ethical rules in online surveys. After defining and discussing the main ethical principles applicable in "cyberspace," the study explained the main differences among various types of research. The results of an online investigation of 50 active Web-based questionnaires were then presented and analysed.

Despite the growing interest in defining and applying ethical principles in online research, there is still much to be done. The research into the real application of ethical principles in online surveys should be extended, in order to investigate more Web-based questionnaires, and to extend the analysis to the questionnaires posted within discussion forums. On the other hand, the work of various interest groups or specialised committees should continue, in order to establish a chart of ethical principles applicable in cyberspace research. The dissemination of information on this subject can also help educate the Internet users to become more knowledgeable regarding the protection of their rights, and the standards of ethical protection that should be provided by online researchers.

REFERENCES

Cho, H., & LaRose, R. (1999). Privacy issues in Internet surveys. *Social Science Computer Review, 17*, 421-434.

Comley, P. (2000). Pop-up surveys: What works, what doesn't work and what will work in the future. *ESOMAR Net Effects Internet Conference.* Dublin, April. Retrieved January 2005, from http://www.virtualsurveys.com/news/papers/paper_4.asp

Comley, P. (2002). Online survey techniques: Current issues and future trends. *Interactive Marketing, 4*(2), 156-169.

Coomber, R. (1997). Using the Internet for survey research. *Sociological Research Online, 2*(2). Retrieved January 2005, from http://www.socresonline.org.uk/socresonline/2/2/2.html

Frankel, M. S., & Siang, S. (1999). *Ethical and legal issues of human subjects research on the Internet.* Washington: American Association for the Advancement of Science.

Hom, W. (2004). *Some rules for online research.* Retrieved January 2005, from http://www.ocair.org/files/knowledgebase/willard/OnlineRes-GuideAb.pdf

Hmieleski, K. (2000). *Barriers to online evaluation. Surveying the nation's top 200 most wired colleges.* New York: IDEA Laboratory - Rensselaer Polytechnic Institute.

Hutchinson, R. (2001). Dangerous liaisons? Ethical considerations in conducting online sociological research. *TASA 2001 Conference.* 13-15 December, The University of Sydney. Retrieved January 2005, from http://www.tasa.org.au/members/docs/2001_12/Hutchinson.pdfIlieva

J., Baron, S., & Healey, N. (2002). Online surveys in marketing research: Pros and cons. *International Journal of Market Research, 44*(3), 361-376.

Komando, K. (2005). *3 reasons to use online customer surveys.* Retrieved January 2005, from http://www.microsoft.com/smallbusiness/issues/marketing/market_research/3_reasons_to_use_online_customer_surveys.mspx

National Institutes of Health. (2004). The Belmont Report: Ethical principles and guidelines for the protection of human subjects of research. *The*

National Commission for the Protection of Human Subjects of Biomedical and Behavioral Research. April 18, 1979. Retrieved January 2005, from http://ohsr.od.nih.gov/guidelines/belmont.html

Schrum, L. (1995). Framing the debate: Ethical Research in the information age. *Qualitative Inquiry, 1*(3), 311-326.

Sharp, K. (2002). *Public sector use of Internet surveys and panels.* White paper. Retrieved January 2005, from http://www.decisionanalyst.com/publ_art/PublicSector.asp

Witmer, D. F. Colman, R., & Katzman, S. L. (1999). From paper-and-pencil to screen-and-keyboard: Towards a methodology for survey research on the Internet. In S. Jones (Ed.), *Doing Internet research: Critical issues and methods for examining the Net* (pp. 145-161). London: Sage.

Zimitat C., & Crebert, G. (2002). Conducting online research and evaluation. *HERDSA 2002 Conference Proceedings*, 761-769.

KEY TERMS

Autonomy: Ethical principle that outlines that prospective participant should be given the respect, time, information, and opportunity necessary to decide whether to enter research or not participate.

Beneficence: Ethical principle that obligates the researcher to secure the well being of all research participants, protecting them from harm, and ensuring that they experience the possible benefits of involvement.

Confidentiality: Ethical principle concerning the obligation of the online researcher to disclose the information provided by a research subject, only within the limits defined by the subject.

Informed Consent: Consent given by the participant to an online survey only after achieving an understanding of the research project context, and of the consequences or risks involved.

Justice: Ethical principle requiring researchers to fairly distribute the benefits and the burdens of participation in research projects among various participants, creating an equitable balance of advantages and disadvantages.

Online Privacy: The capacity of an online user to control the collection and the use of his/her personal information in the digital environment.

Online Surveys: Surveys in which the respondents are using World Wide Web applications to fill in and return questionnaires, using one or more of the following alternatives: complete a questionnaire online on the Internet, whereby it is stored on a server; download the questionnaire from a server and return it by e-mail; or, receive and return the questionnaire by e-mail.

Chapter XIII
Legal and Ethical Concerns of Collecting Data Online

Amanda Sturgill
Baylor University, USA

Pattama Jongsuwanwattana
Yonok University, Thailand

ABSTRACT

International data collection offers the possibility of greater external validity for studies. However, using the Internet to collect information internationally brings concerns related to data privacy for respondents. Nations vary on their privacy protections for citizens' Internet use. Beliefs about data privacy, official policies notwithstanding, can also affect respondents and response rates. This chapter explores these issues and lists issues that should concern the international survey researcher.

INTRODUCTION

Although proposals to conduct survey research via the mail or telephone may generate questions about the content or phrasing of the questions, these methods of data collection are not routinely questioned on the basis of their delivery mechanisms. In fact, these methods of collecting data are commonly used and are, themselves, the subject of research (Dillman, 2001). However, they are not technologically guaranteed to protect respondents' privacy. Even though mail interception and wiretapping are illegal in the United States, this does not guarantee that they do not occur. In other nations, reading mail or e-mail and wiretapping may be legal. It seems difficult for any researcher

using Internet data collection to guarantee security of respondent data.

In recent years, using the Internet as a mechanism for data collection has appealed because it may lower turnaround time for responses, and may also either lower cost or defer cost (for computers, network service, etc.) to either the researcher's organization or the respondent. As the use of the Internet has made multinational data collection much less expensive, it is, therefore, more likely to occur. Including a variety of national and cultural perspectives considered in research may lead to greater external validity of the findings. However, issues involving privacy and access concerns in other nations need to be addressed. Regardless of the *de jure* legality, researchers must also be concerned about the *de facto* security of computer networks in different nations. The beliefs of Internet users about their security also matter, as these beliefs can affect response quality and rate.

GENERAL ISSUES IN DATA PRIVACY

Using the Internet to deliver surveys is desirable for the researcher for a number of reasons. Copying and distribution costs drop a great deal and turnaround time is faster without postal system delays. It is possible to target an individual through electronic mail, while a paper survey might be opened or answered by another member of the household. Data can be extracted electronically, without need for hand coding and entry. But Internet data collection, especially across national boundaries, has repercussions both for the users and for the data that is collected.

It is not difficult to imagine cases where privacy of personal data is important for the respondents from whom data is collected. Studies of socially undesirable behaviors or studies requesting sensitive medical information already compel researchers to provide evidence that they will protect the security of the respondent's data. Collecting that data electronically and/or across borders carries risks that the data can be accessed legally by authorities or illegally by hackers.

In the United States, it appears that electronic communication may be afforded protection under the federal wiretapping statutes (Levary, Thompson, Kot, & Brothers, 2005), which state that taking electronic information either in transit or while in storage is punishable by both a fine and jail time. Although wiretapping statutes (U.S. Code Title 47, Chapter 9) were initially written to cover "aural transfer" of information (subsequently defined as transactions containing the human voice), the finding in Steve Jackson Games, Inc. vs. United States Secret Service in 1993 (Electronic Frontier

Foundation, n.d.) appears to have extended the interpretation of that law to include electronic data transmission. Like most laws relating to computer network communication, this is a case-law finding and not an actual amendment to the U.S. Code. Such precedent can, however, be used to bring suit for interception of electronic mail or Web-based survey responses.

In order to preserve the abilities of law enforcement to investigate crimes carried out using the postal service or electronic communication, both mail theft and wiretapping laws have exceptions that may be important in guaranteeing confidentiality to survey participants. A first exception states that, after following procedures specified under the U. S. Code, law enforcement officers and/or government agents might legally intercept communication if they had just cause to suspect it was being used in the course of an illegal activity. Procedures, including when judicial approval or warrants are required, were loosened with the USA Patriot Act of 2001, and even when afforded, protections are not foolproof (Detroit Free Press, 2005). Mistakes have occurred where legal communications were intercepted and not only read, but entered into the public record. This is evidenced in case-law findings in lawsuits against law enforcement agencies that have improperly intercepted communications (Adams, 2004).

In the U.S., a second exception allows the provider of an electronic service to retain the right to intercept and read communications. This definition includes one's employer who provides the telephone extension, computer, or other connection to an electronic network. An Internet service provider, such as MSN or America Online, is also given that right. Because it is difficult for an individual American to connect to the Internet without using some type of Internet service provider, this exception may mean that most Americans can have their e-mail legally intercepted.

This issue with electronic mail is similar to a weakness in the mail theft statute (Title 18 Chapter 83 section 1708) that covers mail while it is in transit from an authorized mail receptacle, through the postal service, and to an authorized mail receptacle. Generally, this means that it is illegal to steal mail from someone's mailbox. However, once the mail has been delivered to an "authorized agent," it is no longer in the custody of the postal service, and therefore no longer subject to the law. The mail is considered delivered when it reaches the correct address. If one is receiving mail at an organization, the receipt at the organization's address would be delivery to an authorized agent. Therefore, it would be the prerogative of each individual organization to read mail intended for particular employees. This could be important in considering the researcher's ability to maintain confidentiality of mailed surveys that go to persons working for an organization.

Proper access to information can be defined differently in other nations. South Korea has a high level of Internet adoption, due in part to efforts by the government to encourage this adoption (Kim, S., 2002). South Korean human rights activists say residents all accept a loss of privacy when they accept residential registry numbers, which are 13-digit numbers assigned to every South Korean citizen from birth to death (Kim, K, n.d.; Cho, n.d.). This system has been used for more than 30 years, since Japanese colonial rulers first established it in 1968 in order to control the population. This 13-digit number contains a person's sex, birthday, and a place of birth, and is unchangeable for life. When individuals reach the age of 17, they receive government-issued residential ID cards in which new information regarding the holder and family continues to be added. Approximately 140 items of personal information, including fingerprints, are stored under these person-unique numbers. Transactions of daily life are impossible without presenting the card. The personal information stored in the residential registry number system is available for governmental review when requested for law enforcement, criminal investigation, or prosecution.

Korea exemplifies how de jure protection from electronic surveillance may not equal *de facto* privacy. *De jure,* Koreans enjoy data privacy similar to what Americans do. The country's Communication Secrecy Protection Law of 1993 requires court permission before communications can be monitored, including Internet interception. *De facto,* the rise of the Internet in Korea has been accompanied by a rise in permitted surveillance. From 1996 to 1998, court-permitted communication surveillances rose from 2,444 cases to 6,638 cases (Kim, K., n.d.). Also, when matters are considered urgent, governmental monitoring, even without court permission, is possible for 48 hours. When charges are against the National Security Law, surveillance can easily be extended by 6 months.

In addition to direct communication interception, the Korean government also can get information directly. When law enforcement requests it, Internet service providers must provide full access to users' online records. Internet content is also open to governmental censorship. The government can ask for deletion of content considered to be antinational, socially harmful, and so on. Whoever posted the content is then banned from using online communication, suggesting that the government does, in fact, monitor not only the contents of messages, but also their sources. This regulation is the same on PC rooms, which are public, pay, Internet-use sites. These must register their IP addresses with the government. In one way, Koreans enjoy greater freedom. Companies may only legally monitor employee e-mails if they have a written prior agreement from the employee. However, legal stipulations about business e-mail monitoring are not clear, and many confused cases have been appearing (*Korean Economy Daily*, May 2, 2002).

There can be social consequences as well. In the United States, learning about someone's HIV status can damage him or her if that information becomes public (National Women's Health Information Center, n.d.). In 2005, hacking into the cell phone of Paris Hilton, and the publication of her phone number list, led to embarrassment for her and her confidants (Thomas, 2005). In Korea, Lee and Hong (n.d.) noted that social discourse about privacy issues in Korea has been at the fledgling level or nonexistent. And they argued that from the Japanese domination to recent history of authoritarian and military regimes, the people have implicitly taken it for granted that governments can collect personal information for the purpose of surveillance and control of social dissidents. Experiences in the Korean War and the division into communist and capitalist nations increased social anxiety for another war and spurred anticommunist fever.

Conducting a survey in Korea, a nation that has embraced Internet technology, still requires the researcher to know the extent to which communication is legally protected. Since the content of communication has a great deal to do with treatment under Korean law, areas of inquiry need to be compared with what would be unacceptable for Koreans to answer. Similar questions need to be asked for any international study. It is important for both the well being of the participants and the integrity of the study.

The privacy of an individual's responses can affect the quality of data collected. If the respondent believes his or her information may be compromised, they may be more likely to lie or fail to answer some or all of the questions posed. If certain topics are socially taboo or legally forbidden, those topics are not good choices for querying via the Internet. Generally, researchers need to use careful investigation and cultural sensitivity when designing studies to be conducted across international borders.

ISSUES TO CONSIDER

As shown previously, different governments have different views on what is lawful state seizure of data. Changing laws in the United States since September 11, 2001, point out that even within a given country the situation regarding data privacy may be fluid (Siphor & Ward, 1995). The careful researcher will determine how questions might result in consequences for the individual. For example, in the United States, to say that one disagrees with or simply does not like the president does not draw notice from the government. In Europe at the time of the American Revolution, it was a capital crime. And *lese majeste* remains a crime in some nations today (BBC, 2000). Similarly, agencies that send Christian missionaries to the Middle East go to great pains to conceal their identities, for the safety of both the missionaries and the locals with whom they work.

It is not only government interception that must be considered. Individuals such as employers or owners of technology (Internet cafés, ISPs) may have a legal right to examine the communications of others. Hackers have the opportunity to examine data in transit, or to illicitly retrieve data stored on servers, including the researcher's own. Although this might have no legal consequence, it could have devastating personal ones. Being found out as being gay in some Islamic nations could lead to shunning or even mob violence.

In identifying populations for study, the diffusion patterns of Internet technology need to be considered. Although South Korea has wide Internet diffusion, its Asian neighbor, Thailand, has seen more biased adoption. As of March, 2001, according to surveys done in Thailand, 5.64% of Thais used the Internet, mostly in urban areas. The Internet user profile of Thailand 2001, a survey conducted by the National Electronics and Computer Technology Center (NECTEC, 2002), shows that Internet usage is confined largely to the nation's capital. It suggested that 52.2% of the users live in Bangkok, and a further 13.8% in suburban Bangkok. While Internet cafés are now available on busy streets in big Thai cities, rural residents may be left out.

Location is not the only prejudicing factor. Thai Internet users are young. Respondents from 20-29 accounted for 49.1%, followed by 30-39 year-olds (21.5%) and those between 10-19 years of age (18.2%). They are also educated. The survey also found that 60.3% of respondents had bachelor's degrees, while 12.9% had a master's degree. Only 5.7% of the respondents had not completed high school. Regarding English language proficiency, more than 80% of NECTEC respondents claimed that they had fair or better English proficiency.

The diffusion of the technology and sophistication of the participants has a direct effect on the nature of informed consent. In the United States, survey research is not generally required to pass an internal review board. However, providing potentially naïve users with information about the possibility of their data being captured, and about what the researcher plans to do with the data is, at minimum, a courtesy to them. Providing this information may also encourage additional response, if users' concerns are allayed. Information about data security and the opportunity to consent through answering of questions does not require separate forms or paperwork, but can be included in a respondent information statement like the following:

Any answers that you choose to provide in this study will be combined with answers from others in order to make generalizations about SUBJECT OF STUDY. You have a right to choose not to participate in this study by failing to return your questionnaire or by failing to answer any individual question therein. If you choose to participate, your answers will never be reported to anyone in such a way that you personally can be identified. As you may be aware, electronic communication may be subject to interception, legally by your employer or Internet host or illegally by another party while the information is in transit. Therefore, it is possible that your information might be seen by another party and I cannot control whether that happens. If you are concerned about your data

security, I suggest that you print this message, fill out the answers by hand, remove information from headers etc. that identifies you as the respondent and mail the completed survey to the following address:...

CONCLUSION

- Learn about the Internet law and cultural practice in nations you intend to survey
- Learn about the diffusion of the Internet and technical sophistication of your audience
- In designing the study, select electronic distribution of surveys only if the information collected will not subject the respondent to government or social penalty
- Consider a respondent information statement that tells of the risks of Internet research and offers offline response mechanisms
- When survey data are received, store them in a medium that is not connected to a computer network to reduce the risk of data theft.

REFERENCES

Adams, J. (2004). Suppressing evidence gained by government surveillance of computers. *Criminal Justice Magazine, 19*(1), 46-55.

British Broadcasting Company (BBC). (2000). *Two arrested in Anna clampdown*. Retrieved March 21, 2002, from http://news.bbc.co.uk/1/hi/entertainment/594716.stm

Cho, Y-h. *States and personal information*. Retrieved June 5, 2002, from http://www.good-citizen.or.kr/lecture/list.asp?b_number=236&b_code=code2

Detroit Free Press. (2005). PATRIOT ACT: Court ruling on key section is long overdue. *Detroit Free Press*, February 25, 2005. Retrieved February 28, 2005, from http://www.freep.com/voices/editorials/epatact25e_20050225.htm

Dillman, D. A. (2001). *Mail and telephone surveys: The total design method.* New York: Wiley-Intersciences.

Electronic Frontier Foundation (EFF). *Steve Jackson Games vs. Secret Service Case.* Retrieved March 21, 2002, from http://www.eff.org/legal/cases/SJG/

Kim, K-j. *Governmental surveillance and control: Korean experience.* Retrieved June 5, 2002, from http://www.privacy.or.kr/privacy_text.htm

Kim, S-J. (2002). *The digital economy and the role of government: Information technology and economic performance in Korea.* Cambridge: Harvard University.

Korean Economy Daily. (2002). Fear on e-mail monitoring spreads. *Korean Economy Daily,* May 2, 2002. Retrieved June 5, 2002, from http://kr.dailynews.yahoo.com/headlines/tc/20020502/ked/ked2002050203948.html

Lee, J., & Hong, S. *Reconstruction of privacy as the right of counter surveillance: Reacting to states' control and surveillance.* Retrieved March 21, 2002, from http://www.privacy.or.kr/privacy_text.htm

Levary, R, Thompson, D., Kot, K., & Brothers, J. (2005). RFID, electronic eavesdropping and the law. *RFID Journal.* Retrieved February 28, 2005, from http://www.rfidjournal.com/article/articleview/1401/1/128/

National Electronics and Computer Technology Center. (2002). *Thailand domain count and host count* . Retrieved May 28, 2002, from http://ntl.nectec.or.th/internet/domainname/WEB/

National Women's Health Information Center. (n.d.). *Women and HIV/AIDS: Your rights.* Retrieved June 1, 2002, from http://www.4woman.gov/HIV/rights.cfm

Sipior, J. C., & Ward, B. The ethical and legal quandary of e-mail privacy. *Communications of the ACM, 12*(38), 48-55.

Thomas, K. (2005). Paris Hilton and the not so simple life. *USA TODAY,* Feb. 23, 2005. Retrieved February 28, 2005, from http://www.usatoday.com/life/people/2005-02-23-hilton-phone-reaction_x.htm?POE=LIFISVA

U.S. Code Title 47, Chapter 9. (n.d.). Retrieved from http://uscode.house.gov

KEY TERMS

De jure **Legality:** Provisions explicitly provided for by the law.

De facto **Security:** The actual security afforded to respondents, which may involve parties who act outside of the law.

Diffusion Patterns: The way technology is adopted by a population, including characteristics and location of users.

Informed Consent: A statement of the procedures to be used in the study and the potential risks to the participants.

IRB: Internal (or institutional) review board at an institution required by government funding agencies to approve many studies that include human participants in order to protect the participants' rights.

Naïve Users: Persons who use technology, but have little knowledge of the mechanisms by which the technology operates.

Respondent Information Statement: An explicit delineation of security issues included with a survey.

Chapter XIV
Measuring
Internet Dependency

Jaime L. Melton
Pepperdine University, USA

J. Lynn Reynolds
Fuller Theological Seminary, USA

ABSTRACT

Internet dependency measures need to be refined from the previous measurements with regard to media dependency in order to more fully understand relations with the Internet and how the population uses the Internet to facilitate adaptation into a constantly changing culture. The basis for this study will be media system dependency theory; however, there are new concepts that need to be refined in order to build a greater understanding of how dependencies vary with types of media. The application included in this chapter tries to identify how users of the Internet learn information about culture and, therefore, facilitate their adaptation into the information age. With regard to Internet dependency, findings show that Internet goals, unlike those posited in the media system dependency literature (namely, understanding, orientation, and play) were better identified as goals related to information, communication, entertainment, and news.

INTRODUCTION

The Internet serves a wide range of communication roles such as interpersonal communication, group communication, and mass communication, as well as disparate functions ranging from e-mail and interactive games, to chat rooms and Web surfing (Mastro, Eastin, & Tamborini, 2002). Because of the tremendous growth in recent years, there is a strong need for additional understanding of this medium through improved measurement instruments.

This chapter uses media system dependency theory (MSD). This theory has the ability to explain the dual-dependency relationship among the media and social organizations such as political and economic systems (Ball-Rokeach, 1985; DeFleur & Ball-Rokeach, 1989). But more than the macro applications are the implications of the micro or individual media dependencies that scholars have recognized (Ball-Rokeach, 1998; Loges & Ball-Rokeach, 1993; Merskin, 1999). In both instances, the media system is an information system whereby media power or dependency is related to the degree of informational resources that are produced by the media. Dependency relationships that exist among the aggregate media system need to be refined as well as those relationships with a specific medium such as the Internet.

REVIEW OF LITERATURE

Morris and Ogan (1996) propose scholarship focused on the Internet may be less due to the fact that as a newer medium, scholars have confined studies to more traditional forms of media that are more conforming to existing models and theories, such as those in the uses and gratifications literature. However, MSD looks at individuals as problem solvers. As problem solvers, individuals are goal oriented and motivated to seek out information to achieve their goals. Unlike needs as used in uses and gratifications (U&G) applications, goals are vulnerable to external influences. MSD goes beyond U&G to account for the social environment, and how an individual's goal to understand, to orient themselves, and play in this environment is impacted by the media's control over the informational resources needed to attain those goals (Ball-Rokeach, 1998). This opens up multiple focal points that expand many relationships within society. Specifically, the Internet may be:

(a) one-to-one asynchronous communication, such as e-mail; (b) many-to-many asynchronous communication, such as . . . electronic bulletin boards; (c) synchronous communication that can be one-to-one, one-to-few, or one-to-many, and can be organized around a topic . . . such as chat rooms; and (d) asynchronous communication generally characterized by the receiver's need to

seek out the site in order to access information that may involve many-to-one, one-to-one, or one-to-many source-receiver relationships. (Morris & Ogan, 1996, p. 43)

When all of these possible relationships are considered, it makes individuals wonder not only how they functioned before the Internet, but also what would be the best way to frame these relationships in order to provide societal insight. Unfortunately, little measurement explains how this dependency has evolved.

With regard to micro-MSD relations, individuals are goal oriented, and may form dependencies with the media as a means of achieving these goals (Ball-Rokeach, 1985; Ball-Rokeach, 1998; Ball-Rokeach, Rokeach, & Grube, 1984; DeFleur & Ball-Rokeach, 1989, Loges & Ball-Rokeach, 1993, Merskin, 1999). The media typology goals identified that motivate individuals to utilize the media are understanding, orientation, and play. An individual's media dependency strengthens, based on the media's ability to produce relevant content that satisfied these goals. Similarly, the media's ability to produce cognitive, affective, and behavioral effects depends on the degree of usefulness the media has in achieving specific goals.

MSD seeks to answer, "Why, when and how are the media powerful regarding individuals and interpersonal networks and with what consequences? (Ball-Rokeach, 1998, p. 27). The major assumptions behind MSD are that: (a) society can only be understood in knowing the relations among its parts; (b) humans are motivated to achieve understanding, orientation, and play goals; (c) to attain those goals, one must seek informational resources such as the media either as a whole or through individual mediums; (d) the power of the media stems from control over desired resources that individuals, groups, or society need in order to attain their goals; (e) a change in one dependency will affect other related dependencies; (f) the construction of knowledge is held at the macrolevel;

therefore, individual or interpersonal knowledge is limited to the dissemination of information via the media; (g) media production occurs and is influenced in the macrolevel; and lastly, (h) the media controls the information resources central to the individuals success in goal attainment—the individual does not control the resources that the media system needs to attain its goals (Ball-Rokeach, 1998).

The foundational premise within a micro-MSD relation is the individual need for goal attainment through the utilization of various resources (Ball-Rokeach, 1985; Ball-Rokeach, 1998; Ball-Rokeach et al., 1984; DeFleur & Ball-Rokeach, 1989; Loges & Ball-Rokeach, 1993; Merskin, 1999). Media behavior is then shaped by the media's ability to provide the resources necessary for goal attainment: "those resources being the capacity to (a) create and gather, (b) process, and (c) disseminate information" (Ball-Rokeach, 1985).

Dependencies may be formed based on the perceived utility of the media's ability to fulfill one's goals. Ball-Rokeach and colleagues (1984) state, "a person's media dependencies should be a function not only of his or her goals . . .[but] of the individual's perceptions of the goal-related utility of media resources" (p. 6). The media serves to fulfill understanding goals or knowledge-gathering goals and also orientation (behavior) and play goals.

Media Dependency Typologies

When guided by an understanding dependency, individuals may be motivated by self-understanding or social understanding goals. They may consume media that will aid in the interpretation of self, or they may seek information from the media as a means of gaining a better understanding of their social environment or community. Orientation dependencies include individual goals in seeking appropriate action and interaction. Action orientation refers to goals of obtaining "guides"

to individual behavior, whereas interaction goals refer to actions involving more than one person (DeFleur & Ball-Rokeach, 1989, p. 306). Orientation dependencies tie to understanding dependencies in that individual actions are a result of the way that the media constructs the social situation (Ball-Rokeach et al., 1984).

Interaction goals seek to answer, "What shall I say? What are they like? How should I behave?" (Ball-Rokeach et al., 1984, p. 9). Media dependencies of this nature are likely to result when individuals choose not to seek counsel from within the social group, or when it is too costly to seek out expert advice (Ball-Rokeach et al., 1984, p. 9).

Play dependencies refer to motivations for relieving stress. Motivations are driven by "pleasure, aesthetic enjoyment, excitement, or relaxation" goals that are achieved through exposure to media content (Ball-Rokeach et al., 1984, p. 10). Melton, Reynolds, and Reynolds (2005) summarize original data that gives insight into how the Internet is used by college students participating in an international study-abroad program. Morris (1996) and other researchers have applied MSD theory to study various motivations for Internet use to gratify needs (Flanagan & Metzger, 2001; Leung, 2001; Papacharissi & Rubin, 2000). Ball-Rokeach (1989) contends that the Internet is not in a class by itself, but rather part of the existing media system. Ball-Rokeach (1998) contends that continued growth of the Internet will only extend the assimilation of this medium into the existing media system; thereby, extending the media systems utility in goal attainment. Furthermore, she states that the power of interpersonal communication will remain unbalanced, whereas the macro-producer-consumer relations will continue to dominate.

The foundational premise within a microMSD relation is the individual need for goal attainment through the utilization of various resources (Ball-Rokeach, 1985; Ball-Rokeach, et al., 1984; DeFleur & Ball-Rokeach, 1998; Loges & Ball-

Rokeach, 1993; Merskin, 1999). According to MSD, individuals are goal oriented and depend on the media to fulfill these goals. Goals, in this sense, suggest a problem-solving orientation, meaning individual goals are meant to address specific problems and, therefore, influence media behavior (Ball-Rokeach, 1985; Ball-Rokeach et al., 1984;). Thus, media behavior is shaped by the media's ability to provide the resources necessary for goal attainment; "those resources being the capacity to (a) create and gather, (b) process, and (c) disseminate information." (Ball-Rokeach, 1985).

According to MSD, individuals may have three types of goal-related media dependencies. More specifically, motivation to consume the media is derived from an individual's understanding, orientation, and play goals (Ball-Rokeach, 1985; Ball-Rokeach et al., 1984; DeFleur & Ball-Rokeach, 1998; Loges & Ball-Rokeach, 1993). These goals, while extensive, may be fulfilled by any one media function. In other words, they are not "mutually exclusive since any media message may serve more than one dependency" (Ball-Rokeach, 1985; Ball-Rokeach, et al., 1984, p. 7).

Measuring MSD

Media system dependency theory was tested in 1984 by Ball-Rokeach, Rokeach, and Grube. Their measure consisted of 11 items related to television behavior, and was intended to measure the three media typologies. Participants in their sample were asked to respond to questions such as "how do you use television to decide what to buy and where to buy it" (Ball-Rokeach, et al., 1984). Conducting a varimax rotation factor analysis, items were collapsed into factors that became combined media typologies (social understanding, self-understanding, and orientation play) (Ball-Rokeach, et al., 1984).

In August 2000, 51% of all U.S. households owned a computer (NTIA, 2000). Of those households, registered Internet users reached 42%; a 58% increase from December 1998 (NTIA, 2000). During a typical day, 68 million people log on to the Internet (Pew Internet, March 2000-2004). On average, users spend nearly 8 hours a month online, "visiting approximately 12 unique sites and over 300 pages of content" (Mastro, et al., 2002, p. 158). The Internet serves a wide range of communication roles such as interpersonal communication, group communication, and mass communication, as well as disparate functions ranging from e-mail and interactive games, to chat rooms and Web surfing (Mastro et al., 2002)

Papacharissi and Rubin (2000) assert that the Internet provides both "interactive/social and informational/task-oriented dimensions" (Papacharissi & Rubin, 2000, p. 179). Depending on individual need, individuals will select a particular function based on the accessibility and perceived capacity to fulfill a particular need. How the Internet is utilized is also dependent upon the individual characteristics of the user (Papacharissi & Rubin, 2000). The question that needs to be asked is how do participant students use the Internet to learn?

Ball-Rokeach and colleagues (1984) evaluated media dependency based on motives for television consumption. Although this application section is looking specifically at Internet dependency, the 11-item MSD scale is relevant. Reliabilities for each of the media typologies were assessed after conducting a varimax rotation factor analysis. Three factors emerged: (a) social understanding (.69), (b) self-understanding (.54), and (c) orientation-play (.68).

Specific Application

To construct the Internet dependency measure used in this application (Melton et al., 2005), eight items were adapted from Ball-Rokeach and colleagues (1984) assessment of media dependency. The remaining items were developed from the "daily Internet activities" measured in the Pew Internet and American Life Project (March 2000-2004).

In total, this measure was composed of 29 items in which participants were asked to indicate how often they use the Internet for various Web-related media activities such as sending e-mail, surfing the Web, and making decisions for evening and weekend recreation. Responses were assessed based on a five-point scale (1= Very Often, 5 = Never).

Procedures

The measure used to assess the proposed hypotheses was an online survey distributed to the student sample by their respective administrators. The administrators facilitated the study by forwarding an e-mail message from the researcher explaining the purpose of the study, and a link to the online survey. The percentage of the total population (1,243 students) who had received the e-mail once they had returned from their absence from campus was 25% ($N = 314$)

Using SPSS, several statistical measures were employed. A principle component factor analysis was utilized to determine the emergent Internet typologies from the Internet dependency measure. First, a varimax factor rotation method was employed, resulting in eight factors with eigenvalues greater than 1.0. Further reducing the data, an oblique promax factor rotation method was then utilized in two iterations that ultimately resulted in four significant factor loadings. To assess the relationships between the independent and dependent variables, a correlation matrix was produced. The coefficients for anxiety and attributional confidence were standardized using z-scores, and then evaluated to determine the critical value. The critical value was calculated with the intent of finding any correlation between the resultant Internet dependency typologies and the point at which either uncertainty control or anxiety control processes were enacted among survey participants.

RESULTS

The data collected for the Internet dependency measure was subjected to a principle component analysis using a varimax factor rotation structure that resulted in eight factors with eigenvalues greater than 1.0. Using an oblique promax rotation method, the data was reduced to five factors. Items that either failed to load or revealed secondary factor loadings were discarded, and the data was further subjected to a principle component analysis using an oblique promax rotation method that resulted in four significant factor loadings. See Table 1 for the factor analysis structure and Table 2 for factor variance.

Factor one. The first factor that emerged from the four-factor structure included the items, "decide where to go for evening and weekend recreation" (.89), "get travel information" (.87), "use an online search engine to find information" (.67), "decide what to buy and where to buy it" (.63), "conduct an Internet search to answer a specific question" (.61), and "search for a map or driving directions" (.60). In this factor, two of the items from the MSD measure emerged: "decide where to go for evening and weekend recreation" and "decide what to buy and where to buy it." When the measure was devised, Ball-Rokeach and colleagues (1984) labeled these media activities as social-play and action-orientation goals, respectively. Social-play goals are centered on achieving enjoyable interaction. The media serves these goals as being a catalyst for the interaction. An action-orientation goal relates to the media's utility in effecting a specific action. In their analysis, these items were collapsed with other items as an orientation-play goal.

The factor loadings in this structure only moderately fit these descriptions. From the wording of the items, it cannot be determined, necessarily, that these Internet activities are being utilized to serve social-play or action-orientation goals. It could be argued that "get travel information" or "search

Table 1. Factor analysis structure for Internet dependency

Typology assigned	Items: How often do/did you use the Internet to . . .	Factor 1	Factor 2	Factor 3	Factor 4
Information	Decide where to go for evening and weekend recreation	**0.89**	-0.09	-0.06	-0.13
	To get travel information	**0.87**	-0.10	0.03	-0.09
	Use an online search engine to find information	**0.67**	-0.08	0.10	0.20
	Decide what to buy and where to buy it	**0.63**	0.32	-0.21	0.07
	Conduct an Internet search to answer a specific question	**0.61**	0.07	0.05	0.17
	Search for a map or driving directions	**0.60**	-0.06	0.25	-0.10
Communication	Take part in an online group that you consider yourself a member of	0.04	**0.82**	-0.03	-0.07
	Visit an online support group	-0.11	**0.81**	-0.09	0.01
	Chat in a chat room or participate in an online discussion	-0.09	**0.75**	0.13	-0.14
	Express your opinions (e.g. discussion group, online bulletin boards)	-0.01	**0.66**	0.08	0.04
	Learn more about yourself	0.10	**0.47**	0.10	0.13
Entertainment	Download other files such as games, videos, or pictures	-0.03	-0.06	**0.91**	-0.03
	Share files with others	0.09	-0.08	**0.72**	-0.13
	Watch a video clip or listen to an audio clip	0.11	0.08	**0.65**	0.08
	Play a game	-0.14	0.22	**0.63**	0.07
	Have something to do when nobody else is around	0.16	0.22	**0.43**	0.04
News	To obtain news	-0.05	-0.08	0.05	**0.97**
	Find out what is/was happening in the world	-0.09	-0.13	0.13	**0.96**
	Find out what is/was happening in your community	0.07	0.13	-0.25	**0.79**

for a map or driving directions" could facilitate a social-play goal, but it is not conclusive from this analysis. Likewise, using a search engine and conducting an Internet search do not specify any specific action, or whether a social-play goal is being served. It is possible that these activities were sought for informational purposes only, not to engage in any action or social play. Based on these findings, the commonalities between each of these items suggest that an information-seeking goal is being served. Therefore, the media typology assigned for Factor one is information.

Factor two. The significant factor loadings that emerged in factor two were, "take part in an online group that you consider yourself a member of" (0.82), "visit an online support group" (.81), "chat in a chat room or participate in an online discussion" (.75), "express your opinions (e.g., discussion group, online bulletin boards)" (.66), and "learn more about yourself" (.47). In this factor, two items from the MSD measure emerged, although they were the weakest factor loadings in factor two. These items were, "express your opinions" and "learn more about yourself." The original media typologies assigned to these items by Ball-Rokeach et al. (1984) when they developed the MSD measure were interaction orientation and self-understanding respectively. Interaction-orientation goals involve seeking information to effect successful interaction (e.g., "What shall I say?"

Table 2. Table of variance for Internet dependency media typologies

Media typology	Eigenvalue	% of Variance	Reliability
Information	6.342	33.376	.83
Communication	2.061	10.846	.75
Entertainment	1.788	9.409	.87
News	1.236	6.503	.80

"What are they like?"), while self-understanding involves information seeking to better oneself (Ball-Rokeach et al., 1984, p. 9). In the MSD study, the item "express your opinions" was condensed under the typology of self-understanding. In comparing each of the other significant factor loadings against these typology descriptions, it appears that the factor loadings in factor two (e.g., participating in an online chat room or support group) could serve a wide array of functions that are not necessarily specific to self-understanding or even effective social interaction. Therefore, factor two was labeled communication.

Factor three. Five significant factor loadings emerged in factor three. These factors were, "download other files such as games, videos, or pictures" (.91), "share files with others" (.72), "watch a video clip or listen to an audio clip" (.65), "play a game" (.63), and "have something to do when nobody else is around" (.43). The MSD item that emerged with this factor was, "have something to do when nobody else is around." This item was originally identified as a solitary play media typology, but condensed in their analysis as an orientation-play item. Play goals, according to the literature on MSD, are related to "fantasy escape" for enjoyment, recreation, or to alleviate stress (Ball-Rokeach, et al., 1984, p. 10). To some degree, the significant factor loadings could be play related. However, given the multifaceted nature of the Internet, it was found that there is a strong entertainment component, the possible goals having to do with being entertained (e.g., downloading a video clip) or to entertain others (e.g., sharing files). Therefore, factor three was labeled entertainment.

Factor four. Factor four contained three significant factor loadings. These items were, "to obtain news" (.97), "find out what is/was happening in the world" (.96), and "find out what is/was happening in your community" (.79). The latter two items, "find out what is/was happening in the world" and "find out what is/was happening in your community" were items adapted from the MSD measure. These items were identified as social-understanding goals by Ball-Rokeach and colleagues (1984). A social-understanding goal involves information gathering to make sense out of one's social environment. Of the four factors, this factor is the most aligned with the MSD media typologies. However, it is argued that the goal of social understanding is too broad for this factor. In this factor, "obtain news" achieved the highest factor loading. Furthermore, staying abreast of happenings around the world and in one's community is essentially a form of news gathering. Therefore, this factor has been labeled more specifically as news.

"How do students studying abroad use the Internet to learn about the host culture?" The findings of this analysis confirm that students studying abroad use the Internet. Based on the factor loadings, students used the Internet to fulfill information, communication, entertainment, and news goals.

Dependency Goals

The Internet-dependency measure revealed that the subjects were using the Internet to fulfill specific Internet-related goals. The findings of the oblique promax factor rotation revealed four factors, or

Internet typologies, associated with participants' Internet behavior. In comparing the resultant factors to the MSD literature, it was found that there did not appear to be a true fit between these factors and the MSD media typologies (namely, understanding, orientation, and play goals). While it may be argued that the some of the findings of this analysis could be labeled using these typologies, it is the contention of the authors that the significant factor loadings from this analysis are better identified using labels that connote more specific goal-related behavior. A plausible reason is that the MSD media typologies were identified after examining television use. Given the Internet's ability to deliver specific information, perform disparate tasks, and serve many functions, this medium's utility is quite different than television; the key difference being the way that users are able to interact with the medium (Mastro et al., 2002). For example, understanding or orientation goals, whether social or self-understanding, or action- or interaction-orientation goals, these typologies are seemingly too broad to characterize Internet users' goals. While it may be true that users (that is, students) could be logging on to obtain information about their social environment or to engage in appropriate action, the Web enables users the ability to obtain highly targeted information that they may tailor to their needs. Through the use of search engines, users can search for answers to specific questions, topics, or special interest areas. In general, users can obtain information on just about anything that is in cyberspace. "There is . . . abundant evidence that the Internet is now the primary means by which many people get key information" (Pew Internet, 2002b, p. 3).

Likewise, the media typology for play goals does not truly capture what was found in this analysis against items that were related. The MSD literature states that play goals are related to fantasy escape or the alleviation of stress. This seems to connote a passive activity. Solitary play goals for example are motivated by the mere act of seeking pleasure or enjoyment. The significant factor load-ings in this analysis that could somewhat relate to solitary play suggested that a more active goal was being served: either to be entertained (e.g., downloading files such as games) or to perhaps entertain others (e.g., sharing files with others).

Another significant finding of this analysis is that Internet users, particularly student, are utilizing this medium to fulfill communication goals. Unlike television, the Internet enables users to communicate through various platforms such as sending instant messages or participating in chat rooms. There is an interpersonal component, whether it is "one-to-one, one-to-few, or one-to-many" (Morris & Ogan, 1996, p. 43) that is not capable through other traditional media. It is likely that these activities had a stronger importance among the sample as a means to keep touch with their family and friends back home. Additional study involving the Internet as an interpersonal platform is needed. This is particularly warranted among student travelers, tourists, or immigrants who are separated by large distances from friends and family who were the participants in the application study discussed above. The findings of the Internet dependency measure confirm that participants (students) have dependency relations with the Internet for various goals, specifically, communication, information, entertainment, and news.

CONCLUSION

Information, communication, entertainment, and news needs will continue to be met by use of the Internet. New media typologies must be developed to more accurately reflect the exact tendencies as they evolve. The Internet serves such a variety of functions that terms like understanding orientation and play should be revised to better reflect specific activities. As different generations become more and more savvy, the general populations will need to be studied to see how these activities are being diffused into society.

REFERENCES

Ball-Rokeach, S. J. (1973). From pervasive ambiguity to a definition of the situation. *Sociometry, 36,* 378-389.

Ball-Rokeach, S. J. (1985). The origins of individual media-system dependency. *Communication Research, 12*(4), 485-510.

Ball-Rokeach, S. J. (1998). A theory of media power and a theory of media use: Different stories, questions, and ways of thinking. *Mass Communication & Society, 1*(1/2), 5-40.

Ball-Rokeach, S. J., & DeFleur, M. L. (1976). A dependency model of mass-media effects. *Communication Research, 3,* 3-21.

Ball-Rokeach, S. J., Rokeach, M., & Grube, J. (1984). *The great American values test: Influencing behavior and belief through television.* New York: Free Press.

DeFleur, M. L., & Ball-Rokeach, S. J. (1989). *Theories of mass communication* (5th ed.). Needham Heights, MA: Allyn & Bacon.

Flanagen, A. J., & Metzger, M. J. (2001). Internet use in the contemporary media environment. *Human Communication Research, 27,* 153-181.

Leung, L. (2001). Gratifications, chronic loneliness and Internet use. *Asian Journal of Communication, 11*(1), 96-119.

Loges, W. E., & Ball-Rokeach, S. J. (1993). The effect of media dependency relations and values on newspapers readership. *Journalism Quarterly, 70,* 602-614.

Mastro, D. E., Eastin, M. S., & Tamborini, R. (2002). Internet search behaviors and mood alterations: A selective exposure approach. *Media Psychology, 4,* 157-172.

Melton, J. L., Reynolds, R. A., & Reynolds, J. L. (2005, May). *Anxiety/uncertainty management, cultural adaptation, and Internet dependency among international students.* Paper presented at the International Communication Association conference, New York.

Merskin, D. (1999). Media dependency theory: Origins and directions. In K. Viswanath, & D. Demers (Eds.), *Mass media, social control, and social change* (pp. 77-98). Ames: Iowa State University Press.

Morris, M., & Ogan, C. (1996). The Internet as mass medium. *Journal of Communication, 46,* 39-50.

National Telecommunications and Information Administration Annual Report (NTIA). (2000). Retrieved October 5, 2003, from http://www.ntia. doc.gov/ntiahome/annualrpt/2001/2000annrpt. htm

Papacharissi, A. & Rubin, A. M. (2000). Predictors of Internet use. *Journal of Broadcasting & Electronic Media, 44*(2), 175-196.

Pew Internet & American Life Project Surveys. (2000-March 2002). *Daily Internet activities.* Retrieved March 31, 2003, from http://www.pewinternet.org/reports/chart.asp?img=Daily_A8.htm

Pew Internet & American Life Project Tracking Surveys. (March 2000-Present a). *Daily Internet activities.* Last updated June 2004. Retrieved July 3, 2004, from http://207.21.232.103/trends/ Daily_Activities_4.23.04.htm

Pew Internet & American Life Project Tracking Surveys. (March 2000-Present b). *Internet activities.* Last updated June 2004. Retrieved July 3, 2004, from http://207.21.232.103/trends/Internet_Activities_4.23.04.htm

Pew Internet & American Life Project. (2002a, September 15). *The Internet goes to college: How students are living in the future with today's technology.* Retrieved March 31, 2003, from http://www.pewinternet.org/reports/toc. asp?Report=71

Pew Internet & American Life Project. (2002b, December). *Counting on the Internet: Most expect to find key information online, most find the information they seek, many now turn to the Internet first*. Retrieved March 31, 2003, from http://www.pewinternet.org/reports/toc.asp?Report=80.

KEY TERMS

Internet Dependency: Relates to an individual's reliance on the media as an information resource to fulfill their goals.

Media Dependency Goal Types: Three types of media dependency goals have been identified: understanding, orientation and play goals.

Media Effects: A degree of change influenced by the degree of utility the media serve cognitively, affectively, and behaviorally for the individual.

Uses and Gratifications: A framework that seeks to identify how individuals use the media.

Chapter XV
Online Advertising Metrics

Ginger Rosenkrans
Pepperdine University, USA

ABSTRACT

Accurate and consistent metrics are critical for determining online advertising effectiveness, and for the growth of online advertising spending. There are a variety of ways to measure online advertising effectiveness, and this chapter explains common online advertising metrics to measure effectiveness, such as page impressions, ad impressions, clicks, visits, unique visitors, path analysis, conversion rates, and recency measures. This chapter also presents online metrics challenges, as well as encourages researchers to employ other pricing and metrics models besides the CTR (click-through)/CPC (cost per click) and CPM (cost per thousands) models.

INTRODUCTION

The Internet, which has been fueled by the efforts of disparate disciplines, has become an essential medium for advertisers and businesses since some of the first online ads began to appear on Web sites in 1994 (Adams, 1995; Hyland, 1998; Reed, 1999; Zeff & Aronson, 1996). Accurate and consistent metrics are critical for determining online advertising effectiveness. Additionally, measurement accuracy and consistency are essential factors for the growth of online advertising spending (Internet Advertising Bureau, 2004).

Although there are no industry-wide metrics standards (Chen & Wells, 1999; Hoffman & Novak, 2000; Maddox, 2002; Menn, 2000), the Internet Advertising Bureau (IAB) has provided the industry with recommended guidelines in 1999, 2002, and 2004 for standardizing measurement. Additionally, the Joint Industry Committee for Web Standards (JICWEBS), an international independent body, provides recommended Web metrics standards for most countries. Adoption of measurement guidelines can result in more meaningful Web advertising metrics for advertisers. One of the goals is to get the online advertising industry to use the same terminology when selling, purchasing, or evaluating the performance of online advertising.

COMMON WEB METRICS

The choice of a Web metric depends on the measurement objective and the advertiser's budget, technology, and time limits (Bhat, Bevans, & Sengupta, 2002). Some common Web metrics include: (1) page impressions, (2) ad impressions, (3) clicks, (4) visits, (5) unique visitors, (6) path analysis, (7) conversion rate, (8) frequency, and (9) recency.

Page impressions. Flat-fee exposure pricing was the earliest online advertising pricing model (Hoffman & Novak, 2000c). Flat-fee pricing can be implemented with or without online traffic (users who visit a Web site). For example, host sites charge advertisers a flat fee per month for posting ads on their sites. Advertisers are provided with basic overall site traffic and not the details of traffic (e.g., traffic during a certain time of day). Providing accurate traffic measurement is critical because advertisers use this information to evaluate the effectiveness of their ad's exposure on the site. Flat fees can be converted into a cost per thousands (CPM) pricing model (Hoffman & Novak, 2000). The CPM pricing model is impressions based. Page impressions are a measurement of the number of responses from a Web server to page requests from users' browsers (Bhat et al., 2002; Internet Advertising Bureau, 2004). They are an estimate of how many pages are served in a time period, and are a good indicator of a Web page's exposure (Bhat et al., 2002). CPMs are impression/exposure-based models that consist of a fixed price for a given period of time (Hoffman & Novak, 2000c). CPM measurements must be filtered to remove robot (i.e., bot or software agent) activity and error codes (Internet Advertising Bureau, 2004). Reliable filtration procedures are essential to accurate page-impression measurements.

Ad impressions. Ad impressions measure the response of a delivery system to an ad request from a user's browser (Bhat et al., 2002; Internet Advertising Bureau, 2004). This metric measures the overall exposure of an online ad. Although this measurement is not an indicator of user involvement, this metric provides advertisers with measurement of an ad's success in terms of brand recognition or brand visibility. The CPM pricing model is applied to ad impressions. The CPM model counts the number of visitors exposed to an online ad (e.g., banner ad) on a particular site, and site traffic is made available to the advertiser (Hoffman & Novak, 2000). The advertiser is charged a flat fee or CPM for exposure. Ad impressions do not track user involvement with an ad. When measuring users' exposures (i.e., ad impressions metric) to an ad, there is no guarantee that ads are actually viewed by users (Bhat et al., 2002). Reliable filtration of bot activity and autorefreshed pages are essential to accurate ad impression measurements (Bhat et al., 2002; Internet Advertising Bureau, 2004).

Clicks. The Internet Advertising Bureau (2004) states there are three kinds of clicks: click-through, in-unit click, and mouse-over (e.g., mouse rollover, or user rolls mouse over ad). These three actions are referred to as clicks. A click-through is when a user initiates action by clicking on an ad and the click-through whisks the user to another online location, such as another browser window or Web site. Click-throughs are tracked and reported by an ad server, and it is imperative that bot activity is excluded to ensure accurate and reliable metrics. The cost-per-click (CPC) model or click-through rate (CTR) remains one of the most important media pricing metrics for the Internet (Chatterjee, Hoffman, & Novak, 2003). Click-throughs are based on the number of clicks divided by the number of ads requested or clicked on by users during a time period (Bhat et al., 2002). Click-throughs are behavioral, and are an accountable measure for online advertising (Chatterjee et al., 2003; Kania, 1999; "Online Advertising," 2000; Young, 2000). The advantages of click-through metrics are that they are easy to observe, and they indicate a behavioral response (Chatterjee et al., 2003; McLuhan, 2000). Additionally, click-throughs indicate an immediate interest in the advertised brand (Lawrence, 2000; Singh & Dalal, 1999). In-unit clicks and mouse-overs are other ad interactions or behavioral measures (Internet Advertising Bureau, 2004). Mouse-overs or in-unit clicks may not necessarily usher a user to another site or browser window. The type of clicks (i.e., click-through, in-unit click, mouse-over) measured should be reported with disaggregated detail. To ensure accurate and reliable metrics, it is critical to exclude robot activity.

Visits. A visit or a committed visitor is a measurement of one user session at a Web site (Bhat et al., 2002; Dainow, 2004; Joint Industry Committee for Web Standards, 2005). For the metric to be accurately counted as a visit, it must have 30 consecutive minutes of activity that can be attributed to a single browser for a single session (Internet Advertising Bureau, 2004). A visits metric is an estimate of the number of visits to a site (Bhat et al., 2002). Visits metrics can be used to measure a site's overall popularity.

Unique visitors. Unique visitors or users represent the number of actual people (filtered bot activity) with one or more visits to a site. This measurement provides advertisers with information on the number of people they are reaching with their message. This is another indicator of a site's popularity (Bhat et al., , 2002). Bhat, Bevans, and Sengupta (2002, p. 3) purport that this measurement. provided by the IAB. can "create confusion" because there are three ways to implement it. The use of cookies is one technique for tracking unique users. A cookie, which is a file on a user's browser, identifies the user's browser. There are two kinds of cookies: (1) persistent cookies and (2) session cookies. Persistent cookies are temporary and are erased when the user exits a browser, and session cookies remain on the user's hard drive until they expire or until the user erases them.

Path analysis. Path analysis charts the paths navigated by users (Bhat et al., 2002). It is an aggregate-level measure and does not identify individual users; however, this metric extends beyond the measures of popularity or exposure. It allows advertisers to examine what users did on the site.

Conversion rate. One of the most critical online measures is the conversion rate (Dainow, 2004). A conversion event occurs when a user follows through on an action within the Web site, such as filling out a form, requesting to opt-in a newsletters, downloading a whitepaper, or completing a credit card payment process (Carrabis, 2005; Dainow, 2004). The conversion rate is the percentage of users who followed through the action, or the ratio of visitors to buyers (Dainow, 2004; Roche, 2005). The overall average conversion across the Internet is 2% (Dainow, 2004). A conversion rate that dips below 2% indicates a site needs improvement. Abandonment occurs when users do not complete an action (e.g., complete a credit card transaction to purchase a product online). Each form has an abandonment rate that is the percentage of users who accessed a page with a form, but did not complete it. The conversion and abandonment metrics provide insight into site design. To reduce abandonment, forms should have fewer questions. If the abandonment rate is OK but the conversion rate is low, this metric provides information on the overall quality of visitors: visitors/committed visitors rate and bounce rate.

The bounce rate metric is the percentage of users who first arrive at a site, scan it, and then leave (Dainow, 2004). Controlling the bounce rate is matching the initial appeal of the site to what users are searching for on the Web. This metric provides insight that users did not think the site offered what they wanted. This metric provides a different insight from the abandonment rate, which reveals that users did not commit because they did not think the product offered what they wanted.

Frequency. A frequency metric involves calculating the average number of times a visitor returns to a Web site (Bhat et al., 2002). Generally, frequency is a measure of user loyalty in the Web context.

Recency. The recency metric captures the interval between Web site visits (Bhat et al., 2002). An average is executed by calculating the intervals between current and previous visits of each visitor. A higher recency figure represents greater user attraction to the site (Bhat et al., 2002; Maity & Peters, 2005). A high recency figure generally indicates a greater loyalty among users. This metric is one way to reflect a site's stickiness. Site stickiness usually refers to the measurement of Web site attractiveness (Maity & Peters, 2005). A stickiness metric is often reported as the average minutes per month visitors spend at a site. Stickiness can also be measured through user frequency, unique visitors, or average time for each unique visitor (Bhat et al., 2002). Maity and Peters (2005) purport that this metric can be misleading, because if visitors cannot find certain information due to navigation difficulties, they might spend a lot of time on the site.

ONLINE METRICS CHALLENGES

Although the Web is one of the most measurable mediums (Bagla, 2004), Web analytic tools are still evolving. Not all measurements are alike. Many definitions exist for the same terms, some proposed guidelines are too vague for precise measurement, and there is a lack of comparability and unique systems that do not allow scaleable auditing (Bhat et al., 2002; Hoffman & Novak, 1997; Menn, 2000). This has resulted in rampant cheating of online ad click-through rates and Web site traffic results to advertisers, investors, and the public (Menn, 2000).

Metrics standards do not exist, which often result in inflated or inaccurate measurements. Brandt Dainow (2005a, 2005b), CEO of Think Metrics, asserts that ad measurement precision is not possible. He purports that Web analytics software is statistics and they have margins of error. Additionally, it is a new industry that has its challenges, yet it is improving with time.

Since there are no industry-wide metrics standards, inaccurate measurements are often reported (Chen & Wells, 1999; Menn, 2000). As more Web sites pay for customers to click on ads (i.e., CPC model), hackers can run programs to send false clicks through online ads. The inflated results for number of impressions and online ad click-throughs persist, especially as ad networks charge advertisers based on the number of click-throughs or use the CPC/CTR model.

Many in-house traffic metrics systems do not exclude bot traffic (almost 40% of total traffic) that sort through the Web on behalf of Internet search engines. A bot is a shortened term for robot, and is a term that has become interchangeable with software agent to indicate that software can be deployed to find information on the Internet and report back with it (Robb, 2000; Venditto, 2001). After a bot is given directions, it will sift through the avalanche of data on the Internet to bring back answers. Bot software helps users and companies find information online. There are several specialized bots to simplify users' needs, such as shopbots, spiders or crawlers, surveillance bots, news bots, and more (Luh, 2001; Middlebrook & Muller, 2000; Proffitt, 2001; Robb, 2000; Sandoval, 2000; Venditto, 2001; White, 2000). Bots can automatically log on a site every 30 seconds on up to seven different sites simultaneously (Sandoval, 2000). Additionally, bots can increase the traffic of a site or an ad (Luh, 2001; Manly, 2000; Middlebrook & Muller, 2000; Sandoval, 2000; Zick, 1998). A Web page that has 20 geographical elements on it can be counted as registering 20 page impressions or just one. Traffic variances can be inflated due to bot intervention (Chen & Wells, 1999; Menn, 2000). There are no metrics tools that can distinguish, track, and report the number of click-throughs from bots and the number of click-throughs from actual visitors. Although the robot exclusion standard (RES) exists, there is no government agency or international standards organization that oversees the bot industry (Middlebrook & Muller, 2000; Solomon, 1999a). Bots can ignore directives in a robots.txt file (Luh, 2001; Middlebrook & Muller, 2000; Solomon, 1999a; Solomon, 1999b).

Since there are no bot regulations, one of the challenges for accurate online advertising metrics is to filter bot intervention in Web and online advertising measurements, and ensure that a robots.txt standard programming file or software is employed for bot exclusion (ABC Interactive, 2001; Luh, 2001; Prosise, 1996; Solomon, 1999a). Other methods to bar bots from entering a host Web site include identifying and blocking the transmission control protocol/Internet protocol (TCP/IP) address of a bot, blocking Web users whose browsers hide their home addresses, and contacting the company deploying a bot (Middlebrook & Muller, 2000; Solomon, 1999a). Even with all the recommendations for implementing bot filtration, bots can still enter a site and inflate click-throughs and page impressions because there are no standards. Thus, this exposure and response metrics conundrum leads to (1) the need of developing software or metrics tools that filter bots or identify which activities are from bots or from actual users, (2) explore new methods for measuring ad effectiveness, and (3) explore other pricing models.

In addition to the challenges of filtering bot activity from Web metrics, the use of cookies for unique visitor counts can become inaccurate due to users deleting cookies. Three to five percent of visitors block session-only cookies, and spyware programs are designed to delete third-party cookies (Anfuso, 2005; Dainow, 2005).

Software can present other metrics challenges, such as inaccuracy in page impressions with SWF files and caching (Dainow, 2005). Flash files are SWF files, and most log analysis software count an SWF file as a page impression. If there are Flash animations within pages and the log analysis reflects Flash as both full-page impressions and page elements, these present inaccurate metrics. In addition to SWF files that present challenges in metrics software efficacy, caching can affect accurate page impressions. According to the Internet Advertising Bureau (2005), copying an online ad or Web page for later reuse is done in the user's browser and on proxy servers. When a user strikes the "back" button on the browser, it is caching or saving pages and it is not reflected in the log analysis; thus, it provides inaccurate ad or page impressions (Dainow, 2005).

Wake turbulence can affect Web page tracking because software tools do not report this type of user behavior (Dainow, 2005). Page-based tracking software counts each page when a user exits a site by clicking on the back button. Visits can end with a series of one or two-second page impressions in reverse order from the first half. This wake turbulence increases the average number of page impressions per visitor and reduces the average page duration.

CONCLUSION

There is a panoply of ways to measure online advertising effectiveness. Software can provide response rate metrics such as page impressions, ad impressions, clicks, and conversions. Advertisers have an advantage to advertising online over traditional methods because of the tracking possibilities. Metrics can be used for evaluating exposure, popularity, stickiness, user loyalty, reach, and behavioral responses. Although software tools are evolving to provide more accurate and precise measurements, metrics challenges persist. Some of the challenges in online metrics include filtering bot activity, the use of cookies for counting unique visitors, measuring page impressions with SWF files and caching, and dealing with wake turbulence as it affects page impressions and page durations. The CPM and CPC models remain important media pricing metrics for the Internet; however, researchers should not ignore other pricing and metrics models for measuring online advertising effectiveness.

REFERENCES

ABC Interactive. (2001). *How to tell whether your online ad has been served per the guidelines.* Retrieved May 14, 2001, from http://www.abcinteractiveaudits.com/news/white_paper_2331.htm

Adams, M. (1995, November 13). Brands of gold. *Mediaweek*, 30-32.

Anfuso, D. (2005, May 12). *Moving from metrics to results.* iMedia Connection. Retrieved May 15, 2005, from http://www.imediaconnection.com

Bagla, G. (2004, January 20). *Analyzing Web analytics.* iMedia Connection. Retrieved January 20, 2004, from http://www.imediaconnection.com

Bhat, S., Bevans, M., & Sengupta, S. (2002, Fall). Measuring users' Web activity to evaluate and enhance advertising effectiveness. *Journal of Advertising, 31*(3) 97-106.

Carrabis, J. (2005, July 15). *Usability studies 101: Defining visitor action.* iMedia Connection. Retrieved July 15, 2005, from http://www.imediaconnection.com

Chatterjee, P., Hoffman, D. L., & Novak, T. P. (2003). Modeling the clickstream: Implications for Web-based advertising efforts. *Journal of Marketing Science, 22*(4), 520.

Chen, Q., & Wells, W. D. (1999, September/October). Attitude toward the site. *Journal of Advertising Research, 39*(5), 27.

Dainow, B. (2004, November 2). *Web analytics 101.* iMedia Connection. Retrieved July 14, 2005, from http://www.imediaconnection.com

Dainow, B. (2005a, March 7). *Things that throw your stats* (Part 2). iMedia Connection. Retrieved July 14, 2005, from http://www.imediaconnection.com

Dainow, B. (2005b, March 3). *Things that throw your stats* (Part 1). iMedia Connection. Retrieved July 14, 2005, from http://www.imediaconnection.com

Hoffman, D. L., & Novak, T. P. (1997). *New Metrics for New Media.* Retrieved February 22, 3000, from http://w3j.com/5/s3.novak.html

Hoffman, D.L., & Novak, T. P. (2000a, May/June). How to acquire customers on the Web. *Harvard Business Review*, 179-188.

Hoffman, D. L., & Novak, T. P. (2000b, May/June). *When exposure-based Web advertising stops making sense (and what CD Now did about it).* Owen Graduate School of Management, E-Commerce Lab, Vanderbilt University. Retrieved May 24, 2000, from http://www.ecommerce.vanderbilt.edu

Hoffman, D. L., & Novak, T. P. (2000c). Advertising pricing models for the World Wide Web. In D. Hurley, B. Kahin, & H. Varian, *Internet publishing and beyond: The economics of digital information and intellectual property.* Cambridge, MA: MIT Press.

Hyland, T. (1998). *Why Internet advertising?* IAB. Retrieved March 22, 1999, from http://www.iab.net

Internet Advertising Bureau (2004, September). *Interactive audience measurement and advertising campaign reporting and audit guidelines.* Retrieved January 2005, from http://www.iab.net

Internet Advertising Bureau. (2005). *Terms and definitions.* Retrieved July 11, 2005, from http://www.iab.net

Joint Industry Committee for Web Standards. (2005). *Global standards.* Retrieved July 20, 2005, from http://www.jicwebs.org/standards.html

Kania, D. (1999, March 9). Order up! Serving up targeted banners. *ClickZ.* Retrieved January 28, 2000, from http://www.search.com/Articles/0309991.shtml

Lawrence, S. (2000, June 12). Beyond banner clicks. *The Standard.* Retrieved June 20, 2000, from wysiwys://2/http://thestandard.com/research/metrics/display/0,2799,15855,00.htm

Luh, J. C. (2001, April 12). No bots allowed. *Interactive Week.* Retrieved April 30, 2001, from http://www.zdnet.com/intweek/stories/news/0,4164,2707542,00.html

Maddox, K. (2002, February). IAB issues Net ad metrics standards. *B to B, 87*(2), 14.

Maity, M., & Peters, C. L. O. (2005, January-March). A primer for the use of Internet marketing research tools: The value of usability studies. *Interactive Marketing, 16*(3), 232-247.

Manly, H. (2000, December 24). There's no accounting for Web site watchers. *Boston Globe*, p. C12.

McLuhan, R. (2000, June 22). Ways to make clicks measure up. *Marketing*, 35.

Menn, J. (2000, April 17). Web firms may vastly inflate claims of hits. *Los Angeles, Times*, p. A1, A8, A9.

Middlebrook, S. T., & Muller, J. (2000, November). Thoughts on bots: The emerging law of electronic agents. *Business Lawyer, 56*(1), 341-370.

Online Advertising Effectiveness Study. (1998). *Internet Advertising Bureau.* Retrieved January 19, 2000, from http://www.iab.net

Oser, K. (2005, March 14). Marketers fume over click fraud. *Advertising Age, 76*(11), 34.

Proffitt, B. (2001, January 1). Surveillance bots scope out competitors, misinformation. *BotSpot.* Retrieved February 17, 2001, from http://bots.internet.com/news/feature010501/htm

Prosise, J. (1996, July). Crawling the Web. *PC Magazine.* Retrieved May 16, 2001, from http://www.zdnet.com/pcmag//issues/1513/pcmag0045.htm

Reed, M. (1999, April 29). Going beyond the banner ad. *Marketing*, 25-26.

Robb, D. (2000, June). Bots and search tools. *Government and Computer News, 19*(3), 30.

Roche, J. (2005, January 12). *Conversion is the new acquisition.* iMedia Connection. Retrieved July 14, 2005, from http://www.imediaconnection.com

Sandoval, G. (2000, December 8). Bots snarl sites as shoppers seek PlayStation 2. *Cnet News.* Retrieved April 30, 2001, from http://news.cnet.com/news/0-1007-200-4049034.html?tag=prntfr

Singh, S. N., & Dalal, N. P. (1999, August). Web home pages as advertisements. *Communications of the ACM, 42*(8), 91-98.

Solomon, K. (1999a, November 22). Stop that bot! *The Industry Standard.* Retrieved May 14, 2001, from http://www.thestandard.com/article/0,1902,7627,00.htm

Solomon, K. (1999b, November 15). Revenge of the bots. *The Industry Standard.* Retrieved January 24, 2001, from http://www.thestandard.com/article/article_print/0,1153,7624,00.htm

Venditto, G. (2001). What's a bot? *BotSpot.* Retrieved January 26, 2001, from http://www.botspot.com/bot/what_is_a_bot.htm

White, E. (2000, October 23). E-commerce (a special report): The lessons we've learned—comparison shopping: No comparison—shopping bots were supposed to unleash brutal price wars; why haven't they? *Wall Street Journal*, p. R18.

Young, S. (2000, April). Getting the message: How the Internet is changing advertising. *Harvard Business School Bulletin.* Retrieved May 19, 2000, from http://workingknowledge.hbs.edu/pubexprin…%20Internet%20is%20Changing%20Advertising

Zeff, R., & Aronson, B. (1996). *Advertising on the Internet.* New York: John Wiley and Sons.

Zick, L. (1998, April 12). *Automatic indexing: Web bots.* School of Library and Information Sciences, IUPUI. Retrieved May 16, 2001, from http://www.dochzi.com/1505/ai.htm

KEY TERMS

Abandonment: Users who fill out credit card or other forms and do not complete or submit them (Dainow, 2004).

Bots/Robots: Terms that have become interchangeable with agent to indicate that software can be sent on a mission to find information on the Internet and report back with it (Robb, 2000: Venditto, 2001).

Bounce, Bounce Rate: The percentage of users who first arrive at a site, scan it, and then leave (Dainow, 2004).

Click-Throughs, Clicks, or Click-Through Rates (CTR): The click rate focuses on understanding the effectiveness of online advertising, and it is a count of the number of times a user clicks on an ad in a Web site and successfully arrives at an advertiser's Web site (Hoffman & Novak, 1997; Young, 2000).

Conversion, Conversion Event, Conversion rate: The percentage of site visitors who commit to action, such as signing up for a newsletter, filling in a contract, completing a credit card transaction, downloading information (Dainow, 2004; Roche, 2005).

Cookie: Cookies are a technique for tracking users, and a cookie is a file on a user's browser that identifies the user's browser (Anfuso, 2005; Internet Advertising Bureau, 2005). There are two types of cookies: persistent cookies and session cookies. Session cookies are temporary and are erased when the browser exits. Persistent cookies remain on the user's hard drive until the user erases them or until they expire.

CPC: Cost-per-click pricing model (Hoffman & Novak, 2000b). The payment on an online ad is based on the number of times a visitor clicks on it. Payment on a click-through guarantees a visitor was exposed to an online ad and actively decided to click on it and become exposed to the target communication (Hoffman & Novak, 2000c).

CPM: Cost per thousand impressions for a particular site or ad exposure (Hoffman & Novak, 2000; Kania, 1999; "Online Advertising," 2000).

Frequency: Calculating the average number of times a visitor returns to a Web site determines the metric of frequency (Bhat et al., 2002).

Impression: The number of times an ad is rendered for viewing ("Online Advertising," 2000). One impression is equivalent to one opportunity to see (OTS) an ad by a Web user. Visitors are exposed to an online ad on a particular site (Hoffman & Novak, 2000c; Young, 2000). For example, it is considered an impression when a banner ad is on a page.

Page View: The number of times a particular Web page is presented to users (Hoffman & Novak, 1997).

Prospect Rate: The percentage of users who viewed a site's forms, or other desired action, but didn't take action (Dainow, 2004).

Recency: The recency metric captures the interval between Web site visits (Bhat et al., 2002).

Scanning Visitor: A user who first arrives at a site and scans it (Dainow, 2004).

Stickiness: Site stickiness usually refers to the measurement of Web site attractiveness (Maity & Peters, 2005).

Visit, Committed Visitor, Committed Visitor Rate: A visit is one session at a site, and it refers to a user who first arrives at a site and spends time reading the site's content (Bhat et al., 2002; Dainow, 2004).

Chapter XVI
Measurements in E–Business

Damon Aiken
Eastern Washington University, USA

ABSTRACT

This chapter is designed to answer two fundamental questions related to research on electronic surveys and measures. First, what are some of the major measures specifically related to e-business? Second, what makes Internet research methods different from off-line research methods? The chapter partly delineates what makes Internet research methods distinctive through its discussion and separation of the most common measures. This separation not only provides the framework for the chapter, but it distinguishes research for understanding the evolving e-consumer from measures related to the new paradigm for e-business strategy. In total, 17 different measures are discussed. The chapter concludes with a discussion of emerging issues in e-business metrics, and possibilities for future research.

INTRODUCTION

The Internet has emerged as the very foundation for business communications worldwide. Indeed, in the instant that it takes to read these words, millions of people are shopping on the Internet, checking the status of orders and shipments, investigating stock prices and mortgage rates, and browsing and bidding in a new realm of online auctions. The Internet has transformed the physical marketplace into a virtual marketspace (Varadarajan & Yadav, 2002); it has created a shift from reasonably well-informed buyers to worldly Web-enabled e-consumers (Bakos, 1997); and, it has accelerated business into an information age

wherein issues of technological expertise, privacy, security, and control are now essential aspects of business (Glazer, 1991; Hoffman, Novak, & Peralta, 1999).

Marketing practitioners, strategists, and researchers cannot deny the critical changes that have occurred in the realm of global business communications. Most have come to realize that online retailing is distinctive and that it requires a great deal of new research. Interactive communications and transactions now occur together in a single virtual medium that has increased risks for online consumers, and has placed a heavy communications burden on sellers whose Web site effectiveness is affected by a multitude of

Table 1. Summary of measures in e-business

Measurements for understanding e-consumers	Measurements for e-business strategy
Online trust	Exposures
Privacy	Impressions
Control of information	Hits
Cognitive effort	Visits
Information search	Clicks
Flow	Path analysis
	Conversion
	Frequency
	Recency
	Average time per visit
	Stickiness

design characteristics (Geissler, Zinkhan, & Watson, 2001). Internet consumers are placed in a unique inference-making position in which information asymmetry abounds. The task at hand now, for researchers and practitioners alike, is to accurately measure, analyze, and interpret online behaviors.

The purpose of this chapter is to introduce the topic of e-business measurement, and delineate some of what makes Internet research methods different from off-line research methods. The chapter separates measures for understanding the evolving e-consumer from measures related to the new paradigm for e-business strategy (a separation derived from the work of Biswas and Krishnan, 2004). The measures discussed in this chapter are graphically displayed in Table 1. The chapter concludes with a discussion of emerging issues in e-business metrics, and possibilities for future research.

Internet technologies are like an arms race in which both sides develop increasingly powerful weapons. (Bakos, 1998, p. 41)

MEASUREMENTS FOR UNDERSTANDING E-CONSUMERS

Understanding how the Internet has influenced consumer psychology is a critical task for business people. Speaking of the transformative nature of the Internet, it appears that businesses and consumers alike are now "armed" with previously unthinkable advances in information acquisition, classification, evaluation, and storage. In the unusual context of the Internet, key traditional elements of business exchange are noticeably absent, such as personal, nonverbal cues, and physical contact with products (Keen, Wetzels, de Ruyter, & Feinberg, 2004). In an effort to understand the Internet consumer, business researchers have begun to study notions of online trust, privacy, issues of control of personal information, cognitive effort and information search, and flow. Many of these issues are interrelated and, given that we are still in the early stages of Internet research, the topics need further exploration and insightful analysis.

Online trust. Internet marketing researchers have reported that, regardless of the number of privacy policies or "high-tech" encryption systems, what Web consumers really want is "… another type of exchange—characterized by an explicit social contract executed in the context of a cooperative relationship built on trust" (Hoffman et al., 1999; p. 82). This finding is both a recognition of the uniqueness of the Internet as a computer-mediated business environment, and an allusion towards the critical importance of trust in any Internet relationship. A consumer wishing to shop or purchase over the Internet needs to trust the e-tailer, but also needs to trust the Internet itself as a mode of shopping.

A small but growing subset of the business and marketing literature has attempted to define and measure the concept of trust in a computer-mediated environment (CME) (Handy, 1995; Hine & Eve, 1998; Jarvenpaa & Tractinsky, 1999; McKnight & Chervany, 2002). New definitions of trust in the CME reflect particular concerns about risk, reliability, privacy, and control of information. Milne and Boza (1999) operationalize trust in terms of an affective privacy element as "the expectancy of a customer to rely upon database marketers to treat the consumer's personal information fairly" (p. 8). Through unique processes of interactive communication, consumers must achieve a level of trust that surpasses perceptions of personal vulnerability (Aiken, Liu, Mackoy, & Osland, 2004). Inasmuch as trust requires a cognitive and affective leap of faith (a movement beyond calculative prediction—see Williamson, 1993), trust in the Internet implies, to some extent, behaviorally overcoming a concern for privacy. To take action in the face of risk is to engage in trusting behavior. Thus, much of the research on trust seems to derive three primary dimensions: (1) the affective/emotional element, (2) the cognitive/rational element, and (3) the behavioral element.

Privacy. Recent research reveals that concern for privacy is the most important consumer issue facing the Internet, ahead of ease-of-use, spam, security, and cost (Benassi, 1999). In the off-line world, consumers think nothing of giving their phone numbers or home addresses to seemingly disinterested servers, cashiers, and sales clerks. However, Internet consumers worry about everything from excessive spam e-mails and intrusive cookie files, to costly credit card fraud and perilous identity theft.

Measuring perceptions of privacy, as well as the e-consumer's felt need for privacy, is a critical issue in e-business. Researchers have observed that privacy is a multidimensional concept, and plays a critical role in fear of purchasing online (Hine & Eve, 1998; Sheehan & Hoy, 2000). Much of the concern for privacy may stem from fear of the unknown (Hoffman et al., 1999). Online consumers often cite feelings of helplessness while shopping on the Internet (Hine & Eve, 1998).

Control of personal information. Issues of control further substantiate the unique nature of Internet business relationships. Degrees of interactivity between consumer and e-business become a communicative "tug-of-war" as consumers strive for varied levels of control just as businesses strive to gather more and more strategic information (Yadav & Varadarajan, 2005). User control over personal information, over the actions of a Web vendor, and over the Internet site itself all relate to issues of trust. Additionally, control over the actions of a Web vendor affects consumers' perceptions of privacy and security of the online environment (Bhatnagar & Ghose, 2004; Hoffman et al., 1999). Consumers often guard their personal information carefully. Hoffman and Novak (1998) note that "Virtually all Web users have declined to provide personal information to Web sites at some point, and close to half who have provided data have gone to the trouble of falsifying it" (p. 1). Consequently, perceptions and levels of control become key measures in e-business.

Cognitive effort and information search. Many researchers have noted that decision making is both task dependent (Bettman, Johnson, & Payne, 1990; Maule & Edland, 1997) and context dependent (Bettman, Luce, & Payne, 1998; Wright, 1974). Given that both the decision task and the decision context are different in a CME; new research has just begun to measure cognitive effort, search characteristics, and decision-making processes. Weiner et al. (Weiner, Deighton, Gupta, Johnson, Mellers, Morwitz, & O'Guinn,1997) note, "The ability of [Internet] consumers to sort on attributes and make reasoned decisions at home about which brands to choose … has the potential to change decision processes and ultimately brand choice" (p. 291). These authors also reason that customization, searching, and sorting will drastically change decision making on the Internet. Within a decision context, cognitive effort relates to the mental resources required, as well as to the individual resources available. *Cognitive effort* can be thought of as information load that deals with how cognitive processes handle incoming stimuli (information), matching the cognitive resources required with the cognitive resources available. The experience, skill, and amount of resources a decision maker has are negatively correlated with the cognitive effort required in the decision task (Bakos 1997; Garbarino & Edell, 1997).

Cognitive effort, within the context of Internet decision making, can be seen from two perspectives. First, it seems logical that cognitive effort could be *reduced* within the CME. Certainly, consumer search costs have been drastically lowered with the assistance of the Internet (Bakos, 1997). This premise allows price and product information to be readily gathered, analyzed, and compared. Furthermore, one could argue that there is less noise when shopping on the Web compared to shopping in a crowded, information-packed retail outlet. Additionally, people can gain experience and skill in utilizing the Internet as a shopping tool. As experience and skill grow, less cognitive effort may be required to gather, sort, and analyze attributes of a choice set. However, a second perspective yields precisely the opposite conclusions: that, as a rule, cognitive effort is persistently *increased* for Internet decision makers. It seems reasonable that users are required, by necessity of the medium, to hold more information in working memory. More cognitive resources are needed to "surf" from Web page to Web page, recording, analyzing, and maintaining information in memory. Further, given the wealth of information available on the Web and the relative ease of searching for additional facts and advice, one could summarily argue that increases in cognitive effort are the norm. The sheer volume of Web advertising is a critical noise factor that would seem to rival the distractions of any retail environment. Internet consumers' may routinely have their decision processes clouded by information overload. Future research should strive to resolve this issue.

Flow. Flow is not only useful in describing general human-computer interactions (Csikszentmihalyi, 1990), it is also an important construct in the study of Internet navigations. Hoffman and Novak (1996) have ascribed the flow experience

to Web behavior, measuring the loss of self-consciousness in an essentially blissful encounter. In this situation, *flow* can be defined as the state occurring during Web navigations characterized by (1) a seamless sequence of responses facilitated by interactivity, (2) an intrinsically enjoyable experience, (3) accompanied by a loss of self-consciousness that is (4) self-reinforcing (Novak, Hoffman, & Yung, 2000). Of course, flow is not only a difficult concept to identify, it is also a difficult concept to measure. E-business researchers have just begun to study the effects of consumers entering (and Web sites facilitating) the flow experience (Richard & Chandra, 2005).

Just as human experiences are evolving because of the Internet's influence, so too are the possibilities and methods of commerce evolving. (Parasuraman & Zinkhan, 2002, p. 294)

MEASUREMENTS FOR E-BUSINESS STRATEGY

The evolution of business and communications has transpired at lightning speed. The Internet has made the collection of data faster, easier, and less costly than ever before in the history of business. Consequently, a new paradigm is emerging in terms of e-business research strategy (see Hoffman & Novak, 1997) wherein the challenge is no longer in the painstaking meticulousness of data collection, but rather it emerges as researchers strive to "mine" truly meaningful information, insights, and predictions from figurative "mountains" of data. Over the last decade, e-business researchers have made valiant attempts to measure consumer actions in an effort to more strategically communicate with and influence Internet consumers. Studies have measured primary actions (i.e., initial exposures, impressions, hits, and visits), secondary actions (i.e., what happens next in terms of clicks and path analyses), transforming actions (i.e., consumer conversions), and "involving" actions (i.e., Web site stickiness). Measures of all types of consumer actions directly relate to strategic changes in site design as well as alterations to multiple elements of the marketing mix.

Exposures, impressions, hits, and visits. A wealth of strategic measures evaluate e-consumers' primary actions including exposures, impressions, hits, and visits. The simple essence of measuring exposures entails measuring frequency counts of Web traffic by page. This is an important matter for advertisers as they convert fees into cost per thousand (CPM), and partially evaluate advertising according to the number of people exposed. Page impressions deal with counting the number of Web pages requested by users' browsers (Bhat, Bevans, & Sengupta, 2002). Hits are essentially similar measures of user actions. Finally, put plainly, visits count the number of user-sessions at a Web site. This is an important measure because businesses can track trends, charge advertisers accordingly, modify their sites and servers, and so forth.

Clicks and path analysis. A second set of measures attempts to interpret the paths of Web consumers. Researchers note that the sheer number of clicks may be important as to time spent on a Web site, the length of time a user is exposed to an ad, and the overall level of interest expressed in average time per visit. Researchers have measured click-throughs and click-through rates for some time. Essentially, this is when a potential e-consumer clicks on an advertisement and is taken, via hyperlink, to another online location (i.e., another Web site, another e-tailer, etc.). Path analysis provides strategic insight into the popularity of various pages, the ease (or difficulty) of navigating a site, and general navigational trends. Often, this type of data is labeled *click-stream* data as it measures the series of links that a user goes through when steering through the Web (Rayport & Jaworski, 2002)

Conversion. A third topic of strategic measures relates to tracking *conversion rates*. Conversion basically implies the completion of some action

by an e-consumer (Rayport & Jaworski, 2002). For example, conversion events include completing a membership form, requesting a newsletter, opting in to receive future e-mails and updates, filling out online forms, and so forth. A conversion rate measures the number of visitors who come to a Web site and take action relative to the total number of visitors to the site (Bhat et al., 2002). Conversion rates are of strategic importance because of their abilities to bring the customer closer to the business, converting and escalating a new and heightened level of involvement and perhaps loyalty.

Stickiness. A final topic of strategic Internet business measures is that of Web site *stickiness*. Web site stickiness relates the notion of user involvement to an evaluation of how attractive and memorable a site is (Gladwell, 2000). Stickiness can also be evaluated according to the frequency of site visits, the recency between visits, and the average time per visit (Bhat et al., 2002). The attractiveness of this metric is that it makes a good deal of intuitive sense, and that it encompasses multidimensional aspects of a site experience. However, there may be a misconception in simply evaluating length of time on the site as a measure of stickiness. In this case, researchers may be mislabeling time as stickiness, as opposed to patience spent searching through a complex and perhaps frustrating Web site.

Thus, operationaliztions, or measures, are the means by which we attempt to capture a moonbeam and hold it in our hands. (Straub, Hoffman, Weber, & Steinfield, 2002, p. 228)

EMERGING ISSUES IN E-BUSINESS MEASUREMENTS

Online interviewing and focus groups. Purely quantitative analyses of clickstream data and Internet survey research methods are limited in their abilities to enlighten us. Web surveys have notoriously low response rates, and are often suspect in their abilities to gather a representative sample (Dillman, 2000). Simple frequency counts of consumer actions yield very shallow data. Since technology has sped up the transmission of Internet content, and advances in software have dramatically enhanced Web design and graphics, researchers have expanded the use of online qualitative research. For instance, it is not uncommon to hold online focus groups wherein respondents can interactively participate in virtual forums. Participants can evaluate prototypes, respond to potential advertisements, and hold meaningful, insightful conversations about various aspects of e-business. Furthermore, online interviewing is growing in popularity. This is a way to effectively reach some very narrow groups of respondents and gather very rich, powerful data. Online interviews also allow for greater flexibility, follow-up questions, and provide greater depth of analysis. Qualitative Internet research is certainly an emerging field.

Content analysis. Again, as advances in technology, hardware, and software progress, researchers have begun to analyze Internet content more directly and more precisely (Boush & Kahle, 2004). The essence of content analysis is to measure words and phrases throughout a page, a site, a chatroom, a blog, and so forth. Researchers have detected meaningful patterns in the data, made fitting interpretations, and derived strategic insights for future actions. Researchers have even coined a new phrase to describe the word-of-mouth communication over the Internet. Dubbed word on-line (WOL), researchers have noted the powerful influence of the online community and the ever-expanding number of conversations (Granitz & Ward, 1996).

Continuing challenges in electronic survey research. As technological advances make electronic survey research easier, faster, and cheaper, a number of challenging issues arise. First, the issue of low response rates must be addressed. Surely a nonresponse bias must be affecting some research results. Second, asking the right questions and recording the right answers from the right respondents has become increasingly difficult. We cannot simply continue to make up in quantity of data what we knowingly lack in quality of data. We must strive to keep e-business research meaningful and strategically useful. Finally, we must develop a viable communications framework that encompasses the interactivity of e-business, the informational asymmetry that abounds, as well as the unique perspectives of Internet users and e-businesses. Within a sound framework, valid, reliable, and relevant metrics will emerge as the new standard.

Future research. The emergence of the Internet as the foundation for business communications worldwide has given rise to a wealth of truly spectacular measurement tools. Business researchers now have access to an abundance of data that, just a few years ago, might have been deemed unimaginable. Furthermore, they have the research tools to analyze and interpret mass quantities of information; thereby, giving valuable meaning to seemingly chaotic data. Researchers can now track consumer responses and measure psychological issues in a multitude of forms. Straub, et al. (2002) not only provide an expert synopsis of existing metrics, but also provide excellent foresight into numerous e-business metrics that require further exploration, examination, and validation. The likely "next step" in online business metrics will be the measurement of the Internet consumption experience. Some major research questions arise, including (1) What makes the Internet consumption experience so different? (2) Which off-line behavioral/communications/business theories apply to the online context and which need to be altered? (3) What information processing and decision-making theories apply to the CME? (4) Which metrics apply to the online business-to-business context?

REFERENCES

Aiken D., Liu, B., Mackoy, R., & Osland, G. (2004). Building Internet trust: Signaling through trustmarks. *International Journal of Internet Marketing and Advertising, 1*(3), 1-17.

Bakos, Y. (1997). Reducing buyer search costs: Implications for electronic marketplaces. *Management Science, 43*(12), 1676-1692.

Bakos, Y. (1998). The emerging role of electronic marketplaces on the Internet. *Communications of the ACM, 41*(8), 35-42.

Benassi, P. (1999). TRUSTe: An online privacy seal program. *Communications of the ACM, 42*(2), 56-59.

Bettman, J., Johnson, E., & Payne, J. (1990). A componential analysis of cognitive effort in choice. *Organizational Behavior & Human Decision Processes, 45*, 111-139.

Bettman, J., Luce, M. F., & Payne, J. (1998, December). Constructive consumer choice processes. *Journal of Consumer Research, 25,* 187-217.

Biswas, A., & Krishnan, R. (2004). The Internet's impact on marketing: Introduction to the JBR special issue on "Marketing on the Web - Behavioral, strategy and practices and public policy." *Journal of Business Research, 57*, 681-684.

Bhat, S., Bevans, M., & Sengupta, S. (2002). Measuring users' Web activity to evaluate and enhance advertising effectiveness. *Journal of Advertising, 31*(3), 97-106.

Bhatnagar A., & Ghose, S. (2004). Segmenting consumers based on the benefits and risks of Internet shopping. *Journal of Business Research, 57*, 1352-1360.

Boush, D. M., & Kahle, L. (2004). What, and how, we can learn from online consumer discussion groups. In C. Haugtvedt, K. Machleit, & R. Yalch (Eds.), *Online consumer psychology: Understand-* *ing and influencing behavior in the virtual world* (pp. 101-121). Mahwah, NJ: Lawrence Erlbaum Associates.

Csikszentmihalyi, M. (1990). *Flow: The psychology of optimal experience.* New York: Harper and Row.

Dillman, D. (2000). *Mail and Internet surveys: The tailored design method.* New York: John Wiley and Sons.

Garbarino, E. C., & Edell, J. A. (1997). Cognitive effort, affect, and choice. *Journal of Consumer Research, 24*, 147-158.

Geissler, G., Zinkhan, G., & Watson, R. T. (2001, April). Web home-page complexity and communication effectiveness. *Journal of the Association for Information Systems, 2*, 1-46.

Glazer, R. (1991). Marketing in an information-intensive environment: Strategic implications of knowledge as an asset. *Journal of Marketing, 55*(Oct.), 1-19.

Gladwell, M. (2000). *The tipping point.* New York: Little, Brown and Company.

Granitz, N. A., & Ward, J. C. (1996). Virtual community: A sociocognitive analysis. *Advances in Consumer Research, 23*, 161-166.

Handy, C. (1995, May-June). Trust and the virtual organization. *Harvard Business Review, 73*, 40-50.

Hine C., & Eve, J. 1998). Privacy in the marketplace. *The Information Society, 14*(4), 253-262.

Hoffman, D., & Novak, T. (1996). Marketing in hypermedia computer-mediated environments: Conceptual foundations. *Journal of Marketing, 60*, 50-68.

Hoffman, D., & Novak, T. (1997). A new marketing paradigm for electronic commerce. *The Information Society, 13*, 43-54.

Hoffman, D., & Novak, T. (1998). Trustbuilders vs. trustbusters. *The Industry Standard.* Retrieved Aug, 2003, from http://www.thestandard.com/articles/article_print/0,1454,235,000.html

Hoffman, D., Novak, T., & Peralta, M. (1999). Building consumer trust online. *Communications of the Association for Computing Machinery, 42*(4), 80-85.

Jarvenpaa, S. L., & Tractinsky, N. (1999). Consumer trust in an Internet store: A cross-cultural validation. *Journal of Computer-Mediated Communications, 15*(2), 1-35.

Keen C., Wetzels, M., de Ruyter, K., & Feinberg, R. (2004). E-tailers vs. retailers: Which factors determine consumer preferences. *Journal of Business Research, 57,* 685-695.

Kirmani, A., & Rao, A. R. (2000). No pain, no gain: A critical review of the literature on signaling unobservable product quality. *Journal of Marketing, 64,* 66-79.

Maule, J. A., & Edland, A. C. (1997). The effects of time pressure on human judgment and decision making. In R. Ranyard, W. R. Crozier, & O. Svenson (Eds.). *Decision making: Cognitive models and explanations* (pp. 189-204). London: Routledge.

McKnight, H. D., & Chervany, V (2002). What trust means in e-commerce customer relationships: An interdisciplinary conceptual typology. *International Journal of Electronic Commerce, 6*(2), 35-59.

Milne, G. R., & Boza, E. (1999). Trust and concern in consumers' perceptions of marketing information management practices. *Journal of Interactive Marketing, 13*(1), 5-24.

Novak, T., Hoffman, D., & Yung, Y. F. (2000). Modeling the flow construct in online environments: A structure modeling approach. *Marketing Science, 19*(1), 22-42.

Parasuraman, A., & Zinkhan, G. M. (2002). Marketing to and serving customers through the Internet: An overview and research agenda. *Journal of the Academy of Marketing Science, 30*(Fall), 286-295.

Rayport, J. F., & Jaworski, B. J. (2002). *Introduction to e-commerce.* Boston: McGraw-Hill.

Richard, M. O., & Chandra, R. (2005). A model of consumer Web navigational behavior: Conceptual development and application. *Journal of Business Research, 58,* 1019-1029.

Sharma A., & Sheth, J. N. (2004). Web-based marketing: The coming revolution in marketing thought and strategy. *Journal of Business Research, 57,* 696-702.

Sheehan, K. B., & Hoy, M. G. (2000). Dimensions of privacy concern among online consumers. *Journal of Public Policy and Marketing, 19*(1), 62-73.

Straub, D. W., Hoffman, D. L., Weber, B. W. , & Steinfield, C. (2002). Toward new metrics for net-enhanced organizations. *Information Systems Research, 13*(3), 227-238.

Varadarajan, P. R., & Yadav, M. S. (2002). Marketing strategy and the Internet: An organizing framework. *Journal of the Academy of Marketing Science, 30*(4), 296-312.

Weiner, R., Deighton, J., Gupta, S., Johnson, E., Mellers, B., Morwitz, V., et al. (1997). Choice in computer-mediated environments. *Marketing Letters, 8*(3), 287-296.

Williamson, O. E. (1993, April). Calculativeness, trust, and economic organization. *Journal of Law and Economics, 36,* 487-500.

Wright, P. (1974). The harassed decision maker: Time pressures, distractions, and the use of evidence. *Journal of Applied Psychology, 59*(5), 555-561.

Yadav, M. S., & Varadarajan, P. R. (2005). Interactivity in the electronic marketplace: An exposition and implications for research. *Journal of the Academy of Marketing Science, 33*(4), 585-604.

KEY TERMS

Click-Stream: The series of links that a user goes through when using the Internet (Rayport & Jaworski, 2002).

Cognitive Effort: Information load that deals with how cognitive processes handle incoming stimuli (information) (Bettman et al., 1990).

Conversion Rates: A frequency measurement of the completion of some action(s) by an e-consumer as a proportion of the total number of visitors to site (Bhat et al., 2002; Rayport & Jaworski, 2002).

Flow: The state during Web navigations characterized by (1) a seamless sequence of responses facilitated by interactivity, (2) an intrinsically enjoyable experience, (3) accompanied by a loss of self-consciousness that is (4) self-reinforcing (Novak, et al., 2000).

Stickiness: Sometimes a subjective/attitudinal measurement of how attractive and memorable a site is (Gladwell, 2000). Stickiness can also be evaluated according to the frequency of Web-site visits and the average time spent per visit (Bhat et al., 2002).

Chapter XVII
Measurement in Public Relations

Renée A. Botta
University of Denver, USA

ABSTRACT

Although public relations has been an established field for more than 100 years, standardized measures have only recently been introduced. In an attempt to make public-relations practitioners more accountable and to demonstrate the value and effectiveness of public relations in an era of downsizing, scholars and practitioners have called for more rigorous, reliable, valid, and quantifiable measures for evaluation. In addition, the contribution of public relations is also being measured in terms of the relationships built between an organization and its public. This chapter will review those measures and discuss the development and usage of online surveys and measurements in public relations. Finally, the chapter will conclude with a discussion of the future of measurement in public relations.

INTRODUCTION

Although measurement in public relations has come a long way, it is still in its infancy. For years, measurement consisted of counting the number of press releases written or the number of news clips that mention the organization. However, these measures are not valid in assessing the extent to which public-relations practitioners achieve their objectives (e.g. inform, educate, build relationships with, or change the opinions, attitudes, or behaviors of a target audience). In other words, they are not really measuring what they would like to claim they are measuring.

According to Lindenmann (2005), public-relations academics and practitioners have been

talking about measurement for nearly 60 years. He specifically traces it back to an article, published in 1947, that talked about measurement within the context of the question "Why campaigns fail." Some scholars argue better measures must be developed, while other scholars, such as Lindenmann, argue the measures exist but practitioners are not using them.

From my perspective, the biggest problem in the PR field is NOT that adequate PR measurement and evaluation tools and techniques do not exist and that they need to be invented. There are many different methodological tools and techniques available that are already being utilized in the field. In my view, the three major issues that we, in the public-relations field need to address pertaining to PR measurement and evaluation are these:

1. *We need to more effectively train public-relations practitioners and counselors on how to measure and evaluate public-relations effectiveness.*
2. *We need to do a better job of building public-relations measurement and evaluation components into our various ongoing communications programs and activities.*
3. *We need to do a better job of convincing senior management of the importance of allocating appropriation funds to support PR evaluation efforts.* (Lindenmann, 2005, p. 9)

In the past decade, academics have been pushing for better measurement development, in part due to the increased need for public-relations programs to be accountable to management and its bottom line. Indeed, when cost-saving measures are introduced in an organization, one of the questions is, in what measurable ways do public-relations activities and programs make or save money for this organization. A push for measurement, in terms meaningful to management, helped to increase the need for better measurement and more formal research methods. The field responded. For example, according to Wright (1998), the use of formal research methods in the Public Relations Society of America's (PRSA) Silver Anvil award winners for best public-relations campaigns rose from 25% in 1980 to 40% in 1989 to over 75% in 1998. Of course, these are the best of the best in the field. Conducting formal research is costly, and many organizations do not budget for formal research. Thus, the average practitioner too often may still rely on news clips as measurement, as if the placement of public-relations material gives any indication of whether publics are made aware of, paid attention to, understood, remembered, or acted upon the information.

Turning our gaze from the best public-relations campaigns in the field to the average practitioner,

Katherine Delahaye Paine, founder of a public-relations measurement firm, said the average percentage of a public-relations budget devoted to measurement and evaluation jumped from 1% to 5% from 1994 to 2004, (as quoted in Wilcox, Cameron, Ault & Agee, 2005). She projects it will grow to 10% over the next decade. On Paine's Website, she cites a CyberAlert 2005 measurement survey as having revealed that money budgeted for public-relations measurement ranged from 26% of the respondents who said they have no budget, to 23% of the respondents who have more than $1,000 per month to spend on measuring whether they have achieved their objectives. Additionally, although 75% of the respondents reported measuring results for their campaigns, 68% of those said their measurement consisted of counting news clips (http://www.themeasurementstandard. com/issues/1105/contents1105.asp).

As argued by Stacks (2002), "public-relations research should be programmatic by nature; that is, the research should be a continuous process that continually assesses an organization's position among its publics on a variety of outcome measures" (p. 20). As Stacks further notes, most formal research in public relations, when it does happen, is reactive rather than proactive. Moreover, measuring the impact of public-relations practices has become a question of fundamental importance in need of social scientific methodology including benchmark studies that use valid and reliable measures of knowledge, comprehension, perception, attitude, opinion, and behavior. Stacks (2002) also argues that in order to facilitate a stronger drive toward continuous formal research in public relations, the familiar RACE acronym used in public relations, which stands for the linear research, action and planning, communication, and evaluation process, needs to be changed to ERASE, a circular method in which "continued evaluation leads to research that leads to action (or objectives) that leads to strategy that leads to evaluation that leads to more research, and so forth." (p. 22) In other words, public-relations practitioners need to recognize that they do not start over with each project; rather, a new project has to be started within the framework of what was learned from previous projects. Research in public relations is generally considered either formative or summative (program evaluation); however, as Stacks points out with his circular model, it needs to be an ongoing process. Witte, Meyer and Martell (2001) describe three types of evaluation that provide a better fit for the ERASE model: Formative evaluation happens in the planning stages of a campaign and includes evaluating what was learned from previous campaigns, process evaluation occurs during a campaign, and outcome or summative evaluation occurs after the campaign is finished (pp. 95-97). When formal research is a part of the everyday cycle of public relations, practitioners will be much more likely to use valid measures.

Examining the most common measures used by practitioners reveals that they are much more interested in applied research than theoretical research. A range of measures is available that fit this practical need. However, those most commonly used tend to measure something other than that intended. For example, as already discussed, the most commonly used measurement tool is gathering clips from electronic and print news that mention the organization. This tool is commonly used to measure productivity, audience reach, audience exposure, media placement or recognition, advertising equivalency, and message dissemination.

As a measure of productivity (i.e., public-relations effort), the number of news clips does not tell you how much effort practitioners put into getting those news clips published. Additionally, such a measure encourages practitioners to publish anything anywhere, regardless of whether it reaches a target audience and what it might say to the audience, yielding a counterproductive measurement of quantity rather than quality. Other measures of productivity include the number of hours worked and the number of news releases

generated, both of which also encourage quantity rather than quality. More importantly, the point of measurement in public relations is to assess the effectiveness or impact of public-relations activities and programs, and no measure of productivity will tell you that.

Print clips and electronic-media mentions are also inaccurately used as a measure of audience reach and message exposure. For example, practitioners equate circulation figures with audience reach and call it media impressions. However, assuming a news clip in a publication with a circulation of 100,000 equates an audience reach of 100,000 is problematic because we cannot assume that all 100,000 of the people who subscribe to the publication saw the information. This measure does not tell us how many were reached or were exposed to the message and thus, it is not a valid measure. The most accurate way to measure message exposure would be through observation: we watch the audience to see if they are exposed to the message. However, such observation is nearly impossible. Thus, a proximal measure is necessary. One example of a proximal measure for audience exposure is audience recall, or the extent to which the target audience remembers hearing or seeing the message. To measure recall, the practitioner contacts members of the audience and asks them about their message exposure. To clarify whether respondents are simply agreeing rather than actually remembering, practitioners may ask the respondents to freely recall all messages they remember hearing from or about the organization, or they may ask if the respondent recalls having heard several different messages, only one of which was the actual message disseminated. Although message recall is not the same as message exposure, it offers a better assessment of whether the audience was exposed to the message than circulation figures.

As a measure of media placement or recognition, practitioners must go beyond simply counting clips, and more systematically look at what the clips say and what type of audience the clips reach. In other words, when we examine media placement, we need to assess the type of outlet in which it was placed, the audience typically reached by the outlet, and the extent to which the message has a positive, negative, or neutral valence toward the organization.

Media clips are also used to measure what is called advertising equivalency, which places a dollar value on media placement. Practitioners count the column inches or seconds-of-airtime earned, and multiply the total by the advertising rate the media outlet charges to determine how much it would cost to buy that space. For example, if the press release resulted in an 8-inch news story on page 2 of the Sunday business section, the cost to place an 8-inch ad on page 2 of the Sunday business section would be the advertising equivalency. Public-relations practitioners often use this measure as a means for how much money the organization saved by not having to purchase that space. However, a mention of the organization in a news clip is not the same thing as an advertisement in which the content is controlled by the organization; thus, the measure is not a valid assessment of advertising equivalency because the news clip is not at all equivalent to an ad. Practitioners will often argue that although the content of the message is not controlled by the organization, it is perceived as more credible by the public and thus, valuable. Granted, it may be important for a practitioner to use media clips as a measure of something, but practitioners must be careful about what they claim this information is measuring.

News clips are also used to measure the accurate dissemination of messages (i.e. to what extent did the placed message remain intact). In addition to counting the number of clips, practitioners examine the content of the message. An exact match to the message released is not required; what practitioners are most interested in is whether they received positive coverage with a

prominent mention of the organization. The most reliable and valid way to measure this concept is through a systematic content analysis of all media placement in which a set of variables is consistently quantified. Such a measure indicates not only how many news clips were generated, but what percentage of those clips were positive and what percentage of those clips appeared in media outlets that reach key publics. Remsik (2000) suggests creating a barometer for news clips in which a set of variables addresses the value of the publication in/on which the clip appeared, with value being a combined measure of the type of publication and who it reaches, assessed against the type of publication and the audience needed for a specific objective. The barometer would also contain a measure of the content in the message. I suggest that the content variables minimally include the overall valence of the clip (i.e. positive, negative, neutral), the number of sources used in the clip categorized by valence (e.g. number of sources who said something positive about the product, the service, the organization, the issue), and the number of times the organization is mentioned categorized by valence (e.g. number of times the organization is mentioned in negative context). Other variables of interest may also be operationalized and measured. Although a systematic content analysis of media placements can be a good indicator of how the message was disseminated, practitioners must be cautious not to assume that because a message was accurately disseminated, it had any impact on their publics. They will need to use other measures to determine message impact.

The measures described so far are basic, and do not provide the practitioner with any information about how the message was received by the target audience. Because understanding how the target audience responds to the message is key to understanding the value of public relations, more accurate measures must be utilized.

Table 1. Measuring attitudes toward an organization

Reputation (Kim, 2001)

Respondents record the extent to which they agree/disagree with each of the following statements on a Likert Scale:

1. This organization has the ability to attract, develop, and keep talented people.
2. The organization uses corporate assets very effectively.
3. The organization is innovative in its corporate culture.
4. The organization is financially sound enough to help others.

Reputation (Smith, 2005)

Place an "X" at the appropriate location in the following listing to indicate how you would describe (add organization name, product/service). The closer your mark is to one of the two terms, the more you feel that term applies to how you would describe the organization (or a specific product or a service provided by the organization).

Contemporary	___:___:___:___:___:___:___	Traditional
High Tech	___:___:___:___:___:___:___	Low Tech
Efficient	___:___:___:___:___:___:___	Inefficient
High Quality	___:___:___:___:___:___:___	Low Quality
Essential	___:___:___:___:___:___:___	Luxury
Worthless	___:___:___:___:___:___:___	Beneficial
Routine	___:___:___:___:___:___:___	Innovative

Corporate reputation (Lee, 2004)

Responses were recorded on a nine-point Likert scale.

Perceived corporate dynamism (alpha .86)

1. The company often has new ideas in providing services to customers.
2. This company generates creative products.
3. The company is internationally competitive.
4. Managers in this company are receptive to different ideas.
5. The company is a modern enterprise.
6. The products of this company are innovative.
7. The company is advanced in technology.

Perceived quality of products and services (alpha .86)

1. The company's products are reliable.
2. The services provided by the company are outstanding.
3. The quality of the products of this company is outstanding.
4. The services provided by this company are professional.
5. The company is credible.

Perceived corporate management (alpha .78)

1. The chief executive officer is a good leader.
2. The chief executive officer has strong leadership.
3. The company is a moral company.
4. The company has a good management system.
5. Managers in this system are flexible.

Perceived advertising and marketing activities (alpha .77)

1. This company's advertisements about its products (including TV ads, radio ads, newspaper print ads, magazine print ads) are well executed.
2. The company has excellent marketing strategies.
3. The company's advertisement and promotion techniques are attractive.
4. There is a lot of media coverage of this company.

Perceived treatment to employees (alpha .85)

1. The company provides good benefits to employees.
2. The company treats its employees kindly.
3. Employees are highly valued by the company.

Perceived social responsibility (alpha .75)

1. This company is devoted to donating money for charity.
2. This company is generous in donation to social causes.
3. This company is a good public citizen.

MEASURING MESSAGE IMPACT OR EFFECTIVENESS: ATTITUDES

The two audience impact categories of predominant interest for public-relations practitioners are attitudes and behaviors; to what extent did the message change the attitudes of the target audience (e.g., do they think more positively of the organization than they did before the image campaign), and to what extent did the message change the behaviors of the target audience (e.g.,did they do something as a result of seeing the message). Practitioners must identify the attitude of interest and then choose the response options. (See Table 1.) The first type of response commonly used is called a Likert scale, in which the target audience responds to statements that illustrate the attitude (e.g., the like/dislike of a product or service, or an opinion statement about an issue or an organization) with the extent of agreement or disagreement on a five- or seven-point scale (strongly disagree, disagree, neutral or no opinion, agree, strongly agree for five-point scale with very strongly agree/disagree added for a seven-point scale). The second type of response commonly used is called a semantic differential scale, which uses bipolar adjective descriptors to measure attitudes toward the organization, the product, the service, the issue, and so forth. Rather than listing a discrete set of terms for the respondent to chose, an odd number of spaces (generally 5-9) fall between the opposite set of adjectives, and the respondents place an X in the space that best represents where their attitude fits (see Table 1).

Arlene Fink (1995) recommends five other types of response options to use for rating scales: endorsement (def true, true, don't know, false, def false), frequency (always, very often, fairly often, sometimes, almost never, never), intensity (none, very mild, mild, moderate, and severe), influence (big problem, moderate problem, small problem, very small problem, no problem), and comparison (much more than others, somewhat more than others, about the same as others, somewhat less than others, much less than others).

Table 1 illustrates sample measures for one attitude that has been explored recently in public relations: organizational reputation. Public-relations scholars have chosen to talk about reputation rather than image because reputation is something assigned by a public, whereas image is something assigned by the organization. Kim measured reputation as a dimension of a public's perception of the organization (2001) and on its own (2000). Kim (2000) found that reputation impacts revenue change in Fortune 500 companies: a more positive reputation was associated with increased revenues from one year to the next. Lee (2004) developed a much more in-depth measure of corporate reputation specific to public-relations definitions and needs. Lee's measure was designed to account for 10 dimensions as well as overall reputation. An exploratory factor analysis revealed seven factors, six of which were ultimately found to be important dimensions of corporate reputation for the Hong Kong sample. Lee's measure must be cross-validated with other samples in Hong Kong as well as around the world; however, it provides an example of how in-depth an attitude may be measured.

Regardless which of the attitude measures practitioners use, the best method for determining whether public-relations activities have had an impact on those attitudes is through benchmark studies in which the attitudes are measured prior to a message campaign, and again after the message campaign is complete. The extent to which there is a change in the attitudes of those who reported being exposed to the message is used as an indicator that the message changed their attitudes.

MEASURING MESSAGE IMPACT OR EFFECTIVENESS: BEHAVIORS

Measurement for audience behaviors in response to public-relations activities can be as simple as counting the number of attendees at an event, the requests for information, or the amount of donations; more complex measures that require formal surveys in which respondents are asked to report their behaviors and behavioral intentions before, during, and after a campaign are also used. In deciding which measures to use, the key to good measurement of behavior is linking what is measured to what the practitioner hoped to achieve, and assessing if the measure is a stable indicator of the desired behavior. For example, if the objective of holding a promotional event is to increase the use of organizational services, measuring the number of attendees is not a valid measure. Measuring the change in use of services before and after the event is a better measure, although the practitioner can still not be sure the change of use in services is due entirely, or at all, to the event. Practitioners can get a better idea of the connection if they can find out whether those who initiated or dropped services after the event did so because they had either attended or heard about the event, and if that made a difference in their decision to use services.

Table 2. Measure for type of public-relations model practiced in an organization (Grunig, 1984, 1992)

Press agentry model

1. The main purpose of my organization/agency's public relations is to get publicity about my organization/client.

2. In public relations, we mostly attempt to get favorable publicity into the media and to keep unfavorable publicity out.

3. We determine how successful a program is from the number of people who attend an event or use our products and services.

4. In my organization/agency, public relations and publicity mean essentially the same thing.

Public information model

1. In public relations, nearly everyone is so busy writing news stories or producing publications that there is no time to do research.

2. In public relations, we disseminate accurate information, but do not volunteer unfavorable information.

3. Keeping a clipping file is about the only way we have to determine the success of a program.

4. In my organization/agency, public relations is more of a neutral disseminator of information than an advocate for the organization or mediator between management and publics.

Two-way asymmetrical model

1. After completing a public-relations program, we do research to determine how effective the program has been in changing people's attitudes.

2. In public relations, our broad goal is to persuade publics to behave as the organization wants them to behave.

3. Before starting a public-relations program, we look at attitude surveys to make sure we describe the organization in ways our publics would be most likely to accept.

4. Before beginning a program, we do research to determine public attitudes toward the organization, and how they might change.

Two-way symmetrical model

1. The purpose of public relations is to develop mutual understanding between the management of the organization and publics the organization affects.

2. Before starting a program, we do surveys or informal research to find out how much management and our publics understand each other.

3. The purpose of public relations is to change the attitudes and behavior of management as much as it is to change the attitudes and behavior of publics.

4. Our organization/agency believes public relations should provide mediation for the organization, to help management and publics negotiate conflicts.

Table 3. Measuring excellence in public relations (Rhee, 2002)

Direction of communication (Cronbach's alpha .66)

1. One-way communication

   a. Information flows out from this organization, but not into it

   b. We speak more than we listen in doing public relations

   c. Public-relations programs in this organization involve one-way communication from the organization to its publics.

   d. Most public-relations programs in this organization are designed to disseminate information to the publics. *(removed from scale to improve alpha)*

2. Two-way communication

   a. Public-relations programs in this organization involve two-way communication between the organization and publics.

   b. We listen to the opinions of the publics.

   c. Before carrying out public-relations or communications activities, we first conduct research to understand how the public feels about certain issues.

   d. After conducting public-relations or communications activities, we conduct evaluations of those activities.

Purpose of communication – asymmetric (Cronbach's alpha .58)

1. We do programs or projects to persuade publics to agree with the organization's point of view.

2. We do programs or projects to persuade publics to behave as the organization wants them to behave.

3. In doing public relations, we try to provide only information that will help the public to see the organization more favorably.

Purpose of communication – symmetric (Cronbach's alpha .71)

1. We not only try to change the attitudes and behaviors of members of the public, but we also try to change our attitudes and behaviors.

2. Before making final decisions or adopting policies, we seek the opinions of those groups or individuals that will be affected by the decision or policy.

3. We believe public relations should provide mediation for the organization – to help management and publics negotiate conflict.

4. We consider the opinions of members of the public and try to change our behaviors and policies.

Ethical communication (Cronbach's alpha .63)

1. Ethical

   a. The information we provide is factual

   b. We consider the interests of the public as much as organizational interests.

   c. We take into account the effects of the public-relations activities or communication activities on the public.

   d. We explain our motivations or why we do things to the public.

2. Unethical

   a. When doing programs or projects, we avoid disclosing negative information about our organization/company.

   b. We believe the role of public relations is to promote the interests of the organization, even if the organization's decisions have negative effects on the publics.

   c. We try to avoid dialogue with the public when organization makes unpopular decisions.

   d. In our public relations, we believe that favorable information should be disseminated, but unfavorable information should be kept from the public.

Interpersonal communication (Cronbach's alpha .70)

1. We offer valuable gifts.

2. We use face-to-face communication.

3. We contact government offices in person.

4. We communicate in person with the public.

5. We hold banquets.

6. We attend meetings.

Table 3. Measuring excellence in public relations (Rhee, 2002) (continued)

Mediated communication (Cronbach's alpha .71)
1. We distribute news releases.
2. We use advertisements.
3. We hold news conferences.
4. We use mass media, such as television and radio broadcasts, newspapers, or magazines.
5. We offer information and news briefings.
6. We give speeches.
7. We stage events, tours, open houses.
8. We distribute flyers, pamphlets, magazines, or other printed materials that represent the company.

BEYOND MEASURING MESSAGE EFFECTIVENESS: THE PUBLIC-RELATIONS PROCESS

In addition to measuring outcomes, for the past 20 years, public-relations scholars have been focused on examining the process of public-relations activities. Grunig (1984; 1992) situational theory describes four models of pr practice: in the press agent/publicity model, practitioners follow the old propaganda model of public relations; in the public information model, practitioners see public-relations' goal as disseminating information from the organization to its publics; in the two-way asymmetric model, communication between the organization and its publics is two-way, but the practice of public relations is still focused on persuasion and advocacy; and in the two-way symmetric model, two-way communication is combined with collaboration between an organization and its public. Grunig posited that more effective and "excellent" public-relations organizations practice the two-way symmetrical model of public relations in which an equally balanced dialogue was ongoing between an organization and each of its publics. He argued that only the two-way symmetrical model of public-relations benefits both the organization and its publics. Table 2 lists items used to measure the extent to which each of the four models is practiced. The public-relations process has been examined in

this context around the world (See Grunig, 2001 for a discussion).

Grunig (2001) later pushed for examining best practices rather than trying to fit an organization into one of the four models. He described four dimensions that he felt were most important to measuring excellence: symmetry (collaboration) vs. asymmetry (advocacy), or the "extent to which collaboration and advocacy describe public-relations strategy or behavior" (2001, p. 17); one-way communication (monologue) vs. two-way communication (dialogue), or the use of asymmetrical vs. symmetrical forms of research; use of both mediated and interpersonal communication; and, ethical practices.

Using Grunig's dimensions, Rhee (2002) created a measure to assess excellence in the practice of public relations in South Korea (See Table 3). Rhee measured both one- and two-way communication as part of the same scale, symmetric and asymmetric communication as separate scales, and interpersonal and mass communication tactics as separate scales. Although other items seem to focus on the quality of public-relations practice, the items for mass and interpersonal communication seem to indicate that quantity is more important than quality because there is no consideration for whether those tactics helped achieve objectives. It seems odd for an indicator of excellence to rely on the act as sufficient, regardless of the quality of the act. Grunig (2001) argued that "the most

Table 4. Measuring relationship outcomes (Hon & Grunig, 1999)

Control mutuality
1. This organization and people like me are attentive to what each other says.
2. This organization believes the opinions of people like me are legitimate.
3. In dealing with people like me, this organization has a tendency to throw its weight around. (Reversed)
4. This organization really listens to what people like me have to say.
5. The management of this organization gives people like me enough say in the decision-making process.

Trust
1. This organization treats people like me fairly and justly.(integrity)
2. Whenever this organization makes an important decision, I know it will be concerned about people like me. (integrity)
3. This organization can be relied on to keep its promises. (dependability)
4. I believe that this organization takes the opinions of people like me into account when making decisions. (dependability)
5. I feel very confident about this organization's skills. (competence)
6. This organization has the ability to accomplish what it says it will do. (competence)

Commitment
1. I feel that this organization is trying to maintain a long-term commitment to people like me.
2. I can see that this organization wants to maintain a relationship with people like me.
3. There is a long-lasting bond between this organization and people like me.
4. Compared to other organizations, I value my relationship with this organization more.
5. I would rather work together with this organization than not.

Satisfaction
1. I am happy with this organization.
2. Both the organization and people like me benefit from the relationship.
3. Most people like me are happy in their interactions with this organization.
4. Generally speaking, I am pleased with the relationship this organization has established with people like me.
5. Most people enjoy dealing with this organization.

Exchange relationships
1. Whenever this organization gives or offers something to people like me, it generally expects something in return.
2. Even though people like me have had a relationship with this organization for a long time, it still expects something in return whenever it offers us a favor.
3. This organization will compromise with people like me when it knows that it will gain something.
4. This organization takes care of people who are likely to reward the organization.

Communal relationships
1. This organization does not especially enjoy giving others aid. (Reversed)
2. This organization is very concerned about the welfare of people like me.
3. I feel that this organization takes advantage of people who are vulnerable. (Reversed)
4. I think that this organization succeeds by stepping on other people. (Reversed)
5. This organization helps people like me without expecting anything in return.

excellent communication functions seem to practice all forms of public relations more extensively than do the less excellent functions," (p. 17) and so maybe more is better. What must be clarified, however, is whether it is simply a variety of tactics, or if a variety of high quality tactics is what works best; I suspect it is the latter.

Another problem with Rhee's (2002) assessment of excellence is that the reliability scores for the excellence dimensions were not very good, particularly for the asymmetric dimension and, to a lesser extent, the ethical communication and the direction of communication dimensions. Huang (2001) may have found similar reliability problems in the scales because ethical practices and symmetrical communication were collapsed into one factor and the one-way communication items were dropped. Like Rhee, Huang's communication tactic items simply measure whether the tactics were undertaken, and not whether they had an impact.

As part of the switch from measuring which public-relations model is practiced by an organization to measuring the extent to which an organization practices indicators of excellence, Grunig now backs a mixed-motives model that takes into consideration when an organization needs to practice asymmetrical (advocacy) communication. Symmetry is in the middle and describes a win-win situation, whereas asymmetry falls on either side with either the publics' position winning or the organization's position winning. Rhee's results, which indicated that excellent public-relations activities are both symmetrical and asymmetrical, two-way, ethical, mediated, and interpersonal, support this new model.

BEYOND MEASURING MESSAGE EFFECTIVENESS: THE ORGANIZATION-PUBLIC RELATIONSHIP

The focus on the relationship between an organization and its public began in the mid-1980s when Cutlip, Center and Broom (1985) defined public relations as "that management function that identifies, establishes, and maintains mutually beneficial relationships between and org and its publics."

Three ways to measure this relationship have received the most discussion and evaluation: measurement through observation of the organization-public relationship, measurement of a public's perception of the quality of the organization–public relationship, and measurement of a public's perception of the type of organization-public relationship.

Observation measurement of the organization-public relationship has proved difficult in terms of reliability and validity; however, scholars have been working toward an accurate model

for observation. (For more discussion, please see Bridges & Nelson, 2000; Broom, Casey, & Ritchey, 2000; Coombs, 2000; Kruckeberg, 2000; Lucarelli-Dimmick, 2000; Wilson, 2000). Hon and Grunig (1999) and Bruning and Ledingham (1998) developed measures for the quality of the relationship between an organization and its public. Both research teams developed their measures by first looking at successful measures of interpersonal relationships. Hon and Grunig (1999; See Table 4) used four dimensions of successful interpersonal relationships that they said could be applied with equal success to relationships between organizations and their publics. The first dimension is control mutuality, or the degree to which the parties in a relationship are satisfied with the amount of control they have over the relationship. Some degree of power imbalance is natural, but the most stable, positive relationships exist where the parties have some degree of control in influencing the other. Willingness to give up some control is based on trust, which is the second dimension. Trust is the level of confidence that both parties have in each other, and their willingness to open themselves to the other party. The three most important considerations of trust are integrity, which is when an organization is seen as just and fair; dependability, which is when publics believe the organization will do what it says it will do; and, competence is the belief that the organization has the ability to do what it says it will do. The next dimension is satisfaction, which is the extent to which both parties feel favorably about each other, and positive expectations about the relationship are reinforced. Each party believes the other is engaged in positive steps to maintain the relationship. After satisfaction is commitment, which is the extent to which both parties believe and feel the relationship is "worth spending energy to maintain and promote" (p. 3).

In addition to the four dimensions borrowed from interpersonal communication, Hon and Grunig (1999; See Table 4) added two dimensions to account for what is more specific to

Table 5. Organization-public relationship factors (Bruning & Galloway, 2003)

Anthropomorphis
1. Company A is open about its plans for the future,
2. I feel that I can trust Company A to do what it says it will do,
3. Company A shares its plans for the future with customers, and
4. Company A seems to be the kind of organization that invests in its customers.

Coefficient alpha was 0.84.

Professional benefit/expectation
1. Company A is not involved in activities that promote the welfare of its customers,
2. Company A does not act in a socially responsible manner,
3. Company A is not aware of what I want as a customer,
4. Company A does not see my interests and the company's interests as the same,
5. I think that Company A is not honest in its dealings with customers, and
6. Company A is not willing to devote resources to maintain its relationship with me.

Coefficient alpha was 0.85.

Personal commitment
1. I am committed to maintaining my relationship with Company A,
2. I feel very strongly linked to Company A, and
3. I want my relationship with Company A to continue for a long time.

Coefficient alpha was 0.87.

Community improvement
1. I feel that Company A supports events that are of interest to its customers,
2. I think that Company A strives to improve the communities of its customers, and
3. I think that Company A actively plays a role in the communities it serves.

Coefficient alpha was 0.87.

Comparison of alternatives
1. The alternative providers of electricity are excellent companies
2. I think other providers of electricity could fulfill my needs.
3. I would not feel very upset if Company A were no longer my provider of electricity.

Coefficient alpha was 0.72.

Overal, cofficient alpha for the revised 18-item scale was 0.89.

---

the relationship between an organization and its public. Scholars have come to see and use these additional dimensions as measures of the type of relationship (e.g. Hall, 2006; Hung, 2005). The first type is exchange relationship, in which partners exchange benefits. In other words, the organization gives something beneficial to a public because it knows it already has, or will in the future receive, something beneficial from that public. The second type is communal relationship, in which providing benefits to the other is based on concern for the welfare rather than exchange; nothing is expected in return.

Relationship dimensions were measured with a series of agree/disagree statements (using a 1-9 scale). In the initial test of the measure, Hon and Grunig (1999) used five different types of orga-

nizations, and found that all but one dimension had an average Cronbach's alpha over .80 (alphas ranged from .81-.93). The exchange relationship dimension tested at an average alpha of .70 (ranging from .62 to .78). Since the original test, the dimensions have been retested for both reliability and validity. Table 4 includes the shortened list of items used by Hon and Grunig. The control mutuality, commitment, satisfaction, and communal relationships dimensions remain reliable when shortened to four items. The last item listed in those dimensions can be removed without sacrificing the integrity of the scale.

A number of scholars have used just the four quality dimensions. For example, Kim and Chan-Olmsted (2005) examined trust, mutual control, satisfaction, and commitment, and found that satisfaction was the only significant predictor of brand attitude.

When Hon and Grunig (1999) developed the measure, they recognized that it measures a one-sided perception of the relationship from the perspective of the public, and said that, eventually, scholars will need to measure the perception of the relationship from both sides: measuring the extent to which a gap exists. In the future, they also suggest measuring the relationship through observation rather than through self-reported perceptions.

Ledingham and Bruning (1998) also tapped interpersonal indicators of relationship quality, measuring trust, openness, involvement, investment, and commitment. Later, Bruning and Ledingham (1999) developed another measure for the organization-public relationship. Rather than a list of the indicators of the quality of the relationship, they developed a scale that measured the public's perception of the type of relationship held with the organization: professional, personal, and community. Rather than measuring the quality of the relationship in terms of individual dimensions, this new measure gave a snapshot of the overall status of the relationship. The initial test included three statements for each of their previously measured dimensions (trust, openness, involvement, investment, and commitment), as well as three statements for each of the dimensions argued for by Grunig, Grunig, and Ehling (1992; reciprocity, mutual legitimacy, and mutual understanding).

Bruning and Galloway (2003) later described the typology measure as focusing on key publics' attitudes and expectations about the organization's personal, professional, and community relationships. Bruning and Galloway (2003) updated the scale by adding two more sets of measures: the degree of structural commitment, and the degree of personal commitment. Structural relationship commitment focuses on whether members of a public feel other organizations are appealing and/or could satisfy their needs, whereas personal commitment focuses on levels of dedication to the organization. As shown in Table 5, two of the structural commitment questions loaded with one of the personal commitment questions to form a new factor the authors labeled "comparison of alternatives." Bruning and Galloway argued that "when combined with the other two questions in this dimension, it appears that (the structural commitment) question focuses on comparing the feelings that respondents would have if they were to leave the relationship. Thus, the dimension now compares (a) the quality of the other companies, (b) the ability of other companies to fulfill the respondent's needs, and (c) the feelings that the respondent would have if he/she switched providers" (p.316). Three of the original personal commitment items loaded together and thus, the dimension was named personal commitment. Three of the original community relationship items loaded together and the dimension was renamed community improvement, and six of the professional relationship items loaded together and the dimension was renamed professional benefit/expectation. Finally, two items from the original personal relationship dimension and two items from the original community relationship dimension loaded together to form a new factor the authors labeled "anthropomorphis," because it deals with the organization displaying human qualities.

What is difficult about the measures produced by Bruning and his colleagues is that because they allow the statistics to define the factors with each new sample rather than confirming and validating factors created from theoretical concepts and previous research, they change the dimensions based on each new sample. Thus, the measures are currently neither generalizable to other samples, nor are they useful to practitioners or other researchers. Another problem with their latest measure is a test of one of the dimensions, content validity; I could just as easily argue that their anthropomorphis dimension is a measure of perceived transparency of an organization. The worry here is that they have created a reliable, but not valid, measure for this sample, and the question of whether the measure would remain reliable when given to another sample is unknown. If they can validate this new measure with additional samples and continue to find solid reliability, then the measure will prove useful in the future.

Kim (2001) attempted to develop another measure of relationships for public relations. Using the interpersonal communication, marketing, and public-relations literature on relationships, he developed a questionnaire with 113 items. His initial test dropped 57 questions due to "irrelevancy (mean scores less than 1.5, some scores reversed)" (p.804). However, the initial test involved undergraduate students offering their perceptions of a hypothetical company. Many of the items dropped seem to be less about their relevance to measuring a relationship between an organization and one of its publics, and more about the fact that it would be difficult for someone to assess such things about a hypothetical company. For example, the items that measured the extent to which the students exchange benefits with the organization, the extent to which the company is sincere, the extent to which they feel confident about the organization's operations, and most of the interpersonal relationship questions were dropped. Kim does an excellent job with the rest of the analysis, testing, cross-validating, and confirming his dimensions; however, because the first step removed so many potentially relevant items, the remaining dimensions may be reliable but, as an overall measure of the public-organization relationship, the measure does not appear to be valid.

Hon and Grunig (1999) found good reliability and validity with their measure in their initial tests. Others have also used these measures and continued to find good reliability and validity. Another benefit of using Hon and Grunig's measure is that the perception scores for each dimension can be used in a practical sense to tell an organization how it needs to improve the relationship with this public. For example, when an organization scores low on control mutuality, it means they need to

"develop symmetrical strategies for empowering publics and maintaining relationships in which publics feel they have little control ... these organizations need to consider ways of increasing the involvement of publics in organizational decision-making." (pp. 31-32). At this point, it is clear that relationship measurement will continue to be refined by scholars and practitioners in the coming years.

MEASURING PUBLIC RELATIONS ON THE WEB AND USING THE WEB FOR MEASUREMENT

The Web has become an important public-relations tool in achieving objectives; thus, measurement has also become an issue. Practitioners have fallen back on some of the same types of measurement miscalculations with the Web as they have conducted in print and electronic evaluation. For example, many practitioners use the number of hits on a Web site to indicate media impressions; however, they do not assess whether those hits are times when someone has come to the site to have a look, or because the site automatically comes up as the last site visited, or a home page from which users simply move on without really looking at the page. Just because my television was on channel 7 when I turned it on, does not mean I paid any attention to, or was even made aware of, what was on that channel before I quickly changed it to channel 6. As with all measures of media impressions, the practitioner must ask what it really tells you. Some organizations have tracking systems that tell them how long a user stayed on the site, which pages were accessed, from what site they arrived, and to what site they departed. Such information can be particularly helpful if connected to a mention in an online news clip. The extent to which mentions of the organization on the Web lead to visits to the organization's Web site is an additional impact practitioners have had a difficult time measuring for print and electronic mentions. Although the

Web can sometimes allow practitioners to assess a certain level of impact from those mentions, a mention of the organization in a newsgroup, blog, or online news clip must still be systematically analyzed for the content and context of that mention. Practitioners need to perform systematic analyses of blogs and other Internet postings in order to keep track of how their organization is being received by various publics. Many scholars and practitioners have begun to recognize the public-relations power of blogging. Measurement of this new tactic must keep step with its use and potential impact. Thus, practitioners should also examine the extent to which key publics are aware of, exposed to, paid attention to, learned from, and/or had their attitudes and behaviors changed as a result of such blogs.

The Web can also help practitioners conduct more cost-effective research. Web surveys on the organizations home page can allow practitioners to assess visitors' attitudes and behaviors. Practitioners must recognize the segment of the audience who is visiting their Web site and willing to complete a survey, and not try to generalize to a broader public. Organizations can also send out e-surveys to customers and other key publics' whose e-mail they have. At minimum, organizations must allow for feedback on their Web sites.

CONCLUSION

Measurement in the field of public relations has come a long way in a short time, and yet much is still to be learned. Scholars continue to develop measures and encourage practitioners to use them. This chapter has not addressed every measurement used in the field: such breadth could not be covered in just one chapter. However, this chapter does cover measures most often used by practitioners and most heavily discussed by scholars. As a final note for practitioners, take Stack's advice and think of research as an ongoing process. Going beyond measurements of message impact allow for ongo-ing assessment of the concepts most important to the practice of effective public relations such as a key public's perception of the organization's reputation, relationships between the organization and its publics, and issues management. Crises can be averted, opportunities can be utilized, problems can be addressed, relationships can be improved and maintained, and the management function of public relations can be affirmed.

REFERENCES

Bridges, J. A., & Nelson, R. A. (2000). Issues management: A relational approach. In J. A. Ledingham & S. D. Bruning (Eds.), *Public relations as relation management: A relational approach to the study and practice of public relations* (pp. 95-115). Mahwah, NJ: Lawrence Erlbaum Associates.

Broom, G. M., Casey, S., & Ritchey, J. (2000). Concept and theory of organization-public relationships. In J. A. Ledingham & S. D. Bruning (Eds.), *Public relations as relation management: A relational approach to the study and practice of public relations* (pp. 3-22). Mahwah, NJ: Lawrence Erlbaum Associates.

Bruning, S. D., Castle, J. D., & Schrepfer, E. (2004). Building relationships between organizations and publics: Examining the linkage between organization-public relationships. *Communication Studies, 55*(3), 435-446.

Bruning, S. D., & Galloway, T. (2003). Expanding the organization–public relationship scale: Exploring the role that structural and personal commitment play in organization-public relationships. *Public Relations Review, 29,* 309-319.

Bruning, S. D., & Ledingham, J. A. (1999). Relationships between organizations and publics: Development of a multidimensional organization-public relationship scale. *Public Relations Review, 25,* 157-170.

Coombs, W. T. (2000). Crisis management: Advantages of a relational perspective. In J. A. Ledingham & S. D. Bruning (Eds.), *Public relations as relation management: A relational approach to the study and practice of public relations* (pp.73-93). Mahwah, NJ: Lawrence Erlbaum Associates.

Cutlip, S. M., Center, A. H., & Broom, G. M. (1985). *Effective public relations* (6th ed). Englewood Cliffs, NJ: Prentice Hall.

Fink, A. (1995). *The survey kit: 2. How to ask survey questions.* Thousand Oaks, CA: Sage Publications.

Grunig, J. E. (1984). Organizations, environments, and models of public relations. *Public Relations Research and Education, 1*(1), 6-29.

Grunig, J. E. (1992). *Excellence in public relations and communication management.* Hillsdale, NJ: Lawrence Erlbaum Associates.

Grunig, J. E. (2001). Two-way symmetrical public relations. In R. L. Heath (Ed.), *Handbook of public relations* (pp. 1-19). Thousand Oaks, CA: Sage Publications.

Grunig, L. A., Grunig, J. E., & Ehling, W. P. (1992). What is an effective organization? In J. E. Grunig (Ed.), *Excellent public relations and communication management: Contributions to effective organizations* (pp. 65-89). Hillsdale, NJ: Lawrence Erlbaum Associates, Inc.

Hall, M. R. (2006). Corporate philanthropy and corporate community relations: Measuring relationship building. *Journal of Public Relations Research, 18*, 1-21.

Hon, L. C., & Grunig, J. E. (1999). *Guidelines for measuring relationships in public relations.* Gainesville, FL: The Institute for Public Relations.

Huang, Y. (2001). Values of public relations: Effects on organization-public relationships mediating conflict-resolution. *Journal of Public Relations Research, 13*, 265-301.

Hung, C. F. (2005). Exploring types of organization-public relationships and their implications for relationship management in public relations. *Journal of Public Relations Research, 17*, 393-426.

Kim, Y. (2000). Measuring the bottom-line impact of corporate public relations. *Journalism and Mass Communication Quarterly, 78*, 273-291.

Kim, Y. (2001). Searching for the organization-public relationship: A valid and reliable Instrument. *Journalism and Mass Communication Quarterly, 78*, 799-815.

Kim, J., & Chan-Olmsted, S. M. (2005). Comparative effects of organization-public *relationships* and product-related attributes on brand attitude. *Journal of Marketing Communications, 11*(3), 145-170.

Kruckeberg, D. (2000). Public relations: Toward a global profession. In J. A. Ledingham & S. D. Bruning (Eds.), *Public relations as relation management: A relational approach to the study and practice of public relations* (pp.145-157). Mahwah, NJ: Lawrence Erlbaum Associates.

Ledingham, J. A., & Bruning, S. D. (1998). Relationship management in public relations: Dimensions of an organization-public relationship. *Public Relations Review, 24*, 55-65.

Lee, B. K. (2004). Corporate image examined in a Chinese-based context. *Journal of Public Relations Research, 16*(1), 1-34.

Lindenmann, W. K. (2003). *Guidelines for measuring the effectiveness of PR programs and activities.* Gainesville, FL: The Institute for Public Relations.

Lindenmann, W. K. (2005). *Putting PR measurement and evaluation into historical perspective.* Gainesville, FL: The Institute for Public Relations.

Lucarelli-Dimmick, S. (2000). Relationship management: A new professional model. In J. A. Ledingham & S. D. Bruning (Eds.), *Public relations as relation management: A relational approach to the study and practice of public relations* (pp. 117-136). Mahwah, NJ: Lawrence Erlbaum Associates.

Remsik, J. (2000). You can really measure your pr impact. *Total communication measurement, 2*, 3.

Rhee, Y. (2002). Global public relations: A cross-cultural study of the excellence theory in South Korea. *Journal of Public Relations Research, 14*, 159-184.

Smith, R. D. (2005). *Strategic planning for public relations* (2nd ed.) (pp. 29-66). Mahwah, NJ: Lawrence Erlbaum Associates.

Stacks, D. W. (2002). *Primer of public relations research.* New York, NY: The Guilford Press, 3-32, 127-149.

Wilcox, D. L., Cameron, G. T., Ault, P. H., & Agee, W. K. (2005). *Public relations strategies and tactics* (7th ed.) (pp. 191-2070). Boston, MA: Allyn and Bacon.

Wilson, L. J. (2000). Building employee and community relationships through volunteerism: A case study. In J. A. Ledingham & S. D. Bruning (Eds.), *Public relations as relation management: A relational approach to the study and practice of public relations* (pp. 137-144). Mahwah, NJ: Lawrence Erlbaum Associates.

Witte, K., Meyer, G., & Martell, D. (2001). *Effective Health Risk Messages.* Thousand Oaks, CA: Sage Publications.

Wright, D. K. (1998). *Research in strategic corporate communications.* New York, NY: the Executive Forum.

KEY TERMS

Alpha: An overall measure of how well a group of items measures the same characteristic. Scales are composed of items measuring the same general concept (we ask for some information more than once and in different ways). Researchers examine whether there is sufficient consistency between how people answer the related items. The alpha provides a numerical indicator that ranges from .00 (no consistency among the items) to 1.00 (perfect consistency).

Confirmatory Factor Analysis: A statistical analysis to test theories and hypotheses about what factors or dimensions (set of items) are expected for a set of items.

Content Validity: Items in a scale accurately represent what the scale is said to measure

Cross-Validation: The accuracy of a measure is tested with a different sample than it was first developed.

Exploratory Factor Analysis: A statistical analysis conducted on a set of items to determine what factors or dimensions (set of items) evolve.

Measurement Reliability: Measuring something in a consistent and stable manner. A matter of whether a particular measurement technique applied repeatedly to the same object or person would yield the same results. Does not ensure accuracy.

Measurement Validity: Does your empirical measure adequately reflect the real meaning of the concept? Are you measuring what you think you are measuring: how well does your measure fit/actually reflect/match your conceptual definition, how well does your measure really tap into the concept as defined. Measurement reliability is numerical, whereas measurement validity is more conceptual

Proximal Measures: Less direct indicators of a concept that are thought to approximate more direct measures. Proximal measures are assumed to have some degree of correlational or predictive validity to the concept of interest.

Chapter XVIII
Measuring Intrinsic Motivations

J. Lynn Reynolds
Fuller Theological Seminary, USA

ABSTRACT

Numerous instruments have been created over the last several decades for measuring both extrinsic and intrinsic values, as they are made manifest in Western culture. Although many of these instruments are well balanced and have strong internal validity, more progress needs to be made specifically with the items being used. If this can be done, then it may be possible for a great leap of progress in measuring the intrinsic values. It is very difficult to gain understanding about how to bridge the small differences in subcultures if surveys continue to gloss over delicate areas that are the very reasons for subculture disagreements. This chapter reviews current measurement instruments for measuring both extrinsic and intrinsic values. It gives a sample of a specific study, and makes a call for improved intrinsic instruments in the future.

INTRODUCTION

Different religious and nonreligious groups within the various subcultures of society want to understand the internal motivations operating in conjunction with decision-making behavior. Within marketing research groups, there is always a need to have a better understanding about consumer values and their effect on behavior. Among religious groups and nonprofit organizations, there is a need to understand the deep-seeded beliefs that drive constituents. Once the values that are important to specific groups are measured, it is easier to relate to these subcultures and build bridges to other aspects of society, no matter what the specific goal. As religious or spiritual variables are more fully conceptualized in different instruments, scholars will be able to more fully explain key ideas that have previously escaped

explanation. This chapter will highlight specific instruments that measure internal concepts that need to continue to be researched. However, readers should investigate Hill and Hood (1999), Koenig, McCullough, and Larson (2001), and Plante and Sherman (2001).

EARLY RESEARCH

Allport and Ross (1967), who researched both the intrinsic and extrinsic motivations, felt that the intrinsically oriented participants brought everything in their lives in concert with their religious beliefs. These authors saw the intrinsically motivated as those who lived out their religion. The nine intrinsic religiosity items in their measure included: "If I were to going a church group I would prefer to join a bible study group rather than a social fellowship," and "Quite often I have been keenly aware of the presence of God or the Divine Being." Donahue (1985) saw the usability with regard to Christian denominations, but felt that measures of religiousness were the primary significance of the variables used.

One of the most important instruments, to date, is the intrinsic religious motivation scale (IRMS) by Hoge. Hoge's scale (1972) has been helpful for communication researchers. It has 10 items that focus on motivations behind faith and religion. Two of these include: "My religious beliefs are what really lie behind my whole approach to life," and "One should seek God's guidance when making every important decision." Many different religious groups have been able to use this scale because it is fairly general. Benson, Dehority, Garman, Hanson, Hochschwender, & Lebold (1980) found that when Hoge's scale is used, it helps to predict nonspontaneous helping (e.g., volunteering), and so the possible variety of uses for this instrument have probably not been fully explored. In addition, scales such as Hoge's survey help toward the understanding of information processing within the area of health communication and health risks (See Egbert, Mickley, & Coeling, 2004).

The Duke religion index (DUREL) (see Koenig, Meador, & Parkerson, 1997) expertly used key items to measure religious variables related to health outcomes. The level of reliability and consistency that was found in various studies indicated that this measure has a great deal of potential with regard to connecting religious variables with other health patient samples. One of the reasons that this is so exciting is because it gives added insight with regard to attitudes and feelings related to altruism.

RECENT APPLICATIONS

Others have designed original items to measure very specific beliefs. In Reynolds and Reynolds

(2000), the goal was to explore the Christian concepts that might make men embrace an ecumenical ideal in terms of a group of concepts (There were no female respondents.). A survey was written to intentionally use ideas that have been potentially disruptive with regard to massive agreement with American culture. Several brainstorming sessions were held with ministers, former ministers, and lay people. There were 34 items that seemed key. Life issues, as well as doctrinal and traditional issues, were used. The items are identified in the factor analysis groupings given in Table 1. The respondents scored the questions from one to five, with one as "strongly disagree" and five as "strongly agree."

Demographics were collected with regard to church background: Evangelicals (10%), Baptists (19%), Traditionalists (16%), Nondenominational (31%), and Other (24%). Respondents were clergy, church lay leaders, church members, frequent attendees, and occasional attendees. They were self-identified by race as 4% Asian Americans, 1% African Americans, 3% Hispanic, and 88% Caucasians. They fell into conservative (72%), moderate (27%), and liberal (1%) groups with their self-report of religious beliefs. Specifics included Table 1.

In addition to these findings, beliefs about spiritual gifts were also measured in this study.

Table 1. Factor analysis

Biblical Basics	
Item	Loading
Mary was a virgin.	.89
Jesus rose from the dead.	.90
Jesus was divine.	.86
Hell is not a metaphor.	.74
God acts directly now.	.73
Conservative Doctrine	
The rapture will occur before the tribulation.	.80
The strict biblical account of creation is true.	.76
Infant baptism is against the Bible.	.75
The rapture will, in fact, occur.	.71
Scripture is never in error.	.68
One's political position should be consistent with one's Christian beliefs.	.67
Jesus will return within the next few years.	.64
Women leaders in the church goes against the Bible.	.64

Overall, in all of the participants, older men were more positively correlated toward all three groups. Education level was positively related only to the Biblical Basics group. There were no differences among denominations. This specific kind of research allows researchers to see how various demographic variables, such as education, function with religiosity and spirituality measures.

This group of participants was unique in that they had participated in a cultural phenomena (belonging to the men's group called The Promise Keepers), and this allowed them to respond without feeling bound by specific community pressures of their home groups. Because they were filling out the survey from a posted Web site, they may have felt free to respond more anonymously than they had ever felt at any time in their life. This is one of the advantages of electronic measurement.

SENSE OF SELF

It has been found that religiosity and spirituality affect individuals through their sense of self (Blaine, Trivedi, & Eshleman, 1998). Religion should not be ignored in research studies because of the prominent way it influences the self-concept, and molds the way participants think about their lives. This area should not be ignored any more than socioeconomic status or race or gender should be ignored.

It would be unfair, in this chapter, to overlook the spiritual well-being scale (SWB) by Paloutzian and Ellison (1982) because of how widely it has been used as a sociopychometric instrument. In addition, Moberg (1984) has developed a longer instrument with 13 related subscales. A wide array of groups beyond religious groups, (AIDS patients and the elderly, for example) make for one of the reasons why this instrument is so widely accepted as an excellent choice for measurement. The Paloutzian and Ellison (1982) scale measures both Religious Well-Being (a religious well-being), and another component that shows how one's purpose, spiritually, and one's satisfaction with life fit together. Sample items include "My relationship with God helps me not to feel lonely," and "I believe that God loves me and cares about me." On the Existential Well-Being subscale, sample items are "I feel very fulfilled and satisfied with my life," and "I feel a sense of well-being about the direction my life is headed in." The reliability, internal consistency, and construct validity has held up in nursing research (Boivin, Kirby, Underwood, & Silva, 1999). This instrument has been so popular in health-related research that it will probably continue to aid researchers in understanding the health and spirituality connection.

CONCLUSION

Both researchers and religious leaders alike must make strong use of the opportunities that the current technology provides (such as posting surveys on Web sites used by their constituents), and make use of specific databases used by their organizations to survey various groups for answers that provide insight into what is going on: the spiritual ebb and flow of the culture. The deep internal motivations, when captured online, reduce the trappings of religious denominations, and there is more freedom to be anonymous and allow for a depth of self-disclosure in the answers not found in face-to-face responses.

REFERENCES

Allport, G. W., & Ross, J. M. (1967). Personal religious orientation and prejudice. *Journal of Personality and Social Psychology, 5,* 432-443.

Benson, P. I., Dehority, J., Garman, L., Hanson, E., Hochschwender, M., & Lbold, C. (1980). Interpersonal correlates of nonspontaneous helping behavior. *Journal of Social Psychology, 110,* 87-95.

Blaine, B. E., Trivedi, P., & Eshleman, A. (1998). Religious belief and the self-concept: Evaluating the implications for psychological adjustment. *Personality and Social Psychology Bulletin, 24*, 1040-1052.

Boivin, M. J., Kirby, A. L., Underwood, L. K., & Silva, H. (1999). Spiritual well-being scale. In P. C. Hill & R. W. Hood (Eds.). *Measures of religiosity* (pp. 382-385). Birmingham, AL: Religious Education Press.

Donahue, M. J. (1985). Intrinsic and extrinsic religiousness: Review and meta-analysis. *Journal of Personality and Social Psychology, 48*, 400-419.

Egbert, N., Mickley, J., & Coeling, H. (2004). A review and application of social scientific measures of religiosity and spirituality: Assessing a missing component in health communication research. *Health Communication, 16*(1), 7-27.

Hill, P. C., & Hood, R. W., Jr. (Eds.) (1999). Measures of religiosity. Bermingham, AL: Religious Education Press.

Hoge, D. R. (1972). A validated intrinsic religious motivation scale. *Journal of the Scientific Study of Religion, 11*, 369-376.

Hood, R. W. (1975). The construction and preliminary validation of a measure of reported mystical experience. *Journal of the Scientific Study of Religion, 14*, 29-41.

Koenig, H. G., McCullough, M. E., & Larson, D. B. (2001), *Handbook of religion and health*. New York: Oxford University Press.

Koenig, H. G., Meador, K., & Parkerson, G. (1997). Religion index for psychiatric research: A 5-item measure for use in health outcomes studies [Letter to the Editor]. *American Journal of Psychiatry, 154*, 885-886.

Moberg, D. O. (1984). Subjective measures of spiritual well-being. R*eview of Religious Research, 25*, 351-359.

Paloutzian, R. F., & Ellison, C. W. (1982). Loneliness, spiritual well-being and the quality of life. In L. A. Peplau & D. Perlman (Eds.), *Loneliness: A sourcebook of current theory, research and therapy* (pp. 224-237). Wiley-Interscience.

Plante, T. G., & Sherman, A. C. (Eds.). (2001). *Faith and health: Psychological perspectives*. New York: Guilford.

Reynolds. J. L., & Reynolds, R. A. (2000). Ecumenical promise keepers: Oxymoron or fidelity? In D. S. Claussen (Ed.). *The Promise Keepers: Essays on masculinity and Christianity*. Jefferson, NC: McFarland & Company, Inc.

KEY TERMS

Concepts Involved in Religiousness and Spirituality: This involves the cognitions, emotions, and behaviors with regard to searching for the sacred.

Extrinsically/Intrinsically Motivated: The extrinsically motivated person sees his religion as useful, but the intrinsically motivated person walks out his religion.

Organizational Religiousness or Nonorganizational Religiousness: The ability to indicate how often a person attends church or religious meetings vs. how often they spend time in activities like prayer or studying the Bible.

Religiousness: Society's belief that an organized group does certain practices relating to God.

Spirituality: Individual experiences that relate to a higher power; also, experiences that culminate in adding purpose in life.

Chapter XIX
Measuring Disagreement

Brian Whitworth

Massey University (Auckland), New Zealand

ABSTRACT

Agreement is an important goal of computer-mediated and face-to-face groups. This chapter suggests a measure of disagreement in groups facing limited choices, as in a multichoice questionnaire. It defines a disagreement score between two people, then takes one person's disagreement as the average of their pair-wise scores with the rest of the group, and finally, defines the group disagreement as the average of its member's disagreement. This gives a standard disagreement scale (from 0 to 1) for any group response pattern, for any size group, facing any number of choices. It can be inverted to give agreement, though this does not necessarily predict group coalescence. It is encouraging that when the method is extended to ranked, interval, or ratio scale data, it is equivalent to the score variance, and that it also matches an ecological diversity measure. Unlike variance, this measure can be used with categories, and gives both individual and group values. Being standard, it offers a single score in cases where the group size and number of choices faced is unknown, for example, online computer-based group feedback. Examples are given of how the measure can be used.

INTRODUCTION

Many real-life tasks are "equivocal," or ambiguous, so no amount of information analysis will resolve them (Daft, Lengel, & Trevino, 1987). They require the group to "enact" agreement, that is, create it without rational basis, for example, one cannot (today) find convincing reasons to drive on the left side of the road or the right (the Romans chose the left so the sword arm faced oncoming strangers), but it is still crucial that we all drive on the same side.

Agreement may be as important a group output as task resolution and decision quality (Maier, 1963). A group must first agree to even create a decision with any quality. An individual making a rational decision can be correct or incorrect, but groups have an additional possibility: unable to agree. This is illustrated in Figure 1, showing a group whose members (the small arrows) have choices in a decision space. In 1a, their decisions cancel out, giving no net group decision. Only in 1b, with agreement, does the group as a whole decide (large arrow). Two thousand years ago, Aesop expressed the social value of agreement:

A lion used to prowl in a field where four oxen also dwelt. Many a time he tried to attack them; but whenever he came near they turned their tails to one another, so whichever way he approached them he was met by the horns of one of them. At last however they fell a-quarrelling among themselves, and each went off to pasture alone in a separate corner of the field. Then the lion attacked them one by one and soon made an end to all four. (Aesop's Fables, ca. 600BC)

Agreement can be considered an independent output of social activity, distinct from task quality or quantity (Whitworth, Gallupe, & McQueen, 2000). If agreement is important, that powerful social processes maintain it is not surprising. Forty years ago Asch gave subjects a simple perceptual task, to choose the longer of two lines (Asch, 1952). They completed the task correctly 99% of the time when acting alone. However, when given the same task in a group where six other group members had chosen the clearly shorter line as longer, 76% of subjects went along with the group for at least one of six trials. The conformity effect had surprising strength in the face of unequivocal contradictory sensory evidence. In the autokinetic effect, a stationary point of light appears to move when viewed in total darkness (Sherif, 1936). People viewing such lights alone

arrive at stable (but different) estimates of how the light moves, but when they view it publicly in a group, their estimates converge until they closely resemble each other. The same process caused the dropping of idiosyncratic behavior in groups. Speech samples of five-person groups over 4 months showed metaphor usage idiosyncrasies decreased, until a single metaphor category dominated (Owen, 1985). Conformity research suggests that generating agreement is one of the more important things that groups do when they interact.

Modern software is becoming more social, for example, chat, bulletin boards, online voting and reputation systems, common spaces, and e-mail lists. If agreement is important for physical social interaction, it is also important for electronic social interaction. However, current research in computer-mediated communication (CMC) is at best confusing. Meta-analyses of groupware research suggest that while it sometimes improves task performance (Dennis, 1996; Pinsonneault & Kraemer, 1989), it often reduces or has no effect on agreement and confidence (Fjermestad & Hiltz, 1999; McGrath & Hollingshead, 1991; McLeod, 1992). A major groupware review concluded: "It is obvious that the relative lack of ability to reach consensus is a problem for groups using GSS (group support systems)." (Fjermestad & Hiltz, 1999). This matches earlier findings that while computer support improves task performance, it often reduces or has no effect on agreement (Mc-

Figure 1. Agreement and social action

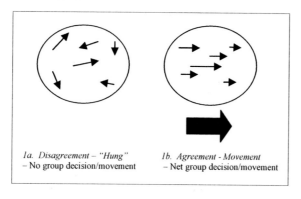

1a. *Disagreement – "Hung"*
– No group decision/movement

1b. *Agreement - Movement*
– Net group decision/movement

Grath & Hollingshead, 1991; McLeod, 1992). A comparison of face-to-face (FTF) and computer-mediated communication groups found no task quality differences, but while seven of eight FTF groups reached consensus, only one of eight CMC groups did so (Adrianson & Hjelmquist, 1991). In a collaborative writing task, computer-mediated groups had substantially more difficulty coordinating their work than FTF groups, the authors concluding: ". . . the major problem, achieving consensus about how to proceed, seems much less amenable to technological intervention." (Kraut, Galegher, Fish, & Chalfonte, 1992). Computer groups seem to take significantly longer to reach consensus than face-to-face groups (Hollingshead, 1993), and consistently report lower satisfaction (Straus, 1996). The suggestion is that computers support task rather than social interaction (Hiltz, Johnson, & Turoff, 1986; Ho & Raman, 1991; Siegel, Dubrovsky, Kiesler, & McGuire, 1986).

One conclusion from these findings is that the low agreement is due to the low computer communication bandwidth, implying that rich, video-style communication will enable social agreement. Many millions of dollars have been spent developing hardware and software to increase electronic media richness. However, recent evidence suggests another view, as strong computer-mediated agreement can be created with lean interaction (Whitworth, Gallupe, & McQueen, 2001), and some studies report computer-mediated groups generate *more* consensus than FTF interaction (Lea & Spears, 1991; Postmes & Spears, 1998). The key to consensus, it is proposed, is the communication channel linkage (one-to-one, one-to-many and many-to-many), rather the channel richness (Whitworth et al., 2000).

In the resolution of an important and complex issue like how online groups generate agreement, measurement is critical. Research cannot proceed unless the construct in question is defined. We analyze the construct of disagreement, and present a new measure suitable for computer-mediated interaction.

DEFINITION

Agreement on a physical level can be conceived as sameness of behavior, as in a herd or flock that moves together (in a cohesive way). Its value is that without behavioral agreement, herd members would wander apart, and the herd would cease to exist as a social unit. Likewise, agreement on an intellectual level can be seen as sameness with respect to intellectual "positions"; for example, given a choice between say buy, hold or sell. When individuals choose the same position, we say they agree. When they choose different intellectual positions, we say they disagree. However, even given this construct, how to measure it is not obvious.

A simple measure is *commonality:* the number of people who choose a common option (Lorge, Fox, Davitz, & Brenner, 1958, p364). This, however, only uses the choices for the majority option, and ignores the variation among the rest. Another method is to instruct the group to reach *consensus* or unanimity; then calculate the percentage of unanimous groups (Sniezek, 1992). This also ignores relevant information, namely the degree of agreement in groups who achieve less than complete unanimity. Some experiments with electronic groups used a measure of group agreement derived from the mathematics of fuzzy set theory (Spillman, Spillman, & Bezdek, 1980), and calculated by computer program (Sambamurthy & Chin, 1994; Tan, Wei, & Krishnamurthy, 1991; Watson, DeSanctis, & Poole, 1988,). However, this measure requires interval data, not the nominal data produced by questionnaires (Tan, Teo, & Wei, 1995). For example, it could not apply to the buy, sell, or hold case mentioned previously. It also requires the group data provide voting probabilities for the options. A measure will now be proposed that does not require known voting probabilities. It uses the actual group response pattern, and also applies to nominal data (where people choose from a set of nonnumerical options).

Table 1. Definition of terms

Term	Meaning
N	Number of group members.
K	Number of response options.
A, B, C,...	Different response options.
f_j	Number who chose the *jth* option.
d_{ij}	Disagreement between one person who chose option *i*, and another who chose *j*, where *i* and *j* are undefined.
d_i	Disagreement of one person choosing option *i* with the rest of the group.
D	Average disagreement of the group.

Table 2. Individual disagreement (d) for N=5, K=4

Individual	Rest of group	d	a
A	AAAA	0.0	1.0
A	AAAB	0.25	0.75
A	AACD	0.5	0.5
A	ABBC	0.75	0.25
A	BCCD	1.0	0.0
A	BBBB	1.0	0.0

The core construct proposed is that *the disagreement between two group members is the distance apart of their positions on the given issue*. Naturally, two people may disagree on one issue but not on another. This common-sense concept applies both physically and intellectually. In a herd moving together, the distance apart of its members is small. Likewise, when many people in a group choose the same intellectual position, their intellectual distance apart is also small. The basic terms that will be used are defined in Table 1, given a group of N people facing K discrete choices.

INDIVIDUAL DISAGREEMENT

Consider N group members facing K mutually exclusive choices A, B, C, ... ($N > 1$, $K > 0$). For example, suppose five people must select one of four colors. We first define the disagreement between two people, then the individual's disagreement with the rest of the group, then the group disagreement as the average of the individual disagreements.

What is the disagreement (d_{ij}) between any two people? From this construct, if they choose different colors the disagreement is one, and if they choose the same color it is zero:

$$d_{ij} = 1 \text{ if } i \neq j, \text{ else } d_{ij} = 0$$

This is just the disagreement between two people, but for a given person, their pair-wise disagreements with the rest of the group can be averaged. An individual's disagreement (d_i) is then the sum of their disagreements with each other group member, divided by the number of pairs (N-1):

$$d_i = \frac{1}{(N-1)} \sum_{1 \leq j \leq K} d_{ij} f_j$$

where f_j is the number of people who chose option *j*. If everyone chooses the same option, there is no disagreement ($d_i = 0$), while if everyone chooses different options, there is maximum disagreement ($d_i = 1$). Table 2 shows how **d** varies for five people choosing from four colors: A, B, C, and D.

In this case, an agreement inverse can be calculated: $a = 1 - d$. This measure matches the use of the index of the actual number of mutual friendships in a group divided by the number of possible mutual friendships as "one of the best indicators of a group's cohesion" (Dimock, 1986, p. 123).

GROUP DISAGREEMENT

The group disagreement (**D**) is now the average of the disagreements of all its members:

$$D = \frac{1}{N} \sum_{1 \leq i \leq K} f_i d_i$$

$$= \frac{1}{N(N-1)} \sum_{1 \leq i \leq K} \sum_{1 \leq j \leq K} d_{ij} f_j f_i$$

Table 3. Group disagreement (D) for N=5 and K=4

Group response	Example	D	A
Unanimous	AAAAA	0.0	1.0
All but one	AAAAB	0.4	0.6
3-2 split	AAABB	0.6	0.4
3-2 majority	AAABC	0.7	0.3
Hung group	AABBC	0.8	0.2
Maximum disagreement	AABCD	0.9	0.1

Table 4. Maximum D by N for low K

Group size	Number of Options			
	K = 2	K = 3	K = 5	K = 10
2	1.000	1.000	1.000	1.000
3	0.667	1.000	1.000	1.000
5	0.600	0.800	1.000	1.000
10	0.556	0.733	0.889	1.000
100	0.505	0.673	0.808	0.909
1,000	0.501	0.667	0.801	0.901

The minimum **D** value (0) is when all group members agree (see Table 3). The maximum value of 1.0 (everyone disagrees) is impossible with five group members but only four choices, as some people must agree. The line at D = 0.75 indicates where the group moves from being "hung" to having majority agreement. An inverse measure (of agreement) can again be calculated: **A = 1 − D**.

ADVANTAGES

The advantages of **D** and **d** as measures of group and individual disagreement are

1. **Simple: D** and **d** can be calculated manually for small groups. Just average each person's pair-wise disagreements; then average for the group; for example, for three people, each person can have an average disagreement (with two others) of 0.0, 0.5, or 1.0. In the first case, they disagree with no one, in the second they disagree with one other, and in the last they disagree with both others. **D** is then the average of the **d** values for all the group members.
2. **Sensitive:** This measure shows all levels of disagreement, not just majority; for example, a group response of *AAABC* (**D** = 0.7) shows more disagreement than a group response of *AAABB* (**D** = 0.6).
3. **Valid:** The core construct has content validity, based on a meaningful definition of disagreement.

4. **Scaled:** The measures offer a fixed scale, from 0 (unanimity) to 1 (everyone disagrees), for any group size or number of choices, allowing comparisons between different numbers of people and choices.
5. **Adaptable:** Can measure at group (**D**) or individual level (**d**), depending on the research unit.

Maximum D

For a few choices, as the group gets bigger the maximum disagreement decreases (Table 4). The maximum of 1.0 is only possible if each person can make a different choice. If there are more group members than choices (N > K), then it is impossible for everyone to disagree, and the maximum **D** is less than 1. In general, as *N* gets very large, D_{max} tends towards *1 - 1/K*. For example, in the case where there are two solution choices (*K* = 2), as *N* becomes very large, D_{max} tends to 0.5.

Measure Properties

This measure may say something about the nature of groups. When one person disagrees in a group of five, they go from disagreeing with no one to disagreeing with everyone, and their individual **d** changes from *0.0* to *1.0* (Table 2). Such a major change, from zero disagreement to maximum disagreement, can be expected to be difficult, and perhaps is why conformity is so powerful. Likewise, one dissenter moves the group **D** almost half the scale (**D** = *0.4*) (Table 3); so for a small group, one person disagreeing is a major event. This effect reduces as group size increases: in a group of 10, the **D** change is *0.2*, and for a group of 100, it is only *0.02,* that is, one person's dissension has less impact on larger groups.

Though its maximum varies with the number of choices, **D** itself is independent of K. A group response pattern AAABB has a disagreement of 0.6, whether the group faces two choices, four choices, or a thousand. However, disagreement depends on $N;$ for example an individual in a polarized pair facing two choices has a disagreement of 1.0, but a person in a polarized group of 1,000 has only half that disagreement (because 499 people agree with them). Given this property, the measure can compare groups of different sizes, which is useful when research cell groups have missing members.

Numeric Data

This measure can also apply to ranked, interval, and ratio scale data, as its concept of distance apart still applies. It just means giving disagreement scores beyond 0 and 1; for example, when selecting a color from lime green, mint green, sea green, and deep purple, the lime green to purple distance could be taken as 2, while the lime green to mint green disagreement is taken as 1. When this is done for interval data, it is gratifying that **D** can be shown to be equal to twice the variance (Whitworth & Felton, 1999). The doubling occurs because averaging the **d** values counts each pair-wise disagreement twice, once for each

participant. That **D** also works for interval data suggests it is a valid measure for categorical data (where a variance cannot normally be calculated). This approach also gives individual disagreement measure, while in contrast, one cannot normally calculate the "variance" of a single data point, still less regard the total variance as the average of individual point "variances."

Further support for the generic nature of this measure comes from mathematical ecology. Simpson's measure calculates the ecological diversity of a habitat with N creatures and K types of species (Pielou, 1969, p. 223). If all creatures are of the same species, the diversity is low, whereas if each animal is a different species, the diversity is high. This measure can be shown to equate to the group disagreement **D** (Whitworth & Felton, 1999). It is interesting that two such different situations, each with different logics, can give equivalent mathematical formulae. *Perhaps there is a higher dispersion concept that incorporates disagreement, variance, and ecological diversity as specific cases.*

Choices that are not Mutually Exclusive

The logic presented here can be extended to the case where the choices are not mutually exclusive. Suppose a group faces choices where each option can be accepted or not, and the group can accept any, all, or none of the options. Each option can be considered a yes/no choice in itself, and **D** can be calculated for that option. The choices can be

Table 5. Probability distribution for N=5, K=4

Group Response	Example	Group Disagreement	P ( )
Unanimous	AAAAA	0.0	4/1024
All but one	AAAAB	0.4	60/1024
3-2 split	AAABB	0.6	120/1024
3-2 majority	AAABC	0.7 mean = 0.75	240/1024
Hung group	AABBC	0.8	360/1024
Maximum disagreement	AABCD	0.9	240/1024

Table 6. Probability distribution for N=6, K=4

Group Response	Example	Disagreement	P ( )
Unanimous	AAAAAA	0.00	4/4096
All But 1	AAAAAB	0.33	72/4096
All But 2 Solid	AAAABB	0.53	180/4096
All But 2 Split	AAAABC	0.60	360/4096
All But 3 Solid	AAABBB	0.60	120/4096
All But 3 Split 1:2	AAABBC	0.73	1440/4096
All But 3 Equi-Split	AAABCD	0.80	480/4096
Hung Group	AABBCC	0.80	360/4096
Max Disagreement	AABBCD	0.87	1080/4096

compared according to the agreement each generates. Averaging these values over all the options will give a measure of the group disagreement for the choice set as a whole.

Probability Distribution

Assuming all solution options are equally likely to be chosen by all group members gives the probability distribution shown in Table 5, for $N = 5$ and $K = 4$. The **D** distribution is positively skewed, as there are more ways a group can disagree than they can agree. The mean **D** value is 0.75, halfway between a 3-2 majority and a hung group (see the line in Table 5). The Table 5 probabilities reflect a null hypothesis that all solution options are equally likely, either because subjects do not know which option is correct (a difficult choice), or find the choices equally attractive (an unbiased choice). By contrast, for an easy problem like $2 + 2 = ?$, the response pattern will differ significantly from the Table 5 probabilities.

Table 6 represents the same values for $N = 6$ and $K = 4$, where again the 0.75 value represents the movement from majority to indecision. In a similar way, tables can be derived for any combination of N and K.

Limitations

These measures must be used carefully in situations where causality is unclear, as agreement can be a cause as well as an effect. For example, studies show the first person advocating a position better predicts the group final decision than predecision group preferences (McGuire, Kiesler, & Siegel, 1987). The first advocate seems to influence or "lead" the rest of the group. Yet when no prior discussion was allowed, their "influence" disappeared. The first advocate was actually reflecting rather than directing the group, like a group process tuning fork (Weisband, 1992). The caution is not to assume causality in a group interaction.

D is a process-independent measure of disagreement, and makes no assumptions about how a group state came about. Equally, it need not predict future group states, though it may be used in models that do. For example, in a group of eight facing four choices, a polarized split (AAAABBBB) gives a relatively low disagreement of **D** = 0.57, while a majority of five with the rest of the group split over all options (AAAAABCD) gives a higher disagreement of **D** = 0.64. Yet the latter is more likely to reach consensus based on a normative process. That polarized groups, where the group splits into two opposing subgroups, show relatively high agreement is not a problem with the measure, as each pole contains many pair-wise agreements. This is shown when a polarized group splits into two, as then, each group has full agreement (for each new group, **D** = 1.0). Group disagreement and the likelihood of consensus seem two different dimensions, one measuring the current state, and the other predicting a future state.

EXAMPLE APPLICATIONS

This measure can be used wherever agreement is an important outcome for groups facing categorical choices. Some examples are:

1. **Diagnostic Situations:** For example, online doctors diagnose a patient's condition.
2. **Expert Analyses:** For example, online experts assess disaster prevention options.

3. **Leadership Selection:** For example, bulletin board members elect a leader
4. **Product Evaluations:** For example, a group of customers selecting a product

Whether it is three doctors with different diagnoses, or three computers with different space shuttle launch decisions, the issue of agreement arises commonly when groups choose then act. Agreement here is the precondition for correctness, as a group must first agree to be wrong or right. Indeed, in some cases, making a choice may be more important than the choice made. The measure **D** is especially useful for online interaction, because it is standard and can always be calculated, even if N and K are unknown at first. For example, in a diagnostic case, the number of doctors and diagnoses may be initially unknown. Whether for 7 people making three choices or 10 people making two choices, **D** produces a single summary score, suitable for graphical display, for example, a bar graph.

The measure can also be used in cases where agreement is a secondary group measure. For example, students can, after reading a textbook chapter for homework, answer online multichoice questions on various topics prior to class. This can tell an instructor which topics are unknown, and be used to direct valuable class time. The primary computer generated measure is the % correct for each question, but the computer could also generate disagreement as a secondary measure. For example, low correct but low disagreement suggests the majority understood something, but were perhaps fooled by a distractor, while low correct and high disagreement suggests no common understanding at all. Since most multiple-choice questions are categorical, not ranked, a statistical variance cannot be calculated here. Correctness and disagreement for category data can be compared to mean and variance for interval data. There are many cases where current measures provide choice means, but it would be useful to also know the group disagreement, for example,

reputation systems tell how many people like you choose a given book, but not how many people like you do not.

This measure can be used in dynamic online social interaction, where the agreement output can be fed back into the system as an input; for example, selecting an online board or project leader. Voting for a leader is as important for online interaction as for face-to-face, yet most bulletin boards are appointed dictatorships. Why not elect online leaders democratically? One reason is that voting is more complex than it appears. For three or more choices, it may be impossible to translate individual choices into a valid group choice, as Arrow's paradox formally states (Arrow, 1963). To give a simple example, suppose two candidates support the majority 60% view but split that vote, getting 30% each. A third minority candidate may then get the highest vote of 40%, even though the majority oppose their view. Some suggest this is how Hitler came to power. One way to avoid this problem is to repeat the vote. Face-to-face voting is usually such an expensive procedure that this is not an option, although the Vatican cardinals repeat vote until a decision is reached. In online voting, repeating a vote is much easier as the computer collects and counts the votes. To computerize online voting, one needs some measure of whether the group is done, or needs to vote again. An automated measure of agreement could trigger the group to vote again or not. In some cases, trivial candidates could be deleted, eventually giving a binary vote where Arrow's paradox does not apply. Agreement should not be thought of as a static quantity, but as an evolving group dynamic where people affect people in a recursive way (Hoffman & Maier, 1964).

Finally, the individual level of this measure can tell individuals how much they disagree with the group on a given topic. Such feedback about what others think is naturally important to people in a social setting (Whitworth et al., 2000). In a study of voting before discussing, high disagreement was used to trigger the topics a group needed to talk about (Whitworth & McQueen, 2003). This focused the group on topics they disagree on, and let them ignore topics they already agreed upon. While one might expect such feedback to create conformity, it can also be a springboard for change. The authors found cases where individuals who disagreed with the entire group used the ensuing discussion to convince the others of their point of view. If one knows an idea generates disagreement, it can help the person know they must make a good case for it to succeed. It should not be assumed that group dynamics work only one way.

A RESEARCH EXAMPLE

The following illustrates how **d** and **D** can be used in dynamic online groups. Anonymous on-line groups had to decide a group response to 12 multichoice questions, each with four response options. The groups had three voting rounds, and between each round, members were told how their choice compared with the others. For example, they could find themselves in the minority (**d** $\geq$ *0.75*) or in the majority (**d** < *0.75*). First, they voted without seeing how others voted. On their second vote, however, they saw the group first vote, and likewise on the third vote, they could see their group's second votes. Each round, subjects could change their vote if they wanted to. Table 7 shows how the % who changed their position varied with individual group disagreement (Whitworth & Felton, 1999). Overall, only about a quarter of subjects changed their initial vote, but in general, the more subjects disagreed with the rest of the group, the more likely they were to change their original position.

But the individual disagreement (**d**) alone was not the sole predictor. It also depended on the degree the rest of the group agreed to disagree with them. A **D** score, called **Drest,** was calculated *for the other four members* of the group. Table 8 shows the possible **d** and **Drest** combinations; for example, *AAAAB* is an individual (in bold)

who chooses option A and finds one other group member disagrees with them. Note that not all combinations of **d** and **Drest** are possible. Table 9 shows the percentage vote change broken down by **d** and **Drest,** with the subject numbers in brackets. It suggests individuals change their initial vote depending not only on how many disagree with them, but also on how much the others agree among themselves:

1. For **d = 0.0,** there is a low probability that another solution will be accepted, as three group members would have to change position. Only 1% of those who found that everyone else agreed with them changed their position.

2. For **d = 0.25,** the alternative probability has increased, though only slightly, as two group members would have to change position. The percentage vote change also rises slightly, though it more than doubles the amount for **d = 0.0.**

3. For **d = 0.5,** the subject is still in the majority. If the opposing two agree, their alternative position could form a majority if the voter changed to it. The vote change likelihood is twice as high if the others agree (8.3%) than if they disagree (3.8%).

4. For **d = 0.75,** the individual is now in a minority of two, so vote change rises dramatically to 35%. Again, it is higher if the others all agree (45%) than if they disagree (15%). Even if they disagree, the vote change is still twice that found than when **d = 0.5.**

5. When **d = 1.0,** the subject disagrees with everyone else, so are unlikely to form a majority. In this case, four disagreeing with the subject produces no more effect than three, so perhaps a normative threshold has been reached. In this case, the maximum vote change pattern is ABBCC, where two other options compete for the group majority, that is, where the group member has the casting vote.

Table 7: Percent vote change by individual disagreement

Vote 2	Individual disagreement				
	0.0	0.25	0.5	0.75	1.0
% changed vote	0.8%	2.0%	7.1%	36.3%	72.6%
N	479	403	368	355	551

Table 8. Vote patterns, individual by rest of group disagreement

	Rest of group disagreement				
Individual disagreement	0.0 AAAA	0.5 AAAB	0.67 AABB	0.83 AABC	1.0 ABCD
0.00 Disagree with no one	AAAAA				
0.25 Disagree with one		AAAAB			
0.50 Disagree with two				AAABB AAABC	
0.75 Disagree with three		BAAAB		BAABC	BABCD
1.00 Disagree with all	DAAAA	DAAAB	DAABB	DAABC	

Table 9. Vote change by d & Drest

	Rest of group disagreement (Drest)				
Individual disagreement (d) when choosing option A	0.0 AAAA	0.5 AAAB	0.67 AABB	0.83 AABC	1.0 ABCD
0.00 Disagree with no one	1.0% (1625)				
0.25 Disagree with one		2.9% (886)			
0.50 Disagree with two			8.3% (289)	3.8% (261)	
	AAAA	ABBB	BBCC	ABBC	ABCD
0.75 Disagree with three		45.0% (238)		25.3% (190)	14.7% (34)
	BBBB	BBBC	BBCC	BBCD	ABCD
1.00 Disagree with all	66.1% (369)	68.4% (247)	77.0% (61)	60.3% (78)	

The above suggests the following propositions on how group members create agreement:

1. **Inertia:** Individuals will tend to maintain their previously adopted position (about 75%).
2. **Isolation:** Individuals will change if their current position is unlikely to form a majority (0-45%).
3. **Conformity:** Individuals will change if an alternative option is likely to form a majority (2-20%).

A small amount of random change can also be expected to occur, at about 1%. These propositions could form the basis of a computer simulation of normative group behavior.

CONCLUSION

Disagreement is an important group output; for example, a group may resolve an issue by majority vote, yet still spend time discussing to reduce disagreements. If groups see agreement as important, then it is important to measure it. Facilitators can use online agreement measures taken prior to a meeting to adapt their meeting style for groups with higher disagreement. A group may find feedback on whether their agreement is going up or down over time useful. Quantifying the agreement a meeting produces can make it easier to justify the time groups spend generating agreement. These measures are particularly suitable in computer-mediated groups, where disagreement can be computer calculated. A standardized measure of group disagreement can be used in a wide variety of online situations.

REFERENCES

Adrianson, L., & Hjelmquist, E. (1991). Group processes in face-to-face and computer-mediated communication. *Behaviour and Information Technology, 10*, 281-296.

Arrow, K. (1963). *Social choice and individual values* (2nd ed.). London: Yale University Press.

Andrews, P. H. (1992). Group conformity. In R. S. Cathcart & L. A. Samovar (Eds.), *Small group communication: A reader* (pp. 205-213). Dubuque, IA: Wm C. Brown.

Asch, S. E. (1952). *Social psychology.* New York: Prentice Hall.

Daft, R. L., Lengel, R. H., & Trevino, L. K. (1987). Message equivocality, media selection, and manager performance: Implications for information systems. *Management Information Systems Quarterly, 11*, 354-366.

Dennis, A. R. (1996). Information exchange and use in small group decision making. *Small Group Research, 27*(4), 532-550.

DeSanctis, G., & Gallupe, R. B. (1987). A foundation for the study of group decision support systems. *Management Science, 33*(5), 589-609.

Dimock, H. G. (1986). *Groups: Leadership and group development*. San Diego: University Associates.

Fjermestad, J., & Hiltz, R. (1999). An assessment of group support systems experimental research: Methodology and results. *Journal of Management Information Systems, 15*(3), 7-149.

Hiltz, S. R., Johnson, K., & Turoff, M. (1986). Experiments in group decision making: Communication process and outcome in face-to-face versus computerised conferences. *Human Communication Research, 13*(2), 225-252.

Ho, T. H., & Raman, K. S. (1991). The effects of GDSS and elected leadership on small group meetings. *Journal of Management Information Systems, 8*, 109-134.

Hoffman, L. R., & Maier, N. R. F. (1964). Valence in the adoption of solutions by problem-solving groups: Concept, method, and results. *Journal of Abnormal and Social Psychology, 69*(3), 264-271.

Hogg, M. A. (1992). *The social psychology of group cohesiveness*. London: Harvester, Wheatsheaf.

Hollingshead, A. B. (1993). Information, influence and technology in group decision making. Unpublished doctoral dissertation, University of Illinois, Urbana-Champaign.

Kraut, R., Galagher, J., Fish, R., & Chalfonte, B. (1992). Task requirements and media choice in collaborative writing. *Human Computer Interaction, 7*, 375-407.

Lea, M., & Spears, R. (1991). Computer-mediated communication, de-individuation and group decision making. *International Journal of Man-Machine Studies, 34*, 283-301.

Lorge, I., Fox, D., Davitz, J., & Brenner, M. (1958). A survey of studies contrasting the quality of group performance and individual performance. *Psychological Bulletin, 55*(6), 337-372.

Maier, N. R. F. (1963). *Problem solving discussions and conferences*. New York: McGraw-Hill.

Marckwardt, A. H., Cassidy, F. G., & McMillan, J. G. (Eds.). (1992). *Webster comprehensive dictionary: Encyclopedic edition*. Chicago: J. G. Ferguson Publishing Company.

McGrath, J. E., & Hollingshead, A. B. (1991, January). *Interaction and performance in computer assisted work groups*. Paper presented at the Conference on Team Decision Making in Organizations, University of Maryland.

McGuire, T. W., Kiesler, S., & Siegel, J. (1987). Group and computer-mediated discussion effects in risk decision making. *Journal of Personality and Social Psychology, 52*(5), 917-930.

McLeod, P. L. (1992). An assessment of the experimental literature on electronic support of group work: Results of a meta-analysis. *Human Computer Interaction, 7*, 257-280.

Owen, W. F. (1985). Metaphor analysis of cohesiveness in small discussion groups. *Small Group Behaviour, 16*, 415-424.

Pielou, E. C. (1969). *An introduction to mathematical ecology*. New York: John Wiley.

Pinsonneault, A., & Kraemer, K. L. (1989). The impact of technological support on groups: An assessment of the empirical research. *Decision Support Systems, 5*, 197-216.

Postmes, T., & Spears, R. (1998). Deindividuation and antinormative behaviour: *A meta-analysis. Psychological Bulletin, 123*(3), 1-22.

Reeves, B. N., & Lemke, A. C. (1991, Jan). The problem as a moving target in cooperative system design. In *1991 HCI Consortium Workshop*.

Sambamurthy, V., & Chin, W. (1994). The effects of group attitudes towards alternative GDSS designs on the decision-making performance of computer-supported groups. *Decision Sciences, 25*(2), 215-241.

Sherif, M. (1936). *The psychology of social norms*. New York: Harper.

Siegel, J., Dubrovsky, V., Kiesler, Kiesler, S., & McGuire, T. W. (1986). Group processes in computer-mediated communication. *Organisational Behaviour and Human Decision Processes, 27*, 157-187.

Sniezek, J. (1992). Groups under uncertainty: An examination of confidence in group decision making. *Organizational Behaviour and Human Decision Processes, 52*, 124-155.

Spillman, B., Spillman, R., & Bezdek, J. (1980). A fuzzy analysis of consensus in small groups. In P. P. Wang & S. K. Chang (Eds.), *Fuzzy sets: Theory and application to policy analysis and information systems* (pp. 291-308). New York: Plenum.

Straus, S. G. (1996). Getting a clue: The effects of communication media and information distribution on participation and performance in computer-mediated and face-to-face groups. *Small Group Research, 27*(1), 115-142.

Tan, B. C., Teo, H. H., & Wei, K. K. (1995). Promoting consensus in small decision making groups. *Information and Management, 28*(4), 251-259.

Tan, B. C., Wei, K., & Krishnamurthy, S. R. (1991, May). *Effects of support and task type on group decision outcome: A study using SAMM*. Paper presented at the Proceedings of the 24th Hawaii International Conference on System Sciences, Honolulu, HI.

Watson, R. T., DeSanctis, G., & Poole, M. S. (1988, Sep). Using a GDSS to facilitate group consensus: Some intended and unintended consequences. *Management Information Systems Quarterly, 12*(3), 463-478.

Weisband, S. P. (1992). Discussion and first advocacy effects in computer-mediated and face-to-face decision making groups. *Organizational Behavior and Human Decision Processes, 53*, 352-380.

Whitworth, B., & Felton, R. (1999). Measuring disagreement in groups facing limited choice problems. *THE DATABASE for Advances in Information Systems, 30*(3 & 4), 22-33.

Whitworth, B., Gallupe, B., & McQueen, R. (2001). Generating agreement in computer-mediated groups. *Small Group Research, 32*(5), 621-661.

Whitworth, B., & McQueen, R. J. (2003). Voting before discussing: Electronic voting as social interaction. *Group Facilitation, 3*(1), 4-15.

KEY TERMS

Computer-Media Properties: The computer medium has different properties from a physical one; for example, *asynchrony* (the message sending and receiving can be independent of time). Another property is *media richness,* the ability of a medium to convey meaning. An important media property when enacting agreement is *linkage,* which can be one-to-one, one-to-many, or many-to-many. One-to-one occurs when two people converse, one-to-many occurs with any broadcast or speech, but many-to-many is less-well known. An example is a choir: each singer hears everyone else, and each contributes to the total sound. This is possible because air allows sound signals to merge, so many sounds can combine into one sound. **Normative Interaction** means the whole choir can move off key, but individuals will not. Many-to-many computer-mediated communications can occur if the information system is designed correctly, and allows many-to-many exchange of merged group member position information (Whitworth et al., 2001).

Computer-Mediated Communication (CMC): In face-to-face interaction, information is exchanged by physical world activity. In computer-mediated communication, a computer network replaces the physical world as the medium of communication. In one sense, all technology operates in a physical environment, but in another sense, the technology is the environment through which communication occurs. In this view, telephone, CMC, and face-to-face (FTF) are all just communication environments. FTF communication is just as mediated (by the physical world) as CMC is mediated by technology.

Disagreement, Group: The degree that members of a group adopt different positions, whether physical positions, as with a herd, or intellectual positions, as with a group voting on an issue (See **Group**). If everyone adopts the same position, then the disagreement is zero.

Disagreement, Individual: The degree that one member of a group adopts a different position from the rest of the group.

Equivocality: Can mean any ambiguity or uncertainty that involves two or more choices, but in information systems, it generally means uncertainty that cannot be resolved by gathering or analyzing information (Daft, Lengel, & Trevino, 1987), for example:

1. Social decisions, like how people greet each other, that are enacted by social norms, where "right" is simply what everyone does.
2. Relational decisions, like who to marry, where how one decides affects the outcome; for example, if one commits to another that commitment can make the decision "right."
3. Wicked problems where what is unknown is not just the problem but its context, as when a group must decide how it will make decisions before it can begin to make a decision (Reeves & Lemke, 1991).

In equivocal situations, groups enact decisions using **Normative Interaction**.

Group: Though there are many definitions of "group" (e.g., see Hogg, 1992, p. 4), a generally accepted one is any set of people who consider themselves to be a group (DeSanctis & Gallupe,

1987). The group in this sense emerges from the perceptions of its members as being part of it, and so is distinct from a simple aggregate or set of entities.

Normative Interaction: Normative interaction is a social process whereby members try to match their behavior to what they see as the group position. This "conformity" seems the prime force generating agreement in groups. Unlike rational analysis, it does not need verbal interaction, and unlike interpersonal interaction, it works with any size group. Social identity theory (Hogg, 1992) offers a psychological basis, namely that members identify with groups to which they belong; for example, U.S. citizens identify themselves as "American," even though that group contains millions. Normative interaction requires that group members are aware the position of the rest of the group, each individual is carefully "positioning" themselves so as not to be out of step with the rest of the group, maintaining the identity of the group and consequently, their own identity as a part of that group. A high-linkage medium can do this. See **Computer-Media Properties**.

Chapter XX
Measuring Cognitive Load

Nanette M. Hogg
University of Nebraska at Kearney, USA

ABSTRACT

Cognitive load theory describes learning, in terms of a processing system, when all too often, working memory is overloaded and learning is impeded. Measuring cognitive load is an important component of research in the area of information processing. The design, delivery, and administration of an instrument, as well as its reliability and validity, are discussed as a solution to the measurement of cognitive load. A nine-point subjective rating scale ranging from very, very low (1) to very, very high (9) measures cognitive load, defined as the mental effort needed to complete a task. It is a replica of the instrument used by Paas (1992) and Paas and van Merriënboer (1994). The measurement instrument can be used both on paper and on the Web.

INTRODUCTION

Cognitive load theory (Sweller, 1988; 1994) is an instructional theory, based on the discipline of cognitive science, that describes learning in terms of a processing system, the working memory, and a storage system, which is long-term memory. Information is stored in long-term memory after working memory processes it. Working memory, however, is extremely limited in both capacity and duration, making it difficult to process complex information. These limitations may be increased due to poorly designed instruction and instructional materials, thereby, obstructing the learning process.

BACKGROUND

Cognitive load is defined as the processing of information that occurs in working memory. For example, while learning the English language, word meanings, word types, (nouns, verbs, adjectives, and adverbs), and word order must be considered. Word meanings, types, and order are all single elements that can be learned individually and processed in short-term memory. As the individual elements are learned, a building block of information forms a schema to categorize information that combines the interaction of the single elements. For example, the building block could include the adjective "green" that describes a noun and the placement of that adjective before the noun. The term "green tree" is the interaction of two elements, the adjective and noun. When multiple elements that interact are categorized, they can form a schema. In this example, an entire grammatically correct sentence can be constructed with each word interacting correctly with the other words. When each word must be considered as well as the interaction with the other words, a great amount of processing would occur in the working memory. When the schemata for the English language are in place, the sentence is constructed without having to process the individual elements and the interaction of those elements.

Cognitive load theory (CLT) promotes ways to design instructional materials to reduce cognitive load on the working memory. The basis of this theory states that when extra burdens are placed on the working memory, the limited capacity prevents schemata acquisition. When too much information is readily available or the materials are poorly designed, burdensome restraints are placed on the limited space of the working memory and learning is impeded. Learning may fail, not necessarily due to the complexity of the information, but because of the way the instruction is presented, wasting the use of cognitive resources. Sweller (1988) suggested that in order for learning to take place, information must be processed in the working memory and stored in long-term memory, which is unlimited and holds huge numbers of schemata. Instructional materials should be designed in such a way as to minimize the use of working memory resources in order to facilitate an increase in the construction of the schemata.

Cognitive load theory indicates that working memory must organize and process information before schemata are constructed. Then, once schemata are constructed, the individual must use the knowledge. This can be accomplished efficiently through transfer or automation. Transfer occurs when one or more schemata are consciously brought into working memory as a single element and applied to a new or different situation. Automation occurs when the schemata are unconsciously

used in a situation. Continuing with the same example, the process of sentence construction is somewhat automatic for most English-speaking people, so the word types and word order do not need to be considered. The cognitive processing of elements can occur anywhere on a spectrum from complete conscious control to full automation. Prior to automation, cognitive processing can take place with conscious control. Sweller (1994) tells us that with time and practice, a specific process can become automated. Once a schema is fully automated, it is stored in long-term memory and can act as a single element in a more complex task. At the fully automated level, the more complex task also can act as an element in yet a more complex task. Cognitive load and the working memory resources are greatly reduced when automation occurs, so more working memory is available to process other information.

Cognitive load can be classified into categories and discussed as levels of processing in the working memory. Intrinsic cognitive load is the processing in working memory that must occur for the task at hand, such as the task of processing the elements to learn the English language. Intrinsic cognitive load cannot be determined by the number of elements. It can only be determined by the interactivity between the elements, no matter if the number of elements is small or large. Learning information that is not based on knowledge of other elements has low intrinsic cognitive load and does not require much processing in the working memory. This type of learning is usually in a serial fashion, or in isolation, such as the colors. The color green is learned and the color red is learned without interaction between the two or without interaction with other elements. A higher level of intrinsic cognitive load is required when the task at hand needs simulation of new information or previous knowledge. The adjectives and nouns are known; now the sentence must be constructed using previously known elements and perhaps new elements, such as order. Intrinsic cognitive load is difficult to measure and unlikely to be controlled, especially since the number of interacting elements that must be learned simultaneously is an estimate based on the knowledge of the learner.

Theorists recently have begun to distinguish between two other types of cognitive load: extraneous and germane cognitive load (Van Gerven, Paas, van Merriënboer, & Schmidt, 2000, 2002). Extraneous cognitive load does not contribute to learning. Extraneous cognitive load would be additional processing that results from other factors, such as the design of the instructional materials. For example, if the word types: nouns, verbs, or adjectives, their rules, their placement in the sentence, and the dual meanings of the words, are all presented together, the design of the material would be adding to the extraneous cognitive load for a novice. When a learner must deal with poorly designed or poorly organized materials, cognitive processes are used to assimilate the materials, leaving little or no resources to devote to learning.

Unlike extraneous cognitive load, germane cognitive load, the more recent term, refers to the processing capacity used to construct schema. The goal would be to have enough space in working memory to allow for germane cognitive load to process the types of words, which words and their location would be used in the sentence. This processing can begin the construction of the schema. Germane cognitive load is closely related to extraneous cognitive load because it can be manipulated or promoted as a result of instructional design. Working memory must process the intrinsic and extraneous cognitive load, leaving the remainder of the capacity for germane cognitive load. While intrinsic cognitive load cannot be reduced, altering the design of the instructional materials can decrease extraneous cognitive load. Reducing extraneous cognitive load will increase cognitive capacity. "The more cognitive capacity, the more germane cognitive load can be imposed on the learner" (Van Gerven et al., 2000, p. 516). Sweller, van Merriënboer, and Paas (1998) point out that germane cognitive load can reflect the

effort that contributes to the construction of schemata, and "appropriate instructional designs decrease extraneous cognitive load but increase germane cognitive load" (p. 259).

The focus of cognitive load theory in several of these studies is the development of instruction and instructional materials that could reduce extraneous cognitive load and promote germane cognitive load, that is, schema acquisition. The studies on variability are of special interest because the results showed the effect can increase germane cognitive load, while keeping extraneous cognitive to a minimum. Germane cognitive load is relevant to learning and benefits schema

Figure 1. Three types of cognitive load are present during learning. Intrinsic cognitive load is determined by the interactivity of the elements in the task. The designs of the instructional materials contribute to germane or extraneous cognitive load.

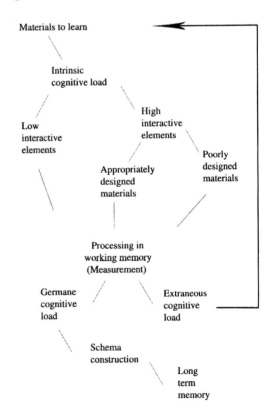

construction. However, it is important to keep in mind that modification to instructional materials is appropriate only for tasks with high intrinsic cognitive load, determined by the amount of interacting elements. If items are learned in a serial fashion, or in isolation, instructional design may not be an issue. However, students using learning materials that include high interactive elements may experience cognitive overload; thereby, benefiting from first learning those elements in isolation before attempting to understand the interaction among the elements. Figure 1 shows the distinct types of cognitive load during the flow of information. The flow starts with intrinsic cognitive load based on the materials to learn, and proceeds through working memory to long-term memory. Extraneous cognitive load is present when the elements are interacting with each other and the design of the instruction is poor. Extraneous cognitive load may impede schema construction and thereby, obstruct learning. Measuring cognitive load can help identify materials that are inappropriate for the learner.

MEASURING COGNITIVE LOAD

The early work with the cognitive load theory was limited by problems of measuring cognitive load. Measuring cognitive load for a majority of the research prior to 1992 was based on student performance. Sweller (1988) used a secondary

task as a computation model to provide evidence that cognitive load could be reduced. A secondary task required the subject to respond to or complete a different activity, other than the primary task. Response time and completion of the secondary task were considered the amount of cognitive load, placed on the learner, as a result of the primary task. Secondary tasks could be difficult to administer and jeopardized the primary task performance. Physiological measures, including heart rate, and brain and eye activity, were additional measures of cognitive load. These measurements, which could be costly and intrusive, were not readily available, and were found to be unreliable, detecting and measuring only large differences in cognitive load. Chandler and Sweller (1991, 1992) also used processing time of instruction, which they suggested was a valid, indirect measure of cognitive load. A direct measure of cognitive load was needed for research studies.

Cognitive Load Rating Scale

Concerned with the interference from a secondary task, Paas (1992) used a subjective technique, based on rating scales of task difficulty, that allowed the participant to rate the mental effort needed to complete the primary task. Since that time, subjective and physiological measurement techniques have been used in studies of cognitive load. Since the original use of the subjective rating scale (Paas, 1992; Paas & van Merriënboer,

Figure 2. A cognitive load rating scale appears on a computer screen each time a participant is asked to rate their mental effort

Please rate your mental effort required to complete this question:

1	2	3	4	5	6	7	8	9
very very low mental effort	very low mental effort	low mental effort	minimal mental effort	neither high nor low mental effort	some mental effort	high mental effort	very high mental effort	very very high mental effort
O	O	O	O	◉	O	O	O	O

1993), a variety of labels and point systems have been attempted using a Likert scale to measure cognitive load. Results have varied greatly due to the use of altered rating scales.

The subjective rating scale, shown in Figure 2, was a replica of the rating scale for measuring perceived mental effort used by Paas (1992) and Paas and van Merriënboer (1994). The rating scale was a 9-point Likert scale labeled from 1 as very, very low to 9 as very, very high mental effort, with 1 indicating the lowest perceived mental effort and 9 indicating the highest required mental effort. This subjective rating scale is now used frequently and has been verified as reliable.

Reliability and Validity

Paas (1992) compared measurement techniques for mental effort and found the subjective rating scales as reliable, highly correlated with objective measures, valid, nonintrusive, and, most important, sensitive to relatively small differences in cognitive load. According to Paas and van Merriënboer (1993), the intensity of effort being expended by learners can be considered the essence of a reliable estimate of cognitive load. Marcus, Cooper, and Sweller (1996) support Paas' (1992) view of subjective measures of task difficulty. They recommend the subjective measure over secondary tasks. They agreed that secondary tasks intrude on the primary task performance. The validity and reliability of the subjective rating scale to measure cognitive load will remain stable when the wording remains the same and no physical activity is required from the subject (Marcus et al., 1996). In 1994, Paas, van Merriënboer and Adam's evaluation of subjective and physiological measurement techniques showed that this subjective rating scale was sensitive to relatively small differences in cognitive load, and that it was valid, reliable, and nonintrusive, concluding that this subjective rating scale was the most promising measurement technique for use in research of the cognitive load theory. Since

1996, research that has measured the cognitive load placed on subjects has used this rating scale. To date, no better method of rating has been found, and the validity and reliability of the original 9-point Likert scale has been very consistent.

Rating Scale Administration

Marcus et al., (1996) gave three recommendations for subjective ratings of mental effort. The rating scale should be administered immediately after the task; the wording of the scale should be considered carefully; and the rating should require minimal, if any, physical activity, since participants may confuse mental and physical workload. The scale meets these requirements in both print and on the Web. The rating scale of the perceived mental effort, that is, cognitive load, can be recorded for each section of instructional material, each task, or each test question; any item that needs cognitive load measured. The electronic administration of the rating scale has many advantages over the printed version. The printed rating scale can be placed after any items with the assumption that the participant will record the perceived mental effort. However, a computerized administration can provide additional features. The electronic Likert scale, like the printed copy, needs to be consistent throughout the entire program, and as simple as possible. When the scale is set up as radio buttons and displayed on a Web page, the user can click with the mouse to make a choice, can change the choice, but can be restricted to one choice. The computerized system can also prevent the next item from appearing until the mental effort is recorded.

FUTURE STUDIES

Paas and van Merriënboer (1993) developed a measurement of training efficiency that has been used to determine relationships between subjective ratings of mental effort and performance scores.

Training efficiency is an additional measure that is widely used and is both reliable and easily obtainable for experimental conditions. Paas and van Merriënboer used it to predict the total effect on cognitive load when one study was attempting to both decrease extraneous cognitive load and increase germane cognitive load. "The calculation of training efficiency is based on the standardization of raw mental effort scores and performance scores across conditions to z-scores" (van Merriënboer, Schuurman, de Crook, & Paas, 2002, p. 16). Since the performance scores are a standard, reliable measurement, and subjective ratings of mental effort are shown to be also, training efficiency should become another important consideration for measuring work in the cognitive theories. An example of the training efficiency measure can be seen in the work of Tuovinen and Sweller (1999) using a FileMaker Pro database. It is reasonable to think that a time component could also be incorporated into the training efficiency measurement, as computerized systems are readily available to collect time sensitive data.

CONCLUSION

Working memory is extremely limited in both capacity and duration, making it difficult to process complex information. Measuring cognitive load is essential to the understanding of the learning process. Secondary task and physiological measures are not appropriate, whereas a subjective rating scale meets the criteria for a reliable measurement of cognitive load. Additional measurements can be developed based on the rating scale.

REFERENCES

Chandler, P., & Sweller, J. (1991). Cognitive load theory and the format of instruction. *Cognition and Instruction, 8*(4), 293-332.

Chandler, P., & Sweller, J. (1992). The split-attention effect as a factor in the design of instruction. *British Journal of Educational Psychology, 62,* 233-246.

Kalyuga, S., Ayres, P., Chandler, P., & Sweller, J. (2003). The expertise reversal effect. *Educational Psychologist, 38*(1), 23-31.

Leung, M., Low, R., & Sweller, J. (1997). Learning from equations or words. *Instructional Science, 25*(1) 37-70.

Marcus, N., Cooper, M., & Sweller, J. (1996). Understanding instructions. *Journal of Educational Psychology, 88*(1), 49-63.

Paas, F. G. W. C. (1992). Training strategies for attaining transfer of problem-solving skill in statistics: A cognitive-load approach. *Journal of Educational Psychology, 84,* 429-434.

Paas, F. G. W. C., & van Merriënboer, J. J. G. (1993). The efficiency of instructional conditions: An approach to combine mental-effort and performance measures. *Human Factors, 35,* 737-743.

Paas, F. G. W. C., & van Merriënboer, J. J. G. (1994). Instructional control of cognitive load in the training of complex cognitive task. *Educational Psychology Review, 6,* 51-71.

Paas, F. G. W. C., van Merriënboer, J. J. G., & Adam, J. J. (1994). Measurement of cognitive load in instructional research. *Perceptual and Motor Skills, 79,* 419-430.

Sweller, J. (1988). Cognitive load during problem solving: Effects on learning. *Cognitive Science, 12,* 257-285.

Sweller, J. (1994). Cognitive load theory, learning difficulty, and instructional design. *Learning and Instruction, 4,* 295-312.

Sweller, J., van Merriënboer, J. J. G., & Paas, F. G. W. C. (1998). Cognitive architecture and instructional design. *Educational Psychology Review, 10*(3), 251-296.

Tuovinen, J. E., & Sweller, J. (1999). A comparison of cognitive load associated with discovery learning and worked examples. *Journal of Educational Psychology, 91*(2), 334-341.

Van Gerven, P. W. M., Paas, F. G. W. C., van Merriënboer, J. J. G., & Schmidt, H. G. (2000). Cognitive load theory and the acquisition of complex cognitive skills in the elderly: Towards an integrative framework. *Educational Gerontology, 26*(6), 503-521.

Van Gerven, P. W. M., Paas, F. G. W. C., van Merriënboer, J. J. G., & Schmidt, H. G. (2002). Cognitive load theory and aging: Effects of worked examples on training efficiency. *Learning and Instruction, 12*(1), 87-105.

van Merriënboer, J. J. G., Schuurman, J. G., de Croock, M. B. M., & Paas, F. G. W. C. (2002). Redirecting learners' attention during training: Effects on cognitive load, transfer test performance and training efficiency. *Learning and Instruction, 12*(1), 11-37.

KEY TERMS

Automation: Automation of schema is an optimal circumstance during learning that occurs when a schema is brought into the working memory unconsciously or bypasses working memory altogether.

Cognitive Load: Cognitive load is the total of extraneous, germane, and intrinsic cognitive load. It is the total processing that occurs in working memory.

Extraneous Cognitive Load: Extraneous cognitive load is the cognitive load placed on the learner, usually as a result of instructional design and or task organization.

Germane Cognitive Load: Germane cognitive load refers to the processing capacity in the working memory used to construct schema.

Interacting Elements: Interactive elements can be likened to the ingredients in the instructional material. Low interaction consists of learning a single ingredient (element), whereas high interaction consists of learning ingredients (elements) and their interaction with other ingredients and therefore, must be learned simultaneously rather than as individual elements (Kalyuga, Ayres, Chandler, & Sweller, 2003).

Intrinsic Cognitive Load: Intrinsic cognitive load is the cognitive load in the working memory that results from the task at hand.

Schema: Schema (plural: schemata) is a cognitive construct that categorizes information according to the manner in which it will be used (Leung, Low, & Sweller, 1997). This definition is based on the schema theory of the early 1980s that states that cognitive construction permits an individual to treat multiple elements of information as a single element, categorized according to the manner in which it will be used (Marcus et al., 1996). Multiple elements should refer to those that interact with each other.

Transfer: Transfer occurs when one or more schemata are consciously brought into working memory and processed to be applied to a new or different situation.

Chapter XXI
Surveying Online Scholarship

J. D. Wallace
Lubbock Christian University, USA

ABSTRACT

Part of the importance of descriptive studies, such as surveys, is the identification of directions and issues that can be pursued in future research. Surveying online scholarship helps scholars to identify component features of their fields reflecting where research scrutiny and deficiencies reside. Online access is providing users with the ability to survey exhaustive datasets available previously to a relatively few information scientists. Because of the relative newness of this level of access, scholars outside information and library science are just beginning to wrestle with issues that have a mature but somewhat obscured literature available. This chapter describes technologies, components, and possible analytical techniques related to some of these struggles. Specifically, it addresses their use in examining trends, producers, artifacts, and concepts of scholarly communication. Additionally, it provides a targeted application of these components to the literature concerning computer-mediated communication.

INTRODUCTION

The original "reality television show" was not "Survivor" or any of a number of other so-called "reality" shows. For many, the original reality television show was sports television. It has all the attributes of reality TV (no script, drama, relatively economical production costs); however, it tends not to be viewed as reality television because it does not fit the current manifestation model. For this author, the original "online research" was not Web-based surveys, or any of a number of current manifestations. It was database research in the university library (Wallace, 1999). It has many of the attributes of online research (computer use, data from distributed locations, methodological

strengths and weaknesses). While Web-based online research is substantial, the current Web-centric manifestation may tend to obscure some of the more obvious and prolific forms of research in computer-mediated environments.

To be sure, the publication, procurement, and production of online research is fraught with many of the difficulties inherent in computer-mediated communication (CMC). As early as 1984, Kiesler, Siegel, and McGuire offered the generic distinction that "electronic communication differs from any other communication in time, space, ease of use, audience, and opportunity for feedback" (p. 1127). McClure (1991) puts the implications in a clearer light when he states that: "The advent of CMC has created new communication needs

(Hellerstein, 1985, 1986) and has encouraged the emergence of patterns of communicative change which did not previously exist" (p. 58).

SURVEYING SCHOLARLY COMMUNICATION

There are any number of ways to review a literature, from simple compilation of bibliographies to more sophisticated meta-analytical and bibliometric techniques. The publication manual of the American Psychological Association articulates the usefulness of reviews in: " ... organizing, integrating, and evaluating previously published material..." (American Psychological Association, 2001, p. 7). All of these methods have inherent strengths and weaknesses. Choosing among them is often determined by ends desired, resources available, and value for resources expended. The following sections discuss three broad categories of describing and synthesizing literature: qualitative, quantitative, and bibliometric. Then it expands the discussion to include a more comprehensive treatment of scholarly communication.

Qualitative literature examination. Some of the most common qualitative examinations of literature include bibliographies and literature reviews. The existence of bibliographies concerning CMC supports its position as an increasingly prevalent area of study. Extensive bibliographies both accompany literature reviews, and are a source of publication themselves (e.g., Romiszowski, 1992). Possibly because the individuals who study CMC tend to be users, they seem to avail themselves of the Internet as an outlet. The Internet provides a number of notable bibliographies containing hundreds of references specifically targeting the CMC literature base (e.g., Shah, 1999; Walther, 2004). These reviews bring with them the informed view of their respective authors. These views often disseminate nuances of the relevant and significant, while discarding the unnecessary. The weakness of bibliographical description is that, while they do

contain many pertinent examples of a given field, they do little to tell about the general make-up of what the examples include. Also, bibliographies are typically more closely aligned to the research forays of their producers than to a generalizable literature (Chung, 1994; Rubincam, 1987).

Rosenthal (1991) points out that even the most rigorous reviews have difficulty in providing more than cursory descriptions. Moreover, these reviews are seldom exhaustive and hardly replicable, two qualities that help the scholastic community agree on a characterization of a field of study. While subjective reviews have value for the reasons previously stated, there is little chance for a common description of a literature to emerge. Quantitative methodologies are generally thought to be a less subjective approach to describing literatures as a whole, increasing the chances for a common description (Ely, 1990; Everett & Pecotich, 1991).

Quantitative literature examination. Content anaylsis is one way to develop a treatment of quantitative literature examinations. It has been articulated for almost half a century, and has long predominated in some literatures (Berelson, 1952; Dick & Blazek, 1995). There are any number of source materials for this technique (e.g., Holsti, 1969; Krippendorf, 2004). Content analysis can provide a preliminary glimpse into the strength of the purveyance of topic, word, or author within a given area. However, traditional content analysis tends to fall short in describing complex relationships within a sampling frame (Dick & Blazek, 1995; Everett & Pecotich, 1991; Krippendorf, 2004). This technique, with its widest interpretation, includes many of the bibliometric techniques to be discussed subsequently. Generally, however, it is thought of in reference to simple frequency comparison.

Another quantitative method is meta-analysis of literature in a particular area. Meta-analytic studies are able to discern consistent levels of significance over a range of literature. Their focus, by design, must be confined to a narrowly defined variable, experimented upon in comparable conditions. Moreover, they are dependent on that literature to provide a large enough database to make a credible generalization (Hunter & Scmidt, 1990; Rosenthal, 1991). Forays using this procedure, such as Walther, Anderson, and Park (1994), lack sufficient studies to deliver more than a preliminary glimpse into an area of study such as CMC. Emerging specialties, like CMC, benefit from a broader range of analytical approaches in order to decipher the chaotic dynamics often inherent in their makeup (McCain & Whitney, 1994).

Survey techniques are useful both from a descriptive and historical point of view. They can help pinpoint a topic's core, demarcating in what journals a topic is most likely to reside. This core can, in turn, be used to examine what are the dominant issues in relation to a topic. Borgman and Rice (1992) recount a number of studies utilizing surveys to establish core journals by examining "... journals read by those surveyed (Coblans, 1972; Dansey, 1973, Hansen & Tilbury, 1963; Swicher & Smith, 1982), a survey of authors publishing in one journal of where else they publish (Meadows & Zaborowski, 1979; Reeves & Borgman, 1983) ..." (p. 398). Surveys can help establish an informed consensus about what an area of study includes, and establish prominent issues within a field (Schloegl & Stock, 2004). While more in tune with quantitative description, surveys have structural weaknesses that seem to predominate their use. These have included a number of methodological drawbacks such as subjectivity of opinion, nonresponse, and rater bias toward a particular entity (Everett & Pecotich, 1991; Jobber & Simpson, 1988).

Bibliometric analysis. As more research shifts to online venues, it seems natural to investigate that research utilizing the very tools required for access. Library information science provides a host of techniques that are well suited for this enterprise. Under the category of bibliometrics, one can describe the overall aspects of online literature in a quantifiable, interpretable, and reliable manner (Hinze, 1994; McCain & Whitney, 1994; Moed, 1989; Paisley, 1989; Tijsen, 1992; Ungern-Steenberg, 1995). Lievrouw (1990) states that "bibliometric studies are of interest to communication researchers because scholarly communication artifacts result directly from a process that involves, first, the authors' expression of their own and others' expert ideas" (p. 61). The genesis of this statement came from a revision of Lievrouw (1989), where the strength of communication analysis is because scientific articles are "written according to a strict set of convention" (p. 616). Secondly, the " ... appearance of the article in print is usually taken to indicate that communication has also occurred among the author and the evaluators" (p. 617). Online and Internet research is starting to approach a point that library science had realized early in their development. There is an integration among persons, networks, and institutions (Wellman, 2004).

Pritchard's (1969) definition of bibliometrics is widely accepted as an authority on defining the basic assumptions (Borgman, 1989; Tijssen, 1992). One rendering of the definition simply refers to bibliometrics as the " ... mathematical and statistical analysis of patterns that arise in the publication and use of documents" (Diodato, 1994, p. ix). Arguably, it could be considered a form of content analysis. However, Paisley (1989, p. 707) distinguishes bibliometrics from content analysis because it uses a categorical system based on "extrinsic facts" about the publication (e.g., when, where, who, etc.). Content analysis, on the other hand, is more intrinsic in nature because " ... of the need to develop coding categories based on a theory of the relationship of the text to intentions, effects, and the symbolic environment" (p. 707)[1]. Regardless, bibliometrics has taken a prominent role in the description of scholarly literature's communication patterns (Borgman, 1989; Diodato, 1994; Jarneving, 2005; Rice et al., 1996).

A number of techniques, familiar to most social scientists, have been employed to help analyze the bibliometric structure of a literature and, subsequently, the field it represents. These include traditional statistical methodologies such as cluster analysis, factor analysis, multidimensional scaling, and multiple linear regression (e.g., Campanario, 1995; Frandsen, 2005; Spasser, 1997).

While structural methodologies are varied, examination has traditionally been based on two forms of data analyses. Probably the best recognized technique is citation analysis (Borgman, 1989; Diodato, 1994). Currently, the most used forms of citation analyses are cocitation analysis and bibliographic coupling. Both provide useful examinations with some differentiation in their final descriptions (Jarrneving, 2005). Cocitation analyses examines when journals, articles, or authors are cited together. Bibliographic coupling examines when "two documents each have citations to one or more of the same publication(s)" (Diodato, 1994, p. 12).

The second area of analyses is commonly called co-word analysis. Instead of examining the relationship between citations, co-word analysis examines "the co-occurrence of two or more words in one document or in different documents" (Diodato, 1994, p. 54). It is more focused on the content of a research area as opposed to the internal relationships of the literature (Cambrosio, Limoges, Courtial, & Laville, 1993). Co-word analysis has been described as particularly useful in the actual content of the research in a particular field of study (Callon, Courtial, & Laville, 1991; Courtial, 1994; Hinze, 1994; Ungern-Steenberg, 1995). It has a particular strength in the articulation of disjoint literatures such as CMC (Stegmann & Grohmann, 2005).

Local vendors of research, such as Proquest, are starting to provide their users with bibliographic data such as cocitations. Research in the past has revealed component features of an area of study including density of literature, core journals, and frequency and relationships between a variety of concepts (e.g., publications, key words, citations, authors, and universities).

COMPONENTS OF SCHOLARLY COMMUNICATION

Borgman (1989) gives an overview of the bibliometric techniques and their relation to social science, in general, and communication specifically, with a ". . . model for the intersection of bibliometric and scholarly communication" (p.586). The model puts the variables studied by the technique into three categories: artifacts, producers, and concepts. While bibliometric theory provides guidance in terms of artifacts, producers, and concepts, it does not present an absolute methodology. Defining any sampling frame is difficult, and literature domains are no different in this respect. Because producers and artifacts are so closely linked, their definitions are necessarily intertwined. Producers are simply the authors of the selected artifacts. However, artifacts can be defined as any number of forms of scholarly communication. Conceptually, they could range from working papers to books (Borgman, 1989). The issue involved is deciding how far to extend the analysis (Schloegl & Stock, 2004). Following is a description of some of the more accessible terminology and analytical techniques available to scholars that may not be as familiar to those outside of information science.

Artifacts. Artifacts are the output of the producers. They can include either direct or indirect representations of the communication activities of the producers. Commonly, they are reified as publications and convention papers of the producers. Borgman (1990) considers artifacts as foundational to the study of scholarly communication.

Most studies that use the individual article or book as a unit of analysis are considering the artifacts as the message, or the embodiment of an idea. Studies that use the journal as a unit of analysis are likely to view the artifact as the channel through which producers communicate with one another (p. 16).

Concerning analysis, one of the major defining characteristics or laws in bibliometrics is Bradford's law[2]. Formulated by Samuel Clement Bradford in 1934, this law states that a few journals will produce a large number of the articles, while a large number of journals will produce relatively few articles in a literature (Diodato, 1994). Core journals in bibliometrics have long been identified by Bradfordian analysis (Brookes, 1969; Diodato, 1994; Egghe, 1990; Goffman & Warren, 1969).

Diodato (1994) gives a general description on how the analysis is typically executed.

- identify many or all items (usually articles) published in this field;
- list the sources (usually journals) that publish the articles (or items) in rank order beginning with the source that produces the most items; and
- while retaining the order of the sources, divide this list into groups (or zones) so that the number of items produced by each group of sources is about the same (pp.16-17).

What this typically generates are zones with roughly the same number of articles produced by an increasing number of journals. The zone with the least number of journals contains the set of core journals. While it is generally thought that zones beyond the core zone must contain a greater number of journals, the question becomes, "how are these zones decided?" Zones could range from 2 to n, where n is the number of articles sampled. Bradford's original conceptualization recommended the use of three zones.

Because of predictable attributes, it should come as no surprise that journals have long been considered a strong entry point for bibliometric analysis, particularly for structural characteristics of a field or discipline (Campanario, 1995; Glaenzel & Moed, 2002; Price, 1965). Scholarly and academic journals are preferred over more popular outlets because of a more rigorous treatment of the subject at hand. They are the primary conduit to communicate theories, research methods, and research results of a given field of study. Furthermore, journals are easily accessible, searchable, and analyzable due to their predominance in storage mediums such as database vendors. Database vendors, such as the Institute for Scientific Information (ISI), provide access to thousands of scientific and social scientific journals with some bibliometric analysis tools included in the system (Schloegl & Stock, 2004). Data from these vendors typically can be accessed, purchased, and analyzed for a fee that is absorbed by either an individual or institution. Some researchers consider this a cost-effective vehicle for database acquisition (Ingwersen & Christensen, 1997). More fine-grained analyses consider issues involving how much weight to give various journals. Indicators range from frequency to more to advanced analyses that calculate journal impact (Glaenzel & Moed, 2002; Schloegl & Stock, 2004). Typically, libraries provide less extensive research capabilities from vendors such as ProQuest and EBSCO than ISI.

Producers. Producers are generally regarded as individual or corporate authors of scholarly communication. Frequency has long been utilized as an indication of producers' contributions (Brooks, 1989; Callon et al., 1991; Rice, Chapin, Pressman, & Funkhouser, 1996.) Frequency of publication at first seems to be straight foreword, but on closer examination produces many problems. Can you use frequency as a valid indicator of an author's contributions to literature (Glaenzel & Moed, 2002; Lindsey, 1980; Nicholls, 1989; Schloegl & Stock, 2004)? This issue has, at its' core, what the data is going to be used for. Even though it has been shown to be strongly correlated with peer judgments, compelling questions remain about how much weight this single factor should have on decisions of promotion or tenure (Cronin & Overfelt, 1994; Glaenzel & Moed, 2002; Narin, 1976; Schloegl & Stock, 2004). However, from a literature examination point of view, the artifact's value is stronger and less contentious.

Another contributor to these difficulties is the idea of multiple authorships. There are primarily three ways used to calculate frequency of authorship: complete, adjusted, and straight count (Diodato, 1994; Lindsey, 1980; Nicholls, 1989). Complete count is where an author is credited with a publication, regardless of where their name resides in a multiple authorship. Adjusted count gives the author fractional credit for a publication based on the number of coauthors. A single author would receive a count of one, dual authors would receive a count of one-half, and so on. Straight count only considers the first author. All others are not counted, making first authorship the only visible data in this kind of counting. It is considered the "simplest and least labor intensive" (Cronin & Overfelt, 1994, p. 61). The way that the count is obtained directly effects calculations and application of Lotka's law.

Lotka's law is another of the major laws in bibliometrics (Diodato, 1994). It is similar to Bradford's law except it involves authors instead of journals (Diodato, 1994). Lotka (1926) proposed that a relatively few number of authors would be prolific while most would not be. Generally, Lotka considered the amount of authors to contribute one entry to be about 60%. Burnham, Shearer, and Wall (1992) recount a figure close to 94% for authors contributing two or less journals.

The count impacts the analytical results, and many authors recommend the use of either complete or adjusted counts for a variety of ethical and pedagogical reasons (Glaenzel & Moed, 2002; Nichols, 1989; Schloegl & Stock, 2004). Straight count has the advantage of parsimony and efficiency. Adjusted and complete counts have the advantage of inclusion and granularity .The task of identifying core authors or producers of scholarly communication is fundamentally different from examining an individual author's strength of contribution. In this regard, after examining 70 empirical authorship distributions, Nichols (1989)

reluctantly concludes that Lotka's law is robust when either complete or straight count is used.

Concepts. Concepts are terms or words used by the producers themselves. This could include words in titles and text. It can also include: "assigned terminology or classification added through the publication process and studies that focus on the purpose or motivation of a citation" (Borgman, 1989 p. 588). These concepts can be used to help describe a structure that approximates the flow of ideas as they emerge, move, or fade within scientific or other communities (Borgman, 1989, 1990; Hinze, 1994; Paisley, 1989; Stegmann & Grohmann, 2005).

Concepts, by definition, need to have a direct link to the producers and artifacts (Borgman, 1989). While, technically, any word written by the producer can be considered a concept, some verbiage is considered negligible in value (Courtial, Callon, & Sigogneau, 1984; Dick & Blazek, 1995; Stegmann & Grohmann, 2005). Typically, key words are "indexing terms assigned to documents by an indexing service or by the authors of the documents." (Diodato, 1994, p. 54). Using key words and, specifically, the ". . . analysis of the co-occurrences of the key words used to index articles and other documents" (Ungern-Steenberg, 1995) has been described as particularly useful in the actual content of the research in a particular field of study (Callon et al., 1991; Stegmann & Grohmann, 2005). They can provide data typically aligned with content anaylsis, such as frequency of occurrence of a specific concept. Additionally, they provide relationship information that is seen as critical in describing scientific inquiry.

Courtial, Callon, and Sigogneau (1984) provide a brief description of the theory underlying the relevance of this relationship information. It is built on the premise that scientific inquiry is built on a series of problems that hinge upon their relationship with each other. It does not matter that there are often contradictions and conflicts involved as the problems are cast into the networks or "problematisations" by their various producers. This is considered representative of how research forms the basis on which scientific inquiry advances. "Co-word analysis represents an attempt to map the evolution and temporary stabilization of such problematisations" (Courtial, et al., 1984, p. 47). Some researchers make a distinction between co-word analysis and classification analysis. However, Hinze (1994) states that "it is assumed that coassigned classification codes or common key words reflect linkages between the papers concerned, and therefore, also between the underlying scientific and technological activities" (p. 354). Co-word analysis is seen as highly complimentary to more traditional historical and descriptive techniques (Cambrosio et al., 1993). As such, it is seen as an acceptable method for the identification of the conceptual base in which concepts reside (Courtial, 1984).

A glimpse into the semantic content of articles can be provided by a simple count of key word or indexing terms (Rice et al., 1996; Stegmann & Grohmann, 2005). Key words and indexing terms are considered more conservative in their estimation of the content of the article, and have a higher degree of stability than other indicators, such as the text itself or titles (Leydesdorff, 1997; Rice, et al., 1996). A higher frequency of key words indicates a greater number of journal articles addressing a particular subject area. A greater number of journal articles would suggest a particular problematisation being more dominant in the field (Courtial, 1994; Larsen & Levine, 2005; Stegmann & Grohmann, 2005). Breaking down such frequency counts by years helps establish the emergence and diminishing of such problematisations over time.

Using a CMC Exemplar for Bibliometric Issues

Identifying the domain. Because CMC is dispersed across a number of literatures, a single database such as ABI/INFORM might be inappropriate for a research frame (McCain & Whitney, 1994). One parsimonious solution suggested for this problem is to find a professional database that cuts across disciplinary lines (Spasser, 1997). However, an appropriate professional database does not appear to be readily apparent for CMC. Spasser (1997) offers guidance in this direction, suggesting that "... the problem could be approached, through the parallel analysis of combined databases with different disciplinary orientations, corresponding collectively, to the area under investigation ..." (p. 94). Multiple databases would appear to be a better treatment of this analysis, particularly when aligned with a range of perspectives. With the CMC artifacts being operationalized, a typical and appropriate operationalization of the producers is the authors of those artifacts (Borgman, 1990). Therefore, multiple databases provide a research frame from which to draw the artifacts, the level of analysis is at the journal level, and the producers are the authors of those journals.

Relationship of concepts. Because the ultimate dataset is perceived to be too large to be useful, some sort of parameters will have to be established. The literature provides many relevant examples from which to glean guidance. Rice et al. (1996) demarcated a frequency dataset of the top 200 terms. Courtial uses a linkage algorithm to reduce key word data by a factor of 10. Hinze (1994) used terms that occurred in at least 10 journals, capturing the majority of the total terms used. All of these methods would provide indications of where attention is being focused on CMC in the literature base. Once a dataset has been established, traditional data reduction techniques such as factor analysis, cluster analysis, multidimensional scaling, or regression derivatives can be utilized. As with all such techniques, algorithms and application impact such issues as level of granularity and typicality of results.

CONCLUSION

Part of the importance of descriptive studies is the direction and issues that can be pursued in future research. Many of these issues can be aligned with major categories within this chapter. The categories included descriptions of components and possible analytical techniques useful in examining trends, producers, artifacts, and concepts of scholarly communication. Bibliometric, information science, and communication scholars believe that this kind of analysis exposes characteristics and trends of scholarly communication (Borgman & Rice, 1992; Larson & Levine, 2005; Stegmann & Grohmann, 2005). Additionally, it provided a cursory application of those components to scholarly communication concerning CMC. This is important because of the accelerated changes in online research. Application of these techniques is quickly moving from a nicety engaged in by library science practitioners to a necessity of those from any background that would find literary analysis contributory to their respective field.

REFERENCES

American Psychological Association (APA). (2001). *Publication manual of the American Psychological Association* (5th ed.), Washington, DC: APA.

Berelson, B. (1952). *Content analysis in communication research*. Glencoe, IL: The Free Press.

Borgman, C. L. (1989). Bibliometrics and scholarly communication: Editors note. *Communication Research, 16*(5), 583-599.

Borgman, C. L. (Ed.). (1990). *Scholarly communication and bibliometrics*. Newbury Park, CA: Sage.

Borgman, C. L. & Rice, R. E. (1992). The convergence of information science and communication: A bibliometric analysis. *Journal of the American Society for Information Science, 43*(6), 397-411.

Brookes, B. C. (1969). Bradford's law and the bibliography of science. *Nature, 224*, 953-956.

Brooks, T. A. (1989). Core journals of the rapidly changing research front of "superconductivity." *Communication Research, 16*(5), 682-694.

Burnham, J. F, Shearer, B. S., & Wall, B. C. (1992). Combining new technologies for effective collection development: A bibliometric study using CD-ROM and a database management program. *Bulletin of theMmedical Library Association, 80*, 150-156.

Callon, M., Courtial, J. P., & Laville, F. (1991). Co-word analysis as a tool for describing the network of interactions between basic and technological research: The case of polymer chemistry. *Scientometrics, 22*(1), 155-205.

Cambrosio, A., Limoges, C., Courtial, J. P., & Laville, F. (1993). Historical scientometrics? Mapping over 70 years of biological safety research with co-word analysis. *Scientometrics, 27*(2), 119-14.

Campanario, J. M. (1995). Using neural networks to study networks of scientific journals. *Scientometrics, 33*(1), 23-40.

Chung.Y. K. (1994). Bradford's distribution and core authors in classification systems literature. *Scientometrics, 29*(2), 253-269.

Courtial, J. P. (1994). A co-word analysis of scientometrics. *Scientometrics, 31*(3), 251-260.

Courtial, J. P., Callon, M., & Sigogneau, M. (1984). Is indexing trustworthy? Classification of articles through co-word analyses. *Journal of Information Science, 9*, 47-56.

Cronin, B., & Overfelt, K. (1994). Citation-based auditing of academic performance. *Journal of the American Society for Information Science, 45*(2), 61-72.

Diodato, V. (1994). *Dictionary of bibliometrics.* New York: Haworth Press.

Dick, J., & Blazek, J. (1995). The nature of the discipline: A bibliometric study of communication with some comparisons to library reference/information work. In J. B. Whitlatch (Ed.), *Library users and reference services* (pp. 289-304). New York: Haworth Press.

Egghe, L. (1990). A note on different Bradford multipliers. *Journal of the American Society for Information Science, 41*(3), 204-209.

Ely, D. P. (1990). Trends and issues in educational technology, 1989. In G. J. Anglin (Ed.). *Instructional technology* (pp. 34-58). Englewood, CO: Libraries Unlimited Inc.

Everett, J. E., & Pecotich, A. (1991). A combined loglinear/MDS model of mapping journals by citation analysis. *Journal of the American Society for Information Science, 42*(6), 119-146.

Frandsen, T. V. (2005). Journal interaction: A bibliometric analysis of economic journals. *Journal of Documentation, 61*(3), 385-401.

Glaenzel, W., & Moed, H. F. (2002). Journal impact factors measures in bibliometric research. *Scientometrics, 53*(2) 171-193.

Goffman, W., & Warren, K. S. (1969). Dispersion of papers among journals based on a mathematical analysis of two diverse medical literatures. *Nature, 221*, 1205-1207.

Hinze, S. (1994). Bibliographical cartography of an emerging interdisciplinary discipline: The case of bioelectronics. *Scientometrics, 29*(3), 353-376.

Holsti, O. R. (1969). *Content analysis for the social sciences and humanities.* Reading, MA: Addison-Wesley.

Hunter, J. E., & Schmidt, F. L. (1990). *Methods of meta-analysis: Correcting error and bias in research findings.* Newbury Park, CA: Sage.

Hyland, K. (2003). Self-citation and self-reference: Credibility and promotion in academic publication. *Journal of the American Society for Information Science and Technology, 54*(3), 251-259.

Ingwersen, P., & Christensen, F. H. (1997) Data set isolation for bibliometric online analyses of research publications: Fundamental methodological issues. *Journal of the American Society for Information Science, 48*(3), 205-217.

Jarneving, B. (2005). A comparison of two bibliometric methods for mapping of the research front. *Scientometrics, 65*(2), 245-263.

Jobber, D., & Simpson, P. (1988). A citation analysis of selected marketing journals. *International Journal of Research in Marketing, 5*, 137-142.

Kiesler, S., Siegel, J., & McGuire, T. W. (1984). Social psychological aspects of computer-mediated communication. *American Psychologist, 39*(10), 1123-1134.

Krippendorf, K. (2004). *Content analysis: An introduction to its methodology* (2nd ed.). Beverly Hills: Sage.

Larsen, T. J., & Levine, L. (2005). Searching for management information systems: Coherence and change in the discipline. *Information Systems Journal, 15*(4), 357-381.

Leydesdorff, L. (1997). Why words and co-words cannot map the development of the sciences. *Journal of the American Society for Information Science, 48*(5), 418-427.

Lievrouw, L. H. (1989). The invisible college reconsidered: Bibliometrics and the development of scientific communication theory. *Communication Research, 16*(5), 615-628.

Lievrouw, L. H. (1990). Reconciling structure and process in the study of scholarly communication. In C. Borgman (Ed.), *Scholarly communication and bibliometrics* (p. 59-69). Newbury Park, CA: Sage.

Lindsey, D. (1980). Production and citation measures in the sociology of science: The problem of multiple authorship. *Social Studies of Science, 10*, 145-162.

Lotka, A. J. (1926).The frequency distribution of scientific productivity. *Journal of the Washington Academy of Sciences, 16*(12), 317-323.

McCain, K. W. (1989). Mapping authors in intellectual space. *Communication Research, 16*(5), 667-681.

McCain, K. W., & Whitney, P. J. (1994). Contrasting assessments of interdisciplinarity in emerging specialties. *Knowledge: Creation, Diffusion, Utilization,* (3), 285-306.

McClure, C. R. (1991). *The national research and education network (NREN): Research and policy perspectives* (ERIC Document Reproduction Service No. ED341371). Norwood, NJ: Ablex Publishing

Moed. H. F. (1989). *The use of bibliometric indicators for the assessment of research performance in the natural and life sciences.* Leiden, The Netherlands: DWSO Press.

Narin, F. (1976). *Evaluative bibliometrics: The use of publication and citation analysis in the evaluation of scientific activity.* Cherry Hill, NJ: Computer Horizons.

Nicholls, P. (1989). Bibliometric modeling processes and the empirical validity of Lotka's law. *Journal of the American Society for Information Science, 40*(6), 379-385.

Paisley, W. (1989). Bibliometrics, communication, and communication research. *Communication Research, 16*(5), 701-718.

Price, D. J. (1965). Networks of scientific papers, *Science, 149*, 510-515.

Pritchard, A. (1969). Statistical bibliography or bibliometrics? *Journal of Documentation, 25*, 348-350

Rice, R. E. (1990). Hierarchies and clusters among communication and library and information science journals, 1977-1987. In C. Boreman (Ed.), *Scholarly communication and bibliometrics* (pp. 138-153). Newbury Park, CA: Sage.

Rice, R. E., Chapin, J., Pressman R., Park, S., & Funkhouser, E. (1996). What's in a name? Bibliometric analysis of 40 years of the journal of broadcasting (& electronic media). *Journal of Broadcasting & Electronic Media, 40*, 511-539.

Romiszowski, A. J. (1992). *Computer-mediated communication: A selected bibliography.* Englewood Cliffs, NJ: Educational Technology Publications.

Rosenthal, R. (1991). *Meta-analytic procedures for social research* (Rev. ed.). Newbury Park, CA: Sage.

Rubincam, I. (1987). Frequently cited authors in the literature on computer application to education. *Journal of Computer Based Education, 14*, 150-167.

Schloegl, C., & Stock, W. G. (2004). Impact and relevance of LIS journals: A scientometric analysis of international and German-language LIS jounals—Citation analysis vs. reader survey. *Journal of the American Society for Information Science and Technology, 55*(13), 1155-1168

Shah, R. (1999). *CMC bibliography.* Retrieved August 15, 2005, from http://www.rajivshah.com/CMCbiblio.html

Spasser, M. A. (1997). Mapping the terrain of pharmacy: Co-classification analysis of the international pharmaceutical abstracts database, *Scientometrics, 39*(1), 77-97.

Stegmann, J., & Grohmann, G. (2005). Hypothesis generation guided by co-word clustering. *Scientometric, 56*(1), 111-135.

Tijsen, R. J. W. (1992). *Cartography of science: Science metric mapping with multidimensional scaling*. Leiden, The Netherlands: DWSO Press.

Ungern-Steenberg, S. (1995, August). *Applications in teaching bibliometrics*. Libraries of the Future. 61st International Federation of Library Associations and Institutions Conference Proceedings.Istanbul, Turkey, August 20-25. Retrieved January 30, 1999, from http://www.nlc-bnc.ca/ifla/IV/ifla61/61-ungs.htm

Wallace, J. D. (1999). *An examination of computer-mediated communication's scholarly communication*. Unpublished doctoral dissertation, University of Oklahoma.

Walther, J. B. (2004). *CMC bibliography*. Retrieved from http://www.people.cornell.edu/pages/jbw29/docs/471_Things_to_Read.html

Walther, J. B., Anderson, J. F., & Park, D. W. (1994). Interpersonal effects in computer-mediated interaction: A meta-analysis of social and antisocial communication. *Communication Research, 21*(4), 460-487.

Wellman, B. (2004). The three ages of the Internet: Ten, five and zero years ago. *New Media & Society, 6*(1), 123-129.

KEY TERMS

Artifacts: Artifacts are any number of forms of scholarly communication. Conceptually, they could range from working papers to books.

Bibliographic Coupling: Bibliographic coupling is where two documents each have citations to one or more of the same publication, but do not have to necessarily cite each other.

Bibliometrics: The mathematical and statistical analysis of patterns that arise in the publication and use of documents.

Bradford Partitions: These partitions are used in library and information science to establish core journals. The process ranks journals from most to least prolific in terms of number of articles produced concerning a subject. They are then divided into three or more "zones" that have roughly the same number of articles. The zone that has the least journals is used to identify the "core" journals for a subject area.

CMC: An acronym standing for computer-mediated communication.

Cocitation Analyses: The analysis of journals, articles, or authors that are cited together in an article or articles.

Concepts: Concepts are terms or words used by the producers themselves. This could include words in titles and text, or assigned terminology such as key words.

Core Authors: Core authors are generally established through a well-articulated benchmark that exceeds two publications.

Core Concepts: Core concepts are the relatively few concepts that account for a large amount of problematisations under study.

Core Journals: Core journals are generally established through a well-established benchmark such as Bradford partitions.

Co-Word Analyses: The analyses of the co-occurrence of two or more words in one document or in different documents.

Problematisations: Scientific inquiry is built on a series of problems that hinge upon their relationship with each other. Problematisations are the networks of these problems generated in scholarly discourse by their various producers.

Producers: Producers produce scholarly communication. Technically, they can be either readers or authors, but generally are identified as the authors of selected artifacts.

ENDNOTES

[1] Paisley's argument appears to be directed at the application of content analysis. At a broader level, bibliometric variables are easily included at either the manifest or latent content level (Holsti, 1969). Furthermore, Diodato defines content analysis as "an analysis of the textual and non textual elements of a document" (1994, p. 50). This definition also suggests that bibliometrics are content analytic techniques.

[2] Diodato (1994, p. 99) defines bibliometric laws as "... descriptions or hypotheses about patterns that seem to be common in the publication and use of information. They are not the formal, highly validated laws we associate with the physical sciences."

Chapter XXII
Computer–Mediated Communication Research

J. D. Wallace
Lubbock Christian University, USA

ABSTRACT

This chapter asks "What is meant by computer-mediated communication research?" Numerous databases were examined concerning business, education, psychology, sociology, and social sciences from 1966 through 2005. A survey of the literature produced close to two thousand scholarly journal articles, and bibliometric techniques were used to establish core areas. Specifically, journals, authors, and concepts were identified. Then, more prevalent features within the dataset were targeted, and a fine-grained analysis was conducted on research-affiliated terms and concepts clustering around those terms. What was found was an area of scholarly communication, heavily popularized in education-related journals. Likewise, topics under investigation tended to be education and Internet affiliated. The distribution of first authors was overwhelming populated by one time authorship. The most prominent research methodology emerging was case studies. Other specific research methodologies tended to be textually related, such as content and discourse analysis. This study was significant for two reasons. First, it documented CMC's literature historical emergence through a longitudinal analysis. Second, it identified descriptive boundaries concerning authors, journals, and concepts that were prevalent in the literature.

INTRODUCTION

Computer-mediated communication (CMC) involves a wide number of characteristics involving human communication. It also includes systems, methods, and techniques that are typical of online environments. Therefore, one would rightfully expect definitional difficulties both technological and methodological. Wallace (1999) extensively surveyed the literature concerning CMC and found relatively few definitions. While differences abounded in the definitions found, the one constant was the use of the computer as an intermediary device. The centrality of the computer and communication layers human characteristics and technological issues.

Levinson (1990) suggests that in order to understand a device or a technique, not only should we take a microscopic view through research and examination, but we should also take a more macroscopic view. A survey of the scholarly communication might help provide a different perspective. Hopefully, it would reveal some of the larger areas of inquiry concerning online research in general, and computer-mediated communication specifically. This macroscopic survey would enable researchers and scholars to more efficiently coordinate their own activities with outlets and concepts that have the most pressing need for their contributions. It has the additional benefit of documenting CMC's developmental features that can be compared with future research or differing methodologies.

Similar to other such studies, the purpose of this chapter is provide an overview of the CMC scholarly literature, and to "identify its component features in providing a tangible means of identification" (Dick & Blazek, 1995, p. 291). Likewise, it is not to determine the magnitude that CMC occupies as a discipline, field, specialty, or subspecialty area. For purposes of literary description, the term "field" is not a cataloguing designate, but rather a convenient moniker under which CMC scholarship resides. CMC is often described in the literature as a field. However, designates of specialty, or subfield are probably more accurate.

Simply put, the statement of the problem is: "what are trends in computer-mediated communication research?" Definitions and descriptions of current literature on the subject reflect views that are selective and often disparate. Rather than revisit debatable definitional issues, an arguably more objective approach will be used as the focus of this inquiry. Specifically, what authors, journals, concepts, and research issues possibly populate the CMC domain?

Certainly, a number of conceptual problems would be introduced with any kind of predictive examination (Hargittai, 2004). Therefore, exploratory and descriptive procedures seem more appropriate than postulating hypotheses. With this in mind, the original question concerning CMC has, as one possible answer, a bibliometric analysis into the nature of the field. Bibliometrics is the ". . . mathematical and statistical analysis of patterns that arise in the publication and use of documents" (Diodato, 1994, p. ix).

Library and information science have long used bibliometrics for this kind of analysis. They have a body of literature supporting their validity and reliability. Moreover, bibliometric procedures provide the means upon which relationships of theoretical inquiry can be based. Borgman & Rice (1992) state that: "Bibliometric data are particularly useful for studying longitudinal trends in scholarly disciplines because of the massive datasets that can be utilized. Virtually no other method provides as comprehensive coverage of a topic in scholarly communication" (p. 400).

Journal articles appear to be reasonable and available artifacts for identifying this area. This is done for three reasons. First, their affiliation with the bibliometric theory of problematic network analysis provides support for their representation of scholarly activity. (Coutial, 1994; Courtial, Callon, & Sigogneau, 1984). This theory views scholarly communication and literature as a series of problematisations that reflected the underlying intellectual discourse. Journal articles are seen as the primary artifact from which to extract elements of that discourse. Second, analyses of journals do not consume the financial resources inherent in more exhaustive treatments. Third, their online availability makes this current analysis easier to replicate and contrast when used as a benchmark upon subsequent research.

Research questions. One advantage of surveying the field is to let the "field" define itself as it exists in the extant literature. In this regard, almost 40 years of archival data was examined by combining the results of a previous survey (Wallace, 1999) with this 2005 examination. Hopefully, this will offer a more comprehensive look at how CMC research is viewed through a database analytic lens. As search engines replace annotated bibliographies and other indexical instruments, the nature of the scholarly profile produced through this lens becomes more critical.

In regard to the above literature framework, this chapter poses four research questions concerning the computer-mediated communication research. These questions are general in nature, and align themselves theoretically with artifacts, producers, and research concepts. The conceptual issues are somewhat more complex than general identification and demarcation that led to the creation of a fourth research question. Simply put, the research questions posed are:

- **RQ1:** What are the primary journals of CMC literature, both past and present?
- **RQ2:** Who are the producers of CMC literature, both past and present?
- **RQ3:** What are the CMC concepts being examined in scholarly journals?
- **RQ4:** How do the current research concepts of CMC relate to other topics in the field?

Research question 1: Journals. Research question 1 addresses the scholarly journals representing literature concerning computer-mediated communication. Specifically, it will identify these artifacts by the analysis of frequency data and an identification of core journals across several disciplines. Common databases were set up both in the previous and the current study so that frequency and other component features could be identified.

One advantage of using journals over other artifacts, such as citations, is that they are believed to contribute to minimizing threats to validity (Cronin & Overfelt, 1994; Glaenzel & Moed, 2002; Hyland; 2003; Schloegl & Stock, 2004). Cites often go to secondary sources (obfuscating the real influence), and authors often do not hold the opinions that citation patterns attributed to them. Once frequency counts are established, a number of other component features can be derived, such as prolific and core journals. This may provide indicators of publication patterns that can be used to target future scholarship.

Research question 2: Authors. Research question 2 looks at producers of CMC's scholarly communication. It will be addressed by the analysis of frequency data concerning authorship. Frequency of author publication rate will give a glimpse into the most prolific authors, and has been indicative of some of the major theoretical contributions of bibliometrics (Cronin & Overfelt, 1994; Nicholls, 1989; Rice, Chapin, Pressman, Park, & Funkhouser., 1996).

Research question 3: Concepts. Research question 3 identifies the more prominent areas of focus in regard to CMC research. It will be addressed by the analysis of indexical key words from the master database. Indexical key words were chosen as concepts because they have demonstrated useful in identifying research trends in other studies (Callon, Courtial, & Laville, 1991; Cambrosio, Limoges, Courtial, & Laville, 1993; Stegmann & Grohmann, 2005). Key words stand for indicators of scholarly problematisations that are being articulated in the literature (Courtial, 1994; Callon et al., 1991)

Research question 4: Relationship of research concepts. Research question 4 investigates how the research concepts of CMC relate to topics in the field. It will be addressed through coword analysis. This is generally done by analyzing the proximity that key words and other concepts have with one another (Diodato, 1994; Larsen & Levine, 2005; Stegmann & Grohmann, 2005).

METHOD

In order to produce a literature survey that spans almost 40 years, two studies were combined. A more recent analysis of CMC research extended a previous CMC literature study (Wallace, 1999). The previous study's data was collected in June of 1998, for 1997 and prior, utilizing the indexes of ABI/INFORM, ERIC, Psychlit, Social Science Index, and Sociofile. The more recent study's data was collected in August of 2005. EBSCO was used as a common vender in the 2005 study. Academic Search Complete, Communication & Mass Media, Business Search Premier, ERIC, PsychInfo, and PsychArticles were selected as databases. The selected databases are considered prominent resources in the areas of business, education, psychology, and the social sciences. Furthermore, these databases are noted for their strong research affiliations, and have an intuitive link with CMC. A key word search of the respective databases was done for the variable "computer-mediated communication.." Both hyphenated and unhyphenated variations of the term "computer-mediated" were used to insure breadth of coverage.

Each of the databases had idiosyncratic characteristics that made identical survey techniques, across all databases, impossible. However, all methodologies adhered to the following guidelines. Databases were examined to see if there were any inherent journal markers that would enable the extraction of journal articles. Books, book reviews, conference papers, and other nonjournal materials were eliminated through either filters or inspection. Extraneous information and fields were eliminated. Documents were then placed into a common file. Procedures were similar for both studies, and a relatively exhaustive description is available in Wallace (1999).

Data Analysis

Journals. The data file was examined in terms of journal frequency. From this, it could be determined the identity of CMC journals and how they were positioned in terms of the overall literature as defined by this chapter. Subsequently, Bradford-type partitions were derived to identify the core journals.

Bradford partitions are where journals are ranked from most to least prolific in terms of number of articles produced concerning the subject under scrutiny. They are then divided into

"zones" that have roughly the same number of articles. Predictably, the journals that produce the most articles have the least number of journals in their zone. The zone that has the least journals is used to identify the "core" journals for a subject area. Bradford recommended the use of three zones (Diodato, 1994). The previous study serendipitously arrived at three zones through a somewhat more complex procedure. These zones had a relatively equal number of journal articles with the core zone containing a relatively few prolific journals. For comparative purposes, the more current study utilized three zones as well.

Authors. The 2005 analysis of authors was also restricted by comparative constraints. The previous study used the straight count method of authorship. The straight count method identifies all the first authors from the journal database. Therefore, both studies used straight count to extract authors for analysis.

After authors were extracted from the master database, they were then rank ordered, and standardized. Frequency and cumulative data was then calculated. The CMC authors were then analyzed from an "authors x number of contributions" format.

Concepts. Frequency of problematisations overall were calculated and analyzed for segmentation. This is not only critical for this research question, it is imperative for RQ4. Both Hinze's (1994) "10 journals or more" and Rice et al.'s (1996) "top 200 key words" were considered exemplars in this regard. The decision was made to view the distribution in terms of which kind of demarcation was most efficient while capturing the majority of the distribution. Fifty percent was considered the benchmark on which to base the comparisons. This is an area where the literature distribution must be known to be able choose the more efficient method. If neither of the previously mentioned methods surpassed the 50% benchmark, then the literature would be deemed too disparate to determine more prominent terms.

Once segmentation was determined, then the core key words were longitudinally examined for their visibility. The previous study examined key words concerning 1997 and prior. The more recent study surveyed the literature from 1997 through 2005. The overlap was intentional as many databases' literatures are not well represented in their last year of analysis (Egghe, 1990). Indicators of this "droop" were present in the previous 1997 survey.

Relationship of research concepts. The above concepts were then scanned for more familiar research affiliated terminology. Terms that appeared methodological, or had the term "research" as a component-attached term were extracted. Establishing relationships was done through cluster analysis. A number of clustering procedures have been used in the analyses of emerging fields. The complete linkage method (furthest neighbor) was considered an appropriate procedure because of its rigor over the single linkage method and its comparability to the previous study (Aldenderfer & Blashfield, 1984; Hinze, 1994, Wallace, 1999). The lack of knowledge of current granularity of findings also makes this procedure well suited. (McCain, 1989; Spasser, 1997). As with other studies, similarity between concepts was measured using a Pearson relation procedure. (e.g., Hinze, 1994; McCain, 1989; Spasser, 1997).

RESULTS

The 1997 CMC study generated 611 unique article references for 1997 and prior. Four hundred and fifty-nine, or about 75%, tended to be education related as indicated by their ERIC affiliation. The current examination started from a more mature 1997 dataset through 2005. It generated 1,326 unique article references. Nine hundred and fifty-three, or about 72%, tended to be education related as indicated by their ERIC affiliation.

The following sections survey journal publication trends for CMC, identify some of the

more common terminology within that survey, and then narrow that terminology to research-affiliated terms and concepts clustering around those terms.

Artifacts: Survey of Core Journals

A Bradfordian-type analysis was done both in the more current and the previous study (Table 1). In the 1997 study, journals had to produce six or more articles total to be considered core. In the 2005 study, journals had to produce 11 or more articles.

While roughly the same number of journals were considered core in both studies, only six journals were recognized as core in both studies. These were

American Journal of Distance Education, Computers & Education, Computers and Composition, Educational Media International, Information Society, Internet Research, Journal of Educational Computing Research, and TechTrends. A cursory look at journal affiliation reveals that the journals are largely education affiliated. Two notable exceptions are Information Society and Internet Research (see Table 2).

Productivity of these core journals ranged, in the earlier research, from a high of 16 to a low of 6. The more recent research frequency was appreciably higher ranging from a high of 34 to a minimum threshold level of 11.

To give an idea how this distribution might be comparable to other literature descriptions, in terms of longevity, it was tracked over time. While no journals appear till 1984, databases were

Table 1. Core journal distribution

Zones	Early Journals	Early Articles	Recent Journals	Recent Articles
1	22*	195	25*	430
2	54	196	101	427
3	153	195	360	426
*6 or more articles			*11 or more articles	

Table 2. Survey of core journals for CMC

1966-1997	1997-2005
Behaviour and Information Technology	British Journal of Educational Technology
Canadian Journal of Educational Communication	Business Communication Quarterly
Communication Education	CALICO Journal
Communication Research	CyberPsychology & Behavior
Computers in Human Behavior	Distance Education
Educational Technology	Distance Education Report
Educom Review	Indian Journal of Open Learning
Human Communication Research	Instructional Science
Interpersonal Computing and Technology	Internet and Higher Education
Journal of Communication	Journal of Adolescent & Adult Literacy
Journal of Computer-Mediated Communication	Journal of Computer Assisted Learning
Learning and Leading with Technology	Journal of Educational Technology Systems
Organization Science	Journal of Instruction Delivery Systems
	Journal of the American Society for Information Science
	New Media & Society
	Quarterly Review of Distance Education
	Small Group Research

searched in previous years. The most far-ranging search occurred in ERIC, which started in 1966. Records were also examined from ABI/INFORM, Psychlit, Sociofile, and Social Science Index in 1986, 1971, 1971, and 1983, respectively. All databases were producing articles by 1986

Producers: Survey of Core Authors

Three or more references were used to demarcate core authors in both studies. This formulation has the benefit of fitting within the general contention that authors producing one or two articles have the vast majority of the distribution and should be excluded from consideration (e.g., 94% by Burnham, Shearer, & Wall 1992; 83% by Keenan, 1988). On the other hand, because the production numbers were low in general, using more than three was considered too severe a threshold for the respective studies.

The CMC literature examined was heavily weighted toward authors producing only one article. The early 1997 research had 506 different first authors producing 611 different references. Close to 96% of the authors had one or two pub-

lications. They accounted for 87% of the articles produced. The 21 core authors were published in 54 different journals producing 80 different articles. The 2005 survey had a similar distribution, with 1,169 authors producing 1,326 different articles. However, the core authors produced a somewhat smaller 8.5% of the articles. Specifically, there were 31 authors that produced 113 articles in 71 different publications. Only Joe Walther was included in both previous and recent sets of core authors (Table 3).

Concepts: Survey of Key Terms

First, to contextualize the conceptual survey concerning CMC, it is useful to understand the scope of the current and previous examination. The previous study had 1,787 unique problematisations (indexical terms) contributing to a total dataset of 6,898 terms. The 2005 study had 2,700 unique problematisations contributing to 12,935 total terms.

The overall datasets were then examined for more dominant concepts. Both Hinze's and Rice's methods detailed earlier surpassed the

Table 3. Survey of CMC first authors

1966-1997 Authors		1997-2005 Authors	
Adrianson, Lillemor	Phillips, Gerald M.	Abrams, Zsuzsanna Ittzes	Li, Qing
Baym, Nancy K.	Rice, Ronald E.	Arbaugh, J. B	MacDonald, Lucy
Collis, Betty	Riel, Margaret	Baron, Naomi S	Riva, Giuseppe
Dyrli, Odvard Egil	Rojo, Alejandra	Belz, Julie A	Rourke, Liam
Harris, Judith B.	Schrum, Lynne	Benbunan-Fich, Raquel	Saba, Farhad
Hiltz, Starr Roxanne	Snyder, Herbert	Caverly, David C.	Savicki, Victor
Lea, Martin	Valacich, Joseph S.	Fahy, Patrick J	Selwyn, Neil
Mantovani, Giuseppe	Walther, Joseph B.	Flanagin, Andrew J.	Trentin, Guglielmo
Matheson, Kimberly	Weinberg, Nancy	Gu,guen, Nicolas	Tu, Chih-Hsiung
McMurdo, George	Zack, Michael H	Hampton, Keith N.	Vrooman, Steven S.
Olaniran, Bolanle A		Haythornthwaite, Caroline	Walther, Joseph B.
		Herring, Susan C	Warnick, Barbara
		Johnson, E. Marcia	Wellman, Barry
		Kling, Rob	Wilson, E. Vance
		Kock, Ned	Wolfe, Joanna
		Lee, Lina	

Table 4. Common core terms for CMC

Term	Difference	Freq 2005	Rank 2005	Freq 1997	Rank 1997
Computer-Mediated Communication	210%	960	1	457	1
Higher Education	250%	510	2	204	2
Internet	206%	287	3	139	3
Distance Education	322%	245	4	76	8
Computer-Assisted Instruction	198%	212	5	107	6
Foreign Countries	268%	153	7	57	14
Educational Technology	317%	152	8	48	18
Computer Uses in Education	219%	151	9	69	10
Online Systems	332%	146	10	44	19
Electronic Mail	78%	107	12	137	4
Information Technology	139%	71	19	51	17
Computer Networks	51%	70	20	136	5
Teleconferencing	111%	69	21	62	12

50% threshold. The previous study used Hinze's (1994) demarcation, and identified 116 core terms. They accounted for more than 3,684, or 53%, of the total indexical terms mentioned. However, Hinze's demarcation was primarily used because the previous study's emphasis was on the totality of the conceptual base. Since the 2005 study was designed specifically to identify research affiliations within that base, Rice et al.'s (1996) more liberal "top 200 terms" was utilized. This accounted for 7,827 or roughly 60% of the entire conceptual set.

While a complete discussion of the core terminology would be unwieldy at best, a physical inspection of the two studies indicated about 30% of the totality of terms is included in the 21 most prominent descriptors. With the admitted conces-

sion that computer-mediated communication is the search term predicating the study, these terms still provide an overview of some of the more dominate themes that have emerged in the CMC literature. Table 4 details both studies with the count and rank of terminology that occurred.

Thirteen of the 21 terms appeared in both studies. As would be expected, even with rank differentiation, the more recent study has substantially more contributions. Online systems had the highest overall percentage increase. Decreases were only observed concerning the terms electronic mail and computer networks.

There were eight terms that were not reciprocal (Table 5). The overwhelming number of these fell in the bottom half of the rankings where predominance was not as stable.

Table 5. Unique core terms for CMC

2005	Freq 2005	Rank 2005	1997	Freq 1997	Rank 1997
World Wide Web	175	6	Telecommunications	100	7
Telematics	142	11	Information Networks	72	9
Second Language Learning	93	13	Interpersonal Communication	67	11
Student Attitudes	90	14	Computer Applications	57	13
Teaching Methods	83	15	Adulthood	53	15
Second Language Instruction	82	16	Computers	52	16
Online Courses	81	17	Experimental Theoretical	42	20
Interaction	78	18	Group Dynamics	42	21

Table 6. Survey of research terms

Concept	1997	2005
Case Studies	29	37
Communication Research	38	36
Comparative Analysis	21	32
Content Analysis	17	14
Discourse Analysis	14	28
Educational Research	5	23
Evaluation Criteria	3	11
Evaluation Methods	7	31
Literature Reviews	11	15
Pilot Projects	9	11
Research	5	14
Research Methodology	12	11
Surveys	14	17
Use Studies	21	14

The more exhaustive 2005 analysis was used to identify research-affiliated terms to be inlaid within respective conceptual maps of the two studies. The research-affiliated concepts are listed for both the 1997 and 2005 research studies in Table 6. The highest number of scholarly articles was connected with the term communication research.

The top-ranked term was communication research for the 1997 survey and case studies for the 2005 survey. As would be expected, most concepts were identified at higher levels in the larger, more recent study. However, there were some exceptions to this trend. These included communication research, research methodology, and use studies.

Conceptual Map of CMC Research Methodologies

Research question 4 was explored in two ways. First was the identification of prominent problematisations within each of the previously identified research affiliated terms. This was done by setting a somewhat arbitrary four-occurrence threshold that had to be surpassed. What follows is a more lexical description of those relationships. Clearly, terms that are more numerous are not necessarily strongly related, and terms strongly related are not necessarily more numerous. Below are topical areas that were most dominant when the respective research problematisations were used as filters. Because of the magnitude of higher education occurrences, it was included in almost all categories.

Communication research. Both studies included higher education, Internet, communication behavior, and group dynamics as areas of foci. Additionally, the 2005 study included interpersonal relationships, student attitudes, and World Wide Web. The 1997 conceptual set was relatively extensive including the following terms:

- Adulthood
- Communication
- Communication Social Aspects
- Computer Applications
- Computer Assisted Instruction
- CMC Systems
- Computer Networks
- Computers
- Decision Making
- Electronic Mail
- Group Decision Making
- Interpersonal Relations
- Organizational Communication
- Social Interaction
- Telecommunications

Case studies. Both studies included the indexical terms higher education, Internet, distance education, foreign countries, computer-assisted instruction, and electronic mail. The 2005 study also had World Wide Web, instructional effectiveness, online systems, information technology, college students, literacy, and teacher role. The 1997 study was more writing oriented with computer networks, teaching methods, writing research, student attitudes, collaborative writing, technical writing, and writing instruction.

Evaluation methods. Only higher education and computer-assisted instruction appeared prominently in both studies when evaluations methods was used as a filter. However, no other terms, except for the previously mentioned higher education, reached a level of predominance in the

1997 study. The 2005 conceptual set was relatively extensive including the following terms:

- Collaborative learning
- Distance education
- Foreign countries
- Instructional effectiveness
- Interaction
- Internet
- Online systems
- Research methodology
- Student attitudes
- Student evaluation
- Teaching methods
- Teleconferencing
- World Wide Web

Comparative analysis. Dominant concepts in both studies included higher education, distance education, and computer-assisted instruction. The 2005 study also had face-to-face communication, interaction, instructional effectiveness, interpersonal communication, nontraditional education, second-language instruction, and second-language learning. The 1997 study had more dominant terms including computer networks, futures of society, teleconferencing, electronic mail, and experimental theoretical.

Discourse analysis. Higher education and interpersonal communication was the only dominant concept in both studies. The 2005 dominant concepts included communication behavior, Internet, language research, second-language instruction, second-language learning, sex differences, and written language. Only two additional terms were dominant in the 1997 study. These were computer-assisted instruction and computer networks.

Educational research. The term educational research did not have sufficient mentions to be considered in the dominant term analysis for the 1997 study. The dominant terms for the 2005 study included higher education, computer-assisted instruction, cooperative learning, distance education, educational technology, Internet, nontraditional education, online systems, and World Wide Web.

Surveys. There were no dominant terms included in both studies other than higher education. The 2005 study featured student attitudes, distance education, and World Wide Web, while the 1997 study featured Internet, computer networks, electronic mail, teleconferencing, information networks, and scholarly communication.

Literature reviews. Distance education was a dominant term in both studies concerning literature reviews. The 2005 study also included community and information technology. The 1997 study additionally had higher education, computer networks, electronic mail, and teleconferencing.

Research. When used as a filter, the singular term, research, did not have sufficient mentions of any terminology to be included in this analysis.

Table 7. Longitudinal research term comparison

2005 - research clusters	1997- research clusters
Case studies	***Case studies***
Literacy	group discussion
computer literacy	graduate study
Tutoring	writing instruction
Communication research	***Communication research***
communication behavior	Organizational communication
Discourse analysis	interpersonal communication
classroom communication	Computers
Comparative analysis	***Discourse analysis***
face to face communication	microcomputers
interpersonal communication	man machine systems
	Computer attitudes
Content analysis	Computer literacy
Research methodology	
Evaluation methods*	***Comparative analysis***
	learner controlled instruction
Survey	
electronic mail	***Content analysis***
ethics	***Research methodology***
	research needs
Use studies	
computer use	***Survey***
undergraduates	Teleconferencing
technology utilization	foreign countries
	Use studies
Literature reviews	
Community	***Literature reviews***
	tables data
	Questionnaires.
	*=not enough for 1997 analysis

Use studies. Higher education, Internet, and electronic mail were dominant in both studies. Additionally, the 2005 study featured the term World Wide Web. The 1997 study's dominant concepts were more ranging, including communication thought transfer, computer networks, foreign countries, online systems, tables data, telecommunications, and teleconferencing.

Content analysis. Only higher education was identified for both studies. The only additional dominant term for the 2005 study was Internet. Terms for the 1997 study included electronic mail, interpersonal communication, research needs, and tables data.

Pilot project. There were no dominant mentions of terminology in both studies except for higher education. Additionally, the 2005 study included foreign countries and educational technology. The 1997 study had electronic mail.

Evaluation criteria. Evaluation criteria did not have sufficient enough mentions for dominant term analysis in the 1997 study. The dominant affiliated terms with the 2005 study included higher education, computer-assisted instruction, distance education, Internet, and online systems.

Research methodology. There was no overlap in dominant terms. The 2005 study had distance education and interaction, and the 1997 study had higher education, computer networks, and electronic mail.

The second way research question 4 was explored was to examine strength of affiliation through cluster analysis. This was thought to provide some clues as to which core terms were most closely related to particular research problematisations. Some of the linkages were clearly methodological (Table 7). However, not all terms were included in both analyses due to the number of occurrences when research term filters were applied. Table 7 identifies clusters of research and affiliated co-occurring terms that appeared in at least one of the studies. Clustered terms tend to be conceptual sets that journal articles focus upon.

Aside from terms that were affiliated across both studies, there were terms that only appeared in the 2005 analysis. These relationship clusters included:

- **Educational Research:** Distance education, nontraditional education, computer-assisted *instruction, and educational practices*
- **Evaluation Criteria:** Feedback, course content, and course development
- **Pilot Project:** Information services, library services, reference services, user needs, information, and electronic libraries
- **Research:** Communication

DISCUSSION

This chapter analyzed "what is meant by computer-mediated communication research?" While a number of suitable answers exist for this question, it chose to let the "field" define itself as it exists in the extant literature concerning business, education, psychology, and the social sciences. In this regard, almost 40 years of archival data was surveyed. Wallace's study of 1997 and prior literature was combined with this 2005 examination to offer a look at how CMC research is viewed through a database analytic lens. Because of the interdisciplinary nature of computer-mediated communication (CMC), a parallel analysis of multiple databases from different perspectives was used (Ingwersen & Christensen, 1997; McLaughlin, 1994; Spasser, 1997). It should be noted that as database sophistication increases regarding education, business, and social life in general, this kind of lens may become more crucial.

The descriptive nature of this study necessarily dictated a balance between rigor and latitude. Several limitations must be considered in this respect. These include generalization, design limitations, and theoretical assumptions. First, operationalization of the domain should clearly impact the use of the findings. Therefore, results from this analysis do not claim to identify characteristics of CMC beyond the domain examined. Second, the selection of cluster analysis over other classifying procedures has a number of inherent limitations. This was considered a necessary condition given the emerging nature of the field. Emergence (or lack of emergence) of clusters will have to be weighed against the nonrandom nature of their partitioning (Aldenderfer & Blashfield, 1984). Third, the design was somewhat restricted in order to have a longitudinal comparison. The above limitations were addressed in the traditional way for descriptive studies. Detailed explanations, including supporting literature, were provided for choices made.

CONCLUSION

This survey of computer-mediated communication literature revealed three interesting trends. The first trend is a paradoxical turbulence and stability common in literature surveys. This pattern was somewhat present for articles, journals, authors, concepts, and research affiliations. The total articles doubled while the number of core journals remained relatively constant. Both the overall production of articles and the production of core journals increased by 217%. Despite this increase, the number of core journals producing those articles only advanced by 3, from 22 to 25.

The total number of core authors producing more than two articles also had relatively little growth, while there was a virtual turnover in actual author names. Joe Walther was the only author to emerge in both surveys. Core authorship increased by an anemic 30%, from 21 to 31. When considering total articles produced, core author production actually shrank from 13% in the 1997 survey, to 8.5 % in the 2005 survey. The top 21 terms in both studies accounted for 30% of the total indexical terms. Eight of those terms were not reciprocal. Most of the unique terms can be attributed to shifts in the more turbulent bottom half of the distribution. However,

telecommunications and information networks were ranked seventh and ninth, respectively, in the 1997 survey, and were not prominent in the 2005 study. One interesting note is that while "World Wide Web" was not a core terminology in the 1997 study, it was identified as the number one emerging concept. In the 2005 survey, it was firmly established as sixth in overall mentions. Communication research and discourse analysis were the only research affiliated terms that fell within the top 21 terms of both surveys.

The majority of the previously identified research terminologies emerged in both studies, but were not related to the same issues. Nine out of the 14 research affiliated terms emerged in both surveys. Serendipitously, the only two terms that were related to each other were also research affiliated. These were content analysis and research methodology. The terms educational research, literature reviews, research, pilot projects, and evaluation criteria were exclusive in that they did not overlap with any of the other dominant research terms.

The second trend is that literature tended to have an online and higher education focus. Five hundred and ten articles were higher-education related. Internet was the second most populous descriptor, with 287 articles. Furthermore, World Wide Web had 176 articles, and online systems had the highest percentage increase with 146 articles. Besides articles, both surveys indicated in excess of 70% of the journals were related to education. Core journals were also highly education and Internet related.

Higher education was also connected with almost all research terminology for both surveys. The only exceptions were the terms research, research methodology, and literature review for the 2005 survey. The 1997 study had higher education absent for educational research, evaluation criteria, and the singular term, research. While the 1997 survey results could be attributed to low production numbers, this was not the case with the 2005 results. Other problematisations with similar production numbers managed to have at least four articles with a higher education affiliation.

The third trend emerged through a post hoc analysis of the 2005 dataset that was not conducted in the 1997 study. Journals were examined to see if they affiliated with any of the dominant research terminology. Most journals were affiliated with a single prominent research term. Eight were affiliated with two terms, and only the journal Internet Research involved three terms that included comparative analysis, evaluation criteria, and use studies. The appendix describes the research affiliation as indicated by key word term, journal that it was published in, and the count of articles in a journal concerning a particular research term.

FUTURE RESEARCH

Clearly, this study detailed CMC research as an area that tended to be education and "Internet" affiliated. Furthermore, the computer-mediated communication literature prominently used a number of textual analysis techniques, such as content and discourse analysis. Noticeably absent were articles focused on possible experimental techniques, ethnographies, and focus groups. This does not mean that these were not tools used in the literature, merely that they were not the focus of the more prominently presented research articles (Schneider & Foot, 2004). Surveys also had a surprisingly diminutive presence. Certainly, there are both specific and extensive treatments of online survey methodology (e.g., Andrews, Nonnecke, & Preece 2003; Katz & Rice, 2002). However, the current examination suggests a need for this and other volumes to specifically localize methodological issues relevant to computer-mediated and online communication.

With the exception of Joe Walther, core authors had completely overturned. While Nicholls concedes the robustness of the straight count, an exhaustive identification of authorship might more fully answer questions concerning ranking issues, shifting authorships, and omissions (Cronin & Overfelt, 1994; Nicholls, 1989).

One general consideration is that indexed literature does not always reflect the centrality of artifacts and producers. The current analysis focused on work being produced without discrimination in regard to usage. Identification of CMC's literature usage patterns might provide complementary information to the current study. Furthermore, it would help shed light on whether theoretical or pragmatic issues are driving CMC's scholarly communication.

Another important consideration is that it is unlikely that people engaged in CMC are overwhelmingly involved in education-related phenomena (Katz & Rice 2002; Papacharissi & Rubin, 2000). If the study of CMC is to more accurately reflect current usage patterns, it should be aggressively broadened in other areas. Conceptual linkages exposed by this analysis are formative at best. Future studies should rigorously examine both the linkages and the conclusions in regard to their longevity and stability.

However, while conceding a number of caveats, this study does identify component features of past and more recent computer-mediated communication research. These resources are readily available online through many library services and outside vendors. Therefore, CMC and "online" researchers can use these features to identify research redundancies, and opportunities to consider, and hopefully more efficiently advance, the scholarship of the field.

REFERENCES

Aldenderfer, M. S., & Blashfield, R. G. (1984). *Cluster analysis*. Newbury Park, CA: Sage

Andrews, D., Nonnecke. B., & Preece, J. (2003). Electronic survey methodology: A case study in reaching hard-to-involve Internet users. *International Journal of Human Computer Interaction, 16*(2), 185-210.

Borgman, C. L., & Rice, R. E. (1992). The convergence of information science and communication: A bibliometric analysis. *Journal of the American Society for Information Science, 43*(6), 397-411.

Burnham, J. F, Shearer, B. S., & Wall, B. C. (1992). Combining new technologies for effective collection development: A bibliometric study using CD-ROM and a database management program. *Bulletin of the Medical Library Association, 80,* 150-156.

Callon, M., Courtial, J. P., & Laville, F. (1991). Co-word analysis as a tool for describing the network of interactions between basic and technological research: The case of polymer chemistry. *Scientometrics, 22*(1), 155-205.

Cambrosio, A., Limoges, C., Courtial, J. P., & Laville, F. (1993). Historical scientometrics? Mapping over 70 years of biological safety research with co-word analysis. *Scientometrics, 27*(2), 119-14.

Courtial, J. P. (1994). A co-word analysis of scientometrics. *Scientometrics, 31*(3), 251-260.

Courtial, J. P., Callon, M., & Sigogneau, M. (1984). Is indexing trustworthy? Classification of articles through co-word analyses. *Journal of Information Science, 9,* 47-56.

Cronin, B., & Overfelt, K. (1994). Citation-based auditing of academic performance. *Journal of the American Society for Information Science, 45*(2), 61-72.

Dick, J., & Blazek, J. (1995). The nature of the discipline: A bibliometric study of communication with some comparisons to library reference/information work. In J. B. Whitlatch (Ed.), *Library users and reference services* (pp. 289-304). New York: Haworth Press.

Diodato, V. (1994). *Dictionary of bibliometrics.* New York: Haworth Press.

Egghe, L. (1990). A note on different Bradford multipliers. *Journal of the American Society for Information Science, 41*(3), 204-209.

Glaenzel, W., & Moed, H. F. (2002). Journal impact factors measures in bibliometric research. *Scientometrics, 53*(2) 171-193.

Hargittai, E. (2004). Internet access and use in context. *New Media & Society, 6*(1), 137-143.

Hinze, S. (1994). Bibliographical cartography of an emerging interdisciplinary discipline; The case of bioelectronics. *Scientometrics, 29*(3), 353-376.

Hyland, K. (2003). Self-citation and self-reference: Credibility and promotion in academic publication. *Journal of the American Society for Information Science and Technology, 54*(3), 251-259.

Ingwersen, P., & Christensen, F. H. (1997) Data set isolation for bibliometric online analyses of research publications: Fundamental methodological issues. *Journal of the American Society for Information Science, 48*(3), 205-217.

Katz, J. E., & Rice, R. E. (2002). *Social consequences of Internet use: Access, involvement and interaction.* Cambridge, MA: MIT Press.

Keenen, M. (1988). Report on the 1987 membership survey. *Journal of Finance, 43,* 767-777.

Larsen, T. J., & Levine, L. (2005). Searching for management information systems: Coherence and change in the discipline. *Information Systems Journal, 15* (4), 357-381.

Levinson, P. (1990). Computer conferencing in the context of the evolution of media. In L. M. Harasim (Ed.), *Online education: Perspectives on a new environment* (pp. 3-14). New York: Praeger.

McCain, K. W. (1989). Mapping authors in intellectual space. *Communication Research, 16*(5), 667-681.

McCain, K. W., & Whitney, P. J. (1994). Contrasting assessments of interdisciplinarity in emerging specialties. *Knowledge: Creation, Diffusion, Utilization,* (3), 285-306.

McLaughlin, M. (1994). *Announcing the Journal of Computing Mediated Communication.* Retrieved January 30, 1999, from http://sunsite.unc.edu/cmc/mag/1994/jul/jcmc.html

Nicholls, P. (1989). Bibliometric modeling processes and the empirical validity of Lotka's law. *Journal of the American Society for Information Science, 40*(6), 379-385.

Papacharisi, Z., & Rubin, A. M. (2000). Predictors of Internet use. *Journal of Broadcasting and Electronic Media, 44*(2), 175-196.

Rice, R. E., Chapin, J., Pressman, R., Park, S. & Funkhouser, E. (1996). What's in a name? Bibliometric analysis of 40 years of the Journal of Broadcasting (& Electronic Media). *Journal of Broadcasting & Electronic Media, 40,* 511-539.

Schloegl, C., & Stock, W. G. (2004). Impact and relevance of LIS journals: A scientometric analysis of international and German-language LIS journals—Citation analysis vs. reader survey. *Journal of the American Society for Information Science and Technology, 55*(13), 1155-1168.

Schneider, S. M., & Foot, K. A. (2004). The Web as an object of study. *New Media & Society, 6*(1), 114-122.

Spasser, M. A. (1997). Mapping the terrain of pharmacy: Co-classification analysis of the international pharmaceutical abstracts database. *Scientometrics, 39*(1), 77-97.

Stegmann, J., & Grohmann, G. (2005). Hypothesis generation guided by co-word clustering. *Scientometric, 56*(1), 111-135.

Wallace, J. D. (1999). *An examination of computer-mediated communication's scholarly communication.* Unpublished doctoral dissertation, University of Oklahoma.

KEY TERMS

Artifacts: Artifacts are any number of forms of scholarly communication. Conceptually, they could range from working papers to books.

Bibliographic Coupling: Bibliographic coupling is where two documents each have citations to one or more of the same publication, but do not have to necessarily cite each other.

Bibliometrics: The mathematical and statistical analysis of patterns that arise in the publication and use of documents

Bradford Partitions: These partitions are used in library and information science to establish core journals. The process ranks journals from most to least prolific in terms of number of articles produced concerning a subject. They are then divided into three or more "zones" that have roughly the same number of articles. The zone that has the least journals is used to identify the "core" journals for a subject area.

CMC: An acronym standing for computer-mediated communication or computer mediated communication.

Co-Citation Analyses: The analysis of journals, articles, or authors that are cited together in an article or articles.

Concepts: Concepts are terms or words used by the producers themselves. This could include words in titles and text, or assigned terminology such as key words.

Core Authors: Core authors are generally established through a well-articulated benchmark that exceeds two publications.

Core Concepts: Core concepts are the relatively few concepts that account for a large amount of problematisations under study.

Core Journals: Core journals are generally established through a well-established benchmark such as Bradford partitions.

Co-Word Analyses: The analyses of the co-occurrence of two or more words in one document or in different documents.

APPENDIX: 1997-2005

Journal	Count	Journal	Count
Case studies		*Evaluation methods*	
Computers and Composition	2	American Journal of Distance Education	2
Educational Media International	2	Instructional Science	2
Internet and Higher Education	2	Quarterly Review of Distance Education	2
Journal of Computer Assisted Learning.	2	Educational Technology & Society	2
		Computers & Education	2
Communication research		Journal of Educational	2
Human Communication Research	3	Computing Research	2
Computers and Composition	3	Distance Education	2
Public Relations Review	2	Performance Improvement.	2
International Review of Research in Open and Distance Learning	2	*Literature reviews*	
Business Communication Quarterly	2	ARIST	6
Journal of Computer-Mediated Communication	2	*Evaluation methods*	
Written Communication	2	Internet Research	2
Comparative analysis		*Pilot project*	
Internet Research	3	Educational Media International	4
Computers & Education	3		
		Research	
Content analysis		Journal of Language & Social Psychology	2
Educational Computing Research	2		
Instructional Science	2	*Survey*	
		Educational Media International	2
Discourse analysis		American Journal of Distance Education	2
Computers and Composition	6		
CALICO Journal	3	*Use studies*	
Research on Language and Social Interaction	3	Internet Research	5
Written Communication	2		
		Research methodology	
Educational research		The Journal of the American Society for Information Science	2
British Journal of Educational Technology	2		
Internet and Higher Education	2		
Journal of Adolescent & Adult Literacy	2		
Quarterly Review of Distance Education	2		
Community College Journal	2		

Section II
Survey Software

In this second section of the Handbook of Research on Electronic Surveys and Measurements, *the focus is on software services and programs that should be of strong value to those who do research with, on, or about electronic-based communication platforms.*

Chapter XXIII
Mixed–Mode Surveys with Netservey

Savvas Papagiannidis
University of Newcastle upon Tyne, UK

Feng Li
University of Newcastle upon Tyne, UK

ABSTRACT

Mixed-mode approaches are often used to boost response rates and reduce costs. Still, they can increase the complexity of designing, deploying, and managing a survey, especially when combining online and off-line methods, and when the number of modes and recipients increases. This article presents a prototype of a mixed-mode solution that can handle both online and off-line modes, freeing the researcher from the survey's practicalities, especially deploying the survey and collecting the responses. The solution can handle Web, e-mail and postal surveys, using advanced digital printing technology, although in principle, any channel can be utilised.

BACKGROUND

Mixed-mode surveys are often used to overcome the shortcomings of using a single mode, and also to test the assumptions about the sampling, and the reliability and validity of the research methodologies used. On the other hand, multiple modes can increase the complexity of designing, deploying, and managing a survey, as the researcher will need to possess the technical skills and the resources required to run a survey over the selected modes.

Netservey (the name comes from serving surveys online) is a mixed-mode solution that can handle both online and off-line modes, freeing the researcher from the survey's practicalities, especially deploying the survey and collecting the responses. Netservey began as a tool to organise Web surveys by one of the authors. Dr.Papagiannidis was often asked to build bespoke surveys that often required a lot of programming time and effort. The solution was then coupled with a digital print technology and was presented as a commercial solution, winning the 2004 Enterprise Challenge, the business plan competition organised by the University of Newcastle upon Tyne.

The solution can handle Web, e-mail, and postal surveys; although in principle, any channel could be added. The biggest challenge that Netservey faces, when it comes to fulfilling these modes, is to automate the logistics of postal surveys: "the questionnaire has to be printed, envelopes to be stuffed, mailing labels and postage to be applied, and then the survey can be mailed to participants; these all cost money and time" (Huang, In Press). This process dominates the administration of the survey, especially when it comes to large research projects or repeated surveys. Netservey's ability to handle postal surveys is very innovative and can resolve most of the logistics of mailing a survey, irrespective of the sample's size, differentiating it from other online survey solutions.

Of course, this does not imply that digital modes, even the most established ones, like fax, do not pose their own set of challenges when it comes to administering surveys. "Skills and time required for handling differed between the three methods (fax, e-mail, and mail); faxing about 50 copies took several hours, time that could have been saved had we sacrificed the personalised introductory letter" (Quinn, Robinson, & Parham, 1998). For more complex modes, like the Web, "the rapidity of technological change requires that researchers have technology support in developing, testing, and implementing their surveys" (Hayslett & Wildemuth, 2004). Such support increases the cost and time required to implement a new project.

Netservey aims to alleviate the shortcomings of each mode, allowing the researcher to select modes without having constraints imposed by his/her skill set, time, and budget.

SETTING UP A SURVEY WITH NETSERVEY

The management of a survey is carried out online using simple forms. The first step in the setting-up process is completing a form with the survey's options. These include, among others, the dates to begin and finish the collection of responses,

the number of responses to accept, whether the survey is currently accepting responses or not, a password to protect the survey from uninvited responses, and various mode-related options.

Netservey, by default, assumes that all modes are to be used. If this is not the case, the researcher should not distribute the survey over one of the modes. For example, if no responses are to be received via the Web, then the researcher should not advertise the survey's Web address.

BUILDING A SURVEY

Netservey can handle multiple modes by breaking a survey's structure into objects that are stored in a database. These objects are then put together to generate the survey for a specific mode. For example, the solution can output a survey in HyperText Markup Language (HTML) format in order to generate its Web version, or in a portable document format (PDF) format in order to print it and mail it.

When starting to build a survey, the user is presented with the option of using a wizard to create the survey's structure, or to create a very simple survey that can then be edited accordingly. The time needed to build a survey depends on its complexity, especially the number of questions. Each survey consists of areas, sections, question groups, questions, question options, and question keys. These are the building blocks that come together to generate the questionnaire, as shown in Figure 1.

Areas are used to separate question groups that cover different topics. For example, a survey may have an area covering the main research topics, and a second area with questions aiming to gather personal information about the participant.

Sections are used for conditional logic. A section carries the questions to be asked, while the groups of questions that the section contains correspond to an answer of the conditional logic question. A section may contain one or more groups

Figure 1. Breaking a survey into objects

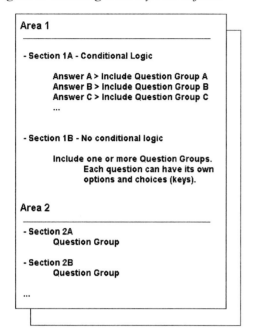

Area 1

- Section 1A - Conditional Logic

    Answer A > Include Question Group A
    Answer B > Include Question Group B
    Answer C > Include Question Group C
    ...

- Section 1B - No conditional logic

    Include one or more Question Groups.
    Each question can have its own
    options and choices (keys).

Area 2

- Section 2A
    Question Group

- Section 2B
    Question Group

...

of questions that may be part of the conditional logic or not.

A group may contain one or more questions. If a group is part of the conditional logic, its questions will only be asked if the answer selected matches the answer associated with the group. This type of interactive filtering only takes place in the Web version of a survey.

Netservey supports 15 types of questions:

- **Open Ended:** One line and multiple lines
- **Multiple Choice:** One answer, one answer-menu, dichotomous, multiple answers
- **Matrices:** One answer, multiple answers, spreadsheet
- **Scales:** Likert, rating, semantic differential, Stapel
- **Other:** Rank order, constant sum

Finally, question options and question keys are used to save information about questions that have predefined options. For example, when adding a multiple-choice question, the researcher

has to specify the question's options, that is, the choices.

The survey options are automatically applied to the modes based on their properties. For example, if a survey contains conditional logic, this will make the Web version filter out the questions that do not apply. Also, on the Web, the solution can force the participant to complete all required questions before continuing, ensuring that no incomplete answers are received. These are not options that are available, for example, for paper surveys, as this is not an interactive mode!

DISTRIBUTION

Once the survey structure is ready, distribution and data gathering are performed automatically. It should be noted that once a response has been received, the survey's structure cannot be changed.

The researcher can use the sampling database to add details for each participant and send out invitations. Each participant can have a mode preference that can allow for individual distribution. When it comes to Web and e-mail surveys, distribution is simply achieved by making the URL of the survey known. For example, the researcher may add a link on a Web site, or send out e-mails to the participants with a link to the survey. Distribution of postal surveys, though, is not as easy, and this is one of the features that make Netservey special.

The solution outputs a PDF that is imported into a collateral fulfilment solution, that is a solution that allows for short-run print on demand, via the Web, which undertakes the mailing (Papagiannidis & Li, 2005). This is through an exclusive collaboration with Gaia Fulfilment. The mailing solution then arranges for full-colour printing and next-day distribution in the United Kingdom. When Gaia Fulfilment makes the necessary arrangements for global printers to be added in their network, Netservey will be able to distribute surveys globally within a few days (normally next day, if a local printer exists). Even for the smallest postal surveys, Netservey can save money, time, and effort, which can be diverted into the design, monitoring, and analysis of the survey and the data gathered.

The biggest challenge when generating PDF files automatically is that the presentation and layout will not be as optimised as they would have been had the PDF files been produced manually. Still, this can be counteracted, to some extent, by the convenience factor of not having to manually design and output the PDF file. Also, Netservey does not require the user to have any software installed on their computers to create the PDF version of the survey, which would have resulted in additional costs. Researchers, especially those who seek total control of their postal survey, are encouraged to upload a manually created PDF file, instead of using the one that the solution outputs, which can then be mailed using Gaia's mailing solutions.

The collateral fulfilment solution offers access to an enhanced electoral roll (requires licence) that consists of 46 million UK records, and includes lifestyle data that can be used for sampling purposes. There are also other databases that could be used on a "pay-as-you-go" basis or the users could upload their own data sets. The participants' details can be used to personalise the surveys, although this may require additional work by the digital print support staff, depending on the level of customisation. Most often, this will simply involve addressing the covering letter to the participant. This only needs the PDF to leave an empty "window" on a predefined position, so that the address can be superimposed on the document. The ability to personalise a survey is of great importance, as it can have an impact on the response rates, but also on the answers one may receive to sensitive questions (Joinson, Woodley, & Reips, in press). On the other hand, this may not necessarily be the case when dealing with other modes, for example e-mail (Porter & Whitcomb, 2003). Another advantage of collateral

fulfilment is that the researcher only needs to print what is required, preventing waste and reducing costs. If only one member of the samples prefers to complete a postal questionnaire, then only one questionnaire will be printed and mailed. This can result in substantial cost benefits, as the researcher only has to pay for what was actually printed and posted.

Cover letters can be included, if needed, while follow-up letters and postcards can be arranged separately via the collateral fulfilment solution. Mailed follow-ups could be a good way of addressing the negative connotation that e-mails may have, which can easily be misunderstood as unsolicited e-mail (spam).

Another point of interest is that as Netservey offers the researcher the ability to add responses, mainly in order to enter responses gathered via postal surveys, the solution could be used for structured interviews, for example, over the phone.

Finally, Netservey's approach to decomposing a survey and then building it for a specific mode allows for adding more modes in the future. For example, Netservey could fax a survey or even take responses via digital-TV and mobile phones. As most digital modes support mark-up languages, such as HTML or XML (eXtensible Markup Language), Netservey could potentially distribute surveys over all of them.

RELIABILITY

Each mode has its own characteristics that the researcher has to take into consideration. In many cases, electronic surveys were found to be generally comparable to print surveys in most respects, provided the researcher evaluated their key advantages and challenges (Boyer, Olson, Calantone, & Jackson, 2002; Hayslett & Wildemuth, 2004; Knapp & Kirk, 2003; McCabe, Boyd, Young, Crawford, & Pope, 2005; Morrel-Samuels, 2003). On the other hand, there is also evidence that there are considerable differences between the different modes that could be the outcome of many variables, for example sampling (Cobanoglu, Warde, & Moreo, 2001; Grandcolas, Rettie, & Marusenko, 2003; Roster, Rogers, Albaum, & Klein, 2004).

As Netservey acts only as the means of building and distributing a survey, it does not increase or decrease the reliability of conducting a survey over a specific mode, provided the researcher appreciates the advantages and challenges of each mode. This argument is also supported by the fact that Netservey, although designed as a mixed-mode tool, does not necessarily have to be used as one; hence, mode-related differences only apply to the planning stage when the researcher has to select a mode to conduct the survey. Still, even in the single-mode case, the researcher must understand and fully appreciate the selected mode's attributes.

VALIDITY

Netservey inherits the validity issues that mixed-mode approaches have. Still, as is the case with reliability, it is up to the researcher to appreciate the distinct characteristics of the modes used, and ensure the validity of the gathered data. This is well summarised by Morrel-Samuels' (2003) words on good practices when using Web surveys: "as any good carpenter knows, it's important to be clear about the differences between a wooden yardstick and a steel ruler— especially if you intend to use both to build your house."

Equally, validity issues arise when the researcher faces mode dilemmas due to barriers associated with each mode. For example, if the employment of a Web survey calls for technical skills that the researcher does not have, then Web surveys may not be used even if it could be beneficial for the project. With Netservey lowering many of these barriers and making multiple modes available through one interface, the effects of mode-selection decisions are minimised, which could indirectly affect the reliability and validity of the data gathered.

RESULTS

For digital modes, Netservey can collect data and store them directly in the database. It also provides the researcher with a facility to input responses gathered by postal questionnaires. All responses stored in the database can be used to perform basic analysis in real time. Netservey can perform a set of simple statistical functions, but more complex analysis should be done with more advanced software packages.

Although Netservey's primary aim is not to analyse, but gather data, the level of analysis that the solution provides can be useful to monitor the survey and help identify patterns, while data gathering is still in process. Analysis could potentially be performed on responses gathered via all modes, if the modes do not call for a separate design, or via a specific mode, allowing each mode's effectiveness to be benchmarked separately.

The prototype has so far been used in a number of academic projects. A mixed-mode approach was used once. A PDF file, consisting of a cover letter and the survey, was manually prepared and sent out using the mailing solution to about 400 recipients. In the cover letter, participants were asked to consider completing the survey online, and one of them did so. In all other cases in which Netservey was used, the questionnaires were only deployed over the Web. The solution's usage, so far, highlights the point made before about validity and reliability, that is, that the researcher must be clear about the implications associated with mode selection: using mixed modes is not a panacea for research challenges.

COMMENTARY

Netservey is a data-gathering solution that can automate many of the practicalities of undertaking mixed-mode surveys. The solution is unique in its innovative use of collateral fulfilment in order to enable postal questionnaires. The solution can be used in both academic- and commercial-related projects, reducing the technical and resource-related barriers of mixed-mode surveys. Although the researcher is not assumed to possess any technical skills, he/she is expected to be able to assess mode-related effects.

From the participant's point of view, the ability to switch modes can be an incentive to complete a survey. This switch can take place without any intervention by the researcher; for example, when a participant receives a postal survey, the covering letter may include a link to the Web version, which can be used instead of the postal one.

Netservey encourages the use of Web surveys, provided the researcher and the respondent have no mode preferences, and that this does not affect the reliability of the response. This is due to the following reasons:

1. Results are validated in real time; hence, if the responder is expected to answer a question or provide an answer in a specific format, the solution can ensure that the predefined rules are adhered to before adding the answer to the database, preventing incomplete or incompatible answers.

2. As results are immediately stored in the database, the analysis can commence in real time, allowing the researcher to monitor the progress of the survey.

3. To receive e-mails, one must have an Internet connection, which suggests that, most probably, access to the Web is also available. In such cases, the Web version could have been used instead of the e-mail one. Similarly, providing a link within a postal survey can encourage participants to complete the survey over the Web. It is then up to them to select a mode based on their preferences.

4. Postal surveys result in greater administration overheads for the researcher, with most of the time spent entering the responses into the database. The Web version stores answers directly into the database and as a result, there are no extra requirements for time and effort, which can translate to significant costs, depending on the number of responses. It also prevents potential errors in the data input process.

5. The Web allows for more interactive surveys that could include audio and video files. If multimedia are to be used for a survey though, the survey must be custom built.

Netservey plans to add new modes in the future, allowing for more complex mixed-mode projects to be undertaken, but also to enhance distribution of invitations and follow-ups.

COST

Netservey is a subscription-based service, with prices depending on the amount and type of usage. Printing and distribution of surveys is charged separately, as this depends on the mailing options selected. Complimentary accounts are provided for specific types of research, as part of Netservey's social responsibility policy.

LOCATION

Netservey is available at http://www.netservey.com. Customised solutions and private installations for organisations that seek complete control over the solution can be arranged. More information about collateral fulfilment and online demonstrations of the solutions can be found at: http://www.gaia-fulfilment.co.uk.

REFERENCES

Boyer, K. K., Olson, J. R., Calantone, R. J., & Jackson, E. C. (2002). Print vs. electronic surveys: A comparison of two data collection methodologies. *Journal of Operations Management, 20*(4), 357-373.

Cobanoglu, C., Warde, B., & Moreo, P. J. (2001). A comparison of mail, fax and Web-based survey methods. *International Journal of Market Research, 43*(4), 441-452.

Grandcolas, U., Rettie, R., & Marusenko, K. (2003). Web survey bias: Sample or mode effect? *Journal of Marketing Management, 19*(5/6), 541-561.

Hayslett, M. M., & Wildemuth, B. M. (2004). Pixels or pencils? The relative effectiveness of Web-based vs. paper surveys. *Library & Information Science Research, 26*(1), 73-93.

Huang, H.-M. (in press). Do print and Web surveys provide the same results? *Computers in Human Behavior.*

Joinson, A. N., Woodley, A., & Reips, U.-D. (in press). Personalization, authentication and self-disclosure in self-administered Internet surveys. *Computers in Human Behavior.*

Knapp, H., & Kirk, S. A. (2003). Using pencil and paper, Internet and touch-tone phones for self-administered surveys: Does methodology matter? *Computers in Human Behavior, 19*(1), 117-134.

McCabe, S. E., Boyd, C. J., Young, A., Crawford, S., & Pope, D. (2005). Mode effects for collecting alcohol and tobacco data among 3rd and 4th grade students: A randomized pilot study of Web-form vs. paper-form surveys. *Addictive Behaviors, 30*(4), 663-671.

Morrel-Samuels, P. (2003). Web surveys' hidden hazards. *Harvard Business Review, 81*(7), 16-18.

Papagiannidis, S., & Li, F. (2005). Management and delivery of digital print via the Web: A case study of Gaia fulfilment. *International Journal of Cases of Electronic Commerce, 1*(1), 1-18.

Porter, S. R., & Whitcomb, M. E. (2003). The impact of contact type on Web survey response rates. *Public Opinion Quarterly, 67*(4), 579-588.

Quinn, J. E., Robinson, L. C., & Parham, E. S. (1998). Evaluation of electronic and fax methods for survey research. *Journal of the American Dietetic Association, 98*(9, Supplement 1), A56.

Roster, C. A., Rogers, R. D., Albaum, G., & Klein, D. (2004). A comparison of response characteristics from Web and telephone surveys. *International Journal of Market Research, 46*(3), 359-373.

KEY TERMS

Collateral Fulfillment: Collateral fulfilment is the management and delivery of digital print via the Web; a very innovative approach to printing with many advantages over traditional printing methods. With collateral fulfilment, one can achieve variable print of a single document, preventing wastage and set up costs.

Digital Modes: Modes that are based on a digital channel for their distribution such as online surveys and faxed surveys.

Mixed-Modes Surveys: Mixed-modes surveys are surveys conducted over a number of different modes such as the Web, e-mail, postal surveys, telephone, and so forth.

Online Surveys: Surveys conducted over the Internet, mainly e-mail, and Web surveys.

PDF: PDF (portable document format) is a platform-independent document format created by Adobe (http://www.adobe.com). As PDF documents are platform-independent, they should look and print the same on a variety of computing platforms.

Spam: Unsolicited e-mail, often sent for commercial purposes.

Web Surveys: HTML and Scripting Languages: In order to build a Web survey, the researcher must have the required technical skills. These can range from simple HTML coding to more advanced scripting languages, for example PHP, Perl, or ASP.

XML: XML (eXtensible Markup Language) is a mark-up language for interchange of structured data, standardised by the World Wide Web Consortium. It can be used to pass on information; for example, information about the structure of a survey, from one system to another.

Chapter XXIV
Design and Development of an Electronic Survey System

Bruce Aaron
Accenture, USA

Samir Desai
Accenture, USA

ABSTRACT

Within the Accenture Corporation, the CDO (capability development organization), which manages human resource development, designed and implemented an electronic survey system (ESS) as a component of the system that manages learning within the company. This chapter discusses the relationship of the organizational learning infrastructure, and the use of survey software (ESS) within the mission of human resource development.

BUSINESS CONTEXT FOR THE DEVELOPMENT OF AN ELECTRONIC SURVEY SYSTEM

Accenture is a global management consulting, technology services, and outsourcing company. Given the nature of the company's core capabilities and services, the importance of Accenture's employees to the company's success is sharply defined, and the development of human capital is a priority for the organization. Accenture's CDO (capability development organization), which manages human resource development, designed and implemented an electronic survey system (ESS) as a component of the system that manages learning within the company. The relationship of

this learning infrastructure and ESS, within the mission of the CDO, is shown in Figure 1.

The ESS operates in the performance measurement function, and helps determine progress against key performance indicators for Accenture's learning strategy. In order to achieve that strategy, Accenture designed and implemented an integrated e-learning infrastructure, known internally as *myLearning*. The *myLearning* system serves the delivery vehicle function in the company's e-learning strategy.

Several factors led to the design and implementation of *myLearning* at Accenture, including (a) pressure to contain training and development costs, (b) an increasingly dispersed workforce, (c) advances in e-learning tools and Internet technol-

Figure 1. CDO capability blueprint

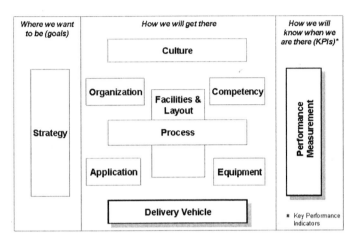

Figure 2. Accenture learning management

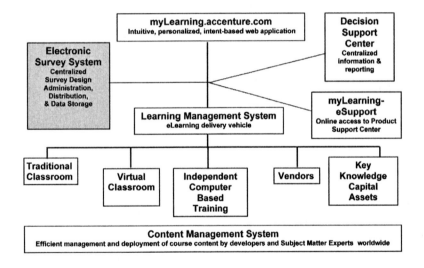

ogy, and (d) a learning strategy requiring point delivery of learning and knowledge assets.

The company, which was delivering instructor-led training (ILT) and distributed online training in a ratio of about 70% to 30%, respectively, set a target of reversing that ratio (70% online, 30% ILT) with the implementation of *myLearning*. This target was achieved, and the system provides online learning management to over 100,000 employees, resulting in savings of $125 million in the first 3 years of implementation. The ESS is a critical component of this infrastructure, shown in Figure 2.

Through the *myLearning* LMS, employees locate and access learning and knowledge assets that meet their immediate needs or are prescribed for their individual profiles. Through the ESS, a wide range of survey data is collected to determine the effectiveness of these assets. Survey data are merged with data from other systems, including training projections, costs, attendance, and usage, to provide a wide range of learning metrics and reports in the decision support center (DSC).

STRATEGY AND THE DESIGN OF ELECTRONIC SURVEY SYSTEMS

The ESS exists to address particular business questions. These fundamental issues are the first consideration in design of an ESS. The fundamental goals and the role of survey data in addressing performance against those goals can be illustrated by the V-model, a conceptual map showing the relationship between business needs, metrics, and solutions (Aaron, 2004a, Waddington, Aaron, & Sheldrick, 2004). A general form of the V-model for human resource development is shown in Figure 3.

In practice, the V-model helps ensure that solutions (at the bottom of the model) and measurement (the right side of the model) link to the important fundamental questions or needs of the enterprise (upper left of the model). In Accenture's *myLearning* system, the integration of survey data and data from other systems is crucial for meaningful measurement. Survey and test data typically are most useful at the middle levels of the model (when evaluating participant perceptions or skills). However, they are irrelevant to other metrics near the bottom of the model (relating to delivery status) or the top relating to business results and ROI—(return on investment) (Aaron, 2004b). For the latter, the most credible data

typically come not from surveys, but from other systems, including financial (e.g., for capturing costs) and human resources databases. Additionally, survey data are typically analyzed by other factors, such as demographic variables pulled from other systems.

In our experience, design and implementation of an ESS begins with fundamental questions about what is going to be measured. Once the measurement architecture is defined, the data architecture is addressed by identifying the data needed to construct measures. With these requirements established, system design and development is addressed. Therefore, key considerations for designing and implementing an ESS relate to (1) measurement architecture (2) data architecture, and (3) system design and development. Inherent in each of these are trade-offs between cost and benefit.

KEY CONSIDERATIONS FOR ELECTRONIC SURVEY SYSTEMS

Measurement Architecture

At Accenture, measures needed for making decisions about the training and development of employees include data from survey responses

Figure 3. Human resource development V-model

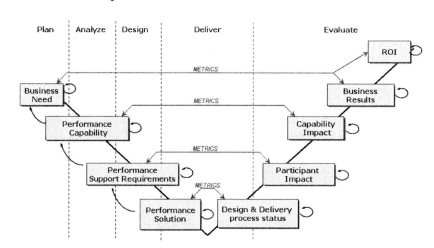

and knowledge tests. These are collected by the ESS. Data are also collected from the *myLearning* learning management mystem (LMS) and other internal systems. The principles and considerations for the design and development of an ESS generalize to other, nonlearning contexts.

Data collected by an ESS are unique in that they are generated by respondents through carefully constructed stimuli (survey or test items). Decisions about the types of stimuli the ESS can present are needed, given the wide variety of possible item formats, and benefit will need to be weighed against cost. In testing higher-level knowledge and skill, for example, innovative item formats (e.g., simulations and object manipulation in virtual environments) are useful, but expensive. Well-written multiple-choice items can assess higher-level knowledge and application effectively and objectively, at a relatively low cost (Carey, 1988).

In our experience, an effective approach is to start simply and build iteratively. For example, test item formats in the first release of the ESS were limited to text-based questions and multiple-choice or alternative response (e.g., "True/False") response sets. Our experience and success with the system led to additional funding for the next release, and included critical but cost-efficient enhancements. For test item formats, the greatest incremental value came from increasing flexibility in formats for questions, rather than responses. This included a randomization feature that allows us to randomly administer test (or survey) items to individual respondents from defined sets of items. This can greatly reduce instrument length, saving time and increasing response rates. Given reasonably large samples, randomization provides sufficient data across a wide range of domains for program evaluation decisions, and even individual decisions when the items are calibrated using an item response theory (IRT) measurement model (e.g., the Rasch model) (Rasch, 1980). Item calibration involves fitting the data to a model that places items (and persons) on a single unidimen-

sional scale, such that differing samples of items can provide reliable estimates on the same scale (Wright & Masters, 1981).

Another enhancement to the presentation of questions was the addition of rich text format, graphics, and URL links in question fields. This feature is particularly effective in increasing the level at which knowledge and skill can be assessed. For example, a scenario and spreadsheet of simulated data can be presented in an item that requires a relatively complex cognitive operation from the respondent.

The same features are available for presenting survey items and test items; test items are scored according to a key (correct response) associated with each item. In addition to the standard list format (stacked scale responses with clickable selection buttons), important features in designing survey response sets are dual scales and multiple selections. Dual-scale items allow two ratings per item stem. For example, a course evaluation survey might include items in which a "Before Training" and "After Training" self-assessment scale are collected for particular learning objectives of a course. Or, in a competency study, a respondent might provide ratings of "Importance to Role" and "Frequency of Application" for each of a set of performances. Multiple selection items ("select all that apply") are convenient for respondents and, essentially, are a set of dichotomous items ("checked/not checked", "true/false", etc.) when stored the database. For dual-scale and multiple-selection items, each rating is stored in a separate variable.

All measurement is based on comparison, and particular comparisons and benchmarks that guide decisions should be identified in the measurement architecture. These comparisons typically require standard metrics provided by a common or equated set of items. The need for standardization must be balanced against the need for customization. We accomplish this with a small bank of survey items that measure general domains such as overall satisfaction, strength of recommendation to peers, effectiveness of the learning environment, increase in knowledge or skill, and relevance to work. By leveraging a large data set and calibrating these items, we can offer a menu of common items to survey designers who select those that best meet their needs, while providing a standard across all surveys. In addition to these standard items, project sponsors may include unique items.

Another simple, but important, guideline for designing ESS measurement is collection of qualitative data. The measurement architecture should collect open-text comments with the same consideration for standardization and customization that apply to quantitative data, and recognition that quantitative and qualitative research are complementary endeavors with similar important roles in inference and decision-making (King, Keohane, & Verba, 1994).

Data Architecture

After defining measurement architecture for the ESS, identify the specific data that need to be collected, aggregated, and reported. Approaching data architecture before clearly analyzing the business rationale and measurement architecture can lead to costly redesign and opportunity costs due to gaps in the information needed to support ongoing business decisions. Also, it might be tempting to proceed to system design and development after completing the measurement architecture, but important data design issues need to be addressed to prevent rework down the road. While it is our experience that an iterative approach to ESS development is most efficient and effective, it is very important to get the foundational data model correct. In the end, the purpose of an ESS is to collect *data* to support measurement and analysis. Giving the architecture of those data due consideration is crucial to success. Following are important considerations and common pitfalls in developing the data architecture for an ESS.

Data formats. A basic aspect of data architecture is determining the data formats for the various questions, scales, results, and metadata that need to be collected and aggregated. Consider whether the codes or decodes should be stored, if responses are stored in string or integer format, the lengths allowed for qualitative data strings, and whether data need to be saved as "blobs" to account for nontextual elements. Getting these issues right the first time will prevent costly rework, and reduce the chance of losing data due to format incompatibility.

Data timeliness. Ideally, survey data would be available for analysis in real time. However, obtaining and aggregating data immediately is expensive and operationally intensive, so carefully consider how current the data truly need to be. Typically, data outdated by a day or a week are sufficient, especially when much of the analysis is based on trends. While some data might be more urgent, do not assume that all data share this urgency. For example, if the measurement architecture calls for assessment of a learning asset for various career levels, and career levels update once a month, then updating career level more often is wasted effort. Of course, it is important to design the data architecture to keep parallel data in sync.

Data accuracy. Perfect data accuracy seems like a natural expectation. However, perfect accuracy can, in fact, be too expensive. In our ESS, the quality and cleanliness of some data is dependent on other source systems we do not have resources to control. Of course, a high degree of accuracy is very important for the data to be trustworthy for decision making. In our experience, there are three key aspects to achieving high data accuracy. First, a full and accurate understanding of the rules used to generate data elements is crucial. For example, when measuring trends across fiscal years, what determines the year to which those survey data are assigned: when the course was completed, when the survey was delivered or completed, or when the survey was returned? Second, it is important in ensuring accuracy to minimize manual steps in the overall process. For example, variability in the way that a question is manually associated with a content domain can lead to inaccurate measurement of that content domain. Third, adequate testing is crucial. Unlike a transactional system where finite steps can be identified for test conditions, an ESS can easily have millions of possible data values and aggregations. It is unlikely that each value can be tested for accuracy. Therefore, it is important that the process for obtaining the data is tested, and a substantial segment of the data is included in formal testing. It is also important to have continual validity testing conducted by users familiar with the data.

Data redundancy. Consider what would happen if you were to lose the ESS data due to system failure, or miss collection of a data set due to system downtime. Also, establish the importance of the decisions that need to be made based on the data. For example, for legally mandated employee education, it might be necessary to ensure 100% data collection and redundancy. This would be very expensive for all data, so it is important to determine the need for redundancy across all measurement areas.

Historical data. Is trend analysis required by the measurement architecture? If so, and the analysis factors will change (e.g., job role, organizational unit), then those data values need to be captured and stored at time of survey submission. All dimensions could be stored at point of submission, but data storage is operationally expensive. For each saved dimension, it will be important to maintain historical data. For example, if area codes are saved, and districts restructure area codes due to shifts in population, it would need to be determined if and how to update the historical data. One way to reduce this impact is to store off codes instead of decodes. For example, the literal names of business units may change, but their representative code or value may be held constant. By saving the code and pulling the decode (the literal name of the unit matched to the code) at the point of reporting or analysis, historical data do not need to be updated.

Metadata. Perhaps the most important data architecture considerations relate to metadata. Put simply, metadata are data about some part of the ESS data architecture that are not directly collected from the individual. Metadata are typically demographic or organizational data that are universal in nature. It is important to import metadata from the appropriate sources, and not to reinvent them. For example, if measurement calls for analysis by country, what should be the source of the country data values? Will you ask the individual? If so, will they type it in, or select from a list? If they are to select from a list, where will those values come from? Will they be the same values that another survey uses? How do you ensure one common list of countries? Either you will need to create a metadata store in the ESS data warehouse or, preferably, you will need to pull the values from a global data store. This is especially important if the measurement architecture calls for analysis of survey responses crossed with other data elements. The most common cause of manual, expensive postprocessing of data is mismatches in common demographics due to different sources of metadata.

These are the key considerations for the data architecture phase of ESS development. Time invested here is well spent. It is important to involve people who are familiar with the type of data being processed, as well as experienced database architects who can work together to ensure a solid data architecture.

SYSTEM DESIGN AND DEVELOPMENT

Requirements. In determining requirements for the ESS, gather input from various stakeholders, but maintain a strong central vision for the future direction of the ESS, in order to balance these needs. As with any system implementation, it typically is not feasible to deliver all requirements in the first release of the product. Therefore, establish a central group that can clearly drive the most important, valuable requirements first, and then iterate through other requirements in future releases. The primary business requirements for the *myLearning* ESS address (1) survey design, (2) survey delivery, (3) survey data collection, (4) data storage, and (5) data processing. To that might be added reporting requirements, although in our context (as shown in Figure 2), these are addressed in the design of the DSC, which is a separate system.

Survey design tool. To design electronic survey forms and limit variability in the input data due to manual processes, it is important to consider implementing a survey design toolset. The survey design tool is used to create surveys, items, scales, context, formatting, and data mapping. A key decision will be how much to invest in this component of the ESS. Building a highly intelligent, broadly usable survey design tool is expensive. Our experience suggests the benefit of first investing in the delivery, storage, and reporting of the data, and training central staff on a robust, but somewhat arcane, survey design tool, rather than designing the tool for the masses. The survey design tool populates the database with the attributes of the survey, and defines the relationship of the survey to the items. It controls what is delivered to end users, and is populated with actual data, both to define the survey to users, and to deliver data to the database.

Survey delivery. Once created, the survey needs to be delivered to the end user. In many environments, the typical channel is e-mail. However, delivery might also be paper based (and require OCR, optical character recognition, technology), or via the phone or mobile device. The delivery mechanism(s) of the survey will drive significant requirements related to the way that the survey is created from the database and delivered to the end user.

Another key consideration is the timing and frequency of the survey delivery. In our experience, delivering the survey at or soon after the conclusion of the target experience or very soon afterwards, promotes the highest response rate. In order to increase response rates, consider sending reminders, and/or resending the survey for some period of time until the user responds.

Survey data collection. Once the survey is completed and returned by the end user, the data need to be uploaded to the database. If delivered online, this occurs as a live transaction. If there is a requirement for completing surveys offline, another mechanism must be used to initiate the data upload.

It is also important to answer other questions relating to survey design. Can the user submit the survey more than once? If so, what response values are saved: the latest, the average, or the highest? Can questions be left blank (and how will rules be implemented for treating missing data from tests differently than those from surveys)? Are comments required? All of these considerations influence the data and processes for uploading to the database.

Data storage. The data must be stored in an environment that allows for update, and also allows for data access and reporting. For a medium to large set of data with global reach, a data warehouse might be needed. For smaller sets of data, a basic database might be sufficient. Data architecture requirements will typically determine the type of data store needed.

Data processing. Once the data are stored to the data warehouse, additional processing might be necessary. The data need to be placed in an environment providing access and analysis. Typically, a separate reporting database is necessary, from which standard reports are built. But standard reports do not always meet decision makers' needs, and ad hoc tables should be used to allow users to access and manipulate data as needed. For example, ad hoc statistical analysis might require flat files (one record per person, one column per variable) containing analysis variables from several relational database tables.

Each of these functional areas of the ESS involves many other technical considerations. For *myLearning* and the ESS, stability and scalability are very important. Given the dynamic nature of resources, we chose an open architecture and a platform with sufficient backing and support. Important technical considerations that were taken into account include the following:

1. **Open vs. Proprietary:** Should an open architecture be built, or a custom, proprietary system that better meets immediate needs?
2. **Build vs. Buy:** Does an off-the-shelf product meet the business requirements, or will a custom system need to be built? Or can a baseline product be purchased and customized?
3. **Scalability:** It is important to look to the future. How large will the system need to be? How much data will need to be supported in the future? How many end users will exist in the future?
4. **Data Warehouse:** Is a full-fledged data warehouse needed? Will there be a need for segmented data stored in data marts? What is the anticipated data volume?
5. Security—how much security is required? Is the data sensitive; is it restricted?
6. **ETL:** What extract, transform, and load processing will be needed? From how many systems will the ESS import data? How often? Are the source data in a format that is usable, or will they need to be manipulated?
7. **Reporting:** In *myLearning*, reporting is implemented through a separate system (the DSC), but in other contexts, technical constraints based on reporting requirements might need to be considered in designing an ESS.

CONCLUSION

An ESS can provide uniquely valuable insight for assessing the impact of organizational strategy and informing decisions. The suggestions provided here, based on Accenture's experience in designing and implementing *myLearning*, can be used to guide strategic planning, measurement architecture, data architecture, design, and development of electronic survey systems.

REFERENCES

Aaron, B. C. (2004a, May). *How to turn evaluation requests into performance improvement*. Paper presented at the International Conference and Exposition of ASTD, Washington, DC.

Aaron, B. C. (2004b). Using the V-model for human performance ROI. *ROI Network News, 3(I)*. Carey, L. M. (1988). *Measuring and evaluating school learning*. Boston: Allyn and Bacon.

King, G., Keohane, R.O., & Verba, S. (1994). *Designing social inquiry*. Princeton, NJ: Princeton University Press.

Rasch, G. (1980). *Probabilistic models for some intelligence and attainment tests*. Chicago: MESA press.

Waddington, T., Aaron, B., & Sheldrick, R. (2004). Guerilla evaluation: Adapting to the terrain and situation. In A. Armstrong (Ed.), *Instructional design in the real world: A view from the trenches* (pp. 136-159). Hershey, PA: Information Science Publishing.

Wright, B. D., & Masters, G. (1982). *Rating scale analysis*. Chicago: MESA press.

KEY TERMS

Data Mart: A specialized data repository providing quick access for particular users and applications.

ETL (Extract, Transform, Load): Process or type of application that assists in gathering and integrating data from various sources for storage in a database.

Item Calibration: Estimation of an item's position on a variable along which persons are measured. Persons are measured, and items calibrated, along the single dimension that they define simultaneously.

Item Response Theory (IRT): A theory for performance on an instrument that relates the measure of a person on the variable of interest, and the position of the item on the same variable, usually by a logistic function that resembles the cumulative normal distribution.

Key Performance Indicator: A measure used to monitor progress in achieving objectives.

Learning Management System (LMS): A system (typically based on Internet technology) that delivers, manages, monitors, and reports student-learning events.

Metadata: Data, existing at a higher level of abstraction than raw operational data, that describe the latter in terms of entities, attributes, or relationships that have meaning at the business or organizational level.

ROI (Return on Investment): A currency measure used to determine the percentage of original investment in an initiative that is gained, using a formula of the form: [(Benefits – Cost / Cost) ×100].

Stem: The part of a test or survey item that poses the problem or question.

Chapter XXV
Open Source Surveys with Asset

Bert G. Wachsmuth
Seton Hall University, USA

ABSTRACT

At Seton Hall University we developed Asset, a Web-based academic survey system and evaluation tool to design, administer, and analyze surveys. This free, open-source project is widely used at our institution, and has even been approved for electronic voting. Other universities have also successfully deployed the project. In this article, we will introduce the Asset system, describe its design principles and capabilities, and compare it to similar tools. We will include a discussion of sample surveys using Asset, and briefly describe the requirements for installing the system.

INTRODUCTION

Since its beginning in the early 1990s the World Wide Web has been used to gather data. During the early stages, custom-made CGI scripts were used to collect and process data from Web pages containing simple forms. Today, form generation, data collection, and processing is routinely done using elaborate Web-optimized tools with acronyms such as PHP, ASP, JSP, or Servlets, and sophisticated database servers for background processing and data storage. From an abstract programming perspective, there is little difference in handling an online business such as *Amazon.com*, processing airline tickets and flight reservations, or distributing and evaluating online surveys for

educational or scientific purposes. In each case, a mechanism must exist to (a) design and manage the information to present, to (b) collect the information efficiently from the customer, and to (c) manage, evaluate, and analyze the collected data.

In this paper I will discuss *Asset*, the academic survey system and evaluation tool developed at Seton Hall University. *Asset* is an open source online survey management system that is freely available to anyone affiliated with an educational institution, and can be installed under a GNU-like license on any server. At Seton Hall, *Asset* has been used since 2002, and is currently managing over 500 active surveys with almost 1.5 million data points. It is also used as the official electronic voting system for the university. In addition, *Asset* has been installed at institutions such as Creighton School of Pharmacy and Health Professions, Raritan Valley Community College, and others. I will discuss the capabilities and limitations of *Asset*, talk about *Asset*'s technical requirements, and conclude with a discussion on lessons learned.

ASSET CAPABILITIES

Asset conceptualizes two types of users:

- A **registered user** can create and manage online surveys and analyze or download existing data. Registered users need an *Asset* username and password, and they must login to the *Asset* system to manage their surveys and associated data. A registered user can create and own any number of surveys.
- An *Asset* **subject** is an individual who fills out a survey created with *Asset* by visiting a specific URL. The authentication a subject needs to provide to take a survey depends on the survey parameters set by the survey owner.

When a registered user logs in to *Asset* using a standard Web browser, he/she sees a list of surveys he/she owns. He/she can edit existing surveys, create new ones, or analyze or download data for existing surveys. Any number of the following survey elements can be combined into a survey (see Figure 1):

- Multiple-choice questions with an optional text field to capture user input
- Groups of multiple-choice questions in table form, with the same choices per row, with an optional text field to capture user input
- Groups of questions in table form with choices mapped to a numeric scale
- Numeric fields that allow entry of arbitrary numbers
- Text fields that allow entry of arbitrary text
- Group of questions in table form where each row contains a text field for arbitrary text entry

Asset's main design criteria is simplicity; thus, some more elaborate survey elements present in other online systems, such as, for example, con-

Figure 1. Some of Asset's survey elements, displayed in "edit" mode

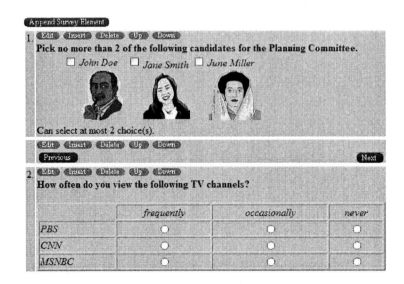

Figure 2. Asset-generated online frequency chart

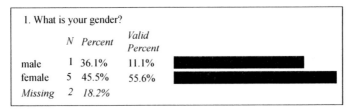

1. What is your gender?				
	N	Percent	Valid Percent	
male	1	36.1%	11.1%	
female	5	45.5%	55.6%	
Missing	2	18.2%		

Figure 3. Asset-generated online contingency table

Contingency Table

(row): **What is your gender?**
by (col): **PBS**

	frequently	occasionally	never	Totals
male	66.7% 2	33.3% 1	0.0% 0	100.0% 3
female	60.0% 3	20.0% 1	20.0% 1	100.0% 5
Totals	62.5% 5	25.0% 2	12.5% 1	100.0% 8

The contingency table shows observed counts as well as *row percentages*. The number of missing observations is 3 (27.3%)

stant sum questions, are not available. However, *Asset* surveys can include two types of passive elements to enhance the look of a survey:

- Page-break elements to divide longer surveys into a sequence of pages
- Text elements to insert static text into a survey.

All elements can contain HTML formatting code, which allows for inclusion of formatted text and images.

Elements are combined into surveys with various properties, including an automatic closing date and one of the following authentication schemes:

- Anonymous surveys without using any authentication

- Password-protected surveys authenticated using an arbitrary username and a survey-specific password
- List-based surveys and list-based anonymous surveys.

List-based authentication offers the most flexibility. The survey owner can create a list of subjects allowed to take a particular survey. Each subject can have a custom-made username and password, or can, optionally, be linked to a standard, institution-wide LDAP-based username and password combination, if available.

Once a survey is created, it is assigned a unique URL that can be distributed to the intended target audience via e-mail or other communications, or can be embedded in existing Web pages. If a survey has a list-based access scheme, *Asset* can automatically send e-mail reminders to all subjects on the access list who have not yet completed the associated survey.

A subject takes the survey by visiting the associated URL, providing the required authentication, and filling out the online form representing the survey elements.

Registered users can monitor the data for existing surveys as it arrives, except for anonymous surveys, which must close first before any data becomes available. *Asset* provides simple online descriptive statistics such as frequency charts, measures of central tendency and variation, as well as contingency analysis with associated Chi-square statistics (see Figures 2 and 3). All results can be filtered to restrict the analysis to specific subsets. For a more detailed analysis data can be downloaded in CSV or SPSS-compatible format.

To try *Asset* as a guest user, visit http://tltc. shu.edu/servlets/asset.Asset

ASSET **AS VOTING TOOLS**

One of the more interesting uses of *Asset* is as a voting tool. A voting ballot can be considered a survey where (a) only authorized people vote, (b) authorized people can vote at most once, and (c) the vote is anonymous. *Asset* satisfies these requirements as follows:

- The survey representing a voting ballot is created with list-based authentication and marked as anonymous.
- When a subject accesses the survey, authentication is performed against the associated access list. When the list is based on institution-wide LDAP authentication, the subject can use the normal username and password combination. If the list shows that the authenticated subject did not yet take this particular survey, they can continue.
- When the subject submits the survey (ballot), an entry is made in the access list that the subject took the survey (voted). At the same time, the username and other identifying information is removed from the survey data and the survey data is entered into the database.

Thus, *Asset* knows who voted, when they voted, and what was voted for, but any relation between the vote and the subject information has been removed and cannot be recovered. In addition, all survey results are blocked from view until the survey closes to prevent the survey owner from continuously monitoring results.

It should be noted that when a survey system is used for voting, it is essential that the software performs as advertised. *Asset*, in particular, is

an open-source project, so anyone with some programming knowledge can verify that identifiable information, such as name and IP number, is indeed removed from anonymous surveys before the data is entered into the database. This verification process was important for *Asset*'s acceptance as the electronic voting system of Seton Hall University.

TECHNICAL ASPECTS

Asset is based on free tools, and is an open-source project. It is written exclusively in Java, and uses the Java Servlet 2.4 specifications. It has been written to work with the database program MySQL version 3.4 or later, but can be modified to work with other database servers. A configuration file is included to allow easy installation under the Apache Tomcat Web server.

While anyone affiliated with an educational institution can obtain an unrestricted account on Seton Hall's *Asset* system, the *Asset* system can be installed on other servers without any restrictions. The advantages of installing *Asset* locally are:

- All data is physically stored locally at the institution housing the software, greatly improving data security.
- *Asset* can be configured to work with existing local authentication schemes such as LDAP authentication, if available.
- Additional survey elements can be created to address particular needs.
- *Asset* can be reconfigured to match an institution's overall look and feel.

Asset can be downloaded from http://www. cs.shu.edu/thinklets/General/Asset/ including detailed installation instructions. The system can be adjusted to specific circumstances by editing a few constants. If desired, however, any part of the source code may be edited to fit particular needs.

Requesting an account on Seton Hall's system requires no technical knowledge or download, simply send electronic mail to surveys@shu.edu.

OTHER ONLINE SURVEY MANAGEMENT SYSTEMS

A variety of online survey management systems exist; Table 1 lists some of the more common ones. Most are comparable to each other but differ in

- **Payment Scheme:** Several systems in Table 1 offer basic services free, but require membership fees to access advanced features such as data downloads. Others use advertisement to recover their costs.
- **Types of Survey Elements Offered:** Most services offer similar elements to the ones discussed previously, but some feature more sophisticated elements (such as constant sum elements).
- **Level of Visual Sophistication:** Many services allow configuration of the look and feel of surveys via themes and/or custom logos, and they differ in the way form elements are rendered.

- **Build-in Logic:** Some services allow logical statements to be added to a survey, for example to skip a group of questions based on the answer to other questions.

In contrast, *Asset* differs from the systems listed in Table 1 in two main aspects:

- It is a free, open source system that can, if desired, be installed on other servers. The program can be verified and customized, and any submitted data is completely owned by the institution housing the software, greatly improving data security.
- Registered user accounts and list-based authentication can be tied to existing authentication schemes, such as LDAP directories, so that users and subjects can use existing usernames and passwords. This provides increased authentication convenience, which allows Asset to be used as a voting system.

LESSONS LEARNED

The *Asset* survey management system has been a resounding success. While the advantages of this

Table 1. Online survey management systems

Active Web survey (http://www.webintel.net/websurvey4)	Apian software (http://www.apian.net)
Asset (tltc.shu.edu/servlets/asset.Asset)	Cool surveys (http://www.coolsurveys.com)
CustomerSat (http://www.customersat.com)	EZSurvey (http://www.raosoft.com)
Greenfield online (http://www.greenfieldonline.com)	Hosted survey (http://www.hostedsurvey.com)
Infopoll (http://www.infopoll.net)	Inquisite (http://www.inquisite.com)
InSite (http://www.insitesurveys.com)	InstantSurvey (http://www.netreflector.com)
LiveSurveys (http://www.livesurveys.com)	mantaINSIGHT (http://www.mantacorp.com)
Mercator (http://www.mercatorcorp.com)	ObjectPlanet (http://www.objectplanet.com/Surveyor)
Perseus (http://www.perseus.com)	PollCat (http://www.pollcat.com)
PollPro (http://www.pollpro.com)	StatPac (http://www.statpac.com)
StatSurvey (http://www.statsurvey.com)	SumQuest (http://www.sumquest.com)
SuperSurvey (http://www.supersurvey.com)	Survey Select (http://www.sajasoftware.com)
Survey System (http://www.surveysystem.com)	SurveyCrafter (http://www.surveycrafter.com)
SurveyGold (http://www.surveygold.com)	SurveyHeaven (http://www.surveyheaven.com)
SurveySaid (http://www.surveysaid.com)	SurveySite (http://www.surveysite.com)
SurveyTrends (http://www.surveytrends.com)	SurveyView (http://www.surveyview.com)
Surveywire (http://www.surveywire.com)	Zoomerang (http://www.zoomerang.com)

online system are obvious, we also learned some unexpected lessons. In particular:

- Many online surveys are poorly designed. They are unnecessarily long, questions are not grouped into logical units, and terms are not adequately explained. One recent *Asset* survey, for example, asked subjects "Would you use the Jitney to get to the Village?", but did not explain what the *"Jitney"* was.
- Researchers frequently mark questions as mandatory so that a subject cannot submit a survey without providing a response to such questions. While a careful and sparse use of mandatory questions can improve the return rate for key questions, overuse simply results in subjects opting out of a survey entirely and not submitting any data.
- Users do not spend enough time to carefully design and research questions, and they do not fully understand the implications of selecting a particular type of question. One survey, for example, asked: "What are your thoughts about starting a campus sponsored shuttle system", inviting an open-ended response. Then, after thousands of responses were received, the overwhelming and uncategorized data became unwieldy. Categorizing it after the fact requires expensive (human) resources (and judgment calls) that a researcher is likely not prepared to handle.

These issues are not program or, in fact, technology related; they apply any time researchers create surveys. But the ease of use and cost effectiveness of an online survey system allows poorly designed surveys to be disseminated to a large number of subjects quickly, resulting in possible survey fatigue.

To alleviate some of these problems, we found it essential to increase the oversight of the Human Subjects Review Board, and to expand training and education in survey design. Proper guidance, enhanced training, and a simple online survey management system have to go hand in hand to allow for the successful use of online surveys.

KEY TERMS

Active Server Page (ASP): Active server pages are dynamically created Web pages that include programming code in a scripting language such as Visual Basic or JavaScript. ASP pages require properly configured Web servers. ASP technology is closely tied to Microsoft. For more information, see http://www.asp.net/

Common Gateway Interface (CGI): The common gateway interface is a specification for transferring information between a World Wide Web server–usually received via a Web form–and a program, called a CGI script, designed to accept and return data in a specified format. For more information, see http:// hoohoo.ncsa.uiuc.edu/cgi/overview.html

GNU General Public License (GPL): The GNU GPL (general public license) is a commonly used license for free software, regulating the rights and obligations of users of that software. For more information, see http://www.gnu.org/copyleft/gpl.html

Human Subjects Review Board (HSRB): A Human Subjects Review Board is an administrative body responsible for review and approval of research involving human participants. Virtually all colleges and universities in the US have an HSRB, which must be consulted prior to administering any survey.

HyperText Markup Language (HTML): A collection of tags to format and annotate documents on the World Wide Web. For more information, see http://www.w3.org/MarkUp/

IP Number: The Internet protocol number is a numeric identifier that uniquely identifies every system connected to the Internet. For more information, see http://en.wikipedia.org/wiki/IP_address

Java Server Page (JSP): Java server pages are Web pages that include programming code in a variant of Java. JSP pages require a specially configured Web server, and are translated "on the fly" into Java servlets. JSP technology is tied to Sun Microsystems. For more information, see http://java.sun.com/products/jsp/

Lightweight Directory Access Protocol (LDAP): The lightweight directory access protocol regulates how to specify and access directory information. Many educational institutions and corporations store user directory information, such as name and password, in LDAP-readable format. For more information, see http://www.openldap.org/

Online Survey Management System: An online survey management system is a Web-based tool that allows (a) the creation and logical maintenance of surveys, (b) handles the dissemination of surveys, and (c) manages and analyzes existing data online.

PHP: PHP is a recursive acronym that stands for "PHP: hypertext preprocessor." It is a general-purpose scripted computer programming language that can be embedded into Web pages. It requires a Web server configured to properly process PHP statements. For more information, see http://www.php.net/

Servlet: Servlets are programs written in Java that run on a specially configured Web server, similarly to CGI scripts. Servlet technology is tied to Sun Microsystems. For more information, see http://java.sun.com/products/servlet/

URL: A uniform resource locator is a descriptor to locate information on the World Wide Web. Any document or resource available on the Web has a URL by which it can be viewed or accessed. For more information, see http://www.w3.org/Addressing/

Web Form: A Web form is an online, formatted portion of a Web page containing active fields for user interaction such as text fields and checkboxes. Data entered in forms is processed by CGI programs or other scripted computer languages.

Chapter XXVI
Web Survey Methodology (WebSM) Portal

Katja Lozar Manfreda
University of Ljubljana, Slovenia

Vasja Vehovar
University of Ljubljana, Slovenia

ABSTRACT

The chapter describes a Web portal, dedicated to survey research, using modern information-communication technologies, especially the WWW. Although supported by EU since 2002, it provides worldwide visitors information on events (e.g., scientific meetings, calls for papers, projects), software, and literature on the methodology and implementation of Web surveys. The most valuable databases are the bibliography (including over 2,000 entries) and software/services databases (including over 500 entries).

INTRODUCTION

The "WebSM portal" (http://www.websm.org) is dedicated to the use of new technologies in survey data collection. Initially (since 1998), it was concentrated on the methodological issues of Web surveys, and the title WebSM (Web survey methodology) originates from this initial orientation. Now it covers a broader area of interaction between modern technologies (Internet, mobile phones, digital TV, etc.) and survey data collection. It presents a global reference point for survey data collection using modern information-communication technologies (ICTs), especially the WWW.

The work on WebSM portal started in 1998 at the University of Ljubljana, Slovenia. It was internationally oriented already from the beginning by presenting content in English. The researchers involved had been studying Web surveys since 1996, when they performed one of the first Web questionnaire design experiments (Vehovar & Batagelj, 1996). A similar Web site existed also at ZUMA, Germany as part of the activities of the German Online Research Association; however, its content was in German. The authors of both sites, together with other partners (Linkoeping University in Sweden and University of Bergamo in Italy) in 2002 joined in a thematic network formed within the EU fifth framework program (Contract HPSE CT 2002 50031, acronym: WebSMSite). The involved researchers have published on Web survey methodology in several international scientific journals, in monographs by established international publishers, have had several invited talks at international scientific conferences, and have taken active role in organizing sessions on Internet surveys at international scientific meetings.

The basic mission of this academic portal is to:

- provide all target groups (students, professionals, users from academic, public, and business sector) information related to Web survey methodology and to the impact of other new technologies on survey process,
- stimulate the communication and interaction between them,
- integrate and increase the research cooperation, and
- enforce more efficient implementation of ICTs in the practice of survey research organizations.

Over the last few years, the portal has been presented at some of the largest international conferences on survey methodology and/or statistical analysis. Response from visitors has been positive, particularly owing to the extensive bibliographic references constituting the largest source of references in this field.

PORTAL STRUCTURE AND CONTENT

The portal individual Web pages consist of a variable central part and upper menu. Behind, there are several databases (bibliography, authors, software/services, sources, events) with information that displays on individual Web pages.

Central part. The central part of the introductory Web page (homepage) offers latest information on several issues:

1. *News* on the use of new ICTs for survey research, but also other research methods (online qualitative research, automated electronic measurement, etc.). They include calls for papers, information on paper competitions, and other related information.
2. *Events* relates to the database of events, such as scientific meetings (workshops, conferences), tutorials, courses where Web surveys or other survey modes using new ICTs are the main or one of the topics.
3. *Forum* is a platform for communication among the portal visitors. Recently, topics such as problems of unsolicited e-mails, standards for online panels, discussion on particular software products, size of the Internet survey industry, representativeness and reliability of online surveys, and so forth, have gained interest.
4. *Bibliography* relates to the database of bibliographic references dedicated to Web surveys and other uses of new ICTs in social science research.
5. *Software* relates to the database of software products that are used for conducting Web surveys.
6. *Guides, standards, and best practices* relates to the list of guides and standards on how to conduct Web surveys (and Internet research on general) prepared by professional organizations and academics.

The posts in the above categories are ordered in chronological order, with the latest on the top. Few entries for each category are listed on the homepage, and others are accessed by clicking dedicated links.

Upper menu and databases. The upper menu is fixed for all portal Web pages. It links to several databases supporting the whole portal. The largest and probably the most valuable for the visitors is the already mentioned *Bibliography database*. It includes over 2,500 references to relevant monographs; papers in scientific journals, edited monographs or conference proceedings; conference presentations and other manuscripts. Where available, links to full manuscripts are provided (by linking to external databases, such as Proquest, OCLC First Search, etc., to conference or other Web sites). When available, contact information of the authors is also listed. As already mentioned, few most recently included entries are listed in the central part of the portal homepage.

The portal offers two search options through the bibliography database. The visitor can use the list of bibliography entries ordered in several categories, accessible from the menu. Lists of entries across some thematic categories (e.g., Costs, Measurement, Mode comparisons, Noncoverage & Sampling , Nonresponse, Questionnaire design, Solicitation & Incentives, Weighting & Imputation), across data collection mode (e.g., Web, e-mail, mobile phone, WebTV surveys, etc.), and across the survey topic or geographical region are available. In addition, lists of entries by year of publication or bibliographical type is also available from the menu. List of entries on topics that do not deal directly with new ICTs in survey methodology, but are somewhat related (e.g., online qualitative research, Internet ethical issues, usability studies, general survey methodology) are also available.

The second search option, accessible through the link »Browse bibliography«, allows the visitors to search the database using keywords. Most of them are the same as this. The search based on year of publication, bibliographic type, target population, sampling method, and survey sponsor is added. In this way, it is possible to generate, for example, a list of journal articles published since 2004, dealing with questionnaire design in Web surveys. The visitor can choose the number of hits displayed on the Web page, and the sort option (by title, author, source, and year of publication).

When clicking an individual entry in the bibliography list, the abstract and link to full text (when available) is displayed. Clicking on the author(s) or source links to the related databases. The *Authors database* includes over 1,000 authors that have at least two bibliography entries in the bibliography database. Clicking on the author displays the other bibliography entries by this author, a »send e-mail« option, and URL address of homepage (if available). Similarly, clicking on the source links to the *Sources database* results in display of other bibliography entries from the same source and link to the source Web site (if available).

The upper menu links to another database, that is, *Software/Services database* of companies that offer software packages for implementing Web surveys. Clicking on the software product in an alphabetical list results in displaying additional information, such as URL address; contact e-mail; language of the interface; code availability (close/open source); whether it is for free, free with chargeable upgrades or only chargeable; whether a demo/trail version of the package is available; whether it is a stand-alone or hosting solution; and where the company has its offices. Also here, the »Browse software« allows the visitors to search among packages using keywords.

We must stress that the listed software packages do not encompass all existing products. Whenever information on such a product reaches the portal administrators, the list is updated. In addition, the WebSM portal does not guarantee the quality of work by listed companies. However, efforts are made to gather and add software evaluations. The evaluation includes testing the product whenever a demo/test/trial version of the software is available, and including additional information regarding the software by vendors themselves (by completing the WebSM questionnaire on software characteristics). The WebSM team is extensively working on upgrading the Software database to offer additional information that would help the visitors in the choice of appropriate software for their needs.

The *Community* section in the upper menu links to the *Events database*, including information of events (conferences, workshops, tutorials, seminars, etc.) interesting for the portal visitors. Information on time, place, and URL address is displayed when an event entry in the list is clicked. As already said, few most recent entries are displayed also in the homepage.

The other links in the *Community* section offer a list of professional Web sites from related areas; a list of online discussion groups (e-mail lists, forums, etc.) with discussion on Internet research, as well as general survey methodology or Internet-related issues; and a list of codes of ethics and guides of professional research associations that are relevant for researchers using Web surveys.

The other links in the upper menu has more administrative purposes, linking to the portal homepage (*Home*), description of the portal and their authors (*About*), contact information (*Contact*), and forum (*Forum*).

SEARCH OPTIONS

Besides the already mentioned searches through the Bibliography, Software, and Events databases, a simple Search option through the whole site content simultaneously, using keywords (in the upper left side of the Web pages), is available. The hits are displayed in categories based on the databases. For example, entering the name of a particular author will display hits in the categories *News/Posts, Events or Forum* if his/her name is included in any of these posts; the category *Authors* from the Authors database; the category *Bibliography* from the Bibliography database; the category *Articles, papers, files* where actual full texts are displayed, and so forth. The search

engine browses through all HTML files of the WebSM portal, and also through text or PDF files included in the WebSM databases.

COMMUNICATION WITH PORTAL VISITORS

The information on the WebSM portal is available free of charge for all visitors. Additionally, visitors can register (using the link on the upper right corner of the Web pages) and subscribe to News, Events, and/or Forum entries. Whenever a new entry in any of these categories is added to the portal, they are notified through e-mail.

HOW THE INFORMATION IS COLLECTED

A variety of online sources are used for adding content to the WebSM portal: professional organizations, research institutions and universities, other organizations and individuals dealing with Web surveys, but also with survey research in general, statistics, and/or Internet use. Their Web sites, newsletters, and online discussions are checked periodically. Information is sometimes also received directly from interested individuals that have content to be published on the portal.

REFERENCES

Vehovar, V., & Batagelj, Z. (1996, June). *The methodological issues in WWW surveys.* Paper presented at CASIC '96, San Antonio. Retrieved from http://www.ris.org/casic96/

KEY TERMS

Computerized Self-Administered Questionnaire (CSAQ): Computer-based questionnaire completed by the respondent him/herself, without the presence of an interviewer. Examples of such questionnaires are Web questionnaires, e-mail questionnaires, disk-by-e-mail questionnaires, and so forth.

E-Mail Survey: An Internet survey mode where a survey questionnaire is sent by e-mail to respondents. It can be sent within the message itself, and respondents respond by marking their responses in the reply message. Or it can be sent as an attachment file, including the questionnaire to be downloaded, and run on the respondent"s computer.

Internet Survey: Broad term for all surveying modes implemented through one or more Internet services. These include World Wide Web (Web surveys), e-mail (e-mail surveys), WebTV (WebTV surveys), and so forth.

Web Questionnaire: Questionnaire implemented as an interactive or static Web form, based on hypertext markup language (HTML). Respondents access and complete it using a Web browser.

Web Survey: Most widely used Internet survey mode implemented using World Wide Web. Respondents access and complete Web survey questionnaires using a Web browser. Their responses are automatically sent via the Internet to a data server and stored on it.

Chapter XXVII
Web–Based Survey Software for Academic Research

Hallie D'Agruma
University of New Hampshire, USA

Erika A. Zollett
University of New Hampshire, USA

ABSTRACT

The features of Datacurious, a Web-based survey software program designed specifically for academic research, are examined in this article. Web-based data collection has been deemed an effective, reliable, and safe method of data collection, while also saving researchers time, effort, and cost, and reducing data entry error. Recent developments in Web-based survey software systems allow data to be collected through relatively simple, easy-to-use interfaces, making the technology accessible to researchers with little to no technical expertise. Datacurious, available online at http://www.datacurious.com, utilizes an intuitive and user-friendly interface with broad capabilities in its survey designer. Programming enables researchers to adhere to ethical guidelines for surveying human subjects. Technical features of Datacurious ensure survey participant privacy and confidentiality and provide options for informed consent, incentive, and debriefing pages. Datacurious also allows researchers to control entry to online surveys. Providing a flexible and robust Web-based survey platform, Datacurious accords to Web-design standards in survey design, while being responsive to the needs of the academic research community.

INTRODUCTION

The growth of the Internet has generated interest in the potential of using the Web for data collection (Kittleson, 1997; Schaefer & Dillman, 1998; Schleyer & Forrest, 2000; Schmidt, 1997; Stanton, 1998). Researchers have begun to move towards conducting more Internet research using online surveys, and the results of these studies can be found in many popular academic journals (Granello & Wheaton, 2004). There has been less discussion in the research community about the process of data collection online (Granello & Wheaton, 2004). Online surveys have been implemented via e-mail and Web-based technology (through Web pages). Data collection through Web-based technology has been deemed an effective method of data collection for a variety of methodological reasons, as well as for its efficiency and cost effectiveness (Birnbaum, 2004; Cho & LaRose, 1999; Crawford, 2002; Granello & Wheaton, 2004; Hewson, Laurent, & Vogel, 1996; Kiesler & Sproull, 1995; Kraut et al., 2004; Schleyer & Forrest, 2000; Schmidt, 1997; Sills & Song, 2002; Wyatt, 2000). While data collection through Web-based technology is arguably one of the best methods of conducting survey research, there has been little review of the various methodological and technical approaches researchers may use in collecting their data online through Web pages (Granello & Wheaton, 2004; Schmidt, 1997). Furthermore, few attempts (Crawford, 2002) have been made to review current applications available for Web-based data collection. Thus, this chapter will review the features of Datacurious, a survey software program enabling Web-based data collection for academic research. It will also evaluate the program according to its ability to maximize the advantages of online data collection, while minimizing the disadvantages.

Until recently, researchers who wished to collect data on the Internet through Web-based technology required sophisticated technical knowledge (Schmidt, 1997) because online surveys were often developed utilizing specialized programming languages. In the past few years, comprehensive software systems have been developed that enable Web-based data collection through relatively simple, easy-to-use interfaces, making publishing surveys online possible for researchers with little to no technical expertise (Crawford, 2002). With the emergence of comprehensive software systems for Web-based data collection, there has been no clear consensus about what constitutes a good survey design application (Crawford, 2002). Crawford (2002) proposed several specifications for a good quality Web-based data collection system: adherence to Web survey design standards, flexibility, and robustness. Furthermore, in his article, Crawford

(2002) discusses the necessity for researchers to find programs that contain the tools necessary to meet their particular research needs. Given the fact that many comprehensive software systems have been developed by technical programmers, not necessarily researchers engaged in academic research, this point is particularly important. One advantage offered by a Web-based data collection program, such as Datacurious, is that it was developed in collaboration with academic researchers. The authors of this chapter worked closely with the principal programmer with design requirements and specifications and supervised beta-testing of the product by a variety of research teams at a large west coast university. The net result is a program that includes a wide range of features that accounts for key methodological issues in survey research and adheres to the ethical requirements related to conducting human subjects research.

Datacurious is an interactive Web-based data collection program that can be found online at http://www.datacurious.com. Researchers utilizing Datacurious may visit the Web site and gain full access to the survey design program and publisher without purchasing any software on compact disc or downloading any software programs. The only requirement is a Web browser to access the application. Surveys are designed through a Web interface and published online for the purposes of data collection. Datacurious hosts the surveys throughout the data collection process and stores all collected data for researchers, which may then be downloaded onto their personal computers. Thus, researchers do not require a dedicated Web server to host surveys, which reduces the resources, and thus cost, associated with implementing online surveys. One of the benefits of Datacurious is that new users may visit the Web site, create a secure personal account, and gain full access to the survey designer, allowing researchers to test the program's compatibility with their research needs prior to purchasing any survey product(s).

SURVEY DESIGN

Survey design is essential to creating effective online surveys and collecting unbiased data (Couper, Traugott, & Lamias, 2001). Research has shown that low response rates may be related to poor survey design (Morrel-Samuels, 2003). In order to meet the demands of researchers with limited technical skills who wish to create sophisticated online surveys, Datacurious utilizes an intuitive and user-friendly interface, with broad capabilities, in its survey designer. Researchers are given the opportunity to import their survey questions and answers from a spreadsheet or text file, formatted according to simple specifications, into Datacurious. Once imported, the questions and answers may be customized, for aesthetic and methodological considerations, into a final version for publishing online. Researchers may also utilize the survey designer to build the survey by manually entering each question and answer choice using the Web interface, which also provides options for formatting the look, feel, and functionality of the survey. With Datacurious, researchers may design surveys with an unlimited number of questions and answer choices. Surveys may incorporate multiple sections and subsections, with the option of adding a title(s), headings, subheadings, instructions, and additional pages to suit a wide range of research purposes.

The survey designer supports the development of additional text fields and/or pages for the purposes of obtaining informed consent, communicating instructions, sharing information, gathering identifying information, offering incentives, providing resources, and so forth. Many of these survey designer features have been built to fulfill generic research protocols common to a variety of disciplines, yet the features are flexible enough to allow researchers to use the tools to customize the offerings in ways that will help them meet their individualized research needs, an important attribute of a good quality Web-based data collection system (Crawford, 2002). For example, with

Web-based data collection, the process of gaining informed consent is complicated by the fact that there may be considerable distance between the researcher and the participant, unlike in traditional laboratory experiments (Kraut, Olson, Banaji, Bruckman, Cohen, & Couper, 2004). For this reason, Datacurious offers a feature that allows researchers to create an informed consent page with a "click to accept" button, giving participants an opportunity to express their understanding and agreement with the aims and guidelines of the research study (Kraut et al., 2004) and requiring them to take some action to indicate their consent as recommended by Schmidt (1997).

Another fully customizable feature is the incentive page, which may be utilized by researchers to offer potential participants incentives for participation. Incentives have been shown to have a positive effect on response rates for mail surveys (Church, 1993), which might suggest a similar relationship for Web-based surveys. Researchers interested in offering incentives benefit from the technology employed by Datacurious that allows for incentive use without compromising participants' privacy. With the incentive feature, researchers may collect identifying information (e.g., name, e-mail, address, phone number, etc. ...) that will be stored in a unique database kept completely separate from the participants survey responses. The entries into this database are also randomly ordered so as to prevent matching across databases. Furthermore, identifying information will only be made available for viewing once a predetermined response threshold is met (set by the researcher), to ensure that enough participants have responded to the survey so that it is not possible to hypothesize links between participant identity and response. Therefore, researchers may offer respondents the ability to participate in their research without revealing their identity. It seems logical that the assurance of privacy in the offering of incentives may actually enhance the effectiveness of incentives in attracting potential participants to research studies. While the incentive feature provides a method for collecting identifying information from participants in a way that prevents identity from being linked to survey response, nothing precludes researchers who wish to collect identifying information from participants as part of the study from incorporating questions and answer choices about identity into the survey itself.

FORMATTING

Datacurious' formatting options offer researchers the capability to design surveys in accordance with the Web survey design standards articulated by Crawford (2002). Several font styles, with specifiable type size and color, are supported by Datacurious, including sans serif styles, which have been deemed important by Nielson (2000). Selection of font may differ across the survey to make distinctions between various types of information (e.g., titles, headers, instructions, questions, answers, etc. ...). Background color may be set by the researcher to allow for the use of contrasting color for emphasis, another feature of Web surveys highlighted as useful by Nielson (2000). Datacurious does not require use of a predetermined graphical interface (Crawford, 2002), which reduces download time and extraneous distractions (Couper et al., 2001), yet Datacurious allows researchers to import images into their survey if desired.

Question types may be selected by the researcher, including radio, Likert, checkbox, list, and text, with single- and multiple-answer selection options. Range checks and data format checks are possible by choosing a question type that allows for preset answer choices, such as radio, checkbox, and list formats. Range checks and data format checks are key validation capabilities available in good quality Web-based data collection systems (Crawford, 2002). In the survey designer, question numbers may be enabled or disabled. Researchers may mandate respondents to answer specific questions that may increase the usability of online survey data (Crawford, 2002; Couper et al., 2001; Morrel-Samuels, 2003), and require respondents to answer all questions on a page or in a survey, eliminating invalid or missing data (Schleyer & Forrest, 2000; Stanton, 1998). Question order may be fixed to encourage respondents to answer questions in a predetermined order, improving upon paper–and–pencil surveys in which participants can flip back and forth filling out questions and changing answers at will. Another option that Datacurious provides, which has been deemed important by Crawford (2002), is randomization of answer choices. Furthermore, multiple questions may be placed on a page, a Web survey design standard enumerated by Couper, Traugott, & Lamias (2001), and surveys may be created in one page or multiple-page formats. Page numbers may be added to enhance usability if a multiple page format is chosen. Researchers may also customize navigation labels to designate page forward, page back, and close window. Upon survey completion, researchers may also incorporate a page containing debriefing materials, or redirect the Web browser to other Web pages that may provide important resources, consistent with ethical guidelines for debriefing subjects (American Psychological Association, 2002). Another optional customization is to utilize Web browser redirect to provide debriefing or resources for those participants who indicate a wish to drop out of a study.

The Datacurious survey designer is built for ease of use. For example, examples of each question type are provided to clarify available options. Questions and answer choices, as well as other customizable text fields for titles, headers, instructions, and so forth, may be moved, edited, or deleted according to evolving design specifications. Entire pages from the survey may also be moved or deleted, if desired. In addition, answer choices that have been defined by the researcher may be saved and reused to save time and energy in the development process when the same answer set is used multiple times. Researchers may also view how their survey will appear to respondents, at any time during the design phase, by clicking "test."

PUBLISHING

When researchers complete the design phase, they may choose to publish their surveys, making them available for data collection on the Web. Each published survey receives a unique record locator (URL) or Web address that may be sent to potential participants to direct them to where they can complete the survey online. The URL is not accessible via search engines, allaying common concerns regarding how to control entry to online surveys (Stanton, 1998). With Datacurious, it is possible to access surveys 24 hours a day, 7 days a week, making data collection available at anytime at your participants' convenience, which is one of the advantages of online data collection (Birnbaum, 2004).

With the Datacurious survey publisher, researchers have the option to indicate a survey expiration date, so that users cannot respond to a survey after a certain date and time. They may also choose to limit the number of responses to their survey(s). By not utilizing these optional features, researchers may collect data from their surveys indefinitely. If research needs require the readministration of the same survey, or to make modifications to an existing survey after it has been published, Datacurious also provides researchers with the option to copy an existing survey and to republish it.

DATA COLLECTION

Data collection on the Web offers many unique advantages, including the ability to expand sample sizes (Birnbaum, 2004; Kraut et al., 2004; Schmidt, 1997); build heterogeneity into samples with respect to age, education, income, social class, geographic location, and nationality (Birnbaum, 2004; Cho & LaRose, 1999; Kraut et al., 2004; Schleyer & Forrest, 2000; Wyatt, 2000); recruit specialized samples with characteristics not common in traditional samples pulled from the undergraduate college population (Birnbaum, 2004; Kraut et al., 2004); reach low incidence and/or nonclinical populations (Alexander & Trissel, 1996; Borer, Hebert, & Breshears, 1996; Granello & Wheaton, 2004); and establish asynchronous contacts with participants on the move (Hewson, Laurent, & Vogel, 1996). Additionally, Web-based surveys are less effort to conduct than other types of surveys requiring human intervention (Kraut et al., 2004). There is no need to personally give instructions, introduce the experiment, and supervise data collection (Kraut et al., 2004).

By publishing surveys online with Datacurious, researchers are able to effectively collect data on specific target groups on the Internet. Recruiting methods must be selected that maximize the ability to generalize results to populations of interest (Granello & Wheaton, 2004). Just as with paper-based survey research, there is no simple way to gather truly random data that can be generalized to the population at-large. Even if it were possible to collect data across all Internet users, this sample would be biased because most Internet users are white, married, and highly educated (Graphics, Visualization, and Usability Center, 1999; Stanton, 1998; U.S. Dept. of Commerce, 2002). However, research has shown that the Internet is becoming increasingly diversified over time (U.S. Dept. of Commerce, 2002).

After data is collected, it is stored by Datacurious in a secure database that is password protected, giving researchers the ability to log in to their personal accounts and view their results at any time. Researchers may gain virtually instant access to their incoming data. Datacurious may be configured to send e-mail alerts to a specified e-mail address when a survey has been completed. Researchers have found this feature to be invaluable in monitoring the response rates without having to log in and check for results on a recurring basis. Research has shown that data collected through Web-based data collection systems tend to be returned quite quickly (Birnbaum, 2004; Cobanoglu, Warde, & Moreo, 2001; Couper et al., 2001; Granello & Wheaton, 2004). Data is also virtually ready to be analyzed, as no data entry is necessary, which reduces time, effort, cost, and data entry error (Birnbaum, 2004; Granello & Wheaton, 2004; Kiesler & Sproull, 1995; Kraut et al., 2004; Schmidt, 1997; Wyatt, 2000). Results may be viewed online in several easy-to-read formats. Furthermore, with Datacurious results may be downloaded into a spreadsheet or text file that can be easily imported in many of the common statistical software packages for data analysis, such as SPSS, another advantage of Web-based data collection (Birnbaum, 2004; Granello & Wheaton, 2004).

Datacurious enables researchers to view incomplete surveys to analyze when participants left the survey, to better understand drop-out rates. Research has shown that drop-out rates may be higher in Web-based research than in lab studies (Birnbaum, 2004; Kraut et al., 2004). Higher drop-out rates may suggest that participants involved in Web-based research experience less social pressure or embarrassment than those in the lab studies (Birnbaum, 2004), strengthening the internal validity of the study. Drop-out rates for online surveys have been said to be reduced when participants provide a short password to enter the study (Heerwegh & Loosvelt, 2002). Enabling passwords with Datacurious will be discussed later in this chapter.

PERFORMANCE

To function smoothly, a Web-based data collection program must be designed to support multiple respondents completing surveys simultaneously at any time of day (Crawford, 2002). Datacurious utilizes a dedicated Web server with a wide band Internet connection, capable of handling tens of thousands of users at any one time. It is, thus, able to host thousands of surveys running simultaneously at once. In addition, to address the technical problems that may interfere with participants accessing and taking online surveys (Granello & Wheaton, 2004), Datacurious utilizes standard HTML constructs to render survey Web pages that can be viewed in old and new versions of various Web browsers with consistent formatting. Datacurious is also designed to deliver Web pages quickly, even over slow dial-up Internet connections and slower computers. It achieves this quick delivery by eliminating superfluous cosmetic programming. Therefore, Datacurious exhibits the robustness necessary to withstand high-volume usage on a continuous basis, a key component of a good quality Web-based data collection system (Crawford, 2002).

DATA INTEGRITY

Research has shown that Web-based surveys may actually promote candor regarding sensitive issues because of the absence of human experimenters, whose presence in lab studies may preclude open sharing (Bailey, Foote, & Throckmorton, 2000; Kiesler & Sproull, 1995). In addition, data integrity appears to be strengthened by the fact that participants may feel less social pressure to complete the surveys outside of the lab environment (Birnbaum, 2004; Erdman, Klein, & Greist, 1995; Kiesler & Sproull, 1995; King & Miles, 1995; Walsh, Kiesler, Sproull, & Hesse, 1992). Participants are also less likely to be solely undergraduates, who may be receiving extra credit for completing surveys, which also may improve the data integrity (Reips, 2000).

It also has been suggested that the anonymity of the Internet, combined with the promise of confidentiality given to participants in research studies, may lead to the taking on of fictitious identity (Birnbaum, 2004) and frivolous participation, demonstrated by high drop-out rates, as well as malicious intent (Kraut et al., 2004). Malicious intent refers to disingenuous participation that may surface through multiple submissions by the same individual, widespread dissemination of the URL, and other behaviors that may undermine the study's integrity (Birnbaum, 2004; Kraut et al., 2004; Schmidt, 1997). Although research has shown that malicious intent is not common (Birnbaum, 2004), researchers wishing to safeguard against such potentialities may utilize record comparison (i.e., to search for identical responses submitted in succession that may indicate multiple submission) with Datacurious, in addition to the suggestion made by Birnbaum (2004) to simply inform participants to submit their answers only once, which they found to be an effective means of controlling multiple submissions. Date/time stamps are also logged by Datacurious and can be made available to researchers. Identifiers may also be collected from participants in order to determine if duplicate entries have been submitted by the same person. Offering another level of assurance, one-time passwords may be created by researchers to control that participants only enter the sample once (Birnbaum, 2004; Couper et al., 2001; Stanton, 1998). Other suggestions for controlling widespread dissemination of the URL include informing participants not to forward the URL on to associates and explaining the participant criteria required to complete the survey.

PASSWORDS

Datacurious offers researchers the ability to create passwords and define their usage characteristics (e.g., one time, multiple use, and unlimited use). One-time passwords have been heralded as a mechanism to control entry into the sample (Schmidt, 1997; Stanton, 1998), allowing only invited participants to take the survey, as one-time passwords are discontinued after one use. They also may decrease the number of multiple submissions (Birnbaum, 2004; Couper et al.,

2001), particularly when combined with record comparison. Passwords have also been associated with increased sense of confidentiality (Couper et al., 2001), lower drop-out rates (Heerwegh & Loosvelt, 2002), and greater substance on sensitive issues (Heerwegh & Loosvelt, 2002). They have also been found to not limit response rates, particularly when usernames are not utilized, and passwords are kept short (i.e., four digits) (Heerwegh & Loosvelt, 2002).

CONFIDENTIALITY AND PRIVACY

Designed with the academic research community in mind, Datacurious acknowledges and takes its commitment to confidentiality very seriously. Research has shown that people using the Internet are more likely to provide information when they do not have to identify themselves (AT&T Labs, 1999), due to a high level of concern about confidentiality and privacy on the Internet (AT&T Labs, 1999; O'Neil, 2001). Research has shown that 80%-90% of Internet users are somewhat or very concerned about threats to personal confidentiality and privacy (AT&T Labs, 1999; O'Neil, 2001). Although online surveys are no more risky than off-line surveys (Kraut et al., 2004), it appears that the greatest risk to participants of online research studies is a breach in confidentiality, due to unintended data sharing, or in privacy as a result of invasive programs that log information about users covertly. The researcher can often reduce risk by not asking for identifying information, or by keeping this data separate from the survey responses (Kraut et al., 2004). Datacurious offers this capability through its incentive feature. Furthermore, Datacurious stores data in a secure, password-protected database that is only accessible through personal login. Data will, under no circumstances, be shared with any third parties or associates; researchers have complete ownership of their data. Once the research study is concluded, researchers may request that the data be deleted from Datacurious' database. Datacurious also supports secure socket later protocols (SSL), an encryption mechanism that protects data in transit for an additional layer of security to be implemented by the researcher, if desired. Some research has suggested that encryption may be beneficial in cases where sensitive material is collected (Cho & LaRose, 1999). Additionally, Datacurious utilizes random identification numbers to link together the multiple pages of a participant's survey responses, instead of relying on other commonly employed methods like collecting personal identifiers, using session cookies, or tracking IP addresses (Kraut et al., 2004). Datacurious was designed specifically to ensure that it would not collect any unauthorized information from participants that might identify participants unknowingly when they complete surveys, which would be a violation of their privacy rights. The risks of collecting such information outweigh the benefits. For example, IP addresses may impinge on participants' confidentiality without necessarily providing reliable information about identity (Birnbaum, 2004).

Research has shown that despite the risks to confidentiality and privacy with online surveys, most people accept assurances of anonymity (Conboy, Domar, & O'Connell, 2001). Thus, it is useful to provide participants with a brief explanation regarding confidentiality, when securing informed consent, to detail how their identifying information and responses will be protected, which may increase confidence and boost participation.

If your data collection requirements stipulate that no third party may have access to data, researchers may elect to license the Datacurious survey software to run on their own server, giving them complete control of the data and its usage.

COST

Web-based data collection has been said to reduce survey cost (Granello & Wheaton, 2004; Kraut et al., 2004; Kittleson, 1997; Schleyer & Forrest, 2000; Schmidt, 1997; Sills & Song, 2002; Wyatt, 2000), specifically by minimizing the need for lab space and dedicated equipment (Birnbaum, 2004); reducing the need for travel to collect data from diverse samples; and limiting the use of paper, office supplies, and other materials associated with mailings (Birnbaum, 2004; Schmidt, 1997). Moreover, the cost to collect data online with a Web-based data collection system such as Datacurious may offer researchers a substantial discount when compared to mail and telephone surveys (Cobanoglu et al., 2001; Schleyer & Forrest, 2000). Cobanoglu, Warde, and Moreo (2001) found that mail surveys, on average, cost $1.93 per participant, whereas telephone surveys can cost even more, ranging from $40-$100 per participant. Schleyer and Forrest (2000) found that their mail survey was more expensive than their Web survey by virtue of the fact that mail surveys are a function of sample size. Datacurious offers a competitive pricing structure that is comparable with other products with similar capabilities. Cost is assessed, per survey, based on both the number of responses (sample size) and number of questions in the survey (survey size). Upgrades are available for surveys with response rates that go beyond initial projection. For a midsized survey, prices range from around $200-$300, which comes out to be less than $.50 per participant. All packages include e-mail support.

Subscription packages may also provide savings for researchers collecting data on multiple surveys annually. The subscription package offers yearly, unlimited usage of the Datacurious site, with unlimited designing and publishing capabilities, free upgrades, and e-mail support services. Finally, for researchers with research protocols that dictate that they have complete control over their data, Datacurious offers an attractive alternative: product licensing. Product licensing allows researchers the ability to acquire the survey designer and publisher and its data collection and storage capabilities to be hosted on their own Web server.

A full support package is included with the price. More information about product licensing can be found at http://www.datacurious.com

FUTURE DEVELOPMENTS

Datacurious is committed to future development to make its survey software even more attuned to the needs of the academic research community. For example, Datacurious is working to incorporate functionality that would allow researchers to design and implement surveys that are even more interactive and flexible in nature. Researchers with a desire to present participants with a "question tree" would gain the ability to direct participants to particular follow-up questions, depending on their response to an initial differentiating question. It has been suggested that this type of functionality would be a huge benefit to researchers, who would even have the ability to embed true experiments in surveys by changing up questions, as well as instructions or scenarios, based on participant responses to earlier items (Crawford, 2002; Kraut et al., 2004; Wyatt, 2000).

Datacurious is also developing a mechanism to allow users to leave and return to their survey without losing data by virtue of a login system with user-created passwords; thus, it will minimize interruption, a long considered potential hazard of online surveys (Morrel-Samuels, 2003).

Another new feature that will enhance Datacurious' ability to serve as a methodologically sound tool for researchers will be its ability to control for order effects. Researchers will be given the ability to have components of their surveys randomly presented to participants. Order IDs will also be supplied to each possible order, such that researchers will be able to conduct data analysis to rule out or better understand the effects of order.

To further enhance the ease of participation, Datacurious will be adding even more formatting options. Currently, researchers have the ability to enable a page progress indicator that reads "Page X of X," to give participants an idea of survey length. To expand upon this offering, Datacurious plans to provide a pictorial progress meter, which has been said to increase the overall ease of completing online surveys (Couper et al., 2001; Morrel-Samuels, 2003).

CONCLUSION

Web-based data collection offers researchers a viable method of collecting data, with many improvements over traditional means of conducting survey research through the mail or in the laboratory. Results have been shown to be consistent across these divergent methodological approaches (Birnbaum, 2004), and data quality on the Web appears to be uncompromised, on par with that of traditional paper-based surveys (King & Miles, 1995; Stanton, 1998). It is critical, though, for a Web-based data collection to be responsive to the needs of the academic research community. The Datacurious program, reviewed in this chapter, provides a good quality product that allows for the adherence to Web design standards in survey design, while being both flexible and robust, qualities that have been said to be essential in the creation of effective Web-based surveys (Crawford, 2002).

REFERENCES

Alexander, R. B., & Trissel, D. (1996). Chronic prostatitis: Results of an Internet survey. *Urology, 48*, 568-574.

American Psychological Association (2002). *Ethical principles of psychologists and code of conduct.* Retrieved January 10, 2005, from http://www.apa.org/ethics/code2002.html

AT&T Labs. (1999, April 14). *Beyond concern: Understanding net users' attitudes about online privacy.* Retrieved January 31, 2005, from http://www.research.att.com/resources/trs/TRs/99/99.4/99.4.3/report.htm

Bailey, R. D., Foote, W. E., & Throckmorton, B. (2000). Human sexual behavior: A comparison of college and Internet surveys. In M. H. Birnbaum (Ed.), *Psychological Experiments on the Internet* (pp. 89-117). San Diego, CA: Academic Press.

Birnbaum, M. H. (2004). Human research and data collection via the Internet. *Annual Review of Psychology, 55*, 803-832.

Borer, M. J., Hebert, T. E., & Breshars, D. (1996). Cost and demand analysis of excimer laser use: First World Wide Web Internet survey of the interest in refractive surgery. *Journal of Cataract Refractive Surgery, 22*, 709-712.

Cho, H., & LaRose, R. (1999). Privacy issues in Internet surveys. *Social Science Computer Review, 17*(4), 421-434.

Church, A. H. (1993). Estimating the effect of incentives on mail survey response rates: A meta-analysis. *Public Opinion Quarterly, 57*, 62-79.

Cobanoglu, C., Warde, B., & Moreo, P. J. (2001). A comparison of mail, fax, and Web-based survey methods. *International Journal of Market Research, 43*, 441-452.

Conboy, L., Domar, A., & O'Connell, E. (2001). Women at mid-life: Symptoms, attitudes, and choices, an Internet-based survey. Maturitas, 38, 129-136.

Couper, M. P., Traugott, M. W., & Lamias, M. J. (2001). Web survey design and administration. *Public Opinion Quarterly, 65*, 230-253.

Crawford, S. (2002). Evaluation of Web survey data collection systems. *Field Methods, 14*(3), 307-321.

Daley, E. M., McDermott, R. J., McCormack Brown, K. R., & Kittleson, M. J. (2003). *American Journal of Health Behavior, 27*(2), 116-124.

Erdman, H., Klein, M., & Greist, J. (1995). The reliability of a computer interview for drug use/abuse information. *Behavior research methods and instrumentation, 15*(1), 66-68.

Granello, D. H., & Wheaton, J. E. (2004). Online data collection: Strategies for research. *Journal of Counseling & Development, 82*, 387-393.

Graphics, Visualization, and Usability Center. (1999). GVU's tenth WWW user survey. Retrieved May 8, 2005, from http://www.gvu.gatech.edu/user_surveys/survey-1998-10/tenthreport.html

Heerwegh, D., & Loosveldt, G. (2002). Web surveys: The effect of controlling survey access using pin numbers. *Social Science Computer Review, 20*(1), 10-21.

Hewson, C., Laurent, D., & Vogel, C. (1996). Proper methodologies for psychological and sociological studies conducted via the Internet. *Behavior Research Methods, Instruments, & Computers, 28*, 186-191.

Kiesler, S., & Sproull, L. S. (1995). Response effects in the electronic survey. *Public Opinion Quarterly, 50*, 402-413.

King, W. C., & Miles, E. W. (1995). A quasi-experimental assessment of the effect of computerizing noncognitive paper-and-pencil measurements: A test of measurement equivalence. *Journal of Applied Psychology, 80*(6), 643-651.

Kittleson, M. (1997). Determining effective follow-up of e-mail surveys. American *Journal of Health Behavior, 21*(3), 193-196.

Kraut, R., Olson, J., Banaji, M., Bruckman, A., Cohen, J., & Couper, M. (2004). Psychological research online: Report of Board of Scientific Affairs' Advisory Group on the conduct of research on the Internet. *American Psychologist, 59*(2), 105-117.

Morrel-Samuels, P. (2003, July). Web surveys' hidden hazards. *Harvard Business Review*, 16-17.

O'Neil, D. (2001). Analysis of Internet user's level of online privacy concerns. *Social Science Computer Review, 19*(1), 17-31.

Reips, U.-D. (2000). The Web experiment method: Advantages, disadvantages, and solutions. In M. H. Birnbaum (Ed.), *Psychological Experiments on the Internet* (pp. 89-117). San Diego, CA: Academic Press.

Schaefer, D. R., & Dillman, D. A. (1998). Development of a standard e-mail methodology: Results of an experiment. *The Public Opinion Quarterly, 62*(3), 378-397.

Schleyer, T. K. L., & Forrest, J. L. (2000). Methods for the design and administration of Web-based surveys. *Journal of the American Medical Informatics Association, 7*, 416-425.

Schmidt, W. C. (1997). World-wide Web survey research: Benefits, potential problems, and solutions. *Behavior Research Methods, Instruments, & Computers, 29*(2), 274-279.

Sills, S. J., & Song, C. (2002). Innovations in survey research: An application of Web-based surveys. *Social Science Computer Review, 20*(1), 22-30.

Stanton, J. M. (1998). An empirical assessment of data collection using the Internet. *Personnel Psychology, 51*, 709-725.

U.S. Department of Commerce. (2002). *A nation online: How Americans are expanding their use of the Internet.* Washington, DC: U.S. Government Printing Office.

Walsh, J. P., Kiesler, S., Sproull, L. S., & Hesse, B. W. (1992). Self-selected and radomly selected respondents in a computer network survey. *Public Opinion Quarterly, 56*, 241-244.

Wyatt, J. C. (2000). When to use Web-based surveys. *Journal of American Medical Informatics Association, 7*, 426-430.

KEY TERMS

Data Format Checks: The process by which data is assessed for correct format (e.g., numbers vs. letters).

Internet Protocol (IP) Addresses: A unique number used by computers to refer to each other when sending information through the Internet.

Malicious Intent: Disingenuous participation by participants who deliberately undermine the integrity of the study.

Range Checks: The process by which data is assessed for fitting into an appropriate range (e.g., 1-100).

Record Comparison: The process by which different rows of data may be compared to determine if duplicate data was submitted by the same party.

Secure Socket Layer (SSL): A protocol developed to transmit private documents over the Internet that encrypts data transferred between a client and a server.

Uniform Resource Locator (URL): Refers to the Web address where a specific resource on the Internet is located.

Chapter XXVIII
Comparison of
Online Surveys Tools

Gerd Beidernikl
Center for Education and Economy Research & Consulting, Austria

Arno Kerschbaumer
Center for Education and Economy Research & Consulting, Austria

ABSTRACT

This chapter compares two major online survey tools made in Germany: Rogator and Formgen. Both are of a very high standard, and can be highly recommended for carrying out professional online surveys in any social or psychological science setting. This chapter compares the technical functions, the graphical representation, and the usability of both providers.

INTRODUCTION

Modern telecommunication technologies have had major impact on social research methods. Especially, the World Wide Web offers an inexpensive way to reach thousands of respondents for data gathering. But it is not only the distribution of questionnaires that is an advantage of the Internet. The medium offers a number of new possibilities to present information as well: Pictures, sound and movies can be implemented in questionnaires. Additionally, it is possible to define a logical structure in the questionnaires and let the respondent be guided through the form. Filter questions and ramifications allow a dynamic structure of the survey such as it could never be implemented in paper-and-pencil surveys.

In the meantime, numberless specialized software tools are available, offering the possibility to design and manage online surveys in a very easy way without the need for expert knowledge in Web page programming. The two German software packages, Rogator G3 (from Rogator AG, www.rogator.de) and Formgen (from pilotdata GmbH, www.formgen.de), are among the most elaborated online survey tools in the German-speaking countries. Main fields of appliance are inter- and intranet questionnaires for product tests, employee surveys, evaluation, quality management, and market analysis. The software also meets the

Figure 1. Example of Rogator questionnaire

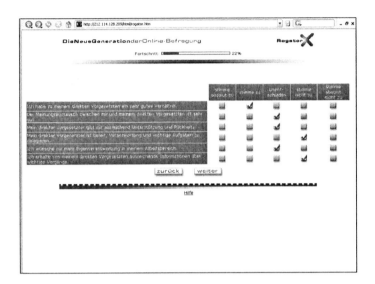

needs of psychological testing in multiple settings and CATI settings (computer-assisted telephone interview). These two major online survey tools will be assessed in the following.

TECHNICAL REMARKS

Both Formgen and Rogator work with any modern system environment, such as Windows, with connection to the Internet and an installed Web browser.

In Formgen, questionnaires are regularly built online via a browser (Web interface), so there is no need to install additional software into a workstation. It is possible to design and run surveys on a host-server or, in case someone wants to run surveys or his/her own server, to install Formgen on a standard Web server running the J2SE environment (min. JDK 1.2), a JSP engine and an SQL database (Oracle 8.05, MS SQL server 7.0 or MySQL).

For designing questionnaires with Rogator, a basic software package has to be installed into a desktop computer. The questionnaire is built offline on the local workstation and then uploaded on a host-survey server.

In general, basic computer knowledge is sufficient to create and manage a survey. Both software packages offer the possibility for customization by HTML and Javascript. In Formgen, the whole HTML code is accessible for modifications, while in Rogator, HTML or Javascript code has to be saved as a .txt file that then can be embedded in the page.

LAYOUT AND GRAPHICAL DESIGN

Both programs, Formgen and Rogator, allow adapting the online questionnaires graphically to nearly every layout. The realization of, for example, corporate identity style therefore becomes quite easy, even for nonprofessional layouters. The implementation of logos, and the use of specific colors and background pictures are standard features. The two online survey tools provide a library with predefined and practically proved layouts. Furthermore, both software packages offer the possibility of embedding multimedia objects like audio and video files, as well as flash animations.

Figure 2. Example of Formgen questionnaire

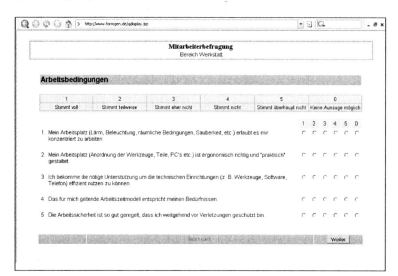

One major difference between the two online survey tools lies in the layout possibilities and the graphical realization of the questions and answers themselves. While Formgen uses the standard radio button and check box style, Rogator offers more flexible design possibilities in this regard: animated buttons (they even allow to upload self-made checkboxes, e.g. emblems of companies). In general, the high quality of the questionnaires' design is a plus for the Rogator software. Filling in questionnaires designed in Rogator is rather more like using a Windows application than clicking on a Web-page. A disadvantage of the Rogator software is that only one question per page can be displayed in the browser, whilst Formgen has no limitations.

LOGICAL STRUCTURE

The big advantage of online surveys, in comparison to paper questionnaires, is a dynamic logical structure: It is possible to implement filters, ramifications, randomization of questions and answers, as well as online validating mechanisms (e.g., restrictions, limitation of answers, or real-time check of postal codes). Both software packages offer plenty of possibilities for this purpose and are of equal functionality. The setting of this logical structure uses either a graphical drag and drop solution, or an easy-to-learn syntax programming language.

QUESTIONS AND ANSWERS

In both tools, different basic question types, such as single choice, multiple choice, matrix (for scaled answers), open questions (text field), are offered to build up the survey. It is even possible to let the respondents disseminate a predetermined number of scores (e.g., 100 pts.) to a given number of answers to weight different options according to his/her opinion (10:30:20:40). The overall sum of the questions is validated by the tools.

Rogator offers one additional very attractive way of answering option: so called sliders. This means a scale (with normally three to seven answer categories like "I totally agree" to "I totally disagree") becomes a continuum between two extremes, where the respondents can indicate their opinion by analogy with a volume slide control.

Both tools offer the possibility to store questions in a so called "question library." This feature makes it easy to use questions again in another survey context by simply uploading them again.

SURVEY MANAGEMENT AND REPORTING

There are mainly two possibilities to organize an online survey: E-mail invitations to a specified group of persons (providing the link and access codes) or an open survey with pop ups and links implemented in Web pages to attract visitors. Formgen as well as Rogator is applicable to both survey types. For the distribution via e-mail it is possible to create unique access codes for each test person to identify their answers. Both tools offer functionalities to administrate online panels as well. This means that the organization of serial surveys among a given set of respondents becomes easy.

Both programs allow the download of data of the carried-out survey for further data analysis in standard spreadsheet formats; for example, EXCEL or SPSS. Aside from the raw data from the

questionnaires, additional data, such as the start and end time for the survey, the duration of filling it in, the IP address of the respondent, and so forth, is stored to the file. Answers of respondents are saved immediately, so that in case participants abort the survey, at least all given answers can be used for analysis.

A very interesting feature of both programs is real-time statistics about the survey. The researchers can get a quick overview of the complete quota of the survey and, on midterm results, at any time.

SPECIAL FEATURES

As already shown, both programs are powerful tools to design, administer, and operate online surveys. Nevertheless, some particularities of the programs might make an important difference in special research contexts.

The highly elaborated design possibilities (even for nonexperts) surely are a big strength of Rogator; especially, the very attractive design of

Table 1. Comparison of main features

FEATURE	FORMGEN	ROGATOR
Questionnaire design	Online	Off-line
Survey management	Host or own server	Host server
Security, passwords, encryption	X	X
Panel administration, serial letter	X	X
E-mail surveys, pop-up surveys	X	X
Sampling and quota functions	X	X
Question archive	X	X
Survey statistics/online reporting	X	X
Individual layouting	X	X
Implementation of multimedia	X	X
Number of questions per site	Not limited	Only one
Dynamic structure (randomization & rotation of answers, validation...)	X	X
Saving of aborted questionnaires	X	X
Progress bars	X	X
Graphical buttons and sliders	Limited	X
Multilingual survey settings	X	X
Import of questionnaires and addresses	X	X
Export of data to Excel and SPSS	X	X
PDF download of results	X	no
Off-line application (e.g., for event surveys)	X	no

answer buttons should be highlighted. Questionnaires designed with Formgen tend to look a little bit old-fashioned in comparison.

On the other hand, Formgen has implemented some very innovative features. The possibility to download statistics on running surveys as a PDF-document would be one example. Another useful functionality is to carry out surveys off-line (e.g. at an event).

Some of the main features of both programs are summarized in the following table.

CONCLUSION

All in all, we can characterize both Formgen and Rogator as excellent online survey tools, highly recommendable for carrying out professional online surveys in any social or psychological science setting. Due to the fact that both software packages offer very similar functionalities, a decision over them may depend on special research contexts, price, and personal preferences. Therefore, the online testing possibilities offered by both companies can be recommended.

Concluding, we would like to note that both companies offer consulting services to help customers in carrying out surveys. These services include help for survey design and layouting, as well as small customizations.

KEY TERMS

CATI / CAPI: Computer assisted telephone interview (CATI) is a telephone surveying technique in which the interviewer follows a script provided by a software application. The software is used for inputting the answers of the proband as well. Computer assisted personal interview (CAPI) is similar to CATI, except that the interview takes place in person instead of over the telephone.

Dynamic Structure: Online surveys do not stringently follow a linear structure from first to the last question. It is possible to implement branching according to different target groups, or according to user attributes. Examples: Probands owning a car are asked to fill in five questions more than people without a car. Persons below the age of, for example, 16, are not even asked whether they own a car because they are too young. Males are not asked whether they are pregnant or not. The point is the proband does not notice that the online survey converts according to his/her questions. He/she does not have to skip questions. The questionnaire itself modulates according to filter questions.

Filter Questions: Questions that influence the progress of the online survey and the number responding order of the following questions.

Host Server: A Web hosting service is a type of Internet hosting service that provides individuals, organizations, and users with online systems for storing information, images, video, or any content accessible via the Web. Web hosts are companies that provide space on a server they own for use by their clients, as well as providing Internet connectivity.

Validation: In general, validation is the process of checking if something satisfies a certain criterion. In the regard of collecting data via an online survey, validation means that the tools are able to check the input of the users by certain criteria of correctness, defined by the researchers. Examples are age—is the age between 0 and 100; zip-codes—has the user entered a valid zip-code regarding the geographic area of the survey target group; e-mail addresses—has the user entered an e-mail address containing an @,and so forth. If the answer is incorrect, the proband is reminded to control his/her answer. In paper-and-pencil surveys, these validation procedures are not possible, as the questionnaire is filled out independently by the proband.

Chapter XXIX
SurveyTracker E-Mail/ Web Survey Software

Eun G. Park
McGill University, Canada

ABSTRACT

This chapter offers an introductory description of SurveyTracker software. Comparisons are made to competitor software programs. The central focus is an explanation of the functions, features, and advantages of the software application.

INTRODUCTION

SurveyTracker is one of the most popular software applications in the current field of online survey, developed from Pearson NCS Inc., and currently registered from Training Technologies, Inc. This company provides the integrated and powerful SurveyTracker line of software applications on survey, including SurveyTracker, SurveyTracker Plus, SurveyTracker E-Mail/Web, SurveyTracker Plus E-Mail/Web and Survey-by-Disk. One advantage of using this comprehensive software is to provide many functions as one module, and offer flexibility and extensibility for prewritten survey modules, specialized training, survey design and distribution services, and survey consulting.

As an introductory description of SurveyTracker, this chapter explains the functions, features, and advantages of the software application. The software supports functional requirements that educational software needs, including survey authoring and design, interface, data management, and multiple electronic and paper data collection technologies. It can especially integrate all forms of data collected from e-mails in text and images, the Internet, networks, and scanning forms. This software can be easily applicable to a variety of survey-based research on schools, higher education, government, business, and healthcare.

FUNCTIONS

The latest versions of the SurveyTracker line of software are SurveyTracker E-Mail/Web 4.5, SurveyTracker Classic 4.5, and SurveyTracker E-Mail/Web Network 4.5. These software applications support several advantageous features in terms of interface, data management, reporting, and distribution.

Interface. SurveyTracker is based on user-friendly and graphic-based design so that users can design a survey form with the overview, questions, notes, sections, and a summary, quickly and easily with a simple click of the mouse. Users can get screen views as designed and displayed in the mode of what-you-see-is-what-you-get in 32-byte interface. Regarding editing, the software is flexible, with text-editing functions including character sets, fonts, color, size, and other editing settings. Graph provides enhanced color support, a variety of data marker shapes, and improved flexibility. Convenient shortcuts and standard text-editing functions allow survey designers to create and modify texts fast. It displays overall updates of ongoing projects. The built-in question library is chosen by a drag-and-drop interface. The built-in image library also provides quick access to commonly used graphics. Users can create global layout settings for all current and future surveys.

Data collection and management. File import is fast and easy from the previous version or other software applications. Data and report export is easy for use in Microsoft Office and other products. Automatic recording of returned surveys is possible to directly send reminder messages. The survey forms and reports are printed, distributed, collected, and read back into SurveyTracker. There are many options for creating, managing, distributing, responding to, analyzing, and reporting from response data. Spreadsheet-style data collection for rapid manual data entry can be changed to different layouts. The data collection screen offers instant electronic survey retrieval, and convenient manual response entry for paper-based surveys. Open-ended questions can be coded for quantitative data analysis, or printed out verbatim in a report. Regarding coding, the built-in codebook supports up to 300 codes per question, as defined as single response or multiple response for multiple code entry. Automatic filtering and batch reporting are possible for the Web. It is easy to customize score values after data collection. Identification bar codes on scannable forms and unique lithocodes on each survey are used to trace printed forms. A number of statistical analyses are built in, such as frequency, variance, minimum, sum, maximum, skewness, range, correlation, chi-square, standard deviation, significance, and so on. SurveyTracker can analyze through manual configuration or auto-filtration for maximum reporting flexibility. Tables and graphs for reports are used with multitable forms. All distribution is handled by conducting multiple distributions. E-mail responses can be sent directly through e-mail systems.

Access and retrieval. A single source database holds all project information for faster access and better organization. The message library allows users to store and retrieve survey and report notes/instructions, as well as distribution.

SYSTEM REQUIREMENTS

To install SurveyTracker, systems require an IBM PC or compatible with at least a Pentium® 200 MHz processor (Pentium class processor running at 300MHz or better strongly recommended), at least 64MB RAM (128MB or more is strongly recommended), in Microsoft Windows 95, 98 SE, ME, Windows NT® or 2000 (Professional), at least 100MB hard disk space (more may be needed depending on the size of the survey and the number of respondents).

FEATURES FOR EDUCATIONAL RESEARCH

SurveyTracker has competitive advantages over the following three aspects:

Flexibility. Most of all, SurveyTracker can support a variety of survey forms. It is compatible with traditional paper surveys, e-mail surveys, and Web surveys. Each respondent opens a program on the disk to access and complete the survey. When the survey is returned, the survey administrator reads it into SurveyTracker. Survey answers are created in SurveyTracker and then converted to scannable forms, using the fully integrated features of the other software application. In network environments, surveys are possible to distribute on network or placed on a disk individually. Surveys can also be carried in intranet or extranet. Paper surveys directly support optical mark recognition scanners and data sheets.

Compatibility. Different survey forms are compatible with Web survey forms. For example, disk surveys, and html-based e-mail surveys deliver the same look and feel directly to the respondent's e-mail inbox. The software works directly with a personal computer's e-mail system to send out the survey questionnaire in text-based messages, form-based messages, or html-based message.

Extensibility. The new SQL database engine handles millions of records for larger projects, audience lists, and more extensive reporting. Audience supports up to 200 fields per record. It is easy to enter a list of potential respondents directly, and to import an existing list from another software program up to 1.6 million people in an audience list. The audience list can be narrowed down as well. Users can create surveys with six scales per question up to 300 choices per scale. SurveyTracker includes a comprehensive library of prewritten questions and scales. Scale types in SurveyTracker include horizontal numerical, Likert, multiple choices, semantic differential, fixed sum, forced ranking, ordinal, and paired comparison.

COST AND LOCATION

Information on price and additional consulting services is available at the Web site of Training Technologies, Inc (http://www.SurveyTracker.com).

COMMENTARY

Currently, there are other survey software applications that are available in the market. For example, popular alternatives include WebSurveyor 5.0, Perseus SurveySolutions, Ultimate Survey, and WebSurveyor. Among them, SurveyTracker is recommended as a better way to integrate all forms of separate surveys, and to maximize many compatible functions. Next step will be needed to examine their comparative usage and implementation in depth on how to apply these software applications' functions to research on schools, higher education, government, business, and healthcare for ultimate results.

REFERENCES

KeySurvey (n.d). Retrieved March 1, 2005, from http://www.keysurvey.com

Perseus SurveySolutions (n.d). Retrieved March 1, 2005, from http://www.perseus.com

SurveyTracker (n.d.). Retrieved March 1, 2005, from http://www.SurveyTracker.com

Ultimate Survey (n.d). Retrieved March 1, 2005, from http://www.prezzatech.com

WebSurveyor 5.0 (n.d). Retrieved March 1, 2005, from http://www.websurveyor.com

KEY TERMS

Compatibility: The ability of two or more systems or components to perform their required functions while sharing the same hardware or software environment.

Extensibility: A property of a system, format, or standard that allows changes in performance or format within a common framework, while retaining partial or complete compatibility among systems that belong to the common framework.

Flexibility: The ease with which a system or component can be modified for use in applications or environments other than those for which it was specifically designed.

Online Survey: To conduct a statistical survey by means of online tools or methods in the procedures of survey, such as data gathering, data analysis, summary reports, distribution of results, and so forth.

What-You-See-is-What-You-Get (WYSIWYG): A user interface that allows the user to view something very similar to the end result, while the document or image is being created.

Chapter XXX
Open Source Survey Software

Jason D. Baker
Regent University, USA

ABSTRACT

One of the significant advances in software design afforded by the Internet has been the open source movement, an effort to collaboratively create software and make it widely and freely available to the on-line community. Although the open source movement started with Unix-like computer operating systems, it has expanded to include a wide variety of software programs, including tools to publish and analyze online surveys. This chapter introduces the open source movement, and then profiles three leading open source survey programs: php Easy Survey Package (phpESP), PHP Surveyor, and the Moodle course management system.

BACKGROUND

The open source movement has its roots in the Unix community and, in particular, the development of the GNU Project back in 1984. The goal of this idealistic group of software developers was to create an entirely free Unix operating system so users would not be dependent on commercial versions from Sun, IBM, and others. Here is the introduction from the GNU Web page:

The GNU Project was launched in 1984 to develop a complete Unix-like operating system which is free software: the GNU system. (GNU is a recursive acronym for 'GNU's Not Unix'; it is pronounced 'guh-NEW'.) Variants of the GNU operating system, which use the kernel Linux,

are now widely used; though these systems are often referred to as 'Linux,' they are more accurately called GNU/Linux systems. (http://www.gnu.org)

Since then, the movement has grown far beyond computer scientists writing operating system code, and has become an ideology in which people freely contribute to content that is made freely available, and where changes are not only acceptable, but encouraged, just as long as the results are offered back to the community. In many ways, it is a sophisticated countercultural response to the limitations of copyrights and patents. As Raymond (1998) declared, "Perhaps in the end the open-source culture will triumph...simply because the commercial world cannot win an evolutionary arms race with open-source communities that can put orders of magnitude more skilled time into a problem."

Not surprisingly, the open source approach has moved beyond computer operating systems into high-demand computer and Internet-based applications, including survey software. For those individuals or organizations unable or uninterested in paying commercial hosting companies to administer online surveys and tests, there are open source equivalents. Popular open source survey programs include the php Easy Survey Package (phpESP) and PHP Surveyor. For educational-style tests, the Moodle open source course management system is one of the more popular.

PROFILES AND COMMENTARY

phpESP, PHP Surveyor, and Moodle are all open source programs that run on Unix Web platforms and make use of the php scripting language and the MySQL database system. Each of these programs can be installed using their respective Web-based installation programs. Additionally, many Web hosting providers offer one-click installation of various open source programs through a menu-driven program called Fantastico De Luxe. Fantastico generally comes bundled with phpESP, PHP Surveyor, and Moodle, along with other useful open source programs. Once installed, all three programs can be administered via a Web-based interface.

phpESP is the older of the survey programs and features a number of basic and advanced online survey functions. To create a survey, one first configures the general survey details, along with the look and feel of the survey template, and then populates the survey with individual questions. A variety of question types are supported including yes/no, multiple choice, check boxes, Likert-style scales, short answer, and even essay (although open-ended questions cannot be tallied the same way as multiple-choice and other

fixed questions). Once all of the questions and answer options are entered and ordered, the user can test the survey before publishing it for real. Once activated, the survey administrator can view individual and aggregate results through the management interface, as well as download the results for analysis in Excel, SPSS, or similar programs. The strength of phpESP is its varied features, extensive development history, and simplicity of code modification. The weakness of the program is that it lacks detailed documentation and thus, can be confounding to basic computer users.

PHP Surveyor possesses many of the same survey features as phpESP, but couples them with a significantly richer administration interface that makes the program more accessible to novices. In addition to 20 different question types ranging from multiple choice and checkboxes to Likert-style scales and flexible arrays (which permit custom text descriptors in each point along the scale), PHP Surveyor supports open or closed surveys. Open surveys can be completed by anyone visiting the Web site, while closed surveys require registration or invitation to participate. Furthermore, the survey administrator can preregister selected users and send out e-mails to solicit participation in the online survey. PHP Surveyor also supports branching surveys, which enable different follow-up questions to be presented based on answers to previous questions, and uses a templating feature to change the look and feel of online surveys. Survey responses can be reviewed online or downloaded for more in-depth statistical analysis. While still under heavy development, PHP Surveyor is likely to become a leading open source survey program because of its rich feature set and relative ease of use.

Unlike phpESP and PHP Surveyor, Moodle is not strictly a survey program, but rather is an open source course management system (CMS). Moodle can be considered an open source equivalent to commercial CMSs like Blackboard or WebCT and thus, is designed for instructional purposes. It includes features to post course syllabi, documents, grades, and hold online class discussions. In addition, however, Moodle includes robust online quiz and survey modules that can be used to administer online assessments or surveys. The quiz module enables instructors to set up assessments, along with the correct answers, so students can complete these and have their scores provided instantly. The survey module includes predefined surveys that can be used with online courses, and also supports the development of custom surveys. Results can be viewed online, or downloaded in Excel or comma-separated value format. Since Moodle is designed for online courses, complete with student accounts and registration, it is less ideal for a public survey than either phpESP or PHP Surveyor, but has many more options if one is integrating such online tests and surveys into coursework.

COST

All three programs are open source and available at no cost. In addition to the free download, the source code is also freely available, and can be changed as desired.

LOCATION

phpESP is available at http://phpesp.sourceforge.net

PHP Surveyor is available at http://www.phpsurveyor.org

Moodle is available at http://www.moodle.org

REFERENCES

Dougiamas, M., & Taylor, P. (2003). Moodle: Using learning communities to create an open source course management system. In P. Kommers & G. Richards (Eds.), *Proceedings of World Conference on Educational Multimedia, Hypermedia and Telecommunications 2003* (pp. 171-178). Chesapeake, VA: AACE.

Kaskalis, T. H. (2004). Localizing and experiencing electronic questionnaires in an educational Web site. *International Journal Of Information Technology, 1*(4), 187-190.

Rapoza, J. (2005). Open-source survey tool phpESP stands test of time. *eWeek*. Retrieved December 15, 2005, from http://www.eweek.com/article2/0,1895,1749890,00.asp

Raymond, E. S. (1998, March). The cathedral and the bazaar. *First Monday, 3*(3). Retrieved February 15, 2005, from http://www.firstmonday.org/issues/issue3_3/raymond/

KEY TERMS

Course Management System: A computer software program designed to support the delivery of online instruction. Popular CMSs include Blackboard, WebCT, and Moodle.

Database: A software package for storing information in a searchable and relational structure. Popular databases include Oracle, MySQL, SQL Server, and Access.

Open Source Software: An approach to software development where multiple individuals collaboratively write code and release both the source code and resulting program to the online community. Anyone is then permitted to freely use the software and modify the code, provided that such modifications are again made available in a public release of the code.

Unix: A popular computer operating system. Many Web servers run on Unix-based systems.

Section III
Instrument Profiles of Interest to Survey Researchers

In the third section of the Handbook of Research on Electronic Surveys and Measurements, *the focus is on the profiles of specific measurements or measurement processes related to or of value for survey research on or about the use of electronic-based communication platforms.*

Chapter XXXI
Hyperlink Analysis

Mike Thelwall
University of Wolverhampton, UK

BACKGROUND

Hyperlink analysis is a collection of techniques that researchers can use to identify patterns in the hyperlinks between collections of Web sites. The purpose can either be to investigate linking behaviour within a given community, or to use links as a convenient data source with which to investigate an aspect of, or a reflection of, a wider behaviour type. An example of a direct application is investigating the types of links used in political Web sites (Foot, Schneider, Dougherty, Xenos, & Larsen, 2003; Park, 2003). Examples of indirect applications include using links between university Web sites to identify highly connected pairs of sites (Thelwall, 2002b), and using links to access whether the Web publishing of highly rated scholars is better than that of others (Thelwall & Harries, 2004). There are two general approaches used in hyperlink analysis. The first is a content analysis of the hyperlinks themselves, categorising them by their context in their source Web page and using the categorisation results for a descriptive analysis of why hyperlinks are used in the chosen set of Web sites. The second general approach for hyperlink analysis is to choose a set of Web sites relevant to a research question and then count links between all pairs of sites within the set,

then applying statistical techniques to identify or verify a pattern in the link counts. Below is a set of findings from hyperlink analyses that illustrate potential uses.

- Hyperlinks in U.S. senatorial campaign Web sites do not follow a systematic policy of link creation, but tend to connect to affiliated organisations rather than to topical debates (Foot et al., 2003).

- Hyperlinks are affected by geographical considerations; for example, closer university Web sites tend to interlink more than distant ones (Thelwall, 2002a).

- International patterns of informal scholarly communication, as reflected by hyperlinks, tend to reflect international patterns of formal scholarly communication, in the form of citations (Thelwall & Smith, 2002).

- Although hyperlinks tend to connect documents concerning similar topics, the cross-topic hyperlinks are a useful source of information about the connections of academic research (Björneborn, 2004).

- Identifying central Web sites in a given network can be useful to illuminate the informal relationships between different organisations, such as political pressure groups (Garrido & Halavais, 2003).

The rest of this section outlines the three main stages of a typical hyperlink analysis. These are problem identification, data collection, validation, and pattern identification.

Problem identification. As introduced, the purpose of a link analysis can either be to study links and linking practices in a particular context, or to use links as a device through which to study another related phenomenon. Having decided upon the purpose of a link investigation, the next step is to identify the Web sites to be studied. In some cases this may be straightforward, if time consuming. Examples include UK universities, Australian computer science departments, German psychologists' personal home pages. In all these cases, membership of the target set is relatively unambiguous, although there would be problems over what constitutes a computer science department and a psychologist. Identification of relevant sites can be achieved through off-line or online lists and Google searches to find the Web sites or pages.

In some cases, the identification of the Web sites may be more complex and part of the research design. For example, a study may wish to investigate Web use around a social or political issue, finding Web sites as part of an ongoing process of identifying relevant online material, usually with a degree of human judgement about whether a site is deemed relevant or not (e.g., Foot et al., 2003; Hine, 2000). Even in cases where judgement is required, it would be good practice to design guidelines to help decide when a site should be included.

Data collection. There are three sources of link data, each suitable in different circumstances.

- Manual link identification is appropriate when there are not too many pages to check, and also when the pages need to be visited by a human for other purposes, such as the classification of links or other aspects of the page as part of a content analysis exercise.

- Commercial search engine advanced interfaces can be used to count either the number of links to a Web site or a Web page, or to count the number of pages in one site that contain a link to another. For example, the command linkdomain:wlv.ac.uk AND domain:bham.ac.uk when entered in AltaVista's advanced search on January 4, 2005 returned 98 as the number of Birmingham University (bham.ac.uk) pages containing a link to at least one Wolverhampton University (wlv.ac.uk) page. It would be clearly impractical to visit all Birmingham University Web pages to check for links to a Wolverhampton University page, and so this advanced search facility makes possible types of research that would not be practical with manual checking. In particular, the interlinking between a set of large Web sites could be investigated, as could counts of links to a set of Web sites or pages. The results from commercial search engines must be treated with caution, however. They do not index every Web page, so their results may be underestimates (Lawrence & Giles, 1999). Moreover, they may fail to recognise links in pages that they do visit because of the technology used to embed the links in the page (Thelwall, 2004). For some studies, it will also be relevant that search engine coverage of the Web is biased in favour of older sites, better linked sites, and U.S. sites, in addition to other problems and biases. In summary, search engine data does not have a high degree of (internal) validity: it should be taken as suggestive rather than definitive. Nevertheless, search engines can provide valuable data for link analysis.

- Personal crawlers can be tasked to visit Web sites and identify their links, providing a partial solution to the coverage problems of search engines. They solve the problem of biases in site coverage, and have the additional advantage of being more fully under the control of the researcher, who can determine when each site is visited, and ensure that the same version of the crawler is used on all sites. This does not circumvent the problem of missing some pages (those not linked to), and missing some links that are embedded with technologies such as Java, JavaScript, and Macromedia Flash (Thelwall, 2002c). Personal crawlers are particularly useful for counting links between collections of Web sites. They cannot be used for counting links to Web sites from the rest of the Web because they could only get this data from crawling the rest of the Web, which is impractical. Since commercial engines can be used for this, some previous research has used personal crawlers for intersite links, and AltaVista for counts of links to a site.

Pattern identification. Here is a list of examples of methods for identifying patterns in link data.

- Link type classification can be used for pattern identification, even if it is not needed for validation. It can be used to report the percentage of links of different types in the data set.
- Simple network diagrams can be used to display the interconnectivity between Web sites, for visual pattern identification. For a small number of sites, perhaps up to 15, this can be achieved with a network diagram with arrows between sites having thickness proportional to the number of links between the sites. For a large number of sites, this will produce an unreadable diagram and so, other techniques can be used that do not display the links directly, but organise the network or display the Web sites in ways that reflect their connectivity. Examples include pathfinder networks and multidimensional scaling (Thelwall, 2002b).

- Mathematical modelling can also be used as a form of pattern identification. Like correlation testing, this can involve external data, using it to build a model to predict link counts; for example, using linear regression or curve fitting techniques (e.g., Thelwall, 2002d). Note, however, that link counts are derived from a very skewed distribution (Barabási & Albert, 1999); hence, fitting a model may be difficult, or logarithmic transformations may first be needed. An example of a simple mathematical model that does not need an external data source is one that predicts the count of links between a pair of Web sites to be proportional to the product of the number of pages in the source and target Web site. Linear regression can be used to estimate this proportion, and an application of this type of modelling would be to identify pairs of Web sites that interlink significantly more or less than predicted by the model.

RELIABILITY

Link count data is not reliable in the sense of being repeatable. Not only is the Web constantly evolving, with new pages being added and old ones modified or deleted, but changes in publishing technology, such as HTML versions and Web content management tools, can also have a significant impact upon the way in which the Web is used. Nevertheless, correlations with external data sources can be used as evidence that link counts are at least not random, and a track record of significant link-based results points to the fact that the temporal reliability issue should not be fatal (Thelwall, Vaughan, & Björneborn, 2005). The reliability of the link analysis may be ensured by publishing the raw link data online, however.

VALIDITY

Validity checking is an issue for link data, and is one that needs to be addressed in each study with the techniques described, and with reference to the research question. Because of the enormous variety of uses of the Web, validity is likely to be not high in many cases, suggesting either triangulation with other approaches, or the use of link analysis for exploratory research. It is particularly suited to exploratory research because of the ease of data collection and its nonintrusive nature.

Link data needs to be validated if it is to be used to make inferences about other phenomena that are hypothesised to be related to links. One type of validity check, content analysis, should be always possible and normally desirable, whereas another, correlation testing, is not always possible. Both should be used, if possible.

Link type content analysis is a classification exercise to group the links in the data set into different categories. Often, the categories will relate to the apparent function of a link or the apparent reason for its creation, but ultimately, the categories must be determined by the research question. The purpose of the exercise is to assess the extent to which the links in the data set reflect the assumptions in the research design. For example, an assumption that links represent collaborative ties should be tested by a classification exercise that would estimate the percentage of links that reflect collaborative ties. This is not necessary if no assumptions are made (i.e. the research question is about linking rather than assuming that links reflect some other process).

The link type content analysis should be conducted broadly in line with standard content analysis techniques (e.g., Neuendorf, 2002), but a random sample of not more than 160 links should be used, because the increased accuracy of a larger sample is not appropriate in the context of a fast evolving Web (Thelwall, 2004). Ideally, however, two classifiers will conduct the exercise, to allow cross-checking of results, and an initial pilot exercise will be used to determine appropriate classification categories and descriptions.

Correlation testing, a form of external validity check, is correlating the Web site inlink counts with another source of data about the owners of the Web site that is hypothesised to be connected. For example, a hypothesis that links to a university Web site, reflecting its research capability, could lead to a correlation test between university Web site inlink counts and a university research productivity measure. A positive result serves both to partially confirm the hypothesis and to partially validate the lack of significant bias in the link count data collection exercise. Care must be taken to normalise for size, if the Web sites studied do not have similar sizes.

RESULTS

Link data collection may produce either a list of links, or a series of counts of links to Web sites that can then be analysed in various ways: the instrument results are not just the raw link count or link classification data, but its analysis. The parameters used in data collection also form part of the results. The information to be reported if a link crawler is used is the Web sites crawled, the crawling policy (e.g., whether duplicate pages were ignored), and a list of areas that were excluded from the crawl. If a commercial search engine is used, then the Web sites, search syntax, and query date should be reported. Although this information does not allow the experiment to be exactly duplicated because of changes in the Web over time, it allows others to challenge key aspects of data collection that they may have reason to disagree with.

COMMENTARY

Link analysis can be used to investigate link creation or link types as an end in itself. It is also useful in situations where links are an aspect of the phenomenon being studied, such as the Web sites of a group of political organisations. It may also be used in some circumstances to track non-Web phenomena that are difficult to observe directly, such as informal scholarly communication, provided that adequate validity safeguards are made.

Link analysis is particularly suited to initial exploratory investigations because it is relatively quick to carry out, but is not likely to return results with a high degree of reliability and validity. It can also be used as part of a triangulation strategy.

COST

All the necessary tools for link analysis are free.

LOCATION

For automated data collection, there is a free Web crawler at http://socscibot.wlv.ac.uk/ that comes with software to conduct a range of link analyses. For network diagrams, the free software Pajek is recommended (http://vlado.fmf.uni-lj.si/pub/networks/pajek). There are also some archives of link data collections, including http://cybermetrics.wlv.ac.uk/database/, that contain collections of links related to university Web sites.

REFERENCES

Barabási, A. L., & Albert, R. (1999). Emergence of scaling in random networks. *Science, 286,* 509-512.

Björneborn, L. (2004). *Small-world link structures across an academic Web space—A library and information science approach.* Copenhagen: Royal School of Library and Information Science.

Foot, K., Schneider, S., Dougherty, M., Xenos, M., & Larsen, E. (2003). Analyzing linking practices: Candidate sites in the 2002 US electoral Web sphere. *Journal of Computer Mediated Communication, 8*(4). Retrieved February 5, 2004 from http://www.ascusc.org/jcmc/vol8/issue4/foot.html

Garrido, M., & Halavais, A. (2003). Mapping networks of support for the Zapatista movement: Applying social network analysis to study contemporary social movements. In M. McCaughey & M. Ayers (Eds.), *Cyberactivism: Online activism in theory and practice* (pp. 165-184). London: Routledge.

Hine, C. (2000). *Virtual ethnography.* London: Sage.

Lawrence, S., & Giles, C. L. (1999). Accessibility of information on the Web. *Nature, 400,* 107-109.

Neuendorf, K. (2002). *The content analysis guidebook.* London: Sage.

Park, H. W. (2003). Hyperlink network analysis: A new method for the study of social structure on the Web. *Connections, 25*(1), 49-61.

Thelwall, M. (2002a). Evidence for the existence of geographic trends in university Web site interlinking. *Journal of Documentation, 58*(5), 563-574.

Thelwall, M. (2002b). An initial exploration of the link relationship between UK university Web sites. *ASLIB Proceedings, 54*(2), 118-126.

Thelwall, M. (2002c). Methodologies for crawler-based Web surveys. *Internet Research: Electronic Networking and Applications, 12*(2), 124-138.

Thelwall, M. (2002d). A research and institutional size based model for national university Web site interlinking. *Journal of Documentation, 58*(6), 683-694.

Thelwall, M. (2004). *Link analysis: An information science approach.* San Diego: Academic Press.

Thelwall, M., & Harries, G. (2004). Do better scholars' Web publications have significantly higher online impact? *Journal of American Society for Information Science and Technology, 55*(2), 149-159.

Thelwall, M., & Smith, A. G. (2002). A study of interlinking between Asia-Pacific University Web sites. *Scientometrics, 55*(3), 335-348.

Thelwall, M., Vaughan, L., & Björneborn, L. (2005). Webometrics. *Annual Review of Information Science and Technology, 39*, 81-135.

Van Couvering, E. (2004). *New media? The political economy of Internet search engines.* Paper presented at the Annual Conference of the International Association of Media & Communications Researchers, Porto Alegre, Brazil.

KEY TERMS

A (Site) Inlink: A link to a Web site from a different Web site.

A (Site) Outlink: A link from a site to a different Web site.

Hyperlink Analysis (Link Analysis): The analysis of Web hyperlinks for the purpose of identifying communities underlying the Web pages or hyperlinking practices within Web communities.

Interlinking: Linking between two or more Web sites.

Chapter XXXII
Web Site Experience Analysis

Mihaela Vorvoreanu
University of Dayton, USA

BACKGROUND

The Web site experience analysis (WEA) (Vorvoreanu, 2004) is a research protocol used to evaluate the experience of visiting a Web site. Currently, the dominant approach to Web site evaluation is usability, which is primarily concerned with ease of use (Brinck, Gergle, & Wood, 2002; Nielsen, 1993, 2000a; Nielsen & Norman, 2000; Nielsen & Tahir, 2002; Spool, 1999). While ease of use is an essential part of the experience of visiting a Web site, the Web site experience cannot be reduced to usability alone. Meanings, perceptions, and attitudes are also significant aspects of the Web site experience. Take the example of an emergency preparedness Web site such as Ready America (U.S. Department of Homeland Security, 2004). A usability evaluation of this Web site would assess whether information is easy to find, the site is easy to navigate, and so forth. WEA would take usability into consideration, but would also address other aspects of the Web site experience, asking questions such as: Did the Web site visitors understand the information? Were they persuaded? Were they scared? How likely are they to take the actions recommended? Did they perceive the Web site as credible? What are their understandings of the Web site authors' intentions?

In short, WEA taps into the communication aspect of visiting a Web site. Its purpose is to create a map of the user's Web site experience, complete with meanings, perceptions, and interpretations.

The WEA research protocol is directly derived from a framework of the Web site experience (Vorvoreanu, 2004) that incorporates results of several user behavior studies (Berkun, 1999; Brinck et al., 2002; Cockburn & McKenzie, 2001; Koyani & Bailey, 2002; National Telecommunications and Information Administration, 2002; Nielsen, 1999a, 1999b, 2000a, 2000b, 2000c, 2003a, 2003b; Paul, 2000; Shedroff, 2001; Spool, 1999). The framework conceptualizes two interrelated dimensions of the Web site experience: the spatial one—the Web site virtual space; and the temporal one—the sequence of user perceptions, cognitions, and behaviors a Web site visitor experiences during a Web site visit. The spatial dimension of the Web site experience includes a classification of Web site elements and components. The temporal dimension is broken down into three main phases of the experience: first impression, exploration, and exit. The exploration phase is further broken down into two steps: orientation and engagement. The two dimensions of the Web site experience are explained in more detail elsewhere (Vorvoreanu, 2004, 2005).

The purpose of the WEA research protocol is to produce a map of a user's Web site experience by observing how the connections between the spatial and the temporal dimensions are activated. For each phase of the temporal dimension, WEA contains one or more questions exploring the connections with the spatial dimension. For example, user behavior research shows that in the first few seconds of looking at a Web page, users form a quick assessment of the quality and usefulness of the Web site. Therefore, the questions corresponding to the first impression phase ask users to rate their perceptions of the Web site's quality, and to provide an account of the specific Web site elements their perceptions are based upon.

WEA contains items for all phases and steps of the Web site experience, except for the engagement step. During the engagement step, users engage in information learning and evaluation, while at the same time trying to maintain their orientation on the website (Eveland & Dunwoody, 1998, 2000). Different batteries of items can be used with the engagement step to assess different communication goals. For example, in an analysis of corporate Web sites, Vorvoreanu (2004) used a battery of items assessing aspects of organization-public relationship building. This battery of items can be replaced with items assessing learning, persuasion, or other user perceptions. WEA's built-in modularity was intended to provide the flexibility needed to assess the experience of visiting various types of Web sites.

RESULTS

WEA is available as a computer-based questionnaire that Web site users fill out as they visit the Web site to be evaluated. WEA requires switching between two computers, one used to visit a Web site, the other to complete the questionnaire. The questions for each phase of the Web site experience are presented on a separate page. WEA also includes a preliminary background questionnaire.

The data collected through the computer-based questionnaire is sent to a database. The data is a combination of quantitative ratings and open-ended answers that research participants type in. Overall, the data provides a map of the Web site experience. WEA makes it possible to identify how users perceive a Web site, what they understand, what conclusions they draw.

COMMENTARY

To date, the instruments available for studying and evaluating Web sites are mostly concerned with Web site usability. WEA is the only systematic, theory-derived research protocol available for assessing the overall experience of visiting a Web site. WEA is ideal for assessing user perceptions before launching a Web site. WEA points to the specific Web site elements that users base their interpretations upon, and makes it easy to alter the Web site in order to achieve different perceptions. For example, certain Web site elements might be intended to be perceived as playful and family-oriented. WEA can assess whether the Web site's public actually perceives them positively or negatively, and provides detailed accounts of these perceptions.

The caveat, of course, is that individual perceptions vary, and so it is theoretically problematic to generalize from a sample of users who completed WEA to a larger population. Theory argues that groups of people who share experiences, interests, and backgrounds, known as interpretive communities, tend to also share interpretations and perceptions (Fish, 1980, 2001). Therefore, in order to use WEA effectively, it is important to start with a well-defined interpretive community, or Web site public. A public is defined here as an interpretive community (Fish, 1980, 2001) who shares a set of assumptions, interpretations, and values (Botan & Soto, 1998), interests (Dewey, 1927), and cognitions and behaviors (Grunig & Hunt, 1984). It is important to keep in mind that

WEA results should not be generalized across interpretive communities, or publics.

COST

WEA is free for academic use.

LOCATION

WEA is available from the author on demand.

REFERENCES

Berkun, S. (1999). *The importance of simplicity: Create ease of use without losing power*. Retrieved 3/20, 2002, from http://msdn.microsoft.com/library/default.asp?url=/library/en-us/dnhfact/html/humanfactor8_4.asp

Botan, C. H., & Soto, F. (1998). A semiotic approach to the internal functioning of publics: Implications for strategic communication and public relations. *Public Relations Review, 24*(1), 21-44.

Brinck, T., Gergle, D., & Wood, S. D. (2002). *Usability for the Web: Designing Web sites that work* (1st ed.). San Francisco: Morgan Kaufmann Publishers.

Cockburn, A., & McKenzie, B. (2001). What do Web users do? An empirical analysis of Web use. *International Journal of Human-Computer Studies, 54*(6), 903-922.

Dewey, J. (1927). *The public and its problems*. Chicago: Swallow Press.

Eveland, W. P., & Dunwoody, S. (1998). Uses and navigation patterns of a science World Wide Web site for the public. *Public Understanding of Science, 7*, 285-311.

Eveland, W. P., & Dunwoody, S. (2000). Examining information processing on the World Wide Web using think-aloud protocols. *Media Psychology, 2*, 219-244.

Fish, S. (1980). *Is there a text in this class?* Cambridge, MA: Harvard University Press.

Fish, S. (2001). Yet once more. In J. Machor, L. & P. Goldstein (Eds.), *Reception study: From literary theory to cultural studies* (pp. 29-38). New York: Routledge.

Grunig, J. E., & Hunt, T. (1984). *Managing public relations*. New York: Holt Rinehart and Winston.

Koyani, S. J., & Bailey, R. W. (2002). *Searching vs. linking on the Web: A summary of the research*. Rockville, MD: Office of Communications—National Cancer Institute.

National Telecommunications and Information Administration. (2002). *A nation online: How Americans are expanding their use of the Internet*. Retrieved 12/12, 2002, from http://www.ntia.doc.gov/ntiahome/dn/

Nielsen, J. (1993). *Usability engineering*. Boston: Academic Press.

Nielsen, J. (1999a). *"Top ten mistakes" revisited three years later*. Retrieved 03/25, 2003, from http://www.useit.com/alertbox/990502.html

Nielsen, J. (1999b). *Usability as barrier to entry*. Retrieved 06/08, 2004, from http://www.useit.com/alertbox/991128.html

Nielsen, J. (2000a). *Designing web usability*. Indianapolis, IN: New Riders.

Nielsen, J. (2000b). *Drop-down menus: Use sparingly*. Retrieved 06/04, 2004, from http://www.useit.com/alertbox/20001112.html

Nielsen, J. (2000c). *Eyetracking study of Web readers*. Retrieved 03/25, 2003, from http://www.useit.com/alertbox/20000514.html

Nielsen, J. (2003a). *Investor relations website design*. Retrieved 03/27, 2003, from http://www.useit.com/alertbox/20030218.html

Nielsen, J. (2003b). *PR on websites: Increasing usability*. Retrieved 03/27, 2003, from http://www.useit.com/alertbox/20030310.html

Nielsen, J., & Norman, D. A. (2000). *Web-site usability: Usability on the Web isn't a luxury*. Retrieved 03/24, 2003, from http://www.informationweek.com/773/web.htm

Nielsen, J., & Tahir, M. (2002). *Homepage usability: 50 websites deconstructed*. Indianapolis, IN: New Riders.

Paul, C. (2000). *When Web pages don't work: Steps you can take to improve the user experience on the Web*. Retrieved 03/25, 2003, from http://www-106.ibm.com/developerworks/web/library/web-work.html

Shedroff, N. (2001). *Experience design*. Indianapolis, IN: New Riders.

Spool, J. M. (1999). *Web site usability: A designer's guide*. San Francisco: Morgan Kaufmann Publishers.

U.S. Department of Homeland Security. (2004). *Ready America*. Retrieved 10/11, 2004, from http://www.ready.gov

Vorvoreanu, M. (2004). *Building and maintaining eelationships online: A framework for analyzing the public relations Web site experience*. Unpublished doctoral dissertation, Purdue University, West Lafayette, IN.

Vorvoreanu, M. (2005, November). *Online organization-public relationships: An experience-centered approach*. Paper presented at the Annual Convention of the National Communication Association, Boston.

KEY TERMS

Interpretive Community: A group of people who share interpretive strategies

Public: A group of people who share a set of assumptions, interpretations, values, interests, cognitions, and behaviors.

Usability Evaluation: A research protocol designed to test the ease of use of a Web site, software, or other user interface.

Web Site Experience: The sequence of perceptions, cognitions, and behaviors experienced by users in response to, and interaction with, a Web site's constitutive elements.

Chapter XXXIII
Bit–Wise Coding
for Exploratory Analysis

Thomas O'Daniel
Monash University, Malaysia Campus, Malaysia

INTRODUCTION

Getting data to yield their insights can be hard work. This is especially true with survey data, which tends to be oriented toward the presence or absence of characteristics, or attitude relative to some arbitrary midpoint. A good example of the first comes from surveying the Web by looking at Web sites: Ho (1997) analysed the value-added features used by 1,800 commercial Web sites to form a profile of commercial use of the Web within various industries; the U.S. Federal Trade Commission (2000) examined the characteristics of the privacy policy on 426 Web sites; West (2004) looked at 1,935 national government Web sites for 198 nations around the world, evaluating the presence of various features dealing with information availability, service delivery, and public access. A good example of the second comes from any number of studies that use the "Likert scale."

These studies are characterised by (a) large sample sizes and (b) an analysis that must incorporate a large number of "indicator" and "categorical" variables. Coding and analysis should be considered at design time: not only "what information to collect" but also "how to store it" and "how to use it." This is particularly true with Web-based surveys using HTML forms, since the data can be stored automatically without the intermediate step of transcribing the answers from paper questionnaires into the computer. Getting a relevant graphical view of the data is often essential, since the human eye is a powerful analytical tool. The help files that come with statistical analysis applications explain particular techniques, but the importance of coding is often obscured by the description.

Most multivariate statistical methods are built on the foundation of linear transformations: a weighted combination of scores where each score is first multiplied by a constant and then the products are summed. This combines a number of scores into a single score. For example, in multiple regression analysis, linear transformations are used to find weights for several independent or predictor variables such that the regression line expresses the best prediction of the dependent or criterion variable.

In surveys like the ones mentioned, it is easy to have a large number of variables that merely indicate the presence or absence of a trait. The goal of the technique presented here, "bit-wise coding," is description rather than prediction, using groups of these variables. The essence of the method is to code each variable as zero or one, multiply by a power of two, and sum the products to achieve a single score. The key difference between this and a linear transformation is that the constants (weights) are assigned sequentially, so the resulting score uniquely represents a combination of attributes.

The real power of this method lies in the fact that no data is lost: the score represents a "profile" of each observation, and a frequency histogram represents the "popularity" of each profile within the sample. *A priori*, peaks offer insight into *multicollinearity*, which occurs when two variables are highly correlated, or if one variable has a high multiple correlation with others. Many analysis techniques are sensitive to multicollinearity, and it is often not immediately apparent when many variables are involved. Valleys and missing values represent combinations that are infrequently (or never) present. Outliers may be the result of (a) observations that are truly not representative of the general population or (b) undersampling of actual group(s) in the population. In both cases, they will distort the analysis, so outliers must be examined and the observations deleted (cautiously) if deemed unrepresentative–at the expense of sample size.

In this entry, we will look at the essence of the technique using a group of simple "yes/no" categorical variables, move on to using dummy-coded variables to represent several states, and finally, discuss appropriate methods for using these scores. It is assumed that we are using some statistical software that represents the data spreadsheet style: each column as a variable and each row an observation. The definition section provides a short list of multivariate techniques and the appropriate types of data.

THE BASIC TECHNIQUE

To begin, assume the following variables have been used in a study similar to the ones mentioned, and that they have been coded as (one = has) (zero = does not have) the characteristic. Each variable is assigned a power of 2 as its weight,

the weight is multiplied by zero or one, and added to the total.

16	Privacy Policy
8	Advertisements for Other Companies
4	Return Policy
2	Online Ordering
1	Online Payment

Thus, a final value of (say) 20 means that this Web site has a privacy policy and a return policy (16+4), but no other features; furthermore, *no other combination of features will yield a score of 20.* A site with all of these features will have a score of 31, and a site with none will have a score of zero. It is also important to note that since every score represents a unique combination of features, the arithmetic mean is meaningless: a score of 3 means the site has Online Ordering and Online Payment, which does not represent the midpoint between a site that only has Online Ordering (2) and a site that only has a Return Policy (4).

This technique can be called "bit-wise" because it is the technique used by the computer internally to deal with groups of binary digits (bits). The powers of two are assigned sequentially, so the order of the bits we are combining becomes important. Unfortunately, bit ordering has long been a subject of controversy in the computer world. The "Little-Endians" want binary numbers to look like positive integers, where the leftmost digit is the most significant: (001 < 010 < 100). The "Big-Endians" want to lay out the bits like the x-axis of a traditional two-dimensional graph, with the origin (left) as zero, thus (100 < 010 < 001). This is the sort of thing that gets people (even computer scientists) annoyed and possibly confused. For a rather detailed but still amusing explanation, see Cohen (1981).

The happy reality is that it does not matter as long as the order used is consistent. These examples have the "low" bits on the right and the "high" bits on the left: thus, 10100 would be the binary representation of 20 in this example.

The simple reason for choosing this order is that this is the order used in the "ASCII" table, and it is easy to find small utilities that show binary equivalents of ASCII characters: such tables commonly showing combinations of 8 or 16 bits are often included in computer science textbooks along with tables of the powers of two. This sort of reference cuts down the mental agility required to interpret the combination of features that a particular score represents.

USING INDICATOR VARIABLES

While the examples here use a limited number of bits, in reality, there is no limit to the size of the score. The only caveat is that as more variables are combined into a single bit-wise score, the more the score begins to represent individual observations.

The general formula is:

t += ((2^p)/2) * v
where
t is the total
p is the bit position, starting at one
v is zero or one

which looks a little cryptic if you are not a programmer. Spreadsheet style, with the variables coded in columns A through E and the first data in row 1, in cell F1, the formula would look like:

= (((2^5)/2) * a1) + (((2^4)/2) * b1) + (((2^3)/2) * c1) + (((2^2)/2) * d1) + (((2^1)/2) * e1)

which can be copied down the column for all observations.

The next step is to look at a frequency histogram for column F. In theory, any number between 0 and 2^p is a valid combination of characteristics. There are several things to look for:

- **Powers of 2:** These represent the observations with *only one* of the set of characteristics
- **Odd Scores vs. Even Scores:** The score will be odd If and Only If the lowest-order bit is set (e.g., from this example, the site has Online Payment).
- **Largest Scores:** In the example, any score above 16 means that the site has a Privacy Policy AND some other characteristic.
- **Peaks and Valleys:** Peaks represent the combinations of characteristics that are most frequently observed, and are, thus, most likely to drive subsequent analysis. Valleys represent combinations that are infrequently observed (outliers), and missing values represent combinations that were never observed.

There is one thing NOT to look for:

- Normality of the distribution. Since weights are assigned sequentially, *changing the order of the bits only changes the scores, not their relative frequency.* If one frequency histogram looks "normal," it is easy to rearrange the bits to make it look "exponential," and rearrange again to make it "two-peaked." The essential point is that *combining the variables in any order is an equivalent representation of the data.* This critical characteristic of the method will be covered in more detail, because the frequency distribution can only be used "As-Is" with some specific analytical techniques.

USING DUMMY CODED VARIABLES

Dummy coding is a technique commonly used for variables with more than two states, in order to use them with multivariate statistical techniques that allow categorical variables (see the definitions section as follows). Consider a variable that might be called "Prices":

```
0 0 = 0  No prices are shown
0 1 = 1  prices are shown in USD only
1 0 = 2  prices are shown, but Not in USD
1 1 = 3  prices are shown in both USD and some
other currency
```

Survey data also commonly includes "Likert scale"'data: variables with six states, that can be represented using three binary digits. The trick here is to code the *middle* of the scale as the *highest bit*, which is easily converted to a positive/negative scale suitable for a regression equation (in this case, by subtracting 4).

```
0 0 0 = 0  ( -4 ) Missing Data
1 0 0 = 4  ( 0 )  Neutral
1 1 0 = 6  ( 2 )  Strongly Agree
0 1 0 = 2  ( -2 ) Strongly Disagree
1 0 1 = 5  ( 1 )  Agree
0 0 1 = 1  ( -3 ) Disagree
1 1 1 = 7       Unused
0 1 1 = 3       Unused
```

This example emphasises the symmetry of the bits, in practice, since $-2 > -3$ it might be useful to code them slightly differently.

Two scores can be combined into a single bit-wise score using this general formula:

$$c = (H * (2\char94 b)) + L$$

where

c is the combined (new target) score
L and H are bit-wise scores
b is the number of bits in L

This is easier to see in "real time." For example, L is a three-bit score, H is two-bit; c will have L as the lower bits and H as the higher bits. The desired outcome has five binary digits, so c will always be less than or equal to 31 ($2\char94 5 = 32$ minus one because counting really starts at zero).

Since there are 3 bits in L: $2\char94 3 = 8$
Since there are 3 bits in L: possible values are 0,1,2,3,4,5,6,7
Since there are 2 bits in H: $2\char94 2 = 4$
Since there are 2 bits in H: possible values are 0,1,2,3
for H * ($2\char94 3$) possible values are 0, 8, 16, 24 which can be added to any possible value of L

Using this approach, any number of indicator and dummy-coded variables can be combined into a single score.

MORE FORMAL ANALYSIS

While an informal (visual) analysis of the frequency histogram of bit-wise scores is a useful exploratory technique, more formal analysis is, perhaps, desirable in order to identify patterns of variables that can be combined into a single variable, and also to identify outliers. Comparing two groups is one form of analysis where bit-wise scores can be used "As-Is," without further manipulation. If the sample can be divided into two independent groups, the similarity of the frequency distributions of the bit-wise scores can be compared *using non-parametric tests*. Frequency distributions of scores based on two different combinations of variables can be compared to check multicollinearity: if the distributions are similar, they measure the same thing. Meaningful comparisons can also be made between a distribution, excluding observations suspected to be unrepresentative and a distribution that uses them.

Most common statistical techniques are either based on the normal distribution or on distributions that can be derived from it. The normal distribution is defined by a function that has only two parameters: mean and standard deviation. A characteristic property of the normal distribution is that 68% of all of its observations fall within a range of ±1 standard deviation from the mean, and 95% fall within a range of ±2 standard deviations.

Methods that rely on the estimation of parameters (the mean and the standard deviation) are known as *parametric* methods, and are only appropriate with *interval* and *ratio* data, where equally spaced intervals on the scale can be compared in a meaningful manner.

This is obviously not the case using bit-wise encoding, where every score has a unique meaning and the arithmetic mean is "meaningless." Nonparametric techniques make no assumption about normally distributed data: generally, they use the ranks, or order, of the data rather than the data values themselves, which makes them appropriate for *nominal* and *ordinal* data. Bit-wise scores are nominal data: it would be a fatal error (analytically speaking) to treat the bit-wise scores as interval or ratio data.

Most statistical packages will offer two non-parametric tests for comparing two independent groups: the Mann-Whitney U test and the Kolmogorov-Smirnov test. The Mann-Whitney test tests the null hypothesis that there is no difference in the medians of the groups (sometimes expressed as testing the equality of the central tendency). The Kolmogorov-Smirnov test is actually a generalised procedure that tests the null hypothesis that the population distribution from which the data sample is drawn conforms to a hypothesized distribution. In this case, the hypothesized distribution is the distribution of the other group rather than (say) normal or chi-square. It is advisable to run both of these tests, because they have different sensitivities relative to each other. More specifically, the Kolmogorov-Smirnov two-sample test is more sensitive to the overall shape of the distribution, while the Mann-Whitney U test is affected more by the differences in mean ranks (location).

Nonparametric methods are considered less powerful than their parametric counterparts, which means they are less flexible in terms of types of conclusions that they can provide. Under normal circumstances, nonparametric results cannot be generalized to the population. In the case of comparing two groups using frequency distributions of bit-wise scores it might be justifiable to argue that since the sample size is large, the frequency of a given set of characteristics in the sample is representative of the population as a whole. However, this sort of argument should be presented cautiously, backed up by a number of different views of the data and other evidence.

CONCLUSION

Quantitative research must start from qualitative judgments on what research questions are to be pursued, and may rely on qualitative insights for the interpretation of results. Data must be "good" for their intended use; inferences can only be as good as the data allow. The most engaging characteristics of this technique are the immediate visualisation of the interaction between groups of nominal and ordinal variables, and the ability to incorporate individual variables coded in this manner directly into other multivariate analysis techniques. This means that the technique is extremely useful at the initial stages of the analysis, especially for identifying groups, outliers, and complex interactions of covariates that may not be easily identified using other techniques like cluster analysis or factor (principle components) analysis. While there are limits on the utility of these scores as input for further analysis, they can provide valuable insight into similarity between groups in a subdivided sample.

REFERENCES

Cohen, D. (1981). On Holy Wars and a plea for peace. *IEEE Computer Magazine, 14*, 48-54.

Federal Trade Commission. (2000). *Privacy online: Fair information practices in the electronic marketplace*. A Federal Trade Commission Report to Congress. Retrieved May 26, 2000, from http://www.ftc.gov/reports/index.htm#2000

Ho, J. K. (1997). Evaluating the World Wide Web: A global study of commercial sites. *Journal of Computer-Mediated Communication, 3*(1).

West, D. M. (2004). *Global e-government.* Brown University Center for Public Policy, 2004. Retrieved October 21, 2004, from http://www. InsidePolitics.org/egovtdata.html

KEY TERMS

"Bit-Wise Coding": An informal name for the technique of treating a number of CATEGORICAL variables as a single binary number. The goal is description rather than prediction: a Bit-Wise 'score' represents a unique combination of values. While it is a less formal technique than factor analysis and cluster analysis, the frequency histogram of Bit-Wise scores can be used in similar ways for data reduction, as well as investigating the effects of multicollinearity and outlying observations.

Linear Probability Models: Linear probability models (often referred to as logit analysis) estimate the relationship between a single CATEGORICAL dependent variable and a set of METRIC OR CATEGORICAL independent variables. However in many instances, particularly with more than two levels of the dependent variable, discriminant analysis is the more appropriate technique.

Metric Data: Metric (or continuous) data has a constant unit of measurement, indicating exact differences between points on a scale: Ratio data have a true zero point, such as weight; Interval data lack a true zero point, such as a thermometer. Categorical (or nominal) data indicate the presence of an attribute, but not the exact amount: Indicator data simply indicates presence or absence; Ordinal data indicates the relative position in an ordered series without an absolute baseline and without indicating the exact difference between points on a scale.

Parametric and Nonparametric Methods: Parametric methods make assumptions based on the normal curve, or some curve that can be derived from it such as t, F, or Chi-square. Nonparametric methods make no assumptions based on the normal curve, and are considered less powerful than parametric methods. Most parametric tests have nonparametric counterparts that generally use the ranks, or order, of the data rather than the data values themselves.

Chapter XXXIV
Measurement of End–User Computing Satisfaction

Rodney A. Reynolds
Azusa Pacific University, USA
(on leave from Pepperdine University, USA)

BACKGROUND

Doll and Torkzadeh (1988) developed their measure of end-user computing satisfaction because "decision analysis" (examination of specific uses of computer applications in decision making) is "generally not feasible" (p. 259), but that satisfaction is a reasonable surrogate for assessing use. Doll and Torkzadeh claim that evidence from other studies support an expectation that satisfaction leads to use (as opposed to use leading to satisfaction). The Doll and Torkzadeh study focused more on broad notions of systems and applications (Mini- or mainframes, microcomputer applications, analysis, and monitor applications).

The end-user computing satisfaction scale is a multidimensional instrument. Doll and Torkzadeh (1988) started with 40 items, and reduced those first to 18 items, and then reduced the scale further to a final set of 12 items. The dimensions of the end-user satisfaction scale are content, accuracy, format, ease of use, and timeliness.

Aladwani (2003) reviewed the existing measures of information satisfaction and found the Doll and Torkzadeh (1988) measure to be less limited by particular context or application than other measures are. Aladwani applied the end-user computing satisfaction scale to assess student satisfaction with e-mail. McHaney and Cronan (1998) used the end-user computing satisfaction scale to assess responses to computer simulations.

RELIABILITY

Doll and Tofkzaheh (1988) report an overall reliability (alpha) of .92 for the end-user computing satisfaction scale. The reliabilities for the specific dimensions are: Content, .89; Accuracy, .91; Format, .78; Ease of use, .82; and Timeliness .82. Torkzadeh and Doll (1991) demonstrated high test-retest reliability for the end-user computing datisfaction scale.

VALIDITY

Doll and Torkzadeh (1988) conducted a multi-trait-multimethod approach to assess the validity of the end-user computing satisfaction scale, and reported strong convergent and discriminant validity. They report a criterion-related validity coefficient of .76. Doll and Weidong (1997) and also McHaney, Hightower, and Pearson (2002) replicated the original factor analytic structure with a confimatory factor analysis. McHaney, Hightower, and Pearson (2002) demonstrated the utility of the end-user computing satisfaction scale to test for differences between competing applications, features, and technologies. Lee and Kim (1995) demonstrated that end-user computing satisfaction predicts information system acceptance and job satisfaction.

RESULTS

Researchers typically sum the items on the entire scale or on the respective dimensions to achieve composite scores. Researchers in the literature on the end-user computing satisfaction scale do not commonly report using factor score coefficients when calculating scores.

COMMENTARY

Doll and Torkzadeh (1991) responded to concerns raised about the end-user computing satisfaction scale. They indicate that most of the concerns are misunderstandings or unreasonable demands that exceed normal standards for measurement development and use. The scale is clearly one of the more popular instruments in the literature on technology usage.

COST

The end-user computing satisfaction scale is readily available in print (Doll & Torkzadeh, 1988). The MIS Quarterly holds the copyright on the original publication, so researchers should consult that journal before assuming any rights to the use of the instrument.

LOCATION

Doll, W. J., & Torkzadeh, G. (1988). The measurement of end-user computing satisfaction. *MIS Quarterly, 12*, 259-274.

An electronic version of the instrument is available from the author of this profile, so long as the user takes personal responsibility for protecting the rights of the copyright holder.

REFERENCES

Abdinnour-Helm, S. F, Chaparro, B. S., & Farmer, S. M. (2005). Using the end-user computing satisfaction (EUCS) instrument to measure satisfaction with a Web site. *Decision Sciences, 36*, 341-363

Aladwani, A. M. (2003). A deeper look at the attitude-behavior consistency assumption in information systems satisfaction research. *The Journal of Computer Information Systems, 44*, 57-63

Doll, W. J., & Torkzadeh, G. (1988). The measurement of end-user computing satisfaction. *MIS Quarterly, 12*, 259-274.

Doll, W. J., & Torkzadeh, G. (1991). The measurement of end-user computing satisfaction: Theoretical and methodological issues. *MIS Quarterly, 15*, 5-10.

Doll, W. J., & Weidong, X. (1997). Confirmatory factor analysis of the end-user computing satisfaction instrument: A replication. *Journal of End User Computing, 9*, 24-31

Lee, S. M., Kim, Y. R., & Lee, J. (1995). An empirical study of the relationships among end-user information systems acceptance, training, and effectiveness. *Journal of Management Information Systems, 12*, 189-202.

McHaney, R., & Cronan, T. P. (1998). Computer simulation success: On the use of the end-user computing satisfaction instrument: A comment. *Decision Sciences, 29*, 525-536.

McHaney, R., Hightower, R., & Pearson, J. (2002). A validation of the end-user computing satisfaction instrument in Taiwan. *Information & Management, 39*, 503-512

Torkzadeh, G., & Doll, W. J. (1991). Test-retest reliability of the end-user computing satisfaction instrument. *Decision Sciences, 22*, 26-37.

KEY TERMS

Accuracy: The degree that information or processes [on a computer system or Web page] are correct or true.

Computer or Web Satisfaction: Overall summary sense that a computer system or Web page offers appropriate and efficient worth.

Computer or Web Use: Seeking to fulfill goals or gratifications by use of computer and Web-based technology

Content: The subject material available (as distinct from the form of the material), particularly through a computer system, Web page, and the related database

Ease of Use: The perception that the layout and design of a computer system or Web page is uncomplicated, understandable, and usable

Format: The presentation and layout of material or "output"

Timeliness: The perception that information is up-to-date and on time.

Chapter XXXV
Web Credibility Measurement

Rodney A. Reynolds
Azusa Pacific University, USA
(on leave from Pepperdine University, USA)

BACKGROUND

Several researchers (e.g., Carter & Greenberg, 1965; Flanagin, & Metzger, 2000; Fogg, 2002; Johnson & Kaye, 2004; Newhagen & Nass, 1989) discuss or mention the concept of media or Web credibility. The classic concept of credibility (typically attributed to Aristotle's *Rhetoric*) identifies credibility as a multidimensional perception on the part of the receiver that the source of a message has a moral character, practical wisdom, and a concern for the common good. Warnick (2004) points out that the "authorless" nature of the online environment complicates the use of traditional analyses of credibility.

The most common set of Web credibility scales cited in the research are the Flanagin and Metzger (2000) items. The five Flanagin and Metzger scale items address the believability, accuracy, trustworthiness, bias, and completeness of the information on the Web site. Other researchers have added other items such as fairness or depth of information. Flanagin and Metzger used a 7-point response format with anchors for each term (e.g., "Not At All Believable" to "Extremely Be-

lievable"). Other researchers have used a 5-point response format.

Fogg (2002) indicates a slightly different approach adopted at the Stanford University Web credibility project (Fogg cites Danielson, in press, as the most current overview on Web credibility). In the Stanford studies, the researchers asked participants to examine many different characteristics from a number of Web sites, and rate each characteristic on the degree that the characteristic contributed to the "believability" of the Web site. The Stanford approach basically replicated the Flanagin and Metzger (2000) Web credibility features, but extended the list of features to include items related to operation or navigation on the site (e.g., organization of site, access or contact, ease of use, updating, excesses in promotional content, and errors of any form).

RELIABILITY

Flanagin and Metzger (2000) report an average Web credibility reliability across four different types of information (news, entertainment, commercial, and reference) of alpha = .91 (p. 523).

VALIDITY

There is relatively little information on the validity of the measurement of Web credibility. Flanagin and Metzger (2000) point out that the major limitation of their study is the nonrepresentative sample of Web users. The Stanford Web credibility project is certainly broader in the representation of the variety of Web pages. There is a clear need for a comprehensive and systematic assessment of the validity of Web credibility measurement.

RESULTS

In the typical research study on Web credibility, the researchers sum the items to obtain a single Web credibility score. Researchers often report comparisons of both items and totals across different types of media or information.

COMMENTARY

It seems questionable to use single items to measure what appear to be complex perceptions on each dimension of Web credibility. The argument is a foundational question about the ability to fit the verbal universe to the observational universe (Miller & Boster, 1989, p. 19). A single word can seldom sum up the breadth or depth of most concepts. The concept of "accuracy," for example, has at least five major synonyms that capture substantively different aspects worthy of attention. When respondents check off "Not At All Accurate" when rating a Web page, we might wonder if the concern is with incorrect information, incomplete information, or just the meticulousness in the information provided. On a more pragmatic note, it is difficult to assess internal consistency (reliability) of ratings on a dimension with a single rating scale for that dimension. Textbooks that cover the basics of measurement often illustrate the point with some reference to assessing a person's skills based on a single performance. While Pedhazur and Schmelkin (1991, p. 101) warn that increasing scale length may artificially increase reliability estimates, we cannot forget Epstein's (1979) dictum about having an adequate number of questions to adequately represent the measured concept.

COST

There are various versions of the Web credibility scale items readily available in print.

LOCATION

Various versions of the instrument are available in print, but there is sufficient information in this chapter for most researchers to construct their own versions of the scale. The original description is in Flanagin and Metzger (2000). An electronic version of the instrument is available from the author of this profile, so long as the users take personal responsibility for protecting the rights of anyone who might claim to hold a copyright to the scales.

REFERENCES

Carter, R. E., & Greenberg, B. S. (1965). Newspapers or television: Which do you believe? *Journalism Quarterly, 42,* 29-34.

Danielson, D. R. (in press). Web credibility. To appear in C. Ghaoui (Ed.), *Encyclopedia of Human-Computer Interaction*. Hershey, PA: Idea Group.

Epstein, S. (1979). The stability of behavior: On predicting most of the people most of the time. *Journal of Personality and Social Psychology, 37,* 1097-1126.

Flanagin, A. J., & Metzger, M. J. (2000). Perceptions of Internet information credibility. *Journalism and Mass Communication Quarterly, 77,* 5J5-540

Fogg, B. J. (May 2002). *Stanford guidelines for Web credibility.* A research summary from the Stanford Persuasive Technology Lab. Stanford University. Retrieved January 26, 2006, from http://www.webcredibility.org/guidelines

Johnson, T. J., & Kaye, B. K. (2004). For whom the Web toils: How Internet experience predicts Web reliance and credibility. *Atlantic Journal of Communication, 12*(1), 19-45.

Miller, G. R., & Boster, F. J. (1989). Data analysis in communication research. In P. Emmert and L. L. Barker (Eds.). *Measurement of communication behavior* (pp. 18-39). New York: Longman.

Newhagen, J., & Nass, C. (1989). Differential criteria for evaluating credibility of newspapers and TV news. *Journalism Quarterly, 66,* 277-284.

Pedhazur, E. J., & Schmelkin, L. P. (1991). *Measurement, design, and analysis: An integrated approach.* Hillsdale, NJ: Erlbaum.

Warnick, B. (2004). Online ethos: Source credibility in an "authorless" environment. *American Behavioral Scientist, 48*(2), 256-265.

KEY TERMS

Bias: The perception that content represents a particular preference or perspective without offering a fair representation of alternative views.

Completeness of Information: The perception that information is an extant representation of the available information.

Media Credibility: The perception that a channel of information or a specific media agency tends toward conveying believable, accurate, and trustworthy content.

Site Navigation: The degree of difficulty experienced when a person maneuvers through the links and connections on a Web site.

Web Credibility: The perception by a Web user that the "source" and the content on a Web page is believable, accurate, and trustworthy.

Chapter XXXVI
Constructivist Online Learning Environment Survey

Jason D. Baker
Regent University, USA

BACKGROUND

Understanding the psychosocial classroom environment has been important in both traditional face-to-face courses and online education. Trickett and Moos (1974) pioneered the use of postcourse self-report instruments to measure the classroom environment through the classroom environment scale. More recently, Taylor and Maor (2000) developed the Constructivist Online Learning Environment Survey (COLLES) to examine the students' perceptions of the online learning environment in light of social constructivist pedagogical principles.

The 24-item, Likert-type COLLES instrument is a popular measure for examining online learning environments for a least two reasons. First, it measures the online learning environment along constructivist categories, which makes it in line with the dominant pedagogical philosophy for online instruction. Second, the COLLES instrument is freely included in the survey module of Moodle, the most popular open source course management system available. This makes it particularly convenient for online instructors to use COLLES in their teaching and research.

COLLES assesses the learning environment using six scales:

- **Relevance:** How relevant is online learning to students' professional practices?
- **Reflection:** Does online learning stimulate students' critical reflective thinking?
- **Interactivity:** To what extent do students engage online in rich educative dialogue?
- **Tutor Support:** How well do tutors enable students to participate in online learning?
- **Peer Support:** Is sensitive and encouraging support provided online by fellow students?
- **Interpretation:** Do students and tutors make good sense of each other's online communications? (http://surveylearning.moodle.com/colles/)

Each of these scales is represented by four items. In filling out the form, an individual indicates the relative frequency (ranging from almost never to almost always) that different activities occur in the online course.

An individuals' score on the COLLES is determined by summing responses across all six scales (24 items). In addition, six scale scores can be calculated (4 items each). Thus, an overall constructivist learning environment score and a separate score for relevance, reflection, interactivity, tutor (instructor) support, peer support, and interpretation.

The COLLES instrument is self-report and takes about 10-15 minutes to complete. There are preferred and actual forms of the instrument available. According to the authors:

Which form of the COLLES to administer depends largely on timing and purpose. Typically, we administer the preferred form early in the teaching semester, after allowing a couple of weeks to pass while students become familiar with our online learning requirements. Then, in the final week of semester, we administer the combined form (preferred and actual) (http://surveylearning. moodle.com/colles/).

COMMENTARY

The COLLES is a significant instrument to support online learning within a constructivist pedagogical framework. The constructs that it measures are useful for the teacher and researcher alike. Furthermore, the simplicity of the instrument, the availability of both preferred and actual versions, and the ease of access make the COLLES an extremely attractive instrument for online learning research. The lack of detailed validity and reliability testing bundled with the instrument itself is disconcerting, although perhaps explained by the relative newness of the instrument and the extensive validation of similar learning environment instruments. Nevertheless, the popularity and accessibility of the COLLES warrants additional research into this instrument to support its continued usage in academic research and practice.

COST

The COLLES is free to take and use online.

LOCATION

The preferred and actual forms of the COLLES are available online at

http://surveylearning.moodle.com/colles/

The COLLES is also bundled with the Moodle course management system, available at: http://www.moodle.org

REFERENCES

Byer, J. L. (2000). Measuring the positive effects of students' perceptions of classroom social climate on academic self-concept. *Journal of Social Studies Research, 24*(1), 25-34.

Fraser, B. J. (1998). Classroom environment instruments: Development, validity and applications. *Learning Environments Research: An International Journal, 1*(1), 7-33.

Dougiamas, M., & Taylor, P. C. (2002). Interpretive analysis of an Internet-based course constructed using a new courseware tool called Moodle. *Proceedings from the Higher Education Research and Development Society of Australasia 2002 Conference.* Perth: HERDSA. Retrieved from http://www.ecu.edu.au/conferences/herdsa/main/papers/nonref/pdf/MartinDougiamas.pdf

Taylor, P. & Maor, D. (2000, February 2-4). Assessing the efficacy of online teaching with the Constructivist On-Line Learning Environment survey. In A. Herrmann & M. M. Kulski (Eds.), *Flexible futures in tertiary teaching. Proceedings of the 9th Annual Teaching Learning Forum.* Perth: Curtin University of Technology. Retrieved

November 6, 2005, from http://lsn.curtin.edu. au./tlf/tlf2000/taylor.html

Trickett, E. J., & Moos, R. H. (1974). Personal correlates of contrasting environments: Student satisfaction in high school classrooms. *American Journal of Community Psychology, 5*, 93-102.

Walker, S. (2003, April). *Distance education learning environments research: A short history of a new direction in psychosocial learning environments*. Paper presented at the Eighth Annual Teaching in the Community Colleges Online Conference, Honolulu, HI. Retrieved from http://education. ollusa.edu/mtt/presentations/TCC_2003/

KEY TERMS

Constructivism: An educational philosophy that emphasizes the learner's active role in acquiring and developing one's own knowledge and understanding. This contrasts with other approaches that may emphasize the transmission of information or observable behaviors.

Course Management System: A computer software program designed to support the delivery of online instruction. Popular CMSs include Blackboard, WebCT, and Moodle.

Online Learning Environment: The computer-mediated space in which online distance education occurs. An online learning environment has both technological characteristics (e.g., asynchronous, Web-based) and psychosocial characteristics (e.g., collaborative, independent).

Open Source Software: An approach to software development where multiple individuals collaboratively write code and release both the source code and resulting program to the online community. Anyone is then permitted to freely use the software and modify the code, provided that such modifications are again made available in a public release of the code.

Chapter XXXVII
Celebrity–Persona Identification Scale

William J. Brown
Regent University, USA

Mihai C. Bocarnea
Regent University, USA

BACKGROUND

The *celebrity-persona parasocial identification scale* (CPI) is designed to measure how media consumers develop identification with celebrities or popular fictional characters. Identification is defined as a persuasion process that occurs when an individual adopts the behavior or attitudes of another individual or group based on a self-defining relationship (Kelman, 1961, p. 63). Identification is a psychological orientation through which individuals define themselves based on their group membership and derive "strength and a sense of identity" from the affiliation (Kelman, 1961, p.64).

Identification is a fundamental process of social change that has been discussed by several important theorists and social scientists. Freud (1922, p. 29) defined identification as "the earliest expression of an emotional tie with another person." Lasswell (1965) also discussed the concept, referring to mass identifications such as nationalism. Johnson, Johnson, and Heimberg (1999) traced the concept of identification to both Freud and Lasswell.

According to Burke, identification occurs when one individual shares the interests of another individual or believes that he or she shares the interests of another (1969, p. 180). Burke noted that two individuals could be joined and still be distinct. He conceptualized identification as compensatory to division (Burke, 1969, p. 182). Burke used another concept, consubstantiality, to further explain identification, positing that things are consubstantial when they share the same nature of substance (Burke, 1969, p. 180). In a pragmatic sense, identification is simply the common ground held by people in communication (Rosenfeld, 1969). Although Burke focused on the efforts of speakers to identify with their intended audiences, identification is also a way in which an audience member can say to a communicator, "I am like you" or "I have the same interests as you" (Cheney, 1983, p. 147).

Identification has been studied in a number of mediated contexts (see Woodward, 2003), especially with regards to sports fans (Basil, 1996; Basil & Brown, 2004; Matviuk, 2006). Fans frequently view a team or a player as an extension of themselves. A significant body of research has explored identification and sport fan affiliation because identification provides a foundation for understanding many of the unique psychological processes associated with sport fans.

Identification is often confused or entangled with parasocial interaction. Although both parasocial interaction and identification are both forms of audience involvement, they are distinct processes (Brown, Basil, & Bocarnea, 2003b, Brown & Fraser, 2006). Parasocial interaction often predicts identification because people commonly seek to adopt the values, beliefs, and behaviors of celebrities and media persona whom they admire. However, there are examples of celebrities that fans have strong parasocial interaction with, and yet the fans do not want to be like that person (Matviuk, 2006).

RELIABILITY

The CPI has been found to be very reliable, achieving Cronbach alpha reliability scores of .87 or higher (Bocarnea, 2001; Matviuk, 2006). Brown, Basil and Bocarnea (2003a) used many of the scale items in their study of identification with Princess Diana, and achieved an alpha coefficient of .87.

VALIDITY

Several studies have been conducted of identification with celebrities (Basil, 1996; Fraser & Brown, 2002) using many of the items in the CPI scale. Construct and criterion-related validity has been supported in studies by Bocarnea (2001), Brown, Basil and Bocarnea (2003b), and Matviuk (2006). Identification with baseball star Mark McGwire predicted increased desire to use androstenedione and to support child abuse prevention, while identification with soccer legend Diego Maradona predicted increased awareness of drug abuse and increased support for drug prevention programs. Identification has also been predicted by strong parasocial relationships with well-liked celebrities (Brown et al., 2003b).

RESULTS

The CPI online survey includes the 20 items of the Likert-type scale. Participants are asked to rank their level of agreement with statements about their identification with celebrities on a five-level scale: strongly disagree, disagree, neutral, agree, and strongly agree.

The online instrument was created and published using SurveySuite. This survey generation tool, provided by the University of Virginia, is located at http://intercom.virginia.edu/Survey-Suite. After a 14-day free trial period, an annual fee is required to continue the service. The service includes online survey creation and administration, and tallying results. Additionally, all data collected are made available in a format compatible with any statistical software. Such statistical software is required for any analyses beyond summarized descriptive statistics.

Given the fact that CPI data are usually combined with measurements of other conceptual variables in media studies, no demographic data are collected. The simple design allows potential users to combine CPI data with other variables of interest, ensuring the good portability of a modular instrument. Furthermore, minor editing allows the instrument to be adapted to the celebrity or media persona of interest.

The self-reported instrument takes about 5 minutes to complete. Participation is anonymous. All results are kept confidential.

COMMENTARY

The CPI instrument is available for anyone to use. However, in order to use the Web form for research, those interested are advised to contact the CPI authors to get a research code that participants can include in the demographic area of the form in order for the MGS authors to be able to extract the requested data from the database. The contact information is provided at the survey site.

COST

The CPI is free to take and use online.

LOCATION

The CPI scale is located online at: http://intercom.virginia.edu/SurveySuite/Surveys/celeb_ident

REFERENCES

Basil, M. D. (1996). Identification as a mediator of celebrity effects. *Journal of Broadcasting & Electronic Media, 40*, 478-495.

Basil, M. D., & Brown, W. J. (2004). Magic Johnson and Mark McGwire: The power of identification with sports celebrities. In L. R. Kahle & C. Riley (Ed.*), Sports Marketing and the Psychology of Marketing Communication* (pp. 159-174)*.* Mahwah, NJ: Lawrence Erlbaum Associates, Inc.

Bocarnea, M. C. (2001). *Mediated effects of celebrities: Cognitive and affective paths of processing information about Princess Diana's death.* Doctoral dissertation, Regent University, Virginia.

Brown, W. J., Basil, M. D., & Bocarnea, M. C. (2003a). Social influence of an international celebrity: Responses to the death of Princess Diana. *Journal of Communication, 53*, 587-605.

Brown, W. J., Basil, M. D., & Bocarnea, M. C. (2003b). The influence of famous athletes on public health issues: Mark McGwire, child abuse prevention, and androstenedione. *Journal of Health Communication, 8*, 41-57.

Brown, W. J., & Fraser, B. P. (2006). Global identification with celebrity heroes. In S. Drucker & G. Gumpert (Eds.), *Heroes in a Global World*. Cresskill, NJ: Hampton Press.

Burke, K. (1969). *A rhetoric of motives*. Berkeley, CA: University of California Press.

Cheney, G. (1983). On the various and changing meanings of organizational membership: A field study of organizational identification. *Communication Monographs, 50*, 342-362.

Fraser, B. F., & Brown, W. J. (2002). Media, celebrities, and social influence: Identification with Elvis Presley. *Mass Communication & Society, 5*(2), 183-206.

Freud, S. (1922). *Group psychology and the analysis of ego*. New York: Norton. Johnson, Johnson & Heimburg (1999).

Johnson, W. L., Johnson, A. M., & Heimberg, F. (1999). A primary- and second-order component analysis of the organiztional identification questionnaire. *Educational and Psychological Measurement, 59*, 159-170.

Kelman, H. (1961). Process of opinion change. *Public Opinion Quarterly, 25*, 57-58.

Lasswell, H. D. (1965). *World politics and personal insecurity*. New York: Free Press.

Matviuk, M. A. C. (2006). *The social influence of sports celebrities: The case of Diego Maradona.* Doctoral dissertation, Regent University, Virginia.

Rosenfeld, L. B. (1969). Set theory: Key to understanding of Kenneth Burke's use of the term "identification." *Western Speech, 33,* 175-183.

Woodward, G. C. (2003). *The idea of identification.* Albany, NY: State University of New York Press.

KEY TERMS

Celebrity: Heavily mediated person that is the focus of intense public interest.

Identification: The persuasion process that occurs when an individual adopts the behavior or attitudes of another individual or group based on a self-defining relationship; can be a form of audience involvement.

Media Involvement: Cognitive, affective, and behavioral participation induced in an individual by the media through media exposure.

Media Persona: Real person or a popular fictional character to whom media consumers react.

Chapter XXXVIII
Technology Acceptance Model

Mary McCord
Central Missouri State University, USA

BACKGROUND

The technology acceptance model (TAM) (Davis, 1989) measures perceived usefulness and perceived ease of use as predictors of a user's *intent* to use computer technology, and their *actual* usage on the job. The measure first appeared in 1989, in an *MIS Quarterly* article by Fred Davis, and in a coauthored article in *Management Science* (Davis, 1989; Davis, Bagozzi, & Warshaw, 1989). Extending the theory of reasoned action (Ajzen & Fishbein, 1980) to technology, perceived usefulness (U) is defined as "the degree to which a person believes a particular system would enhance his or her job performance." Perceived ease of use (EOU) is defined as "the degree to which a person believes that using a particular system would be free of effort." "Usage intentions" (BI) was measured through self-predicted future usage, and "user acceptance" was measured through self-reported current usage.

Although information technology is adopted to improve employee performance, these gains are often lost or diminished by users' unwilling to accept and use the information system. Davis wanted to understand why users rejected or accepted information technologies, to better predict,

explain, and increase user acceptance. The TAM model has since become one of the most established models for predicting user acceptance.

The 12-item, Likert-type TAM instrument is considered one of the most robust and parsimonious models for predicting user acceptance. After some introduction to the new technology, respondents are given the short TAM questionnaire. The model assesses end-user acceptance of a *particular* technology, by regressing the construct PU and PEU on usage intentions (BI), and eventually, on user acceptance (actual usage). Acceptance is predicted via the strength of the coefficient regression. The instrument is self-report, and takes about 10 minutes to complete. The model is outlined next.

RELIABILITY

Extensive research supports the technology acceptance model's reliability and internal consistency. In the first year TAM was introduced, Davis was involved in two publications that outlined four studies that measured reliability and validity. In these first studies, the Cronbach alpha reliability coefficients for perceived usefulness ranged

Figure 1. TAM model

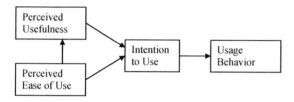

from 0.92-0.98, reliability for ease of use ranged 0.90-0.94, and reliability for (behavioral) intent to use ranged 0.84-0.90 (Davis, 1989; Davis et al., 1989). Intent to use did strongly correlate with actual usage, increasing from 0.35 to correlation of 0.63 by the one study's end.

VALIDITY

In the original TAM study from 1989, convergent and discriminant validity were strongly supported and tested using the multitrait-multimethod analysis (MTMM). Convergent validity measures the extent to which items comprising a scale behave as if they are measuring a common construct. Items that measure the same construct will be highly correlated. For perceived usefulness, the monotrait-heteromethod correlations were all (100%) significant to the .05 level. For ease of use, 95.6% of the monotrait-heteromethod correlations were significant; hence, convergent validity was supported. Discriminant validity measures the ability of an item to differentiate between two objects being measured. So, an item in the construct "perceived usefulness" should not correlate too highly with the same item when the technology being measured is different. In measuring discriminant validity, perceived usefulness (involving 1800 correlations/comparisons) was 100% confirmed. For ease of use, 97% of the comparisons were confirmed, representing a high level of discriminant validity (Davis, 1989).

In the original studies mentioned, TAM explained 47% - 51% of a user's intent to use. In subsequent studies, TAM has consistently predicted 0.40% of the variance in a user's intent or actual use of a particular technology. Perceived usefulness, especially, is a stable predictor of usage intentions, with standardized regression coefficients averaging around 0.6 (Venkatesh & Davis, 2000). Over time, ease of use (EOU) has less impact on usage (the technology is learned and ease of use is less important with experience). At time 1, EOU seems to have a direct effect on intent to use (BI), but when the test is repeated, EOU is entirely indirect via usefulness (U).

As stated, several researchers have replicated Davis's original studies, further validating his questionnaire instrument. The original technologies studied (Davis, 1989; Davis et al., 1989) were electronic mail, a text editor, word processing, and graphics software. TAM was extended to different technologies (electronic and voice mail, word processing, a spreadsheet, and a graphics package) (Adams, Nelson, & Todd, 1992; 1992) where it maintained reliability. Test-retest reliability was validated by Hendrickson, Massey, and Cronan (1993) using a database management system and a spreadsheet. Over time, user acceptance of several different technologies has been tested, and support for TAM's construct validity has accumulated.

ONLINE RESULTS

Perhaps because the instrument is so short, this author could find no examples of the use of TAM in an online Web survey. Even when the technology being assessed was Web usage, or online learning technology such as BlackBoard (Landry, Griffeth, & Hartman, 2006), the survey method of the pretest and posttest may not be online.

COMMENTARY

Extensions to the model (TAM2) (Venkatesh & Davis, 2000) explain perceived usefulness and usage intentions in terms of social influence and cognitive instrumental process. TAM and TAM2 later became part of the unified theory of acceptance and use of technology (UTAUT) (Venkatesh, Morris, Davis, & Davis, 2003). The UTAUT has outperformed each of the eight individual models it integrated (adjusted R^2 of 70 percent) (Venkatesh et al., 2003).

REFERENCES

Adams, D. A., Nelson, R. R., & Todd, P. A. (1992; 1992). Perceived usefulness, ease of use, and usage of information technology: A replication; perceived usefulness, ease of use, and usage of information technology: A replication. *MIS Quarterly, 16*(2), 227-247.

Ajzen, I., & Fishbein, M. (1980). In I. Ajzen, M. Fishbein (Eds..), *Understanding attitudes and predicting social behaviour* (1st ed.). Englewood Cliffs, NJ: Prentice-Hall.

Davis, F. D. (1989). Perceived usefulness, perceived ease of use, and user acceptance of information technology. *MIS Quarterly, 13*(3), 318-340.

Davis, F. D., Bagozzi, R. P., & Warshaw, P. R. (1989). User acceptance of computer technology: A comparison of two theoretical models. *Management Science, 35*(8), 982-1003.

Hendrickson, A. R., Massey, P. D., & Cronan, T. P. (1993). On the test-retest reliability of perceived usefulness and perceived ease of use scales. *MIS Quarterly, 17*(2), 227-230.

Landry, B. J. L., Griffeth, R., & Hartman, S. (2006). Measuring student perceptions of BlackBoard using the technology acceptance model. *Decision Sciences Journal of Innovative Education, 4*(1), 87-99.

Venkatesh, V., & Davis, F. D. (2000). A theoretical extension of the technology acceptance model: Four longitudinal field studies. *Management Science, 46*(2), 186.

Venkatesh, V., Morris, M. G., Davis, G. B., & Davis, F. D. (2003). User acceptance of information technology: Toward a unified view. *MIS Quarterly, 27*(3), 425-478.

KEY TERMS

Perceived Ease of Use: The degree to which a person believes that using a particular system would be free of effort.

Perceived Usefulness: The degree to which a person believes a particular system would enhance his or her job performance.

User Acceptance: Self-reported current usage of a particular system.

Usage Intentions: The self-prediction of future usage of a particular system.

Chapter XXXIX
Celebrity–Persona
Parasocial Interaction Scale

Mihai C. Bocarnea
Regent University, USA

William J. Brown
Regent University, USA

BACKGROUND

The *celebrity-persona parasocial interaction scale* (CPPI) is designed to measure how media consumers form parasocial relationships with celebrities or popular fictional characters. A parasocial relationship is defined as an imaginary interpersonal relationship between a media consumer and a media persona (Horton & Wohl, 1956). Persona can be real people, such as actors, athletes, and performing artists; or they can be fictional characters, such as Susan in the television serial *Desperate Housewives*, a character played by actress Teri Hatcher; or Indiana Jones, a character in the film, *Raiders of the Lost Ark*, played by actor Harrison Ford.

The CPPI is derived from several other published parasocial action scales, including Rubin, Perse, and Powell (1985), Cole and Leets (1999), and Auter & Palmgreen (2000). While most parasocial interaction scales are designed to measure the strength of parasocial relationships that

develop through television viewing, the CPPI is particularly targeted to celebrities whose exposure far exceeds television programs alone.

Parasocial interaction is one kind of mediated involvement that occurs through enduring or repeated exposure to famous people, both real and fictional. The concept of involvement assumes that media consumers are active rather than passive receivers of information. Two types of involvement conceptualized by Rubin and Perse (1987) are (1) a motivational state that reflects the attitudes that people bring with them to the communication situation, and (2) the cognitive, affective, and behavioral participation induced by the media during media exposure (i.e. becoming emotionally and intellectually involved with a character while watching a film or television program).

Repeated exposure to media persona through the mass media creates a sense of friendship or intimacy in media users (Levy, 1979). Audience members commonly look to media personalities as "friends" and those with whom they feel "comfortable."

The concept of *parasocial interaction* was extended by Brown and his colleagues (see Brown & Basil, 1995; Brown, Basil, & Bocarnea, 1998; Brown, Duane, & Fraser 1997; Fraser & Brown, 2002) beyond what occurs between television personalities and television viewers. Their work demonstrates that individuals establish parasocial relationships with celebrities through many years of exposure to a variety of media. Audiences develop parasocial relationships with sports celebrities through their attendance of sports events, and by watching televised sports, movies, and commercials featuring sports celebrities (Brown & Basil, 1995; Brown et al., 1997; Matviuk, 2006).

RELIABILITY

The reliability of the CPPI is similar to that of other parasocial interaction scales, producing Cronbach coefficient alpha that typically range from .80 to .90. Factor analytic analyses of the scale items yield single factors with generally high factor loadings with single factor solutions (Bocarnea, 2001; Brown, Basil, & Bocarnea, 2003a; Matviuk, 2006).

VALIDITY

The criterion—related validity of the CPPI, that is, its effectiveness to predict theoretically hypothesized outcomes, is good. CPPI items consistently predict identification with popular celebrities (Bocarnea, 2001; Brown, Basil, & Bocarnea, 2003b; Matviuk, 2006). CPPI items also are predicted by media exposure to celebrities and persona (Babb & Brown, 1994; Basil & Brown, 1997; Brown, Basil, & Bocarnea, 2003a, 2003b; Rubin & Mchugh, 1987). Construct validation regarding the inferences of the unobserved vari-

ables also is satisfactory. As noted earlier, factor analysis of CPPI items reveals that parasocial interaction can be validly measured as a single conceptual variable.

RESULTS

The CPPI online survey includes the 20 items of the Likert-type scale. Participants are asked to rank their level of agreement with statements about their parasocial interaction with celebrities on a five-level scale: strongly disagree, disagree, neutral, agree, and strongly agree.

The online instrument was created and published using SurveySuite. This survey generation tool, provided by the University of Virginia, is located at http://intercom.virginia.edu/SurveySuite. After a 14-day free trial period, an annual fee is required to continue the service. The service includes online survey creation and administration, and tallying results. Additionally, all data collected are made available in a format compatible with any statistical software. Such statistical software is required for any analyses beyond summarized descriptive statistics.

Given the fact that CPPI data are usually combined with measurements of other conceptual variables in media studies, no demographic data are collected. The simple design allows potential users to combine CPPI data with other variables of interest, ensuring the good portability of a modular instrument. Furthermore, minor editing allows the instrument to be adapted to the celebrity or media persona of interest.

The self-reported instrument takes about 5 minutes to complete. Participation is anonymous. All results are kept confidential.

COMMENTARY

The CPPI instrument is available for anyone to use. However, in order to use the Web form for research, those interested are advised to contact the CPPI authors to get a research code that participants can include in the demographic area of the form in order for the MGS authors to be able to extract the requested data from the database. The contact information is provided at the survey site.

COST

The CPPI is free to take and use online.

LOCATION

The CPPI is available online at http://intercom.virginia.edu/SurveySuite/Surveys/celeb_parasoc

REFERENCES

Auter, P. J. (1992). TV that talks back: An experimental validation of a parasocial interaction scale. *Journal of Broadcasting & Electronic Media, 35*(2), 173-181.

Auter, P. J., & Palmgreen, P. (2000). Development and validation of a parasocial interaction measure: The audience-person interaction scale. *Communication Research Reports, 17*, 79-89.

Babb, V., & Brown, W. J. (1994, July 11-15). *"Adolescents' development of parasocial relationships through popular television situation comedies*. Paper to be presented to the 44th Annual Conference of the International Communication Association, Sydney.

Basil, M. D., & Brown, M. J. (1997). Marketing AIDS prevention: Examining the differential impact hypothesis and identification effects on concern about AIDS. *Journal of Consumer Psychology, 6*, 389-411.

Brown, W. J., Basil, M. D., & Bocarnea, M. C. (1998, July). *Responding to the death of Princess Diana: Audience involvement iwth an international celebrity*. Paper presented at the International Communication Association Conference, Jerusalem, Israel.

Bocarnea, M. C. (2001). *Mediated effects of celebrities: Cognitive and affective paths of processing information about Princess Diana's death*. Doctoral dissertation, Regent University, Virginia.

Brown, W. J., & Basil, M. D. (1995). Media celebrities and public health: Responses to "Magic" Johnson's HIV disclosure and its impact on AIDS risk and high-risk behaviors. *Health Communication, 7*, 345-371.

Brown, W. J., Basil, M. D., & Bocarnea, M. C. (2003a). Social influence of an international celebrity: Responses to the death of Princess Diana. *Journal of Communication, 53*, 587-605.

Brown, W. B., Basil, M. D., & Bocarnea, M. C. (2003b). The influence of famous athletes on public health issues: Mark McGwire, child abuse prevention, and androstenedione. *Journal of Health Communication, 8*, 41-57.

Brown, W. J., Duane, J. J., & Fraser, B. P. (1997). Media coverage and public opinion of the O.J. Simpson trial: Implications for the criminal justice system. *Communication Law and Policy, 2*(2), 261-287.

Cole, T., & Leets, L. (1999). Attachment styles and intimate television viewing: Insecurely forming relationships in a parasocial way. *Journal of Social and Personal Relationships, 16*, 495-511.

Fraser, B. P., & Brown, W. J. (2002). Media, celebrities, and social influence: Identification with Elvis Presley. *Mass Communication & Society, 5*, 185-208.

Horton, D., & Wohl, R. R. (1956). Mass communication and para-social interaction: Observations on intimacy at a distance. *Psychiatry, 19*, 215-229.

Levy, M. R. (1979). Watching TV news as parasocial interaction. *Journal of Broadcasting, 23*(1), 177-187.

Matviuk, M. A. C. (2006). *The social influence of sports celebrities: The case of Diego Maradona.* Unpublished doctoral dissertation. Virginia Beach, VA: Regent University.

Rubin, A. M., & Perse, E. M. (1987). Audience activity and soap opera involvement: A uses and gratifications investigation. *Human Communication Research, 14,* 246-268.

Rubin, A. M., Perse, E. M., & Powell, R. A. (1985). Loneliness, parasocial interaction, and local television viewing. *Human Communication Research, 12,* 155-180.

Rubin, R. B., & McHugh, M. P. (1987). Development of parasocial relationships. *Journal of Broadcasting and Electronic Media, 31,* 279-292.

KEY TERMS

Celebrity: Heavily mediated person that is the focus of intense public interest.

Media Involvement: Cognitive, affective, and behavioral participation induced in an individual by the media through media exposure.

Media Persona: Real person or a popular fictional character to whom media consumers react.

Parasocial Relationship: A form of audience involvement in which media consumers build imaginary interpersonal relationships with a media persona.

Chapter XL
Organizational Culture Profile

Katty Marmenout
McGill University, Canada

BACKGROUND

The organizational culture profile (OCP) is an instrument initially developed by O'Reilly, Chatman, and Caldwell (1991) to assess person-organization fit. The tool can be useful as well in assessing organizations in need of culture change, distinguishing subcultures, and evaluating potential fit in mergers and acquisitions.

Person-organization fit is a useful predictor of job satisfaction and organizational commitment, which in turn affect performance. The OCP is considered an important instrument to measure the fit between individual's preferences and organizational cultures. Traditional measures of person-situation fit used a limited set of descriptions and situations, thus failing to take into account idiosyncratic differences between individuals and situations, depending on salience and relevance. An additional advantage of the profile is that it allows the assessment of individuals and situations using a common language.

Culture is understood as a system of shared symbols and meanings (Alvesson, 2002). Accord-

ing to Schein's (1984) well-established model, organizational culture is composed of different levels with artifacts and creations at the visible level, values at the next level, and finally, basic underlying assumptions at the core, below the conscious level of culture. The attraction-selection-attrition framework (Schneider, Goldstein, & Smith, 1995) posits that organizational members perpetuate an organization's values by virtue of attraction to similar individuals (Newcomb, 1960), selection of similar recruits, and departure of ill-fitted individuals. As person-organization fit is a useful predictor of job satisfaction and organizational commitment, the congruency between the values of the individual and the organization may be particularly relevant to organizations.

The OCP contains 54 value statements (see appendix) that are to be sorted by the participants and reflect the following seven factors: (1) innovation; (2) stability; (3) people orientation; (4) outcome orientation; (5) easygoing; (6) detail orientation; (7) team orientation. First, a representative sample of organizational members are requested to complete the instrument by sorting the value statements into nine categories according to how characteristic they find them to the firm. Adkins and Caldwell (2004) used a sample of 52, but others have used as few as 14 individuals (Sheridan, 1992). Once the organizational profile information is so gathered, individual members can take the survey in order to measure their fit with the organization. The same instrument measures fit, only this time by sorting the items according to desirability of the item.

In both cases, following the Q-sort approach (Block, 1961), respondents are asked to categorize the statements and to assign a specified number of statements to each category (most characteristic/desirable = 2 statements, quite = 4 statements, fairly = 6 statements, somewhat = 9 statements, neither characteristic/desirable neither uncharacteristic/desirable = 12 statements, somewhat uncharacteristic/undesirable = 9 statements, fairly = 6 statements, quite = 4 statements, most = 2 statements). O'Reilly et al. (1991) used the following instructions for the organizational measure: "Important values may be expressed in the form of norms or shared expectations about what's important, how to behave or what attitudes are appropriate. Please sort the 54 values into a row of nine categories, placing at the one end of the row those [items] that you consider to be the most characteristic aspects of the culture of your organization, and at the other hand those [items] that you believe to be the least characteristic ..." (p. 495) and the following for the individual fit instrument "How important is it for this characteristic to be a part of the organization you work for?" (p.496). The instrument takes 20-30 minutes to complete.

RELIABILITY

Research supports that the OCP is internally consistent and reliable. Adkins and Caldwell (2004) report coefficient alpha scores between .85 and .96 for 5 different profiles. Sheridan (1992) used

as few as 14 to 19 members per organization, and observed .23 as the median interclass correlation for OCP dimensions, which is low but not inconsistent with other measures used in climate research.

VALIDITY

The literature (Adkins & Caldwell, 2004; O'Reilly et al., 1991) suggests that the measure of person-organization fit has not only discriminant validity, but also substantial predictive validity, and is therefore useful to organizations.

RESULTS

In order to establish the organizational culture profile for the organization surveyed, item-by-item averages of scores (most characteristic = 9, least characteristic = 1) are calculated to obtain the overall profile. Then the individual responses are correlated with this organizational profile to measure person-organization fit. For a sample of 136 respondents, observed correlations ranged from -.52 to .48 (Adkins & Caldwell, 2004). Person-organization fit scores can be compared across individuals in order to assess which individual's desired culture is more congruent with the organizational culture in place.

COMMENTARY

The organizational culture profile is a multi-purpose instrument that can be used to evaluate the culture of the organization as a whole, for example, as a diagnostic instrument before a change intervention. It can be useful to compare subcultures within the same organization (Adkins & Caldwell, 2004), or to evaluate culture fit prior to a merger. Person-organization fit determination can be useful for applicant selection or evaluation of employee socialization. Although these cross-sectional measurements are valuable, one should be aware that they are diagnostics. They should be used to inform appropriate socialization, realistic job previews, transparent change management, communication, and other process-related approaches intended to foster values that are attractive to most individuals.

COST

The OCP can be used and implemented online using customizable online survey tools such as http://www.surveymonkey.com/

REFERENCES

Adkins, B., & Caldwell, D. (2004). Firm or subgroup culture: Where does fitting in matter most? *Journal of Organizational Behavior, 25*(8), 969-978.

Alvesson, M. (2002). *Understanding organizational culture*. London: Sage.

Block, J. (1961). *The Q-sort method in personality assessment and psychiatric research*. Springfield, IL: Thomas.

Newcomb, T. M. (1960). *Personality and social change: Attitude formation in a student community*. New York: Holt Rinehart & Winston.

O'Reilly, C., Chatman, J., & Caldwell, D. (1991). People, jobs, and organizational culture: A profile comparison approach to assessing person-organization fit. *Academy of Management Journal, 34*, 487-516.

Schein, E. H. (1984). Coming to a new awareness of organizational culture. *Sloan Management Review (pre-1986), 25*(2), 3-16.

Schneider, B., Goldstein, H. W., & Smith, D. B. (1995). The ASA framework: An update. *Personnel Psychology, 48*, 747-779.

Sheridan, J. E. (1992). Organizational culture and employee retention. *Academy of Management Journal, 35*, 1036-1056.

KEY TERMS

Culture: A system of shared symbols and meanings.

Organizational Culture: Shared symbols and meanings held by organizational members, with artifacts and creations at the visible level, values at the next level, and basic underlying assumptions at the unconscious level.

Person-Organization Fit: The extent to which an individual's preferences are aligned with, or complement organizational characteristics.

APPENDIX: ORGANIZATIONAL CULTURE PROFILE ITEMS

1. Flexibility
2. Adaptability
3. Stability
4. Predictability
5. Being innovative
6. Being quick to take advantage of opportunities
7. A willingness to experiment
8. Risk taking
9. Being careful
10. Autonomy
11. Being rule oriented
12. Being analytical
13. Paying attention to detail
14. Being precise
15. Being team oriented
16. Sharing information freely

17. Emphasizing a single culture throughout the organization
18. Being people oriented
19. Fairness
20. Respect for the individual's right
21. Tolerance
22. Informality
23. Being easy going
24. Being calm
25. Being supportive
26. Being aggressive
27. Decisiveness
28. Action orientation
29. Taking initiative
30. Being reflective
31. Achievement orientation
32. Being demanding
33. Taking individual responsibility
34. Having high expectations for performance
35. Opportunities for professional growth

36. High pay for good performers
37. Security of employment
38. Offers praise for good performance
39. Low level of conflict
40. Confronting conflict directly
41. Developing friends at work
42. Fitting in
43. Working in collaboration with others
44. Enthusiasm for the job
45. Working long hours
46. Not being constrained by many rules
47. An emphasis on quality
48. Being distinctive-different from others
49. Having a good reputation
50. Being socially responsible
51. Being results oriented
52. Having a clear guiding philosophy
53. Being competitive
54. Being highly organized

Chapter XLI
Measuring Online Flow

Damon Aiken
Eastern Washington University, USA

BACKGROUND

Examination of the flow construct began almost 20 years ago. Csikszentmihalyi has written extensively on this notion, loosely described as attaining an intrinsically enjoyable "optimal experience" (Csikszentmihalyi, 1977, 1990, 1997). Flow requires people to be completely and totally immersed in an activity. Time will stand still and nothing else will seem to matter (Mannell, Zuzanek, & Larson, 1988). Flow is important because it has a relatively clear set of antecedents and consequences that have significant implications for Web commerce.

While flow has been studied in a broad range of contexts including sports, work, shopping, games, and computer use, researchers are only now beginning to study flow during consumer Web navigations. Hoffman and Novak (1996) have ascribed the flow experience to Web behavior, measuring the loss of self-consciousness in an essentially blissful encounter. In this situation, flow is defined as the state occurring during Web navigations characterized by (1) a seamless sequence of responses facilitated by interactivity, (2) an intrinsically enjoyable experience, (3) accompanied by a loss of self-consciousness that is

(4) self-reinforcing (Hoffman & Novak, 1997). Web consumers who achieve the flow experience are so acutely involved in the act of online navigation that thoughts and perceptions not relevant to navigation are filtered out completely: the consumer is immersed in the computer-mediated interaction. Self-consciousness disappears, the consumer's sense of time becomes distorted, and they achieve an internalized sense of gratification (Novak, Hoffman, & Yung, 2000).

One of the most comprehensive and methodologically sound measurements of online flow was recently conducted by Novak et al. (2000). These researchers utilized a structural modeling approach to test a model of flow that embodied multiple antecedent components. Additionally, the researchers combined multiple past studies into a wide-ranging measurement instrument. The instrument contained sets of variables measuring flow (directly), focused attention, involvement, playfulness, positive affect, skill, telepresence, and time distortion. While a few scale items were dichotomous, most were intervally scaled Likert-type questions. The researchers used data collected from a large sample, fit a series of structural equations, and also tested relationships with key consumer behavior and Web-usage variables.

RELIABILITY

Research supports the model of online flow. Confirmatory factor analyses show appropriate levels of goodness-of-fit and root-mean-squared errors of approximation. Further, composite reliabilities estimated from the model (as well as from the revised model) were greater than 0.75.

VALIDITY

The data support the construct validity of the online flow scale. The model has been cross-validated using multiple samples. Moreover, the model has been used to accurately estimate relationships with outcome variables such as Web shopping and various Web applications.

RESULTS

Essentially, the work of Novak et al. (2000) provides empirical evidence and establishes reliability and validity in a comprehensive framework. A compelling online customer interface (i.e., a flow experience) was found to correlate with fun, recreational and experiential uses of the Web, expected use in the future, and the amount of time spent online. However, flow was negatively associated with using the Web for work-related activities. Interestingly, greater online "challenge" corresponded to greater focused attention, alluding to the importance of Web site design. Contrary to hypotheses, higher levels of interactive speed were not associated with greater levels of flow.

COMMENTARY

No doubt precise measurements of such an imprecise Web-consumption phenomenon are extremely difficulty. The difficult, elusive, and perhaps ethereal, Internet flow concept *can* be accurately measured and modeled. Novak et al. (2000) do an excellent job in synthesizing past research, applying it to the Internet context, and modeling antecedents and consequences. It seems that where their research falls short is in the evaluation of Web site design as a facilitator of flow. Researchers have just begun this next step in understanding flow, that is, to study the effects of consumers entering (and Web sites facilitating) the flow experience, as well as understanding the intricacies of Web navigation while in flow (see Richard & Chandra, 2005).

LOCATION

Novak et al.'s (2000) work on measuring and modeling the flow concept can be seen in *Marketing Science, 19*(1), 22-42.

REFERENCES

Csikszentmihalyi, M. (1977). *Beyond boredom and anxiety.* San Francisco: Jossey-Bass.

Csikszentmihalyi, M. (1990). *Flow: The psychology of optimal experience.* New York: Harper and Row.

Csikszentmihalyi, M. (1997). *Finding flow: The psychology of engagement with everyday life.* New York: Basic Books.

Hoffman, D., & Novak, T. (1996). Marketing in hypermedia computer-mediated environments: Conceptual foundations. *Journal of Marketing, 60*, 50-68.

Hoffman, D., & Novak, T. (1997). A new marketing paradigm for electronic commerce. *The Information Society, 13*, 43-54.

Mannell, R. C., Zuzanek, J., & Larson, R. (1988). Leisure states and "flow" experiences: Testing perceived freedom and intrinsic motivation hypotheses. *Journal of Leisure Studies, 20*(4), 289-304.

Novak, T., Hoffman, D., & Yung, Y. F. (2000). Modeling the flow construct in online environments: A structure modeling approach. *Marketing Science, 19*(1), 22-42.

Richard, M. O., & Chandra, R. (2005). A model of consumer Web navigational behavior: Conceptual development and application, *Journal of Business Research, 58*, 1019-1029.

KEY TERMS

Online Flow: The state occurring during Web navigations characterized by (1) a seamless sequence of responses facilitated by interactivity, (2) an intrinsically enjoyable experience, (3) accompanied by a loss of self-consciousness that is (4) self-reinforcing.

Online Interaction: A sense that a Web page or environment is responsive (e.g., the speed with which pages load), options or choices seem natural and intuitive, and there are an appropriate range of response options.

Online Playfulness: An attitude of being imaginative, creative, and spontaneous while on the Web.

Online Time Distortion: Losing track of time while on the Web.

Telepresence: A potent sense of being part of, and directly engaged in, an online environment.

Chapter XLII
Personal Report of Communication Apprehension

Robert H. Woods, Jr.
Spring Arbor University, USA

BACKGROUND

The personal report of communication apprehension (PRCA-24) (McCroskey, 1982) measures communication apprehension. Communication apprehension (CA) first appeared in James McCroskey's 1970 research note in *Communication Monographs*. Communication apprehension is defined as the level of fear or anxiety associated with either real or anticipated (oral) communication encounters. McCroskey was interested in a person's *trait* or dispositional anxieties across all or most communication situations. Recent investigations have expanded CA to include *state-like* communication apprehension, or anxiety associated with particular communication contexts and events.

The 24-item, Likert-type PRCA instrument is the most popular and valid measure of *trait-like* CA. It assesses a person's CA in four separate communication contexts: public, small group, meeting, and interpersonal. Each of these contexts is represented by six items. In filling out the form, an individual indicates the level of anxiety he or she feels about participating in various oral communication situations in one of these four contexts.

An individual's CA score on the PRCA-24 is determined by summing responses across all four contexts (24-items). In addition, four generalized-context scores can be calculated (6-items each). Thus, an overall CA score and a separate score for each communication context may be computed.

A "high" range is between 80-120, and a "low" range is between 24-50. A "high" score means that you report more anxiety related to oral communication than most people do. A "low" score means that you report less anxiety related to oral communication than most people do.

The instrument is self-report and takes about 10-15 minutes to complete.

RELIABILITY

Research supports that the PRCA-24 is internally consistent and reliable. Alpha reliability coefficients ranging from .93-.95 have been reported (McCroskey, Beatty, Kearney, & Plax, 1985). Alpha coefficients are only slightly lower for the four communication contexts (McCroskey & Beatty, 1984). Moreover, test-retest coefficients greater than .80 have been reported (Rubin, Graham, &

Mignerey, 1990), indicating that the measure is stable across time.

VALIDITY

Construct and criterion validity of the PRCA-24 have been supported. Scores in each of the four areas (public, small group, meeting, and interpersonal) predicted *state* anxiety experienced in a public speaking context (McCroskey & Beatty, 1984). This finding was replicated for the public speaking component of the PRCA-24 (Beatty, 1987, 1988; Beatty, Balfantz, & Kuwabara, 1989; Beatty & Friedland, 1990). Scores on the public speaking portion of the PRCA-24 have predicted speech duration (Beatty, Forst, & Stewart, 1986) and avoidance/withdrawal behavior (Beatty, 1987). Students with high CA who anticipated interaction reported lower recall of lecture material than did those not anticipating social interaction (Booth-Butterfield, 1988).

Finally, PRCA-24 total scores are negatively correlated (-.70) with assertiveness (McCroskey, et al., 1985).

COMMENTS

Other instruments have been developed to measure communication apprehension. Many of these instruments are similar to the PRCA-24. For example, a popular alternative to the PRCA-24 is the communication anxiety inventory (CAI) (Booth-Butterfield & Gould, 1986). The CAI includes two separate scales designed to measure trait and state CA. The CAI assesses an individual's predispositions to experience anxiety in three contexts: interpersonal, small groups, and public speaking. The PRCA-24 is recommended as a way to assess trait-like CA, given its high reliability and validity.

LOCATION

The PRCA-24 may be completed online at http://www.wadsworth.com/communication_d/templates/student_resources/053456223X_hamilton/survey/prca.html. The PRCA-24 instrument is launched in a new window.

A welcome page appears that gives users two options. By selecting the first option, users can respond to the 24-item instrument and receive a personal report assessment of their CA. This option also allows them to e-mail the results to themselves and their instructors. Finally, by selecting the first option, individual responses are anonymously entered into a database of responses of all users who have visited the site. The second option allows the user to view how all individuals completing the PRCA-24 at this site have responded.

Clicking on the first option described above opens another page that includes the 24-item PRCA survey. Before answering the 24 questions, users must indicate gender and select a location from which they are taking the survey (one of the 50 states or "outside the United States"). Students may then answer each of the 24 questions by clicking one of five Likert-style serial button options: Strongly Agree, Agree, Undecided, Disagree, Strongly Disagree.

At the end of the survey, users click on "Submit My Data." The data will only be submitted if all questions have been answered. If any item, including the demographic questions (gender and location), have not been answered, a notice in red font will appear, just below the "Submit My Data" button, directing the user to complete the missing item(s).

The results are reported on a separate page in table format according to each of the four contexts: public, small group, meeting, and interpersonal. An overall CA score is also provided. A brief explanation of subscale and overall scores is provided just below the table. A place for Student Name/e-mail and Faculty Name/e-mail is provided just above the table of results.

Versions of the PRCA-24 that are nonscoring can also be found online: http://plaza.ufl.edu/dnagy/GEB5215/PRCA-24.htm, and http://www.usm.maine.edu/com/prca.htm

REFERENCES

Beatty, M. J. (1987). Communication apprehension as a determinate of avoidance, withdrawal and performance anxiety. *Communication Quarterly, 35*, 202-217.

Beatty, M. J. (1988). Situational and predispositional correlates of public speaking anxiety. *Communication Education, 37*, 28-39.

Beatty, M. J., Balfantz, G. L., & Kuwabara, A. Y. (1989). Trait-like qualities of selected variables assumed to be transient causes of performance state anxiety. *Communication Education, 38*, 277-289.

Beatty, M. J., Forst, E. C., & Stewart, R. A. (1986). Communication apprehension and motivation as predictors of public speaking duration. *Communication Education, 35*, 143-146.

Beatty, M. J., & Friedland, M. H. (1990). Public speaking state anxiety as a function of selected situational and predispostional variables. *Communication Education, 39*, 142-147.

Booth-Butterfield, S. (1986). The communication anxiety inventory: Validation and state- and context-communication apprehension. *Communication Quarterly, 34*, 194-205.

Booth-Butterfield, S. (1988). Inhibition and student recall of instructional messages. *Communication Education, 37*, 312-324.

McCroskey, J. C. (1970). Measures of communication-bound anxiety. *Speech Monographs, 31*, 79-84.

McCroskey, J. C. (1982). *An introduction to rhetorical communication* (4th ed.). Englewood Cliffs, NJ: Prentice Hall.

McCroskey, J. C., & Beatty, M. J. (1984). Communication apprehension and accumulated communication state anxiety experiences: A research note. *Communication Monographs, 51*, 79-84.

McCroskey, J. C., Beatty, M. J., Kearney, P., & Plax, T. G. (1985). The content validity of the PRCA-24 as a measure of communication apprehension across communication contexts. *Communication Quarterly, 33*, 165-173.

Rubin, R. B., Graham, E. E., & Mignerey, J. T. (1990). A longitudinal study of college students' communication competence. *Communication Education, 39*, 1-14.

KEY TERMS

Communication Apprehension: The level of fear or anxiety associated with either real or anticipated (oral) communication encounters.

State Anxiety: Communication apprehension associated with particular communication contexts and events.

Trait Anxiety: Communication apprehension across all or most communication situations.

Chapter XLIII
Reactance Proneness Assessment

Lijiang Shen
The University of Georgia, USA

James P. Dillard
The Pennsylvania State University, USA

INTRODUCTION

The theory of psychological reactance (Brehm, 1966; Brehm & Brehm, 1981; Wicklund, 1974) has often been called upon to explain the failure of persuasive attempts, and/or the "boomerang effect" in persuasion (Buller, Borland, & Burgoon, 1998; Burgoon, Alvaro, Grandpre, & Voulodakis, 2002; Grandpre, Alvaro, Burgoon, Miller, & Hall, 2003; Ringold, 2002). The theory contends that any persuasive message may arouse a motivation to reject the advocacy. That motivation is called reactance. Reactance may be considered to be an aversive motivational state that functions to reinstate an individual's perceptions of autonomy. Although initially investigated as a state phenomenon, it has become evident that individuals are likely to vary in their trait propensity to experience reactance. Individual differences in reactance proneness offer a useful means of segmenting target audiences, especially in the context of health communication, because individuals most at risk

for various health threats are also the individuals most likely to experience reactance when exposed to persuasive messages about that health risk (e.g., Bensley & Wu, 1991).

THE THEORY OF PSYCHOLOGICAL REACTANCE

The theory of psychological reactance contends that any persuasive message will likely be viewed as a threat to freedom, and therefore arouse psychological reactance. Psychological reactance is "the motivational state that is hypothesized to occur when a freedom is eliminated or threatened with elimination" (Brehm & Brehm, 1981, p. 37). Reactance produces a desire, possibly in the form of anger and negative cognition combined (Dillard & Shen, 2005), to restore one's attitudinal or behavioral freedom, that directly causes the failure of the persuasive attempt.

REACTANCE AS AN INDIVIDUAL DIFFERENCE

Psychological reactance was first conceived as situation specific (Brehm, 1966; Wicklund, 1974). Most of the reactance research was done on situational reactance, such as alternative restriction and forced choice, and in social influence settings (see Burgoon et al., 2002 for a review). However, Brehm and Brehm (1981) recognized that reactance could be conceptualized as a trait too, a position that is consistent with the theory's assumption that people vary in the strength of their needs for autonomy and self-determination (Wicklund, 1974). Scholars have sought to develop instruments to assess individual differences in reactance proneness in two fields: social psychology (e.g., Hong & Faedda, 1996; Hong & Page, 1989; Merz, 1983) and counseling and therapy (e.g., Dowd, Milne, & Wise, 1991).

Scholars in both areas recognize the utility of the trait reactance construct. It has found to be a significant predictor of failure in persuasion (e.g., Dillard & Shen, 2005; Imajo, 2002) and resistance to interpersonal influence (e.g., Sachau, Houlihan, & Gilbertson, 1999) in social psychology. In the realm of clinical counseling and therapy, it has been found to predict inpatient treatment and outcomes (e.g., Frank, Jackson-Walker, Marks, Van Egeren, Loop, & Olson, 1998), resistance to physician advice (e.g. Graybar, Antonuccio, Boutilier, & Varble, 1989), and resistance to therapy (Robin, Kumar, & Pekala, 2005; Seemann, Bulboltz, Jenkins, Soper, & Woller, 2004). With their applications on the rise, an alarming issue remains: The unidimensionality of the scales has not been well established (but see Shen & Dillard, 2005). In order to apply these scales to assess trait reactance proneness in surveys and other research; and to meaningfully interpret results from such research, we need to validate their dimensions and assess their validity and reliability.

The next section of this chapter will review the historical development of reactance proneness measures. Unidimensionality of a measure must be established before it can be applied as a whole scale that will be evaluated by three criteria: (a) item content, (b) associations among the items, and (c) associations between the items and external variables (DeVellis, 1991; Hunter & Gerbing, 1982).

EVALUATION OF REACTANCE PRONENESS SCALES

Merz's Questionnaire for the Measurement of Psychological Reactance

Merz (1983) developed the first self-report measure of reactance proneness, questionnaire for the measurement of psychological reactance (*QMPR*), which contained 18 items that loaded on four factors (see Tucker & Byers, 1987 for a detailed description). In our estimation, the (from German to English translation of) QMPR items not only exhibit good semantic correspondence with the reactance construct (i.e., they possess face validity), but also constitute a reasonable sampling of that conceptual domain (i.e., they possess content validity). Adding another reactance scale to the QMPR did not result in an improvement (Woller, 2000).

Although Merz's initial study showed promising results, later factor analyses on the English translation of the scale yielded inconsistent factor structures (see, Donnell, Thomas, & Buboltz, 2001; Hong & Ostini, 1989; Tucker & Byers, 1987). Whether German speakers have different perceptions about reactance than English speakers remains an empirical question; however, these studies indicated that the English version of QMPR lacks internal consistency, although possible "translation loss" (Tucker & Byers, 1987) cannot be ruled out as a cause. There has been no documented test of association between QMPR items and external variables. Due to these limitations, the utility of the QMPR is limited; however, it laid the basis for further development and refinement of an instrument to assess reactance proneness.

Dowd's Rherapeutic Reactance Scale

Dowd et al. (1991) developed the 28-item therapeutic reactance scale (*TRS*) for clinical purposes. The scale has been widely used in the field of counseling and therapy (e.g., Baker, Sullivan, & Marszalek, 2003; Buboltz, Woller, & Pepper, 1999; Dowd & Wallbrown, 1993; Johnson & Buboltz, 2000; Seemann et al., 2004; Seibel & Dowd, 2001), despite that there has been little evidence for the unidimensionality of the scale.

First, several of the TRS items exhibit poor correspondence with the theoretical construct of reactance. For example, higher score on the TRS scale reflects a lessened desire to impress and to be socially appropriate. This is inconsistent with the definition of psychological reactance (Brehm & Brehm, 1981). Free behavior in reactance theory does not have to be antisocial norms, nor does it have to be competitive (e.g., Item 23: "I consider myself as more competitive than cooperative") or be more powerful than others (e.g., Item 20: "It is important to me to be in a powerful position relative to others"). On the contrary, people might utilize psychological reactance for impression management (Wright & Brehm, 1982). Labeled as behavioral reactance and verbal reactance, the TRS also fails to capture the motivational properties of psychological reactance. These indicate that the TRS is limited in face validity and content validity as a measure of reactance proneness.

Second, the TRS is also limited in internal consistency. The two factors lacked a simple structure in Dowd et al. (1991): Some items exhibited similar loadings on both factors, and some items showed low loadings on both factors. The factor analytic study by Buboltz, Thomas, and Donnell (2002) yielded a four-factor structure that suggested that the scale is psychometrically unstable. Moreover, there has not been a confirmatory factor analysis that validates the factor structure of the scale.

Third, there have been efforts to assess the construct validity of the TRS vis-à-vis external variables (e.g. Baker et al., 2003; Buboltz, Williams, Thomas, Seemann, Soper, & Woller, 2003; Dowd & Wallbrown, 1993; Dowd et al., 1991; Dowd, Wallbrown, Sanders, & Yesenosky, 1994; Johnson & Buboltz, 2000; Seibel & Dowd, 2001). In the absence of evidence of unidimensionality, support for the external validity of the whole scale from these studies was rather limited.

In conclusion, the TRS has substantial and statistical limitations, and is in need of further refinement as a measure of reactance proneness (see also Buboltz et al., 2002). Continued use of TRS as a whole scale seems unwarranted. We recommend that data involving TRS should be interpreted with caution and at the level of subscales at the best.

Hong's Psychological Reactance Scale

Dissatisfied with existing measures, Hong and Page (1989) translated (German to English) and revised Merz's (1983) questionnaire, thereby creating the 14-item Hong psychological reactance scale (*HPRS*). The first investigation of the scale structure yielded a four-factor solution whose factors were labeled Freedom of Choice, Conformity Reactance, Behavioral Freedom, and Reactance to Advice and Recommendations. Subsequent efforts produced a similar four-factor structure and retained the same labels for the four factors, despite there being slight differences in the factor structure matrix (Hong, 1992). Hong and Faedda (1996) also reported a four-factor solution, though, again, there were some substantial variations in structure vis-à-vis previous work. Hong and Faedda decided to remove three items because they showed severe cross-loadings, resulting in the 11-item version of the HPRS. The four factors were also labeled differently: Emotional Response toward Restricted Choice, Reactance to Compliance, Resisting Influence from Others, and Reactance to Advice and Recommendations.

As an offspring of Merz's QMPR, the HPRS corresponds well to the theory of psychological reactance (Brehm & Brehm, 1981) and captures both the affective and cognitive elements in reactance (Dillard & Shen, 2005). In another word, the scale possesses face validity and content validity. However, evidence for the validity of HPRS from Hong and her colleagues (Hong, 1992; Hong & Faedda, 1996; Hong & Page, 1989) was limited in that (a) all their factor analytic studies were exploratory and (b) evidence from the association between items and external variables (Hunter & Gerbing, 1982) was lacking.

So far, there have been two confirmatory analyses on the HPRS (Shen & Dillard, 2005; Thomas, Donnell, & Buboltz, 2001). The confirmatory work reported by Thomas et al. (2001) provided strong evidence that the appropriate first order four-factor structure was oblique, not orthogonal. However, they also rejected the possibility of second-order unidimensionality, and recommended that without a major revision to the scale, the use of HPRS should be discontinued. Shen and Dillard (2005) came to a different conclusion. They argued that the conclusion to reject the second-order unidimensional factor structure could be an overinterpretation of a small decrement in model fit because Thomas et al. (2001) had power in excess of .99 when fitting the models. Their secondary analyses of Thomas et al. (2001) data, with sample sizes adjusted for appropriate level of power verified the problem of overinterpretation. Moreover, their confirmatory analyses of their own data (11-item version) indicated that the four first-order scales were reducible to a single factor on the second order, and that such a second-order unidimensional structure was invariant across three independent samples. These results provided strong evidence for the internal consistency of the HPRS.

In addition, Shen and Dillard (2005) also provided evidence for the external consistency of the HPRS. Consistent with the theory of psychological reactance, each of the four first-order factors and the second-order factor were positively correlated with perceived threat to freedom, and negatively associated with attitude toward, and intention to comply with, the message advocacy. Moreover, the magnitude of association between the external variables and the second-order factor was greater than any first-order factors. Although not reported in Shen and Dillard (2005), their data also showed that the first-order factors (r ranging from .18 to .25, p<.05) and second-order factor (r=.28, p<.05) were positively associated with the behavioral approach system (BAS), which corresponds to appetitive motivation, but not with the behavioral inhibition system (BIS) (r=-.00, n.s.), which correponds to aversive motivation. Although these correlation coefficients could have been inflated because the HPRS data were collected after participants being exposed to the messages, this parallelism was notable with respect to the variables that are part and parcel of reactance theory: perceived threat to freedom, attitude, and behavioral intention. These correlation coefficients demonstrated the construct validity of the HPRS

The HPRS also demonstrated satisfactory reliabilities in Shen and Dillard (2005): Alphas ranged from .75 to .80 across three samples, which was similar to those reported in the literautre (e.g., Hong, 1992; Hong & Faedda, 1996; Hong & Page, 1989).

CONCLUSION

This chapter introduces reactance proneness as a potential means of audience segmentation in the context of persuasion and social influence, and health communication in particular. The unidimensionality of three reactance proneness scales, Merz's QMPR, Dowd's TRS, and Hong's

HPRS, were evaluated according to three criteria: item content, internal consistency, and external consistency. It is concluded that the QMPR and the TRS do not demonstrate unidimensional factor structures, and suffer from psychometric instability and lack of validity. Therefore, they are not recommended as valid measures of reactance proneness.

In addition to face validity and content validity, the HPRS demonstrates internal and external consistency, and can be reduced to a unidimensional factor on the second order (Shen & Dillard, 2005) with satisfactory alpha reliability. It is recommended that the HPRS is a theoretically and empirically justifiable measure of reactance proneness. One potential limitation lies in that the HPRS was developed and validated among college students in western cultures: Hong and colleagues (Hong, 1992; Hong & Faedda, 1996; Hong & Page, 1989) in Australia, Shen and Dillard (2005) and Thomas et al. (2001) in the United States. Future studies that use samples from populations more diverse in age and culture, and that test external consistency with more/different criterion variables, should further validate the HPRS.

Hong and Faedda (1996) suggested that three items (Items 4, 10, and 14) should be excluded because of severe cross-loading in their exploratory factor analysis. On the other hand, confirmatory factor analyses (Shen & Dillard, 2005; Thomas et al., 2001) indicated that inclusion of these three items did not significantly impact the factor structure. The 11-item version of the HPRS offers more parsimony and could potentially reduce participant fatigue; while the 14-item version has slightly higher alpha reliability than the 11-item version (cf. Dillard & Shen, 2005; Hong & Faedda, 1996; Shen & Dillard, 2005), which could lead to more statistical power, given the same effect size in the population (DeVellis, 1991). However, such tradeoff should be minimal. Researchers and practitioners can choose either version of the HPRS upon their own discretion.

REFERENCES

Baker, K. D., Sullivan, H., & Marszalek, J. M. (2003). Therapeutic reactance in a depressed client sample: A comparison of two measures. *Assessment, 10,* 135-142.

Bensley, L. S., & Wu, R. (1991). The role of psychological reactance in drinking following alcohol prevention messages. *Journal of Applied Social Psychology, 21,* 1111-1124.

Brehm, J. W. (1966). *A theory of psychological reactance.* New York: Academic Press.

Brehm, S. S., & Brehm, J. W. (1981). *Psychological reactance: A theory of freedom and control.* New York: Academic Press.

Buboltz, W. C, Jr. Thomas, A., & Donnell, A. J. (2002). Evaluating the factor structure and internal consistency reliability of the therapeutic reactance scale. *Journal of Counseling and Development, 80,* 120-125.

Buboltz, W. C., Jr. Williams, D. J., Thomas, A., Seemann, E. A., Soper, B., & Woller, K. (2003). Personality and psychological reactance: Extending the nomological net. *Personality & Individual Differences, 34,* 1167-1177.

Buboltz, W. C., Jr., Woller, K., & Pepper, H. (1999). Holland code type and psychological reactance. *Journal of Career Assessment, 7,* 161-172.

Buller, D. B., Borland, R., & Burgoon, M. (1998). Impact of behavioral intention on effectiveness of message features: Evidence from the family sun safety project. *Human Communication Research, 24,* 422-453.

Burgoon, M., Alvaro, E., Grandpre, J., & Voulodakis, M. (2002). Revisiting the theory of psychological reactance: Communicating threats to attitudinal freedom. In J. P. Dillard, & M. W. Pfau (Eds.), *The persuasion handbook: Developments in theory and practice* (pp. 213-232). Thousand Oaks, CA: Sage.

DeVellis, R. F. (1991). *Scale development: Theory and applications*. Newbury Park, CA: Sage Publications.

Dillard, J. P., & Shen, L. (2005). On the nature of reactance and its role in health communication. *Communication Monographs, 72,* 144-168.

Donnell, A. J., Thomas, A., & Buboltz, W. C., Jr. (2001). Psychological reactance: Factor structure and internal consistency of the Questionnaire for the Measurement of Psychological Reactance. *The Journal of Social Psychology, 141*(5), 697-687.

Dowd, E. T., Milne, C. R., & Wise, S. L. (1991). The Therapeutic Reactance Scale: A measure of psychological reactance. *Journal of Counseling & Development, 69,* 541-545.

Dowd, E. T., & Wallbrown, F. (1993). Motivational component of client reactance. *Journal of Counseling & Development, 71,* 533-538.

Dowd, E. T., Wallbrown, F., Sanders, D., & Yesenosky, J. M. (1994). Psychological reactance and its relationship to normal personality variables. *Cognitive Therapy and Research, 18,* 601-612.

Frank, S., Jackson-Walker, S., Marks, M., Van Egeren, L., Loop, K., & Olson, K. (1998). From laboratory to the hospitals, adults to adolescents, and disorders to personality: The case of psychological reactance. *Journal of Clinical Psychology, 54,* 361-381.

Grandpre, J., Alvaro, E. Burgoon, M., Miller, C., & Hall, J. (2003). Adolescent reactance and antismoking campaigns: A theoretical approach. *Health Communication, 15,* 349-366.

Graybar, S., Antonuccio, D., Boutilier, L., & Varble, D. (1989). Psychological reactance as a factor affecting patient compliance to physician advice. *Scandinavian Journal of Behavioral therapy, 18,* 43-51.

Hong, S.-M. (1992). Hong's psychological reactance scale: A further factor analytic validation. *Psychological Reports, 70,* 512-514.

Hong, S. M., & Faedda, S. (1996). Refinement of the Hong Psychological Reactance Scale. *Educational & Psychological Measurement, 56,* 173-182.

Hong, S. M., & Ostini, R. (1989). Further evaluation of Merz's psychological reactance scale. *Psychological Reports, 64,* 707-710.

Hong, S. M., & Page, S. (1989). A psychological reactance scale: Development, factor structure and reliability. *Psychological Reports, 64,* 1323-1326.

Hunter, J. E., & Gerbing, D. W. (1982). Unidimensional measurement, second order factor analysis, and causal models. In B. M. Staw, & L. L Cummings (Eds.), *Research in organizational behavior,* vol. 4 (pp. 267-320). Greenwich, CT: JAI Press.

Imajo, S. (2002). Reactance proneness, collectivism, uniqueness, and resistance to persuasion. *Japanese Journal of Psychology, 73,* 366-372.

Johnson, P., & Bubolz, W. C., Jr. (2000). Differentiation of self and psychological reactance. *Contemporary Family Therapy: An International Journal, 22,* 91-102.

Merz, J. (1983). A questionnaire for the measurement of psychological reactance. [German]. *Diagnostica, 29,* 75-82.

Ringold, D. J. (2002). Boomerang effect in response to public health interventions: Some unintended consequences in the alcoholic beverage market. *Journal of Consumer Policy, 25,* 27–63.

Robin, B., Kumar, V., & Pekala, R. (2005). Direct and indirect scales of hypnotic susceptibility: Resistance to therapy and psychometric comparability. *International Journal of Clinical & Experimental Hypnosis, 53,* 135-147.

Sachau, D., & Houlihan, D., & Gilbertson, T. (1999). Predictors of employee resistance to supervisors' requests. *The Journal of Social Psychology, 139,* 611-621.

Seemann, E. A., Buboltz, Jr., W. C., Jenkins, S. M., Sopper, B., & Woller, K. (2004). Ethnic and gender differences in psychological reactance: The importance of reactance in multicultural counseling. *Counseling Psychology Quarterly, 17,* 167-176.

Seibel, C., & Dowd, E. T. (2001). Personality characteristics associated with psychological reactance. *Journal of Clinical Psychology, 57,* 963-969.

Shen, L., & Dillard, J. P. (2005). The psychometric properties of the Hong Psychological Reactance Scale. *Journal of Personality Assessment, 85,* 72-79.

Thomas, A., Donnell, A. J., & Buboltz, W. C. (2001). The Hong psychological reactance scale: A confirmatory factor analysis. *Measurement and Evaluation in Counseling and Development, 34,* 2-13.

Tucker, R. K., & Byers, P. Y. (1987). Factorial validity of Merz's psychological reactance scale. *Psychological Reports, 61,* 811-815.

Wicklund, R. A. (1974). *Freedom and reactance.* Potomac, MD: Lawrence Erlbaum Associates.

Woller, K. P. (2000). *The combination of two scales of psychological reactance.* Unpublished doctoral dissertation, Kent State University.

Wright, R. A., & Brehm, S. (1982). Reactance as impression management: A critical review. *Journal of Personality and Social Psychology, 42,* 608-618.

KEY TERMS

Confirmatory Factor Analysis (CFA): The determination of the number of factors and the loadings of measured (indicator) variables on them conform to what is expected on the basis of preestablished theory. Indicator variables are selected on the basis of prior theory and factor analysis is used to see if they load as predicted on the expected number of factors. A minimum requirement of confirmatory factor analysis is that the researcher should hypothesize beforehand the number of factors in the model, but usually also the researcher will posit expectations about which variables will load on which factors.

Exploratory Factor Analysis (EFA): The uncovering of the underlying structure of a relatively large set of variables. The researcher's *à priori* assumption is that any indicator may be associated with any factor. This is the most common form of factor analysis. There is no prior theory and one uses factor loadings to intuit the factor structure of the data.

Internal Consistency: The degree to which each item in a scale relates independently to the rest of the items and how they are related overall.

External Consistency: Also called parallelism. Refers to the degree to which each item in a scale correlated with variables outside of the cluster. The general statement of parallelism is that items in a unidimensional scale should have similar patterns of correlations with items in other clusters, or other traits.

Reactance: The motivational state that is hypothesized to occur when a freedom is eliminated or threatened with elimination.

Reactance Proneness: An individual's trait propensity to experience psychological reactance.

Chapter XLIV
Self–Report Measures
of Discrete Emotions

James P. Dillard
The Pennsylvania State University, USA

Lijiang Shen
The University of Georgia, USA

BACKGROUND

According to appraisal theories of emotion, negative emotions arise from the perception that the environment is in an incongruent relationship with the individual's goals (Dillard, 1997; Frijda, 1986; Lazarus, 1991). In contrast, when an individual judges that the current environment is likely to facilitate his or her goals, positive emotions follow (Frijda, 1986; Lazarus, 1991). However, both within and across these broad categories, individual emotions can be discriminated along several lines (Frijda, 1986; Lazarus, 1991; Oatley, 1992; Roseman, Weist, & Swartz, 1994; Scherer, 1984).

First, emotions vary in terms of their *signal value* (Table 1, column 2). That is, emotions are a source of information regarding the state of the person-environment relationship. For example, surprise follows from the perception of novelty in the environment, and registers that perception in conscious awareness (Frijda, 1986; Lazarus, 1991; Oatley, 1992; Roseman et al., 1994; Scherer, 1984). Emotions also signal the mobilization of psychological and physiological resources correspondent to that person-environment relationship. The subjective experience of an emotion also relays this information to consciousness. In this sense, an emotion may be viewed as a summary readout of the changes taking place in the body (Buck, 1997).

Emotions can be understood further in terms of their *function* (see Table 1, column 3). At the most general level, emotions operate as rudimentary information processing systems designed to deal with a certain, limited set of person-environment relationships. Given a particular understanding of the person-environment relationship, an emotion shifts the organism into a state of being designed to address that relationship (Lazarus, 1991; Oatley, 1992). For example, fear instigates efforts at self-protection, whereas anger provides the motivational basis for subduing the offending stimulus.

Table 1. The signal values, functions, and action tendencies associated with various affects

Affect	Signal Value	Function	Action Tendency
Surprise	Novelty	Orient	Allocate Attention
Anger	Obstacle	Remove Obstacle	Attack /Reject
Fear	Danger	Protection	Revise Existing Plan/Create New Plan
Sadness	Failure	Learning	Review Plan/ Recuperation/Convalesce
Guilt	Transgression	Self-Sanction	Strive to Attain Standard
Happiness	Progress toward Goal	Self-Reward	Bask/Bond
Contentment	Absence of threat	Conserve Resources	Immobility

One of the central premises of most theories of emotion is that these affects are evolutionarily designed to direct behavior. Thus, each emotion has associated with it an *action tendency* of a specific form that aligns with the function of that emotion (Table 1, column 4). Two points in particular are important to understanding the concept of action tendencies. First, although all action tendencies are forms of engagement and withdrawal, particular emotions produce particular variations on these broad themes. For instance, happiness and anger promote quite different types of engagement. And, though sadness and fear may both be considered withdrawal emotions, their behavioral manifestations are notably distinct; sadness is characterized by lethargy while tension is typical of fear. Contentment is a special case in that it is an affect that inspires passivity rather than action. Awkwardly, but accurately stated, its action tendency is one of nonaction.

A second important point bears on the relationship between the emotions and their associated action tendencies. Although statistically significant associations have been reported between particular emotions and the tendency to withdraw or engage (Frijda, Kuipers, & ter Schure, 1989; Roseman et al., 1994), these findings probably are *not* the result of an identity relationship between affect and action tendency that has been measured with error. Rather, they are associations that result from both regularities in the social environment and limits inherent in the affect programs themselves. In fact, we believe that within the limits defined by social regularities and action possibilities, the relationship between affect and action is highly context dependent. Fear, for example, causes freezing in some instances and flight in others. Guilt may prompt efforts to redress the failure, but only if the transgression can be remedied. Thus, when researching the impact of various emotions on persuasion, it is essential to remain cognizant of various contextual factors such as setting, message topic, and response options. It is useful to distinguish emotions in terms of their action tendencies, but equally important to bear in mind that when context is taken into account, tendencies may be translated into distinct forms of behavior.

Over a series of studies, we have developed a set of close-ended scales designed to measure discrete emotions. The scales and their corresponding items are as follows: *surprise* (surprised, startled, astonished), *anger* (irritated, angry, annoyed, aggravated), *fear* (fearful, afraid, scared), *sadness* (sad, dreary, dismal), *guilt* (guilty, ashamed), *happiness* (happy, elated, cheerful, joyful) and *contentment* (contented, peaceful, mellow, tranquil). The 5-point response scale runs from 0 = None of this emotion to 4 = A great deal of this emotion. To facilitate interpretation and to create a meaningful zero point, the items are summed within scales, then divided by the number of items in the scale. Prior to reporting on their emotional state, participants are instructed to focus on "How the message made you feel" or "How you are feeling right now," depending on the aims of the researcher.

RELIABILITY

Typically, alpha reliabilities for the scales are in the .80 to .90 range. In the Dillard and Peck (2001) data, the reliabilities were *surprise* (α = .84), *anger* (α = .88), *fear* (α = .94), *sadness* (α = .82), *guilt* (α = .83), *happiness* (α = .90) and *contentment* (α = .85). Because the scales are intended to assess transient states, test-retest reliability has not been evaluated.

VALIDITY

Confirmatory factor analyses were conducted for each of the studies in which the scales were used (Dillard & Anderson, 2004; Dillard & Kinney, 1994; Dillard, Kinney, & Cruz, 1996; Dillard, Plotnick, Godbold, Freimuth, & Edgar, 1996; Dillard & Peck, 2000, 2001; Segrin & Dillard, 1991; Shen, 2005). All of these same studies show unique and discriminable relationships for each of the scales with some antecedent (such as cognitive appraisals) or some outcome variable (such as perceived message effectiveness). Hence, the evidence for scale validity is quite strong.

RESULTS

Completion of the scales provides a valid and reliable representation of an individuals' emotional state. The scales are not currently posted online.

COMMENTARY

The items are brief and the response scales naturally meaningful. The point of reference (e.g., the message, right now, some specific point in the past, some specific event) can be easily manipulated by varying the instructions that precede the scale. Accordingly, the scales are easy to use and highly adaptable.

COST

The scales may be used without cost for research purposes.

LOCATION

Although the scales are not currently available online, the items are included in this chapter.

REFERENCES

Buck, R. (1997). From DNA to MTV: The spontaneous communication of emotional messages. In J. O. Greene (Ed.), *Message production: Advances in communication theory* (pp. 313-339). Mahwah, NJ: Erlbaum.

Dillard, J. P. (1997). The role of affect in communication, biology, and social relationships. In P. R. Andersen & L. Guerrero (Eds.), *Communication and emotion* (pp. xvii-xxxii). San Diego, CA: Academic Press.

Dillard, J. P., & Anderson, J. W. (2004). The role of fear in persuasion. *Psychology & Marketing, 21,* 909-926.

Dillard, J. P., & Kinney, T. A. (1994). Experiential and physiological responses to interpersonal influence. *Human Communication Research, 20,* 502-528.

Dillard, J. P., Kinney, T. A., & Cruz, M. G. (1996). Influence, appraisals, and emotions in close relationships. *Communication Monographs, 63,* 105-130.

Dillard, J. P., & Peck, E. (2000). Affect and persuasion: Emotional responses to public service announcements. *Communication Research, 27,* 461-495.

Dillard, J. P. & Peck, E. (2001). Persuasion and the structure of affect: Dual systems and discrete emotions as complementary models. *Human Communication Research, 27,* 38- 68.

Dillard, J. P., Plotnick, C. A., Godbold, L. C., Freimuth, V. S., & Edgar, T. (1996). The multiple affective consequences of AIDS PSAs: Fear appeals do more than scare people. *Communication Research, 23,* 44-72.

Frijda, N. (1986). *The emotions.* Cambridge, UK: Cambridge University Press.

Frijda, N., Kuipers, P., & ter Schure, E. (1989). Relations among emotion, appraisal, and emotional action readiness. *Journal of Personality and Social Psychology, 57,* 212-228.

Lazarus, R. S. (1991). *Emotion & adaptation.* New York: Oxford University Press.

Oatley, K. (1992). *Best laid schemes: The psychology of emotions.* Paris: Cambridge University Press.

Roseman, I. J., Wiest, C., & Swartz, T. S. (1994). Phenomenology, behaviors, and goals differentiate discrete emotions. *Journal of Personality and Social Psychology, 67,* 206- 221.

Scherer, K. (1984). On the nature and function of emotion: A component process approach. In K. Scherer, & P. Ekman (Eds.), *Approaches to emotion* (pp. 293-318). Hillsdale, NJ: Erlbaum.

Segrin, C., & Dillard, J. P. (1991). (Non)depressed persons' cognitive and affective reactions to (un)successful interpersonal influence. *Communication Monographs, 58,* 115-134.

Shen, L. (2005). *The interplay of message framing, cognition, and affect in persuasive health communication.* Unpublished doctoral dissertation, University of Wisconsin-Madison.

KEY TERMS

Emotion Action Tendency: Emotion specific forms of engagement and withdrawal and distinct behavioral manifestations.

Emotion Function: How an emotion shifts the organism into a state of being designed to address the person's particular understanding of the person-environment relationship.

Emotion Signal Value: Information regarding the state of the person-environment relationship.

Chapter XLV
The Listening Styles Profile

Stephanie Lee Sargent
Center for AIDS Research (CFAR), Emory University, USA

James B. Weaver, III
Center for AIDS Research (CFAR), Emory University, USA

BACKGROUND

Traditionally, communication scholars have been most concerned with how, when, where, and with whom individuals choose to communicate. While investigating communication events from an encoder perspective is important, it is equally important to investigate communication from a decoder perspective. Many researchers agree that gaining insight into the listening process—how individuals perceive, process, remember and understand oral messages—should enhance our understanding of communication events substantially. There appears to be a good deal of theoretical support for the notion that listening is a multidimensional concept. For example, descriptions of listening constructs such as "appreciative," "critical," "discriminative," and therapeutic" appear throughout the literature. Furthermore, empirical evidence provided by broadly administered listening-performance tests highlights considerable individual differences across divergent constructs such as content, relational, and emotional listening.

Differences in listening styles reflect attitudes, beliefs, and predispositions about the how, where, when, who, and what of information reception and

encoding. Several examples illustrate the diversity of listening styles. Some people prefer listening to factual information or statistics, while others favor personal examples and illustrations. Some are more willing to linger on content, while others prefer concise and to the point presentations. The listening styles profile (LSP-16) was developed to identify an individual's predominant listening style (Watson, Barker, & Weaver, 1995). The listening styles profile is a 16-item inventory designed to assess four distinct listening preferences labeled people, action, content, and time.

The people listening style emerged as a preference where concern for others' feelings and emotions appear paramount. People-style listeners appear to seek out areas of common interest with others and are responsive to their emotions. Action-style listeners prefer to receive concise, error-free presentations, and can become particularly impatient and easily frustrated when listening to a disorganized presentation. Content style listeners, on the other hand, display a preference for receiving complex and challenging information that they can carefully evaluate before forming judgments and opinions. Time-style listeners demonstrate a preference for brief, hurried interactions with others. and tend to let others know how much time they have to listen or how long they have to meet.

RELIABILITY

Watson, Barker, and Weaver (1995) computed two estimates of reliability for each listening style. First, internal consistency was assessed using Cronbach's test. The strongest coefficients emerged for the people (0.62), action (0.64), and time (0.65) oriented listening styles, while the alpha for the content (0.58) style was slightly weaker. Given the small number of items in each listening style, these coefficients suggest a great deal of internal consistency for each listening style (Nunnally & Bernstein, 1994).

The second estimate of reliability was computed using the test/retest procedure, where undergraduate students completed the listening style profile two times and results were compared. These coefficients, derived from the Pearson product-moment correlations, were all moderately high: people, $r = 0.68$; action, $r = 0.75$; content, $r = 0.73$; and time, $r = 0.71$, and significant ($p < 0.0001$) indicating considerable stability in the listening styles measures over time.

Other studies utilizing the listening style profile (LSP-16) have also reported similar reliabilities: people-ranging from 0.60 to 0.76; action-ranging from 0.56 to 0.68; content-ranging from 0.55 to 0.72; and time-ranging from 0.61 to 0.69. Different sample sizes and varying response metrics appear to account for these variations.

VALIDITY

The 16 listening items were subjected to a principal components factor analysis that yielded a four-factor solution and accounted for approximately 50% of the variance. The first factor, labeled people-oriented listening style, was defined by high loadings on four items such as "I focus my attention on the other person's feelings when listening to them." The second factor, labeled action-oriented listening style, was defined by high loadings on four items including "I am frustrated when others don't present their ideas in an orderly, efficient way." Factor three was defined by four items including "I interrupt others when I feel time pressure" and was labeled time-oriented listening style. The fourth factor, labeled content-oriented listening style, was defined by high loadings on four items including "I like the challenge of listening to complex information." The factor loadings for the four indices ranged from 0.57 to 0.80.

In the 10-plus years since the listening styles profile was developed, many researchers have used the instrument successfully in a variety of research projects, further suggesting the instrument's validity. Studies have examined listening styles and empathy (Weaver & Kirtley, 1995), individual differences in listening styles (Johnston, Weaver, Watson, & Barker, 2000; Weaver, Watson, & Barker, 1996; Worthington, 2003), communication apprehension and listening style preferences (Sargent, Weaver, & Kiewitz, 1997), the relationship between listening preferences, communication apprehension, receiver apprehension, and communicator style (Bodie & Villaume, 2003), listening styles and second guessing (Kirtley & Honeycutt, 1996), the listening styles of the Type-A personality (Sargent, Fitch-Hauser, & Weaver, 1997), effect of listening style preference on juror decision making (Worthington, 2001), using listening style preferences to identify sex differences in perceptions of ourselves and our peers (Sargent & Weaver, 2003), and cross-cultural applications (Kiewitz, Weaver, Brosius, & Weimann, 1997).

RESULTS

In completing the LSP-16, respondents are asked to indicate how well each statement applied to them using a five-point scale ranging from "Always" (4), "Frequently" (3), "Sometimes" (2), "Infrequently" (1), and "Never" (0). Scores are summed for the four items measuring each of the four indices: people, action, content, and time. The items comprising the people-oriented listening style are "I focus my attention on the other person's feelings when listening to them," "When listening to others, I quickly notice if they are displeased or disappointed," "I become involved when listening to the problems of others," and "I nod my head and/or use eye contact to show interest in what others are saying." The items which measure the action-oriented listening style are "I am frustrated when others don't present their ideas in an orderly, efficient way," "When listening to others, I focus on any inconsistencies and/or errors in what's being said," "I jump ahead and/or finish thoughts of speakers," and "I am impatient with people who ramble on during conversations." Content-oriented style listeners are identified by high responses on "I prefer to listen to technical information," "I prefer to hear facts and evidence so I can personally evaluate them," "I like the challenge of listening to complex information," and "I ask questions to probe for additional information." Lastly, the four items comprising the time-oriented listening style are "When hurried, I let the other person(s) know that I have a limited amount of time to listen," "I begin a discussion by telling others how long I have to meet," "I interrupt others when I feel time pressure," and "I look at my watch or clocks in the room when I have limited time to listen to others."

COMMENTARY

Taken together, this data suggest that the LSP-16 is a valid and reliable instrument in listening research since it has been used in a number of studies (see Validity). The data at hand also suggest that the listening styles profile (LSP-16) has considerable utility in clinical, training, and research environments for measurement and study of the ways that people prefer to listen.

Readers might also take note of another inventory designed to measure listening preferences. The listening styles inventory (Pearce, Johnson, & Barker, 2003) also categorizes four types of listening styles: active, involved, passive, and detached. While Pearce et al. argue that the inventory was developed as a guide for perceived listening effectiveness in the business environment, its basic structure is essentially the same as the listening style profile (LSP-16).

COST

The LSP-16 is free to those using it for academic research purposes.

LOCATION

The LSP-16 can be found on page 5 of the following article:

Watson, K. W., Barker, L. L., & Weaver, J. B., III (1995). The listening styles profile (LSP-16): Development and validation of an instrument to assess four listening styles. *International Journal of Listening, 9*, 1-13.

REFERENCES

Bodie, G. D., & Villaume, W. A. (2003). Aspects of receiving information: The relationship between listening preferences, communication apprehension, receiver apprehension, and communicator style. *International Journal of Listening, 17,* 47-67.

Chesebro, J. L. (1999). The relationship between listening styles and conversational sensitivity. *Communication Research Reports, 16,* 233-238.

Johnston, M. K., Weaver, J. B., III, Watson, K. W., & Barker, L. B. (2000). Listening styles: Biological or psychological differences? *International Journal of Listening, 14,* 32-46.

Kiewitz, C., Weaver, J. B., III, Brosius, H. B., & Weimann, G. (1997). Cultural differences in listening style preferences: A comparison of young adults in Germany, Israel, and the United States. *International Journal of Public Opinion Research, 9,* 233-247.

Kirtley, M. D. & Honeycutt, J. M. (1996). Listening styles and their correspondence with second guessing. *Communication Research Reports, 13,* 174-182.

Nunnally, J. C., & Bernstein, I. H. (1994). *Psychometric theory* (3rd ed.). New York: McGraw Hill, Inc.

Pearce, C. G., Johnson. I. W., & Barker, R. T. (2003). Assessment of the listening styles inventory. *Journal of Business & Technical Communication, 17,* 84-113.

Sargent, S. L., Fitch-Hauser, M., & Weaver, J. B., III (1997). A listening styles profile of the Type-A personality. *International Journal of Listening, 11,* 1-14.

Sargent, S. L., & Weaver, J. B., III (2003). Listening styles: Sex differences in perceptions of self and others. *International Journal of Listening, 17,* 5-18.

Sargent, S. L., Weaver, J. B., III, & Kiewitz, C. (1997). Correlates between communication apprehension and listening style preferences. *Communication Research Reports, 14,* 74-78.

Verret, M. J. (2000). The impact of buyer/seller listening styles on mutual trust, satisfaction, and anticipation of future interactions. *Dissertation Abstracts International, 61*(6-B), 3328.

Watson, K. W., Barker, L. L., & Weaver, J. B., III (1995). The Listening Styles Profile (LSP-16): Development and validation of an instrument to assess four listening styles. *International Journal of Listening, 9,* 1-13.

Weaver, J. B., III, & Kirtley, M. D. (1995). Listening styles and empathy. *The Southern Communication Journal, 60*(2), 131-140.

Weaver, J. B., III, Watson, K. W., & Barker L. L. (1996). Individual differences in listening styles: Do you hear what I hear? *Personality and Individual Differences, 20,* 381-387.

Worthington, D. L. (2001). Exploring juror's listening processes: The effect of listening style preference on juror decision making. *International Journal of Listening, 15,* 20-37.

Worthington, D. L. (2003). Exploring the relationship between listening style preference and personality. *International Journal of Listening, 17,* 68-87.

KEY TERMS

Action Listening Style: A preference to receive concise, error-free presentations, and to avoid disorganized presentations.

Content Listening Style: A preference for receiving complex and challenging information useful for careful evaluation before forming judgments and opinions.

Listening: How individuals perceive, process, remember, and understand oral messages

Listening Style: The preference to listen for particular content in messages.

The People Listening Style: A preference where concern for others' feelings and emotions appear paramount.

Time Listening Style: A preference for brief, hurried interactions with others, and a tendency to let others know how much time is available for interacting.

Chapter XLVI
Servant Leadership Assessment Instrument

Rob Dennis
VA Medical Center, Ohio, USA

Mihai C. Bocarnea
Regent University, USA

BACKGROUND

The SLAI measures the seven concepts found in Patterson's (2003) theory of servant leadership. According to Patterson (2003), the servant leader (a) leads and serves with love (Winston, 2002), (b) acts with humility (Sandage & Wiens, 2001), (c) is altruistic (Kaplan, 2000), (d) is visionary for the followers (Tangney, 2000), (e) is trusting (Hauser & House, 2000), (f) is serving (Wis, 2002), and (g) empowers followers (Covey, 2002). These are the seven constructs that comprise the servant leadership in Patterson's model. Servant leadership as a theory emerged from Robert Greenleaf's (1977) work. Recent investigations have expanded servant leadership to include identification and assessment servant leadership factors (Dennis & Bocarnea, 2005; Dennis & Winston, 2003; Laub, 1999; Page & Wong, 2000; Patterson, 2003; Russell, 2000; Russell & Stone, 2002).

The 42 items of the servant leadership assessment instrument (SLAI) cover a variety of attitudes and behaviors reflective of the aforementioned research.

RELIABILITY

Research has indicated that the SLAI is internally consistent and reliable. Alpha reliability coefficients ranging from .89 to .92 have been reported (Dennis, 2004) for factors of *love, empowerment, vision,* and *humility*. *Trust* factor, however, has loaded with two items on two second-data collections (Dennis, 2004) and one sample (Irving, 2005). The following alpha coefficients were found, measuring servant leadership at the individual leader level: (a) .92 for the SLAI *love* scale; (b) .92 for the SLAI *empowerment* scale; (c) .86 for the SLAI *vision* scale; and (d) .92 for the SLAI *humility* scale. A Cronbach alpha coefficient could not be calculated for the SLAI trust scale because it only has two items in the scale (Irving, 2005).

VALIDITY

Face and content validity was built into the test development process, following methods set in DeVellis' (1991, 2003) Scale Development Guidelines. The criterion-related validity and construct-related validity of the instrument were established empirically and have been supported (Dennis & Bocarnea, 2005; Irving, 2005).

RESULTS

The Web survey has two parts: one with the 42-item Likert-type SLAI scale, the other with nine demographic questions. The SLAI items are reflective of servant leadership characteristics of a given leader as seen by his or her followers. Participants are invited to indicate their agreement or disagreement with each of the questionnaire items on a 1 to 7 scale: the higher the number, the stronger the agreement with that statement. Statements are reflective of how participants' leader would think, act, or behave. The corresponding items of the seven servant characteristics of a leader are:

1. Loving: items 1.2, 1.7, 1.17, 1.19, 1.21, 1.27;
2. Humble: items 1.8, 1.12, 1.20, 1.22, 1.37, 1.39;
3. Altruistic: items 1.5, 1.9, 1.16, 1.18, 1.23, 1.26;
4. Visionary: items 1.14, 1.32, 1.34, 1.36, 1.40, 1.42;
5. Trusting: items 1.3, 1.10, 1.13, 1.30, 1.31, 1.41;
6. Serving: items 1.1, 1.4, 1.15, 1.29, 1.35, 1.38;
7. Empowering: items 1.6, 1.11, 1.24, 1.25, 1.28, 1.33.

The demographic items in the second part of the Web survey include nine items, 2.1 to 2.9, as follows: age, gender, ethnicity, occupation, tenure at current job, longest job tenure ever, workforce tenure, education, and work situation.

The online instrument was created and published using SurveySuite. This survey generation tool provided by the University of Virginia is located at http://intercom.virginia.edu/SurveySuite.

After a 14-day free trial period, an annual fee is required to continue the service. The service includes online survey creation and administration, and tallying results. Additionally, all data collected are made available in a format compatible with any statistical software. Such statistical software is required for any analyses beyond summarized descriptive statistics.

The instrument is self-report and takes no more than 10 minutes to complete. Individual responses are anonymously entered into a database of responses. All results are kept confidential.

COMMENTARY

Other instruments have been developed to measure servant leadership. However, none of the instruments have measured over three factors of servant leadership. One instrument, the OLA (Laub, 1999) measures servant leadership at the organizational level. The SLAI, given its high reliability and validity, is recommended as a way to assess servant leadership for both self-assessment and group assessment for a leader.

Those interested in using the SLAI online survey in their own research are advised to contact the author to get an additional research code that participants can include in the demographic section of the form in order for the author to be able to detect and extract tagged data sets from the database.

COST

The SLAI is free to take and use online. The SLAI's author, however, encourages those interested in using the instrument to contact him by e-mail. Collaborative research is suggested for further advancing the uses and implications of this new leadership assessment tool.

LOCATION

The SLAI may be completed online at http://intercom.virginia.edu/SurveySuite/Surveys/ServantLdrAssess/

REFERENCES

Covey, S. (2002). Servant-leadership and community leadership in the twenty-first century. In L. Spears (Ed.), *Focus on leadership: Servant leadership for the 21st century* (pp. 27-34). New York: John Wiley & Sons, Inc.

Dennis, R. S. (2004). Servant leadership theory: Development of the servant leadership assessment instrument. *Dissertation Abstracts International, 65*(05), UMI No. AAT 3133544.

Dennis, R., & Bocarnea, M. C. (2005). Development of the servant leadership assessment instrument. *Leadership and Organizational Development Journal, 26*(8), pp. 600-615.

Dennis, R., &. Winston, B. E. (2003). A factor analysis of Page and Wong's servant leadership instrument. *Leadership & Organization Development Journal, 24*(8), 455-459.

DeVellis, R. (1991). *Scale development: Theory and applications.* London: Sage Publications.

DeVellis, R. (2003). *Scale development: Theory and application, 2nd ed.* London: Sage Publications.

Greenleaf, R. (1977). Servant leadership. A journey into the nature of legitimate power and greatness. New York: Paulist Press.

Hauser, M., &. House, R. J. (2000). In E. Locke (Ed.), *Handbook of principles of organizational behavior.* Malden, MA: Blackwell Publishers, Inc.

Irving, J. A. (August 2005). *Exploring the relationship between servant leadership and team effectiveness: Findings from the nonprofit sector.* Servant Leadership Research Roundtable – Regent University. Retrieved March 13, 2003, from http://www.regent.edu/acad/sls/publications/conference_proceedings/servant_leadership_roundtable/2005/proceedings.htm

Kaplan, S. (2000, Fall). Human nature and environmentally responsible behavior. *Journal of Social Issues, 56*(3), 491-505.

Laub, J. (1999). *Assessing the servant organization: Development of the servant organizational leadership assessment (SOLA) instrument.* Dissertation, Florida Atlantic University, ATT 9921922, 60.

Page, D., & Wong, T. P. (2000). A conceptual framework for measuring servant-leadership. In S. AdjGibolosoo (Ed.), *The human factor in shaping the course of history and development* (pp. 69-109). New York: University Press of America, Inc.

Patterson, K. (2003). *Servant leadership: A theoretical model.* Unpublished doctoral dissertation, Regent University, Graduate School of Business.

Russell, R. (2000). *Exploring the values and attributes of servant leaders.* Doctoral dissertation 12, 4856, Vol. 61.

Russell, R., & Stone, G. A. (2002). A review of servant leadership attributes: Developing a practical model. *Leadership and Organizational Development Journal, 23*(3), 145-157.

Sandage, S., & Wiens, T. W. (2001, Fall). Contextualizing models of humility and forgiveness: A reply to Gassin. *Journal of Psychology and Theology, 29*(3), 201-219.

Tangney, J. P. (2000). Humility: Theoretical perspectives, empirical findings. *Journal of Social and Clinical Psychology, 19,* 70-82.

Winston, B. (2002). *Be a leader for God's sake.* Virginia Beach, VA: Regent University-School of Leadership Studies.

Wis, R. (2002). The conductor as servant leader. *Music Educators Journal, 89*(17).

KEY TERMS

Follower: A person that seeks and accepts the guidance of a leader.

Leader: A person that exerts intentional influence over other people to structure and facilitate activities and relationships within a given organization.

Servant Leadership: A theoretical and practical leadership model advocating that the primary focus of leaders is serving the followers.

Chapter XLVII
The Aggression Questionnaire

Christian Kiewitz
University of Dayton, USA

James B. Weaver, III
Center for AIDS Research (CFAR), Emory University, USA

BACKGROUND

We describe two short-form versions of the self-report aggression questionnaire initially developed by Buss and Perry (1992). Often referred to as the Buss-Perry aggression questionnaire (BPAQ), the original inventory consists of 29 items that measure four aspects of trait aggressiveness—anger, hostility, verbal- and physical-aggression—that are typically used both individually and/or combined to create an overall aggressiveness index. The BPAQ is the successor of the Buss-Durkee hostility inventory (Buss & Durkee, 1957).

Perhaps more appropriate for Internet-based research are the AQ-12 and AQ-15 short forms derived from two different efforts to refine the BPAQ. One effort resulted in the AQ-12 (Bryant & Smith, 2001, p. 150), which uses 12 of the original 29 AQ items. The other effort yielded the AQ-15 by drawing from a 34-item AQ revision by the same authors (Buss & Warren, 2000, pp. 13, 65), and also from the AQ-12.

Comparing the AQ-12 and AQ-15 reveals almost identical items for the anger, hostility, verbal- and physical-aggression subscales. The primary difference is that the AQ-15 features an additional three-item subscale that assesses indirect aggression. Respondents typically rate items on both inventories using a Likert-type scale. Both forms can be used with adult/adolescent and normal/abnormal populations. For children, the AQ-15 may be preferable because it has a third-grade readability level. Research has shown both inventories to be quite reliable and valid measures of aggressive tendencies in individuals.

From a conceptual standpoint, anger represents the affective component of aggressiveness, hostility the cognitive component, and verbal-, physical- and indirect-aggression represent the instrumental components (Buss & Perry, 1992; Buss & Warren, 2000). As such, the anger subscales of the AQ-12 and AQ-15 focus on physiological arousal, a sense of control and preparation for aggression, while the hostility subscales tap cognitions related to ill will, injustice, bitterness, social alienation, and paranoia (Bryant & Smith, 2001; Buss & Perry, 1992; Buss & Warren, 2000). The verbal- and physical-aggression subscales pertain to acts intended to cause harm or hurt through quarrelsome and hostile speech or physical force. Finally, the indirect aggression subscale (AQ-15 only) measures the tendency to aggress without direct confrontation (cf. Archer & Coyne, 2005).

RELIABILITY

Although fairly new developments, both the AQ-12 and AQ-15 have been subject to several validation studies in recent years that generally indicate acceptable levels of internal consistency reliability (i.e., Cronbach's Alpha). However, we presently do not know of any studies reporting test-retest reliabilities for the two inventories.

AQ-12. Regarding the AQ-12, Bryant and Smith (2001) report internal reliability estimates from four samples of American (2 samples), British, and Canadian undergraduate students (total $n = 984$). Reliability estimates ranged from .71 to .76 for anger, from .70 to .75 for hostility, from .73 to .83 for verbal aggression, and from .79 to .80 for physical aggression (pp. 155, 162). Because Cronbach's Alpha is sensitive to the number of items included in a given scale, these authors also calculate adjusted Alpha coefficients of .88 to .92 for the four subscales (p. 163) using the Spearman-Brown prophecy formula (cf. Shevlin, Miles, Davies, & Walker, 2000). Alpha values for an overall aggressiveness score were not provided (see remark under *Results*).

Slightly lower reliability coefficients emerge from a study by Tremblay and Ewart (2005) involving four samples of Canadian undergraduate students (total $n = 246$). Here, estimates were .66 for anger, .68 for hostility, .71 and .75 for verbal- and physical-aggression, respectively, plus .78 for the overall aggressiveness score (p. 341). Based on their study results, the authors conclude that "one can safely use the refined AQ scales without much reduction in internal consistency" (p. 344).

AQ-15. For the AQ-15, Buss and Warren (2000, p. 65) report Alpha coefficients of .63 for anger, .72 for hostility, .74 for verbal aggression, .80 for physical aggression, and .62 for indirect-aggres-

sion, plus .90 for the total aggression score for a diverse sample of 2,138 Americans (for details see pp. 30-36). The reliability estimate for the total score from Buss' and Warren's predominantly Caucasian sample (72%) converges with the Alpha coefficient of .85 and .89 reported for two Asian samples ($n = 227$ and $n = 370$) collected by Ang (2005) and Ang and Yusof (2005), respectively, in which the majority of students identified themselves as either Chinese (77% and 84%) or Indian (13% and 9%).

VALIDITY

Research shows substantial evidence for construct, convergent, criterion, and discriminant validity for the AQ-12, while the evidence for the AQ-15 is less abundant due to a lower number of studies having used it so far.

AQ-12. While developing the AQ-12, Bryant and Smith (2001) were careful to provide copious evidence regarding the short form's validity using multiple samples and advanced statistical analyses. These efforts appear to have been fruitful. Specifically, Tremblay and Ewart (2005) conclude from their own confirmatory factor analyses "that the refined [AQ-12] scales with their reduced number of items do not suffer a large reduction in construct validity. In some cases they perform as well as the original AQ scales or better" (p. 342). Moreover, these authors present evidence for criterion-related validity that shows different correlational patterns between AQ-12 subscales and various criteria, such as five-factor personality dimensions and alcohol-related individual differences, in a sample involving Canadian undergraduates.

AQ-15. Evidence for criterion validity comes from a study that used a cut-off score on the AQ-15 to group Asian students into an aggressive and a nonaggressive group, and found higher narcissism scores for aggressive students (medium effect size; Ang & Yusof, 2005). Ang (2005) provides evidence for convergent and discriminant validity in another study with Asian students, showing a positive, moderate relationship between AQ-15 total aggression scores and scores tapping conflict in the student-teacher relationship, while finding no link between AQ-15 aggression and student help seeking.

RESULTS

For both the AQ-12 and AQ-15, respondents' scores are averaged either for individual subscales (three item scores for each subscale), or across all subscales to calculate an overall aggression score. However, Bryant and Smith (2001) actually discourage the use of an overall aggressiveness score because, they argue, it might "obscure differences that exist for individual factors" (p. 163), thus diminishing the AQ's multidimensional approach to aggression (Buss & Perry, 1992; Buss & Warren, 2000; Eckhardt, Norlander, & Deffenbacher, 2004). Both forms do not include any reverse-scored items.

Bryant and Smith (2001) recommend that respondents rate AQ-12 items on a 6-point Likert-type scale ranging from 1 (*not at all characteristic of me*) to 6 (*very much characteristic of me*). This procedure eliminates the midpoint (neutral) category, and forces respondents to decide whether an item is characteristic of them.

In contrast, Buss and Warren (2000) use a 5-point scale ranging from 1 (*not at all like me*) to 5 (*completely like me*) for the AQ-15. The latter authors also provide normative data for the AQ-15 based on a sample of 2,138 individuals, with separate norms for the sexes being presented in three age sets: 9 to 18, 19 to 39, and 40 to 88 years old (pp. 66-71).

COMMENTARY

Altogether, the above data suggest that both the AQ-12 and AQ-15 are internally consistent and valid inventories to assess human aggression. Regarding their reliability over time, however, we were not able to find any studies reporting test-retest reliabilities for these instruments. We also recommend applying the Spearman-Brown prophecy formula (Nunnally & Bernstein, 1994; Shevlin et al., 2000) when calculating Alpha coefficients for the 3-item subscales of these inventories, so to adjust for the coefficient's sensitivity to low numbers of scale items (cf. Bryant & Smith, 2001).

The reader might also want to consider other inventories or AQ versions. A broad review of anger and hostility measures can be found in Eckhardt, Norlander and Deffenbacher (2004). Reviews of the various AQ versions can be found in Bryant and Smith (2001), Buss and Warren (2000), Diamond, Wang, & Buffington-Vollum (2005), Harris (1997,) and Williams, Boyd, Cascardi and Poythress (1996).

The reader might also note that cross-culturally validated versions of the AQ are available. Two recent efforts seem promising. The first one presents a reduced 20-item version of the AQ that is posited to be stable across samples obtained in different countries and even different languages (for details see Vigil-Colet, Lorenzo-Seva, Codorniu-Raga, & Morales, 2005). Interestingly, this version is quite similar to Bryant's and Smith's (2001) AQ-12, with the exception of the hostility scale. The second effort resulted in the shortest AQ version to date, which contains a mere eight items (Gidron, Davidson, & Ilia, 2001). These authors used three samples involving American and Israeli students, as well as Israeli patients (total $n = 453$), to arrive at an AQ short form that features two items from each AQ subscale.

COST

The AQ-12 is free for academic research purposes, as governed under the "fair use" doctrine of US Copyright law (see 17 USC § 107 (2005),

AQ-12 INVENTORY (Bryant & Smith, 2001, p. 150)		
Factor		**Item**
Physical aggression	2.	Given enough provocation, I may hit another person.
	6.	There are people who pushed me so far that we came to blows.
	8.	I have threatened people I know.
Verbal aggression	11.	I often find myself disagreeing with people.
	13.	I can't help getting into arguments when people disagree with me.
	14.	My friends say that I am somewhat argumentative.
Anger	15.	I flare up quickly but get over it quickly.
	20.	Sometimes I fly off the handle for no good reason.
	21.	I have trouble controlling my temper.
Hostility	23.	At times I feel I have gotten a raw deal out of life.
	24.	Other people always seem to get the breaks.
	25.	I wonder why sometimes I feel so bitter about things.

Note. Item numbers correspond with the numbering of items in the original Aggression Questionnaire by Buss and Perry (1992, p. 454) and the numbering scheme used by Bryant and Smith (2001, p. 150). The randomized order for the AQ-12 items suggested by Bryant and Smith is: 11, 23, 8, 25, 21, 14, 15, 2, 13, 24, 6 and 20.

http://www.copyright.gov/fls/fl102.html). For other uses, the reader may want to contact the authors of the original AQ (Buss & Perry, 1992) and/or the abbreviated AQ-12 version (Bryant & Smith, 2001).

As of July 2006, the *Aggression Questionnaire* manual, containing the AQ-15, costs US-$58. The manual can be purchased from Western Psychological Services at https://www.secure.earthlink. net/www.wpspublish.com/Inetpub4/catalog/W-371.htm, or by calling 1-800-648-8857 from the US or Canada or ++1-310-478-2061 from outside the US.

LOCATION

The AQ-12, together with the 1992 AQ, can be found on p. 150 of the following article:

Bryant, F. B., & Smith, B. D. (2001). Refining the architecture of aggression: A measurement model for the Buss-Perry Aggression Questionnaire. *Journal of Research in Personality, 35,* 138-167.

The AQ-15 can be found on p. 65 of the Aggression Questionnaire manual:

Buss, A. H., & Warren, W. L. (2000). *Aggression Questionnaire* (Manual). Los Angeles, CA: Western Psychological Services.

The original AQ can be found on p. 454 of the following article:

Buss, A. H., & Perry, M. (1992). The aggression questionnaire. *Journal of Personality and Social Psychology, 63,* 452-459.

REFERENCES

Ang, R. P. (2005). Development and validation of the teacher-student relationship inventory using exploratory and confirmatory factor analysis. *The Journal of Experimental Education, 74,* 55-73.

Ang, R. P., & Yusof, N. (2005). The relationship between aggression, narcissism, and self-esteem in Asian children and adolescents. *Current Psychology, 24,* 113-122.

Archer, J., & Coyne, S. M. (2005). An integrated review of indirect, relational, and social aggression. *Personality and Social Psychology Review, 9*, 212-230.

Bryant, F. B., & Smith, B. D. (2001). Refining the architecture of aggression: A measurement model for the Buss-Perry Aggression Questionnaire. *Journal of Research in Personality, 35*, 138-167.

Buss, A. H., & Durkee, A. (1957). An inventory for assessing different kinds of hostility. *Journal of Consulting Psychology, 21*, 343-349.

Buss, A. H., & Perry, M. (1992). The aggression questionnaire. *Journal of Personality and Social Psychology, 63*, 452-459.

Buss, A. H., & Warren, W. L. (2000). *Aggression questionnaire* (Manual). Los Angeles, CA: Western Psychological Services.

Diamond, P. M., Wang, E. W., & Buffington-Vollum, J. (2005). Factor structure of the Buss-Perry Aggression Questionnaire (BPAQ) with mentally ill male prisoners. *Criminal Justice and Behavior, 32*, 546-564.

Eckhardt, C., Norlander, B., & Deffenbacher, J. (2004). The assessment of anger and hostility: A critical review. *Aggression & Violent Behavior, 9*, 17-43.

Gidron, Y., Davidson, K., & Ilia, R. (2001). Development and cross-cultural and clinical validation of a brief comprehensive scale for assessing hostility in medical settings. *Journal of Behavioral Medicine, 24*, 1-15.

Harris, J. A. (1997). A further evaluation of the aggression questionnaire: Issues of validity and reliability. *Behaviour Research and Therapy, 35*, 1047-1053.

Nunnally, J. C., & Bernstein, I. H. (1994). *Psychometric theory* (3rd ed.). New York: McGraw-Hill.

Shevlin, M., Miles, J. N. V., Davies, M. N. O., & Walker, S. (2000). Coefficient alpha: A useful indicator of reliability? *Personality & Individual Differences, 28*, 229-237.

Tremblay, P. F., & Ewart, L. A. (2005). The Buss and Perry Aggression Questionnaire and its relations to values, the Big Five, provoking hypothetical situations, alcohol consumption patters, and alcohol expectancies. *Personality and Individual Differences, 38*, 337-346.

Vigil-Colet, A., Lorenzo-Seva, U., Codorniu-Raga, M. J., & Morales, F. (2005). Factor structure of the Buss-Perry aggression questionnaire in different samples and languages. *Aggressive Behavior, 31*, 601-608.

Williams, T. Y., Boyd, J. C., Cascardi, M. A., & Poythress, N. (1996). Factor structure and convergent validity of the Aggression Questionnaire in an offender population. *Psychological Assessment, 8*, 398-403.

KEY TERMS

Aggression: Acts intended to cause harm or hurt through quarrelsome and hostile speech or physical force.

Anger: The affective component of aggressiveness involving intense feelings, physiological arousal, and the preparation for aggression.

Hostility: The cognitive component of aggressiveness. Cognitions related to ill will, injustice, bitterness, social alienation, and paranoia.

Trait Aggressiveness: Where aggression is a persistent characteristic of the individual across contexts, in contrast to state aggressiveness, where the person is responding to a particular situation for a relatively short duration.

Chapter XLVIII
Motivational Gifts Survey

Dorena DellaVecchio
Regent University, USA

Bruce E. Winston
Regent University, USA

Mihai C. Bocarnea
Regent University, USA

BACKGROUND

This motivational gifts survey (MGS) is designed as a seven-scale instrument that measures motivational gifts in order to provide profiles that are useful in person-job fit analysis. The seven factors of the instrument include (a) *encouraging*, (b) *mercy*, (c) *serving*, (d) *teaching*, (e) *perceiving*, (f) *giving*, and (g) *ruling*. The MGS is the first statistically validated gifts survey of its kind. Organizational leaders can use the results of this survey to better place employees and volunteers in ideal job settings that most fully use a person's gifts. In addition, the results of this survey can help individuals understand their motivational gifts and how to best use those gifts, which could contribute to a sense of personal effectiveness and satisfaction.

Bryant (1991), Bugbee, Cousins, and Hybels (1994), Flynn (1974), Fortune and Fortune (1987), as well as Gothard (1986) suggested that motivational gifts are indicators of life purpose, thus valuable to the study of job satisfaction and performance in organizations. It has been proven that there is a relationship between a lack of motivation and an increase in apathy with regard to burnout (Maslach & Jackson, 1984). In support of the relationship between motivational gifts and burnout, Bryant (1991) concluded that people, when using their motivational gifts, may wear out, but they do not burn out.

Phoon (1986) and Lewis (1992) sought to correlate motivational gift tests with the Myers-Briggs type indicator, but offered no conclusive results, and, in fact, Lewis' study contradicts Phoon's work. Choi (1993) also attempted a correlation between temperaments, psychological types, and spiritual gifts, but achieved few significant correlations. Joachim (1984) suggested a correlation between the four temperament types and various motivational gifts and spiritual gifts. However, in Joachim's study, not all motivational gifts appeared to correlate with temperaments.

The motivational gift tests commercially available today (Bryant, 1991; Bugbee et al., 1994; Fortune & Fortune, 1987; Gilbert, 1986; Kinghorn, 1976; Wagner, 1979) are worded to apply to Christians or for use in the church. However, if these gifts are, indeed, general, secular organizations should be able to benefit from assessing them, too. Furthermore, the commercially available gift tests are attitude focused, asking the test-taker to indicate values toward the gift use rather than measuring behavior, which makes the commercially available tests subject to participants reporting higher scores based on belief rather than performance. The MGS is offered as a viable solution to these important shortcomings of the other motivational gift tests.

RELIABILITY

Correlation analyses of the 29 items of the MGS have showed a high level of correlation; thus, an oblique rotation was used in repeated factor analyses on large data sets collected with the instrument. These factor analyses have consistently yielded seven motivational gift factors with acceptable Chronbach alpha reliability coefficients: (a) encouraging, .82; (b) mercy, .89; (c) serving, .68; (d) teaching, .70; (e) perceiving, .80; (f) giving, .67; and (g) ruling, .82.

VALIDITY

There is a paucity of literature in refereed journals documenting any validation of gifts tests. Fortune and Fortune's (1987) instrument is one of the most well-known, published, and copyrighted of the motivational gift tests. Fortune and Fortune's test contains 25 questions per gift. Katie Fortune (personal communication February, 1999) explained that while they administered their motivational test to thousands of people in 32 countries over 24 years, they have not personally published any statistical validation studies. However, Cooper and Blakeman (1994) did examine the Fortune's motivational gift inventory (1987) and found that, despite the apparent strength of the motivational gifts subscales' content validity, reliability fell

in the poor and moderate range, and construct validity was also tenuous. A factor analysis using an oblique rotation supported a three-factor vs. a seven-factor solution. In addition, Cooper and Blakeman found only a three-factor solution rather than the MGS seven-factor solution.

The Naden spiritual gifts inventory, revised in 1988 from its original 1981 form, measures 19 spiritual gifts including the 7 motivational gifts. Naden's subsequent research on his inventory led him to find factors showing clusters of gifts. Each of the functional gifts fall into one of the five clusters: (a) teacher, (b) shepherd, (c) helper, (d) counselor, and (e) leadership. Naden's inventory has test-retest reliability coefficients ranging from .82 to .97 for the five groups. Agreement of experts coefficients range from .87 to 1.00 for the 20 statements in the inventory.

Several authors (Bryant, 1991; Bugbee, et al., 1994; Clinton, 1985; Gilbert, 1986; Hocking, 1992; Kinghorn, 1976) offered their own versions of gift tests. However, the literature shows no evidence of any statistical validation of these tests. The tests cluster into similar groupings.

Clinton (1985) combined three instruments, a personality test, an inward conviction questionnaire, and personal experiences, to confirm the existence of motivational gifts. The results of all three combined reveal one's unique gift combination. Similarly, Bugbee's et al. (1994) assessed three components of passions, spiritual gifts, and personal styles to form a "Servant Profile." Finally, other motivational gift tests did not show convergent results (Bryant, 1991; Hocking; 1992; Gilbert, 1986).

As with any new instrument, the process of validating the MGS has been quite tedious. The MGS authors used a jury of experts from the Schools of Divinity and Business at a private Mid-Atlantic U.S. university to evaluate and modify the survey items. The emerging pool of 120 items was subsequently pretested with 150 graduate students. Next, following a tautological process, the researchers modified the items five more times, in an effort to clearly show the seven factors. Finally, in-depth interviews of 24 individuals were used to modify the individual gift items to more closely represent each of the specific gifts.

RESULTS

The MGS is published online as a Web survey that allows people to access and complete the form, and to receive their results, along with a description of their motivational gifts. The gifts survey is fully automated. Its self-scoring, personal data remain completely anonymous. Individual results and profiles are returned immediately upon completion of the survey. The corresponding items of the seven motivational gifts are

1. encouraging: items 16, 18, 23, 29;
2. mercy: items 7, 12, 13, 22, 26;
3. serving: items 5, 10, 14, 21;
4. teaching: items 6, 11, 19, 25;
5. perceiving: items 8, 15, 20, 28;
6. giving: items 1, 4, 9, 24;
7. ruling: items 2, 17, 19,27.

In addition to the 29 motivational gifts items, the Web form also collects data on gender, type of professional work currently engaged in, type of professional work desired, and what abilities the participant believed that he/she possessed. The open-ended results for current professional work, desired professional work, and abilities represent qualitative data that require separate in-depth analysis.

The self-reported instrument takes about 10 minutes to complete.

COMMENTARY

The MGS is a tautologically built instrument that measures seven motivational gifts using behav-

ioral response measures. This instrument differs from other more popular instruments in that it is the only one statistically tested in terms of reliability and discriminant validity among factors (DellaVechhio, 2000; Winston & DellaVechhio, 2003). Furthermore, the data collected with this instrument from more that 4,000 participants have been normally distributed on all factors (DellaVecchio, 2000; Winston & DellaVechhio, 2003). In order to use this Web form for research, those interested are advised to contact the MGS's authors to get a research code that participants can include in the demographic area of the form in order for the MGS authors to be able to extract the requested data from the database. Collaborative research on more data can only be beneficial to the future advancement of this assessment tool.

COST

This instrument is on the Internet and available for anyone to use.

LOCATION

The MGS is located at http://www.gifttest.org

REFERENCES

Bryant, C. (1991). *Rediscovering our spiritual gifts*. Nashville, TN: Upper Room Books.

Bugbee, B. Cousins, D., & Hybels, B. *Network leader's guide*. (1994). Grand Rapids, MI: Zondervan Publishing House.

Choi, S. D. (1993). The correlation of personality factors with spiritual gifts clusters. Doctoral dissertation, Andrews University. *Dissertation Abstracts International*, 54-06A, 2107.

Clinton, R. (1985). *Spiritual gifts*. Beaverlodge, Alberta, Canada: Horizon House Publishers.

Cooper, S., & Blakeman S. (1994). Spiritual gifts: A psychometric extension. *Journal of Psychology and Theology 22*, 39-44.

DellaVecchio, D. (2000). *Development and validation of an instrument to measure motivational gifts*. Doctoral dissertation, Regent University.

Flynn, L. (1974). *19 gifts of the spirit*. Colorado Springs, CO: Chariot Visitor Publishing.

Fortune, D., & Fortune, K. (1987). *Discover your God-given gifts*. Grand Rapids, MI: Chosen Books.

Gangel, K. (1983). *Unwrap your spiritual gifts*. Wheaton, IL: Victor Books.

Gilbert, L. (1986). *Team ministry: Spiritual gifts inventory questionnaire*. Lynchburg, VA: Church Growth Institute.

Gothard, B. (1986). *How to understand spiritual gifts*. Oak Brook. IL: Institute in Basic Life Principles.

Hocking, D. (1992). *Spiritual gifts*. Orange, CA: Promise Publishing Company.

Joachim, R. L. (1984). Relationship between four temperament types and nineteen spiritual gifts. Doctoral dissertation, Andrews University. *Dissertation Abstracts International, 46-05A*, p. 1239.

Kinghorn, K. (1976). *Gifts of the spirit*. Nashville, TN: Abingdon Press.

Lewis, N. P. (1992). *A correlational study of Myers-Briggs personality types and Naden's spiritual gifts clusters among members of selected southern Baptist churches*. Fort Worth, TX.

Maslach, C., & Jackson, S. E. (1984). Burnout in organizational settings. In S. Oskamp (Ed.), *Applied social psychology annual: Applications in organizational settings*. (vol. 5) (pp. 133-153). Beverly Hills, CA: Sage.

Naden, R. (1990). *Your spiritual gifts manual*, Berrien Springs, MI: Instructional Product Development.

Phoon, C. Y. (1986). *A correlational study of Jungian psychological types and nineteen spiritual gifts*. Unpublished doctoral dissertation, Andrews University.

Wagner, P. (1979). *Your spiritual gifts can help your church grow*. Ventura CA: Regal Books.

Winston, B., & DellaVecchio, D. (2003). *A seven-scale instrument to measure the Romans 12 motivational gifts*. Regent University. Retrieved January 10, 2006, from http://www.regent.edu/acad/sls/publications/other/home.htm

KEY TERMS

Clusters: Naturally occurring configurations of the seven motivational gifts that fit a similar set of work positions; thus, tying to person-job fit.

Motivational Gifts: An individual's intrinsic areas of self-motivation; the seven areas include encouraging, mercy, serving, teaching, perceiving, giving, and ruling.

Person-Job Fit: The physical, mental, emotional, and spiritual match between an individual and the requirements of a specific job.

Chapter XLIX
Queendom Online
Test Repository

Jason D. Baker
Regent University, USA

BACKGROUND

According to Barak and English (2002), the use of Internet-based psychological tests is an extension of computerized testing that emerged in the 1980s (p. 65). As with computerized testing, online psychological tests provide almost instant results, since Likert-style questions can be scored by the computer without additional human intervention. Additionally, customized profiles can be presented along with the resulting scores, enabling the user to draw additional meaning from the selected instrument. An additional benefit of Internet-based measures is the potential for Web sites to serve as clearinghouses containing a myriad of instruments, available to online users for free or on a subscription basis. As a result, numerous online repositories have been developed that offer a variety of psychological tests, ranging from fully validated instruments to individually designed scales. One of the more popular test libraries is the Queendom.com site run by Plumeus, Inc.

Since its founding in 1996, over 90 million people have completed over 400 million tests in nine different languages at the Queendom Web site (http://www.queendom.com). According to

the Queendom home page, the site contains "114 professionally developed and validated psychological tests, 111 Just-for-Fun tests, [and] 230 mind games and quizzes." The five most popular psychological tests are the classical intelligence test, the self-esteem test, the emotional intelligence test, the communication skills test, and the type-A personality test. Just-for-Fun tests include such measures as the snob test, the blind date test, and the party guest test. Mind games and quizzes include puzzles, math problems, memory games, and trivia tests.

The instruments on the Queendom site are varied and include validated psychological tests, psychological tests currently undergoing validation, and less rigorous tests (e.g., those in the Just-for-Fun category) for which such validation is not deemed necessary. The instruments are self-report instruments that generally contain multiple-choice or Likert-style questions.

RELIABILITY AND VALIDITY

For the psychological tests that have been labeled as validated, Queendom states that the test has undergone reliability and validity testing including

Descriptive stats and reference values/norms; correlations with various factors; reliability (Spearman-Brown split-half, Guttman split-half, Cronbach alpha), criterion-related validity (concurrent validity, method of contrasted groups, correlation with other standardized tests); construct-related validity (internal consistency, intercorrelations of subtests, factor analysis, convergent and discriminant validity (http://www.queendom. com/tests/iq/classical_iq_r2_access.html#h).

RESULTS

From the main Queendom page, users have the option to browse the various tests by category, search by keyword, participate in online discussions, submit requests for information, or find additional personal and professional development resources such as therapists. Some content is presented in partnership with the *Psychology Today* magazine. In addition to browsing the available content, users are encouraged to register with Queendom in order to gain access to the basic collection of tests. Additionally, users can pay for additional premium tests and advanced customer support.

When taking online tests, users first log into their accounts, complete the tests online (usually responding to multiple-choice or Likert-style questions by selecting the appropriate bubble), and then submit their results for scoring. At the end of the survey, users are then presented with the results, which are also saved in their user profile.

COMMENTARY

Queendom, and its corporate online twin PsychTests.com, is a valuable repository of self-assessment tools that can be particularly useful for personal and professional development. The lack of specific validity and reliability details is disconcerting to the academic, but probably not to the average visitor. The strength of the Queendom site is the availability of dozens of validated psychological tests, ranging from 5-minute surveys to 60-minute personality profiles, that can be taken and scored instantly for free. While detailed results and more sophisticated tests require the user to purchase a subscription or pay for individual results, the pricing is significantly cheaper than in-person testing services.

The concern with such a battery of tests is that the online user lacks the professional guidance to properly interpret the results and may misuse their scores, despite the disclaimers provided on the site. Additionally, some research suggests that such online instruments have little correlation with more sophisticated measures (e.g., Firmin, Burger, Hwang, & Lowrie, 2005), or that the online survey method itself influences the results more than the constructs ostensibly measured by the instruments (e.g., Roberts, Konczak, & Macan, 2004).

COST

Although some tests can be taken by unregistered visitors, Queendom recommends that users register. Registering with Queendom is free and provides access to numerous "Basic tests," abridged test results, and a personalized online portfolio containing up to five tests with corresponding results. Registered members can also purchase additional credits to take "Advanced tests," view more complete (rather than abridged) test results, and receive additional customer service. Users may also purchase detailed results to individual tests regardless of registration.

LOCATION

The Queendom Web site is available at http://www. queendom.com.

REFERENCES

Barak, A., & English, N. (2002). Prospects and limitations of psychological testing on the Internet. *Journal of Technology in Human Services, 19*(2/2), 65-89.

Epstein, J., & Klinkenberg, W. D. (2001). From Eliza to Internet: A brief history of computerized assessment. *Computers in Human Behavior, 17*(3), 295-314.

Firmin, M. W., Burger, A. J., Hwang, C., & Lowrie, R. E. (2005). Validity of three Web-based IQ tests and the Reynolds Intellectual Assessment Scales. *Proceedings from the American Psychological Society's 17th Annual Convention.* Los Angeles, CA: APS.

Naglieri, J., Drasgow, F., Schmidt, M., Handler, L., Prifitera, A., Margolis, A., & Velasquez, R. (2004). Psychological testing on the Internet, new problems, old issues. *American Psychologist, 59,* 150-162.

Roberts, L. L., Konczak, L. J., & Macan, T. H. (2004). Effects of data collection method on organizational climate. *Applied H.R.M. Research, 9*(1), 13-26.

KEY TERMS

Computerized Testing: The use of computers to administer tests, automatically score them based on a predetermined answer key, and report the results.

Online Testing: A form of computerized testing delivered using the Internet and World Wide Web. The relative ease of publishing material on the Web results in low development and delivery costs associated with online tests, compared to other means of administration such as paper and pencil.

Reliability: The extent to which a measurement is stable over time. An instrument is reliable if it repeatedly produces consistent results under the same conditions.

Validity: The extent to which a construct is authentically measured. An instrument is valid if it actually measures the factors that it purports to measure.

Chapter L
Willingness to Communicate

Sharon Berry
Kadix Systems, LLC, USA

BACKGROUND

The willingness to communicate (WTC) scale (McCroskey & Richmond, 1985) measures a respondent's tendency to approach or avoid initiating communication. The scale is based on Burgoon's (1976) unwillingness to communicate scale, except the construct is worded in positive terms and assumes the respondent is self aware of his/her own approach/avoidance tendencies.

The WTC scale is a 20-item probability-estimate scale (McCroskey, 1992). Eight of the items are fillers, and the remaining 12 are scored to yield a total score and three subscores based on types of receivers (strangers, acquaintances, friends), and four subscores based on communication context (public, meeting, group, dyad). Users indicate the percentage of times they would choose to communicate in each type of situation, from 0 (never) to 100 (always).

A representative sample of receiver/context items is key to establishing a meaningful norm because people may be more willing to communicate with some kinds of receivers and within some kinds of contexts than others.

RELIABILITY AND VALIDITY

Studies have found that the scale is highly reliable. The internal reliability of the instrument's total score ranges from .86 to .95, with a modal estimate of .92 (McCroskey, 1992). Reliability estimates for the subscores are somewhat lower and more variable than those for the total scale. Content and construct validity of the WTC have been supported.

COMMENTS

The WTC has been used in conjunction with other instruments such as the personal report of communication apprehension (PRCA-24) (McCroskey, Fayer, & Richmond, 1985), self-perceived communication competence (SPCC) (Burroughs & Marie, 1990), and the verbal activity scale (VAS) (McCroskey, 1977). Further, McCroskey and Baer (1985) examined the relationship between the WTC and several such constructs. The results indicated a correlation between the VAS and WTC of .41, and one between the PRCA-24 and the

WTC of -.52. The results of this research further support the WTC's construct validity.

The instrument has been used in a variety of studies, including studies on students who are willing to communicate in the classroom (Chan, 1988), and individuals' willingness to communicate with authority figures (Combs, 1990).

LOCATION

The WTC Scale may be completed online at http://www.jamescmccroskey.com/measures/WTC.htm. Instructions for scoring are included.

REFERENCES

Burgoon, J. K. (1976). The unwillingness-to-communicate scale: Development and validation. *Communication Monographs, 43*, 60-69.

Burroughs, N. F., & Marie, V. (1990). Communication orientations of Micronesian and American students. *Communication Research Reports, 7*, 139-146.

Chan, M. B. (1988). *The effects of willingness to communicate on student learning.* Doctoral dissertation, West Virginia University, Morgantown, WV.

Combs, M. J. (1990). *Willingness to communicate: An investigation of instrument applicability to authority target types.* Master's thesis, Ball State University, Muncie, IN.

McCroskey, J. C. (1977). *Quiet children and the classroom teacher.* Falls Church: VA, Speech Communication Association.

McCroskey, J. C. (1992). Reliability and validity of the willingness to communicate scale. *Communication Quarterly, 40*, 16-25.

McCroskey, J. C., & Baer, J. E. (1985). *Willingness to communicate: The construct and its measurement.* Paper presented at the Speech Communication Association convention, Denver, CO.

McCroskey, J. C., Fayer, J., & Richmond, V. P. (1985). Don't speak to me in English: Communication apprehension in Puerto Rico. *Communication Quarterly, 33*, 185-192.

McCroskey, J. C., & Richmond, V. P. (1987). Willingness to communicate. In J. C. McCroskey & J. A. Daly (Eds.), *Personality and interpersonal communication* (pp. 119-131). Newbury Park, CA: Sage.

KEY TERMS

Communication Context: Where communication takes place (a public setting; a meeting; a group; or a dyad).

Types of Receivers: With whom a person communicates (strangers, acquaintances, friends).

Willingness to Communicate: A respondent's tendency to approach or avoid initiating communication.

Chapter LI
Leadership Practices Inventory

Sharon Berry
Kadix Systems, LLC, USA

BACKGROUND

The leadership practices inventory (LPI) (Posner & Kouzes, 2002) was designed to measure what people did when they were at their "personal best" in leading others. Beginning their work in 1983, Posner and Kouzes approached leadership as a measurable, learnable, and teachable set of behaviors. The LPI was created by developing a set of statements describing each of the identified five leadership actions and behaviors: modeling, inspiring, challenging, enabling, and encouraging.

Each statement is based on a 10-point Likert scale, with higher values representing more frequent use of a leadership behavior. The LPI consists of 30 statements, 6 for each leadership action/behavior. Both self and observer forms are available and subject to the same psychometric analyses.

Participating individuals first complete a self (leader) form, and then request 5 to 10 individuals who interact with that person to complete the observer form. The LPI takes 10 minutes to complete, and may be scored by hand or computer.

Over a 15-year period, Kouzes and Posner examined cases of middle and senior level managers in private and public sector organizations. They have expanded their coverage to include community leaders, church leaders, government leaders and others in nonsupervisory positions. A student leadership version is also available (Posner, 2004).

RELIABILITY AND VALIDITY

Research supports that the LPI is internally reliable. The statements pertaining to each leadership practice are highly correlated.

The five scales are generally independent. The five scales corresponding to the five leadership practices do not all measure the same phenomenon. Instead, each measures a different practice.

Alpha reliability coefficients range from .75-.87 in the self form and from .88-.92 in the observer form. Test-retest reliability is high (Posner & Kouzes, 2000).

COMMENTS

The LPI has been applied in studies investigating leadership practices such as work group performance, high- and low-performing schools; the impact of an academic collegiate leadership development program; organizational identification and commitment among nonprofit employees, coaches, church leaders, and pastors involved in establishing new churches; and congregational growth.

Note: Third edition components cannot be used with second edition components of the instrument. The two editions are incompatible, and combining the materials and software will result in false data and inaccurate reports.

LOCATION

Kouzes, J., & Posner, B. (2003). *The leadership practices inventory (LPI): Self instrument.* San Francisco, CA: Jossey-Bass.

Kouzes, J., & Posner, B. (2003). *The leadership practices inventory (LPI): Observer.* San Francisco, CA: Jossey-Bass.

The Leadership Practices Inventory may also be completed online for a cost at http://www.lpionline.com/lpi/helpInfo/aboutLPI.jsp

REFERENCES

Posner, B. Z. (2004, July/August). A leadership development instrument for students: Updated. *Journal of College Student Development, 45*(4), 443-456.

Posner, B. Z., & Kouzes, J. M. (1988). Development and validation of the leadership practices inventory. *Educational and Psychological Measurement, 48*(2), 483-496.

Posner, B. Z., & Kouzes, J. M. (1990). Leadership practices: An alternative to the psychological perspective. In K. Clark and M. Clark (Eds.), *Measures of leadership.* West Orange, NJ: Leadership Library of America.

Posner, B. Z., & Kouzes, J. M. (1993). Psychometric properties of the leadership practices inventory: Updated. *Educational and Psychological Measurement, 53*(1), 191-199.

Posner, B. Z., & Kouzes, J. M. (1995). An extension of the leadership practices inventory to individual contributors. *Educational and Psychological Measurement, 54*(4), 959-966.

Posner, B. Z., & Kouzes, J. M. (2000). *Leadership practices inventory: Psychometric properties.* Retrieved January 27, 2006, from http://media.wiley.com/assets/463/73/lc_jb_psychometric_properti.pdf

Posner, B. Z., & Kouzes, J. M. (2002). *The leadership practices inventory: Theory and evidence behind the five practices of exemplary leaders.* Retrieved January 27, 2006, from http://media.wiley.com/assets/463/74/lc_jb_appendix.pdf

KEY TERMS

Challenging: Seeking innovative ways to change, grow, and improve by experimenting and taking risks.

Enabling: Fostering collaboration by sharing power and discretion.

Encouraging: Recognizing contributions, showing appreciation for excellence, celebrating values and victories, and creating a spirit of community.

Inspiring: Envisioning the future and appealing to shared aspirations.

Leadership Actions and Behaviors: Modeling, inspiring, challenging, enabling, and encouraging.

Modeling: The degree that a person not only sets a personal example with clear personal values and by aligning actions with shared values, but also follows through with monitoring and feedback from others and to others.

Chapter LII
Eysenck Personality Questionnaire

James B. Weaver, III
Center for AIDS Research (CFAR), Emory University, USA

Christian Kiewitz
University of Dayton, USA

BACKGROUND

We describe a newly developed 12-item short form version of the self-report Eysenck personality questionnaire (EPQ), originally developed by Eysenck and Eysenck (1975) and most recently revised by Eysenck, Eysenck, and Barrett (EPQ-R; 1985). The original EPQ consists of 90 items, while the EPQ-R involves 36 items. Both instruments were designed to assess three dimensions of personality: extraversion, neuroticism, psychoticism.

An understanding of the hierarchical model for personality envisaged by Eysenck (1947) facilitates our explication of these personality dimensions. Eysenck's system involved four levels. At the lowest level of this system are singly occurring acts or cognitions. Habitual acts or cognitions are at the second level. The third level is composed of traits, defined in terms of significant intercorrelations between different habitual behaviors. The final level is that of personality types or dimensions, defined in terms of substantial intercorrelations between traits.

Against this backdrop, Eysenck (see Eysenck,1990; Eysenck & Eysenck, 1985) defined extraversion by the observed correlations between the traits sociable, lively, active, assertive, sensation-seeking, carefree, dominant, and venturesome. Neuroticism was defined by the traits anxious, depressed, guilt feelings, low self-esteem, tense, irrational, shy, moody, and emotional. Finally, psychoticism was defined by the traits aggressive, cold, egocentric, impersonal, impulsive, antisocial, unempathic, and tough-minded.

Weaver and his colleagues (see Richendoller & Weaver, 1994; Weaver, 1991) identified two psychometric aspects of both the original EPQ version and the revised EPQ-R that were potentially problematic. First, in their original design, the instruments solicited dichotomous (i.e., yes, no) responses, thus substantially suppressing variance and raising the question of skewness and kurtosis in the distributions of each personality type subscale. Second, several of the original inventory items involved nomenclature that was not well received by contemporary respondents. Consequently, Weaver and his colleagues modified the wording of some EPQ-R items in a progressive series of investigation, so to enhance the meaning for respondents and to permit Likert-type scale responses.

RELIABILITY

Historically, the extraversion (E), neuroticism (N), and psychoticism (P) subscales of the EPQ-R have displayed acceptable levels of internal consistency reliability (i.e., Cronbach's Alpha). In their initial presentation of the EPQ-R, Eysenck, Eysenck, and Barrett (1985) reported reliability estimates ranging from .85 to .90 for extraversion, from .85 to .88 for neuroticism, and from .73 to .81 for psychoticism. These initial estimates have proven consistent across a series of more recent investigations using the Weaver modification of the EPQ-R. Five studies employing large samples (*n* ranging from 635 to 2,466), for example, have yielded reliability estimates ranging from .89 to .91 for E, from .84 to .86 for N, and from .67 to .68 for P (Richendoller & Weaver, 1994; Weaver, 2003; Weaver, 2005; Weaver, Walker, McCord, & Bellamy, 1996; Weaver, Watson, & Barker, 1995).

VALIDITY

Extensive arguments concerning the validity of extraversion, neuroticism, and psychoticism as fundamental dimensions of personality are presented elsewhere (Eysenck, 1990; Eysenck & Eysenck, 1985; Zuckerman, Kuhlman, & Camac, 1988; Zuckerman, Kuhlman, Joireman, Teta, & Kraft, 1993). Considerable evidence is provided in these works establishing the distinctiveness of each personality dimension; highlighting unique interrelationships between these personality measures and various cognitive, behavioral, physiological indices; and demonstrating the in-

tercultural applicability of the Eysenck personality questionnaire.

RESULTS

In order to develop a personality assessment tool more appropriate for electronic-based research, we derived a short-form version of the EPQ (EPQ-SF) from the Weaver modification of the EPQ-R. Specifically, using a very large sample (males, *n* = 2,317; females, *n* = 1,863), responses to the 36-item EPQ-R were solicited on a scale ranging from "Never" (1) to "Always" (5). Factor analysis was then employed to identify 12 items that provided psychometric properties consistent with the longer version.

The resulting EPQ-SF incorporated four items for each of the three personality dimensions. For extraversion, the items included "Are you a talkative person?" "Do you take the initiative in making new friends?" "Are you quiet when you are with other people?" (reversed) and "Do other people think of you as outgoing?" For the neuroticism personality dimension, the items included "Do you ever feel 'just miserable' for no reason?" "Are your feelings easily hurt?" "Are you a worrier?" and "Do you feel lonely?". And, for psychoticism, the items included "Do you prefer to go your own way rather than act by the rules?" "Do you enjoy co-operating with others? (reversed)" "Do you try not to be rude to people? (reversed)" and "Would you like other people to be afraid of you?" Responses can be recorded on a Likert-type scale, such as the 5-point scale used in the example.

The reliability estimates for the subscales of the EPQ-SF emerged as consistent with, but weaker than, those typically observed for the EPQ-R. Specifically, for E (*M* = 3.5, *SD* = .73) the reliability estimate was .81, for N (*M* = 2.8, *SD* = .72) it was .69, and for P (*M* = 2.1, *SD* = .55) it was .60. The acceptability of these coefficients must be judged in light of the fact that only four items were used to compute the reliability estimate for each subscale.

The construct validity of the EPQ-SF is suggested by strong intercorrelations between the three EPQ-SF subscales and the subscales of the EPQ-R (E, r =.91; N, r = .88; P, r = .78; p < .0001 for all).

Subsequent tests for differences between male and female respondents yielded only inconsequential variations in the reliability estimates, the subscale parameter estimates, and the intercorrelations.

COMMENTARY

The EPQ-SF provides the electronic researcher with a convenient tool for assessing the three dimensions of personality isolated by Eysenck. Requiring less than 5 minutes to complete, the EPQ-SF seems ideal for circumstances, such as those often encountered in Internet-based research, where convenience samples can easily disengage from a survey instrument. At the same time, however, at least one caveat must be considered. The EPQ-SF yields lower reliability estimates than the 36-item EPQ-R. Most likely, this discrepancy results from the significantly smaller number of items involved in the EPQ-SF subscales, and may be further accentuated in studies employing smaller sample sizes (Nunnally & Bernstein, 1994). Thus, the researcher is encouraged to carefully evaluate both the advantages and disadvantages when considering the EPQ-SF.

COST

The EPQ-SF is free for academic research purposes, as governed under the "fair use" doctrine of US Copyright law (see 17 USC § 107 (2005), http://www.copyright.gov/fls/fl102.html).

REFERENCES

Beatty, M. J., & McCroskey, J. C. (w/Valencic, K. M.) (2001). *The biology of communication: A communibiological perspective.* Cresskill, NJ: Hampton Press.

Eysenck, H. J. (1947). *Dimensions of personality.* New York: Praeger.

Eysenck, H. J. (1990). Biological dimensions of personality. In L. A. Pervin (Ed.), *Handbook of personality: Theory and research* (pp. 244-276). New York: Guilford Press.

Eysenck, H. J., & Esenck, S. B. G. (1975). *Manual of the Eysenck personality questionnaire.* London: Hodder & Stoughton.

Eysenck, H. J., & Eysenck, M. W. (1985). *Personality and individual differences: A natural science approach.* New York: Plenum Press.

Eysenck, S. G. B., Eysenck, H. J., & Barrett, P. (1985). A revised version of the psychoticism scale. *Personality and Individual Differences, 6,* 21-29.

John, O. P. (1990). The "big five" factor taxonomy: Dimensions of personality in the natural language and in questionnaires. In L. A. Pervin (Ed.), *Handbook of personality: Theory and research* (pp. 66-100). New York: Guilford Press.

Nunnally, J. C., & Bernstein, I. H. (1994). *Psychometric theory* (3rd ed.). New York: McGraw Hill.

Richendoller, N. R., & Weaver, J. B., III (1994). Exploring the links between personality and empathic response style. *Personality and Individual Differences, 17,* 307-311.

Robinson, T. O., Weaver, J. B., III, & Zillmann, D. (1996). Exploring the relationship between personality characteristics and the appreciation of rock music. *Psychological Reports, 78,* 259-269.

Weaver, J. B., III (1991). Exploring the links between personality and media preferences. *Personality and Individual Differences, 12,* 1293-1299.

Weaver, J. B., III (1998). Personality and self-perceptions about communication. In J. C. McCroskey, J. A. Daly, & M. M. Martin (Eds.), *Communication and personality: Trait perspectives* (pp. 95-117). Cresskill, NJ: Hampton Press.

Weaver, J. B., III (2003). Individual differences in television viewing motives. *Personality and Individual Differences, 35,* 1427-1437.

Weaver, J. B., III (2005). Mapping the links between personality and communicator style. *Individual Differences Research, 3,* 59-70.

Weaver, J. B., III, Brosius, H. B., & Mundorf, N. (1993). Personality and movie preferences: A comparison of American and German audiences. *Personality and Individual Differences, 14,* 307-315.

Weaver, J. B., III, Walker, J. R., McCord, L. L., & Bellamy, R. V. (1996). Exploring the links between personality and television remote control device use. *Personality and Individual Differences, 20,* 483-489.

Weaver, J. B., III, Watson, K. W., & Barker L. L. (1995). Individual differences in listening styles: Do you hear what I hear? *Personality and Individual Differences, 20,* 381-387.

Zillmann, D., & Weaver, J. B., III (1997). Psychoticism in the effect of prolonged exposure to gratuitous media violence on the acceptance of violence as a preferred means of conflict resolution. *Personality and Individual Differences, 22,* 613-627.

Zillmann, D., & Weaver, J. B., III (1999). Effects of prolonged exposure to gratuitous media violence on provoked and unprovoked hostile behavior. *Journal of Applied Social Psychology, 29,* 145-165.

Zuckerman, M., Kuhlman, D. M., & Camac, C. (1988). What lies beyond E and N? Factor analyses of scales believed to measure basic dimensions of personality. *Journal of Personality and Social Psychology, 54,* 96-107.

Zuckerman, M., Kuhlman, D. M., Joireman, J., Teta, P., & Kraft, M. (1993). A comparison of three structural models for personality: The Big Three, the Big Five, and the Alternative Five. *Journal of Personality and Social Psychology, 65,* 757-768.

KEY TERMS

Extraversion: The degree to which a person is sociable, lively, active, assertive, sensation-seeking, carefree, dominant, and venturesome.

Neuroticism: The degree to which a person has guilt feelings and low self-esteem, and is also anxious, depressed, tense, irrational, shy, moody, and emotional.

Psychoticism: The degree to which a person is aggressive, cold, egocentric, impersonal, impulsive, antisocial, unempathic, and tough-minded.

Chapter LIII
Personal Report of Intercultural Communication Apprehension

Sharon Berry
Kadix Systems, LLC, USA

BACKGROUND

The personal report of intercultural communication apprehension (PRICA) (Neuliep & McCroskey, 1997) measures the fear people experience when interacting with others from different cultural groups. PRICA was developed by Neuliep and McCroskey, who assessed that because intercultural interaction in the United States is unavoidable, communication apprehension arising from an interethnic context is more acute than other forms of communication fear. PRICA is a derivative of the personal report of communication apprehension (PRCA-24) (McCroskey, 1982), which measures communication anxiety in situational contexts (i.e., dyadic, small group, meeting, or public speaking).

Intercultural communication anxiety is considered a subcategory of general communication apprehension. The 14-item PRICA instrument is a version of McCroskey's original 24-item Likert-type PRCA instrument. While PRCA is one of the most widely accepted measures of trait communication apprehension, the PRICA instru-

ment—designed to fit intercultural aspects—is considered more specific in its definitions than the PRCA.

The 14 statements, half written positively and half written negatively, represent comments people frequently make when interacting with people from other cultures. The person taking the survey considers each statement and identifies the degree to which he/she agrees or disagrees (Strongly Disagree = 1; Disagree = 2; Neutral = 3; Agree = 4; Strongly Agree = 5).

An individual's communication anxiety score on the PRICA scale is determined by summing responses for all the positive statements and then the negative statements. The sum of the individual negative and positive statement results are then subtracted from 42 to obtain the PRICA score.

A score above 52 indicates a "high" level of intercultural communication apprehension, while a score below 32 indicates a person with "low" anxiety. A person with a moderate level of anxiety in intercultural situations will score between 32 and 52. Scores can range from 14 to 70 on the scale.

RELIABILITY

Research supports that PRICA is consistent and stable. Alpha reliability estimates should be above .90 when the PRICA is taken by a native English speaker. However, the reliability estimate may be lower when the instrument is translated into another language.

VALIDITY

The 14-item PRICA instrument was validated by administering it to 369 undergraduate students, 179 males and 174 females, in communication courses at a large eastern university (Neuliep & McCroskey, 1997). Approximately 20% of test subjects were freshmen, 30% were sophomores, 30% were juniors and 20% were seniors. The students averaged 20.2 years in age. The majority (97%) of students tested were Caucasian, 2% were African-American and 1% were identified as Other. As a measure of validity, participants were asked the size of their home town or city, how frequently they traveled outside their home state, the number of people in their home town of the same race, their frequency of contact with people from different countries, and their frequency of contact with people from different races.

The study revealed that PRICA scores were negatively correlated with the frequency of contact with people from other countries, and negatively correlated with the frequency of contact with people of another race; however, the correlation was not statistically significant. In addition, PRICA scores were not significantly affected by the size of the subject's hometown, the racial composition of the locale, or the extent of the subject's travel outside the area. The influence of the subject's hometown may have been mitigated by the influence of the large university environment in which the test was administered.

COMMENTS

Other instruments have been developed to measure communication apprehension. The most closely related to the PRICA is the personal report of interethnic communication apprehension, derived from PRCA-24 and developed by McCroskey and Neuliep. The PRECA is a 14-item instrument for measuring people's anxiety derived from interacting with those of different ethnic backgrounds. Neither PRICA nor PRECA scores are related to verbal aggressiveness.

LOCATION

The PRICA is found online at http://www.james-cmccroskey.com/measures/prica.htm

At the conclusion of the survey, users can score themselves using the step-by-step directions outlined in the scoring section. First, users are to add the scores of items 1, 3, 5, 7, 9, 10, 12. Second, they sum the scores of items 2, 4, 6, 8, 11, 13 and 14. Finally, to obtain their PRICA score, they plug in the totals from the first and second steps into the following formula: PRICA score = 42 – Total from Step 1 + Total from Step 2.

REFERENCES

McCroskey, J. C. (1982). *An introduction to rhetorical communication* (4th ed.). Englewood Cliffs, NJ: Prentice Hall.

Neuliep, J. W., & Daniel J. R. (1998). The influence of intercultural communication apprehension and socio-communicative orientation on uncertainty reduction during initial cross-cultural interaction. *Communication Quarterly, 46,* 88-99.

Neuliep, J. W., & McCroskey, J. C. (1997). The development of intercultural and interethnic communication apprehension scales. *Communication Research Reports, 14*(2), 145-156.

KEY TERMS

Communication Apprehension: The level of fear or anxiety associated with either real or anticipated (oral) communication encounters.

Intercultural Communication Apprehension: The fear people experience when interacting with others from different cultural groups.

Verbal Aggression: Attacking the person's self-concept instead of, or in addition to, the person's position on a topic.

Chapter LIV
Gender Role Inventory

James B. Weaver, III
Center for AIDS Research (CFAR), Emory University, USA

Stephanie Lee Sargent
Center for AIDS Research (CFAR), Emory University, USA

BACKGROUND

We describe a newly developed 14-item inventory designed to measure two dimensions, agency and communion, of gender role self-perceptions. The gender role inventory (GRI-14) emerges as a conceptual and empirical refinement of the Bem Sex Role Inventory (BSRI; Bem, 1976), offering exceptional utility for electronic-based research while overcoming questions about construct validity and psychometric adequacy inherent in the BSRI.

Since its inception, the BSRI has proven a widely used tool for assessing femininity and masculinity in numerous empirical studies and, to a significant extent, has defined the nature of sex role orientation in the research literature. Despite its popularity, however, persistent questions have arisen over whether the BSRI actually measures what it claims to measure (see, i.e., Choi & Fuqua, 2003; Hoffman & Borders, 2001). A highly consistent pattern emerging across a range of factor-analytic studies, for example, is (1) a single femininity factor and two or more complex masculinity factors, (2) a tendency

toward inconsistent item loading across these factors (e.g., over half of the femininity subscale items do not load on the femininity factor), and (3) an unexpectedly low amount of total variance typically accounted for by the primary factors. Concerns such as these, some argue, point to an "initial lack of theoretically defined dimensions of masculinity/femininity measured by the BSRI" (Choi & Fuqua, 2003, p. 884), while others proposed that the BSRI actually measures constructs such as instrumentality and expressiveness (e.g., Bohannon & Mills, 1979; Moreland, Gulanick, Montague, & Harren, 1978).

Balancing both the recognized heuristic value of the BSRI with its demonstrated shortcomings guided our development of the GRI-14. Our conceptual framework is built upon the agency and communion constructs developed by Bakan (1966). Within this framework, with gender role self-perception conceptualized as independent of biological sex, the agentic construct includes characteristics such as goal-orientation, assertiveness, protectiveness, self-activation, and having the urge to master. The communal construct, in contrast, involves characteristics such as selflessness, openness, caring, kindness, and having a desire to be at one with others (Eagly, 1987). Recent research provides empirical evidence illustrating that agentics tend to rely on differentiation in their social sense making, relational problem solving, and social memory, emphasizing their separation from, independent of and, sometimes, opposition with others. Communals, on the other hand, tend to rely upon integration, highlighting their similarities with others; thus, establishing congruity, connectedness, and interdependence in their relationships with others (Markus & Kitayama, 1991; McAdams, Hoffman, Mansfield, & Day, 1996; Tetlock, Peterson, & Berry, 1993; Woike, 1994a, 1994b, 1995).

Building from this conceptual framework, we then identified 14 items from the original BSRI that have emerged from recent research as primary markers for the agentic and communal dimensions (cf., Choi & Fuqua, 2003; Hoffman & Borders, 2001). The seven items tapping the agentic dimension were "willing to take a stand," "strong personality," "have leadership abilities," "dominant," "assertive," "acts as a leader," and "individualistic." The seven items assessing the communal dimension were "eager to soothe hurt feelings," "sensitive to needs of others," "compassionate," "warm," "tender," "sympathetic," and "gentle."

Next, we tested the viability of the agentic and communal conceptual model by subjecting the 14 items to confirmatory factor analyses (CFA). The data for these tests were drawn from a very large sample ($n = 4,179$). Responses to the GRI-14 items were solicited on a scale ranging from "Never" (1) to "Always" (5). As expected, the CFA for the entire sample, as well as those computed within each respondent sex, clearly established the factorial unidimensionality of the agentic and communal constructs.

RELIABILITY

Agentic and communal measures were computed by averaging the responses to the seven items within each subscale. Overall, the two measures (agentic, $M = 3.71$, $SD = .57$; communal, $M = 3.82$, $SD = .62$) yielded very similar descriptive statistics, and were only weakly intercorrelated ($r = .09$, $p = .0001$). Viewed across respondent sex, however, significant differences were apparent, with males ($n = 2,317$) scoring higher on the agentic measure [$t(4,177) = 4.73$, $p < .0001$; males, $M = 3.74$, $SD = .54$; females, $M = 3.66$, $SD = .60$] and females ($n = 1,862$) scoring higher on the communal measure [$t(4,177) = -24.00$, $p < .0001$; males, $M = 3.62$, $SD = .60$; females, $M = 4.06$, $SD = .56$]. The measures were also more strongly correlated for male respondents ($r = .15$, $p = .0001$) than for female respondents ($r = .09$, $p = .0001$).

Reliability estimates for the agentic and communal measures were computed using the Cronbach alpha algorithm. For the entire sample, the reliability estimate for the agentic measure was .82; for the communal measures it was .90. These estimates remained essentially the same within each respondent sex: agentic measure (males, $\alpha = .81$; females, $\alpha = .84$) and communal measure (males, $\alpha = .88$; females, $\alpha = .87$).

VALIDITY

Data from six studies were examined to provide an initial evaluation of the construct validity of the agentic and communal measures. Specifically, the two subscales of the GRI-14 were correlated with measures extracted from the personal report of communication apprehension (Richmond &

McCroskey, 1992), the communicator style profile test (McCallister, 1992), the empathic response style inventory (Richendoller & Weaver, 1994), the fear of intimacy scale (Descutner & Thelen, 1991), the interpersonal communication motives inventory (Rubin, Perse, & Barbato, 1988), the interaction involvement scale (Cegala, 1984), and the receiver apprehension test (Wheeless, 1975). Several strong correlations emerged from these tests that, taken together, revealed a pattern of results consistent with expectations: Agentics perceived interpersonal communication as a device to promote differentiation in their social world, while communals viewed interpersonal communication as a means to foster social integration.

COMMENTARY

The GRI-14 provides the electronic researcher with a convenient tool for assessing two primary dimensions of gender role self-perception: agency and communion. Requiring less than 5 minutes to complete, the GRI-14 seems an ideal replacement for the much longer Bem sex role inventory. Building on insights derived from a range of factor-analytic studies conducted over the last 25 years, the GRI-14 attempts to maintain the demonstrated heuristic value of the BRSI, while incorporating important psychometrically enhancements.

COST

The EPQ-SF is free for academic research purposes, as governed under the "fair use" doctrine of US Copyright law (see 17 USC § 107 (2005), http://www.copyright.gov/fls/fl102.html).

REFERENCES

Bakan, D. (1966). *The duality of human existance: An essay on psychology and religion.* Chicago: Rand McNally.

Bem, S. (1976). Probing the promise of androgyny. In A. G. Kaplan, & J. P. Bean (Eds.), *Beyond sex-role stereotypes: Readings toward a psychology of androgyny* (pp. 48-62). Boston: Brown, Little, & Company.

Bem, S. (1985). Androgyny and gender schema theory: A conceptual and empirical integration. In T. B. Sonderegger (Ed.), *Nebraska symposium on motivation: Psychology and gender* (pp. 179-226). Lincoln: University of Nebraska Press.

Bem, S. (1993). *The lenses of gender.* New Haven, CT: Yale University Press.

Bohannon, W. E., & Mills, C. (1979). Psychometric properties and underlying assumptions of two measures of masculinity/femininity. *Psychological Reports, 44,* 431-450.

Cegala, D. J. (1984). Affective and cognitive manifestations of interaction involvement during unstructured and competitive interactions. *Communication Monographs, 51,* 320-338.

Choi, N., & Fuqua, D. R. (2003). The structure of the Bem sex role inventory: A summary report of 23 validation studies. *Educational and Psychological Measurement, 63,* 872-887.

Descutner, C. J., & Thelen, M. H. (1991). Development and validation of a fear-of-intimacy scale. *Psychological Assessment, 3,* 218-225.

Eagly, A. H. (1987). *Sex differences in social behavior: A social-role interpretation.* Hillsdale, NJ: Erlbaum.

Hoffman, R. M., & Borders L. D. (2001). Twenty-five years after the Bem sex-role inventory: A reassessment and new issues regarding classification variability. *Measurement and Evaluation in Counseling and Development, 34,* 39-55.

Locke, K. D., & Nekich, J. C. (2002). Agency and communion in naturalistic social comparison. *Personality & Social Psychology Bulletin, 26,* 864-874.

Markus, H. R., & Kitayama, S. (1991). Culture and self: Implications for cognition, emotion, and motivation. *Psychological Review, 2,* 224-253.

McAdams, D. P., Hoffmann, B. J., Mansfield, E. D., & Day, R. (1996). Themes of agency and communion in significant autobiographical scenes. *Journal of Personality, 64,* 339-377.

McCallister, L. (1992). *"I wish I'd said that!"* New York: John Wiley & Sons.

Moreland, J. R., Gulanick, N., Montague, E. K., & Harren, V. A. (1978). Some psychometric properties of the Bem Sex-Role Inventory. *Applied Psychological Measurement, 2,* 249-256.

Richendoller, N. R., & Weaver, J. B., III (1994). Exploring the links between personality and empathic response style. *Personality and Individual Differences, 17,* 307-311.

Richmond, V. P., & McCroskey, J. C. (1992). *Communication: Apprehension, avoidance, and effectiveness* (3rd ed.). Scottsdale, AZ: Gorsuch Scarishbrick.

Rubin, R. B., Perse, E. M., & Barbato, C. A. (1988). Conceptualization and measurement of interpersonal communication motives. *Human Communication Research, 14,* 602-628.

Tetlock, P. E., Peterson, R. S., & Berry, J. M. (1993). Flattering and unflattering personality portraits of integratively simple and complex managers. *Journal of Personality and Social Psychology, 64,* 500-511.

Wheeless, L. R. (1975). An investigation of receiver apprehension and social context dimensions of communication apprehension. *Speech Teacher, 24,* 261-268.

Woike, B. (1994a). The use of differentiation and integration processes: Empirical studies of "separate" and "connected" ways of thinking. *Journal of Personality and Social Psychology, 67,* 142-150.

Woike, B. (1994b). Vivid recollection as a technique to arouse implicit motive-related affect. *Motivation and Emotion, 18,* 335-349.

Woike, B. (1995). Most memorable experiences: Evidence for a link between implicit and explicit motives and social cognitive processes in everyday life. *Journal of Personality and Social Psychology, 68,* 1081-1091.

KEY TERMS

Agency Gender Role Self-Perception: Characteristics such as goal-orientation, assertiveness, protectiveness, self-activation, and having the urge to master.

Communion Gender Role Self-Perception: Characteristics such as selflessness, openness, caring, kindness, and having a desire to be at one with others.

Gender Role Self-Perception: One's psychological perception of their gender as opposed to one's biological sex or one's sex role of being masculine or being feminine.

Chapter LV
Internet Motives Questionnaire

Stephanie Lee Sargent

Center for AIDS Research (CFAR), Emory University, USA

BACKGROUND

In the past decade, the growth of the Internet has been undeniable, affecting the way people communicate, interact, and gather information. According to a Nielsen survey conducted in 2002, more than 400 million people use the Internet, demonstrating the swiftness with which this network of computers has changed the way we live and will continue to live. Communication researchers have recognized the importance of studying the Internet as a communication medium (Newhagen & Rafaeli, 1996), but the study of motivations and behaviors associated with Internet use has been limited.

Much of the recent research looking at the motivations associated with Internet use has focused on the relationship between personality types and Internet use and usage. Researchers, for example, have found that those who are more satisfied with their outward, social life preferred to use the Internet for more instrumental purposes (i.e., information seeking) whereas those less satisfied with life, especially those who felt less valued in face-to-face interactions, used the Internet as a substitute for social interactions and to pass time (Papacharissi & Rubin, 2000). Similar interactions were found when externally oriented people (who believe their environment controls them, feel powerless) used the Internet

for inclusion more than internally oriented people (Flaherty, Pearce, & Rubin, 1998). Several studies have demonstrated negative correlations between a leisure services factor (instant messaging and games) and neuroticism (Swickert, Hittner, Harris, & Herring, 2002), and neuroticism and "gathering product and brand information" and "learning, reference, and education" (Tuten & Bosnjak, 2001). Hamburger and Ben-Artzi's (2000) study found that those scoring high on extraversion tended to prefer leisure services (sex Web sites, random surfing), and that those scoring high on neuroticism had a negative association with information services (work-related information, studies-related information.

While these studies examined motivations for Internet use, each study used different motivations, which make comparisons difficult. Thus, Amiel and Sargent (2004) designed an Internet motives questionnaire to examine motivations for Internet use. The original version of the IMQ contains 45 questions compiled and adapted from previous studies (Bourdeau, Chebat, & Couturier, 2002; D'Ambra & Rice, 2001; Papacharissi & Rubin, 2000; Weaver, 2003) that would measure a wide variety of motivations associated with interpersonal and mass media use. The IMQ-45 was reduced to a 12-item version so that it would be easier for researchers to use online.

RELIABILITY

Although the Internet motives questionnaire is a relatively new development, several exploratory studies have demonstrated acceptable levels of reliability (Cronbach's alpha) ranging from 0.64 to 0.80.

VALIDITY

The 45 IMQ questions were conceptually divided into four categories: interpersonal/communication utility, entertainment utility, information utility, and convenience. When a factor analysis was performed, it confirmed that there were four factors. However, the factor analysis was not as clean as it could have been, prompting us to reduce the length of the inventory. The factor analysis had three items loading (alpha's ranging from 0.58 to 0.79) on each of the four factors. Thus, the IMQ-12 was developed. Each of the following statements should be preceded by "I use the Internet . . .".

- **Factor 1-Entertainment:** Because it makes me feel less lonely, To participate in discussions; and To meet new people.
- **Factor 2-Convenience:** Because I can say things online I wouldn't normally say; Because my friends use it; and Because sometimes it's easier to talk online than to tell people
- **Factor 3-Interpersonal/Communication Utility:** To leave messages; Because people don't have to be there to receive a message; and When I need to have a short conversation.
- **Factor 4-Social Utility:** Because I can remain anonymous; Because I can avoid meeting/talking to people; and Because I do things online I wouldn't do in person.

RESULTS

In completing either the IMQ-45 or the IMQ-12, respondents are asked to report which items motivated them to use the Internet based on a nine-point Likert-type scale ranging from "strongly disagree" (1), to "neutral" (5), to "strongly agree" (9).

The first study to use the IMQ-45 examined the relationship between the psychobiological model of personality type (Eysenck & Eysenck 1985) and Internet use and usage motives. A sample of 210 undergraduate students were asked to report on their motives for using the Internet, and how often they engaged in a variety of Internet and Web-based activities. The findings demonstrate distinctive patterns of Internet use and usage motives for those of different personality types. Specifically, those scoring high in neuroticism reported using the Internet to feel a sense of "belonging" and to be informed. Extraverts rejected the communal aspects of the Internet, and made more instrumental and goal-oriented use of Internet services. Finally, those scoring high in psychoticism demonstrated an interest in more deviant, defiant, and sophisticated Internet applications (see Amiel & Sargent, 2004).

COMMENTARY

Taken together, this suggests that the Internet motives questionnaire appears to be a very promising research tool for researchers, whether in electronic form or in pencil-and-paper version.

COST

The IMQ-45 and IMQ-12 is free to those using it for academic research purposes.

LOCATION

In addition to the inclusion of the inventory in this chapter, the IMQ-45 can also be found in the following article:

Amiel, T., & Sargent, S. L. (2004). Individual differences in Internet usage motives. *Computers in Human Behavior*, *20*, 711-726.

However, at this time, the IMQ-12 has only been published in this chapter.

REFERENCES

Amiel, T., & Sargent, S. L. (2004). Individual differences in Internet usage motives. *Computers in Human Behavior*, *20*, 711-726.

Bourdeau, L., Chebat, J., & Couturier, C. (2002). Internet consumer value of university students: E-mail vs. Web-users [Electronic version]. *Journal of Retailing and Consumer Services*, *9*, 61-69.

D'Ambra, J., & Rice, R. E. (2001). Emerging factors in user evaluations of the World Wide Web [Electronic version]. *Information & Management*, *38*, 373-384.

Eysenck, H. J., & Eysenck, M. W. (1985). *Personality and individual differences: A natural science approach*. New York: Plenum Press.

Flaherty, L. M., Pearce, K. J., & Rubin, R. B. (1998). Internet and face-to-face communication: Not functional alternatives [Electronic version]. *Communication Quarterly*, *46*, 250-266.

Hamburger, Y. A., & Ben-Artzi, E. (2000). The relationship between extraversion and neuroticism and the different uses of the Internet. *Computers in Human Behavior*, *16*, 441-449.

Newhagen, J. E., & Rafaeli, S. (1996). Why communication researchers should study the Internet: A dialogue. *Journal of Communication*, *46*, 4-13.

Papacharissi, Z., & Rubin, A. M. (2000). Predictors of Internet use [Electronic version]. *Journal of Broadcasting & Electronic Media*, *44*, 175-196.

Swickert, R. J., Hittner, J. B., Harris, J. L., & Herring, J. A. (2002). Relationship between Internet use, personality, and social support [Electronic version]. *Computers in Human Behavior*, *18*, 437-451.

Tuten, T. L., & Bosnjak, M. (2001). Understanding differences in Web usage: The role of need for cognition and the five-factor model of personality. *Social Behavior and Personality*, *29*, 291-298.

Weaver, J. B., III (2003). Individual differences in television viewing motives. *Personality and Individual Differences*, *35*, 1427-1437.

KEY TERMS

Convenience Internet Motive: Use of the Internet to facilitate communication (say things, access friends, avoid difficult face-to-face encounters).

Entertainment Internet Motive: Use of the Internet to overcome loneliness, participate in discussions, and to meet new people.

Interpersonal/Communication Utility Internet Motive: Use of the Internet to extend beyond the limits of synchronous interactions (e.g., leave messages; allow for schedule and time differences; and limit conversation length).

Social Utility Internet Motive: Use of the Internet in order to remain anonymous, control interpersonal contacts, and allow for experimental social roles.

APPENDIX

Please answer the following questions according to the following scale:

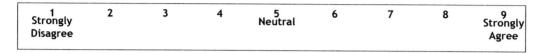

1 Strongly Disagree	2	3	4	5 Neutral	6	7	8	9 Strongly Agree

I USE THE INTERNET

1---Because I can remain anonymous

2---Because I can avoid meeting/talking to people

3---Because it is cheaper

4---Because it is fun

5---Because it makes me feel less lonely

6---To participate in discussions

7---Because it calms me down

8---To leave messages

9---To read about what other users have to say

10---When I have nothing better to do

11---Because it passes the time away

12---Because I do things online I wouldn't do in person

13---To see what is out there

14---To get information for free

15---Because it's a new way to do research

16---So that I can learn about what could happen to me

17---So that I can learn how to do things I haven't done before

18---To find information I can't find elsewhere

19---Because it is enjoyable

20---When I am bored

21---To express myself freely

22---Because it relaxes me

23---To meet new people

24---Because I feel more comfortable talking to people online

25---Because I just like to use it

26---Because it gives me something to do

27---Because people don't have to be there to receive a message

28---To communicate with friends and family

29---Because I can say things online I wouldn't normally say

30---Because my friends use it

31---Because it allows me to do things without leaving my home

32---So I can learn about what is happening in the world

33---It is entertaining

34---When I just want to get away from everything

35---Because it's easy to find things online

36---Because it excites me

37---Because I can always find a computer connected to the Internet

38---When I need to have a short conversation

39---Because sometimes it's easier to talk online than to tell people

40---To look for information

41---To let people know what I think

42---Because it is a comfortable environment

43---To belong to a group

44---Because it's thrilling

45---To purchase products or services

The reduced version, the IMQ-12, consists of the following motivations:

I USE THE INTERNET

1---Because I can remain anonymous

2---Because I can avoid meeting/talking to people

3---Because it makes me feel less lonely

4---To participate in discussions

5---To leave messages

6---Because I do things online I wouldn't do in person

7---To meet new people

8---Because people don't have to be there to receive a message

9---Because I can say things online I wouldn't normally
    say

10---Because my friends use it

11---When I need to have a short conversation

12---Because sometimes it's easier to talk online than to
    tell people

Chapter LVI
Situational Communication Apprehension Measure

Sharon Berry
Kadix Systems, LLC, USA

BACKGROUND

The situational communication apprehension measure (SCAM) was developed by McCroskey and Richmond (1982, 1985) to measure state communication apprehension in any context. This self-report instrument utilizes a 20-item questionnaire to assess how one person felt during a recent interaction with another. Richmond (1978) has also investigated a person's dispositional (trait) anxieties and fears associated with specific situations (state).

The SCAM, a Likert-type measure of state anxiety, asks survey takers to think about the last time they interacted with someone who held a supervisory role over them. Based on that interaction, respondents rate 20 statements—10 describing positive and 10 expressing negative feelings—on an accuracy scale of 1-7. A mark of "7" indicates the statement describing the situation is extremely accurate; a "1" notes the most inaccurate assessment of the interaction.

An individual's score on the SCAM is determined by summing all the positive statements and then summing all the negative statements. The two sums are then added and subtracted from 80. The score should range between 20 and 140. A score below the lower limit or above the upper limit indicates the respondent has made an error.

Because scores on the SCAM are highly dependent on, and variable by, the particular situation, norms for score ranges, means, and standard deviations are hard to define. However, researchers generally accept a score between 39 to 65 as low, 66 to 91 as moderate, and 92 and above as high levels of apprehension.

RELIABILITY

Research supports that SCAM has a measure of high reliability. The alpha reliability of the SCAM ranges from .85 to .90.

VALIDITY

The validity of SCAM's construct and criterion has been supported. Because SCAM is a self-report instrument that gauges a person's apprehension during a recent communication event, validity of the measure increases the less time elapses between the event and the completion of the survey. Scores on the SCAM have helped to assess people's apprehensions in interacting with those who have authority over them, such as a student's interaction with a teacher, an employee's dealings with a boss, or a patient's feeling while talking to a physician.

COMMENTS

Other instruments to measure communication apprehension include the personal report of communication apprehension (PRCA) (McCroskey, 1982). In comparison to SCAM, which measures state apprehension, the PRCA-24 measures trait communication anxiety.

The PRCA, the SCAM, and several demographic questions were administered to 323 non-traditional students (Poppenga & Prisbell, 1996). The study examined trait-like and situational communication apprehension for 212 female and 111 male undergraduate students enrolled in a two-year community college. The students were enrolled in general education requirements at a Mid-western community college. Of these students, 181 were 25 years or under, 142 were older; the mean age of the students was 26.9.

Results indicated a difference between student type and situational communication apprehension. Higher levels of apprehension were reported by the traditional students over nontraditional students.

LOCATION

The SCAM survey is online at http://www.jamescmccroskey.com/measures/scam.htm. The respondent can print out a hard copy of the measure and complete it on paper. Survey takers are provided with a short introduction regarding the survey's scope and intent. A set of directions explain that the following survey intends to gauge how the survey taker felt "the last you interacted with someone who had a supervisory role over you."

For the 20 statements, the test taker is directed to rate responses 1 to 7: a 7 if the statement is "extremely accurate," 6 if "moderately accurate," 5 if "somewhat accurate," 4 if "neither accurate nor inaccurate," 3 if "somewhat accurate," 2 if "moderately accurate," and 1 if "extremely accurate." Respondents are encouraged to mark their answers quickly for the most accurate assessment of their interaction with the other person.

A three-step process for scoring the SCAM follows the completion of the survey.

REFERENCES

McCroskey, J. C. (1982). Oral communication apprehension: A reconceptualization. In M. Burgoon (Ed.), *Communication Yearbook, 6,* 136-170. Beverly Hills, CA: Sage.

McCroskey, J. C., & Richmond, V. P. (1982). *The quiet ones: Communication apprehension and shyness* (2nd ed.). Dubuque, IA: Gorsuch Scarisbrick.

McCroskey, J. C., & Richmond, V. P. (1985). *Communication: Apprehension, avoidance, and effectiveness.* Scottsdale, AZ: Gorsuch Scarisbrick.

Poppenga, J. G., & Prisbell, M. (1996, November). *An investigation into the nature of trait-like and situational communication apprehension of non-traditional undergraduate students.* Paper presented at the annual meeting of the Speech Communication Association, San Diego, CA.

Richmond, V. P. (1978). The relationship between trait and state communication apprehension and interpersonal perception during acquaintance stages. *Human Communication Research, 4,* 338-349.

KEY TERMS

Communication Apprehension: The level of fear or anxiety associated with either real or anticipated (oral) communication encounters.

Situational Communication Apprehension: How a person felt during a recent interaction with another (particularly a powerful other).

State Communication Apprehension: The level of fear or anxiety associated with either real or anticipated (oral) communication encounters in a particular context, such as a group meeting, interpersonal encounter, or a specific type of public forum (as opposed to a generalized trait of apprehension about communication regardless of contexts).

About the Authors

Rodney A. Reynolds is a professor of communication at Azusa Pacific University (and on leave from Pepperdine University in Malibu, CA). Dr. Reynolds teaches classes in research methods, persuasion, and interpersonal relationships. His research includes the persuasive effects of evidence, conversational retreat, and adapting to technology. He was the chair of the Committee on Research Issues for the National Communication Association Task Force on Technology in the Discipline. He is currently serving as the chair of the Communication Theory Interest Group of the Western States Communication Association.

Robert H. Woods, Jr. is a professor of communication at Spring Arbor University, Spring Arbor, MI, where he teaches media ethics and research at the undergraduate and graduate levels. He is licensed to practice law in the Commonwealth of Virginia. He has published journal articles and book chapters on law, distance education, computer-mediated communication, and the pedagogy of online learning.

Jason D. Baker is a professor of education at Regent University, USA where he directs the distance education cognate in the Doctor of Education program. His research interests include faculty and student perspectives toward online learning, social dynamics in the online classroom, and models of effective online learning. He has advised and trained faculty in the use of educational technology, advised numerous organizations on the development of effective online learning programs, and been an active online instructor for the past decade.

* * *

Bruce Aaron manages research and evaluation of workplace learning and performance programs within Accenture. He received his MA in school psychology and his PhD in educational measurement and evaluation from the University of South Florida.

Damon Aiken is an assistant professor of marketing at Eastern Washington University. Dr. Aiken earned his PhD from the Lundquist College of Business at the University of Oregon. His research interests include program context effects in advertising, Internet consumer behavior, the effectiveness of Internet trustmarks, and signaling theory on the Internet.

John M. Artz is a professor of information systems in the School of Business at The George Washington University in Washington, DC. He teaches courses in relational databases, data warehousing, Web-based systems development, and philosophy of science for business and management research. His research interests are in philosophical foundations of information systems, philosophical issues in relational database and data warehouse design and philosophy of science as it applies to information systems research. Dr. Artz has also written many articles on the role of stories in computer ethics.

Gerd Beidernikl is a sociologist. From 1997 to 2002 he studied sociology and new media at the University of Graz. In 2001 he was a research assistant, and since 2002 he has been a researcher at the Center for Education and Economy, Graz (Austria). His main research areas include social network analysis, labor market research, evaluation research, and quantitative surveys.

Sharon Berry is an editor in Kadix Systems' interactive multimedia and training division, Arlington, VA (USA). She has 10 years of experience in editing, writing, graphics design, and production for print and Web-based communications. She has written feature articles for a variety of news publications across industry, government, and nonprofit sectors. Her research interests include online communication and virtual learning.

Mihai C. Bocarnea is a professor in the School of Leadership Studies at Regent University, Virginia Beach, USA. He is an expert in the areas of communication, research methods, quantitative analysis, and statistics. Dr. Bocarnea's research interests include organizational communication, cross-cultural leadership, servant leadership, organizational change, and pedagogy of online learning. Prior to his teaching career, Dr. Bocarnea served as an Internet technology consultant, statistical analyst and consultant, principal researcher, and software engineer.

Renée A. Botta teaches strategic messaging, international and intercultural public relations, health communication, quantitative research methods, and mass communication theory at the University of Denver. Dr. Botta's research focus is on strategic health communication and media effects.

William Brown is a professor of communication at Regent University in Virginia (USA). His academic research interests include media effects, entertainment-education, media personalities, and social influence. His favorite courses include doctoral research methods, entertainment-education campaigns, intercultural communication, and communication theory.

Stephen Burgess is a professor in information systems at Victoria University, Australia. Dr. Burgess has professional memberships in the Information Resource Management Association and the International Association for the Development of the Information Society. His research interests include: the strategic use of IT; small business use of IT; and e-commerce in small business.

Kevin Corley is a professor in the Department of Management at the W. P. Carey School of Business. His areas of research interest include organizational identity and image, employee attachment to the organization, and organizational learning and knowledge management. He is an associate editor of the *British Journal of Management*. He received the William H. Newman Award for Best Paper based on a dissertation at the 2003 Academy of Management meetings, and was a finalist for Best Paper in the Academy of Management Review in 2002. An award-winning undergraduate teacher, Dr. Corley previously taught at Penn State (USA) and the University of Illinois, Urbana-Champaign (USA), as well as conducts a regular seminar on Organizational Identity and Change in the International Executive Masters of Corporate Communication Program at The Rotterdam School of Management (Erasmus University, The Netherlands). Prior to joining academia, he was a change consultant with Ernst and Young, LLP in Chicago.

Hallie D'Agruma, PhD, received her doctorate in counseling/clinical/school psychology from the University of California, Santa Barbara, USA where she engaged in survey research investigating the impact of social factors on psychological development. Her specialization is in the manifestation of eating disorders cross-culturally. She has been most recently employed as a clinical assistant professor in the Graduate Program in Counseling at the University of New Hampshire, USA.

Dorena DellaVecchio served as faculty member at Regent University in Virginia Beach, USA with both the School of Leadership Studies and the Regent Undergraduate School from 2000-2005. Dr. DellaVecchio's research interests include leadership development, autonomous learning, spiritual formation, and motivational gifts. Currently, she serves as a writer, speaker, and consultant in leadership development and curriculum design.

Rob Dennis currently serves as a vocational rehabilitation specialist at the Veterans Administration Medical Center in Dayton, Ohio. He taught courses in rehabilitation counseling for several years at Wilberforce University. His dissertation (2004) was on the development of a servant leadership instrument. Additionally, he recently co-authored an article on this subject, with Dr. Bocarnea, in the *Leadership and Organizational Development Journal* (2005). He is a licensed social worker, licensed counselor, and certified rehabilitation counselor. He is also a member of the American Association of Christian Counselors.

Samir Desai is the product manager for learning systems and virtual learning environments within Accenture. He received his BS in electrical engineering from University of Illinois, Urbana, USA, and MS in computer science from Northwestern University.

James P. Dillard is the head of the Pennsylvania State University Department of Communication Arts and Sciences. Dr. Dillard's research focus is on social influence processes, emotions, and goal seeking.

Rhonda Dixon worked in the IT industry in the financial markets for 20 years in varying positions, for example, system analyst, programmer, and tester. Continuing her education and keeping her skills up to date has been another focus. Rhonda now works part-time as an academic sessional at Victoria University and RMIT University, and also as a contractor in a database development role to the manufacturing and personnel industries. Rhonda's research interests include databases, information systems, and radio frequency identification (RFID).

Călin Gurău is a professor in marketing at Groupe Sup de Co Montpellier, France. Dr. Gurău is a junior fellow of the World Academy of Art and Science, Minneapolis, USA. He worked as marketing manager in two Romanian companies, and he has received degrees and distinctions for studies and research from University of Triest, Italy, University of Vienna, Austria, Duke University, USA, University of Angers, France, and Oxford University, UK. His present research interests are focused on marketing strategies of high-technology firms and marketing strategies on the Internet.

Nanette M. Hogg is a professor of communication at the University of Nebraska at Kearney, where she has taught for 12 years. Her experiences include teaching in public and private school systems, and professional positions in the instructional and informational technology fields. Her area of expertise is multimedia.

Jim Jansen has more than 100 publications in the area of information technology and systems. Dr. Jansen's co-authored a paper in *IEEE Computer* analyzing a 4-year trend in how users search the Web-generated press coverage in over 100 news organizations worldwide, including wire services, cable and network television, radio, newspapers, and commercial Web sites. His 2000 co-authored article published in *Information Processing and Management* has received over 150 citations in outlets such as Proceedings of the ACM SIGIR International Conference on Research and Development in Information Retrieval, Information Processing and Management, and *Journal of the American Society for Information Science and Technology*, among other conferences and journals in a variety of fields. He has received several awards and honors, including an ACM Research Award and six application development awards, along with other writing, publishing, research, and leadership honors.

Karen Jansen specializes in management, with teaching and research in the fields of organizational change and strategic human resource management. Her research broadly explores the process and impact of change on an organization's employees. Her momentum research focuses on identifying momentum triggers, and how momentum trends influence individual attitudes and behavior. She is also interested in the evolution of employee fit with various aspects of the work environment. Professor Jansen's research has appeared in *Organizational Science*; *Organizational Behavior and Human Decision Processes*; and *Journal of Applied Psychology*. She is on the editorial board of *The Journal of Applied Behavioral Science*. She has current research projects with several organizations in the midst of large-scale change (e.g., culture change, lean transformation, and internal branding). Before becoming an academic, Professor Jansen worked for IBM as a systems engineer.

Pattama Jongsuwanwattana is a lecturer in communication at Yonok University in Lampang, Thailand, where her courses focus on broadcasting and electronic media. Her research includes work in cross-national representations in media.

Arno Kerschbaumer studied theology and sociology from 1998 to 2003 at the University in Graz. From 2002 to 2004 Kerschbaumer worked on projects that focused on regional development and since 2004, has been a researcher at the Center Education and Economy, Graz (Austria). Kerschbaumer's main research areas include labor market research (especially IT), quantitative surveys, and regional development.

Christian Kiewitz teaches organizational behavior classes in the Management/Marketing Department in the School of Business Administration and the University of Dayton. Dr. Kiewitz's research interests include: anger, aggression, and emotions in the workplace, work stress, organizational politics and justice, and personality.

Michael Lang teaches in information systems at NUI, Galway. He previously worked in industry as an analyst/programmer. His primary research interest is information systems development, particularly methods, approaches, tools, and techniques for information systems analysis andand design, and information systems education.

Feng Li is chair of e-business development at the University of Newcastle upon Tyne. For nearly two decades, Feng's research has centrally focused on the intersections between information systems and changes in the strategies, business models, and designs of large organisations. A particular focus of his current research is on the Internet and e-business, including e-government and e-learning. He was the editor of the business magazine Europe in China.

Joanna Lumsden is a research officer with the National Research Council of Canada's (NRC) Institute of Information Technology. Prior to joining the NRC, Joanna worked as a research assistant in the Computing Science Department at the University of Glasgow, UK, where she attached both her undergraduate software engineering honours degree and her PhD in human computer interaction. Joanna is also an adjunct professor at the University of New Brunswick in Fredericton, where she teaches graduate courses and supervises a number of graduate students. Among her varied HCI research interests, Joanna conducts research into the development of guidelines for online-questionnaire design.

Qingxiong Ma is a professor of computer information systems at Central Missouri State University. Dr. Ma received his PhD in management information systems from Southern Illinois University at Carbondale. His research interests include information technology adoption/diffusion, electronic commerce, and information security management. His teaching interests include systems analysis and design, data communication, management of information systems, database management systems, and client/server application development.

Katja Manfreda is on the faculty of social science at the University of Ljubljana in Slovenia where Dr. Manfreda is chair of informatics and methodology. Dr. Manfreda is on the organizing committee of the European Survey Research Association.

Katty Marmenout is a doctoral student in the program in management at McGill University.

Mary McCord is a professor of computer information systems in the Harmon College of Business Administration at Central Missouri State University in Warrensburg, MO. After an entrepreneurial career in oil and gas production, she received her PhD in business administration from the University of Oklahoma. Her research areas include e-commerce, service learning, and team-based learning. Dr. McCord's specialty is trust in e-commerce transactions and acceptance of technology.

Jaime Melton manages and supports the development of new business-related activities. She has supported Web development and online advertising initiatives.

Thomas O'Daniel joined the Department of E-Commerce, School of Business and IT at Monash University, Malaysia, in 2000 after having previously taught at Universiti Telekom, University Malaysia Sarawak, and University of Houston. His research interests are information management, and the administration of mission-critical systems.

Savvas Papagiannidis teaches e-management courses at University of Newcastle upon Tyne, UK. He has started and worked for a number of e-business ventures. He is a member of the Institute of Small Business and Entrepreneurship (ISBE). His research interests include e-business, hi-tech entrepreneurship, small businesses, m-commerce, and m-marketing, Internet and other emerging technologies, and online data gathering and research methods.

Eun Park is a professor in the Graduate School of Library and Information Sciences at McGill University. Dr. Park's research interests include digital archives and digital preservation of cultural heritage collections, records management and electronic records management systems, metadata schemes in multidisciplinary contexts, and development and implementation of archival curricula on digital resources

J. Lynn Reynolds is associate director of the Brehm Center for Worship, Theology, and the Arts at Fuller Theological Seminary, Pasadena, California. Dr. Reynolds has degrees in communication from Regent University, University of Hawaii-Manoa, and Abilene Christian University. Her academic interests are in the area where interpersonal communication and internal values are impacted by television, film, and the arts. Her experience includes teaching communication for the University of Hawaii, Old Dominion University, and Pepperdine University.

Lynne Roberts is a research fellow with the Crime Research Centre in the School of Law at the University of Western Australia. Dr. Roberts has conducted a range of qualitative and quantitative research within virtual environments, including conducting surveys. She has published widely on her research in virtual environments, with a focus on social interaction processes online, the integration of on- and off-line life, and measurement and ethical issues.

Ginger Rosenkrans is an advertising professor at Pepperdine University. Dr. Rosenkrans earned her PhD in information systems from the Graduate School of Computer and Information Sciences at Nova Southeastern University in Ft. Lauderdale, Florida. Her research interests include online advertising effectiveness, online advertising metrics and Web analytics, and online ad interactivity and design.

Stephanie Lee Sargent is a research scientist at the Center for AIDS Research (CFAR), Emory University, USA. Dr. Sargent has teaching and research interests in the Internet and society, interpersonal communication, media effects, and gender in communication. Dr. Sargent currently serves as chair of the Communication andSocial Cognition Division of the National Communication Association. Dr. Sargent is a member of several professional and honorary societies including the International Communicaiton Association and Kappa Tau Alpha.

Lijiang Shen is a professor in the Department of Speech Communication at The University of Georgia. His primary area of research considers the impact of message features and audience characteristics in persuasive health communication, message processing, and the process of persuasion/resistance to persuasion; and quantitative research methods in communication.

Mohini Singh is a professor of information technology and e-business at RMIT University, Australia. She has published widely in the areas of e-business and new technology and innovation management. She is the principal editor of two highly regarded books on e-business and serves as a member on the editorial boards of several international journals. She teaches in the MBIT program. She is an invited faculty at the IESEG Graduate School in France to teach e-business management and global issues.

Amanda Sturgill is an assistant professor of journalism at Baylor University. Her research interests include usage of the Web by not-for-profit and ideological organizations and equity of Internet information access.

Mike Thelwall is a professor of information science in the School of Computing and Information Technology at the University of Wolverhampton, UK. He is head of the Statistical Cybermetrics Research Group and a member of the Information and Language Processing Research Institute. His primary academic interest is in developing quantitative methods to analyze Web phenomena, particularly hyperlinking in academic Web sites.

Rodney Turner is a professor in the School of Information Systems at Victory University in Melbourne, Australia. His research interests include training issues, technology transfer in developing nations, and information accessibility. A number of his publications have centered on mathematic and logic ability, and links to information systems training and education.

Vasja Vehovar, PhD, is a professor for statistics at the Faculty of Social Sciences, University of Ljubljana, Slovenia. His main research interests are survey methodology and information in society.

Mihaela Vorvoreanu is a professor in the Department of Communication. Her area of expertise is public relations, with emphasis on new and emerging technologies. Her other interests include international and intercultural communication, theories of persuasion, and communication theory. Dr. Vorvoreanu serves as the faculty adviser for PRSSA (Public Relations Student Society of America). Her research interests include online organization-public relationships, the experience of using new communication technologies, public relations theory, and the internationalization of U.S. academe.

Bert G. Wachsmuth is a professor of mathematics and computer science at Seton Hall University. He received his PhD from Indiana University, where he worked on problems related to the Monge Ampere equation in several complex variables. Dr. Wachsmuth previously taught at Dartmouth College.

J. D. Wallace specializes in organizational communication, research methods, and technology-mediated communication. His most recent research has been in the areas of online immediacy, corporate image restoration, and corporate disaster recovery. Dr. Wallace has authored and coauthored over 30 national and international presentations and publications in the areas of technology-mediated communication, organizational communication and training and development.

James B. Weaver III is a research scientist at the Center for AIDS Research (CFAR), Emory University, USA. His research interests focus on media institutions, media effects, and entertainment functions of the mass media. Dr. Weaver has published extensively and won a number of top paper honors. Weaver is a member of several professional and honorary societies including Phi Beta Delta and Kappa Tau Alpha.

Brian Whitworth is at Massey University (Albany), New Zealand. After degrees in psychology and mathematics, his MA (Hons.) was on the implications of split-brain research. He joined the New Zealand army, did officer training, became senior army psychologist, then moved into operational software and simulations, working with the Australian, Singapore and Malaysian Army War Game Centres. His doctorate on generating agreement in distributed computer-mediated groups used groupware he designed and wrote. For the last decade he has studied how human issues affect computing technology design, evaluation and operation.

Bruce E. Winston is the dean for the School of Leadership Studies at Regent University in Virginia Beach. Dr. Winston's research interests include servant leadership, organizational development and transformation, leadership development, distance education and technology in higher education.

Jiali Ye is a doctoral candidate in communication at Georgia State University in Atlanta, USA. Her research centers on the use of the Internet to form and cope with relationships. She has extensive experience with designing and developing Web pages, Web surveys, and databases.

Erika Zollett is a PhD candidate at the University of New Hampshire. She received a Masters of Environmental Management at Duke University's Nicholas School of the Environment. Erika utilizes survey research to engage fishermen in identifying effective conservation strategies for marine mammals caught in fishing gear.

Index